# The Prairie and the Making of Middle America:

# Four Centuries of Description



by

DOROTHY ANNE DONDORE, Ph. D.

Elmira College

Antiquarian Press, Ltd.

NEW YORK

1961

First published 1926

Reprinted by Antiquarian Press, Ltd. 1961

Library of Congress Catalog Number 61-80-46

Edition limited to 750 copies

To My Mother

and

To My Father

## FOREWORD

When in his essay *The Poet* (1844) Emerson included among his list of subjects still unsung the Western Clearing, he was giving vent to what yet remains a common opinion — that we have neglected our most distinctive and prolific literary theme. Professor Turner and his followers have demonstrated convincingly to us the significance of the Frontier in American History; its influence on literature has never been determined.

This task I set myself a number of years ago, soon coming to the conclusion, however, that sound generalization was impossible without a series of detailed studies dealing with different phases of the frontier — the Forest, the Prairies, the Plains, the Mountains, and the Sea. After completing these I hope to be able to carry out my original idea.

This first book, a unit in itself, outlines the treatment of the Middle West, that rich agricultural region of which the distinctive feature is the Prairie, from the time of its discovery to the present day. The first thing that the study should prove is that, in spite of Emerson's and others' denials, this section has been the subject of numerous and varied interpretations which have reflected all stages of its life. It should further demonstrate the futility of facile generalization concerning the frontier since types from one section were carried over to another and since European romantic traditions shaped many border concepts. The inclusion of historical source materials, ordinarily neglected by the literary historian, will show, I believe, a constant interplay between them and the imaginative treatments, the latter using familiar situations and figures, the former being adorned by some of the most famous creations of the romancers. The survey has been carried beyond the frontier stage to reveal the continuity of tendencies and the significance for social history of the literary treatments of the prairie, regardless of their aesthetic value, which is in many cases relatively slight.

Naturally in such a study the problem is not so much one of finding material as of eliminating it; attempt to treat all the work bearing on the Midland would require not one but many volumes. I trust, however, that this first furrow in the Prairie will indicate the chief interpretations and furnish a guide for further investigations. If the book serves to direct attention to much neglected material and to suggest the flavor of the narratives depicting the Mississippi Valley it will have accomplished its purpose.

In writing the monograph I have incurred many obligations. For early help and encouragement while I was a student and instructor at the State University of Iowa I am indebted to Professors C. F. Ansley (now of the editorial staff of the Encyclopedia Britannica), Nellie S. Aurner, E. N. S. Thompson, Percival Hunt (now of the University of Pittsburgh), Hardin Craig, Benjamin F. Shambaugh, and Arthur Meier Schlessinger (now of Harvard University). Suggestions for material in their special fields were given to me by Professors Gilbert Chinard of Johns Hopkins, Albert Faust of Cornell, A. H. Quinn of the University of Pennsylvania, and Brander Matthews, Professor Emeritus at Columbia. Professor Matthews kindly read some of my proof as well. No work touching upon the frontier could be complete without acknowledgment of the cordial recognition and generous assistance of Dr. Frederick Jackson Turner, Professor Emeritus at Harvard. I am further indebted to Professors Ashley H. Thorndike, William Witherlee Lawrence, and Dixon Ryan Fox of Columbia, who when they read the book in manuscript were enabled through their scholarship and experience to give various helpful hints; to Professor Charles Sears Baldwin, who suggested the narrowing to the Prairie; to Dr. Carl Van Doren, literary editor of the Century Magazine, in whose course in American Fiction I first conceived the idea of writing on the frontier and who made conferences while the book was in progress both stimulating and pleasurable; and most of all to Professor William Peterfield Trent, whose kindly wisdom, thorough scholarship in the fields of history and literature, and sense of form have made his assistance invaluable to me in all stages of this study.

D. D.

TABLE OF CONTENTS

# ILLUSTRATIONS

# THE PRAIRIE AND THE MAKING OF MIDDLE AMERICA: FOUR CENTURIES OF DESCRIPTION

Between the soaring purple ridges of the Alleghanies and the Rockies's white-capped peaks, the sunlit waters of the gulf and our great inland seas, Middle America stretches. Crumpled into the Ozarks and Black Hills, scarred at the Bad Lands as in elemental chaos, eroded at the south and west into strange buttes and great canyons, its main surface yet remains characteristically flat or rolling, evened by the waves of the prehistoric sea beneath which its sedimentary beds were first laid down, smoothed by the massive ice-sheets that advanced resistless in the glacial epochs. In spite of the fact that the mountains make its sunset limits arid plains, that at the time of settlement it was in part shrouded by huge forests centuries old, its characteristic feature is the grass-swathed, fertile expanse of the prairie, parallel to the pampas of the Southland, the broad steppes of Russia. Could the relics of the ancient life speak — the crinoids of Iowa and Indiana, the mastodons' huge bones that awed early visitors to the Licks — they might tell weird tales of the making of a world. Even the modern denizens, the migrant birds that yearly wing their way from their tropic shelters to the north, could pass down from generation to generation a record of new world building, of mysterious change — change that has steadily depleted their numbers, that has diminished their feeding places, that has gashed with man-made structures the harmonious earth covering, formerly broken only by the steely glitter of lakes and streams, the moving dots of wild animals, the camps of the Indian. But although the heavy forests that once mottled it are almost all felled, although the tough prairie sward with its coral-like branching of roots is ploughed up for new crops, although thunderous engines and belching smoke-stacks disturb the peace and quiet of the fertile fields, there still somehow persists the individuality of the territory. The sea of tender green that, flower-spangled, formerly billowed from mountain range to mountain range, much of it tawnied in autumn, ice-bound and snow-clad in winter, has given way to cultivated rectangles of grain, ploughed land, or meadow, straggling villages, the crowded squares of great cities. The transcontinental traveller of today instead of having his way blocked by thousands of grazing or stampeding buffalo, wild game of all sorts, passes herd after herd of blooded cattle, sleek horses, prize pigs. In sections where the periodic burnings formerly confined them to the water courses, trees now grow luxuriantly. Yet changed in detail as are the landscape, the life, and the inhabitants, there still hover over the interior valley the abiding sense of tranquillity, the vast calm of sunlit space and luminous night sky, the freedom of wide-arched horizons, that from the beginning of the written history of the blossoming meadows have dignified and made alluring the swelling vistas of the prairie and that form the dominant notes in the descriptions of the section.

# CHAPTER I

## THE SPANISH AND FRENCH IN THE MISSISSIPPI VALLEY: DISCOVERY AND EXPLORATION

Description of the Midland begins surprisingly early. The horizon of the western world, only recently pushed back, still clung low and threatening; navigators setting sail in their cockle-shell boats over the darkening sea knew not what strange monsters they might encounter; mariners told marvellous tales of voices in the air and demoniac inhabitants; the West Indies were still confused with St. Brandan's Isle and other magic places of antiquity, when Europeans first visited the interior of North America.

Juan Ponce de Leon led the way to discovery with his Floridian quest for the Fountain of Youth. Six years later—in 1519—there is a possibility that the Mississippi's shores were first looked upon by the wondering eyes of white men, although the modern opinion is that it was the Mobile River up which Juan de Pineda sailed. On this stream he found one large Indian town and about forty hamlets filled with kindly natives. The land, he reported, was very good, pleasant, healthful, with ample supplies of provisions, and the Indians wore gold ornaments.[1]

Even this slight hint of riches was enough to set on foot further expeditions—the bootless quests of Lucas Vasquez de Ayllon (1526) and of Panfilo de Narvaez (1528), from the latter of which we have one of the most extraordinary records of exploration in America. Cabeza de Vaca, treasurer and high sheriff of the company, after years of wandering with incredible hardships reached the Spanish settlements. He passed the Mississippi, he first wrote an account of the bison and the great

1 Navarette, M. F.—*Coleccion de los viajes y descubrimientos que hicieron por mar los Españoles desde fines del Siglo XV.*—5 v. 1825-37. III: 148. See also *De Orbe Novo. The Eight Decades of Peter Martyr d'Anghera* tr. by F. A. MacNutt. 1912. P. 63. Bk. I. Fifth Decade. For discussion of the identity of the river see W. B. Scaife—Supplement. *Johns Hopkins Univ. Stud. in Hist. and Pol. Science* v. XIII. 1892.

plains, he first crossed the continent from coast to coast. Yet these distinctions seem slight beside the suffering he endured — hunger so acute that the flesh of dead companions was dried and devoured, torture by the burning sands of summer, intolerable cold in the winter. He found little of the wealth of the Indies — a "hawk-bell of copper, thick and large," a few emeralds and some "fine turquoises that come from the north," near the end of the journey "clear traces of gold and lead, iron, copper, and other metals." Yet that his dream of great treasure still persisted is shown by his statement that Florida was the richest country in the world and by the passage summarizing his journey.

> "In the time we traversed from sea to sea; and from information gathered with great diligence, there may be a distance from one to another at the widest part of two thousand leagues; and we learned that on the coast of the South Sea there are pearls and great riches, and the best and all the most opulent countries are near there."[2]

Others were only too ready to share his visions. The expedition of Coronado in 1540 was directly inspired by Cabeza de Vaca's journey; and his return was in part responsible for the extraordinary eagerness of De Soto's followers.[3]

The explorations of this latter company are particularly important not only because in the official report by Luys Hernandez de Biedma (drawn up 1544, pub. 1841), the narrative of the Gentleman of Elvas (1557), and in Oviedo's account, based on the diary of Rodrigo Ranjel, De Soto's secretary (in *Historia General y Natural de las Indias*, 1547), are shown most characteristically the hopes and failures of the Spaniards, but because in its long years of wandering the steadily diminishing company trampled and devastated the fertile bottom lands of the Mississippi and spent many barren days on the wastes beyond the Great River. Few more tragic stories are found in the history of the West. The return of De Soto, whose

---

2 *Orig. Narr. of Early Amer. Hist. — Spanish Explorers in the Southern United States 1528-1543.* Cabeza de Vaca's narrative ed. by F. W. Hodge. 95, 106, 111, 120. Orig. pub. 1542. His route has been traced by A. F. Bandelier. *Papers of the Archaeological Institute of Amer.* Amer. ser. V. For more recent research see H. Davenport and J. K. Wells — *Southwestern Hist. Quart.* XXII: 111-142.

3 See for instance, French, B. F. — *Hist. Coll. of La.* II: 114, 200.

early career epitomized that of the conquerors of the Southland, the resurrection almost from living death of Cabeza de Vaca, both inspired in men a frenzy for riches. A gorgeous following disembarked on the white sands of the coast — Portuguese who at the first muster "showed themselves armed in very bright armor, and the Castellans very gallant with silk upon silk, with many pinkings and cuts." From the moment of landing, however, the tale was one of disappointment and misery — forced marches through fens; underfoot black mire which sucked up the horses, and loathsome creeping things of the dark; overhead ghostly moss, tangles of rotting vegetation that blocked the way and scratched and dulled the gay apparel; almost continual harassing by the Indians whom the Christians had consistently tortured and oppressed; famine days, winters bitterly cold, and always the will-of-the-wisp pursuit of gold.

The promise of it was ever present.

> "He asked them if they knew or had notice of any rich country where there was gold or silver. They told him they did, and that towards the west there was a province which was called *Cale*; . . . and that there was much gold; and that when those their enemies came to make war with them of *Cale,* these inhabitants of *Cale* did wear hats of gold, in manner of head-pieces."

During his lifetime the iron will of De Soto lashed his company ever on; and even after his death the starving, half-clothed remnant of the once so pompous band grieved at the determination to travel by sea, for "they hoped to find some rich country before they came to the land of the Christians, by that which *Cabeça de Vaca* had told the Emperor: and that was this: That after he had found clothes made of cotton wool, he saw gold and silver, and stones of great value. And they had not yet come where he had been."

Naturally among men of such aims, calloused to all but their own mercenary ends, mention of the soil would be but incidental. And to so large a company, wandering for years with no means of subsistence but food wrenched from the Indians, such mention would be measured in terms of supply. Yet strangely enough through the chronicles of famine and burning and strife gleams the tranquil beauty of the land — waving fields of yellowed maize, the scattered tree-knots of the prairie.

> "There was in the barns and in the fields great store of maize and French beans. The country was greatly inhabited with many great towns, and many sown fields, which reached from the one to the other. It was pleasant, fat, full of good meadows upon rivers. There were in the fields many plum trees, as well of such as grow in *Spain* as of the country; and wild tall vines, that run up the trees; and besides these there were other low vines with big and sweet grapes; but for want of digging and dressing, they had great kernels in them."

And although the fields were laid waste, the grain hacked off, the fruitful meadows seared and trampled with the hoofs of horses and the weight of the chain gangs, through the Spanish desolation, we feel the enduring power of the land.[4]

Of significance from a literary point of view, although unsatisfactory from a historical, is the narrative by Garcilasso Inca de la Vega, (*La Florida del Ynca*, 1605), which, like his Peruvian history, is painted in the most brilliant of hues. The memories of his own youth in America, the wonder tales of his Inca uncle and mother, the braggings of returned De Soto men who wished by their exploits to rival the conquerors of Mexico and Peru, all combined to produce this wondrous vision; to the seeping coast of the gulf he transferred the glories of romance. His Indians, the numbers of which like those of the Spanish he greatly exaggerated, were of a type to delight a poster artist. Sometimes, of course, these epic beings attacked the Spaniards instead of bringing them gifts or offering them land, but even then they frequently aroused the admiration of their opponents by the nobility of their sentiments or the courtliness of their submission.

And as the chronicler lifted into beauty the appearance and customs of the Indians, so he transformed their simple dwellings. Yet in spite of Garcilasso's idealization of his materials, he had after all a pretty shrewd insight into the natures of men. Little notes such as,

> ". . . they thought only of going to Cofaciqui, where

---

4 French — *Hist. Coll. of La.* II: 116, 129, 200, 152. See, also, *Narratives of the Career of Hernando De Soto.* . . . ed. by E. G. Bourne. 2v. 1904.

> they all hoped to enrich themselves. They therefore made long journeys and as the country was beautiful, without rivers or forests, they traversed it in five days,"

or,

> "But the Christians wished not to preach the Gospel to the inhabitants of Florida until they had first conquered the whole,"

do much to throw light on the purpose and conduct of the expedition. The following reveals rather ironically as well his endeavor for accuracy.

> "It is not because I have not tried to learn the distances of the country, but I have not been able to get as exact a knowledge of them as I would wish; for the Spaniards did not think so much of learning the situation of places, as of hunting for gold and silver in Florida."

His book is imaginative, to be sure, and unreliable historically; but even its faults charm by the luxuriance of their fancy. Somehow, too, through all the intricacies of his vision we find true glimpses of the land. The Spaniards camped at times "in very pleasant pastures"; they discovered the plenty of the Mississippi country; in the town of Tula they found "many cowhides dressed with the hair on, and made use of them in the place of bed covers."[5]

The historians say that De Soto ardently desired that Florida, which is vast and fertile, should be inhabited by the Spaniards and especially by those who accompanied him, and that he resolved that he would send faithful persons to inform the inhabitants of Mexico, Cuba, and other countries, that in Florida they had discovered vast regions abounding in everything. Nevertheless the dream of magnificent hoards long submerged all else; and it is doubtful whether Spain ever realized the true significance of this overseas dominion.

---

[5] *History of the Conquest of Florida* tr. from Richlet's condensed French version in Barnard Shipp's *The History of Hernando de Soto and Florida.* 1881, 229 ff. Quot. 343, 325, 274, 421. Theodore Irving's *The Conquest of Florida by Hernando de Soto* (1835) is based largely upon Garcilasso de la Vega's book as is Grace King's *De Soto and His Men in the Land of Florida* (1898). See *Proceed. of the Miss. Val. Hist. Assoc.* V: 148 for an interesting evaluation of De Soto sources by J. R. Swanton and *Miss. Hist. Soc. Proc.* VII: 379ff. for one by T. H Lewis.

Meanwhile far to the north France was sending forth her pigmy handfuls to combat the barbaric distances of the West. Of her first period of indifference to the wealth overseas, of her spasmodic attempts at colonization in Brazil and Florida, of her fisheries and explorations along the coast, we need say nothing. For our purpose it is sufficient to note that slowly but steadily she gained a foothold in Canada; that from the barren waste of Sable Island, past the quiet bay of Tadoussac where the dark waters of the Saguenay, cold from the north, roll between its stern banks into the salt green of the St. Lawrence, along shores, now low, now steep, their tangled pines black against the mountains of the distance, the boats of the venturesome mariners bravely advanced — on to the jutting promontory of Quebec, higher still and higher, till the shelving La Chine rapids barricaded the way.

Even there they were not stopped for long. Champlain after sending out his young adventurer Brulé to winter with the Indians, in 1615 paddled with native guides along the fur trading route, visiting two of the great inland seas which were to prove such important highways to the interior, and describing them and the surrounding country in the clear, direct fashion of the explorer. He also mentions many Indian tribes prominent in middle western history, among them the Gens de Feu "who are distant ten days journey" and whose home later travellers were to find extraordinarily beautiful. His acuteness and sanity rendered his contributions to knowledge of the natives valuable; even more valuable, however, is his conception of the importance of further discoveries.[6]

Champlain's journal furnishes but the prologue, of course; the main drama of the progress to the Prairie and of the establishment there of the Gallic outposts is admirably summarized in the Thwaites series of *Jesuit Relations and Allied Documents* (73 v. 1896-1901). For the writing of a journal was one of the

---

6 *Orig. Narr. of Early Amer. Hist.* — *Voyages of Samuel de Champlain 1604-1618*, ed. by W. L. Grant. 1907. P. 312 Champlain stresses the need of men of means, leisure, and energy for western exploration, and p. 269 he concludes of his desire to obtain complete knowledge of New France that, "there is no better way than, disregarding all storms and difficulties, to have patience until His Majesty shall give the requisite attention to the matter, and meanwhile not only to continue the exploration of the country, but also to learn the language, and form relations and friendships with the leading men of the villages and tribes, in order to lay the foundations of a permanent edifice, as well for the glory of God as for the renown of the French." See p. 303 for mention of the Gens de Feu.

many duties of the laboring missionaries. These reports, transmitted to the superior in Quebec or Montreal, were from 1632 to 1673 combined by him, sometimes with few changes, sometimes with supplements from oral narratives, into a general account of the districts under his control published yearly in France. All are very simple, with the terseness and lack of adornment of men who must jot them down at night in filthy lodges, where smoke palled so thick that they questioned seriously whether the service of God would compel the sacrifice of eyesight, or away in the forest lest the hasty note-taking be interpreted as the casting of spells. But their very brevity gives them charm, and the deeds that they convey need no lustre of words. The intellects that created them were among the best of their century; trained in the severely logical schools of the order, adapted to the analysis and recording of situations at a glance, the Jesuits show in their *Relations* a thoroughness of comprehension of Indian nature, an acuteness of insight into economic and political problems that can be appreciated fully only today.

Their reaction to the land concerns us primarily — their expressions of emotion at the fruitful rolling country to the west and south. The first knowledge was hearsay — fragmentary accounts by trading Indians of the dangers of the route, lakes inconceivably large, great rivers, strange lands, and tribes far beyond their homes. To these as the black-robed fathers pushed farther into the wilderness were added still other accounts of the natives, facts from the priests' own experience, startlingly suggestive thumbnail sketches tucked in among descriptions of savage wars, struggles with the language, and insults of unwilling pupils, such as the following from the Mission to the Nadoussiouek.

> "There are people dwelling to the West of this place, toward the great river named Messipi. They are forty or fifty leagues from this place, in a country of prairies, rich in all kinds of game. They cultivate fields, sowing therein not Indian corn, but only tobacco; while Providence has furnished them a kind of marsh rye which they go and harvest toward the close of Summer in certain small lakes that are covered with it. So well do they know how to prepare it that

it is highly appetizing and very nutritious. They gave me some when I was at the head of Lake Tracy, where I saw them. They do not use muskets, but only bows and arrows, with which they shoot very skillfully. Their Cabins are not covered with bark, but with Deerskins, carefully dressed, and sewed together with such skill that the cold does not enter. These people are, above all the rest, savage and wild,—appearing abashed and as motionless as statues in our presence. Yet they are warlike, and have conducted hostilities against all their neighbors, by whom they are held in extreme fear. They speak a language that is utterly foreign, the Savages here not understanding it at all. Therefore I have been obliged to address them through an interpreter, who, being an infidel, did not accomplish what I might well have wished. Still I succeeded in wresting from the demon one innocent soul of that country,—a little child, who went to Paradise soon after I had baptized it. *A solis ortu usque ad occasum laudabile nomen Domini.* God will give us some opportunity to announce his word there, and glorify his holy Name, when it shall please his divine Majesty to show mercy to those people. They are well-nigh at the end of the earth, so they say. Farther toward the setting Sun there are nations named Karezi—beyond whom, they maintain, the earth is cut off, and nothing is to be seen but a great Lake whose waters are ill-smelling, for so they designate the Sea."

Especially the Iroquois "pushing their way farther down toward the South, without well knowing against whom they bear a grudge, seeking, they know not whom, and declaring war before they have any enemies" furthered the geographical knowledge of the fathers who had the dangerous mission among them. Nor were the priests themselves backward in the matter of exploration. Bancroft's oft quoted assertion that not a cape was turned, not a river entered, but a Jesuit led the way, although inaccurate, is suggestive. With the zeal of the crusaders spurring them on, with the zest for discovery that distinguished the fifteenth, the sixteenth, and seventeenth centuries, with absolute recklessness of self and a fine responsiveness that no austerity could subdue, they rank among our most excellent chroniclers.[7]

[7] *Jes. Rel.* LI:53-55, XLVII:143.

Illustration from the 1707 Dutch edition of Marquette's and Jolliet's Discovery

Most famous among them, perhaps, and certainly most interesting to us is the young priest, Jacques Marquette. His was the true explorer's instinct. In the very first of his letters as he records with rare humility his continuation of the labors of Father Allouez among the numerous tribes that resorted to Saint Esprit, he writes feelingly of his projected mission to the Illinois and the great river near them, which "If the Savages who promise to make me a Canoe do not break their word to me, we shall explore . . . as far as we can. . . ." This undertaking, so long deferred that he had given up all hope of succeeding in it, was brought to pass at last by the decision of Frontenac and Talon to send Jolliet thither. The account of the voyage in frail bark canoes of these two men "fully resolved to do and suffer everything for so glorious an Undertaking," is among the most valuable and the most moving of the documents printed by Thwaites. With a joy so great that it is almost pathetic Marquette records his delight at "This good news, since I saw my plans were about to be accomplished; and since I found myself in the blessed necessity of exposing my life for the salvation of all these peoples. . . ."

Of the trip this fervor is the keynote. In the priest's narrative there is not the cultivation of the men whose self-immolation in surroundings which to every fibre were torture cry martyrdom to us, not the grace of an artist, but the happiness of a boy on a thrilling adventure. This naïve delight rising at times into the purest of apostolic flames, throughout the long journey sensitized his reaction to the wonders about him. The plenty of the wild oats country, the beauty of the Meskousing, the painted rock monsters and the other wonders of the Mississippi, all find in him a sympathetic, we might almost say a too impressionable chronicler. In general, however, his narrative is exceedingly conscientious. Of the general topography of the Mississippi he gives an excellent idea. His account of the customs of the Illinois, of the traces of iron mines, of the bison, and of the peculiarities in appearance and deeds of the Southern Indians, shows him a skilled observer; and his conjecture as to the means of finding the Vermillion or California sea reveals his fitness for the task of explorer. Of the land especially he gives a vivid picture. As we read of the journey between shores constantly varied — "prairies extending farther than the eye can see," lofty trees bordering the river although "the great numbers of wild cattle, which we heard bellowing, lead us to believe that The prairies are near," farther down the graceful canes through which flit many-colored parroquets, with game and fruit in abundance — small wonder, we think, if the travellers found such territories verification of the mediaeval traditions of an Earthly Paradise. But the epochal journey had to come to an end. The evident proximity of the Spaniards, and the probable hostility of their native allies, the conclusion that "beyond a doubt, the Missisipi river discharges into the florida or Mexican gulf," all made advisable a decision to return.[8]

This first voyage, however, marked only the beginning of the Jesuit accounts of the midland. The country of the Illinois, was visited again by the priest to establish the mission he had dreamed of so long. The scenes in which on "a beautiful prairie" he preached to the natives and by two masses, "the only sacrifices ever offered there to God, he took possession of that land in the name of Jesus Christ" are among the most impressive in the history of the church in the West; and his death in the forest, devoted as his life, moved even the priestly chronicler to unusual rhetorical heights. Following it, Allouez set out from De Pere to continue the work of Marquette. His journal of his voyage, the third one to the Illinois, and of his arrival when he at once began to instruct them in the very cabin in which Marquette had lodged, is among the most reliable records of this yet primeval region. Of the loveliness of the landscape and of the reverence with which it filled almost all who looked upon it, the following passage may give illustration.

> "We proceeded, continuing always to coast along the great prairies, which extend farther than the eye can reach. Trees are met with from time to time, but they are so placed that they seem to have been planted with design, in order to make avenues more pleasing to the eye than those of orchards. The base of these trees is often watered by little streamlets, at which are seen large herds of stags and hinds refreshing themselves, and peacefully feeding upon the short grass. We

8 *Jes. Rel.* LIV: 189-91, LIX: 91, 91, 103, 149, 159. The Account of the discovery was first pub. 1681. For a description of the various editions see *Jes. Rel.* LIX: 294-9.

> followed these vast plains for 20 leagues and repeated many times, 'Benedicite opera Domini Domino.' "

And from then on until 1781 when the death of Father Meurin closed the work of the order in the Northwest, the letters, journals, and reports of the hard-working priests built up a clear concept of the land.

The nature of the accounts was determined in part, of course, by conditions. Problems of transportation, for instance, hindered much consideration of the minerals in spite of the fact that the masses of copper on Lake Superior and the possibility of iron were early discussed. The question of livelihood was much more important. For men who had stumbled many years after the famishing tribes of the North with only the inner bark of trees as a stew in the evening or who had subsisted on the gluey black of rock tripe after hours of paddling on the wintry lakes, the plenty of the lands bordering the Mississippi meant inconceivably much. Over and over again are mentioned the abundance of game and the fruitfulness of the soil. Sometimes this is true to such an extent that it is amusing, witness Allouez' account of the food of the Illinois.

> "They live on indian corn and other fruits of the earth, which they cultivate, like the other savages, on the prairies. They eat 14 kinds of roots, which they find in the prairies; they made me eat some and I found them good and very sweet. They Gather from trees and plants 42 different kinds of fruits, all of which are excellent; and catch 25 sorts of fish — among them, the eel. They Hunt the roebuck, the bison, the Turkey, the Wildcat, a species of tiger, and other animals; they Reckon up 22 kinds of these, and some 40 kinds of game and birds."

More often, however, the situation is pathetic. After the gloom of the vast forests where the sun never penetrated and where the possibility of a horrible death lurked always near, the brightness of these grassy meadows afforded ineffable relief. The comparative moderation of the climate, the abundance of food and the ease with which it was obtained, resulted in a high level of intelligence among the savages. The wandering plain tribes, too, whose lives the buffalo made comfortable, showed a hospitality and simplicity that seem unbelievable today. But the thing that moved the missionaries most, seemingly, was the physical charm of the land — the sheer loveliness of leagues of rippling grass and sun-bright flowers, dark bandings of trees, and rivers of enchanting smoothness. On every page it is touched upon, often apparently involuntarily. For these churchly chronicles, so simple in language that the speech-figures of the whole may be counted on the fingers never fail to give some enhancing adjective. "*Pleasant meadows,*" "*a fruitful champayne country,*" "*vast plains stretching farther than the eye can reach,*" these and similar expressions are repeated almost continually. Not until the first fine fervor has a bit worn off do we find words of disparagement, and then they are comparatively slight. On the whole the general traditions among the missionaries seem summed up in the words of Dablon on his journey to the Fire Nation.

> "If the country of this Nation somewhat resembles an earthly Paradise in beauty, the way leading to it may also be said to bear some likeness to the one depicted by our Lord as leading to Heaven."[9]

There were other priests than the Jesuits, however, and of these no one presents a more curious figure or gives a more influential account of the region of the Mississippi than the Recollect friar, Father Louis Hennepin, whose life and writings furnish an extraordinary example of the restless craving for adventure that typifies his age. He says the records of the early missionaries aroused in him "a desire of tracing their Footsteps, and dedicating myself after their Example, to the Glory of God, and the Salvation of Souls." Probably the wanderlust, which caused him to sculk "behind the doors of Victualling Houses, to hear the Sea-men give an Account of their Adventures," was responsible, however, for his setting sail for the beckoning shores of the new continent. There in 1678 he received the formal command of the Recollect provincial to journey with La Salle.[10]

It is the account of this trip in the book, *Description de la Louisiane* (1683) that won for Hennepin fame. At the very

9 *Jes. Rel.* LIX:189, 191, LX:157, 161-3, LV:191.
10 Hennepin, Louis — *A New Discovery of a Vast Country in America* ed. by R. G. Thwaites. 2v. 1903. I: 28, 30.

beginning he shows the difference between himself and his predecessor Marquette, for he is boastful, vain, of a nature far less sensitive and noble. The accounts of the expedition itself are too warped for us to heed save for the few striking sketches he paints — La Salle, for instance, in scarlet coat trimmed with gold going to church with his men while outside the first sailing vessel on the Great Lakes rides at anchor amid a fleet of bark canoes. With his account of the country, however, the matter is different. If for nothing else he would be remembered for the fact that he was the first man to describe in a published narrative the vast cataract of Niagara and the falls of St. Anthony. The accounts were exaggerated, to be sure, in accordance with his usual custom, but in his descriptions of the prairie country we feel a real ring of sincerity. The immense herds of bison seem to have impressed him especially, for he says, "These vast countries are so full of prairies, that it seems this is the element and country of the buffalo." About them he gives very interesting information, not only describing clearly their appearance but mentioning the buffalo trails, picturing the Indian method of hunting by fire, and discussing the use of the beasts.

Nor does he neglect other natural phenomena. We are assured that,

> "Many other kinds of animals are found in these vast plains of Louisiana, stags, deer, beaver and otter are common there, geese, swans, turtles, poules d'inde, parrots, partridges, and many other birds swarm there, the fishery is very abundant, and the fertility of the soil is extraordinary."

For further proof of the richness of this territory,

> "There are boundless prairies interspersed with forests of tall trees, where there are all sorts of building timber, and among the rest excellent oak full like that in France and very different from that in Canada. The trees are of prodigious girth and height, and you could find the finest pieces in the world for ship building. . . . Several kinds of fruit trees are also to be seen in the forests and wild grape vines which produce clusters about a foot and a half long. . . ."

All this wonderland is named for the king, Hennepin states after unctuous flattery, making sure of his majesty's favor by concluding "that the soil is capable of producing all kinds of fruits, herbs, and grain, and in greater abundance than the best lands in Europe" and that "by cultivating the ground, people could subsist there from the second year, independent of provisions from Europe," with other still more glowing promises. The lively style, the vividness of the description of the country and of the manners of the inhabitants made the book immediately popular.[11]

Unfortunately, however, Hennepin was not content with this first success. The egotism and pride that had caused La Salle to send home word that the mendicant was prone to exaggerate and to portray things as he wished them to be,[12] and that had made the friar refuse credit to La Salle, Tonty, Du Lhut, and his companion Michael Ako, all far better men than he, now prompted him to more extreme measures. In 1697 he brought forth at Utrecht another book — *Nouvelle Découverte d'un très grand Pays, situé dans l'Amérique. . . .* In this not satisfied with establishing the conception that he alone had formulated the project of exploring the Mississippi, he actually makes the astonishing statement that he, after leaving Crêvecoeur, had journeyed to the mouth of the Mississippi, from there returning and with his companions making the explorations to the north described in *Louisiane.* The falsity of this contention, contradicting as it does Hennepin's earlier statements, manifestly impossible from his own dates, and supported by the flimsiest of excuses for his long silence, it is useless to discuss. The book seems to have been accepted as a guide, however, by such a man as Iberville, and with the non-critical public it gained an immediate vogue, surely an indication of the interest felt by all Europe in this great new region, the heart of America. Of the portions with which Hennepin was familiar the description was good enough. The experiences in the country to the South, however, appropriated bodily as they are from the narrative of Membré, have a clumsiness and artificiality even more pronounced in the later plagiarism *Nouveau Voyage d'un Païs plus*

11 Hennepin, Louis — *A Description of Louisiana* tr. by J. G. Shea, 1880. 145, 149, 149, 150, 150, 151. For English jealousy of the French discoveries and the missionaries' part therein see *Doc. Rel. to the Col. Hist. of the State of N. Y.* V: 620-1.

12 Margry, Pierre — *Découvertes et établissements des Français dans l'ouest et dans le sud de l'Amérique Septentrionale* (1614-1754). 6 v. 1879-1888. II: 259-60.

*grand que l'Europe* (1698). This latter volume is a mere makeshift attempt to profit by the author's earlier popularity. At the same time was published in London an English arrangement of Hennepin's travels, which combined his two latest volumes with some additional matter under the title of *A New Discovery of a Vast Country in America.* The remainder of the friar's life seems to have been a discredited one, spent in part in an endeavor to return to the wonderland of the West.

In spite of the fact that Hennepin had given us some of the most readable accounts of the Mississippi country as it was first visited by the French, it is a relief to turn from his braggart pretensions to the sincerity of Father Membré, from whose narrative in the quickly suppressed *Établissement de la Foy* . . . (1691) he drew.[13] Membré, like Hennepin, in his veracious and unassuming narrative praises highly the land, "good land, capable of supporting great colonies"; like the former, too, he comments on the abundance of game and fruit. He describes La Salle's ceremony of taking possession and gives a clear conception of the various Indian tribes — the Illinois "wandering, idle, fearful, and dissolute," the pomp of the Taensa. The Natchez, whom Membré mentions briefly and whose customs resembled those of the Taensa, appealed more strongly than any other tribe to the imaginations of the French, and descriptions of them were soon incorporated in the romantic tradition. A long line of writers commencing with the party of La Salle and culminating with Chateaubriand, take up this semi-tropical material, some painting the life of the natives in the most glowing of colors, others politely giving their predecessors the lie. The interest is natural, for although the southern tribes' simple cane buildings were far removed from the golden temples of the Incas, they did represent the highest known civilization of the North American Indians, and their mild and fertile country did permit realization of that concept of savage life Arcadian which long enthralled the imagination.

Father Membré, in direct contrast to Hennepin, makes La

13 Le Clercq, Father Christian — *First Establishment of the Faith in New France* tr. by J. G. Shea. 2v. 1881. Parallel passages from Membré and Hennepin may be found in Sparks' *Life of La Salle.* 1844. Ap. III. p. 168ff. For description of the Taensa see Le Clercq. II: 170 ff, also Margry — *Découvertes et établissements.* I: 567, 600-1. For tribute to the land see Le Clercq. II: 190 and adjacent pages; for description of the Illinois, *Ibid.* 134.

Salle stand out always the great leader of the expedition. By his and others' accounts plus state documents and letters we can trace most of the explorer's career in America — his first journey to the south through the plenty of the smiling land the priests called the "Paradis terrestre du Canada"; his romantic descent of the great river; the founding of the ill-fated gulf colony; and the beginning of the long trip overland. Almost all tend to reveal the greatness of the commander, and all unite in praises of the land. Passages of this latter type, although they contain nothing new, interest us because of the writers — practical men who would stake a good deal for success but who were not moved by undue enthusiasm. Like their forerunners, however, over Louisiana they burst into rhapsody. Douay pencilled his admiration of the territory through which the remnants of the La Salle party passed on their long journey northward.

> "These are the finest and most fertile countries in the world; the soil, which there produces two crops of every kind of grain a year, being ready to receive the plough. From time to time there are vast prairies where the grass is ten or twelve feet high at all seasons; . . . No settler arriving in the country will not find at first enough to support plenteously a large family, or will not, in less than two years' time, be as comfortably settled as in any place in Europe. . . . There might be a very great trade there in all kinds of peltries, tobacco, and cotton. Hemp grows very fine; and as the plains are full of mulberry-trees, which also line the rivers, silk might be raised in abundance. Sugar-canes will succeed there well, and could be easily got by trade with the West Indies, as the European nations have done in Terra-firma, where they are neighbors to Louisiana. Besides the great quantity of wool with which the cattle of the country are loaded, the vast prairies everywhere afford means of raising flocks of sheep, which produce twice a year."

Through the choppy sentences and crude phrasing of Nicolas de la Salle shines his admiration for so fruitful a country, and his enthusiasm is re-echoed in a tone more subdued and cultured in the account of Jean Cavelier, who in spite of the assassination of his brother and the perils that surrounded him had yet a thought for the beautiful prairies studded with little groves at intervals.[14]

The reaction of La Salle himself is, of course, of special interest. As the explorer writes to defend himself from the charges of his enemies or the criticism of his backers, as he chronicles difficulties and discouragements, we get a most poignant glimpse of the hardships of his life, little realized today, and of the gripping quality of the man that made him persist in his project, no matter what stood in his way.[15] Whatever his discouragements, however, when he touches upon the hinterland for which he had such intense enthusiasm his struggles seem repaid; he constantly stresses the ease of colonizing such a country; letters and official records form some of our most impressive memorials to the wealth and beauty of the prairie country.

> "The number of bison is almost beyond belief. I have seen twelve hundred killed in eight days by a single band of Savages. . . . This country is as beautiful and as fertile as Canada is lacking in these qualities. There are not only vast fields of the best land in the world, all ready for cultivation, but in damp places, a quantity of very excellent hemp which I have tested in rope and which is larger than, and as good as, that of France and rots less in the water. The experiments which have been made with French grain and all sorts of vegetables have been very successful. The Indian corn and the tobacco there are of extraordinary size, although what Jolliet said about their sowing two crops is false. . . ."[16]

Many of these La Salle papers were unpublished at the time they were written, having been made accessible to us today by

---

14 Le Clercq. — *First Estab. of the Faith.* II: 278-81. For a typical comment by Nicolas de la Salle see Margry I: 550.

15 It is interesting to note that on his first trip La Salle is described as having "bien de la chaleur pour ces entreprises." Margry — *Découvertes et établissements.* I: 87. He gives the best description of his life, however, when requesting a representative from his backers. "Il n'est pas besoin qu'il soit fort savant, mais fidèle, de fatigue, et qu'il n'aime ny le jeu, ny les femmes, ny la bonne chère, parce qu'il ne trouvera rien de cela avec moy, . . ." (*Ibid.* II:69) and again "Depuis que je suis icy, je n'ay eu ny valets, ny habits, ny cuisine qui ne ressentent plustot la bassesse que le faste, et dès que je verray le moindre rebut out de vostre costé ou du costé de la Cour, je vous asseure que je quitteray tout là, n'y ayant point d'autre attrait à la vie que je mène que celuy de l'honneur, dont je croy ces sortes d'entreprises d'autant plus dignes qu'il y a plus de péril et de peine." *Ibid.* II: 83. See, also, the Memoir for Seignelay where he summarizes his efforts. *Ibid.* III: 18.

16 Margry — *Découvertes et établissements.* II: 244. Similar tributes may be found *Ibid.*, 170, etc.

the careful work of Margry. The journals of two of his followers, however, must be singled out for attention because of their contemporary influence. Joutel's is of especial interest because of the personal ties between him and his commander and because of his candor and modesty. Its greatest praise from an historical point of view was early given by Sieur de Mitchell "who methodiz'd this Journal."

> "We do not pretend here to Criticize upon the Work of Father Hennepin, or that of Monsieur Tonty; but even their own favourers cannot take it ill that this Author does not sometimes say as they do; that he plainly delivers what he saw, and that he exposes to publicke View all the Truths he was an Eye Witness to, without magnifying or inventing."

His journal is valuable, moreover, aside from the light which it throws on the striking figure of the stern commander, as a travel narrative. His humor finds free play in his account of the savages' strange customs, and a genuine feeling for nature manifests itself in his panoramic sketch of the wide-spreading plains and his vivid suggestion of the untrammeled blossoms.[17]

Valuable as is his account, however, far fewer contemporary allusions are made to it than to the work to which Mitchell disparagingly referred — the *Dernières Découvertes dans l'Amérique Septentrionale de M. de la Sale* (1697), which was disavowed by Tonti shortly after its publication.[18] The authentic memoirs of this picturesque leader with the iron hand possess strong appeal by virtue of the simplicity with which he records adventures and hardships, the journey, for instance, during which he and his men lived on wild garlic grubbed up from the snow. His resourcefulness and independence, moreover, give extraordinary force to his praise of the land he explored such as the close of the *Memoir of 1693.*

> "I cannot describe the beauty of all the countries I have mentioned. If I had a better knowledge of them, I should be better able to say what special advantages might be derived

17 Joutel, Henri — *Journal of La Salle's Last Voyage.* Reprint of first Eng. tr. 1714 with the map of the original French ed. 1713. Caxton Club. 1896. French — *Hist. Coll. of La.* I: 85ff. gives a translation, also. Margry prints a fuller version of the Joutel manuscript. III: 91ff.

18 Margry — IV: 365.

from them. As for the Mississippi, it could produce every year 20,000 *ecus'* worth of peltries, an abundance of lead, and wood for ship-building; a silk trade might be established there, and a port for the protection of vessels and the maintenance of a communication with the Gulf of Mexico. Pearls might be found there. If wheat will not grow at the lower end of the river, the upper country would furnish it; and the islands might be supplied with every thing they need, such as planks, vegetables, grain, and salt beef. If I had not been hurried in making this narrative, I should have stated many circumstances which would have gratified the reader, but the loss of my notes during my travels is the reason why this relation is not such as I could have wished."[19]

The pseudo-Tonti relation, however, was the work which exerted great influence in his own time in spite of the fact that it is too inaccurate to be of historic value today. The mere fact that a hack writer would adapt a journal of the kind and forge Tonti's name serves, nevertheless, to reveal wide-spread interest in the discoveries.

Turning from the La Salle party, we find scattered over the early period of French occupation a most picturesque group of explorers, free lances as it were, men who went alone into the great woods and over the fresh water seas in pursuit of riches in furs, power on the frontier, stirring adventure. Probably the most important of these from the point of view of geography and also most representative of the new world itself was the young French Canadian, Louis Jolliet. Mentioned at various times, almost always with praise, as a student and wanderer in the marshy lowlands and down-hanging forests around the Great Lakes, he is described as a person excellently fitted for exploring the Mississippi.[20] Unfortunately because of the wreck which befell him after "he had safely passed more than forty rapids"[21]

---

19 French — *Hist. Coll. of La.* I: 78 and *Ill. Hist. Coll.* I: 164. See also Margry — *Relations et Mémoires Inédits*, 1867, pp. 1-36. Margry prints Tonti's relation of 1864, in his *Découvertes et établissements*, I:573 ff. Tr. by M. B. Anderson, pub. by Caxton Club. 1898. *Relation de la Louisianne et du Mississipi par le Chevalier de Tonti, governeur du Fort Saint Louis, aux Ilinois*, a reprint of the *Dernières Découvertes*, is found in J. F. Bernard's *Relations de la Louisiane, et du fleuve Mississippi.* 1720, and in his *Recueil de Voyages au Nord*, which went through several editions.

20 Margry — I: 255, 263.

21 *Jes Rel.* LVIII: 93.

he has been unjustly deprived of much of the credit of the expedition, and the chart and journal which we today covet have long ago rotted beneath the swirling waters of the St. Lawrence. His oral report has, however, been preserved to us and is important enough to be quoted in part.

> "At first, when we were told of these treeless lands, I imagined that it was a country ravaged by fire, where the soil was so poor that it could produce nothing. But we have certainly observed the contrary; and no better soil can be found, either for corn, for vines, or for any other fruit whatever."
>
> * * * * * * *
>
> "There are prairies three, six, ten, and twenty leagues in length, and three in width, surrounded by forests of the same extent; beyond these, the prairies begin again, so that there is as much of one sort of land as of the other. Sometimes we saw the grass very short, and, at other times, five or six feet high; hemp, which grows naturally there, reaches a height of eight feet.
>
> "A settler would not there spend ten years in cutting down and burning the trees; on the very day of his arrival, he could put his plough into the ground." [22]

So enthusiastic an account by one long used to the discouragements of the wilderness can only make us wish still more for the lost journal of this first Canadian youth to go down the Mississippi.

We do possess fascinating traces, however, of still earlier Frenchmen skimming the leagues of roughened water to the West. The *Jesuit Relations* give us a most picturesque legend — Nicolet wearing a magnificent robe of damask, strewn with flowers and birds of many colors, going forth with confident heart to meet the Chinese and Japanese who had been evolved from the Indian tales of People of the Sea, of hairless traders who journeyed in great canoes. His dreams of bowing mandarins and of Oriental luxury must have been rudely shattered as the naked savages fled screaming from the man who carried

---

22 *Jes. Rel.* LVIII: 105 and 107. For Frontenac's report of Jolliet's return, see *Margry* I:257 ff., and *Doc. rel. to the Col. Hist. of the State of N. Y.* IX:121.

thunder in his hands. Unquestionably his voyage was an epic one. By it a Frenchman had for the first time pierced to the fastnesses of the Northwest. About his nation of gift bearers and wonder workers he must have left with the savages legends as romantic as those we associate with his trip. He pointed the way for later discoveries; and in his solitary penetration of inland sea and tangled forest he made himself one of the most picturesque of those isolated figures with which the literature of exploration in the midlands is filled.[23]

Perhaps impelled by some lingering reminiscences of Nicolet's trip, as well as by the allurements of the "wild men" who brought every year tales of great waters, mysterious peoples, and game untold, the brothers-in-law Radisson and Grosseilliers sought permission of the governor to visit with the trading fleets this wonderful land. Their experiences Radisson has preserved for us in what seems in many ways the quaintest record we have of early America. His naïveté, the very imperfections of his English, his emotional range, all give his journals unique charm. In his pilgrimage through the untracked wilderness he was unoppressed by the sorrow of the missionaries at seeing lost so many souls, yet he had the childlike faith in God which is found today in remote portions of Quebec. Eight days, for instance, he was so tormented with rheumatism he thought never to recover; "at last by means that God and my brother did use, w[ch] was by rubbing my legs w[th] hott oyle of bears and keeping my thigh and leggs well tyed, it came to its former strength." The woodland party he strikingly etches for us—"By this you may see the boldnesse of those buzards that think themselves hectors when they see but their shadowes, & tremble when they see a Iroquoit"; he portrays their hardships.

> "We had scarce to eat a bitt of sault meat. It was pitty to see our feete & leggs in blood by drawing our boats through the swift streames, where the rocks have such sharp points that there is nothing but death could make men doe what we did."

He recognizes the credulity of the natives ("We weare wellcomed & much made of, saying we weare the Gods & devils of the

---

23 *Jes. Rel.* XXIII: 275-9. Margry—I: 47 ff. The voyage of Nicolet has been much discussed by historians. See especially *Wis. Hist. Coll.*

earth.''), but he shows no trace of condescension; and his description of the terrible famine of the Indians is of its kind unexcelled. Driven by the harshness of the winter, the ''churchyard'' gloom of the surroundings, the covetousness and cowardice of the wandering Octanaks he bursts into the denunciations of a Puritan divine, then sinks into the pathos of the morning spectacle of death.

> ''O yee poore people, you shall have their booty, but you shall pay dearly for it. Everyone cryes out for hungar; the women become baren and drie like wood. You men must eate the cord, being you have no more strength to make use of the bow. Children, you must die. ffrench, you called yourselves Gods of the earth, that you should be feared, for your interest; notwithstanding you shall tast of the bitternesse, and too happy if you escape. Where is the time past? Where is the plentynesse that yee had in all places and countreys? Here comes a new family of these poore people dayly to us, halfe dead, for they have but the skin & boans. How shall we have strength to make a hole in the snow to lay us downe, seeing we have it not to hale our racketts after us, nor to cutt a little wood to make a fire to keepe us from the rigour of the cold, w$^{ch}$ is extreame in those countreyes in its season. Oh, if the musick that we heare could give us recreation, we wanted not any lamentable musicke nor sad spectacle. In the morning the husband looks uppon his wife, y$^{e}$ Brother his sister, the cozen the cozen, the Oncle the nevew, that weare for the most part found deade. They languish w$^{th}$ cryes & hideous noise that it was able to make the haire starre on y$^{e}$ heads that have any apprehension. Good God, have mercy on so many poore innocent people, and of us that acknowledge thee, that having offended thee punishes us.''

In happier times he shows ever the vivacity and whimsical gaiety which made the French such successful wood-rovers.

> ''Our songs being finished, we began our teeth to work.''
>
> ''The last guift was in generall for al y$^{e}$ women to love us and give to eat when we should come to their cottages.''

But with all their lightness of spirit and their joy in the woods, the two men were most conscientious and modest about their work of exploration. In spite of the fact that they realized and made evident their own worth, the glory of their discovery they attributed partly to providence.

> "Those great lakes had not so soone comed to our knowledge if it had not ben for those brutish people; two men had not found out y$^{e}$ truth of these seas so cheape; the interest and the glorie could not doe what terror doth att y$^{e}$ end."

Consistently, too, Radisson shows a regard for accuracy that makes his observations valuable. Hearsay evidence he gives as such; scenes which he has witnessed he sketches with a wealth of realistic detail. There are few accounts more suggestive of the Indians' primitive splendor than the passage describing the assembly of the plainsmen.

> "The day following they arrived w$^{th}$ an incredible pomp. This made me thinke of y$^{e}$ Intrance y$^{t}$ y$^{e}$ Polanders did in Paris, saving that they had not so many Jewells, but instead of them they had so many feathers. The ffirst weare yong people w$^{th}$ their bows and arrows and Bucklers on their shoulders, uppon w$^{ch}$ weare represented all manner of figures, according to their knowledge, as of y$^{e}$ sun and moone, of terrestriale beasts, about its feathers very artificialy painted. Most of the men their faces weare all over dabbed w$^{th}$ severall collours. Their hair turned up like a Crowne, and weare cutt very even, but rather so burned, for the fire is their cicers. They leave a tuff of haire upon their crowne of their heads, tye it, and putt at y$^{e}$ end of it some small pearles or some Turkey stones, to bind their heads. . ."

And as vividly as he had sketched the savage welcomers, Radisson outlines the countries and lakes he and his brother-in-law had found. By the desire for exploration the two were always driven on.

> "We were then possessed by the hurrons and Octanac; but our minde was not to stay in an island, but be knowne w$^{th}$ the remotest people."

Therefore they went to the "great and filthy lake of the Hurons," through the sterile lands of the north, down to the plenty of Superior and the regions farther south. There in forests so thick "that it was in some places as dark as in a cellar, by reason of the boughs of the trees" they hunted the "eland $w^{ch}$ is a mighty strong beast, much like a mule, having a tayle cut off 2 or 3 or 4 thumbes long, the foot cloven like a stagge," and the "Buff, a furious animal, of which one must have care, for every yeare he kills some Nadoueseronons." No famine now for the wanderers! One place Radisson compared to the "Buttery of Paris, ffor the great quantity of meat that they use to have there"; everywhere, however, there was plenty.

> "From this place we went along the coasts, $w^{ch}$ are most delightfull and wounderous, for it's nature that made it so pleasant to the eye, the sperit, and the belly."

Ambassadors from the Nadoueseronons, the "Nation of the Beefe," came to greet them with elaborate ceremonies; their treeless plains where "they have no wood, and make provision of mosse for their firing," and their skin tepees, the two Frenchmen visited. "Meddows" they found, too, "that weare squared, and 10 leagues as smooth as a boord." In short, after having spent in their two voyages more than five years in the West Radisson and Grosseilliers went back to civilization grieving that,

> "$y^e$ world could not discover such inticing countrys to live in. This I say because that the Europeans fight for a rock in the sea against one another, or for a sterill land and horrid country, that the people sent heere or there by the changement of the aire ingenders sicknesse and dies thereof. Contrarywise those kingdoms are so delicious & under so temperat a climat, plentifull of all things, the earth bringing foorth its fruit twice a yeare, the people live long & lusty & wise in their way. What conquest would that bee att litle or no cost; what laborinth of pleasure should millions of people have, instead that millions complaine of misery & poverty! What should not men reape out of the love of God in converting the souls heere, . . . It's true, I confesse, that the accesse is difficult, but must say that we are like the Cockscombs of Paris, when first they begin to have wings, imagining that the larks will fall in thir mouths roasted; but we ought [to remember]

that vertue is not acquired w^th^out labour & taking great paines." [24]

Somewhat akin to these daring explorers is the striking figure of Nicholas Perrot, fur trader, interpreter, manager of the Sault Ste. Marie pageant, and commandant of the Northwest, who for thirty-five years wielded enormous influence among the western tribes. Only the end of his life was quiet, the last years of it being spent at Montreal where he wrote his *Mémoire sur les Moeurs, Coustumes et Relligion des Sauvages de l'Amérique Septentrionale.* This in manuscript till 1864 when Reverend Jules Tailhan published it in Paris has been translated in accessible form in Miss Emma Blair's *Indian Tribes of the Upper Mississippi and Region of the Great Lakes* (1911) as have been the parts of La Potherie's *Histoire de l'Amérique Septentrionale* apparently based largely on the lost journals of Perrot.

The value of the information he gives us is very great. To the Jesuits the central valley was "a fine battle-field for those who intend to enter the lists and fight for Jesus Christ." To Perrot, on the other hand, although he had no illusions about it, it was the country of romance, the sombre forests and dry buffalo plains of which absorbed the best efforts of his life. His discussion of the relative providence and the means of subsistence of the various tribes bears the authority of one who has eaten and slept and worked among them; he gives accurate description of practically all the peoples inhabiting the Great Lakes region. On the whole he seems unprejudiced; although he can recognize the better qualities of these denizens of forest and plain, his books are sprinkled with penetrating criticism. The keynote of his work, in fact, is found in his statement about the savages, "In order to succeed with them, it is necessary to know how to manage them; otherwise it is difficult to do anything with them."

And in his accounts of his management we find as much illumination of the savage nature as in the direct descriptions. The figurative speech that was an indispensable accompaniment of all treaty making is scarcely less glowing in these chronicles of the

---

24 *Voyages of Peter Esprit Radisson* . . . ed. by G. D. Scull. Prince Soc. Pub. 1885. 134, 222, 138, 185, 148, 203-4 215, 217, 187-8, 211, 147-8, 134, 156, 156, 156, 217, 189, 207, 220, 191, 150-1. See also *Jes. Rel.* for 1660, repr. by Margry — Découvertes et établissements. I: 53-5.

French frontier than in the later novels of Cooper which were to arouse much criticism; the devices used to induce submission in the savages like the threat to burn the water of the wild oats country enforced by means of blazing brandy, are as picturesque as the speech. Both owe their success to the fact that they are a reflection of the Indian habits of thought; the Gallic imagination entered into and heightened the naïve natural symbolism of the Indian.

Just as Perrot's speech and acts constantly embody the reflexes of savage minds, so he sees through savage eyes the strange new world that surrounds him. It is the Indian, accustomed to privation, daily struggle for his bread, that speaks in the account of the resources of the prairie beginning,

> "The savage peoples who inhabit the prairies have life-long good-fortune; animals and birds are found there in great numbers, with numberless rivers abounding in fish,"

and again,

> "I have already remarked that the savages of the prairies live in a happy land on account of the great number of animals of all kinds that they have about them, and the grains, fruits, and roots which the soil there produces in abundance. . . ."

Perrot gives, to be sure, the ordinary traveller's explanation of the phenomena of a strange land as,

> "The Illinois and their neighbors have no lack of wood for drying their meat; but the Ayoës and the Panys generally use only the well-dried dung of the buffaloes, as wood is extremely scarce among them."

It is, however, his shadowings of Indian opinions of the land that have greatest value, these rising to their height in his account of the native beliefs about the country of the dead. Naturally stress was laid on physical satisfaction in the hereafter; the beautiful country which affords it was unconsciously modelled upon that most fruitful land known to all tribes — the North American prairie. The phenomena there are those mentioned by early visitors to the region of the Mississippi — "a beautiful and fertile land" where the climate is neither hot nor cold, but agreeably temperate. "They say that that land abounds with animals and birds of every kind, and that the hunters while going through it are never in danger of hunger, having only to choose what animals they will attack, to obtain food." The souls pass a river which "abounds with fish, more in number than can be imagined," and they enter finally "a delightful country, in which excellent fruits are found in abundance; and the ground seems to be covered with all kinds of flowers, the odor of which is so admirable that it delights their hearts and charms their imaginations."[25]

The whole work of Perrot with its flashes of humor, its tribute to striking figures among Indians and French, and its picturesque sketches is extraordinarily fascinating. Even more interesting, however, is the *New Voyages to North America* of Louis-Armand, Baron de Lahontan, who in 1683 at the age of seventeen was sent to New France. After various adventures in the East he went, in charge of a detachment, to take command of Fort St. Joseph. At first the beauty of the lake country and the adventurous freedom of the life there gratified him. A rigorous winter and the knowledge that his personal affairs were in an almost irreparable state increased his natural restlessness. He spent the ensuing summer in a series of wanderings, and, having abandoned his post, from Missilimakinak he announced to a friend his decision "to travel through the Southern Countries that I have so often heard of," for "I cannot mew my self up here all this Winter." Then follows in his published manuscript the much discussed account of the fabulous River Long. His later years were changing ones, spent now in France, now in Canada, or in drifting over the old world; always he was dogged, however, by the ill fate and injustice that made him early a cynic.

In one way we may be thankful, nevertheless, for the misfortunes of this talented man; without them there is no doubt that this vivacious correspondence of many years would never have

25 Blair — *Ind. Tribes.* I:252, 113, 119, 124-5, 89, 90, 91. Perrot's work is particularly valuable because so few men of his type left a full personal record. Daniel Greysolon Du Lhut, so-called king of the coureurs-de-bois, who characteristically tells that he undertook the exploration of the country of the Nadouecioux because it was believed to be impossible (Margry — *Découvertes et établissements* VI:20 ff.), although he is one of the bravest figures in the early West has for this reason little interest for the student of literature.

been published, as it was under financial stress in Holland, 1703. Shortly after the Dutch printing Lahontan, under the patronage of the Duke of Devonshire, issued an English translation with some additions. The popularity of the book was immediate and wide-spread; that it was one of the most influential volumes of early travel is evident in its bibliography. The secret of its success it is not hard to find. Keenness of observation, unusual independence and soundness of judgment, a breezy vigor, and forcefulness of figure and epigrammatic statement all combine even now to give the book exceptional vitality.

To the descriptions of the land itself Lahontan adds little. His running comments on the territory are interesting, however, and at times he gives rather extended descriptions like the following.

> "The Lake *Errié* is justly dignified with the illustrious name of *Conti*; for assuredly 'tis the finest Lake upon Earth. You may judge of the goodness of the Climate from the Latitudes of the Countries that surround it. Its Circumference extends to two hundred and thirty Leagues; but it affords every where such a charming Prospect, that its Banks are deck'd with Oak-Trees, Elms, Chestnut-Trees, Walnut-Trees, Apple-Trees, Plum-Trees, and Vines which bear their fine clusters up to the very top of the Trees, upon a sort of ground that lies as smooth as one's hand. Such Ornaments as these, are sufficient to give rise to the most agreeable *Idea* of a Landskip in the World. I cannot express what vast quantities of Deer and Turkeys are to be found in these Woods, and in the vast Meads that lye upon the South side of the Lake. At the bottom of the Lake, we find wild beeves upon the Banks of two pleasant rivers that disembogue into it, without Cataracts or rapid Currents. It abounds with Sturgeon and white Fish. . ."

In the account of the Long River, moreover, fabricated though it is in the main, are found indisputable traces of hunting trips in the North and of real explorers' tales. The fertility of the soil is touched upon as usual; the Indian banquet is typical; he shows the banks of the Wisconsin "adorn'd with Meadows, lofty Trees and Firs"; and the River of his "discovery" gives "a prospect of Meadows'' now and then, filled with wild beeves and deer. The increasing barrenness of the land where ''we could not find a chip of Wood wherewith to warm our selves, or to dress our Victuals; and as far as our Eye could reach, there was nothing to be seen but Fens cover'd with Reeds and Clay, and Naked Fields'' seems to suggest the great plains; and his mention of the salt lake, Indian traditions of the great curiosity to the west. Lahontan's condensed report of his passage from village to village is, however, forced and artificial. Unquestionably he makes no real contribution to the descriptions of the Middle West; and his famous River Long deserves mention only as it reveals the firm place the flat lands had gained in the geography of the French.

His roving habits, however, enabled him to give some valuable sketches of the building of the West. He knew well such famous path breakers as Tonti and Duluth; when he arrived in Canada La Salle had just returned from his exploration of the Mississippi; at Missilimakinac he met Cavelier and the other survivors of the ill fated gulf expedition and suspected from their story that their leader was dead. He describes the latter post and Sault Sainte Marie; he throws interesting side lights on the Jesuit labors for the conversion of the savages; his description of the prodigality and wild revelry of the coureurs-de-bois whom he compares to ''*East-India* Men and Pirates'' does more to convince us of their dissipation than dozens of official or priestly complaints. His plan for concentrating the fur trade and garrisoning the upper lakes to prevent Iroquois raids and the advance of British traders, with his suggestions that the Hugenots be allowed to emigrate to the new world would, if followed, probably have saved French dominion there.

These matters are historically important; but his account of the savages is for literature even more significant, he being the chief promulgator before Rousseau of the doctrine of the natural state. To him, embittered by years of litigation, by unjust detention in America, by official jealousy, the untrammelled life of the Indian appeared the solution of his difficulties. For it he had at the very first an instinctive liking; and to the dashing boy the savages seem to have shown their best side. He mentions their physical comeliness, their bravery, and their skill in the chase; their rhetorical ability likewise appealed to him as did the picturesqueness of their names, their "heraldry," and their hieroglyphics. But these true impressions were soon to be falsified as increasing bitterness at his affairs distorted his view. Then the savage life appeared to him not only a stimulating relief, but a society which afforded correction for European abuses. His progress to such a theory was gradual; but once he had adopted it, nothing about the Indians seemed short of perfection. He ridiculously idealizes the savage love; he stresses the hospitality of the natives; in short, he puts forth every effort to glorify the Hurons. In part Lahontan may have been serious in all this; in part, however, we are sure that with the sarcasm of a Swift he is searing the evils and credulity of civilized man.

It is in the dialogues of Adario that his irony reaches its height. There the Huron chieftain, the Rat, denounces with a clearness and a logical skill which a Greek rhetorician might have envied, the evils of civilization. In his discussion of the Jesuits and the Church Lahontan carries scoffing to an extreme. The ills to which poor civilized flesh is heir and the inability and unwillingness of the so-called physicians to remedy them are contrasted disparagingly with the physical prowess and simple curatives of the Indians. And above all the unjust laws oppressing the poor, the false witnesses, the lawyers who sell their souls for gold, and the corrupt judges are lashed with the whip of scorn. Few of the vices and frailties which the laws were designed to correct, and few of the contradictions and futilities of such laws escape the pitiless attack of the Indian and the ironic defense of the man who most of his life had been wronged. It is truly a crushing picture of frivolity, immorality, social injustice, and inequality of opportunity that the two build up; by the side of it the healthfulness, abundance, and simplicity of the natural state seem very attractive. We feel that Lahontan has made good his threat, ". . . since I can't make use of my Sword, I'll wage War with my Pen," and for the moment we feel like joining Adario in his cry — "Long live the *Hurons*; who without Laws, without Prisons, and without Torture, pass their Life in a State of Sweetness and Tranquility, and enjoy a pitch of Felicity to which the *French* are utter Strangers."[26]

26 Lahontan — *New Voyages to North-America.* 2 v. Ed. by R. G. Thwaites. 1905. 164-5, 164, 319-20, 177, 179, 190, 54, 11, 558.

With this brilliant narrative we may bring to a close the study of the early foreign literature of exploration in the great valley. Not only had it marked the culmination of long centuries of feeling in its glorification of the savage life; it had presented, although much of it was correspondence written without thought of publication, the most sophisticated treatment with which we have dealt. Throughout it displays besides a natural gift for style a conscious effort for the telling phrase; and its classic dialogue brings for the first time the thrilling experiences and wild life of the West under the chastening influence of a definite and polished literary form. It marks, indeed, a period of transition.

In the years that preceded it, however, the nature and resources as well as the life of the Midland had been impressed to an extraordinary extent upon the consciousness of the public. From a few vague rumors of a shadowy hinterland, a place of tradition and dreams, had grown up a substantial travel literature, a literature containing some of the most popular books of the age. From a spot satisfying the physical wants of the Indian and focusing the ambitions of a few white men the Mississippi Basin had become a promised land, offering a magnificent domain to the inhabitants of New France. Its forests and prairies had begun to come into their own.

In these centuries of exploration, these years of introduction to European literatures, certain definite things had become established, certain definite tendencies been marked. Of these it might be well now to take stock. The geographical knowledge of the world had in the first place been greatly extended. The astrologers' cards drawn in their dusky studies, the culmination of mediaeval legend, with which the first Spaniards had been guided, had given way to maps still inaccurate in detail, of course, but based upon actual experience and bringing out clearly the principal physical features. In this change the Spaniards had some share; but the French, a few great souls of whom in spite of discouragement at the court and the continued opposition of commercial interests, persisted in their "useless discoveries," really made the geography of the interior.[27] Alert for new features, they traversed the wilds; priests

27 As illustration of the motives for the explorations, the following sentence about La Salle may be noted. "L'espérance du castor, mais surtout celle de trouver par

wrote back to friends and superiors an explanation of the topography of the country; pioneers like Jolliet sketched after arduous paddling the course of the rivers and lakes they had crossed; rude maps of the Indians drawn in the sand or on bark were copied and elaborated; the Dutch, still in the forefront of printers, placed in their journals the accounts of discovery. And gradually there prevailed the idea that philosophers could no longer locate at will the country of demons or the Garden of Eden and debate to uphold their notions; the new continent had been fairly well outlined and in the vast expanse to the west inland seas, great rivers, and beautiful tributaries watering fertile plains had been found. As a result of actual exploration there grew up a passion for exactness unknown before.[28]

And as the French had contributed chiefly to accuracy of geography in the great inland territory, so they had built up the knowledge of, and interest in, the inhabitants. To most of the Spaniards going out ostensibly to spread the true faith, the natives were, if considered at all, mere chattels for the convenience of superior beings. The imagination is appalled at the records of burning, devastation, pillage, and torture with which their journals are filled, as it is at the system with which bloodhounds and chains were transported to capture and keep in order the wretched slaves. Oviedo criticized the conduct of the De Soto expedition, of course, but he seemed to be actuated more by dislike of the leader than by any compassion for the natives. Garcillaso de la Vega is also an exception, but his exotic imaginings born of Peruvian memories and rainbow visions bear little relation to reality even though he does betray genuine sympathy for the oppressed peoples. His native blood would account for this, probably; certainly the true Spaniard, even though he may like Cabeza de Vaca have lived for years among the Indians, seems to have had for them no fellow feeling. The

icy passage dans la mer Vermeille, où M. de La Salle croyoit que la rivière d'Ohio tomboit, luy firent entreprendre ce voyage pour ne pas laisser à un autre l'honneur de trouver le chemin de la mer du Sud, et par elle celuy de la Chine." Margry — *Découvertes et établissements.* I: 114. Expression of the royal and ministerial disapproval of the discoveries may be found Ibid. II: 309-10, 337, I:256-7, VI: 37. For contemporary opinion in France see *Ibid.* II: 354 ff.

28 Margry prints a letter of 1682, describing the making of some globes for the King, which illustrates this point well, "On a peine encore à mettre sur ces globes la rivière d'Ohio, dont vous avés marqué le cours dans vostre carte. On seroit bien aise de sçavoir s'il y a de bons fondemens de la marquer, comme vous avez fait. *Découvertes et établissements.* II: 276.

French, on the contrary, more than any other race had the power by peaceable means to win the Indians to their own ends. Probably this was due in part to the adaptability and nimbleness of their adventurous spirit; undoubtedly, however, at the root of their success was a genuine interest in the life and ways of these tawny skinned beings.

That this interest was so prolonged and so intense must be attributed in part to the variety of tribes with which the pioneers of New France were in contact — half starved, fur-trapping bands of the north, the bloodthirsty Iroquois, the fishing tribes of the coast. None of them, however, possessed greater appeal, none contributed a more picturesque page to the records of the whites than the fortunate dwellers of prairie and plain. With the coming of the trading fleets from the forests of Wisconsin interest in the Northwest was aroused; there the Nadouessioux, the people of the Wild Oats country, the favored members of the Fire Nation all made striking impression. And before the denizens of the upper valley had fairly become known to the world, the Mississippi explorers revealed a host of new and equally fascinating tribes. The Illinois prompted Marquette to his dream of descending the Great River; the comparatively civilized bands farther south were even more fascinating; the mounted Indians of the plains with their buffalo shields and their hair ropes offered the charm of novelty. Altogether by the close of the period of discovery the place of the Indian had become firmly fixed. The shifting tribes of the great valley had been visited and made known; their appearance, described; their mode of life, fully discussed. And public opinion then as now declared them among the most picturesque features of the land they inhabited. No successful relation was complete without them; a strong interest had been aroused to stay.

Of course unscrupulous writers exaggerated reports about them just as the Indians themselves told wild tales of wonder to keep early voyagers from proceeding further. As the seventeenth century drew near a close, however, stories such as those reported to De Soto's company of the shouts of the Indians in a certain village causing the birds to fall dead to the ground, removed from their mediaeval background, lost credibility.[29]

29 French — *Hist. Coll. of La.* II: 98.

Fabricators of them even received severe criticism, Lahontan, who himself had given one of the most distorted pictures, being, absurdly enough, loudest in his outcries. That the violence of his criticism was due to his hatred of the clergy does not lessen the strangeness of the paradox. Yet his voice is only one of many crying out against the misleading representations of the inhabitants and life of America.[30]

The true customs of the Indians were, nevertheless, so strange to Europeans that there was little need of retouching for effect. The real wonder tales came when travellers wrote about the mineral wealth and precious stones of the Mississippi country. The Spaniards were impelled toward their explorations almost entirely by these legends of untold riches for which the conquests of Mexico and Peru had prepared them. The French, too, were eager to gain treasure. Saint-Lusson was sent toward the west to search for lakes and rivers by which the South Sea might be reached and to seek for copper mines;[31] and each explorer, official or unofficial, deemed it incumbent upon him to give an estimate of the probable mineral wealth. The richness of the Lake Superior region was, of course, early discovered, Radisson commenting upon it and the Relation of 1659-60 stating,

> "It is also enriched in its entire circumference with mines of lead in a nearly pure state; with copper of such excellence that pieces as large as one's fist are found, all refined; and with great rocks, bearing whole veins of turquoises. The people even strive to make us believe that its waters are swollen by various streams which roll along with the sand grains of gold in abundance — the refuse, so to speak, of the neighboring mines."[32]

In the South, too, there grew up legends of fabulous wealth — pearls of finest water but little prized, rivers "more beautiful than the Mississippi . . . in which gold was found in large grains and in dust," which the Indians used "only to make

30 See Gravier's criticism of Hennepin — *Jes. Rel.* LXV: 73 and Lahontan's attack on the Jesuit accounts. *New Voy.* II: 413-4, 523. In turn we might note Father Lemaire's comment on Lahontan in 1714. "On regarde en ce pays, comme des contes faits à plaisir, ce qu'on lit dans le baron de La Hontan de cette partie occidentale de la Louisiane. . ." Margry — *Découvertes et établissements.* VI: 185.

31 *Ibid.*, I: 87-88.

32 *Jes. Rel.* XLV: 219-21. See, also, LXV: 105.

collars and bracelets," but which they valued "less than certain red stones which they put to the same use." [33] Unquestionably such reports were the ones most pleasing in the home land. La Salle painted glowingly the commercial advantages of his discovery, but it took his promises of fortunes in metals to win the ear of the court in his colonizing schemes. Indeed the credulity of the French ministry in this respect gained acceptance even for Sagean's absurd narrative of the Acaanibas, whose king, a descendant of Montezuma, dwelt in an apartment walled in massive gold, and who sent off while he was among them a caravan composed of more than three thousand buffaloes loaded with gold.[34] By the shrewd men on the ground, however, these mines were early judged in the right perspective. Although they at first expected easy profits, they soon realized that the great distance and the almost insuperable obstacles of transportation rendered such discoveries of little avail.[35] It would have been well for France had all agreed with Frontenac and Talon and centered attention on humbler and more reliable sources of wealth.

Among the chief of these were the fertility and abundance of the great valley. To those of us today to whom the wartime boom of prairie farm land was a startling thing it is a revelation to find how enthusiastically and correctly those shrewd pioneers judged the resources of the country. Everyone without exception praised its plenty and productiveness. The importance of its game has, of course, passed today. At a time, however, when men were obliged to travel for months dependent on the provisions they found along the way and when, with ships few and uncertain, self support for a colony was desirable in the extreme, the value of the wild fowl and animals can scarcely be overestimated. In memory of such a time and as a clue to the almost complete extinction of the game once highly praised we might quote a couple of the typical passages.

"Today we saw over 50 bears, and of all that we killed we took only 4, in order to obtain some fat." [36]

---

33 Cavelier's *Account of La Salle's Voyage to the Mouth of the Mississippi* in J. G. Shea's *Early Voyages up and down the Mississippi.* 1861. 25-6. See, also Le Clercq — *First Establishment of the Faith.* II: 280-1.

34 See Margry — *Découvertes et établissements.* VI: 95 ff.

35 *Ibid.*, I: 94-5, 81, 255. See, also, *Wis. Hist. Coll.* XVI: 255.

36 *Jes. Rel.*, 65:105.

"We wanted then neither Powder nor Shot, and therefore we shot at random all that we met, either small birds, or Turtles, and Wood-Pigeons which were then coming from Foreign Countries in so great Numbers, that they did appear in the Air like Clouds."[37]

And these are only extracts chosen at random from among many; almost any page in an early narrative would present similar tributes. Small wonder then that the Indians modelled upon the prairies their hunters' paradise!

Small wonder, too, that the early voyagers regarded its grass-swathed expanse as an agriculturist's heaven! The Mississippi territories, looking "as if they had been already manured," offering "vast meadows" ready for the plough were a revelation to the dwellers in the frozen forests of the North. Over and over again they mention its richness. Marquette remarks upon the valley's productiveness and beauty; Membré describes "the richness and fertility of the plains" which give the Illinois "fields everywhere";[38] Joutel pays tribute to the land; La Salle stresses its possibilities. The enthusiastic Hennepin, not content with the double corn crop described by some, mentions three or four crops in one year and declares of the "vast meadows, which need not to be grubb'd up, but are ready for the Plow and Seed," that "certainly the Soil must be very fruitful, since Beans grow naturally without any Culture." [39] The hunter Lahontan describes the soil as "so fertile that it produces (in a manner without Agriculture) our *European* Corn, Pease, Beans, and several other Fruits that are not known in *France*";[40] and the plenty of the wild-oats "which the prairies furnish naturally" was a common topic. Even the most luke-warm tribute states that although all of the lands in the country of the Illinois "require some Toil and Trouble . . . they can sufficiently recompence in a little time, those who will be at the pains to cultivate them." [41]

Even this faint qualification, however, is so startling an exception to the general comment that it serves to draw attention

37 Hennepin — *New Discovery*, 329.
38 Le Clercq — *First Establishment of the Faith*, II: 134.
39 Hennepin — *New Discovery*, I: 213.
40 Lahontan — *New Voy.*, I: 168.
41 Hennepin — *New Discovery*, II: 630.

to what is the most striking feature of all the exploration literature. This is for the region of the prairies the use of superlatives. With such a type of writing this use may not at first seem distinctive. The basis of all travel volumes is wonder; the writer wishes variously to shock, surprise, amuse, or enchant his readers; he desires to carry them in spirit to the far places he has visited in person, to make them exclaim with Miranda "O brave new world That has such people in't." And for the unskilled writer the most natural method of producing such effects is the use of hyperbole, the sprinkling of his pages with superlatives as freely as he sprinkles his story with marvels. In the Mississippi Valley records, however, there is a difference. Most of its chroniclers of this early period, writing for official purposes to state or church superiors or to intimate friends with no thought of publication have little to gain by such heightening of their emotions. Their praise indicates heartfelt tribute; their glorifying adjectives they seem impelled to use almost without their consciousness or volition. So Marquette even in a moment of such uncertainty as his and Jolliet's approach to the Illinois noticed the beauty of the land. So, too, even in such routine matters as directions for advance, we find indirect praise, "for it is not very difficult to transport Canoes through so fine a country as that prairie."[42] These illustrations are significant because of their context; we find far more exuberant language in any volume we pick up. La Potherie speaks of the Illinois "who are in possession of the most beautiful region that can be seen [anywhere]";[43] even Hennepin, apparently, is unable to find sufficient adjectives. Absolutely every person who enters these regions of delight seems impressed by the fact that they are in quality unexcelled. Cavelier even chronicles the southern Indians' recognition of this fact, for to a request of his brother that they depart with him, they replied that "being in the most fertile, healthy and peaceful country in the world, they would be devoid of sense to leave it and expose themselves to be tomahawked by the Illinois or burnt by the Iroquois on their way to another, where the winter was insufferably cold, the summer without game, and ever in

42 *Jes. Rel.*, LIX: 143.
43 Blair — *Indian Tribes*, I: 288.

war."[44] La Salle's remarks on the "most beautiful region in the world"[45] since he is its great exploiter are possibly the most impressive; neither he nor any of his party excel in praise, however, other chroniclers.

---

44 Shea — *Early Voyages up and down the Miss,* 1861. 29.
45 Margry — *Découvertes et établissements,* II: 174.

# CHAPTER II

## THE SPANISH AND FRENCH IN THE MISSISSIPPI VALLEY: THE COLONIZING CENTURY

With such superlative praise of the fruitful rolling country to the south, we may well wonder why the French did not sooner avail themselves of its showering bounty. In part this undoubtedly was due to the nature of the Canadians; the very characteristics that made for success in the wild roaming life of trader or explorer unfitted them for the patient continued effort necessary for the upbuilding of a colony even in so kindly a region as the Mississippi Valley; the lure of the open, of adventurously won riches in furs, one of the greatest menaces to the stability of the settlements on the St. Lawrence, was also a check to colonization. The court, too, disgusted at the ceaseless expenditures for the northern posts, encouraged establishments as little as it had the advance of the great trail-makers. In 1677, for instance, Colbert writing to M. du Chesneau, refused royal approval to Jolliet's plan for making a settlement in Illinois, stating that it was first necessary to increase the population of Canada.[1] And so for more quiet years the broad expanse of river, wood, and wind-stirred grass lay tranquil under the burning summer sun, the serene mantle of winter; over it the ponderous bison herds peaceably grazed; the Indian tribes, its lords, pursued undisturbed their former avocations. In the lake region, however, tiny fortified posts were erected, largely as centres for the fur trade; and gradually among the Illinois where the black-robed Jesuits were carrying out the project of Marquette, a motley stream of soldiers, traders, farmers trickled in. There around the French fort, on the green ocean of prairie, gray, thick-walled Canadian cabins began to elbow the Indians' mat huts; there one man cherished the superb vision of La Salle.

1 Margry — *Découvertes et établissements,* I: 329.

In September, 1694, we find him, the loyal Henri de Tonti, suggesting to Villermont continuation of the enterprise. The letter, unimportant from a literary standpoint, is significant in that in addition to the mention of the Spanish silver mines, the commerce in skins, the quantity of lead, and the fertility of the country, it sounds a note of warning against the encroachments of the English, a note which was to be a dominant one in the records of the colonizing century. In October, 1697, the Sieur de Louvigny and the Sieur de Mantet submitted a somewhat more detailed plan, stressing particularly the possibility of using the Mississippi as a base for expeditions against the Spanish; and in December of the same year, the Sieur de Rémonville, friend of La Salle, expounded most enthusiastically and convincingly the advantages of a Mississippi settlement.[2] As a result of these efforts Iberville, who had already importuned Pontchartrain, was permitted to gather in 1698 two hundred emigrants.

In the records of his expeditions and endeavours to found the little colony, we find pictured a figure and enterprise as striking in their way as the great one of La Salle. The difference between them is the difference in the centuries; La Salle is the pointing finger, the guide, the maker of new highways; the settlement of the vast regions to which he established claim fate did not permit to him. In Iberville, however, as well as his younger brother Bienville, we have not only the man of action who had distinguished himself against the English, but the stabilizer and administrator. His attitude is not that of a discoverer striking into an untried wilderness, but of the colonizer, the promoter, who with the information of his predecessors at his finger tips, a survivor of the earlier expedition among his company of priests, was seeking the best place to establish his colony.

The documents he has left us, although they are much like those of La Salle — letters, journals, official papers — reflect this difference. As his boats rocked over the Atlantic, we wonder if there was any comprehension on them of the change that had taken place since the first Spaniards had crossed

2 For these memorials see *Ibid.*, IV; 3-5, 9-18, 19-21, 21-43. French in *Hist. Coll. of La.*, VI: 1-16 gives a translation of Rémonville's Memoir.

the great river. No longer was the journey a blind plunging into the unknown; no longer did the company expect to find on the coasts of the gulf the marvels of mediaeval legend; at Pensacola the Spaniards were already established. The Indian remains could be explained; the flare of land fires brought only desire to cultivate acquaintance. There was romance in the meeting with these savage peoples, romance in the dancing and exchange of presents, yet it was the romance of dreams fulfilled, of reality wonderfully surpassing expectation, rather than the sheer exultation in the unknown felt by the earlier explorers.

And as they enter the Mississippi and sing a Te Deum of gratitude this same element is pronounced. The tradition has been built up; the visitors feel no surprise at the abundance of game, the thick cane brakes of the lower river, the flood marks on the tree trunks, the ceremony of the calumet. Constantly they find corroboration of others' reports, even traces of their predecessors — tragically enough the letter of Tonti from the Quinnipissas to La Salle, some engravings, a New Testament, and a gun which the chief "preserved very carefully"; again, the white man's finery.

> "The Chief of the Mongoulachas was clothed with a blue cloak after the fashion of the Canadians, with stockings of the same color, a cravat of a villainous red stuff, that had formerly served as a flag, all of which had been presented to him by M. de Tonty at the time of his descent in search of M. de la Salle."

As we read the description of the chief and his followers we realize that the interest in the savage inhabitants is still strong. Picturesque scenes are constantly suggested — the procession of Indians, each one bearing a wooden cross in his hand, "around the one we had planted, throwing tobacco upon it, and singing after their manner," the dancing till midnight by the flickering light of dried canes. But already there is the hint of disillusionment; little trace was found of some of the feebler tribes; and the fabrications of Tonti's forger had aroused many false hopes. After his visit to the Mongoulachas Iberville who had "met with none of the *Tangipahoes* nor *Quinnipissas* mentioned in the narratives of the Jesuits" concluded they must be false, as well as the writings about Canada, Hudson's Bay, and the return of Sieur Cavalier from the Bay of St. Louis; and disheartened later he jots down,

> "Besides it was time for me to return and look out for a proper place to make a settlement, which hitherto I had been unable to find. Moreover, the fleet was falling short of provisions. I retraced my steps to the *Houmas*, after having gone beyond their village three leagues and a half, very much vexed at the *Recollect*, whose false narrative had deceived every one, and caused our sufferings and total failure of our enterprise, by the time consumed in search of things which alone existed in his imagination." [3]

The real concern, of course, was the location of the settlement. But although Iberville felt he had passed through fine country and although his brother pronounced the lands neighbouring the bay "parfaitement belles à habiter," he seems to have seated the little colony in the most ungenerous of all the barren spots of the coast. There where the sun scorched pitilessly on the blistering wood of the stockade; where the stores had to be ferried wearisomely from the vessels to the shore, where no fresh foods and only brackish waters were obtainable, the company settled down to await the return of the fleet. A desolate ending it was for all the glowing promises, and one rendered more so by the fact that the colonists were content to huddle back and listen to the Spanish deserters' tales of silver mines instead of putting the establishment on a firm basis. The further records of the colony — journals, reports, and letters of the various officials — reveal somewhat similar conditions. In them we see realization of the futility of struggle with bad locations and after much opposition establishment of New Orleans.[4] The papers vary greatly. Always, however, they present the point of view of the colonist; the writers judge the land not merely as an interesting panorama unrolled to explorers but as a means of livelihood. And as the years go by, we see in the statements, formal as they are, a change from the

3 French — *Hist. Coll. of La.*, VII:71, 92; VI:24, 26-7. Margry — *Découvertes et établissements*, IV:259, 267, 120, 121-2. See also 101, 168 for comments on early narratives and 199 for Bienville's praise of the land.

4 Baron Marc de Villiers du Terrage's work, *A History of the Foundation of New Orleans (1717-1722)* tr. *La. Hist. Quar.* III:157 ff., is valuable here.

starving handful at the edge of the basin to a colony prosperous after bitter struggle, with the tiny homes of habitants, cultivated crop squares, already heralds of future greatness.[5]

In the north, too, we find in spite of much quarreling and contradiction record of the permanent establishment of posts, some of them now sites of great cities. The various official papers about them, although they were not intended for publication, give a remarkable amount of information about the early West; and sometimes they are surprisingly ornate, witness the following description of the Detroit region in 1701 by the commandant, M. de la Mothe.

> "The banks are so many vast meadows where the freshness of these beautiful streams keep the grass always green. These same meadows are fringed with long and broad avenues of fruit trees which have never felt the careful hand of the watchful gardener; and fruit trees, young and old, droop under the weight and multitude of their fruit, and bend their branches towards the fertile soil which has produced them. In this soil so fertile, the ambitious vine which has not yet wept under the knife of the industrious vine-dresser, forms a thick roof with its broad leaves and its heavy clusters over the head of whatever it twines round, which it often stifles by embracing it too closely. Under these vast avenues you may see assembling in hundreds the shy stag and the timid hind with the bounding roebuck, to pick up eagerly the apples and plums with which the ground is paved. It is there that the careful turkey hen calls back her numerous brood, and leads them to gather the grapes; it is there that their big cocks come to fill their broad and gluttonous crops. The golden pheasant, the quail, the partridge, the woodcock, the teeming turtle-dove, swarm in the woods and cover the open country intersected and broken by groves of full-grown forest trees which form a charming prospect which of itself might sweeten the melancholy tedium of solitude. There the hand of the pitiless mower has never shorn the juicy grass on which bisons of enormous height and size fatten . . .
>
> "Can it be thought that a land in which nature has distributed

5 For a summary of the change see Mrs. N. M. M. Surrey's *The Commerce of Louisiana under the French Regime 1699-1763*. 1916.

everything in so complete a manner could refuse to the hand of a careful husbandman who breaks into its fertile depths, the return which is expected of it? . . . It is only the opponents of the truth who are the enemies of this settlement, so essential to the increase of the glory of the King, to the spread of religion, and to the destruction of the throne of Baal.''[6]

In contradiction to this, however, we find reports that the land was good for nothing, the fishing very poor, and the hunting between thirty and forty leagues off.[7] Similar disagreements are found in the accounts of the settlement proper, Raudot stating that ''there are only sixty-three houses at Detroit instead of 120, as the said Sr. de La Mothe tells you there are, that as regards the savages, there are about one hundred and fifty huts, in place of 1,200 as the said Sr. de la Mothe informs you; that the whole of the settlers number sixty-three, twenty-nine of whom are married soldiers, while the others are *voyageurs* of the country, and settled here, who go up every year and only have houses within the fort for the purpose of trading.''[8] On the whole the development of all these stations presents a discouraging picture of inefficient agriculture, of quarrels about the fur trade, of friction between ecclesiastical and political authorities, of official graft, and of difficulties with the Indians, increasingly alienated by the machinations of the Iroquois and the cheapness of the English goods.

And, since with the exception of Charlevoix's books and la Potherie's *Histoire de l'Amérique Septentrionale* (4t. 1722), which must have been very influential in spreading knowledge of the northern colony, its struggles and expansion and Indian relations, our knowledge is dependent upon miscellaneous papers and official reports brought together from various state archives,[9] it seems advisable to turn back to Louisiana, which drew the attention of the world more than the Canadian outposts and which boasted several efficient chroniclers. In their works we have a new type of prairie literature. Not only are

6 *Mich. Pioneer and Hist. Coll.*, XXXIII: 111 and 112.
7 *Wis. Hist. Coll.*, XVI: 219; 256.
8 *Mich. Pioneer and Hist. Coll.*, XXXIII: 414.
9 *Wis. Hist. Coll.* XVI, XVII, XVIII, *Mich. Pion. & Hist. Coll.* XXXIII and XXXIV, and *Doc. rel. to the Col. Hist. of the State of N. Y.* IX & X, may be particularly recommended for these.

the earlier traditions preserved, of natural wealth, of picturesque natives, and of a background of beauty, but others are built up. Interest centres now on the adjustment of men to the new land they have made or been compelled to make their homes, on the continuous contact of Indian and white, and, whisperingly at first, later with the violence of open warfare, on the struggle of hostile races for the possession of a continent.

Of these narratives one of the earliest and most fascinating is the *Annals of Louisiana from 1698 to 1722* by M. Penicaut, who entered the service of the king to gratify his "passion for travelling," and for whom the new world had the radiance of romance. With the abandon of the boy that he was he teaches the Indians to use their strange gifts and laughs at their perplexity. With some of the dignity of a boy, too, surveying his Crusoe island, he sets out with his companions for the Mississippi, naming the bays, islands, rivers that are passed. And when at last after crossing through flat lands abounding in game, prodigiously high cypress forests, and grain-bearing cane brakes, he arrives on the borders of the great river, he makes us feel through his simple description all the glory of the moonlight, the delight of camping on the swirling river of his dreams.

He was to have many opportunities to glide between its spongy banks, for on Iberville's return a little party went upstream "changing from one nation to the other, in order not to fatigue them," and meeting among the Natchez M. de St. Cosme. Later, in his capacity as ship carpenter of his Majesty's service he was to become a member of the mining expedition of Le Sueur. It is on this latter trip that he gives us his most adequate picture of the yet primeval charm of the valley—the abundance of deer around the Little Salt River, the village of the Illinois where the beginning mingling of races is evidenced by the presence of "Canadian traders, who were purchasing furs and skins," and numerous missionaries. "All around and beyond the village," he says, "is a prairie, and, in the distance, lofty hills which give a magnificent perspective," and thereafter his mention of these meadow lands is frequent. Opposite the mouth of the Illinois, for instance, begins "a series of the most beautiful and most extensive prairies in the world." His description has no new elements, but already he is looking back upon the first explorers with a feeling of long past time.

> "On the left of these rapids are open prairies, extending ten leagues from, and along the banks of the Mississippi. The grass upon these prairies is like clover, upon which an infinite number of animals browse. After passing these rapids, we found, on the right and left, mines of lead, which are called, to this day, Nicholas Perrot, the name of the person who first discovered them."

Of the roving tribes of the upper territory his account is not worth noticing save that he like most later travellers had a bad word for the Sioux. His real contribution to Indian lore lies in his description of the still little known tribes to the south, the Pascagoulas, for instance, a nation on a comparatively high plane, whose earthen pottery, primitive agriculture, kindness to strangers, and celebrations with "dancing masters" at the head of each band attracted him strongly. On his first visit to the Taensa he had the misfortune to witness a horrible spectacle — parents' sacrifice of their children after the thunder god "had struck the temple, burned all their idols, and reduced the whole to ashes." The Natchez, however, he calls the most civilized of all the tribes; and later he goes into transports about them, having apparently enjoyed to the fullest the stay among them necessitated by the shortage of provisions in the colony.

> "All the pleasures of refined society are observed by the great nobles. They have none of the rude manners of the surrounding nations, and possess all the comforts of life . . . The men and women are well made, and appropriately clothed. The women — among whom are many very beautiful — dress in white linen robes . . . Their language is softer and better modulated than their neighbors . . . They are really very courteous and obliging, and fond of the French. It was really charming to us to behold them dancing at their feasts, arrayed in their beautiful and highly ornamented shirts, and the women in their neat white robes. . . . Their dances are very graceful. . . . After having lighted two large torches, cut from some old pine tree, one is placed

> near the cabin of the chief, and the other on the opposite side of the great square, when, towards sun-down, the master of ceremonies enters, followed by thirty couple, in regular order, who commence the dance at the tap of the drum, and the sound of the voices of the spectators. Each dances, in turn, until midnight when the married men and women retire, and give place to the young people, who keep up the dance until morning . . ."

Indeed the elaborateness of his description makes him one of the most significant of the forerunners of Chateaubriand.

The Natchez were, of course, still largely in their aboriginal state. Even more interesting is Penicaut's description of the peoples already beginning to adopt the ways of the whites, such as the Illinois, with whom alone in the great valley the Jesuits had succeeded in realizing to an appreciable extent their dream of a paternal religious government similar to the one in Paraguay.

> "These Indians are industrious and skillful in cultivating their lands, breaking them up with the plough which they owe to the Jesuits, who have resided among them more than sixty years. This country is one of the most beautiful in all Louisiana. Every kind of grain and vegetables are produced here in the greatest abundance. It is in this country that you may behold the most magnificent prairies in the world. They have horses, which they purchase from the *Cadadoquioux* for merchandize, and pasture them here. They have, also, large numbers of oxen, cows, sheep, etc., upon the prairies. Poultry is abundant and fish plentiful. So that, in fact, they lack none of the necessaries or conveniences of life.
>
> "Near their village are three mills for grinding grain — one wind-mill owned by the Jesuits, and two horse mills, belonging to the *Illinois*. The *Caskaskias* women are very skillful. . . .
>
> "The *Illinois* are very fond of good living, and have frequent feasts among themselves. Their choicest meats are the flesh of dogs, or wolves, which are brought up and fattened in their village. They are, for the most parts, Catholics, and have a very large church in their village which is well arranged in the interior. Besides the baptismal fonts, there

are three chapels, ornamented with a bell and belfry. They regularly attend the services, which the Jesuits have translated from the Latin into their own language.

"They sing, alternately, with the French, the latter in French, and the former, in their own language. . . ."

In spite of the fact that his party was sent there to quell the disorders caused by the coureurs-de-bois, his picture of the community is, indeed, almost as idyllic as that of the exotic life of the Natchez.

Although his description of the Gulf colony is not so full, he does give us many vivid glimpses of its starting life — the inroads of the English, the stir at the coming of the first French girls, who "were very modest and virtuous and who soon found husbands," the distribution of negro slaves, the removal of colonial headquarters "to the rich country bordering on the Mississippi," the arrival of new concessionaires. His gossipy folk history, unfailingly interesting, forms for us the transitional link between the long years of legend and exploration and the colonizing century of the French. In it we have preserved the reactions of the first habitants to the prairies, for of them Penicaut represents the best type. With the enthusiasm of a boy for adventure he unites grave comprehension of the greatness of the task of colonization. Of the spirit in which these founders of Louisiana toiled, no better expression could be wished than the words with which he ends.

"To all those who read these 'Annals,' it will appear that God, in His wisdom, had designed Louisiana for the French, to show forth the power of the holy Catholic religion, and to establish a French empire in America, where the glory of his most Christian majesty might be displayed . . . Since, therefore, we cannot but recognize the hand of God in what he has done in Louisiana, we will now close these 'Annals' in the language of the prophet,

'Blessed be the name of the Lord our God who alone has done all these wonderful works; may his name be praised for ever and ever and may the whole earth be filled with his Glory'."[10]

---

10 French — *Hist. Coll. of La.* VI:35, 56, 65, 66, 67, 68, 58, 88-91, 107-110, 95, 139, 162. See also Margry — *Découvertes et établissements.* V:375 ff.

Other similar chronicles are *Mémoires Historiques sur la Louisiane*, an edition of Dumont's Memoirs by the Abbé Mascrier (2v. 1753),[11] and *Journal Historique de l'Établissement des Français à la Louisiane*, which has been attributed to Bénard de la Harpe,[12] but which was not published till 1831. The first of these quotes Le Page du Pratz pretty extensively. It gives, however, a clear idea of the different French posts in the lower part of the Mississippi Valley, of the size of the various concessions, of the hardships undergone by the early settlers, and of the troubles with the Indians, concluding by discussing measures for putting the colony on a solid basis. The second contains nothing especially novel, but various interesting points are brought out or stressed — the unfortunate refusal to permit the Huguenots to emigrate to Louisiana, the menace of the English, the relations with the Spaniards, sometimes friendly and sometimes hostile, the deleterious changes of administration and policy, and the search for precious metals, sapping much needed energy. Especially full accounts are given of the exploring tours by which la Harpe and others carried the banner of France still further into the midlands. Significant indications of the development of the country are the statistics concerning it in 1724, the mention of visits to plantations and of hunters going down to New Orleans with supplies of salt meat. The Mississippi, when the first explorers descended it a mighty sinuous coil of power for centuries unrestrained, a highway untraversed save by the barks of wandering tribesmen, had begun to take its place as an avenue of commerce.

The change is even more pronounced in Le Page du Pratz's *Histoire de la Louisiane* . . . (3v. 1758), which might be called a pioneer among the many handbooks for immigrants. With a detail frequently wearisome Du Pratz discusses soils, climate, native plants and trees, crops, methods of cultivation, the purchase and treatment of slaves, the development of a concession. Two things account for this prolixity — his desire to give an exact idea of the new land, and the love that he bears for it, evident from the opening pages where he rebuts the charges of

11 Tr. in French — *Hist. Coll. of La.* V:1ff.

12 Villiers du Terrage says this has been incorrectly assigned to Bénard de la Harpe and like Margry attributes it to the Chevalier de Beaurain. *La. Hist. Quar.* III:179. Tr. in French — *Hist. Coll. of La.* III:9 ff.

sterility. He discusses all parts of the country, but he seems particularly drawn by the prairie, now crisped by the burning sun of summer, now tenderly green with the new blading grasses. To him its clustering plants give native simples; its game and fruits, food; its gorgeous flower fabric, beauty.

He lived, as a matter of fact, in one of its most attractive parts, for he soon moved from his original habitation to the country of the Natchez. There white men and red dwelt side by side, apparently, till the advent of the domineering Chopart, in almost ideal companionship. In the community there seems to have been none of the compulsion toward the observance of new and only partially comprehended forms that we feel in even the mildest of the Jesuit missions, none of the broken down warriors or the mongrel bois-brûlées imbued with the evils of two races that disgraced the northern settlements. The Natchez still possessed that primitive vigor that had early awakened the admiration of the French. The dignity of a tribe reputed "the most powerful in North America," the pride of race brought by a long established nobility, traditions carefully handed down from a vague but glorious past by the "Keepers of the Ancient Word," the real beauty of their well ordered villages, the solemnity of their burial processions, their elaborate dances and fêtes all combined to distinguish them.

And in Du Pratz they found a worthy chronicler. Although originally, he confesses, he regarded an Indian as a brute beast, he very early concluded that "it is wrong to call men savages who show good judgment, who reason accurately, who have more prudence, good faith, and generosity than certain civilized nations, who would not suffer comparison between them." For the Natchez he had not only respect but friendship. He learned the language of commoners and nobles; to him were recounted the choicest legends of their past; he knew the intricacies of their rites; he appreciated the demands of their code of honor. And in his books we have the most extensive information about the Natchez as well as the most appreciative tribute to them until the magic pen of Chateaubriand transformed into color and life the details stored up for him.

Du Pratz, most intimate of the chroniclers of the sun-worshipping tribe, was also one of the fullest recorders of their down-

Burial ceremonies for one of the Natchez chieftains. A number of other Indians were strangled that they might accompany him to the Land of the Spirits. From Du Pratz's *Histoire de la Louisiane*. III: 55

fall. The Natchez had many visitors; praises of them and their country drew settlers in such numbers that the company decided to erect a fort. At last greed caused the commandant, already rebuked for his injustice, to demand the surrender for himself of the great village of the Natchez and the removal of the inhabitants to some less favored locality. The uprising that followed and its fatal termination are too well known to be repeated. Too truly did Du Pratz write that "Vengeance is the dominant passion of the natives of America." The tribe he had long exalted and loved was blotted out to his mournful requiem, "Thus was destroyed that tribe, formerly the most brilliant in the colony and the most useful to the French."[13]

The flare of burning buildings, the curdling war whoops were unfortunately to be seen and heard many more times in the valley; and the river which Du Pratz called the great highway of the colony was to be stained like its tributaries with the blood of many tribes and many white men before its possession was settled. The chronicles we have mentioned devote a large amount of attention to the Indian warfare — isolated attacks of the natives, the uprising of the Natchez, the expeditions against the Chickasaws. With the same note, too, Charlevoix's *Histoire et Description Generale de la Nouvelle France* (1744)[14] ends. It is an ironical thing that this most comprehensive of the early accounts of the establishment of France in the western hemisphere appeared so near the turning point in its destinies. The discussion of Louisiana Charlevoix related adequately for the first time to that of the Canadian colony; to his work he brought the knowledge resulting from his own personal observations and the study of his predecessors as well as unusual breadth and a careful historical method. The whole is the culmination of the long years of personal record and simple chronicle that we have traced in part. As we have pointed out, however, the structure so long in building, now only beginning to assume stability and proportion, was before long to disentegrate; Charlevoix's history is at once a summary of past progress and, in its accounts of Indian outrages and troubles with the English, a foreshadowing of the

13 Du Pratz — *Histoire de la Louisiane* II:223, 331, I:88, 182; III:327.

14 Tr. by W. G. Shea, 1866. 6v. Sec. ed. 1900. There were three editions of Charlevoix in 1744, two in 6v. and one in 3.

conflict that was to bring the downfall of French rule in North America.

Already ominous rumblings were heard. The inter-tribal conflicts that for years before the arrival of any European nation had ravaged America were now complicated by the quarrels of the whites. War paint was donned and the tomahawk crimsoned not merely to satisfy native animosities but to carry on the feuds of civilized man. The French traced to the instigations of the traders from Carolina much of the trouble with the southern Indians; in the north the influence of English and Dutch with the Iroquois and the resistance of the Fox Indians were constant sources of terrorization and expense. On the allegiance of the Five Nations England based largely her claim to the West; the recognition of English trading privileges with all Indians formed one of the most troublesome clauses for France in the Treaty of Utrecht. Indeed the success of the rival contestants depended largely on the allegiance of savage tribes; the Five Nations, in particular, long bitter opponents of the French, really wielded the balance in the settlement of the destinies of the midlands of America. The struggle was a protracted one; the stake, a continent; in it we have opposed two widely different policies, two varying types of power. Yet while it was going on there does not seem to have been universal realization of the momentousness of the issues; and even today the events on the western frontier, the ravages of Dumas' raiders, for instance, seem to have made no such impress on the popular imagination as the sacking of Deerfield or the deportation of the Acadians. The conflict remains, however, one of the most important in our history; and from a literary point of view it brought the prairies to the attention of the world in a new light.

In spite of years of neglect the spreading meadows, the dark-shadowed forests were now a prize to be fought for. The eager English pressed through the mountain passes; the French extended forts and posts, zealous to retain the land that they loved. And in the records of the long conflict — reports of combats such as those J. M. Shea brought together in his *Relations Diverses sur la Bataille de Malanguele* (1860), compilations designed to win the sympathy of other nations like J. N. Moreau's *Mémoire con-*

*tenant le Précis des Faits* . . . (1756),[15] discussions of the peace terms, or histories such as Pouchot's *Mémoires sur la Dernière Guerre de l'Amérique Septentrionale* . . . (3v.-1781),[16] we find exaltation of the prize to be won, romantic adventure, and tolling at last the tragic note of defeat, the significance of which was yet barely realized. For the struggle meant not merely possession of the Ohio nor even occupation of the east bank of the Mississippi. In it was involved the future of the continent; by it was sounded the death knell of the Latin races in North America. When in 1760 the English took possession of Detroit to the tumultuous rejoicing of hundreds of leaping savages and in the spring of the following year the posts on the upper lakes saluted one by one the British flag till in the valley of the St. Lawrence and the region of the Great Lakes not a French banner was left floating, the disappointment was only less poignant because less final than at the cession to the United States more than forty years later.

Throughout the consequent parleying and the surrender to the English of the hard-won eastern shore the French were sustained by the thought of the yet almost untouched possibilities of the West; family after family crossed the Mississippi to live under the old faith and according to the old laws. When announcement was made that that territory, too, had been secretly ceded, the blow was indeed a hard one. Yet with the tenacity that keeps the French of Quebec today a separate race they continued their former mode of life, retained in secret the old allegiance. Napoleon's successes and the rumors of the secret cession of Louisiana by Spain brought a triumphant revival of the dream of French dominion in America; only with announcement of the sale to the United States did the vision at last vanish. With

15 An indication of the importance of this work is afforded by its appearance in translation in Phil., Lond., & N. Y. in 1757. One of the N. Y. ed. is repr. in Craig's *Olden Time*. II:142-277 (1848). *The Mystery Revealed; or, Truth Brought to Light* . . . is a Lond. ed. of 1759. Other indications of French popular interest in the contest in Ohio may be found in the song commemorating Braddock's defeat given Appendix I and in the long poem *Jumonville* (1759) by Thomas, a member of the French Academy, which paints the death of the French leader in the most tragic colors and attributes to his "assassination" all of the English troubles during the first part of the war. *Oeuvres Completes de Thomas, par M. Saint-Surin*. V. This has been discussed in the *Hist. Mag.* VI:201-3.

16 Tr. by F. B. Hough. 1866. 2v. A report of the peace negotiations is given in *Mémoire historique sur la negociation de la France & de l'Angleterre*. . . . 1761, issued the same year in London. For French hopes of retaining possession of the West, see *Doc. Rel. to the Col. Hist. of the State of N. Y.* X:1134 ff.

the surrender to the English the end really had come, however. Save for the introductory sections it is a Spanish colony that is described in *La Louisiane Ensanglantée* . . . (1773), a colony bitterly hurt by the betrayal of faith, a colony smouldering with resentment at the tyranny of O'Reilly, and yet a colony by that leader's very act of oppression indubitably Spain's.[17]

Inevitably by all these events the travel literature was tinged. Explorations were continued; intrepid paddlers not only pushed up the main rivers but threaded their branches; long trips were made on foot through the fur-enriched forest, the waving prairie, or the bare sandy plain. Although many of the discoveries were important, the narratives of them are almost entirely official, terse and lacking the first fine glamor. The lure of trade with the Spanish, upon which Crozat based his dreams of great wealth, prompted the romantic trips of Juchereau de Saint Denis, fascinating because of the personal venturesomeness of the leader;[18] it played an important part, too, in the tours of the Mallet brothers and of Bénard de la Harpe, whose descriptions of the country are noteworthy.[19]

The desire for mineral wealth is even more prominent. Instructions from the king, Crozat, and directors of the Western Company emphasized the search for mines. The imposter Sagean and Le Sueur, whose reports of precious metals Featherstonhaugh later scathingly denounced as fables invented to give him influence at the court of France,[20] on a par with Lahontan's remarkable voyage upon the Long River, received a great deal of aid.[21] And in both north and south bootless quests by men ill fitted to recognize the signs of metals absorbed the too scarce energies of the colony.[22] Of the contagion of the fever Du

---

17 Repub. 1776 under the title *État-Présent de la Louisiane*. . . & tr. in French — *Hist. Coll. of La.* V:127 ff. The Préambule says it is edited by the Chevalier de Champigny from the MS. of a deceased English officer, who had lived in Louisiana.

18 Penicaut in Margry V:494ff. also in French VI:114ff. See also Du Pratz — *Hist. de la Louisiane.* I:11-24 & Margry VI:193ff.

19 Margry reprints the *Relation du Voyage de Bénard de la Harpe* in *Découvertes et établissements.* VI:239ff., and extensive use of his reports is made by Penicaut and the author of the *Journal Historique de l'établissement des Français*, which has for a long time been attributed to la Harpe. For explorations of the Mallets see Margry. VI:455 ff.

20 Featherstonhaugh — *A Canoe Voyage up the Minnay Sotor.* I:304.

21 *Jour. Hist. de l'établissement des Français*, 22 ff., 35 ff., etc. French — *Hist. Coll. of La.* III:19, 23, 110, etc. Le Sueur encountered much opposition, especially in Canada, because of the feeling that his search for minerals was a blind to enable him to make a fortune by the fur trade.

22 A considerable amount of lead was secured, but much money was lost by the

Pratz's chronicle forms perhaps the best illustration. Although he had long sharply criticized the quest for precious minerals, he had scarcely set out upon his very amusing discovery when he experienced a violent desire to go farther north than ever before to try to discover some mines, and soon he reports in fairy tale fashion iron and lead mines and traces of gold.[23]

The ancient desire to find the Western Sea was also potent in this century. Bourgmont reported upon the authority of the Indians a nation of little men possessed of much gold and rubies who were thought to be Chinese;[24] Fabruy de la Bruyère was sent to explore the regions supposed to border upon China and Tartary;[25] Du Pratz spun wonderful tales upon Moncacht-apé's trip to the setting sun[26]. In the north numerous posts were established to aid in the finding of the Western Sea, and Charlevoix was sent out by the regent to ascertain the prospects of exploration by way of the upper lakes.[27] The outstanding figure is the Sieur de la Vérendrye, who with his sons devoted his life to the project and who was the first white man to look upon the Rocky Mountains, which he describes as high and for the most part covered with timber. His records, too, are disappointingly meagre although he speaks of magnificent prairies filled with cattle and deer and although in his journal of 1738-9 he mentions the meeting with the fair-complexioned natives, source of much later conjecture. The high hopes aroused by the Assiniboins ("Every day they entertained us with the tale that the whites we were going to see were Frenchmen like ourselves, who said they were our descendants") and la Vérendrye's subsequent disappointment ("I knew from that time on that we had to make an allowance for all we had been told") illustrate the difficulty of reliance upon the Indians for information.[28] The explorer left

failure to insist upon the agricultural development of the colony. There are many mentions of the quest for minerals. Examples may be found *La. Hist. Quar.* I. no. 3, p. 11 ff., *Wis. Hist. Coll.* XVII: 86, 233, 252, 242, 290, 306, XVI: 325, Margry VI:11-12, 182, 183, 190, 393, *Jour. Hist. de l'établissement des Français* 337, Dumont's *Mémoires Historiques* II: 70-1, *Doc. Rel. to the Col. Hist. of the State of N. Y.* IX: 857, etc.

23 Du Pratz—*Histoire de la Louisiane* I:239. Apparently publishers and authors at the time considered a discovery of a new land or people or of gold as important as they do a love story now.

24 Margry—*Découvertes et établissements.* VI:385.

25 Ibid. VI:468ff.

26 Du Pratz — *Histoire de la Louisiane.* III:103ff.

27 *Jour. Hist. de l'Établissement des Français.* 285-6 is interesting here.

28 See *The Explorations of Verendrye and his Sons*, by Warren Upham for a survey of sources, routes, etc. *Proc. of the Miss. Vall. Hist. Assoc.* I:43ff. Quot.

no records, however, comparing in fullness, flavor, or influence with those of the preceding century.

In a similar fashion the embassies to the Indians were usually somewhat dulled in tone, gloomy with the terrors of native warfare or the jealous fear of Spain's and England's power. Bourgmont, to be sure, set out on a picturesque peace-making and exploring mission, passing great prairies with herds of bison so large that it was impossible to count them, visiting the wandering tribes, and giving them presents. But although he creates some idea of the people he sees and the country he traverses, and although he preserves the figurative speeches of the Indian chiefs, the whole lacks the verve that fascinates in the autobiography of Perrot; the description falls into a formula; the hint of Spanish silver mines arouses more fervor than any aspect of the Indian life or feature of the country.[29]

Detailed discussion of this trip, however, belongs in part with the plains. In part it was bound up, too, with the commercial expeditions already mentioned. The journey of Céloron in 1749, one of the most striking expeditions in the east of the valley as Bourgmont's was in the west, is of an entirely different type — an attempt by the energetic marquis de la Galissonière to win back the wavering allegiance of the natives and to hold for his lord the valley of the Ohio. The importance of this region for the French was early realized, Tonti mentioning it, and the Company of the Indies ordering the establishment of a post there in 1726.[30] Yet it had been unfortunately neglected. Governor Vaudreuil in 1745 had urged the ministry in spite of the expense to erect a fort on the Ouabache, for it was of the highest importance not to delay longer in putting bounds to the ambition of the English; and, writing in 1747 of their encroachments, he again stressed the need.[31] The failure of the home government to comprehend the situation, however, and the years of commercial intercourse had given the English undreamed-of power; everywhere Céloron

from pp. 332 & 333 *South Dakota Historical Collections* VII, where all available material is brought together and translated. See Margry VI:58lff. and *Report of the Canadian Archives.* 1889. p. 1 ff. for the originals.

29 For the *Relation du Voyage du Sieur de Bourgmont* see Margry VI:398ff., also 383ff. Dumont gives a rather highly colored account of the Missouri post in his *Mémoires* II:74 and Du Pratz has several chapters on Bourgmont's trip. *Histoire de la Louisiane* III:141ff.

30 Margry → VI: 658-9. See also *Jour. Hist. de l'Établissement des Francais,* 359 for early comment. Juchereau de St. Denis' tannery was early abandoned.

31 Margry → *Ibid.* VI:661-2, 663

meets with traces of the traders, coolness from the Indians, cogent reasoning instead of immediate acceptance of the great white father's message. Very different was his feverish burial of plaques, his eager present giving from the placid sense of possession with which the French had first drifted down the Beautiful River. With the skill of desperation La Galissonière's emissary brings in every possible argument—the promise of traders, troops; the fair treatment the natives had received in the last war fought for their benefit by the French father; the opposing policies in colonization; the Englishmen's hidden purpose to grasp the territories of the Indians. And everywhere he seeks to secure the non-intervention of the Indians or their aid in driving out the intruders; the expulsion of the English "is the means of seeing in your villages a sky ever beautiful and serene."

The response to his words reveals a double tragedy, for, in spite of the stoicism of the chiefs at times there breaks forth the despair of a race already dependent on European commerce and destined to be crushed by the advance of the white men.

> "Consider, my Father, the situation in which we are placed. If you make the English withdraw who furnish us with our necessities, particularly the blacksmith who repairs our guns and our tomahawks, we shall be helpless and exposed to death from hunger and misery on the Beautiful River. Have pity on us, my father; for the present you can not give us what we need. Leave with us at least for this winter or at least until we go on the hunt, the blacksmith and someone who can aid us. We promise you that in the spring the English will go away."

Such outbursts are exceptions, however; usually Céloron is met with politeness, imperturbability, grave promises of decision in the spring. In spite of this baffling sense of defeat he goes on and on, only to realize at last that fair speeches and gifts will no longer avail.

> "All that I can say is that the tribes in these parts are very badly disposed toward the French and entirely devoted to the English. I do not know in what way we can bring them back."[32]

[32] Margry—*Découvertes et établissements* VI:678, 683, 725. There are numerous important articles about Céloron's trip in the various historical publications and

His conclusion was a sorrowful one; in it we find shadowed the overthrow of New France.

The *Jesuit Relations* decrease in importance in this century as other sources of information develop.[33] In their accounts, it is interesting to note, a process of deromanticization seems to have taken place. St. Cosme, for instance, mentions in the most casual manner the painted rock figures that thrilled Marquette. This change is even more pronounced in the letter sent by Father Gravier "from Fort Mississippi, 17 Leagues from its discharge into the Mexican Gulf or sea on The 16th of February 1701." For him there had been little charm in the trip down the Great River. The iron mines, he discovered, were merely "veins of earth, hard and apparently petrified"; the Natchez temple contained no such wonders as the writer of the *Dernières Découvertes* had "invented . . . to embellish his story." And although he does comment on the beauty of the Mississippi and the attractive qualities of the Southern Indians, the praise he gives seems far outweighed by his enumeration of inconveniences — stinging insects, great rains and excessive heat, wretched landings and scanty fare. Father Marest, also, although he lauds the beauty and "charming variety," of the country, "the vast and dense forests, the delightful prairies," finds it incumbent upon him to shatter the idyllic pictures built up by various proselyting papers and the much discussed author of the Pseudo-Tonti relation.

> "I wish that I could give you some information concerning our Missions, that might correspond to the idea which you perhaps have formed of them. What is heard every day in Europe of those immense Countries studded with Towns and Villages, in which an innumerable multitude of Idolaters present themselves

translations of his report *Wis. Hist. Coll.* XVIII:36 ff., *Ohio Arch. & Hist. Quar.* XXIX: 331 ff., and elsewhere. Father Bonnecamps gives an even more mournful summary of the power of the English. *Ibid.* 409-10, *Jes. Rel.* LXIX:185. For the Indians' account of the trip see *The Papers of Sir William Johnson* I:276ff. Many references to it may be found in the New York and Pa. colonial collections, etc.

33 Similar narratives showing the development of the country are those of the Ursulines, pioneer educators of Louisiana. The letters of Marie Hachard, first published in 1728, have been ed. by Gravier under the title *Relation du Voyage des Dames Religieuses Ursulines de Rouen à la Nouvelle-Orleans* (1872). See also *Relation des premières Ursulines à la Nouvelle Orleans et de leur établissement en cette ville.* Par la Rev. Mère St. Augustin de Tranchepain, supérieure. . . . 1859. Both give fascinating glimpses of the spirit of these early nuns and of the new colony. See also Heloise H. Cruzat — *The Ursulines of La., La. Hist. Quar.* II: 5 ff.

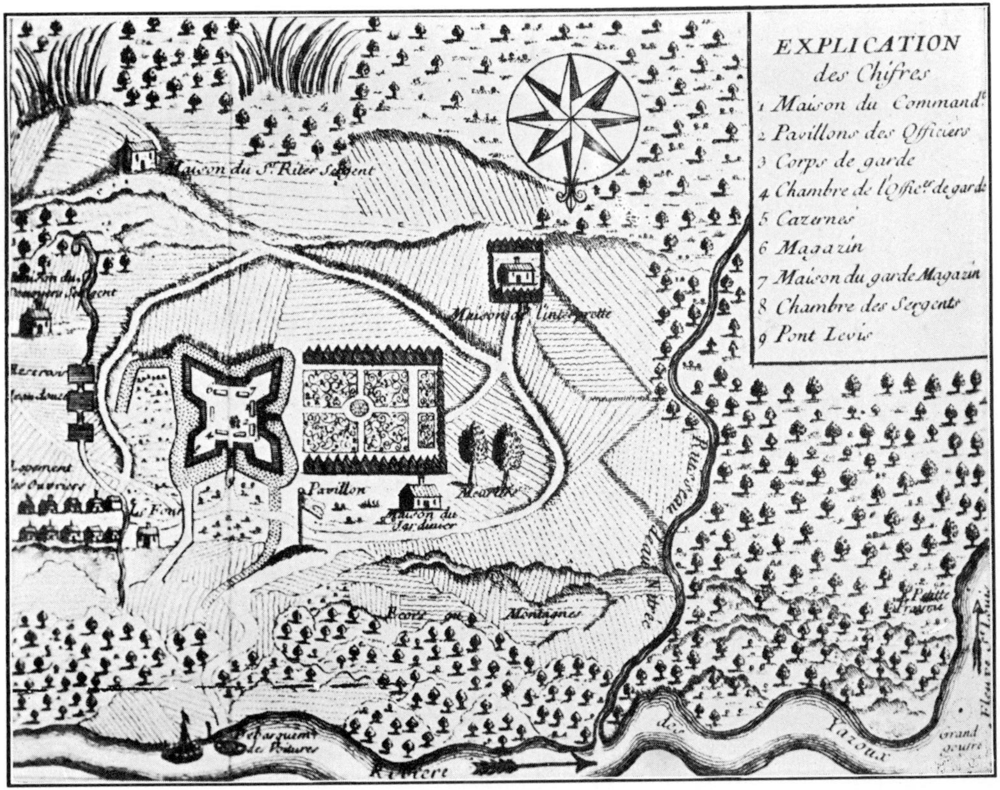


Plan of the Concession of M. le Blanc and his associates from *Mémoires Historiques sur la Louisiane.* II: 85

in crowds to the zeal of the Missionaries, would give room to believe that things here are upon the same footing. Such is very far from being the fact, my Reverend Father; in a great extent of Country, scarcely three or four villages are found. Our life is passed in threading dense forests, in climbing mountains, in crossing lakes and rivers in canoes, that we may overtake some poor Savage who is fleeing from us, and whom we do not know how to render less savage by either our words or our attentions.

"Nothing is more difficult than the conversion of these Savages; it is a miracle of the Lord's mercy; we must first make men of them, and afterward work to make them Christians." [34]

The missionaries continue, however, to give an instructive picture of the development of the country. Gravier records the appearance of an English trader bearing guns and merchandise to alienate the Akansas from the French "and especially from the Missionaries, against whom he bore malice. . . ." He pictures clearly the new posts and gives various interesting anecdotes such as the one concerning the surprise of the Spanish governor, who "through politeness . . . told the Officers that he was visiting the coast to Drive the English away" Poisson portrays in detail the trial of Mississippi voyaging and gives very valuable information as to the colonists in 1727.

"A certain tract of land *granted* by the Company of the Indies to a private individual, or to several persons who have together formed a partnership, for the purpose of clearing that land and making it valuable, is called a 'concession.' These are what were called, when the *Mississipi* was in greatest vogue, the 'Counties' and 'Marquisates' of the *Mississipi*; the concessionaries are, therefore, the gentlemen of this country. The greater part of them were not people who would leave France; but they equipped vessels and filled them with superintendents, stewards, storekeepers, clerks, and workmen of various trades, with provisions and all kinds of goods. They had to plunge into the woods, to set up cabins, to choose their ground, and to burn the cane brakes and trees. This beginning seemed very hard to people not at all accustomed to that

34 *Jes. Rel.* LXV:101, 111, 141, LXVI:223, 219.

kind of labor; the superintendents and their subordinates, for the most part, amused themselves in the places where a few Frenchmen had already settled, and there they consumed their provisions. The work had hardly begun when the concession was ruined; the workman, ill-paid or ill-fed, refused to work, or himself took his pay; the warehouses were pillaged. Do you not recognize in this the Frenchman? It is partly this which has prevented the country from being settled as it should be, after the immense expenditure that has been made for that purpose.

"A smaller portion of land granted by the Company is called a 'habitation.' A man with his wife or his partner clear a little ground, builds himself a house on four piles, covers it with sheets of bark, and plants corn and rice for his provisions: the next year he raises a little more for food, and has also a field of tobacco; if at last he succeeds in having three or four Negroes, then he is out of his difficulties. This is what is called a *habitation,* a *habitant*; but how many of them are as nearly beggars as when they began! . . . . . . . . . . .

"Besides the concessionaries and the habitants, there are also in this country people who have no other occupation than that of roving about: 1st, the women or girls taken from the hospitals of Paris, or from the salpêtrière, or other places of equally good repute, who find that the laws of marriage are too severe, and the management of a house too irksome. A voyage of four-hundred leagues does not terrify these heroines; I already know two of them whose adventures would furnish material for a romance. 2nd, The travelers; these, for the most part, are young men sent to the Mississippi 'for various reasons' by their relatives or by the law, and who, finding that the land lies too low for digging, prefer to hire themselves to row and to ply from one shore to the others. 3rd, The hunters; these at the end of summer ascend the Mississipi for two or three hundred leagues, to the country where there are cattle; they make *plats côtés,* — that is to say, they dry in the sun the flesh that is on the flanks of those animals, — and salt the rest; they also make bear's oil; toward spring, they descend the river and supply the Colony with meat."

From Vivier we have a good account of the condition of

the inhabited Mississippi in 1750—New Orleans and its surrounding plantations, the upper settlements from which are exported fur, bears' grease, salt beef, tallow, tar, and from the Illinois especially flour and pork. He also gives a glimpse of the troubles that come with civilization—the dangers of the liquor traffic ("The Savages—and especially the Illinois, who are the gentlest and most tractable of men—become when intoxicated, madmen and wild beasts"), the religious troubles stirred up by the English who "as well as the French, trade among the Alibamon Savages." Most significant of all it is with fear of the loss of the territory that he closes.

"For the rest this country is of far greater importance than is imagined. Through its position alone, it deserves that France should spare nothing to retain it. It is true that it has not yet enriched the King's coffers, and that convoys to and fro are costly; but it is none the less true that the tranquillity of Canada and the safety of the entire lower part of the Colony depend upon it. Assuredly, without this post there can be no communication by land between Louisiana and Canada. There is another consideration; several regions of the same Canada and all those on the lower part of the river would be deprived of the provisions they obtain from the Illinois, which are often a great resource to them. By founding a solid establishment here, prepared to meet all these troubles, the King would secure the possession of the most extensive and the finest country in north America. To be convinced of this one has but to glance at the well-known map of Louisiana, and to consider the situation of the Illinois country and the multitude of Nations against whom the post usually serves as a barrier."[35]

None of the *Jesuit Relations* can compare in momentousness, however, with the last sad journey down the Mississippi (1763). Not this time with spirits exulting, with hearts joy-filled at each stroke of the paddle, did the fathers skim down the river; not this time did they open eyes wide to the marvels around them and thrill at the lowing of cattle at rest in the prairies. No chanting, calumet-offering savages hailed them in wonder; no

[35] *Jes. Rel.* LXV:117, 165, LXVII:281-5, LXIX:201, 205, 229.

chieftains proffered them welcoming banquets; no pitiful ignorance of kindly disposed peoples stirred them with passionate yearning. For their pioneer Marquette had been entering upon his long-anticipated kingdom; they were expelled from its fertile fields and green pastures. The decision, feared since the arrival of the decree of the Parliament of Paris of August 6, 1761, nevertheless incredulously received from the Council of Louisiana, had been executed with full rigor; cattle had been seized; buildings and furnishings, sold; altar vestments, given away; the chapels, razed; when with a few books, a little clothing and food, and their confiscated slaves, the priests embarked. To them it mattered little that sloops containing many people were now in use on the river, that the banks were domestic with the plantations of white men. They knew only that the season was desolate, the prairie mist-shrouded, the turf sodden-brown, that occasionally friends offered welcome and comfort, but that always they journeyed with the sense of defeat. They were looking their last on the wide-spreading midlands; for them there could be no more thought of a great spiritual empire.[36] And although they were unaware of it, their farewell to the country they had done so much to make known was to be but the precursor of other migrations. The cession to England, just beginning to be realized, was to send slowly but steadily over the river the unfortunate inhabitants of the eastern shore, as down from the north had drifted earlier the scattered families of Acadia.

About the remaining accounts of the period there are two outstanding features. One is the beginning of a true travel literature, the description of a country by men who are visiting it on some definite mission or of their own volition, who are not intimately linked with its destinies as most of the writers so far have been. With the advent of such travellers the second point is inextricably linked. Although on the whole they tend to have greater independence of judgment than the inhabitants or exploiters of a colony, to see things in a clearer, more critical light, nevertheless to some extent their opinions are already formulated by the early relations they have read; they exult or criticize sharply as their preconceptions are surpassed or disappointed;

---

36 *Banissement des Jesuites de la Louisiane* by F. P. Watrin. 1764. *Jes Rel.* LXX:211ff.

in short, reaction to established tradition is exceedingly pronounced.

Of this class of writers Father Charlevoix is one of the most important. His official capacity as well as his stay in the north and his voyage down the Mississippi gave him good opportunity for a study of New France. According to the custom of the time he combined his own observations with others' material in the form of letters addressed to the Duchess de Lesdiguières and published with his history as the *Journal d'un Voyage fait par ordre du Roi dans l'Amérique Septentrionale* (1744). His discussion of the Indians is interesting, for although he pointed out in detail their filth and vices, ironically enough his praise of them as passionate lovers of freedom and as the true philosophers seems to have set the stamp of authority on the cult of nature that with Rousseau as its apostle was to be so influential. Charlevoix's discussion of the French is of even greater significance, for he realized that by their extraordinary adaptability to the life of the open they had both lost and gained. To it he attributes their remarkable endurance, part of their charm, their power of accomplishment under good leaders, but also their readiness to fight, their long periods of indolence and riotous pleasuring, their independence, their extravagance. In addition his thoughtful contrast of English and French characteristics, settlements, and trade does much to explain the results of the later struggle. All these conclusions drawn specifically from the inhabitants of the upper colonies yet apply in a general way to the inmates of the Mississippi Valley; in treating the latter region, he gives, also, an interesting picture of the contact of Indian and white.

The cultivation of the territory is by this time well under way. Although the priest criticizes the emphasis placed upon mines and the carelessness with which the search for them has been made as well as the fatal enticement that draws men to trade with the Spaniards, leaving "the best Lands in the World uncultivated," and although he finds many evidences of shiftlessness and neglect, there are enough of fruitful and well arranged habitations to make "a Lesson for those lazy People, whose Poverty very unjustly disparages a Country which will render a hundred-fold of whatever is sowed in it." To such an extent indeed is this bounteousness of the land marked that Charlevoix already pictures Illinois as the "Granary of *Louisiana,* which it can supply with Plenty of Wheat, though it should be quite peopled down to the Sea." And, it is interesting to note, it is primarily in this utilitarian aspect that he regards the prairies. To the awe inspired by the great forests he devotes one of his most impressive paragraphs, but to the prairies, aside from the discussion of their agricultural possibilities, he renders only such involuntary tribute as is found in the following.

> "On the Left, about sixty Leagues of the River of Bulls, we see the *Moingona* come out of the Midst of an immense and magnificent Meadow, which is quite covered with Buffaloes and other wild creatures."

Yet in spite of the evident fertility of the valley and the development that has taken place within it, Father Charlevoix fails to find many of the tribes and much of the magnificence that he has been led to expect; Garcillaso de la Vega, Hennepin, Lahontan come in particularly for his censure as do all travellers "who make no Scruple to fill their Journals with whatever they hear said, without troubling themselves about the Truth of any Thing." But that it is not merely the Indians that are given misleading representations is evidenced by the following discussion of New Orleans.

> "This city is the first, which one of the greatest Rivers in the world has seen raised on its Banks. If the eight Hundred fine houses, and the five parishes which the Newspapers gave it some time ago, are reduced at present to an hundred Barracks, placed in no very great Order; to a great Storehouse, built of Wood; to two or three Houses, which would be no Ornament to a Village of *France*; and to the half of a sorry Store-house, which they agreed to lend to the Lord of the Place, and which he had no sooner taken possession of, but they turned him out to dwell under a Tent; what pleasure, on the other Side, to see insensibly increasing this future Capital of a fine and vast Country, and to be able to say . . . full of a well-grounded Hope, this wild and desert Place, which the Reeds and Trees do yet almost wholly cover, will be one Day, and perhaps that day is not far off, an opulent City, and the Metropolis of a great and rich Colony."[37]

37 Charlevoix, Father P. F. X. — *A Voyage to North America.* . . 2v. 1766.

Probably Charlevoix was thinking of Bonrepos' *Description du Mississipy* (1720), which grossly exaggerates conditions in the new land and which Villiers du Terrage thinks was printed at the expense of an unscrupulous speculator, perhaps even of the Company.[38] It is an imitation of Vallette de Laudun's *Relation de la Louisiane ou Mississipy,* which gives at the request of a lady information about a country destined to be "the Peru of France." The latter author's praise of the Jesuits and the French officers in their difficult situations is interesting, and his brief account of the country shows some endeavor for accuracy, giving hearsay reports as such. The Illinois country, for instance, is spoken of as "the most beautiful one in the world, full of lead mines, copper, and silver mines."[39]

Such statements were not uncommon in the days of the Law Bubble. A good idea of the kind of reports circulating as fact is afforded by *Le Nouveau Mercure.* The number for September, 1717 mentions on the authority of the Indians mines of gold and silver and the emerald rock to which Dumont scornfully refers; and the letter from the emigrant Duval to his wife printed March, 1719 gives similarly flattering comment. Another letter printed in 1719, this one from the Illinois, says, "We are not among treasures but above them; and we can say without exaggeration that we trample them under foot since there are many rich silver mines over which we walk." Bonrepos states that "Along the upper Mississippi, the mountains are full of gold and silver, copper, lead and quick-silver mines."[40] Maps were made or revised showing the Mississippi region filled with mines and carrying out the fictitious representations of New Orleans.[41] Not only was this true of France; the Company in its first glowing days captured the imagination of the world; presses in England, Germany, Holland, France poured forth pamphlet after pamphlet, probably the first of the many golden promises to immigrants and investors that have made a distinct division of the literature of the prairies.

II:212, 217, 175, 169, I:166, II:207-8. Tr. also in French—*Hist. Coll. of La.* III. Since this chapter was written an excellent reprint of the first London ed. of 1761 ed. by Dr. Louise Phelps Kellogg has been issued by The Caxton Club (1923).

38 *La. Hist. Quar.* III:199.

39 This was included in Bernard's *Recueil de Voyages au Nord.* V. and the corresponding *Relations de la Louisiane et du Fleuve Mississippi.* (1720). It was reissued 1768 at Paris & La Haye, as *Journal d'un Voyage à la Louisiane fait en 1720* . . . For quot. see p. 26, 1731 ed. of *Rec. de Voy.* V.

40 *La. Hist. Quar.* III:199.

41 For reproductions see Ibid. 200, 202.

Some of these like *A Full and Impartial Account of the Company of the Mississippi . . . To which is added a Description of the Country . . . In French and English . . .* (1720) were comparatively moderate in tone even though the title mentioned "the almost incredible advantages thereby accruing" to the French; the majority, however, make the Middle West a veritable Eldorado. The story of the speculation mania that seized upon the people as a result of these advertisements and of their greed for the quick and easy profits that they saw being made all about them, has been told too often to be repeated, picturesque as are the incidents recorded by Duhautchamp and other contemporaries.[42] Law was idolized; story tellers and poets paid homage to the new goddess of Quinquempoix Street.

"J'aime à présent mieux mille fois
Le doux séjour de Quinquempoix,
Que l'Isle de Cythere:
On y fait d'aimables emplois
Sans Contrat, ni Notaire;
L'amour a vendu son carquois,
Pour être Actionnaire."[43]

Even in the height of the frenzy, however, shrewd observers like Defoe in *The Chimera: or the French Way of Paying National Debts Laid Open* or the author of *Faits Fugitifs* in the October, 1719 number of *Le Nouveau Mercure* warned against unstable finance. And when the bubble burst, the paper fortunes proved worthless, the kingdom was once more saddled with debt, there appeared perhaps the most interesting expressions of this most interesting period — recriminations and satires as bitter as the flatteries had been fulsome in the great days of Law. The dismal failure of the scheme was recorded in tracts such as *The Memoirs, Life, and Character of the Great Mr. Law and his Brother at Paris. Down to this Present Year, 1721, with an Ac-*

42 Du Hautchamp — *Histoire du système des finances, sous la minorité de Louis XV. Pendant les années 1719 & 1720 . . .* 6v. in 3. 1739. An invaluable contemporary history, including sketches of Law and the regent, an account of the Mississippi country, of Law's scheme, of the avidity with which the speculation was carried on, of the extraordinary changes in fortune, of the final catastrophe, etc. as well as official documents, songs such as those quoted above, etc. Diarists such as Saint-Simon also give very vivid pictures of the craze.

43 *Le Nouveau Mercure Dec.* 1719. 117. Quoted in Jean Buvat — *Journal de la Régence*, (1865) II: 48.

# MISSISIPPI, OF 'T WYD-BEFAAMDE GOUD-LAND, DOOR DE INBEELDING DER WIND-NEGOTIE.

DIt 's 't wond'ro Miſſiſippi Land
Befaamd door zijne Actie-handel,
't Geen aan den Wind-god is verpand,
En door bedrog en ſnóden wandel
Ontelb're Schatten heeft verkwiſt.
Maar Miſſiſippi, 't is verlóren,
't Is met u achter 't Net geviſt,
Want Schynſchoon, die u van te vóren
Zoo rykelyk heeft afgemaald,
Is nu ontmaskerd, en haar wezen
Word door de Waarheid overſtraald,
't Geen ménig zijn verderf doet vrézen;
Want 't is vergeefs daar Volk geplant,
Daar Goud noch Zilver is te hálen;
De hoop die de Acties bragt in ſtand
Ziet zig met ſchande en ſchaâ betálen,
En Hennepins verréze Geeſt
Schynd elk dit opzet af te ráden,
Die niet te ſtout en onbevreeſt,
Het Zijn wil voor den Schijn verſmáden,
Want 's Konings-kiſt ontbloot van Geld,
Waar in de Rotten ſpélemeyen,
Moeſt door deez' Konſtgreep zijn herſteld,
Al zou het de Onderdaan beſchreyen
(1) Louis leyd naâuw op 't Praal-bed neér,
Wanneer een Schotſſe-wind komt waayen,
En weet zig met een ſchijn van eer
(2) In Orleans zijn raad te drayen;
Hier op word Miſſiſippis naam
Gelijk een Af-god aangebeden
En deez' verdervende Actie-kraam,
Ging boven regt, en deugd, reden.
(3) Toen klom de grootsheyd, wijl men 't Ge
In Huys brengt op een Kruyers-wagen,
Daar 't op de grond leid ongeteld,
Als drek, niet waard om naar te vragen;
Maar ach! die blijdſchap duurt zo kort,
(4) Wijl de Armoede en haar geſpélen
Den Actie-hand'laar overſtort
En doet hem in haar rampen délen;
Dog wijl de uytvinder van dit kwaad,
Zijn valsheid door de vlugt laat blijken,
Zo zal het haat'lyk Actie-zaad
Eerlang ook van de Wéreld wijken,
Want hoe men de Acties ook beziet,
't Is Wind, en Rook, en anders niet.

From *Het Groote Tafereel der Dwaasheid*

*curate and Particular Account of the Establishment of the Mississippi Company in France, the Rise and Fall of its Stock, and Alle the Subtle Artifices Used to Support the National Credit of that Kingdom by the Pernicious Project of Paper-credit. Written by a Scots Gentleman.* (1721). The most horrible descriptions of the country were spread broadcast; exile to the Mississippi was used as a threat and as a means of vengeance. Doggerel verses were posted in public places or ran from lip to lip pilloring the scheme and its founders.

Sarcastic comments had been frequent even in the maddest periods of speculation, witness *Le Misissippi,*

"Aujourdhui il n'est plus question
De parler de Constitution,
Ni de la guerre avec l'*Espagne.*
Un nouveau pays de Cocagne,
Quc l'on nommc Mississipi,
Roule à présent sur le tapis.

"Sans charbon, fourneau, ni soufflet,
Un homme a trouvé le secret
De la pierre philosophale
Dans cette terre occidentale,
Et nous fait voir jusqu'à présent
Que nous étions des ignorants."

or the attacks on Law and his infatuated followers.

"Quand Law jouait à la chance
A Venise, à Parme, à Florence,
On ne s'y fiait que très peu.
Mais aujourd'hui le tour est drôle,
Nous mettons notre argent au jeu
Et nous jouons sur sa parole."

* * * *

"On dit qu'au Mississipi
On a trouvé, chose sûre,
De l'or plus qu'au Potosi,
Ture lure.
Il est bon pour la dorure
Robin ture lure.

"On sait qu'il est dans Paris
Des fous de toute nature,
Mais Law, dans son parti,
En a triplé la Mesure."

It was but natural then that as the dreams of wealth were shattered, the denunciations should grow more and more virulent. *Le Diable Banquier,* the title of one song, is one of the commonest epithets applied to Law. A Satanic genealogy for the whole affair is traced in detail.

"Belzeibuth engendra Law,
Law engendra le système,
Le système engendra la Banque,
La Banque engendra le Mississipi," etc.

*Les Résultats du Système* describes the high prices, the monopolies by gamblers, etc. A *Tocsin* was tolled over the "Maudite nation, faible troupeau de dindes."[44] Tracts like *Le Banquerotteur en désespoir; Das ist, der verzweifflende Banqueroturer* tauntingly repeated the plaints of the victims. Jean Buvat gives a list of book titles in the facetious vein of the eighteenth century.[45] Playing cards and clever cartoons such as compose the suggestive folio *Het groote Tafereel der Dwaasheid, Vertoonende de opkomst, voortgang en ondergang der Actie, Bubbel en Windnegotie, in Vrankryk, Engleland, en de Nederlanden, gepleegt in den Jaare, MDCCXX,* . . . reveal keen comprehension of the absurdities and tragedies of the situation. Altogether the Mississippi received an extraordinary amount of undesirable publicity, excessive praise and excessive blame being equally unfortunate.[46]

About the remaining descriptions of Louisiana there is little to be said. *The Present State of the Country and Inhabitants, Europeans and Indians of Louisiana, on the North Continent of*

44 Raunié, Émile — *Chansonnier Historique du XVIIIe Siècle* . . . 10v. 1879. III:132-3, 139-40, 154, 218, 233, 210, 205.

45 Typical titles are *Les Directeurs de la Retraite, par les sieurs Paris; dédié à M. Law, Journal de la Régence* II:173, *Nouveau Guidon des Finances; par le sieur Law, revu et corrigé par le duc de Bourbon.* Ibid. 344.

46 As official recognition of this fact note the Memoir of La Galissonière on the importance of the Illinois settlements, 1748, "They have perhaps this much in common with everything relating to the Mississippi, that, after having been estimated far above their real value, they can at present barely be looked upon as of any use." *Wis. Hist. Coll.* XVII:493.

A Buffalo Hunt among the Akansas from Bossu's *Nouveaux Voyages dans l'Amérique Septentrionale* . . . 1777.

*America, by an Officer at New Orleans to His Friend at Paris* . . . (1744) gives a harrowing picture of the drunkenness of the soldiery and the waste and dishonesty. Bossu, too, an officer of the marines, asked to be returned to France after his second trip to the colony because of his dissatisfaction with conditions prevailing there. His *Nouveaux Voyages aux Indes Occidentales* . . . (2 t. 1768) betrays some use of Du Pratz and other authorities, but it gives a good account of the tribes and settlements along the Mississippi and of the Illinois colony where he was first stationed as well as of the tricks of the coureurs-de-bois. His work is interesting because he was in America while the war with England was being waged and because in spite of his criticism of the graft and disorders prevailing there he gives high praise to the country, criticizing France for the cession to Spain.[47] His second book *Nouveaux Voyages dans l'Amérique Septentrionale* . . . (1777), a series of letters written to a former comrade in the new world, is chiefly remarkable for its idyllic portrayal of life among the Indians. Pagès, in his *Voyages autour du Monde* . . . 1767 . . . 1776 (2v. 1782) also illustrates the romantic tendencies of these later travellers. He gives a vivid picture in the first volume of New Orleans and its environs, but his dream of discovering the North Pole and his tour among the Indians show suggestively close kinship with Chateaubriand.

It is but natural, however, that visitors to Louisiana should decrease after the cession to Spain, most of the European travellers turning instead to the new nation. Don Antonio de Ulloa's *Noticias Americanas* . . . (1772), chiefly important for his comparison of the phenomena of the two Americas, gives some glimpses of the changes along the Mississippi — the destruction wrought by strong drink among the natives, the increase of negro and white, the mixture of races evident in the half-breed hunters attached to many families, the gay swimming and fishing parties. For the most part, however, his scientific observations offer little to detain us, especially since the greater part of his attention is devoted to South America. The Spanish Archives, however, long

47 Bossu was imprisoned after the publication of this book. Carlyle said Bossu's work had a strange interest to him "like some fractional Odyssey or letter. Only a hundred years ago, and the Mississippi has changed as never valley did; in 1751 older and stranger, looked at from *its* present date, than Balbec or Nineveh!" *Carlyle — Emerson Correspondence.* II:228.

inaccessible to scholars, are revealing a treasure trove of material on the Spanish control of the Mississippi Valley. Some use of this is made in Gayarré's volume dealing with the Spanish Domination (c.1854), and Mr. Louis Houck's *The Spanish Regime in Missouri* . . . (2v. 1909) is excellent in this respect. Reports such as that of Don Pedro Piernas describing the Spanish Illinois Country in 1769 give an excellent idea of the territory, as does Trudeau's report for 1798.[48] Steps were taken to obtain clearer knowledge of the country to the west, as is revealed in the organization by St. Louis merchants of the Spanish Commercial Exploration Company.[49] On the whole the period of Spanish sway seems to have been not a bad thing for the colony. Cultivation of the soil increased, trade developed, life became more luxurious, social cleavages grew more pronounced, amusements in New Orleans became cosmopolitan.

The Spanish control was not entirely peaceful, but the combats that took place and the part Louisiana played in the Revolution must be left to other historians. At the time, however, Spain was naturally unaware of the menace soon to be presented by the new nation, which Carondelet summarized excellently in his report of 1793. After pointing out the changes that had taken place since Spain first gained possession of Louisiana he states,

> "So many advantages are counterbalanced by the unmeasured ambition of a new people, who are vigorous, hostile to all subjection, and who have been uniting and multiplying in the silence of peace, and almost ignored, with a remarkable rapidity from the time of the recognized independence of the United States until the present time . . . . . . . . . . . .
>
> "This vast and restless population, driving the Indian tribes continually before them and upon us, is endeavoring to gain all the vast continent occupied by the Indians between the Ohio and Misisipi Rivers, the Gulf of Mexico, and the Appalachian Mountains. Thus they are becoming our neighbors, while at the same time, they are clamoring threateningly for the free navigation of the Misisipi. If they obtain their pur-

---

48 Houck — *Span. Reg.* I:66 ff., II:247 ff.

49 Ibid. — II:148ff. For report of Trudeau, leader of the first expedition, see *Amer. Hist. Rev.* XIX:299ff. & *Mo. His. Soc.'Coll.* IV:9ff. See also *Notes Supplementary to any ed. of Lewis & Clarke* by F. J. Teggart, *Amer. Hist. Assoc. Annual Report,* 1908. I:183-195.

pose, their ambition will not be limited to this part of the Misisipi. Their writings, and their public papers and speeches, all have as their object the navigation to the Gulf by way of the rivers Misisipi, Movila, Perla, and Apalachicola, which empty into the Gulf; the rich fur-trade of the Misuri; and in time the possession of the rich mines of the interior provinces of the very kingdom of Mexico. Their method of extension and their policy are as much to be feared by Spain as their arms." etc.[50]

The government papers are full of suggestions for combating this danger from importing the unhappy Scioto immigrants to fighting fire with fire and using the Americans to swell the population of the Spanish territories.

Another danger, more productive of literature, had its source overseas. The French minister had come in 1793 with instructions to secure the aid of the settlers beyond the Alleghanies for a raid upon Louisiana and ultimately for revolutionary movements in the other Spanish possessions. The Journal of his agent André Michaux, selected to communicate with the Kentucky leaders (1793) has been published by Thwaites (*E. W. T.* v. III.). General Victor Collot, however, was the man who alarmed the Spanish, Baron de Carondelet reporting December 1, 1796 that the effects of the former's journey were quickly evident, "for, as they advise me under date of October 17, there was formed at San Luis, the capital of the settlements there, after Collot went away, a society to which was given the name of 'Sansculottes,' . . . that it frequently gives public functions and dances, to which invitations are issued without any reserve, under the aforesaid appelation of 'Sansculottes'; and that during these diversions songs are sung that are revolutionary, and that tend to influence the most loyal vassals to rebellion."[51] Collot's device of

50 Houck — *Span. Reg.* II:9ff. quot. 11-12.

51 Houck — *Span. Reg.* II:133-4. It was during this period that General George Rogers Clark used the title of Field Marshal of the French Armies and of the Revolutionary Legions on the Mississippi. Sherrill, C. H. — *French Memories of Eighteenth Century America* (1915), 216, gives Minister Adet's report of his instructions to Collot, who was anxious to do something for France during his enforced stay in America. The first (1805) edition of his book is so rare that I have seen no reference to it. Apparently only a few sheets were bound up, the remainder being used for the 1826 ed., which appeared with the valuable volume of plates. The English translation of the 1826 ed. has been reprinted by O. Lange in his series of Rare Americana (1924). I am indebted to the attendants in the Rare Book room of the New York Public Library for the results of their comparison of the two editions as well as for other courtesies.

concealing his authentic notes and of preparing a special journal filled with praises of Carondelet was fairly successful in spite of his arrest, and his *Voyage en Amérique Septentrionale* . . . (1804) forms one of the most valuable portrayals of the western valley at this period. Naturally he pays particular attention to the French settlements. For the habitants of Illinois he has nothing but hard words, concluding that they have preserved only one French virtue, that of courage, but adding that their country is perhaps the only one of which descriptions had not been exaggerated, it being, indeed, superior to all reports. Of St. Louis his account is more favorable. He found there about six hundred inhabitants, of whom two hundred were capable of bearing arms, all French. As interesting corroboration of Carondelet's suspicions he adds that they have degenerated less than their fellows on the American side, and that the spirit which characterizes the French nation is pronounced among them, of excellent patriots whose life and fortune belong to France. The forts, he states, are in such bad condition and the garrisons so weak that one would think Spain was on the point of abandoning her posts in upper Louisiana. Not only did he discuss fully means of defense, but he made excellent sketches of the existing fortifications and of other points of interest.

His book, however, is only one of an extraordinary group near the close of the century, all brought forth by the expectation that the long lost colony of Louisiana was to be once more under the dominion of France. Popular interest, which had alternately glorified and scorned this land of river-banding forest, dank bayous, and flower-strewn prairies, again was directed toward it. Travellers and officials of various sorts recorded their impressions and experiences; books were issued ostensibly new but in reality a clever compound of former voyagers and historians. Collot was obviously animated by a genuine desire to serve France; Milfort (real name Le Clerc), who says his *Mémoire ou Coup d'Oeil Rapide sur mes Differens Voyages et mon Séjour dans les Nation Crëck* (1802) was written in great haste without his having a chance for revision that it might be of aid in the expedition France was fitting out, although he attained high rank in France, was even then charged with being an adventurer who sought to impose on the first consul; Louis Dubroca's patching together of others' materials to meet the contemporary demand in his *L'Itinéraire des Français dans la Louisiane . . .* (1802) was recognized and denounced by Baudry des Lozières.[52] The contents of these volumes were as varied as their authors — biographical sketches, detailed accounts of plants and animals, praises of the country mingled with statistics of trade, discussions of government, descriptions of the people. To them all, however, certain features are common.

Almost all of them are, of course, essentially handbooks. Made to give information about a colony almost forgotten, they not only discuss its present and future but the brave incidents of its past. The virility of Louisiana's explorers, their versatility and courage, the stamp of their personality upon the affections of the red man, all these receive a praise unknown at the time it was earned. The romance of the region, long founded upon old legend or travellers' tales equally fabulous, now begins to be transferred to the deeds of its promoters. So, too, a change is marked in the facts about the commerce; no longer is the discussion confined to possibilities for the future; elaborate tables are given showing fairly considerable exports, among them manufactures, to balance the former long tally of imports.

All of these things imply, of course, a fairly long history, a colony firmly established, points even more definitely brought out in the descriptions of the valley. No longer is it the Elysian field looked upon by its discoverers or even the sparsely settled region handed over to the Spaniards. The innumerable bison herds that long had blackened in their grazing the valley's rich expanse, had now succumbed to the wilful waste and slaughtering power of the musket or like their Indian hunters had been pushed to the west. The soothing undulations of the virgin prairie were now broken by low-roofed cabins, dignified plantation homes, the huts of slaves, and palisade-like cypress fences; its thick tangled grasses and lacing flower roots were cleft apart by white puffing cotton, indigo, tobacco, cane, and the prim green of corn rows.

The writers are fairly united not only in revealing the development of the country, but in showing differentiation in the various communities. Practically all critics, for instance, condemn the

52 *Voyage à la Louisiane . . . fait dans les années 1794 à 1789 . . .* (1802) 264. American officials charged that the publication and display of these books were part of Napoleon's campaign to popularize his taking over Louisiana.

indolent farming and slovenly housekeeping of the Acadians although they agree that the habitants are kindly and hospitable and that they have many good times among themselves. Collot's patriotic fervor seems to temper his judgment and make him one of the few exceptions to the rule when he speaks of the Acadians "so well known for their industry, their social virtues, and their love for their country."[53] The Germans transported by Law come down as the market gardeners for the city, upon whose industry all writers agree. The colony at the Akansas and to a lesser extent almost all the others have a certain indolent and primitive quality that resulted from the half-savage, hunting life of the habitants and that explains in large degree the quick advance of the Anglo Saxon. This is true even of St. Louis. Only on the spot plucked by blood from the Natchez the traveller finds a city with beautiful homes and at Pointe Coupée a considerable degree of luxury.

New Orleans naturally is urban in character. And yet even it suggests a certain crudeness, a harking back to the early days of snake-infested swamp land, of rudely staked streets and paltry fortifications while it strives for a cosmopolitan atmosphere that makes the caustic Duvallon sneer at the pretensions of the inhabitants. Nevertheless it established traditions of tropic languor and feverish gaiety, of heavy scented blossoms and brilliant costumes, of adventurous meetings and gorgeous fêtes, that make the name yet today connote old world romance, a warmth of blood and gallantry of temper almost unknown in our workaday America. Its promises of greatness are much nearer being fulfilled than when Charlevoix visited it; it has become a commercial centre of importance; its unpaved streets are crowded with Irish, Spanish, English, French so that it is a true tower of Babel, and although most of its houses are low balconied dwellings of wood or brick, it does boast a number of pretentious mansions surrounded by beautiful gardens. The winter is the season of carnival and balls — the "bals pour les dames par excellence" where no one of mixed blood may venture and the celebrated balls "pour les femmes de couleur."[54] The little theatre is built of wood, but

53 Collot — *Voy. en Amér. Sep.* II:123. Aubry had a similar opinion, however; see Villiers du Terrage *Les Der. Années de la Louisiane Fran.* 217.

54 Robin, Abbé C. C. — *Voyages dans l'intérieur de la Louisiane . . . (1802-1806)*. 1807. II:120.

even the critic Duvallon is compelled to admit that he has seen there a number of creditable performances.[55]. Undoubtedly the city was growing steadily in luxury and charm; the influx of foreign fashions, new blood, and the increase of wealth together with the Spanish love of festivity tended to increase the entertainment and show; Robin's description of the short period of French dominion during which "M. Laussat displayed in various brilliant entertainments that gracious elegance which seems to be one of the attributes of the French nature" makes us realize definitely the transformation that had taken place in the little capital.[56]

That with such far reaching changes the condition of the Indians was entirely different goes without saying. Some intermarried with the French; many were destroyed in intertribal wars or the white man's conflicts, still more by the ravages of small pox and strong drink; others went to the yet untamed plains. Many are still found at the trading posts or living as down-at-the-heel neighbors of the whites. From them, however, their native dignity has departed as has their native independence. They are greedy for the white man's goods, and just as the mixed villages made up of the wretched remnants of once proud tribes grow increasingly prevalent so writers tend to blend the Indians in the same way, treating all nations under one general head. Naturally under such circumstances emphasis shifts from delineation of physical appearances and depiction of primitive beliefs, to deliberation over the effects of contact with the Europeans or the apparent futility of the missionaries' efforts. Only with Perrin du Lac do we find the savage tribes of the upper rivers starting forth in bold relief as under the able guidance of an old trader he visits and pencils for us the Sioux, Kansas, and Mahas. The dulling effect of reliance upon other sources and upon observation of half-breeds and enfeebled tribes, the squalidity of whose life is relieved by none of the picturesqueness that makes tolerable the utmost filth is evident in almost all of the passages about the Indians.

All this diminution of the Indian glory entails a rather amusing consequence. It was to the untamed red man for three cen-

55 Duvallon, Berquin — *Vue de la Colonie Espagnole du Mississippi . . . en l'année 1802 . . .* 1803. 30.
56 Robin. II:131. For Laussat's own description see Villiers du Terrage's *Les Dernières Années de la Louisiane Française.* 426-7.

turies that the philosophers and poets of Europe had been turning for their model of the natural man. His society, or lack of it, was the ideal one, his code of honor far superior to the white man's, whose virtues his equally outshone; according to his Spartan rule all youths were to be reared; his skin tepee and thick woods or glossy plain formed a happy exchange for the noisome slums and stately palaces of Europe. How the teeming thousands whom careful cultivation could not support in comfort were to find sustenance irked the philosophers little; the possible discomfort in zero weather of a frail bark cabin or shelter of boughs still less; their business was primarily to see visions, and visions they continued to see as long as the travellers gave them material, regardless of the shoddy that was mixed with the spiritual fabric. But when visitors ceased to proclaim the noble red man, monarch of his stately forests, lord of plains unbounded, then indeed a difficulty arose. It is easy to draw inspiration from a bronze warrior of heroic mould, his sleek locks feather-helmed, his eye alert, his garb rich furs that he himself has trapped; but the same warrior dazed by bad whiskey, muddying some soldier's cast-off finery, is a sadly different story. One may find poetry in a Magdalene; the muse is rare that impels a sonnet to one's scrubwoman!

But mankind must always have its Arcadias; the most likely one for the France of the early nineteenth century was the midland of America; therefore when the degenerate red man failed as ideal, nothing was easier than a shift to the cause of his downfall. The attitude toward the dwellers of the new world is one easy to understand. To a France jaded by the long blood-letting of the Reign of Terror, worn by its struggles for rehabilitation, the peace of the gulf colony appealed from afar. And to the tranquillity derived from contemplation of this far-off haven of refuge was added the exaltation of a war-torn country about to welcome back a long lost child. Nothing was easier than to transfer to the Creoles the idyllic traits that had been in the making since the era of discovery; the cult of the native became the cult of the habitant.

Certain taints of ill repute still lingered, to be sure, around the name of Mississippi. Law's wreck was enduring; Prévost and others had preserved records of the wretched beings forcibly transported. To the true zealot, however, remedy of such a difficulty was easy; in almost as summary a fashion as by the great flood early stains were wiped out and a clean slate presented. The Abbé Raynal assures the reader that the present inhabitants of Louisiana were not descended from the scum of Europe, which France had, as it were, vomited into the new world following the breaking of the Mississippi Bubble. "All these wretched beings perished, fortunately without reproducing."[57] This passage is repeated almost verbatim by Dubroca,[58] and although most writers did not go to such extremes, practically all joined in such idealization of the population of Louisiana as Baudry des Lozières in the following passage.

> "The inhabitants of Louisiana have not lost their innocence; they still have the primeval virtues and that purity of heart which shudders at the thought of crime. Let us guard against sending to them men imbued with the principles which caused our earlier misfortunes." [59]

But unfortunately for the philosophers America was not so inaccessible as most Utopias; and we have incongruously enough beside these visions of spotlessness and charm vivid pictures of brawling, indecent orgies in all night cabarets, high play at cards, examples of egotism, selfishness, tyranny, the results of first hand observation. The tendency was to go rather far to either extreme, and Louisiana suffered by it. Human nature could not then any more than now be neatly sealed in one packet, and dispassionate observers were far too rare.

But although the tendency was to judge one habitant pretty rigidly by another, the land itself suffered by no such general classifications. The prairie indeed is given the most diversified treatment it has had up to this time. Old features are still stressed, of course, — its fruitfulness, a source of livelihood; its openness, a guard against surprise. Travellers picture still its serenely arching sky, its long rippling swells, its dry grass spark-

---

57 Raynal, G. T. F. — *Histoire Philosophique et Politique des Établissements & du Commerce des Européens dans les deux Indes.* (1772-1774). VI:169. It will be remembered that Longfellow drew his conception of the Acadians partly from Raynal. The Abbé's idyllic visions are satirized in a contemporary song, *Voyage en Amérique.* Raunié — *Chansonnier Historique.* X:204ff. Kerlérec may have afforded a source for Raynal's statement. See *Les Dernières Années de la Louisiane Française.*

58 *L'Itinéraire des Fran.* 83-4.

59 Baudry des Lozières, — *Voyage à la Louisiane. . .* 1802. 200-1.

ling into the flames of a prairie fire. Yet after all these are mere elaborations of old attitudes; a more definite step forward is taken when Robin begins his clear detailed discussion of the origin and nature of the prairies, linking the meadows of North America with those of other countries, even bringing in the shepherd peoples of the land of Canaan. His purpose was primarily a scientific one, but he did bring the prairies to mind as a distinct phenomenon more emphatically than had been done up to this time and he did give incidentally many striking glimpses of the vivid green of the marshy lowlands, far vistas of waving grasses and shadowy tree-clumps. Perrin du Lac, like Collot, was particularly impressed by the prairie after traversing the heavy forests that led from the American colonies; he gives us a revelation of the emotion inspired by the open land he was traversing and incidentally one of the first of the many comparisons of the prairie to the sea.

There is something deeply affecting about all this interest in, and detailed description of the land to which France was soon to abandon all claim for ever. Even more touching, however, are the visions created for it. Superlatives are heaped upon it in a manner almost unparalleled even for the Mississippi Valley. Duvallon praises the salubrity and productiveness of the country; Milfort declares that if the Anglo-Americans became masters of the Mississippi before fifty years had elapsed they would dictate the laws of Europe; Dubroca paints a splendid vision of a second France; Baudry des Lozières bursts out in a rhapsody about the loveliness of Louisiana.

> "What riches, what elegance! Nature there is adorned with all her charms, and the breeze wafts voluptuous perfumes! What the poets tell of the Elysian Fields is not a fable; all their divine fancies are realized in these enchanting regions."[60]

In another place he asserts that it is the most magnificent country in the world, needing only men and industry to make it incomparable in its beauty and utility. His interest was probably sincere, but his books are decidedly rhetorical in style, witness his address to the Louisiana martyrs.

"Rise a moment from your tombs, and rejoice with your de-

60 Baudry des Lozières — *Voy. à la Louisiane.* 21-2.

scendants at the happiness of seeing Louisiana given back to the power from which you did not wish to be separated! Dry your tears, have no more regrets; a great man has appeared! He will go among your children as among us, extending his glories and making public felicity flourish in one of the most beautiful regions of the universe. Rely upon his good will as much as upon his power.

"And you also, virtuous citizens, most of you as pure as the air which surrounds you; you who have awaited so long the happiness of becoming French, receive the reward of your affection for a nation which in the bottom of its heart has never forgotten you; may your great and noble souls swell with joy; henceforth you belong to the greatest of nations. . . ."[61]

In the return to the mother country he sees not only ample recompense for ancient wrongs but the avenue to unrivaled prosperity and a true centre for the arts.

All these high hopes, however, were soon dashed to the ground. By the time of publication of several of these volumes the sale to the United States had been announced. Du Lac prefaced his work sadly with an account of the loss, regretting not so much his wasted efforts and time but the troublesome circumstances which compelled the Government to renounce possession "of the most beautiful colony in the world."[62] The Abbé Robin, indeed, made most of his trip after the transfer to the United States, of which he gives us an exceedingly sympathetic picture.

"Meanwhile I saw the French flag descending slowly and at the same time that of the United States rising little by little; soon a French soldier took the first, wrapped it up, carried it back silently to his own ranks, while the American flag remained tangled for a long time in spite of the efforts to raise it, as if it were embarrassed at occupying the place of that one to which it owed its glorious independence. An anxious silence reigned at that moment among all the spectators who flooded the square, who crowded in galleries, balconies, and windows, and it was not until the flag had been hoisted to the top that sudden shrill

61 Baudry des Lozières. *Second Voyage à la Louisiane. . . .* 2v. 1803. I: 336-7

62 Perrin du Lac, F. M. — *Voyage dans les deux Louisianes . . . en 1801, 1802 et 1803. . . .* 1805. X.

cries of *Hurrah* came from the midst of one group who at the same time waved their hats. These cries and this movement rendered the silence and immobility of the majority of the spectators the more mournful; they were the French and the Spanish, much moved, mingling their sighs and their tears.''[63]

With the lowering of the French flag control of Louisiana by the Latin races that had discovered and heralded it was at an end. For three centuries its mighty rivers and erect forests, its slimy bayous and fertile fields had been a possession of Spanish and French. Its buried earth treasurers had focused their dreams of great wealth; its game, of food and riches in peltries; its forests and prairies, of dominion and power. For it men had ventured their lives, enduring inconceivable hardships; on it much blood had been shed; by it had been tested the fixed purpose of La Salle, the unassuming fidelity of Tonti, the spiritual fervor of Marquette, the daring of Jolliet, the steadfastness of Iberville, the tact and wisdom of Bienville. Many picturesque scenes had been enacted in the winning of it; many striking figures had marched in the pageant of conquest. Through it great joy had been felt; the glory of successful achievement, realized; on it much wonder had been expended. The deep note of tragedy, too, had been insistently sounded — the long suffering and almost complete destruction of the first covetous Spaniards, the dooming of La Salle's hopes, the degeneration of a once proud and stately race, the surrender of comfortable homes on one bank of the Mississippi to preserve allegiance to country only to encounter on the other side the rule of aliens, the final shattering by the sale to a young and vigorous nation of all the bright dreams of French empire in America. With so variegated a fabric of great visions and petty cares, of quick gains and sudden loss, of all the hopes and troubles of life not only of an individual but of a nation intensified by contact with the new and unknown West, it is but natural that the imaginative writer whose function it is to select and heighten the experiences of mankind should here find inspiration.

Yet of early Creole literature, much as we wish it, we find very little. What story material the colonial life offered! What a

---

63 Robin — *Voyages dans l'intérieur de la Louisiane.* II:138-9. For further description of the French occupation and final surrender, see Villiers du Terrage — *Les Dernières Années de la Louisiane Française.* 422 ff.

study of character in the reaction of outcast noble, dissolute soldier, dignified governor, to the sun-splashed beauty of the prairie, the sad distances of the delta, the moss-shrouded forest! Unfortunately, however, we have few treatments of these or other phases of the life aside from those we have mentioned. Of poetry, story, or drama there is almost none. Marie Hachard mentions a song which compared New Orleans to Paris;[64] Gayarré tells us that the War of the Jesuits and Capuchins in 1755 gave rise to acrimonious writings, squibs, pasquinades, and satirical songs;[65] Henry Hay in his *Journal* mentions visiting Mrs. Adanker at Detroit and copying off "the two French songs that she made; respecting her Stolen Pigg, — and the Miamies Recollects";[66] some of the negro and Canadian boat songs date back very far; the Missouri Historical Society prints a *Chanson de l'Année du Coup,* said to have been written by the schoolmaster of St. Louis in 1780 when the village was attacked by a considerable number of Indians and Canadians and to have been sung until mixture with the Americans caused relinquishment of the old customs. A couple of stanzas of it might be quoted as illustration of the work of the period.

*Le Gouverneur.*

Courrier, qu'y a-t-il de nouveau?
Tu parais troublé du cerveau:
Les Illinois sont-ils conquis?
Les Anglais ont-ils pris le pays?
Tu parais tout déconcerté;
Quel grand malheur est arrivé?

*Le Courrier.*

Grand Général, tout est perdu.
S'il n'est promptement secouru:
Nous avons été attaqués, —
Nous sommes encore menacés;
Beaucoup de monde ont été tués,
Sans pouvoir secours leur donner.[67]

64 *Rel. du Voy. des dames religieuses Ursulines.* 89-90.
65 Gayarré—*Hist. of La.* II:81.
66 *Wis. Hist. Soc. Proc.* 1914. 247.
67 *Mo. Hist. Soc. Coll.* IV:295 ff. For an example of an old negro field song see King, Grace — *New Orleans* . . . 337.

A more ambitious poem is the one by Julian Poydras de Lalande, in which the daring deeds of Galvez are recited to the God of the Mississippi; *The Indian Father* acted in the governor's mansion in 1753, was afterwards put into verse by Le Blanc de Villeneuve and produced at the Orleans theatre.[68]

Another long poem by Dumont de Montigny describing the Mississippi colony from 1719 remained almost unknown until recently.[69] Yet these, even allowing for the inevitable loss by time, form a comparatively small residue. We are tempted to agree with the warning of the critical Duvallon, himself the author of a book of poems, *Recueil de Poésies d'un Colon de St. Domingue* (1802) that "The air of this region is fatal to the muses."[70] It is only fair, however, to state that the nature of the life was largely responsible for the barrenness of the period — the frequent threat of Indians or of rival Europeans, the pressure of existence, the struggle attendant upon the conquest of even the kindliest of countries. In the later period when conditions became easier, indolence, always a trait of the village hunter and half-breed, was fostered in the wealthier classes by the abundance of negro slaves. The zest for novelty, the gayly adventurous spirit that furthered the exploration of the wilds turned for sport when once the land was conquered to high play, boisterous revel, dancing, and duelling. For the development of any considerable body of Creole literature we have to wait until the latter half of the nineteenth century.

Fortunately in France, mediocre as it might upon occasion be, imaginative expression was not so inhibited. The travellers with their fascinating accounts of strange peoples and costums, in which truth was frequently heightened by fiction, created an in-

---

68 King, Grace — *New Orleans, the Place & the People*. 1895. 126, 79. See also Gayarré — *Hist. of La.* II:65. There must have been a considerable number of colorful processions and spectacles if the following passage from John Pope's *Tour through the United States* . . . (1888 repr. of 1792 ed.) may be trusted. "The French and Spanish Subjects of *Louisiana*, are strict *Romanists*, and therefore, enthusiastically fond of Pageantry in their religious Festivals. This I can avouch from a Procession of Yesterday, when a crucified Redeemer was crucified afresh, in being represented like a Felon, in the Habiliment of a *Jesuit*. The Virgin-Mother was dress'd out *a-la-mode de Paris*; and Traitor *Judas*, for political Reasons, appeared in the Regimental Uniform of a *Spanish* Soldier, under Sentence of Death, for having divulged the countersign to the Enemy in Consideration of a Bribe." 38.

69 See Villiers du Terrage's article on, *Jour. de la Société des Américanistes*. XI. 1914.

70 Duvallon — *Vue de la Colonie Espagnole du Mississippi*. 207. The only poem of Duvallon's of local interest is *Le Colon Voyageur*, a dignified ode paying tribute to the Mississippi.

terest in this type of literature so great that we find a hybrid genre, the *imaginary voyage,* which had appeared at intervals since the days of the ancients developing in the seventeenth century and flourishing to an extraordinary extent in the eighteenth. Many of these pieces have frankly the lure of the märchen depicting strange beings of the air, of fire, under the sea, underground. Others satirize contemporary evils or embody the Utopian concepts while still others work out elaborate topographical allegories. Naturally realistic description is at a premium among them. Yet among the polar icebergs, the frowning precipices, the weird vegetation of other planets that feature the majority of these productions, we find oddly contrasting at intervals such appallingly veracious narratives as *le Naufrage et Aventures de M. Pierre Viaud* depicting shipwreck and horrible suffering on the shores of the gulf;[71] and many of the supposedly fictitious races possess qualities lifted wholesale from the American Indians and the Pacific islanders, or at least from these races as they are portrayed in the conventional idyllized descriptions.

But it is not necessary to go to these curiosities of literature to find traces of the French advance in the West. For their progress is paralleled though sketchily to be sure, by some of the great writers of the Gallic race. Rabelais, for instance, in Pantagruel's famous pilgrimage to the Land of the Bottle shows the influence of contemporary discussion of the Northwest passage and of Cartier's explorations, and his satire of Ouy-dire in the land of Satin is unquestionably one of the most forceful revelations of the change that was taking place in geographic method and ideals.[72] The story of the erring girl left with her lover on the Isle of Demons is included in the *Heptameron* (pr. 1559) by Margaret of Navarre.[73] Various minor theatrical pieces, and exotic narratives such as Marmontel's *Le Huron* (1768), Sauvigny's *Hirza ou les Illinois* (1767), and Voltaire's *L'Ingénu ou le Huron* show the interest of the French in the strange races they encountered in their attempted conquest of the

71 Garnier, C. G. J. — *Voyages Imaginaires, Songes, Visions, et Romans Cabalistiques.* 39v. 1787-9. t. XII.

72 See Tilley, Arthur — *Francois Rabelais.* 1907. p. 204 ff. and Lefranc, Abel — *Les Navigations de Pantagruel,* 1904 for the influence of contemporary discoveries on Rabelais, a point also discussed by Chinard, Gilbert — *L'Exotisme Américain dans la Littérature Française au XVIe. Siècle.* . . 1911. 49 ff. See further Pierre Margry — *Les Navigations Françaises et la Révolution Maritime du XIVe au XVIe Siècle* . . . 1867. 332-341.

73 For the story see Chinard — *Ibid.* 95 ff.

West. J. A. Perreau's *Lettres Illinoises* (1772) suggests the wars between the French and the English, the romance of the daughter of the commandant of one of the French posts and the noble Indian who deserts his people for her sake providing also an interesting foreshadowing of Chateaubriand's theme. For the most part, however, these productions are singularly destitute of local color, their backgrounds being vague and their Indians having as purely savage characteristics only their tribal names, most of them being the philosophical critics of civilized society that Lahontan epitomized in Adario or the courtly youths with whom the later story-tellers have familiarized us.

In several instances, however, the North American possessions received truly noteworthy and extraordinarily influential interpretations. L'Abbé Prévost, whose long and tedious relation of Cleveland emphasized some of the most popular exotic elements, at the close of *Manon Lescaut* (1731) gave one of the most sombre depictions of early Louisiana life. The truth of his portrayal of the various phases of Manon's and des Grieux's sad journey Dr. Pierre Heinrich has demonstrated by citation of official records in his *L'Abbé Prévost et la Louisiane*. The exile of disreputable characters, their conveyance under armed guard to the port of departure, the crowded and comfortless sea voyage, the hasty marriages — all these are ineradicable stains upon the early attempts to build up a colony. The place description is less exact. It is noteworthy, however, that although des Grieux comments on his compatriots' quest for gold, Prévost's description has none of the fictitious glamour which allured the Mississippi speculators. The country offers nothing agreeable at first sight; the vaunted city of New Orleans is but a huddle of poor huts in which the inhabitants live "as in the middle of the sea, that is to say, separated from the rest of the world by immense distances." In it happiness is won not through earthly treasures but through true and self sacrificing love; once the forlorn couple are in disgrace with the governor there is no recourse for them but flight to the English. In the midst of a desolate waste Manon succumbs to her difficulties as did many another woman in the pioneering epoch, her death a fitting end to this tragedy of youthful passion.[74]

74 Prévost, A. F. — *Histoire de Manon Lescaut et du Chevalier Desgrieux.* Nouv.

In sharp contrast to the mutual adoration that brings complete though brief happiness to Prévost's two lovers are the thwarted longings that characterize almost every one of Chateaubriand's personages. Atala, torn intolerably between the intensity of her love and the vow wrenched from her by the over-zealous mother and missionary, kills herself to keep her faith; Chactas is obliged to wait for the hereafter for their union; Amélie seeks the extinction of her sinful attachment to her brother in the convent; Akansie cherishes a criminal passion for Ondouré; Ondouré burns with desire for Céluta; Céluta loves René; and René, loving none, poisons all about him by the aura of his own melancholy. It is this latter feature, the importation of a romantic pessimism, that forms perhaps Chateaubriand's chief contribution to the emotional stores of the prairie. Only to a very minor extent can it be considered due to the ill-fated love of a redskin for a white that is the basis for much of Cooper's tragedy. Chactas' discovery that, "the tragic passions are common to all nations and can be understood by a Natchez as well as a Frenchman"[75] is the key to Chateaubriand's own attitude. An exile, the victim of an unfortunate love affair, from his early years the prey of strange regrets and morbid introspectiveness, it was but natural that the dreamy youth should attribute his own sensitiveness, his own unhappiness to his imaginary creations, in large part a projection of himself.

His conscious literary purpose, moreover, affected directly his reactions. Although he speaks in *Mémoires d'Outre-Tombe* of finding a new muse in America,[76] he states in the preface of *Atala* and repeats in that of *Les Natchez* that when he was very young he conceived the idea of making" an *epic of the natural man*, or of painting the manners of the Savages, linking them with some familiar event." The epic devices of the first division of his *Natchez*, reminiscent of Milton, Homer, and mediaeval Catholi-

éd. préc. d'une notice sur la Vie et les Ouvrages de Prévost par. M. Sainte-Beuve. 1895. 257. There has been much discussion of the historical verity of Manon and much conscientious labor has been expended upon the identification of the characters. To attempt to make the book entirely a thinly veiled narrative of fact is, to my mind, neglecting the ordinary creative processes. It should be enough to show that the exile of Manon was entirely possible at that epoch and that the narrative in general was true to conditions. That this is the case can be proved by reference to only one contemporary authority Buvat — *Journal de la Régence*, ed. by Campardon. I:441, 454, II:1, etc. For songs dealing with abduction and other phases of the settlement of the Mississippi see Appendix I.

75 Chateaubriand — *Les Natchez.* (*Oeuvres.* t. II. 1857.) p. 74.

76 Chateaubriand — *Mémoires d'Outre-Tombe.* Ed. by E. Biré. I:366.

cism, although to the average modern reader they seem anachronistic digressions, tend to lift the American savage to a heroic level. Chauteaubriand yields, also, to the prevailing tendency to philosophize on the differences between civilizations. In the main, however, the luxuriant sense appeals, the idyllic qualities of his Indians and their territories are the results of his own poetic imagination playing on what was already a long established romantic tradition.

As we have pointed out, the Natchez were the most highly civilized tribe with whom the French had any contact, their worship of the sun, their tribal traditions, their white bark robes, their elaborate ceremonials, and their rich and beautiful country making an appeal which none of their chroniclers were able to resist. It was but natural then that a youth so infatuated with the dreams of discovery as to believe himself capable of solving the ancient riddle of the Northwest passage without any provision other than his imagination and courage[77], so steeped in the enthusiastic narratives of travellers that had preceded him, should lavish upon the southern peoples an almost Oriental richness of detail. Unhampered by much actual experience, he was free to forget the sordid aspects of the life of the Indian, to make the bloodthirsty Sioux a gentle pastoral people, the most happy according to Chactas of all those he visited; to depict by the beauty and tenderness of Céluta, the vivid charm of Mila, the serene and kindly wisdom of Chactas, the fraternal loyalty of Outougamiz, the self-sacrificing devotion of Atala, a race of godlike beings who excelled by their virtues as much as Akansie and Ondouré excelled by their crimes most of what we have recorded as characteristic of the American Indian.

There has been much criticism of Chateaubriand's concept of the red man, but his fantastic geography has been ridiculed even more strongly. Studies have been made to show the sources and inaccuracies of his botany and biology so that it is unnecessary for us to go into them. It is important, however, to remember that various types of natural life, extinct today, in the early period enhanced the brilliancy of the Mississippi. We must remember, too, that Chateaubriand carefully suppressed all but the attractive features of the country. The alligators give Céluta an

77 Chateaubriand — *Mémoires*. I:363.

opportunity to display her heroism by her rescue of her child; the rattlesnakes furnish convenient aid to the arch villain in silencing his fellow conspirator; the fearful storm lessens in Atala the power of her resistance to love. Only when they are thus dramatically assets do the threatening phenomena of nature appear; as a rule the prairie stretches sun-warmed, inviting. Huge shade and fruit trees, heavy sward make the forest an attractive place for rambles; flowering shrubs, fragrant plants adorn the banks of the river; apparently no sordid cares for a livelihood ever trouble the native. His thoughts, his customs, his environment are refined into the most delicate and spiritual beauty, being suggested with an elaboration of simile and metaphor that excel even the figurative speech ascribed to him. Chateaubriand is not consciously falsifying when he thus swerves away from reality; seeking refuge from the trials of the Revolution and his personal misery, he gleans attractive details concerning American life wherever he finds them and unmindful of their appropriateness blends them in a lovely poetic fabric that satisfies his own instinct for beauty while it also provides an outlet for his melancholy.

So strong is this harmonizing instinct, indeed, that it more or less tends to obviate even in the whites the stigma of their deeds. Chateaubriand's description of the Natchez probably more than any other single factor has established and helped to perpetuate the tragedy of a vanishing race. Story teller after story teller has followed in his footsteps, each bolstering up his own feeble powers by reliance on the unfailing appeal of the wretched remnant of a once powerful tribe. Yet although Chateaubriand comments repeatedly on the encroachments and dissipations of the whites, although he makes René, the missionary, the noble d'Artaguette align themselves with the Indians against the greed of their countrymen, the lavishness of detail with which he depicts the charms of the life of nature and the emotional crises of his central characters tends to submerge the European aggressions. Save for the sale of Adario and his family, a scene animated by Chateaubriand's bitter hatred of the brutalizing practice of slavery in any form, the tyrannies of the French seem comparatively distant and unreal.[78]

78 All of Chateaubriand's books were published, of course, after the period cov-

And as the vestiges of Latin power in the Midland grow less and less distinct, the tendency to forget whatever of sordidness and oppression there was in the life of the Spanish and French has become more and more pronounced. As the blasé courtiers of le grand siècle found entertainment in the simplicities and naïveté of the natural man, as the strife-weary citizens of the Napoleonic era sought the concept of pastoral peace and content in their long lost colony overseas, so the English-speaking inhabitants of the new nation, amazingly energetic, pre-eminently practical, have relied on these early centuries of alien dominion for historic relief for their own more aggressive materialism. It is, then, in this establishment of the romantic tradition that there is found the chief literary significance of the Latin races on the prairie. The great inland valley that they discovered and explored was a world with the freshness of the dawn upon it, dewy sweet, exceptionally fertile, its bison-pasturing meadows, its dense forests, its placid waterways offering an idyllic background, fascinating vistas for adventure. So forgetting official corruption, desertion and discontent of soldiers, dissipations and greed of coureurs-de-bois, misfortunes and crimes of the transported women, disgraceful quarreling, jealousy, and inefficiency of administrators, we have centred our attention instead upon the truly great achievements, the ardor and daring that gave such brilliancy and verve to the pageant of explorer, missionary, soldier, fur-trader, habitant, and planter, finding there our most colorful history, our most popular field for the word painter of the past. The French and Spanish colonies have and always will have for us extraordinary glamour; over their gentle colonies hovers ever the bewitching haze of romance.

---

ered in this chapter. Since the date of his trip to America is 1791 and since the manuscripts were written long before publication, it has seemed advisable to include the discussion here, particularly since Chateaubriand's work forms a culmination for the early treatments and an inspiration for the later romanticists (See Ch. V.). For the popular reception of *Atala,* an extraordinary illustration of the influence of these works, see his own description. *Mémoires* II:246. His account of his travels in America has not been treated here since it has been proved in part pure fabrication, in part an adaptation of others' work. For the most complete study see G. Chinard's *L'Exotisme Américain dans l'Oeuvre de Chateaubriand.* (1918).

# CHAPTER III

## THE ENGLISH ADVANCE

Turning to the history of the Saxon nation in America, we find no such dauntless early threading of the wilds of a continent, few such picturesque and outstanding figures in the records of interior exploration. England, long the mistress of the seas, was singularly backward in the fifteenth and sixteenth centuries in the matter of maritime advancement. While the ships of Spain and Portugal were rending the veil of mystery that long had hovered over the emerald depths of the ocean, returning from their long voyages with the treasure trove of the Indies, the British remained aloof on their island possessions or clung to their long-established and non-venturesome routes of commerce. So marked was the indifference indeed that even the publication of foreign books of travel was slow, and writers like George Beste in the Epistle Dedicatory to his voyage of Frobisher (1578) commented upon the defect.

"But there hath bin two speciall causes in former age, that have greatly hindered the English nation in their attempts. The one hath bin lacke of liberalitie in the nobilitie; and the other want of skill in the cosmographie, and the arte of navigation. Whiche kinde of knowledge is verye necessary for all oure noblemen, for that wee being ilanders, our chiefest strength consisteth by sea. But these twoo causes are nowe in this present age (God be thanked) very well reformed; for not only hir Majestie now, but all the nobilitie also, having perfect knowledge in Cosmographie, doe not only with good wordes countenance the forward minds of men, but also with their purses do liberally and bountifully contribute unto the same, whereby it cometh to passe, that navigation, whiche in the time of King Henry the 7th was very rawe, and toke (as it were) but beginning (and ever since hath had by little and little continuall increase), is now in hir Majestie's raign growen to his highest perfection."[1]

Yet even in the Elizabethan era, to us English-speaking races, the synonym for all the high hopes, dauntless resolution, daredevil gallantry, and surging imagination that opened wide the portals of the western hemisphere, we find almost no expeditions that concern us directly. Attention centred on the futile search amid the snowy fastnesses of the North for the far-famed western passage, on the achievements of a Drake in encircling the globe, on the exploits of a Hawkins in raiding the Spanish treasure fleets. With such stirring deeds and such valiant figures mirrored against a background of chill blue icebergs, foam-encircled coral islands, or flame-licked, stately galleons long enchanting the reader, is it any wonder that the mind of the race finds it a descent to prosaic everyday to be forced to consideration of the piecemeal progress to the hinterland of the colonies along the Atlantic.

In large part, of course, the geographical conditions with which the English were confronted were responsible for their delay. For them no great rivers or interlocking lake system offered alluring vistas. Instead of making easy progress in a fleet canoe, the explorers were confronted with "great craggy stones in the midst of the river, where the water falleth so rudely, and with such a violence, as not any boat can possibly passe . . ." Newport's and the Company's projects Smith consequently dismissed with contempt.

> "For the charge of this Voyage of two or three thousand pounds, we have not received the value of an hundred pounds. And for the quartred Boat to be borne by the Souldiers over the Falles, *Newport* had 120 of the best men he could chuse. If he had burnt her to ashes, one might have carried her in a bag; but as she is, five hundred cannot, to a navigable place above the Falles. And for him at that time to find in the South Sea, a Mine of gold, or any of them sent by Sir *Walter Raleigh*: at our Consultation I told them was as likely as the rest."[2]

---

1 *The Three Voyages of Martin Frobisher, in Search of a Passage to Cathaia & India by the North-West, A.D. 1576-8*, Repr. from the 1st. ed. of *Hakluyt's Voyages . . . Hak. Soc. Pub.* 1867. 22-3.

2 *Travels & Works of Captain John Smith . . .* ed. by Edward Arber. 2v. 1910. I:6, II:443.

On land if the adventurer did succeed in surmounting one foothill, it was only to discover row after row of rocky summits rising before him, as Glover early testified.

> "There was one Colonel *Catlet*, that was a good Mathematician, who with some other Gentlemen took a Journey to make some further discoveries of the Country to the Westward, and arriving at the foot of the Mountains early in the morning, they left their horses, and endeavoured to gain the tops of the Mountains, which they accomplished about four of the clock in the afternoon, and then looking further forward they discovered other Mountains, whereof they took the altitude and judged them inaccessible; which discouraged them from any further attempts, their design being chiefly to discover whether there were any Rivers that ran into the South-ocean."[3]

The character of the race and the nature and purpose of the colonial organization are also factors to be considered, however. The religious refugees were primarily concerned, of course, with building up a new home in a new land where they could worship God in their own way. The gentlemanly adventurers and wastrels of all sorts who were shipped overseas were looking most of them for an easy method of founding a fortune and lacked the physical stamina and natural affinity with the wilds that were so marked an endowment of the French explorers. In the South tobacco growing soon proved a lucrative occupation; even in the North where agricultural conditions were harder the tenacity of the English led them to wring a living from the soil with a persistency unknown to the majority of the Canadians, whom the long winter and their early initiation into the fascinations of the fur trade tempted into the forests. Consequently we find apparent almost from the beginning of settlement a difference in the two nations that was to determine the later struggle for supremacy. The French, engaging in daring expeditions of many months or even years, soon spun a tenuous web of possession throughout the vast middle valley of the continent. The English with their innate desire for their own possessions established themselves firmly on the coast, then pushed

3 Glover. Thomas — *An Account of Virginia* . . . Repr. fr. the *Phil. Tran. of the Royal Soc.* . . . 1904. 9-10.

westward by single families and by colonies to chop out new homesteads in the wilderness.

Far earlier than we ordinarily realize, however, the mountain barrier was attempted, and Englishmen laid a basis for claim to the West. By the middle of the seventeenth century legislative authorizations for western exploration are recorded; Governor Berkeley actively encouraged discovery; wanderers like Lederer stood in little need of prompting; and some of the most substantial men of Virginia, Colonel Abraham Wood and Colonel William Byrd, in spite of opposition were persistent in their endeavors to open up the interior. Nowhere are the services of literature to history better illustrated, however, than by the oblivion into which without it these early endeavors sank. For the English had no such authentic and comprehensive record of progress as was afforded in Canada by the Jesuit relations. Certain important papers were long buried in state archives; traditional accounts were discredited by the leading historians. Nor can we wonder at this latter fact today; for those early sources of myth — the mines of gold and silver, the hoped for western sea, long established mediaeval beliefs — were as potent factors among the British as among the Spanish or the French. Lederer, dubbed the Lahontan of the English, in his account of his second expedition introduced Indian Amazons; and Batts and Fallam were convinced of their discovery of salt water.

> "It was ebbing Water when we were here. We set up a stick by the Water side but found it ebb very slowly. Our Indians kept such a hollowing that we durst not stay any longer to make further tryal."

Considering the geographic knowledge of the age and the ardor with which the hearts of men were fixed upon the accomplishment of various petted projects, it is small wonder that such misapprehensions arose. Unfortunately acquisition of accurate knowledge tended to discredit entirely early accounts; and popular versions distorting the elements of truth such as are used by Beverley, as well as the fact that the authentic early explorations were combined with what appear to be entirely fictitious ones to bolster up the English claim to the midlands have aided in the corrosive process of time. Surely students of

American history owe a debt of gratitude to Mr. Alvord and Mr. Bidgood who in their volume *The First Explorations of the Trans-Alleghany Region by the Virginians 1650-1674* have combined and evaluated the early records of the trail breakers.

They and their fellow-editors of reprints have done more than give the stamp of historic truth to the expeditions they discuss; they have made accessible the naïve charm of the chronicles, the loss of which in transcription has had something to do with the indifference of the litterateur toward our own heroic legends. Unquestionably the English have lacked the splendid gesture which on the part of the Latin races has made so poignant an appeal to our imagination, a fact of which no better demonstration could be afforded than the simplicity of Batts' and Fallam's taking possession of the new territory three months after the splendid pageant of Saint-Lusson.

> "Early in the morning we went to seek some trees to mark our Indians being impatient of longer stay by reason it was like to be bad weather, and that it was so difficult to get provisions. We found four trees exceeding fit for our purpose that had been half bared by our Indians, standing after one the other. We first proclaimed the king in these words: 'Long live King Charles the Second, by the Grace of God King of England, Scotland, France, Ireland and Virginia and of all the Territories thereunto belonging, Defender of the faith etc.' firing some guns and went to the first tree which we marked . . . with a pair of marking irons for his sacred majesty."

Indian John's ripping out the still warm heart of Needham and with it in his hand turning his face to the East and bidding defiance to the English has in it more of drama than any act of the explorers. Yet these unassuming, matter-of-fact narratives have an appeal all their own. Wood's man Arthur has adventures like those of a "movie thriller"; occasionally there appears unexpected realization of the narrative possibilities of the Indians. Talbot's fulsome dedication to Lord Ashley, one of the Lords Proprietors of Carolina, suggests the wonders conjured up by the dream of the West.

> "In order to which, the Apalataean Mountains (though like the prodigious wall that divides China and Tartary, they

> deny Virginia passage into the West Continent) stoop to your lordships dominions and lay open a prospect into unlimited empires.''

Bland's answer to the Indians attempting to dissuade him from further journeying, although it may involve an element of bluff, has in it a childlike trust worthy of the early missionaries,

> ''we answered him, that we were not afraid to be killed, for that any one of us were able to deale with forty through the protection of our great God, for we were commanded by our king.''

And the deep feeling of Wood's account of the slaughter of his men is equalled only by the emotional ellipsis of a Radisson.

> ''The good suckses of ye last jorney by my men performed gave mee great hopes of a good suckses in ye latter for I never heard from nor any thing after I employed Mr. James Needham past from Aeno an Indian towne two dayes jorny beyond Occhoneeche in safty but now begins ye tragicall scene of bad hap. upon ye 27th of January following I received a flying report by some Indians that my men were killd by ye Tomahitans pasing over theire river as they were returning, now dayly came variable reports of theire miscarige. All Indians spake darkly to hide ye trueth from being discoverd for feare ye guilt of ye mourder would be layd upon them selves . . . soe died this heroyick English man whose fame shall never die if my penn were able to eternize it which had adventured where never any English man had dared to atempt before and with him died one hundered forty-foure pounds starling of my adventure with him. I wish I could have saved his life with ten times ye vallue.''[4]

Nor must the importance of these records for American exploration be slighted. These adventurers, servants, plantation owners, and traders reveal early the presence of a group absorbed in the outlands. By them the line of settlement was early

---

4 Alvord, C. W. & Bidgood, Lee — *First Explorations of the Trans-Alleghany Region by the Virginians 1650-1674.* 1912. 192, 191, 135, 117-8, 214-7. Winsor has written a pamphlet on the Sault Sainte Marie pageant, and there are numerous contemporary references to the impressive taking possession of the country by Saint Lusson. See among others Margry — *Découvertes et établissements* I:92-3, 96-9, *Doc. rel. to the Col. His. of the State of N. Y.* IX:789-790, 803-4, Blair — *Ind. Tribes* I:220 ff., etc. *The Journal & Relation of a New Discovery in Western Virginia* is repr. *Doc. Rel. to the Col. Hist. of N. Y.* III:193 ff.

pushed forward; by them, too, was laid the foundation for still further advance in the exploration of the West. Batts and Fallam by their discovery established a claim to the Ohio of which later pamphleteers were not slow to avail themselves in connection with the Iroquois cession. The great trade routes to the New River and southward to the Cherokees, at this time opened up, were not only economically advantageous but were important politically as we have already seen in the harassing of the French near the mouth of the Mississippi at the instigation of English traders and in the steady percolation of British influence through the Indians of the interior.

Excellent though the start had been, the internal dissensions of the colony, difficulties with the savages, the incessant economic struggle, all tended to check for some time exploration, even use of such knowledge save by the traders. In 1716, however, under that dauntless figure, Governor Spotswood, a band of Virginia gentlemen, servants, and rangers embarked upon the western expedition which, excepting only the later transcontinental tour of Lewis and Clark, undoubtedly has had greatest popular appeal among the English. Just how to explain its extraordinary imaginative effect upon later generations might be difficult for the scientist. Source material is limited, our main dependence for details being John Fontaine's *Journal* in Maury's *Memoirs of a Hugenot Family*. Yet even through Fontaine's brief entries gleam the feasting, the pageantry, the pomp of preparation that made Spotswood's progress akin to the feudal magnificence of the Spaniards before the bearded gulf forests swallowed them up.

> "The Governor had graving irons, but could not grave anything, the stones were so hard. I graved my name on a tree by the river side; and the Governor buried a bottle with a paper inclosed, on which he writ that he took possession of this place in the name and for King George the First of England. We had a good dinner, and after it we got the men together, and loaded all their arms, and we drank the King's health in Champagne, and fired a volley, the Princess's health in Burgundy, and fired a volley, and all the rest of the Royal Family in claret, and a volley."[5]

5 Maury, A. — *Memoirs of a Hugenot Family* . . . 1852. 288-9.

And this "grand air" with which the expedition itself was invested is enhanced for later times by the decoration of the Golden Horse-shoe, which Hugh Jones describes, and which any gentleman was entitled to wear "that can prove his having drunk *his Majesty's Health* upon MOUNT GEORGE."[6] As far as the charting of new territory is concerned, Spotswood's expedition is less important than some of the earlier ones, for he only reached the Valley of the Shenandoah. Aside from the imprint which it made on the popular fancy it is noteworthy, however, for the determination to checkmate the designs of the French, increasing hostility to whom is the distinctive feature of the literature treating the hinterland during the first portion of the century.[7]

To trace the growth of this feeling is not only to view from another angle the national jealousy we have seen among the French but to note important factors in the British policy of expansion. Glover in the Philosophical Transactions of the Royal Society, 1676 accepted with equanimity the opinion that "some *Spaniards* are seated near us upon the back of the Mountains."[8] Clayton in his letter to the Royal Society in 1688 does not seem unduly disturbed by the fact that "a Colony of the

6 Jones, H. — *The Present State of Virginia*. . . . 1724. repr. 1865.

7 Spotswood expresses his motives clearly in the following passage from his *Official Letters* ed. by R. A. Brock (*Va. His. Soc. Pub.* 2v. 1882).

"Tho' I have reason to believe all discontents about the manner of granting of Land are now over, Yet I am humbly of opinion, that her Maj'ty may receive consid'ble service and ye Country great satisfaction, as well as advantage, if permission were given to take up land on one side of James River only, upon the antient conditions of seating and planting. That River, according to the best acco'ts of the Indians, issues from a Lake on ye other side of the great Mountains that ly to the Westward of us, and makes its way through them If such a permission were granted there, while the Lands in other places are under stricter conditions, the people would soon carry on their Settlem'ts to ye very Source of that River, and ye advantages that may reasonably be expected from hence are these: That Whereas the ffrench are endeavouring to settle a communication between Canada and their late Settlements on Mississippi by the way of the Lakes, our people would, by pushing on their settlem'ts in one straight Line along the banks of James River, be able to cutt off that communication and fix themselves so strongly there that it would not be in the power of the French to dislodge them, especially considering how much farther they must travell than we to come at that place, as seems to be manifest by the Discoverys which I have encouraged to be made this fall by a Company of Adventurers, who found the Mountains not above a hundred miles from our Upper Inhabitants, and went up to the top of the highest Mountain with their Horses, tho' they had hitherto been thought to be unpassable, and they assured me . . . that they could have passed over the whole Ledge (which is not large) if the season of the year had not been too far advanced before they set out on that Expedition. And by this means also it is most probable that a very profitable Trade might be established with foreign Nations of Indians, and our Indian Traders would find convenient places of Refreshment without being obliged (as they are now) to travell some hundreds of miles through Desarts before they can vend their Commoditys." I:40-41.

8 Glover — *Acct. of Va.* 10.

French are come down from Canadas, and have seated themselves in the back of Virginia" although he adds that "The French possessing themselves of these Lakes, no doubt will in a short time be absolutely Masters of the Beaver trade, the greatest number of Beavers being caught there."[9] The Coxes, father and son, however, in their various papers advocating their colonizing schemes on the Mississippi and elsewhere, the most notable of which is *Carolana* (1705), repeatedly sound solemn warning against rival nations.

> "By these two last-mentioned rivers, the English may have a ready and easy communication with this and consequently with all the other lakes. If the French should ever settle thereon, which for above twenty years they have endeavored, but have been, in great measure, wonderfully frustrated by the Irocois, our subjects or allies, they might greatly molest, by themselves and their Indians, the colonies of New York, Pennsylvania, Maryland and Virginia; which, I hope, by the wisdom and care of his majesty and ministry, will be speedily prevented."[10]

And as the century progresses the denunciations on both sides of the ocean of the nefarious designs of the French are too numerous for us to do more than mention a few outstanding examples. Colonel William Byrd in his sprightly *History of the Dividing Line Run in 1728,* warns of the need of possession of the mountains as a barrier "lest our good Friends, the French, and the Indians, thro' their Means, prove a perpetual Annoyance to these Colonies" and laments that,

> "Our country has now been inhabited more than 130 years by the English, and still we hardly know any thing of the Appallachian Mountains, that are no where above 250 miles from the sea. Whereas the French, who are later comers, have rang'd from Quebec Southward as far as the Mouth of the Mississippi, in the Bay of Mexico, and to the West almost as far as California, which is either way above 2000 miles."[11]

John Ker of Kersland, whose work is particularly interesting

9 Alvord & Bidgood — *First Explor. of the Trans-Alleg. Reg.* 194.
10 French — *Hist. Coll. of La.* II:249.
11 Byrd, Wm. — *Writings* ed. by J. S. Bassett. 1901. 180, 198.

as a contemporary reaction to the Law scheme, devotes the most striking portion of his second volume of *Memoirs* (3v. 1726) to a history of the French in the interior of America and to an imposing reproof of British neglect, which if continued, he asserts, will cause the ruin of English trade, the harrying of the settlements, and the ultimate driving of the colonists into the Atlantic. Joshua Gee, who in his *The Trade and Navigation of Great Britain Considered,* greatly overestimates the beneficial effects of the transportation of convicts by the French, urges the building of some forts upon the Appalachian Mountains "to secure us the Right of the Mines contained in them, to protect the *Indian* and Skin Trade, and to preserve the Navigation to ourselves of those great Rivers which have their Fountains in the said Hills." [12] Salmon arguing in his volumes dealing with America against the French claims, although he points out the weaknesses in the endeavors of the French to hold by small forces a vast extent of territory and although he feels that fears like Ker's are exaggerated pleads for a policy of union, remarking of Florida that "If we suffer the encroaching *French* to establish themselves there, and drive us from this terrestrial Paradise, when nothing is so easy as to prevent it, by uniting our Forces with the *Spaniards,* both Nations richly deserve to enjoy the Fruits of their supine Negligence." [13] And to close this enumeration, Cadwallader Colden in his *History of the Five Indian Nations of Canada,* stamps with official authority the English fears.

> "The Courage and Resolution of many of these Adventurers are deservedly recorded by the French; but the English give it another Turn, and say it is the Barrenness and Poverty of Canada that pushes the Men of Spirit there, upon Enterprizes, that they would not have attempted, if they had lived in the Province of New York. The chief reason, in my Opinion, however, of the French having so far succeeded beyond the English is, that The Indian Affairs are the particular Care of the Governor and other principal Officers in Canada, who have the greatest Knowledge and Authority; whereas those Affairs in New York are chiefly left to the Management of

12 Gee, J. — *Trade & Nav. of Gt. Brit.* 3d. ed. 1731. 61.
13 Salmon, M. — *Modern History* . . . 1736. XXVIII:449.

a few Traders with the Indians, who have no care for, or Skill in publick Affairs, and only mind their private Interest."[14]

Unquestionably, however, in spite of Colden's disparaging comment the most potent early antidote to the insidious influence of the French was the efforts of these same traders. The part they played in the winning of the West has never been generally accorded the recognition it deserves, a state of affairs that may be explained variously by the fact that the English colonies were never dependent on this source of income as were the settlements in Canada, that the traders as a class were unsparingly condemned, and finally by the fact that they have received no very romantic or extended literary treatments. A quatrain of 1672 demonstrated, however, that the rhymsters of the day were sensitive to this as to other phases of life in the New World.

"Friend, once 'twas Fame that led thee forth
To brave the Tropic Heat, the Frozen North,
Late it was Gold, then Beauty was the Spur;
But now our Gallants venture but for Furs."[15]

---

14 Colden, C. — *Hist. of the Five Ind. Nat.* . . . 2v. 1904. I:21-2.
Most of the preceding quotations were drawn from the popular books of the day. Long before the unofficial writers made much of the danger, however, the colonial documents were filled with warnings against it. See, for instance, Gov. Dongan's *Report*, "Alsoe it points out where theres a great River discovered by one Lassal a French man from Canada, who thereupon went into France, & as its reported brought two or three vessels with people to settle there which (if true) will prove not only very inconvenient to us, but to the Spanish alsoe (the River running all along from our Lakes by the Back of Virginia & Carolina into the Bay of Mexico) . . ." *Doc. Rel. to the Col. Hist. of N.Y.* III:396. Another typical passage is found in Gov. Hunter's communication to the Board of Trade in 1718. "Mr Beresford's representation is very just and no more than what I formerly did lay before the Secry of State at the time we had notice of Mr Crozat's Patent and after the accounts of the new grant. . . . The French have Forts and settlements in many places on the river Mississipi and on the Lakes and claim all the Country and Trade of it as theirs if these settlements continue & prosper the very being of the British Plantations on the Continent will become precarious for by means of these settlements they acquire to themselves the dependances of Numerous Indian Nations and tho the French may be at peace with us in appearance these Indians by ye instigation of their Traders may be prevailed upon to make incursions on the Frontiers of the English Settlements which being all uncovered will be an easy pray and after an attempt of that kind no planter will venture to sit down without the reach of assistance or defence, & so by degrees these Colonies may come to be unpeopled, I know not upon what right the French found their claim neither can I think of any effectual remedy for the evil mentioned but their relinquishing it the next best would be extending our Frontiers, and augmenting our force and Garrisons of which I have heretofore wrote very amply to your Lordships." *Ibid.* V:508. Similar passages are so numerous that it is impossible to cite them.

15 Quoted in Willson, B. — *The Great Company.* I:61.

And in America the commerce soon acquired an importance, adequately to estimate which would require exhaustive investigation of almost every colony.[16]

Even the most superficial study of the records of expansion demonstrates not only the early penetration by the English "bush-lopers" of much of the western part of the continent but the exertion of an extraordinarily far-reaching influence on internal politics and colonial rivalries. Countless scattered references in English and French, moreover, and, in 1755, *The History of the American Indians* "by James Adair, Esquire, a Trader with the Indians and Resident in their Country for Forty Years," built up a picture of venturesome and distinctive life — merchants leading a pastoral existence with their own poultry, stock, and horses amid the friendly villages; long trains of heavily laden pack horses winding their way with tinkling bells and armed escort through the narrow defiles of the mountains, down the leafy forest trails. Unfortunately Adair was too preoccupied with his attempt to prove the Indians the lost tribes of Israel to give us many of the narratives that we today treasure. In his mention of the whites' adoption of native superstitions, of the narrow escapes that he and others experienced, of the "thoughtless young men who were too much attached to the Indian life from an early pursuit in that wild and unlimited country" and who "chose to run any risk, rather than leave their favourite scenes of pleasure" he demonstrates, nevertheless, an adaptation to the savage mode of existence no less striking in many cases than that of the French although infinitely less exploited.[17]

Adair's narrative is based chiefly on his trading life in the South. The most valuable single early record of the "bush-lopers" in the lake country is Cadwallader Colden's *History of the Five Indian Nations,* in which the writer's official position gives especial weight to his account of the English debt to these tribes. Through them British traders were early introduced into the region of the Great Lakes, the comparative cheapness of the

16 Fortunately there is a very large number of careful studies dealing with various phases of the fur trade in American historical publications. Attention may also be called to C. A. Hanna's *The Wilderness Trail.* 2v. 1911.

17 Adair — *Hist. of the Amer. Ind.* 265. *The Journal of Peter Pond* 1740-1775. *Conn. Mag.* X: 239-259 & *Wis. Hist. Coll.* XVIII:314 ff., gives a most vivid picture of a fur trader's wanderings.

latter's goods giving them an advantage which even French tact could not overcome. This advantage Burnet rendered even greater by prohibiting the exportation of Indian goods to Montreal, and although the act caused numerous protests from the wholesalers concerned and was frequently evaded, Colden constantly stresses its benefits in passages like the following.

> "Before this Act passed, none of the people of this Province travelled into the Indian Countries to trade: We have now above forty young Men, who have been several Times as far as the Lakes a trading, and thereby become well acquainted, not only with the Trade of the Indians, but likewise with their Manners and Languages; and these have returned with such large Quantities of Furs, that greater Numbers are resolved to follow their Example."[18]

Incidental mention of the traders is frequent and illuminating. Official agents like Gist and Croghan, for instance, repeatedly testify to their number and power, to say nothing of the French who, through the lower prices of the English and the hostility of certain powerful tribes, saw their hopes of trans-Alleghanian dominion being persistently thwarted. Besides the direct political pressure exerted by these vendors, early observers considered the wood training beneficial in hardening individuals and giving lessons in border warfare, lessons which were soon to be put to use in the bloody strife that for many years unsettled the West.

No estimate of the services rendered by the traders, however,

---

18 Colden — *Hist. of the Five Ind. Nat.* II:25. There are numerous early references to this act, the trade against which it was designed, and the consequent encouragement of English relations with the Indians. See, for instance, *Doc. rel. to the Col. Hist. of N. Y.* V:577-8, 560, 580, 582, 587, 641, 682, 687, 726, 775, 811, VI:750, 1010, etc. Franklin inquired about it, having in mind Pennsylvania problems, and Gov. Burnet lauds it repeatedly. "I have just received news from Albany that the Trade with the French is quite broken and that as the severity of the Act quite discourages the traders from attempting it They are willing at their own charge to begin a trade through our 5 Nations means with the Far Indians, and are going to be at charge and risque for that purpose, even before a regular Settlement is made as proposed which news gives me great satisfaction and is a beginning to a better state of affairs that way that has ever yet been known and of the greatest consequence to the welfare and prosperity of all the British Platations." V:584. Johnson's complaints, however, cause one to realize that the act was not wholly successful. For earlier records of English traders around the Great Lakes see *Col. Doc. rel. to the Hist. of N. Y.* III:442, 466, 476; Lahontan — *New Voyages* I:98-9, 125-6, 127; Blair — *Indian Tribes* I:250-1, 261, etc. Recent studies are Helen Broshar's *The First Push Westward of the Albany Traders, Miss. Val. Hist. Rev.* VII:228 ff., and A. H. Buffinton's *The Policy of Albany and English Westward Expansion, Ibid.* VIII:327 ff.

can offset the harm many of them did among the Indians by their bad rum, conscienceless cheating, and vile living. Their licentiousness called for rebuke not only from outsiders but from the more upright among them. Adair, embittered by the system of general licenses, asserts,

> "While the present ill adapted measures are continued, nothing less than the miraculous power of deity can possibly effect the Indians reformation; many of the present traders are reprobate, white savages."[19]

Gist chronicles a white woman who though grown up in captivity and married to an Indian "still remembers they used to be very religious in New England and wonders how the White Men can be so wicked as she has seen them in these woods."[20] Washington speaks of the great impositions practiced by the traders;[21] Governor Hamilton declares they are "a vile race," "more intent on their private profit than the publick good";[22] Dinwiddie joins in denunciation.

> "Our Indian traders, in general, appear to me to be a set of abandoned wretches."[23]

Yet Dinwiddie inclines enough toward these same evil traders to make strong representations against the French for practicing the same kind of unofficial war that his own men were engaged in, and Colden's lament at the government's trusting the management of Indian affairs very largely to these "rum-runners" is based upon truth. The indifference of people and colonial governments alike left the advance over the mountains to commercial enterprise, a fact that accounts for the meagerness of the published descriptions. Not political agents but the emissaries of the Ohio Company and the fur-buyers were the witnesses to Céloron's discomfiture. Probably it was not merely his station as royal governor but his financial interest in this same Ohio Company that prompted Dinwiddie to take the lead against the so-called invaders.[24] Certainly many of the colonists

19 Adair — *Hist. of the Amer. Ind.* 286.

20 Gist, C. — *Journals* . . . ed. by W. M. Darlington. 1893. 41.

21 Washington, G. — Letter to Dinwiddie, Oct. 17, 1753 in Blanchard, R. — *Discovery & Conquest of the Northwest.* 1880. Ap. p. 5.

22 *Doc. rel. to the Col. Hist. of N. Y.* V:436.

23 Dinwiddie to Hamilton May 21, 1753. Quot. fr. f.n. p. 75 *Jour. of Capt. Wm. Trent* ed. by A. T. Goodman. 1871.

24 *The Official Records of Robert Dinwiddie, Lieutenant Governor of the Colony*

were singularly supine. Croghan's suggestions about frontier problems were so neglected that he wished with all his "hart Some gentleman who is an artist in Philadelphia, and whos Account wold be Depended on, whould have ye Curiosity to take a Journey in those parts" in order to prove to the province (by means of a map) that the lands on which the French were building lay within their jurisdiction.[25] Valuable Indian allies were, according to Johnson's repeated complaints, neglected or wronged. Even after the publication of Washington's journal of his tour to the Ohio in 1753, warning against the immanence of Latin conquest, and his attack on Jumonville, almost no interest could be aroused in a struggle for expansion, and it was with the greatest difficulty that the assemblies, especially that of Pennsylvania, could be forced to vote adequate levies for defence.[26] The defeat of Braddock caused wide-spread consternation, however,[27] and the flight of the terror-stricken frontiersmen before the rifles, tomahawks, and firebrands with which the French and Indians ravaged the border was another potent factor in arousing the dwellers on the sea-board. Of the wide-spread alarm and devastation contemporary letters, journals, and newspapers furnish countless illustrations.

> "ever since the tragical event last July, on the banks of the Monongahela, our frontiers have been ravaged and dispeopled, great quantities of the stock of the back inhabitants driven off by the French and their Indians to Duquesne. Fire, sword and perpetual alarms have surrounded them, persons of every age and sex have fallen a prey to the barbarians, and, in short, the most shocking outrages perpetrated on the western settlements of this colony, and our two next neighbors to the northward. By these means, our frontiers have been contracted in many places 150 miles, and still are drawing nearer and nearer to the centre." [28]

---

*of Virginia, 1751-1758* ed. by R. A. Brock (*Va. Hist. Soc. Pub.* 2v. 1833) form an astonishing testimony to Dinwiddie's zeal and energy.

25 Quot. fr. *E.W.T.* V:72 f.n.

26 Maj. Thos. Mante in his *Hist. of the Late War in N. A.* (1772) gives a good condensed account of the state of mind at this time. p. 45.

27 Unquestionably this received greater publicity than any other episode of the war. For a good summary of contemporary treatments, poetic and prose, see Winthrop Sargent's *Hist. of an Expedition against Fort Du Quesne, in 1755; under Major-General Edward Braddock.* (*Pa. Hist. Soc. Pub.* 1855).

28 Maury — *Memoirs of a Hugenot Family.* 403. *The Papers of Sir William*

Once the seriousness of the situation was realized, paltering was thrown aside, and we have the greatest of those struggles for possession that for a century agitated the continent. With this seven years conflict historians have dealt so comprehensively that the literary student need only note that on the English side as well as on the French it was productive of many interesting journals — the artlessly vivid narrative of the Moravian missionary, Post; the Indian portrayals of the adopted captive, James Smith; Colonel Robert Rogers' account of the surrender of the French forts. Frequently contemporary interest caused such productions to be printed almost at once; again they have been preserved in public or private archives to be sought out and published by the zealous devotee of research. All, however, aid in giving new materials for interpretation of the conquest of the midland, all flash kaleidoscopic pictures before us — red-coats chopping a narrow road through the wilderness, the skilful ambush of the painted savage, the border rangers leading in conquest.[29]

And in another, more formal way the war aided in the upbuilding of a literature of the interior. For the mother country,

---

*Johnson* give many references to the border outrages (II:28-9, 368-9, 439, 443, 468) as do all the colonial documents. See, for instance, *Doc. Rel. to the Col. Hist. of N. Y.* VII:80. In Pennsylvania a large number of pamphlets were printed, lamenting the distressed situation of the province and trying to fix the blame for it. See, for instance, Wm. Smith's *A Brief State of the Province of Pennsylvania* . . . (1755), & *A Brief View of the Conduct of Pennsylvania for the Year 1755* . . . (1756). For French reports of this warfare, see *Doc. Rel. to the Col. Hist. of N. Y.* X:528, 479-80, 406, 408, 423, 435, 398.

29 Of the way in which the war turned public attention to the interior Nathaniel Ames' *Astronomical Diary* gives an excellent illustration. In this *Almanac* for 1758 he states "A Writer upon this present Time says, 'The Parts of *North-America* which may be claimed by *Great-Britain* or *France* are of as much worth as either Kingdom. — That fertile Country to the West of the Appalachian Mountains (a String of 8 or 900 Miles in Length) between *Canada* and the *Missisipi* is of much larger Extent than all *France, Germany* and *Poland*; and all well provided with Rivers, a very fine wholesome Air, a rich Soil, capable of producing Food and Physick, and all Things necessary for the Conveniency and Delight of Life: In fine, the Garden of the World!' — Time was we might have been possess'd of it: At this Time two mighty Kings contend for this inestimable Prize: — Their respective Claims are to be measured by the Length of their Swords. . . . Have we not too fondly depended upon our numbers? . . . Our numbers will not avail till the Colonies are united. . . . If we do not join Heart and Hand in the common Cause against our exulting Foes but fall to disputing amongst ourselves, it may really happen as the Governor of Pennsylvania told his Assembly, 'We shall have no priviledge to dispute about, nor Country to dispute in.' " He concludes with a glowing prophecy as to the future of America. A page from the 1759 almanac is reproduced herewith. *A Brief Chronology of Remarkable Events Relating Chiefly to the Present WAR* in the 1763 issue also treats in rhyme the events of the war in the West. For a later illustration of the way in which the almanacs advertised the West see *Poor Will's Almanack, for the Year of our Lord, 1788* containing *A Journal of an Expedition Undertaken by Patrick Kennedy & Others, from Kaskaskias Village, to the Head Waters of the Illinois River . . . 1773.*

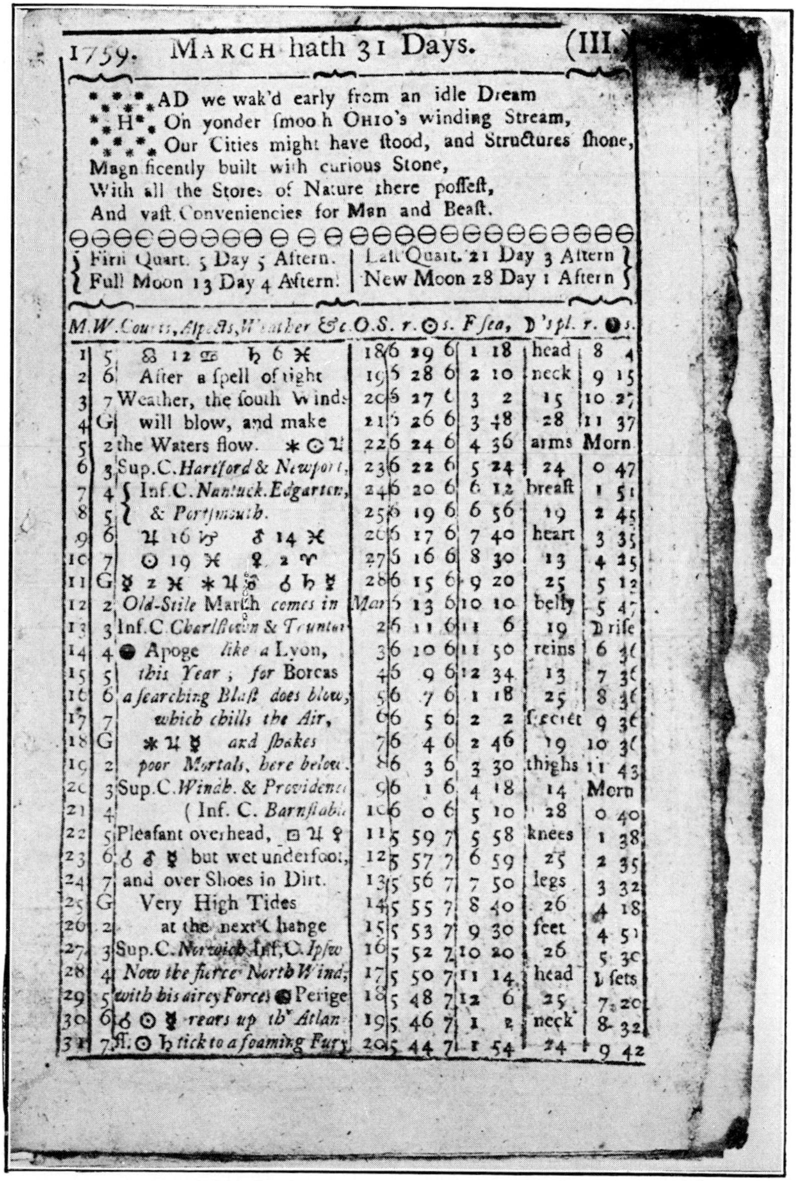

1759. MARCH hath 31 Days. (III.)

HAD we wak'd early from an idle Dream
On yonder smooh h OHIO's winding Stream,
Our Cities might have stood, and Structures shone,
Magn ficently built with curious Stone,
With all the Stores of Nature there possest,
And vast Conveniencies for Man and Beast.

First Quart. 5 Day 5 Aftern. | Last Quart. 21 Day 3 Aftern
Full Moon 13 Day 4 Aftern. | New Moon 28 Day 1 Aftern

| M. | W. | Courts, Aspects, Weather &c. | O.S. | r. ☉ | s. | F sea, | ☽'s pl. | r. ☽ s. |
|---|---|---|---|---|---|---|---|---|
| 1 | 5 | ☊ 12 ♋ ♄ 6 ♓ | 18 | 6 29 | 6 | 1 18 | head | 8 4 |
| 2 | 6 | After a spell of tight | 19 | 6 28 | 6 | 2 10 | neck | 9 15 |
| 3 | 7 | Weather, the south Winds | 20 | 6 27 | 6 | 3 2 | 15 | 10 27 |
| 4 | G | will blow, and make | 21 | 6 26 | 6 | 3 48 | 28 | 11 37 |
| 5 | 2 | the Waters flow. ✱ ☉ ♃ | 22 | 6 24 | 6 | 4 36 | arms | Morn |
| 6 | 3 | Sup. C. *Hartford* & *Newport*, | 23 | 6 22 | 6 | 5 24 | 24 | 0 47 |
| 7 | 4 | Inf. C. *Nantuck. Edgarton*, | 24 | 6 20 | 6 | 6 12 | breast | 1 51 |
| 8 | 5 | & *Portsmouth*. | 25 | 6 19 | 6 | 6 56 | 19 | 2 45 |
| 9 | 6 | ♃ 16 ♑ ♂ 14 ♓ | 26 | 6 17 | 6 | 7 40 | heart | 3 35 |
| 10 | 7 | ☉ 19 ♓ ♀ 2 ♈ | 27 | 6 16 | 6 | 8 30 | 13 | 4 15 |
| 11 | G | ☿ 2 ♓ ✱ ♃ ♂ ☌ ♄ ☿ | 28 | 6 15 | 6 | 9 20 | 25 | 5 12 |
| 12 | 2 | *Old-Stile* March *comes in* | Mar | 6 13 | 6 | 10 10 | belly | 5 47 |
| 13 | 3 | Inf. C. *Charlstown* & *Taunton* | 2 | 6 11 | 6 | 11 6 | 19 | ☽ rise |
| 14 | 4 | ● Apoge *like a* Lyon, | 3 | 6 10 | 6 | 11 50 | reins | 6 36 |
| 15 | 5 | *this Year; for* Boreas | 4 | 6 9 | 6 | 12 34 | 13 | 7 36 |
| 16 | 6 | *a searching Blast does blow*, | 5 | 6 7 | 6 | 1 18 | 25 | 8 36 |
| 17 | 7 | *which chills the Air*, | 6 | 6 5 | 6 | 2 2 | secret | 9 36 |
| 18 | G | ✱ ♃ ☿ *and shakes* | 7 | 6 4 | 6 | 2 46 | 19 | 10 36 |
| 19 | 2 | *poor Mortals, here below*. | 8 | 6 3 | 6 | 3 30 | thighs | 11 43 |
| 20 | 3 | Sup. C. *Windh.* & *Providence* | 9 | 6 1 | 6 | 4 18 | 14 | Morn |
| 21 | 4 | Inf. C. *Barnstable* | 10 | 6 0 | 6 | 5 10 | 28 | 0 40 |
| 22 | 5 | Pleasant overhead, □ ♃ ♀ | 11 | 5 59 | 7 | 5 58 | knees | 1 38 |
| 23 | 6 | ☌ ♂ ☿ but wet underfoot, | 12 | 5 57 | 7 | 6 59 | 25 | 2 35 |
| 24 | 7 | and over Shoes in Dirt. | 13 | 5 56 | 7 | 7 50 | legs | 3 32 |
| 25 | G | Very High Tides | 14 | 5 55 | 7 | 8 40 | 26 | 4 18 |
| 26 | 2 | at the next Change | 15 | 5 53 | 7 | 9 30 | feet | 4 51 |
| 27 | 3 | Sup. C. *Norwich* Inf. C. *Ipsw* | 16 | 5 52 | 7 | 10 20 | 26 | 5 30 |
| 28 | 4 | *Now the fierce North Wind*, | 17 | 5 50 | 7 | 11 14 | head | ☽ sets |
| 29 | 5 | *with his airey Forces* ● Perige | 18 | 5 48 | 7 | 12 6 | 25 | 7 20 |
| 30 | 6 | ☌ ☉ ☿ *rears up th' Atlan* | 19 | 5 46 | 7 | 1 2 | neck | 8 32 |
| 31 | 7 | ☍ ☉ ♄ *tick to a foaming Fury* | 20 | 5 44 | 7 | 1 54 | 24 | 9 42 |

From Nathaniel Ames' *Astronomical Diary* for 1759

usually neglectful of the colonies save for the commercial benefits they afforded her but taught some severe lessons by the catastrophes of the early campaigns, after Pitt came into power threw all her resources into the great contest between nations, of which the struggle on the western border was only a small phase. Magazine articles, maps, plans, journals of campaigns, partisan pamphlets for and against the conduct of affairs, exhortations to increased effort, attempts to fix responsibility for the French encroachments, *The Annual Register*, and in ensuing years compendiums such as John Entick's *General History of the Late War* (5v. 1763-4) all served to emphasize to the public of Britain the importance of her overseas dominion. Though many of these dealt solely with the northern front, the West was by no means slighted, as is indicated by Mitchell's remark about the Ohio, "which is supposed by many, who seem hardly to have heard of any other place in our colonies, 'til they were so alarmed about this, to have been the sole occasion of the present war with the French."[30] Most of these books and pamphlets are comparatively rare now, and most of them have little literary value, being of interest mainly to the specialized student. In them is evident, however, not only consideration of the issues involved between France and Britain, but, a fact of especial interest to us, a discussion of relations and responsibilities between mother country and colonies which was to grow increasingly acrimonious till the Revolution brought at last the much talked of separation.

Not even the successful conclusion of the war made an end of these paper debates, however, for then came discussion of the problem Pitt presented to the representatives of Great Britain in the pithy sentence — "Some are for keeping Canada; some Guadaloupe; who will tell me which I shall be hanged for not keeping?"[31] The great military and naval successes of the British whetted their appetites for spoils; indeed it was only a little after the news of the fall of Quebec that *A Letter Addressed to Two Great Men on the Prospect of Peace* (London, Dec. 1759) appeared, the first tract of many discussing prospective

30 Mitchell, John — *The Contest in America between Great Britain & France. . . .* 1757. 31.

31 Walpole — *Mem. of Geo. III.* 1:26. Quot. fr. Alvord, on whom most of the paragraph immediately following is based.

terms for the treaty. In the pamphlet argument that ensued, party politics and traditional policies played as great a share as the actual territories involved, as Professor W. L. Grant and Professor Clarence W. Alvord have pointed out. For us it is most interesting to note the way in which the writers urge the possession of the Midland, chiefly for protection from the aggressions of the French but also for the economic value of the interior valleys. Statistics, not always an asset to literature, here prove most illuminating. Of the sixty-five pamphlets issued between 1759 and 1763 which are listed in the second volume of *The Mississippi Valley in British Politics,* nine must be ruled out of consideration because of inaccessibility or because of their failure to advance any special territorial claim.[32] Of the fifty-six that remain six especially grasping or hard-hearted authors urge the retention of all conquests, one of them stressing especially Canada; nine put foremost the West Indies; and seventeen, Canada. Although no one was so rash as to ask for Louisiana alone, the propositions involving two or more territories reveal as overwhelming a preponderance for lands on the continent as the single claims. Five demand Canada and the West Indies; two seek Canada, Louisiana, and the West Indies; one, Canada, Louisiana, and Florida; one, Louisiana and the West Indies; and fifteen, Canada and Louisiana. The almost panic fear of French influence with the Indians and the desire to round out British possessions must be considered dominant factors in formulating opinion probably; yet the warmth with which "an unprejudiced Observer," for instance, in *A Letter to a Great M———R, on the Prospect of Peace* (1761) urges colonization of the interior, suggests a growing appreciation of that region as well as fear of trade rivals among the seaboard states, and the rainbow coloring of his picture of Louisiana and that of the ministerial writer who produced *Reflections on the Terms of Peace* leave nothing to be desired.

"The soil is amazingly fertile, the climate mild and salubrious,

---

32 Alvord, C. W. — *The Miss. Vall. in Brit. Pol.* 2v. 1917. II:253 ff. See also W. L. Grant — *Canada versus Guadeloupe, Amer. Hist. Rev.* XVII:735. *Further Pamphlets for the Canada-Guadeloupe Controversy* by C. E. Fryer, *Miss. Val. Hist. Rev.* IV:227 describes additional material found in a special collection of tracts at McGill University. J. Almon — *Biographical, Literary, & Political Anecdotes* . . . 3v. 1797, gives interesting early comment on the controversy.

the land in general elevated, solid, and level, refreshed with breezes, and being interspersed with the most beautiful meadows, afford a most delightful prospect. Look up, you see the horizon clear and serene. Look down, you see nature all the year lavishing profusely the sweetest gifts, on the uncultivated plains. Ask those, Sir, who have been in Louisiana, they will give you the most pleasing ideas of the country and climate, we have had such accounts from the French whose interest it is to conceal its most minute advantages; and so much, that it has occasioned it to be called, in derision, the Frenchman's paradise."[33]

Actual knowledge of, and response to, the beauty of the prairies is, as we have stated, surprisingly slow. In contrast to the lyric descriptions which for years had been available to the French public, in England even the pamphlets lauding the new acquisitions offered for the most part only conventional or warmed-over accounts. Coxe's enthusiasm, it is true, and his careful study of all available sources of information early enabled him to make his Carolana a very tempting place.

"When you come out of the agreeable shade, you see a most beautiful level country, only about six or eight miles distance; there are collins or gentle ascents, for the most part round or oval, crowned with stately trees, which looks more like a work of laborious consummate art than of mere nature; and this on both sides of the river, so far as the acutest sight can reach; in which meadows the wild bulls and kine, besides other beasts, graze, and in the heat of the day retire into these woods for shelter, where they chew the cud."[34]

In 1738, however, we find Keith in his *History of the British Plantations in America* advocating extension over the mountains merely as a developer of trade and a means of increasing the income from quit rents. Ker although he suspends belief in the gold mines near the Mississippi, accounts of which have been published in France, "till that Curious and adventurous Nation shall oblige the World with clearer and more certain Discoveries in that Particular, than any they have yet published" is obliged

33 *A Letter to a Great M———R.* 61-2.
34 French — *Hist. Coll. of La.* II:226.

to place reliance upon them for his geography, stating that, "The Missionaries, and others, who have had the most perfect Knowledge of *Louisiana,* give us so great an Idea of its uncommon Beauties and Productions that one would take it for the *Frenchmen's* Paradise." [35] Gee in spite of the fervor of his belief in the West is limited to such phrases as "that most fertile valley which is watered with the River *Ouerbachee,* and the great River Ohio." [36] Pownall in his *Administration of the Colonies* confines himself to an enumeration of the products of Louisiana. Mitchell, who possessed a thorough knowledge of the issues involved, warns that if the French get possession of the regions "which they are now contending for" they will have "the most fruitful countries of any in all America." [37] Burke, excellent in general as is his discussion of the *European Settlements in America,* drew his information from books. Roberts, appointed by the government to spread knowledge of the Floridas, was obliged to place reliance largely upon Spanish writers. In short Jonathan Carver was meeting a real need when he planned, as he stated in the preface of his *Travels through the Interior Parts of North America, in the Year 1766, 1767, and 1768,* to contribute "as much as lay in my power, to make that vast acquisition of territory, gained by Great Britain, in North America, advantageous to it. It appeared to me indispensably needful, that Government should be acquainted in the first place with the true state of the dominions they were now become possessed of." [38]

Nor were the colonists much better off as far as actual exper-

35 Ker — *Memoirs.* II:38, 36.

36 Gee — *Trade & Nav. of Gt. Brit. Consid.* 60.

37 Mitchell — *Contest in America.* 140. According to him the French had by the Five Nations and the Chicasaws "hitherto been confined to a barren inhospitable soil, in Canada, or to sandy desarts on the mouth of the Missisipi." 140. Other important books were Jefferys' *Natural & Civil History of the French Dominions* (1761) and *The American Gazeteer* (3v. 1762). Practically all the books treated in the first two chapters were translated to afford information about the interior for the English. The prefaces of these translations are significant, but lack of space prevents discussion here.

38 Carver — *Travels* I-II. Carver's book, although it was long influential, has been the subject of considerable controversy of recent years. See Peter Pond's *Journal, Wis. Hist. Coll.* XVIII:341, for an early reference to it. The chief attack was made by Prof. E. G. Bourne — *Travels of Jonathan Carver, Amer. Hist. Rev.* XI:287-302. For defenses and other articles see C. W. Alvord — *Jonathan Carver Vindicated, Mag. of Hist.* May 1913; M. M. Quaife — *Critical Evaluation of the Sources for Western History, Miss. Val. Hist. Rev.* I:167 ff. & his *Jonathan Carver & the Carver Grant, Ibid.* VII:3 ff.; J. T. Lee — *A Bibliography of Carver's Travels Wis. Hist. Soc. Proc.* 1909. 143 ff. and his *Captain Jonathan Carver: Additional Data, Ibid.* 1912. 87 ff.

Sioux Indians from Carver's *Travels through the Interior Parts of North America*, p. 230

ience went than the mother country. The fur traders, of course, were largely inarticulate although their oral accounts must have exerted considerable influence in the development of the West, the *Complete History of the Late War* (1774), for instance, stating that,

> "Whilst agriculture and the maritime commerce flourished on their coasts, the Indian trade drew several of our wandering dealers far into the inland country, and beyond the great mountains. Here they found themselves in a delightful climate, in a soil abundantly fruitful, and watered with many fair and navigable rivers." [39]

and Adair, after his retirement, giving a detailed and admiring account of the middle valley. The main difficulty, naturally, with the narratives that have been preserved is that very few of the early English explorers reached the real prairie country. Yet we have interesting anticipation even in the earliest records of what the reaction was to be. Lederer speaking of the Savanae at the foot of the Appalachians where vast herds of red and fallow deer stood grazing, relates that "their verdure is wonderful pleasant to the eye especially of such as having travelled through the shade of the vast forest, come out of a melancholy darkness of a sudden, into a clear and open skie." [40] Byrd in his *Journey to the Land of Eden* comments with lingering tenderness on that "sweet Place,"

> "a charming Level, of more than a Mile Square, that will bring forth like the Lands of Egypt, without being overflow'd once a year. There is scarce a Shrub in View to intercept your Prospect, but Grass as high as a Man on Horseback." [41]

Salmon, summarizing the experiences of Batts and Fallam, remarks of the trip over the mountains that,

> "In other Places they found large level Plains and fine Savanna's three or four miles wide, in which were an infinite Quantity of Turkies, Deer, Elks, and Buffaloes, so gentle and undisturbed that they had no Fear at the Appearance of the

39 *A Complete Hist. of the Late War, or Annual Register of its Rise, Progress, & Events* . . . 6th ed. 1774. 2.
40 Alvord & Bidgood — *First Explor. of the Trans-Alleg. Reg.* 163-4.
41 Byrd — *Writings.* 306-7.

> Men but would suffer them to come almost within Reach of their Hands."[42]

John Fontaine also gives a somewhat complimentary analysis of the open places.

> "We saw this day several fine tracts of land, and plains called savannas, which lie along by the river side, much like unto our low meadow lands in England, there is neither tree nor shrub that grows upon these plains, nothing but good grass, which, for want of being mowed or eaten down by cattle, grows rank and coarse."[43]

And once the actual invasion of the territory over the mountains had begun, we find even more varied and utilitarian scrutiny. Salley who went with John Howard in 1742 to the Mississippi speaks of the "large spacious open country on each side" of the Alleghany.[44] Gist, sent out by the Ohio Company to find a tract suitable for their purposes, renders repeated tribute to the beauty and fertility of the flowering pastures.

> "All the Way from Shannoah Town to this Place (except the first twenty Miles which is broken) is fine, rich, level Land, well timbered with large Walnut, Ash, Sugar Trees, Cherry Trees &c, it is well watered with a great Number of little Streams or Rivulets, and full of beautiful natural Meadows, covered with wild Rye, blue Grass and Clover, and abounds with Turkeys, Deer, Elks, and most Sorts of Game particularly Buffaloes, thirty or forty of which are frequently seen feeding in one Meadow: In short it wants Nothing but Cultivation to make it a most delightfull Country."[45]

The name *Great Meadows*, immortalized by the combat of Washington, suggests the gratitude with which trader and explorer found abundant grazing for their horses. Smith in his wanderings with the Indians estimated carefully the quality of the land. Rogers to a limited extent in his *Journals* and more elaborately in his *A Concise Account of North America* (1765) discusses the interior, describing the "large plains covered with

---

42 Salmon — *Mod. Hist.* XXXI:14.
43 Maury — *Mem. of a Hug. Fam.* 271-2.
44 Gist — *Journals.* Ap. C. 255.
45 *Ibid.* 47.

tall grass; there being scarce any trees or under-wood upon them for hundreds of miles together," and concluding, "There is perhaps no finer country in the world than that which lies extended on each side of the Misauris, whether we regard the salubrity of the air, or the fertility of the soil." But even some of his descriptions come from hearsay; certainly there is much of convention in his rhapsodic closing remarks on the territory of the Illinois and Missouri Indians.

> "The goodness of the country which they both inhabit, if possible, must render life agreeable and easy to persons who, like them, are content with having the demands of nature answered, without endeavouring to increase these demands by any studied refinement in dress, equipage, or the modes of living. In short, these people, of any upon earth, seem blessed in this world: here is health and joy, peace and plenty; care and anxiety, ambition and the love of gold, and every uneasy passion seem banished from this happy region, at least to a greater degree than in almost any other part of the world." [46]

Yet interesting as are the responses of trader, soldier, land agent, missionary, they sink into insignificance besides that intense longing for possession that was now to form the deepest, most poignant note in the swelling symphony of the land. When the whites first came to America the natives' ignorance of the difference in their methods of livelihood and the thinness of population on the coast made the cession of thousands of acres for the wondrous baubles from overseas a comparatively trivial matter. With the passing of the years, however, the numbers, rapacity, and injustice of the invaders inspired in the Indians an ever increasing sense of bitterness and despair, of which speeches like the following, distorted and condensed as they undoubtedly are by interpreters and transcribers, afford the most moving testimony.

> "We know our Lands are now become more valuable: The white People think we do not know their Value; but we are sensible that the Land is everlasting, and the few Goods we receive for it are soon worn out and gone. For the future, we will sell no lands but when Brother Onas is in the Country;

46 Rogers — *A Concise Acct. of N. A.* . . . 159, 194, 195.

and we will know beforehand, the Quantity of the Goods we are to receive. Besides, we are not well used with respect to the Lands still unsold by us. Your People daily settle on those Lands, and spoil our Hunting. . . ."

"It is customary with us to make a Present of Skins, whenever we renew our Treaties. We are ashamed to offer our Brethren so few, but your Horses and Cows have eat the Grass our Deer used to feed on."[47]

There is no more tragic thing than to read repeatedly in the emotionless pages of colonial records these laments of a diminishing race being pushed slowly, relentlessly from their ancient territories by the utilitarian needs of a numerous and land-hungry people and obliged to contend not only with the problems of normal expansion but with wholesale trickery and fraud. "Pen and ink work," unpardonable deception were responsible not only for traders' unauthorized insertion of grants in their favor in messages the tribes had asked them to write but for such swindles on the part of the proprietors as the scandalous Walking Purchase, and even more than a suspicion of fraud on the part of their natural protectors, the Indian superintendents.[48]

Small wonder then that, as the Indians were forced over the mountains and saw the French and English lust for dominion menacing them there, they threw their forces alternately to the side that seemed to promise them least interference, that they used all the terrible resources of savage warfare to insure their own preservation. Washington in his account of his journey as emissary of Dinwiddie quotes a speech showing the antagonism to the French policy of force.

"Fathers, I desire that you may hear me in civilness: if not, we must handle that rod which was laid down for the use of the obstreperous. If you had come in a peaceable manner, like our brothers the English, we would not have been against your trading with us as they do; but to come, fathers, and

47 Colden — *Hist. of the Five Ind. Nat.* II:86, 88.

48 For a contemporary exposure of these unfortunate conditions see Charles Thomson's *An Enquiry into the Causes of the Alienation of the Delaware & Shawanese Indians from the British Interest.* 1759. Repr. 1867. The *Papers of Sir William Johnson* are filled with the Indians' complaints.

> build houses upon our land, and to take it by force, is what we cannot submit to.
>
> "Fathers, both you and the English are white; we live in a country between; therefore the land belongs to neither the one nor the other; but the Great Being above allowed it to be a place of residence for us; so, fathers, I desire you to withdraw, as I have done our brothers the English; for I will keep you at arm's length. I lay this down as a trial for both, to see which will have the greatest regard to it, and that side we will stand by and make equal sharers with. . . ."[49]

Gist reveals a similar dread of the English.

> "The People in this Town, began to enquire my Business, and because I did not readily inform them, they began to suspect me, and said, I was come to settle the Indians' Lands and they knew I should never go home again safe . . ."[50]

Post with his faithful transcripts of the Indian speeches on his important peace making mission and his record of the natives' alarm when he marked off three acres to be cleared for his garden also brings up this insistent and well-founded fear of the total loss of the land on the part of the red man.[51]

Poor pawns in the struggle for empire that they were, too often cast aside without consideration when they were of no further use although their services in many ways had been decisive in value, it is no wonder that their banded effort of 1763 had a desperation that caused the fall of every fort but two, that terrorized the whole frontier, that defied for years the organized efforts of the British. Franklin's letter to Strahan, June 28, 1763, summarized the contemporary views of the outbreak.

> "Some think it is merely to secure their hunting countries, which they apprehend we mean to take from them by force and turn them into plantations, though the apprehension is

49 Washington — *Jour. of a Tour to the Ohio in 1753* in Blanchard's *Dis. & Conq. of the N. W.* Ap. 14. Johnson makes this same point. *Doc. Rel. to the Col. Hist. of N. Y.* VIII:84-6.

50 Gist — *Journals.* 34.

51 See, for instance, Post, Christian — *Jour. of 1758. E. W. T.* I:215-6. Note also the Indians' criticism of the English methods of making war. *Doc. Rel. to the Col. Hist. of N. Y.* VII:114. Johnson frequently refers to the fears of the natives. See *Ibid.* VII:114, 129-30, 726-7, etc. His own promises contrast most ironically, however, with the real fate of the Indian. *Ibid.* 248.

without ground; others, that too little notice of them has been taken since the reduction of Canada, no presents made them as before; others that they are offended at the prohibition of selling them rum or powder, but I do not find this prohibition has been general, and as to powder, that enough has been allowed them all for their hunting; others, that they acquired a relish for plunder in the late war, and would again enjoy the sweets of it; others that it is the effect of a large belt sent among them by the French commander in the Illinois country before he heard of the peace, to excite them to renew the war and assure them of supplies and assistance; others think all these causes may have operated together. . . ."[52]

Documentary evidence seems to suggest, however, that although the coureurs-de-bois encouraged the belief that a large army was coming from overseas to aid the natives, the French officers who were placed in an extremely difficult position were surprisingly generous in their attempts to pacify the Indians and that the English had themselves to blame for many of their troubles, a fact suggested by Croghan's warning note of March 19, 1763,

> "Since ye reduction of Canada the several Indian Nations this Way has been very jelous of his Majestys growing power in this Country but this last account of so much of North America being added to Great Britain has almost drove them to despair, and by leters from Major Gladwin and Captain Campble it appears that ye Indians over the Lakes are full as many there as on this Side. As to ye News how they may behave I cant pretend to say, but I do not aprove of General Armhurst's plan in distressing them too much at wonst as in my opinion they will not consider consequences if too much distrest, tho' Sir Jeffrey thinks they will . . ."

and driven home by many similar passages in letters, journals, and reports of the time.[53] The dramatic quality of the contest — the natives' holding at bay the victorious red coats who

52 Franklin, B. — *Writings* ed. by A. H. Smyth. 1906. IV:203-4. Note also Colden's denial that there is the "least ground" for the assertion "that the present insurrection has been occasioned by the Indians having been cheated of their lands." *Doc. Rel. to the Col. Hist. of N. Y.* VII:590.

53 The sternness of Amherst's attitude toward the Indians, whom he treated as conquered subjects rather than as allies, brought much criticism. See, *Papers of Sir Wm. Johnson,* III:205, 942, 965, 391-2, 421, 733, 594, 825, 866 ff., etc.

had just wrenched the most sweeping of concessions from the reluctant hands of one of the greatest of European powers —, the number of tribes involved and the intensity of their feeling, above all the wholesome respect inspired by that "firebrand of all the nations," Pontiac, have made the whole episode outstanding in the history of Indian Wars, and productive of numerous striking treatments in literature. The most valuable single source for modern students is the so-called Pontiac Manuscript.[54] In the eighteenth century, however, different aspects of the conspiracy were depicted by contemporary publications, of which we can suggest only a few. Alexander Henry, over-eager to share the rich rewards of the fur trade, barely escaped destruction in the horrible Michilimackinac massacre as he records in his *Travels and Adventures in Canada and the Indian Territories between the Years 1760 and 1776.* The dramatic journal of Captain Thomas Morris, sent as emissary to Illinois, was printed in his *Miscellanies in Prose and Verse* (1791); the account of Bouquet's expedition to subdue the recalcitrant natives gives a clear picture of his military resourcefulness and the reluctant return of the white captives.[55] Major Robert Rogers by his addition to his *Concise Account of North America* (1765) of a conclave with Pontiac unnoted in his *Journals* gives evidence of marked contemporary interest in the great chief, an interest still further testified to by the drama *Ponteach,* by many attributed to him.

This latter effect of the Indians' warfare — self-advertisement of them and their possessions —, although undesired, was certainly attained by them. Their hostility did not prohibit settlement, merely delayed it, while at the same time it centered attention on their territories. As the Ohio during the early part of the Seven Years' War had become a household word, so now Pontiac and the Illinois were on every tongue. And the men who finally attained entrance to the forbidden territory in an official capacity were among the most active in exploiting its charms. Morris in spite of his critical situation responded to the beauty of the prairies.

---

54 See *Journal of Pontiac's Conspiracy* pub. by C. M. Burton (1912), which contains both the French original and a translation.

55 [Smith, Rev. W.] — *Historic Account of Bouquet's Expedition against the Ohio Indians, in 1764.* 1888. (Orig. Pub. 1765).

"Soon after we came into extensive meadows; and I was assured that those meadows continue for a hundred and fifty miles, being in the winter drowned lands and marshes. By the dryness of the season they were now beautiful pastures: and here presented itself one of the most delightful prospects I ever beheld; all the low grounds being meadow, and without wood, and all the high grounds being covered with trees, and appearing like islands; the whole scene seemed an elysium."[56]

Pittman, who made a couple of attempts to reach the Illinois country from the South, made use of his stay in the long-coveted villages, to gather the material for his *The Present State of the European Settlements on the Mississippi* (1770). Croghan in his journal of 1765 stresses repeatedly the fertility of the soil and the value of the flat land's products, emphasizing also the surprising ignorance of the new territory on the part even of a frontiersman like himself.

"On the south side of the Ouabache runs a big bank, in which are several fine coal mines, and behind this bank, is a very large meadow, clear for several miles. It is surprising what false information we had respecting this country; some mention these spacious and beautiful meadows as large and barren savannahs. I apprehend it has been the artifice of the French to keep us ignorant of the country."[57]

And not long after his return he with a number of others formed a company for the exploitation of the region.

That the project was not unique, however, is shown by the following passage in a letter of his to Johnson of March 10, 1764.

"there is Talk of Setleing a Colony from the Mouth of the ohio to the Ilonies which I am Tould Lord Hallifax will Desier My opinion of in a fwe Days."[58]

Indeed almost immediately after the treaty of peace was signed there appeared in Edinburgh a pamphlet called *The Expediency of Securing our American Colonies by Settling the Country Adjoining the River Mississippi* (1763), amusing because of the

56 Morris — *Journal.* *E. W. T.* I:323.
57 *E. W. T.* I:145.
58 Alvord — *Crit. Per.* (*Ill. Hist. Coll. X*) 222-3.

faithfulness with which it sounds the same notes found in the war and pre-war tracts, pre-eminent being the value of the protection thus afforded against the aggressions of the French who, "no doubt, will look with regret, and with a wishful eye upon the fine extensive country they have been obliged to cede. . . ."[59] Franklin's project of barrier settlements may also be mentioned in this connection; but on the whole such discussions are of little intrinsic interest, for the arguments are oft-repeated and the descriptions of the new regions and their products are still drawn mainly from the French. They are valuable reflections of contemporary opinions, however, for although Dr. Johnson with his usual jaundiced attitude toward America wrote of the new possessions that they were at best "only the barren parts of the continent, the refuse of the earlier adventurers, which, the French, who came last, had taken only as better than nothing,"[60] Croghan reported to Johnson, March 30, 1766, that a large portion of England was "New Land mad and every body there has their eye fixt on this Country,"[61] and in America the enthusiasm was even greater. *Reasons for Establishing a British Colony at the Illinois with Some Proposals for Carrying the Same into Immediate Execution* (in Sir William Johnson's letter of July 10, 1766, Board of Trade Papers) relates the advantages of such a project, being interesting for its use of French superlatives (*"The Terrestrial Paradise,"* "the most fertile and pleasant Part of all the Western Territory now in the Possession of the English in North America"), for its mention of the Indians' willingness to sell some of their lands, and for its insistence on the fact that such a colony would not only be the "most likely Way" to prevent Mischiefs of the French but to dispossess the latter "of the remaining Part of Louisiana, should a future War make it expedient."[62] Nor were the earlier claims and plans neglected, as the records of 1763 show.[63] The soldiers

59 *Ibid.* 135.

60 Johnson — *Works* (Lynam ed.). V:414.

61 Quot. p. 111 Carter, C. E. — *The Illinois Country 1763-1774* (Amer. Hist. Assoc. Prize Essays, 1908.) from Johnson MSS. XII. no. 127.

62 Doc. Appendix. *Ibid.* 172 & 175.

63 The best outline of these land schemes is found in Alvord — *The Miss. Val. in Brit. Pol. before the Rev.* As other evidences of the soldiers' interest in speculation we may note that Gen. Amherst in 1762 recommended Detroit as the site of a future colony, that Major Thomas Mante and fifty-nine other officers petitioned to be allowed to establish a colony in Detroit, that Thomas Hutchins under the supervision of Bouquet drew up a paper on Indian warfare, advocating a military settlement for

offered western lands by Dinwiddie as an inducement to enlistment, under the leadership of Washington sent to the king a petition; Lieutenant Colonel Mercer was a personal representative of the Ohio Company in England. The traders and merchants who had suffered severe losses in the Indian Wars also longed for compensation in land. One group of which Franklin was a member proposed to buy the Carolana Grant from Coxe's heirs; speculators of New York talked of a colony on the upper Ohio to be called New Wales, the rumor of their plan causing much bitterness among the Indians according to Johnson.[64] The Walpole Company, the name commonly applied to the Grand Ohio Company, the most powerful among these early combines, had adherents among three political factions and the names of the most prominent men of England and America on its roll, its original plan to purchase two million five hundred thousand acres of land in Viriginia having been expanded to a petition for authority to purchase a tract of twenty millions.

Even before the signing of the treaty of peace, however, the Board of Trade as well as the Ministry seemed to realize the need of a fairer treatment of the Indians with regard to their land, stating, "The granting lands hitherto unsettled and establishing colonies upon the frontiers before the claims of the Indians are ascertained appears to be a measure of the most dangerous tendency," and formulating their attitude in the Proclamation of 1763 which made the mountains the barrier to settlement.[65] Although the policy of the ministry was wavering and unsettled, this being apparently intended merely as a temporary measure, grants were delayed and, although the policy changed, the outbreak of the Revolution soon placed a

---

the protection of the frontiers, that Colden states that in the spring following the submission of Canada "numbers gave in Petitions for licenses to purchase Lands of the Indians on the Frontiers, among which were the Provincial Officers of this Province, in behalf of themselves & of several of their Men. . . . Major Rogers in behalf of himself, his officers and several of his men." *Doc. rel. to the Col. Hist. of N. Y.* VII:491-2. A number of valuable papers about the greed for land and the consequent unrest among the Indians may be found *Doc. Rel. to the Col. Hist. of N. Y.* VII:571, 835. VIII:11, 21, 37, 302, 404. Comments about projected colonies may be found. *Ibid.* VII:605-6, 809, 983. VIII:27, 30-1, 253.

64 "Being naturally inquisitive concerning all our operations they make frequent enquiry's amongst the Inhabitants who understand their Language and read the public papers from whom they have now a report of our intending plant Colonies in the heart of their Country, which notwithstanding all have said to them contributes greatly to their discontent." *Ibid.* 37. See also *Ibid.* VII:959

65 See *Doc. Rel. to the Col. Hist. of N. Y.* VIII:21, 47, etc. & Alvord's *Genesis of the Proclamation of 1763. Wis. Hist. Proc.* 1908. 165 ff.

check for some years on these schemes.[66] For us they are important, partly for the advertising they gave the new territory, mainly, however, for the fact that they early suggest for the Mississippi Valley the large landed interests, and because they foreshadow the later heartless speculation which was to cause so much distress among the immigrants, so much hostility among the squatters. The fertile fields which had delighted the eager eyes of the French explorers, which had filled the Jesuits with visions of a great Christian kingdom, for which the Indian owners had so bitterly fought, now became the prey of the Anglo Saxon financier.

It was not the great land companies, however, that were responsible for the settlement of the West, not the great land companies that succeeded in evading the governmental restrictions for a hunting preserve in the middle of the continent. The people that thoroughly alarmed the Indians by their encroachments, that set at naught the ministerial decrees and the magisterial efforts at enforcement were the frontiersmen, the bold, hardy, and often brutal spirits among the English, the Germans and Scotch-Irish from overseas, who, undaunted by hardship, swarmed in ever-increasing numbers up the narrow valleys, through the mountain passes. Entry after entry gives testimony to their numbers. According to the Indians, they and their dependents were "like Giddy People not knowing what to do."

> "whereever we turned about we saw our Blood, and when our Young men wanted to go a hunting the Wild Beasts in our Country, they found it covered with fences, so that they were weary crossing them, neither can they get Venison to eat, or Bark to make huts for the Beasts are run away and the Trees cut down." [67]

---

66 As a matter of fact practically no attention was paid to this proclamation. Dec. 16, 1766, Johnson reported to the Earl of Shelburne that, "The thirst after Indian lands, is become almost universal, the people who generally want them, are either ignorant of, or remote from the consequences of disobliging the Indians, many make a traffic of lands, and few or none will be at any pains or expence to get them settled, consequently, they cannot be loosers by an Indian War, and should a Tribe be driven to despair, and abandon their country, they have their desire tho' at the expence of the lives of such ignorant settlers as may be upon it." *Doc. Rel. to the Col. Hist. of N. Y.* VII:880-1.

67 *Doc. Rel. to the Col. Hist. of N. Y.* VIII:40. For other complaints see *Ibid.* VII:726-7, VIII:46-7, etc.

Jones, describing his trips to the Ohio in 1772 and 1773, states that "at this time many of the inhabitants were near a famine, occasioned by the multitudes lately moved into this new country."[68] Croghan wrote in October, 1770,

> "What number of families has settled, since the congress, to the westward of the high ridge, I cannot pretend to say positively; but last year, I am sure, there were between four and five thousand, and all this spring and summer the roads have been lined with waggons moving to the Ohio."[69]

Even in the far-off British Parliament Burke stressed the necessity of yielding to the expanding population.

> "But if you stopped your grants, what would be the consequence? The people would occupy without grants. They have already so occupied in many places. You cannot station garrisons in every part of these deserts. If you drive the people from one place, they will carry on their annual tillage, and remove with their flocks and herds to another. Many of the people in the back settlements are already little attached to particular situations. Already they have topped the Appalachian mountains. From thence they behold before them an immense plain, one vast, rich, level meadow; a square of five hundred miles. Over this they would wander without a possibility of restraint; they would change their manners with the habits of their life; would soon forget a government by which they were disowned; would become hordes of English Tartars; and pouring down upon your unfortified frontiers a fierce and irresistible cavalry, become masters of your governors, and your counselors, your collectors and comptrollers, and of all the slaves that adhered to them."[70]

And the lawlessness that Burke thus vividly suggests worked even greater havoc on the western frontier than the number of the settlers. Unquestionably there were some men of fine character among the immigrants, such as the Reverend

---

68 Jones, Rev. David — *A Journal of Two Visits Made to Some Nations of Indians on the West Side of the River Ohio, in the Years 1772 & 1773.* (Sabin repr. II. 1865. Orig. pub. 1774). 29.

69 Quot. from Alvord — *The Miss. Val. in Brit. Pol.* II:113.

70 Burke, Edmund — *Speech on Moving his Resolutions for Conciliation with the Colonies.* 1775. ¶ 50.

David Jones, who tells us that he "from a desire to officiate in the ministry, without dependence upon the people, had views of settling on the east side of the river Ohio, in a province then expected to take place under the propriety of messrs. Franklin, Wharton, Boynton, Morgan and others." [71] Nevertheless most of the frontiersmen seem to have been of a very low and brutal type. Crèvecoeur in his *Letters from an American Farmer* declared, "Thus are our first steps trod, thus are our first trees felled, in general, by the most vicious of our people." [72] According to Johnson, "for more than ten years past the most dissolute fellows united with debtors, and persons of a wandering disposition have been removing from Pensilvania & Virginia &c[a] into the Indian Country, towards & on the Ohio, & a considerable number of settlemen[ts] were made as early as 1765 when my Deputy was sent to the *Ilinois* from whence he gave me a particular account of the uneasiness it occasioned amongst the Indians, many of these emigrants are idle fellows that are too lazy to cultivate lands, & invited by the plenty of game they found, have employed themselves in hunting, in which they interfere much more with the Indians than if they pursued agriculture alone, and the Indian hunters (who are composed of all the Warriors in each nation) already begin to feel the scarcity this has occasioned, which greatly encreases their resentment." [73]

The situation was further complicated by the intense passion for land induced by generations of peasant living. Fully to comprehend the border outrages, to appreciate the passion that caused crimes on the side of the whites as terrible as the atrocities of the savages, we must try to put ourselves in the place of the outlying colonists. The Scotch-Irish driven from Great Britain by religious discrimination and want caused in part by England's narrow economic policy found remedy in going to America as Boswell and other contemporaries testify.

> "We performed, with much activity, a dance which, I suppose, the emigration from Skye has occasioned. They call it

---

71 Jones — *Jour. of Two Visits* . . . VIII.
72 Crèvecoeur, J. Hector St. John — *Letters from an American Farmer* ed. by Ludwig Lewisohn, 1904. 72.
73 *Doc. Rel. to the Col. Hist. of N. Y.* VIII:460.

> *America.* Each of the couples, after the common *involutions* and *evolutions,* successively whirls round in a circle, till all are in motion; and the dance seems intended to show how emigration catches, till a whole neighborhood is set afloat.''[74] ''The bad season for three years past, together with the high price of lands and tythes, have all contributed to the general run to America, and to the ruin of many families, who are daily leaving their houses and lands desolate.''[75]

Once there we find frequent mention of the tenacity with which they grasped the land, the most striking being Secretary Logan's complaint in 1730, that they in an ''audacious and disorderly manner'' settled on the Conestoga Manor, alleging it ''was against the laws of God and Nature that so much land should be idle while so many Christians wanted to labor on it and raise their bread.''[76] The Germans, also enduring severe privations at home and often oppressed by religious intolerance, came to the western hemisphere in infinitely more distressing circumstances. The business of enticing and transporting the immigrants brought wealth to the infamous Newlanders[77] who acted as bait and to the mercenary ship captains who starved and robbed and abused their passengers, but indescribable suffering to the cowed and herded masses who, penned in filthy quarters and doled out the most unedible of rations, died in numbers as great as the African slaves or contracted loathsome diseases, for which no treatment was provided. Even when they were landed in Pennsylvania, their chief destination, their troubles were not at an end. In the case of the Redemptioners, vast numbers of whom were imported each year, families were separated; for each there lay the prospect of many years of sometimes kind but often stern

---

74 Boswell, James -- *Tour to the Hebrides,* ed by R. W. Chapman. Oxford U. P. 1924. 345-6. Entry for Oct. 2, 1773.

75 Ford, H. J. — *The Scotch-Irish in America.* 1915. 195.

76 Quot. *Ibid.* 271.

77 "These man traffickers or Seelen-Hendler, as the elder Saur denominated them, were known to the Dutch as 'Zeilverkoopers,' that is, soul-sellers, but among the Germans themselves more generally as Newlanders. . . . By a show of prosperity they induced the peasants to immigrate, receiving ordinarily a commission of seven dollars per head from the ship owner, their enterprise being so lucrative that it is said in 1749 alone, about one hundred engaged in it." Diffenderffer, F. R. — *The German Immigration into Pa.* . . . Pt. II. *The Redemptioners.* 1900. 189-190. For a first hand account of the disgraceful conditions prevailing on these immigrant ships see the *Narrative of Johann Carl Buettner.* (Heartman's Hist. Ser. I. 16 ff.) Duden warned against the fate of the redemptioners. Letter 31, *Mo. Hist. Rev.* XIII:179-180.

bondage. Certainly it was not strange that when after such trials they finally won a home and a plot of ground for themselves, they clung to it with desperation.[78]

Equally certainly such people were not to be prevented from making a home by the mere presence of a law upon the statute books. Johnson repeatedly complains about their invasions upon the Indians' territories, stating that they "pay as little regard to Government, as they do to title for their possessions. . . ."[79] Dartmouth wrote to Stuart on March third, 1773,

> "I am free to confess that I very much doubt whether that dangerous spirit of unlicensed emigration into the interior parts of America can be effectively restrained by any authority whatever."[80]

Even when officials wished to stop the invaders they were powerless; evicted squatters returned; imprisoned malefactors were freed by mobs of their fellows. The complaints of the Indian chiefs were futile; the attempts of the young Indians to avenge their wrongs by force served as a pretext for the annexation of more territory by the whites.[81] And so for the major portion of the century we have on the western frontier a vicious circle of bloodshed and devastation, the blame for which it is difficult to apportion justly.

The inevitable conflict between Indian and white was complicated at first, of course, by the struggle with the French; after the outbreak of the Revolution by the British incitement of the natives. Allowances must be made, too, for the despair attendant upon the Indian warfare — the pealing out upon the quiet night of the dreaded warwhoop, the burning of the little cabins, built with so much labor and such high hopes, the braining of

---

78 In fact they were more or less obliged to fend for themselves, the great land owners and the legislators who wanted barrier colonies seeming concerned only with their own protection. Salmon put the matter bluntly when he said the frontiers were "a post assigned to the necessitous and hardy *Highlanders* and *Swiss*, who richly deserve the Lands assigned them for securing the rest of the Provinces." *Mod. Hist.* XXXI:586.

79 *Doc. Rel. to the Col. Hist. of N. Y.* VIII:461.

80 Quot. fr. Alvord — *The Miss. Val. in Brit. Pol.* II:141.

81 The belief that Dunmore's War was fought to gain land has been generally held from that time to the present. See *Doc. Rel. to the Col. Hist. of N. Y.* VIII:495, 463 ff., 516; R. G. Thwaites & L. P. Kellogg — *Doc. Hist. of Dunmore's War, 1774* (1905); *Amer. Archives*, 4th. Ser. v. I; Brantz Mayer — *Tah-gah-jute; or, Logan & Cresap.* 1867.

babies, the driving of women and children into captivity, the fiendish tortures, the abandoning of the treasured herds and pitifully few household trinkets at the stealthy sounding of alarm. Even then we cannot excuse the whites' wanton acts of brutality, their consistent breaking of faith, the cold-blooded murder of hostages, the wholesale slaughter of helpless human beings. Foremost in the latter class are the massacres of the unresisting Christian Indians, outcasts from both races, which as depicted by the missionaries and other contemporary historians make the most shameful annals in the approach to the Prairie.[82]

The surprising feature about all this tumult on the border, however, is the way it has sunk into oblivion. The general reader nowadays, for instance, knows nothing of the Black Boys, picturesque as is Smith's description of them.

> "The committee appointed me captain of this company of rangers, and gave me the appointment of my subalterns. I chose two of the most active young men that I could find, who had also been long in captivity with the Indians. As we enlisted our men, we dressed them uniformly in the Indian manner, with breech-clouts, leggins, mockesons and green shrouds, which we wore in the same manner that the Indians do, and nearly as the Highlanders wear their plaids. In place of hats we wore red handkerchiefs, and painted our faces red and black, like Indian warriors. I taught them the Indian discipline, as I knew of no other at that time, which would answer the purpose much better than British. We succeeded beyond expectation in defending the frontiers and were extolled by our employers." [83]

The unassuming self-sacrifice of the Moravians is accorded little of the recognition that justly glorifies the work of the Jesuits. The tempestuous Irishmen, the stolid Germans, the land-craving

---

82 It has seemed impracticable here to give a detailed discussion of the Moravian records, valuable as they are for giving information about the early West and noble as are the missionary efforts they portray. See particularly G. H. Loskiel's *History of the Mission of the United Brethren among the Indians in North America* (1794), *Diary of David Zeisberger* ed. by E. F. Bliss (1885), Heckewelder, John — *A Narrative of the Mission of the United Brethren among the Delaware & Mohegan Indians, from . . 1740, to the close of the year 1808 . . .* (1820); *Ohio Arch. & Hist. Soc. Pub.* XXI:1 ff., XIX:1-173, XVIII:202 ff.

83 *An Account of the Remarkable Occurrences in the Life & Travels of Col. James Smith, . . .* ed. by W. M. Darlington (*Ohio Val. Ser. V*) 1870. 106-7. For different views of some of the exploits described by Smith see *Doc. Rel. to the Col. Hist. of N. Y.* VII:746-7, VIII:186, X:469-70.

Anglo-Saxons of the Alleghany frontier have almost dropped out of sight; for an example of the pioneer or for a typical illustration of border warfare, the modern writer will, almost without exception, turn to Kentucky.

At first thought this idealization of Boone and his fellows seems an unaccountable freak of tradition. Boone was at the outset merely an agent of Henderson, one of the most daring of the great land speculators, whose name and fame have been almost entirely blotted out, however, by the halo surrounding his employee.[84] Before the great scout first looked up on the rich plains that were to be indissolubly connected with his name, Walker and Gist had traversed them, each leaving us interesting journals; John Finley by his enthusiastic accounts inspired Boone; the name of James McBride with the date 1754 was found carved on a tree; John Howard in 1742 had crossed the mountains from Virginia and sailed down the Ohio to the Mississippi where he was captured by the Indians.[85] Consideration, however, reveals various important factors sufficient to account for the pioneer's prestige. Up to this time progress from the seacoast had been fairly steady, a slow and irresistible expansion of the boundaries of civilization. Now after passing southward along the great mountain trough from Pennsylvania

84 Speculators wishing to evade the governmental restrictions on settlement bought land from the Indians, a practice to which the Earl of Halifax refers in his letter to Sir Jeffery Amherst of Oct. 19, 1763.

"I likewise take notice of the intelligence which Governor Boone, (in his letter to you of the 29th of July,) mentions to have received, of many persons, having been authorized to purchase lands of the Indians in the ceded Countries of Florida and Louisiana. As the private purchases formerly made by individuals, have been productive of infinite mischiefs; as His Majesty by Instructions given long since to his Governors, and by his Proclamation lately issued, has forbidden all such purchases and declared that all purchases of lands from the Indians shall be made by the Crown, I must recommend it to you to do your utmost to prevent such a practice from taking place, even in a single instance if it be possible." *Doc. Rel. to the Col. Hist. of N. Y.* VII:571. Nevertheless Henderson as well as others made such a purchase; the fact that his grants were later judged invalid caused Daniel Boone to lose his property and was productive of much trouble in Kentucky. J. F. D. Smyth's contemporary comment is interesting, that for ten wagons of cheap goods Henderson made a purchase from the chiefs of the Cherokees "of a vast tract of territory, equal in extent to a kingdom; and in the excellence of climate and soil, extent of its rivers, and beautiful elegance of situations, inferior to none in the universe." Smyth does not undertake Henderson's justification but admires "his enterprising policy and the vigour and activity of his mind." *A Tour in the U. S. of Amer. 1784.* 2v. I:126, 128. For later discussion see Archibald Henderson — *Richard Henderson & the Occupation of Kentucky, Miss. Val. Hist. Rev.* I:341 ff. & his *The Creative Forces in American Expansion, Amer. Hist. Rev.* XX:86 ff. *An Account of the Proceedings of the Ilinois and Ouabache Land Companies in Pursuance of their Purchases Made of the Independent Natives,* . . . 1796, describes similar activities and asserts the speculators' rights to the lands.

85 See J. S. Johnston — *First Explorations of Kentucky* (Filson Club Pub. XIII).

and up the Virginia valleys into the Piedmont, the daring settlers were to strike off across a steep mountain trail, through heavy forests, to erect their log cabins and wooden palisades in the favorite Indian hunting country wild mile after wild mile from the nearest white stronghold. The type of men and women who thus ventured forth had changed as it must under the exigency of new conditions. The outlying settlers of Pennsylvania at the time of the French and Indian Wars were still so completely under the dominion of their European past that Franklin is said to have obtained from the Germans a superabundance of supplies for the army, partly by the threat of official confiscation but largely by the display of a uniform resembling that of the Hussars. Once an Indian alarm had gone forth, most of the border inhabitants had no thought of anything besides flight. Dallying for property was usually rewarded by scalping, and the war was carried far east of the mountains. The change produced by necessity Smith portrays well in his remarks on Indian warfare.

> "In Braddock's war, the frontiers were laid waste for above three hundred miles long, and generally about thirty broad, excepting some that were living in forts, and many hundreds, or perhaps thousands, killed or made captives, and horses, and all kinds of property carried off: but, in the next Indian war, though we had the same Indians to cope with, the frontiers almost all stood their ground, because they were by this time, in some measure acquainted with their manœuvres; and the want of this, in the first war, was the cause of the loss of many hundreds of our citizens, and much treasure." [86]

And in Kentucky we have perhaps the sturdiest fruit of that contact with the wilderness that developed even in the children amazing adaptability and self-reliance. The repelling of the Indians at Boonesborough and Harrodsburg, the escape of Boone from his Shawnee adopters, the sufferings of the little colony deprived of its slender provision of salt, the slaughter at Blue Licks, each of these could be paralleled or excelled by other single episodes in our history. Yet probably no other district

---

86 *An Account of the Remarkable Occurrences in the Life & Travels of Colonel James Smith.* . . . 157.

could be cited which would furnish so striking a medley of picturesque and heroic elements; and even these have been given especial radiance for the fancy by the vivid colorings of the early historians. Filson's narrative of Boone, stilted as is its phraseology, is, of course, the chief source for the pioneer legend, the dramatic phases of which are well condensed in the following paragraph.

> "To conclude, I can now say that I have verified the saying of an old Indian who signed Col. Henderson's deed. Taking me by the hand, at the delivery thereof, Brother, says he, we have given you a fine land, but I believe you will have much trouble in settling it. — My footsteps have often been marked with blood, and therefore I can truly subscribe to its original name. Two darling sons, and a brother, have I lost by savage hands, which have also taken from me forty valuable horses and abundance of cattle. Many dark and sleepless nights have I been a companion for owls, separated from the cheerful society of men, scorched by the summer's sun, and pinched by the winter's cold, an instrument ordained to settle the wilderness. But now the scene is changed; peace crowns the sylvan shades."

Filson, who declared in the *Discovery, Settlement, and Present State of Kentucky* that "this performance is not published from lucrative motives, but solely to inform the world of the happy climate, and plentiful soil of this favoured region" was also instrumental not only in giving more accurate information about the territory than had existed previously but in establishing the Utopian concept, so prominent a factor in the early travel literature.

> "In your country, like the land of promise, flowing with milk and honey, a land of brooks, of water, of fountains and depths, that spring out of valleys and hills, a land of wheat and barley, and all kinds of fruits, you shall eat bread without scarceness, and not lack any thing in it; where you are neither chilled with the cold of Capricorn, nor scorched with the burning heat of Cancer; the mildness of your air so great, that you neither feel the effects of infectious fogs, nor pestilential vapours. Thus, your country, favoured with the

smiles of heaven, will probably be inhabited by the first people the world ever knew."[87]

And this concept Imlay, one of the most philosophical of the early authors, developed still more elaborately. He opens his letters by assuring his English correspondent that,

> "The task you have given me, however difficult, I undertake with the greatest pleasure, as it will afford me an opportunity of contrasting the simple manners, and rational life of the Americans, in these back settlements, with the distorted and unnatural habits of the Europeans; . . ."

This note he sounds repeatedly throughout the series. Undoubtedly the frontiersmen would have been at as great a loss to detect themselves in his descriptions as they would to recognize the French habitants, for whom they had supreme contempt, but whom Imlay pictures as living

> "in the style of the Patriarchs of old; enjoying the charms of nature, decked in all the soft simplicity which the genial current of the human soul, unsophisticated by the alloy of European artifice, produces in such elegant and fascinating variety. They possessed all the social talents in an eminent degree: and their hospitality was ever enlivened with the charms of wit, and the exhilerating juice of the vine; which grew and flourished to such a degree as to produce wine for exportation."

Of the land his portrayals are equally ornate and impassioned, the following extract being a very fair example.

> "Some few clumps of trees, and a grove here and there, are the only obstructions to a boundless horizon. It is pleasant to behold the deer bounding over the scraggy shrubs which cover the earth. While the setting sun gilds those extensive plains, the mild breezes of a summer's eve, playing upon the enraptured senses, softens the heart to love and friendship. Unperceived, upon some eminence, you may enjoy the sports of wild animals, which here rove unconcerned lords of the field. Heavens! what charms are there in liberty!"

87 Filson, John — *The Discovery, Settlement, & Present State of Kentucky* . . . 1793. (A Supplement to Imlay's *Topographical description of the Western Territory*). 77, 5, 104-5. (Originally published, 1784).

His idealistic views were, of course, given especial circulation by his intimacy with Mary Wollstonecraft and his European popularity; undoubtedly among the intellectuals he did a good deal to promote the fame of Kentucky.[88]

The prominence of that territory was due, however, not only to the printed accounts of Imlay, Fitzroy (*Discovery, Purchase, and Settlement of the Countie of Kentucky, 1786*), and Toulmin, who called his guide book *A Description of Kentucky* (1792) although most of it deals with the East or the United States in general. Its fame grew by oral report among those who, ambitious or discouraged, desired to emigrate to the West, and whose resistless advance in spite of all obstacles has given us the heroic annals of the Wilderness Road.[89]

After the Revolution, even during it, the easy terms of the Kentucky land law, the desire of the soldiers to take up western grants, the possibility of making payments in the depreciated continental currency, and the expanding spirit of nationalism, all caused an unparalleled activity. Once the Indian peril was lessened the river route grew in favor, and Indian commissioners, soldiers, and other travellers constantly testified to the passing of the great broadhorns.

> "In this fleet I am told is 10 large boats with families, slaves, cattle, horses, &c, one among many proofs of the great emigration from the old to the new world, with which all people seem not only pleased but delighted."
>
> "No account from the Shawanese; boats passing daily to the

---

88 Imlay, Gilbert — *A Topographical Description of the Western Territory of North America* . . . 1793. 25, 40, 66. (3d. ed. with great additions 1797, 1st. ed. 1792). Unfortunately for the idyllic pictures of Filson and Imlay the Reverend Francis Asbury, pioneer bishop of the Methodist Church, left in his *Journal* a very different picture of the frontiersmen. Crossing the mountains in 1788, he stated, "This country will require much work to make it tolerable. The people are, many of them, of the boldest cast of adventurers, and with some the decencies of civilized society are scarcely regarded. . . ." (II:36). At Rock-Castle station he found " such a set of sinners as made it next to hell itself." (*Ibid.* 126)

89 See Speed, Thomas — *The Wilderness Road.* 1886. (Filson Club Pub. II). The difficulties are well illustrated in Wm. Calk's Journal (See p. 36) & in an account by Peter Cartwright of his parents' travelling to Kentucky shortly after the Revolution. "It was an unbroken wilderness from Virginia to Kentucky at that early day. . . . There were no roads for carriages, and though the immigrants moved by thousands, they had to move on pack-horses. The fall my father moved there were a great many families who joined together for mutual safety. Besides the two hundred families thus united there were one hundred young men well armed, who agreed to guard the families through the wilderness. We rarely traveled a day, after we struck the wilderness, but we passed some white persons murdered and scalped by the Indians." p. 40.

> falls with goods and families, and by the numbers which pass seem as if the old states would depopulate, and the inhabitants be transported to the new. The greatest danger which I perceive is, that these people consider themselves out of the trammels of law, and have too great a propensity to remain in that lawless situation."[90]

With a rapidity unknown up to that time the population multiplied; less than twenty short years after its founding Kentucky became a state.[91]

Not merely it, however, received attention. Captain Bernard Romans' *A Concise Natural History of East and West Florida* . . . (1775) is a direct invitation to settlement of the region in which Captain Rufus Putnam and other Mississippi adventurers were interested. Not only does he give directions which, if followed, will make travel "through the American *desarts* not so uncomfortable as appears," but he alternately laughs and is vexed at the inaccurate writers about America.

> "Just such nonsense he vends, when he attributes the want of wood in the plains of the north western parts of *America* to barrenness, when experience has taught everyone that they are fertile. . . ."

His picture of the Indians is most unfavorable, "a people not only rude and uncultivated, but incapable of civilization . . ." His book is chiefly striking, however, for the arguments he advances on the necessity of opening up the interior "to the at present crowded Americans." Asking dramatically whether Britain thinks this section will remain unsettled, he answers,

> "No, the prospect is too fine, numbers of families . . .

90 From Gen. Butler's *Journal* in N. B. Craig's *Olden Time.* 1846-8. II:483, 489.

91 Thomas Anburey in his *Travels through Interior Parts of America.* 2v. 1789, gives an amusing explanation of Kentucky's growth. "I think nothing more fully evinces the real distresses of the inhabitants in general, throughout America, and how great the spirit of persecution and oppression reigns throughout all the provinces, as the amazing emigrations to a new settlement, at a place called Kentucky, where the soil is extremely fruitful, and where there are abundance of buffaloes, the country around, for a great number of miles, is an extensive plain, with very few trees growing on it. New discoveries are continually making, as to the vast extent of the continent of America, and in some future day it may be learnt, what the boundaries are to the westward. This new settlement is near a thousand miles from this place, nevertheless, those travelling to it, though to so great a distance, and perhaps have left comfortable houses and plantations, which have been the labor of their whole lives to clear and bring to perfection, appear chearful and happy, pleased with the idea, that they will be free from the tyranny and oppression of the Congress, and its upstart dependants." II:406-7.

> have settled themselves on the lands intended lately for a new province on the Ohio: if i am rightly informed, no less than fifteen hundred families already, and many others not so much as thought of in Britain."

He continues his reasoning in a tone only too characteristic of the settlers.

> ". . . thus it is highly encumbent on Britain to enlarge these limits, or form new provinces; a few paltry tribes of savages who retain the ancient grudge against us are no obstacle; the emigrants will soon bear down those melting remains of a people, who have lost their country, cannot fail to hate us, on that account, and in a kind of despair will rather choose to be destroyed than to incorporate with us." [92]

*The Memoirs and Adventures of Captain Matthew Phelps* . . . (1802) served as an advertisement, though a somewhat undesirable one, of the region around Natchez. The forlorn band who with Clark won the French villages, must have focused observation on the flooded meadows over which they struggled. And the successive harryings by hostile forces sent out from Detroit left no doubt in the minds of the sufferers of the importance of the lake posts. But although the place of the West in the Revolution must be left for the special historian, we may conclude that all these factors combined with the natural spirit of expansion following the war caused an accession of interest in the hitherto neglected regions of the West. The numerous additions to the third edition of Imlay, for instance, illustrate the craving that existed for knowledge of all the inland territory. Bartram who visited the Mississippi, praising the plantations, and showing the Anglo-Saxon immigration (*Travels through North and South Carolina, Georgia, East and West Florida,* 1791) described with luxuriant detail the Floridian prairies. John Pope in 1790-1791 made a *Tour through the Southern and Western Territories of*

---

92 Romans — *Concise Nat. Hist. of E. & W. Fla.* . . . 1775. 190, 180, 46, 222, 216, 217. Somewhat similar reasoning is found in Arthur Young's *Observations on the Present State of the Waste Lands of Great Britain. Published on Occasion of the Establishment of a New Colony on the Ohio* (1773), a pamphlet which well illustrates the change in attitude that had taken place within a decade in England. For an account of the inspection of the West Florida region by the military adventures see S. P. Hildreth — *Biographical & Historical Memoirs of the Early Pioneer Settlers of Ohio* . . . 1852. 38 ff. For proposals for a colony on the upper Mississippi see Houck — *Span. Reg. in Mo.* II:144 ff.

*the United States of North America,* giving a valuable survey of the population at the period and such warm commendation as,

> "Whoever undertakes a Description of the *Walnut Hills,* must have a fertile Imagination, be happy at Landscape Painting, and use Something like Romance, or he will fall infinitely short of that Eulogium which the Place so justly merits." [93]

Isaac Weld, travelling "through the states of North America, and the provinces of upper and lower Canada, during the years 1795, 1796, and 1797" speaks of the "numbers of men prowling aboutt to try and buy cheap land" and going " 'to explore,' as they call it, that is to search for lands conveniently situated for new settlements in the Western country";[94] he pictures also some of the disputed military posts. Earlier than all of these, however, Thomas Hutchins in *A Topographical Description of Virginia, Pennsylvania, Maryland, and North Carolina* (1778) and the *Historical, Narrative, and Topographical Description of Louisiana and West Florida* (1784) gave very detailed and laudatory accounts of the interior, accounts lent especial importance by the fact that he became the official geographer of the United States. His treatment is noteworthy in that he writes constantly with a regard for settlement; not merely the fertility of the soil is discussed but the location of salt springs, stones suitable for milling, and clays for pottery. Such utilitarian needs, however, do not blind him to the beauty of the prairie, as passages like the following demonstrate.

> "This interval land is lovely, has few trees, and is of a very rich soil, yielding shrubs and most fragrant flowers, which added to the number and extent of meadows and ponds dispersed thro' this charming valley, render it exceedingly beautiful and agreeable." [95]

That his work had pronounced influence is evident not only in the number of reprints but in the numerous references to him, or, to take a single example, in the fact that he was called upon to endorse Manasseh Cutler's *Explanation of the Map which*

---

93 Pope, John — *Tour through the Southern & Western Territories* . . . 1792. Repr. for C. L. Woodward. 1888. 28.

94 Weld, Isaac — *Travels through the States of North America* . . . 1795, 1796, & 1797. 2v. 2d. ed. 1799. I:234.

95 Hutchins, T. — *Top. Des. of Va.* . . . ed. by F. C. Hicks. 1904. 107.

*Delineates that Part of the Federal Lands comprehended between Pennsylvania West Line, the Rivers Ohio and Scioto and Lake Erie* (1787) as presenting facts which "are judicious, just, and true," and which "correspond with observations made by me during my residence of upward of ten years in that country." [96]

This pamphlet of Cutler's is an early representative of a large group written to dispel ignorance and to promote settlement of the West, it and the other records of the Ohio Company deserving attention because they reveal a comparatively new type of adventurer in the Midland and a new ideal for settlement. To us their revelation of interest in the West during and after the Revolution in spite of the general ignorance as to the nature of the territory is of especial significance.

Washington is said to have vowed in the dreary days of Valley Forge that "sooner than surrender to the enemy upon any probable terms, he would retire beyond the mountains, and establish another base in the Ohio Valley." [97] Unquestionably the opportunities offered by the hinterland were widely discussed in the army as is evidenced by the petition drawn up by Washington's officers at Newburgh; and when that proved unavailing it was but natural that Putnam and other interested men should form a company. After the war the economic depression made even the more stable portion of the population ambitious to better themselves by emigration. Of the widespread interest in the territory beyond the mountains in spite of the equally widespread ignorance concerning it, the correspondence of Cutler and his associates gives frequent evidence.

"The Ohio country is so little known in this part of the Commonwealth, that the people greatly need information with respect to its situation and the qualities of the lands. They are constantly emigrating into the northern frozen deserts; but were they made sensible of the fertility and temperature of the climate in the Ohio country, they would turn their face to the southward. Such authentic accounts as can be obtained and published from time to time in the newspapers, I am per-

96 W. P. & J. P. Cutler — *Life, Journals & Correspondence of Rev. Manasseh Cutler.* 1888. Ap. C. II:393.

97 Cutler — *Letters & Journals.* 1:142. For a number of articles interesting in this connection see *Ohio Arch. & Hist. Pub.* I. For an early description drawn from *American Husbandry* . . . 1775, see *Ibid.* XXIII:232 ff.

suaded, would be useful, particularly extracts from Captain Hutchins' pamphlet."

"If Congress will accede to either of the propositions proposed by General Putnam I doubt not our company would be immediately filled with valuable adventurers, and a large proportion from this part of the country; for the spirit of emigration never ran higher with us, and the Ohio lands are held in the highest estimation."[98]

The activity of men high in the councils of the nation is also noteworthy, for the public policy in dealing with the interior was involved. Large grants heretofore had been a source of private rather than of public profit; now steps were to be taken to pay off the national debt by means of the fertile lands to the west.[99] Furthermore it was hoped that the mode of settlement would do away with the evils of the past. According to Cutler,

"It is a happy circumstance that the Ohio Company are about to commence the settlement of this country in so regular and judicious a manner. It will serve as a wise model for the future settlement of all the federal lands; at the same time that, by beginning so near the western limit of Pennsylvania, it will be a continuation of the old settlements, leaving no vacant lands exposed to be seized by such lawless banditti as usually infest the frontiers of countries distant from the seat of government.

"The design of Congress and of the settlers is that the settlements shall proceed regularly down the Ohio and northward to Lake Erie. And it is probable that not many years will elapse before the whole country above Miami will be brought to that degree of cultivation which will exhibit all its latent beauties, and justify those descriptions of travelers which

---

98 Cutler — *Letters & Journals.* I:188, 192.

99 All of this material is of a sort demanding detailed investigation impracticable here. Of interest as showing the way estimates of the land affected public policy is the report made by Monroe to Jefferson prior to the organization of the Northwest Territory. "A great part of the territory is miserably poor, especially that near lakes Michigan & Erie & that upon the Mississippi and the Illinois consists of extensive plains wh. have not had from appearances & will not have a single bush on them, for ages. The districts, therefore, within wh. these fall will never contain a sufficient number of inhabitants to entitle them to membership in the confederacy." J. Monroe — *Writings* ed. by S. M. Hamilton. 1898. I:117.

have so often made it the garden of the world, the seat of wealth, and the center of a great empire."[100]

Negotiations were naturally somewhat prolonged; and it was not until Cutler combined forces with Colonel Duer that he was able to consummate the immense purchase. In Duer and his companion financiers, whom Professor Hulbert calls "the best early representative of that class of predatory speculators who in our own day give Wall Street an evil name,"[101] we find somewhat more conventional business types than the honest but rather impractical men that headed the Ohio Company. For us their Scioto speculation, only one among many schemes, is of interest partly because the poet Joel Barlow was the agent selected by Duer to dispose of the lands in Europe, partly because of the romantic atmosphere surrounding the unfortunate French settlers at Gallipolis.[102] Barlow took with him Cutler's pamphlet which was reprinted in Paris, 1789, but for a year met with only indifferent success. In July of 1789 the Bastille was taken, all France, in an uproar. According to Barlow, "The times were propitious for schemes of emigration," and his and Playfair's advertising literature, in which the latter's "good imagination" seems to have run riot, allured people of all classes. Volney in his *Tableau du Climat et du Sol des États-Unis d'Amérique* (1803) gives us the most vivid narrative of the ill-fated scheme, outlining the deceptive promises of the company, the popular enthusiasm ("In the social circles of Paris the sole topic of discussion was the free and rustic life which one could lead on the banks of the Scioto"), the distress attendant upon the arrival of the French in America, his own observation of their unhappy plight, and his feeling that the colony would never prosper.[103] Brissot de Warville, who served, according

100 Cutler — *Letters & Journals.* II:399-400. In connection with this latter passage note Washington's arguments for compact settlement in his letters to James Duane, quot. *Ibid.* I:132 & given in Washington — *Writings.* X:303 ff.

101 Intro. to the *Records of the Original Proceedings of the Ohio Company* ed. by A. B. Hulbert (*Marietta College Hist. Coll.*) LXXXIV. To Professor Hulbert's investigations I owe much in this section.

102 A considerable amount of material about this settlement has of recent years been reproduced. See *Ohio Arch. & Hist. Pub.* III, especiallly 96 ff., for some of the advertising literature. For valuable *Selections from the Gallipolis Papers* made by T. T. Belote during his investigations for his monograph *The Scioto Speculation & the French Settlement at Gallipolis* see *Ohio Hist. & Phil. Soc. — Quar. Pub.* II., no 2.

103 Volney — *Tableau du Climat et du Sol des États-Unis.* 383.

to Volney, to complete the flattering delusion, in his *Nouveau Voyage dans les États-Unis de l'Amérique Septentrionale, fait en 1788* and published 1791, gives glowing praise to the Republican institutions and the freedom of the United States in general as well as particular tribute to the western country, blaming the aristocratic quality of some of the emigrés for their unhappiness. Barlow's biographer Todd also slides over their fate lightly.[104] Brackenridge's picture of the wig-makers, carvers and gilders to the king, and other skilled artisans woefully unfitted for the wilds leaves little doubt, however, of the reality of their sufferings;[105] and Ellicott pronounced Gallipolis the "most miserable" of the places he had yet beheld.[106]

Other companies were formed, of course, to exploit different sections of the Great Valley. Symmes' plan for the Miami Territory was productive of his tract to the "Respectable Public" and other prospectuses.[107] The Illinois and Ouabache Land Companies, the papers of which have lately been edited by Alvord, had their proceedings presented in a couple of early pamphlets (1796; 1803). Morgan issued a circular describing the advantages of his grant at New Madrid.[108] In general, however, the Ohio and Scioto Companies represent the tendencies of all, and are in numerous ways the most outstanding. All the later literature portrays strikingly the seaboard's absorption in the interior, the rise and fall of great land speculations, the flood of immigration from the New England and the middle states as well as the southern that was to be so important a factor in the upbuilding of the West and in the struggle against slavery.

A notable feature of the commercial literature of this time

---

104 Todd, C. B. — *Life & Letters of Joel Barlow* . . . 1886. See pp. 69-73 for an account of Barlow's connection with the company.

105 Brackenridge, H. M. — *Recollections of Persons & Places in the West.* [1834.] 42.

106 Ellicott, Andrew — *Journal* . . . 1814. 13. Numbers of the colonists sickened and died; others went to the older French villages and some to the Spanish territories. In this latter connection see Houck — *Span. Reg. in Mo.* II:5-6, 359 ff., 362-4. Baron de Carondelet states, apropos of this migration, that he has "just concluded a transaction the consequences of which will form an epoch in the annals of this province and of North America," giving glowing promises as to the results of the colony to be established by the French. *Ibid.* 374-5.

107 For the Trenton circular "To the Respectable Public" see *Hist & Phil. Soc. of Ohio — Quar. Pub.* V, no. 3.

108 For a valuable early description of the Morgan settlement and references to him and the circular here mentioned which is printed in Hunt's *Madison* V:331 see E. G. Swem's note *Miss. Val. Hist. Rev.* V:342 ff. See, also, Houck — *Span. Reg. in Mo.* II:275 ff., 286, 294 ff., 310.

is the promise of government protection against the savages. More than paper promises, however, are required to erect adequate defences against despairing tribes of Indians, more than ill-disciplined troops, the scourings of the city streets, to carry war successfully into the territory of the natives. Once the power of the Kentucky settlements was firmly established, the Indians turned their attention to harrying the new denizens of Ohio, attempts at treaty making being in general unavailing. Harmar's campaign, hailed by him and his friends as a success, was regarded by the Indians as an incentive to further aggressions; the disastrous defeat of St. Clair was a shock to the whole country and a serious menace to the out-settlers; only General Wayne, known to fame as Mad Anthony, was able to bring peace to the border. Of the events of these and earlier campaigns and of the heroic episodes and figures developed by the border strife we have numerous early compilations such as McClung's *Sketches of Western Adventure* or Withers' *Chronicles of Border Warfare,* resembling in plan Doddridge's *Notes on the Settlement and Indian Wars of the Western Parts of Virginia and Pennsylvania.* Isolated narratives, too, such as the account of the captivity of William Biggs among the Kickapoo Indians with its vivid picture of the adventurers of many nations upon the plains of Illinois or the *Narrative of the Life & Adventures of Matthew Bunn in an Expedition against the North-western Indians, in the years 1791, 2, 3, 4 & 5,*[109] serve to fill in the outlines of these long years of intermittent hostility. In general rather artless and unsophisticated, offering no such outstanding Indian chieftains as Logan in Dunmore's War, or the later Tecumseh and his brother the Prophet, these accounts of combat and captivity near the turn of the century serve, nevertheless, to add a number of picturesque and dramatic elements to the already all too lurid chronicles of struggle, and to re-echo the tragic note of the loss of the land.

---

109 The seventh edition of Bunn's narrative, one of the most popular books of its type, is reprinted *Buf. Hist. Soc. Pub.* VII:379 ff. For further description of the Indian warfare at this time see W. H. Smith — *Life & Public Services of Arthur St. Clair, . . . with his Correspondence & Other Papers* (2v. 1882); C. J. Stille — *Major-General Anthony Wayne . . .* (1893); *The Remarkable Adventures of Jackson Johonnot . . . who Served as a Soldier in the Western Army . . .* (1791); *O. Arch. & Hist. Soc.* XX:74 ff.; *Wis. Mag. of Hist.* II:41 ff.; *The American Pioneer* I:43 ff., 351 ff., etc.; *Miss. Val. Hist. Rev.* I:421 ff., etc.

The most pathetic thing about all this Indian warfare is that the leaders among the natives realize the inevitably fatal outcome of their efforts. Smith tells how, although the old men encouraged the young warriors to drive the whites into the sea, they themselves knew that this feat was no longer possible; and the record of treaty making in *Putnam's Memoirs* shows this same note of enforced submission.

> "My older Brother,
>
> Consider, were [we] to sell the graves of our Ancestors would not he who gave us life, and placed us on these lands be displeased. I believe there is no son so unworthy of his Ancestors as to sell the graves they are buried in. Were we to sell our lands, we must sell their graves: and the Game which affords us daily subsistance. — We, therefore, wish you never to take our lands by force. — There is nothing will prevent a lasting peace and friendship between us but your attempting to take our Land from us. Fulfil what you have said — Why would I make a new handle for the Axe? I know it would be impossible for us to overcome you in the end. And we believe you have no intention of destroying us. —"[110]

Of the justice of the Indian fears there can be afforded no better illustration than the senate's refusal to ratify the treaty of Vincennes of 1792, the main source of criticism being the clause recognizing the Indian right to refuse sale of the land. All the later records of the valley reveal the steady pushing back of the red men, the influx of the whites, the formation of new states, the expansion of the new nation.[111]

In the two centuries of progress that made the English speaking peoples masters of the eastern half of the continent, that created such types as the fur trader, the squatter, the scout, the renegade, and the speculator, that instead of the fairy tales of the hinterland and the resulting unfortunate disillusionment

110 *The Memoirs of Rufus Putnam* . . . ed. by Rowena Buell. 1903. 356. Such tragic speeches can be paralleled in almost any epoch of the Indian Treaty making, as we have already seen. For poignant later examples see *Annals of Iowa* 3d. ser. XII:321 ff. & *Ia. Jour. of Hist. & Pol.* IX: 408 ff. See, also, *Mich. Pion. & Hist. Coll.* XVII:604.

111 Alexander Wilson, for instance, writes, "This country, notwithstanding the ravages of the French and Yellow fever, is rapidly advancing in power, population, and prosperity. Our boundary is continually extending towards the West, and may yet, after some ages, include those vast unexplored regions that lie between us and the Western Ocean." *Poems & Literary Prose.* 2v. 1876. I:68.

prevailing among the first colonists substituted the careful reports of the United States official geographer, Hutchins, or the philosophical enthusiasm of a traveller like Francis Bailey, whose *Journal of a Tour in Unsettled Parts of North America in 1796 & 1797* (1856) well illustrates the foreign devotion to the cult of nature, it is significant to note the interest in the West felt in high places. Professor Alvord's *Mississippi Valley in British Politics* traces with admirable clearness and erudition the influence of the American interior even on the making and unmaking of ministries. And in America so widespread were the ramifications of the land that we can only hope to suggest its importance by showing the attitude toward the hinterland of three leaders — George Washington, Benjamin Franklin, and Thomas Jefferson.

Of no part of the country could Washington be called more truly the father than of the West. From the time when as a lad he surveyed for Lord Fairfax beyond the Blue Ridge, a trip recorded for us in his *Journal of My Journey over the Mountains*, until the day of his death he was alert to private and national interests there. His letter of October 17, 1753, to Dinwiddie shows his zeal in promoting English claims; therefore it is with no surprise that we find him appointed by the governor emissary to warn the French from the coveted valley of the Ohio. It is notable that even this trip, an affair of state attended with much anxiety, the young officer had ever an eye for the land.

> "We passed over much good land since we left Venango and through several extensive and very rich meadows, one of which, I believe, was nearly four miles in length and considerably wide in some places."[112]

Outgeneralling the French commander by his discovery of the latter's aim, Washington returned hastily to put into shape the journal which according to Professor Hulbert "electrified the world."

Since the reconnoitering mission had been so well accomplished, it was but natural that the zealous young Virginian should be selected to head the troops sent to build forts at the

112 Blanchard — *Dis. & Conq. of the N. W.* Ap. 22.

head of the Ohio with instructions "to be on the Defensive, but if oppos'd by the Enemy, to desire them to retire; if they sh'd still persist, to repel Force by Force."[113] The Journal of this expedition accessible only from the French version in the oft-cited *Précis des Faits* is too well known to be discussed; it is significant chiefly in the light of ensuing developments but also for the youthful ardor which caused Washington to write to a friend apropos of the contest at Great Meadows that the bullets had a charming sound. One of the few who kept their heads in Braddock's shameful rout, Washington's chagrin at that disaster may well be passed over in silence; his later work in defending, or attempting to defend, the frontiers against the hordes of exultant savages whose raids forced the settlers back beyond the Blue Ridge is notable, partly for the commiseration he displays for the wretched white fugitives whose despair he paints in the liveliest of colors, mainly for his formulation at that time of the creed to which he ever after consistently adhered — that the only successful warfare against the American Indian must be an offensive warfare.

With the closing of the French and Indian Wars, we find Washington, not the soldier but the planter and shrewd speculator, intent on gaining his share of the fertile valley "we have labored and toiled so long to conquer."[114] In 1767 in requesting Crawford to seek out good lands for him, he states very frankly his views on the subject.

> "It will be easy for you to conceive that ordinary or even middling lands would never answer my purpose or expectation, so far from navigation, and under such a load of expenses as these lands are encumbered with. No; a tract to please me must be rich . . . and, if possible, level. Could such a piece of land be found, you would do me a singular favor in falling upon some method of securing it immediately from the attempts of others, as nothing is more certain than that the lands can not remain long ungranted, when once it is known that rights are to be had."

* * * * *

113 *Jour of Col. George Washington . . . in 1754 . . .* ed. by J. M. Toner. 1893. 14.

114 *The Writings of George Washington* ed. by W. C. Ford. 14v. 1889-93. II:225.

"I offered in my last to join you in attempting to secure some of the most valuable lands in the King's part, which I think may be accomplished after awhile, notwithstanding the proclamation that restrains it at present, and prohibits the settling of them at all; for I can never look upon that proclamation in any other light (but this I say between ourselves) than as a temporary expedient to quiet the minds of the Indians. It must fall, of course, in a few years, especially when those Indians consent to our occupying the lands. Any person, therefore, who neglects the present opportunity of hunting out good lands, and in some measure marking and distinguishing them for his own, in order to keep others from settling them, will never regain it. . . ."

Butterfield's edition of the correspondence between the two men, the last letter dating a year before Crawford's tragic death, provides valuable historical material in its account of Dunmore's War and the panic caused among the inhabitants, being even more suggestive in its pictures of the struggle for the territory.

"[March 15, 1772]. . . . There will not be a possibility of taking up such a quantity as you want near Fort Pitt, as there are such numbers of people out now looking for land, and one taking another's land from him. As soon as a man's back is turned another is on his land. The man that is strong and able to make others afraid of him seems to have the best chance as times go now."[115]

Washington in his dignified way was no less eager than the men who went out and fought for possession. He bought up the claims of less provident and farseeing soldiers, paid for surveys, kept his fingers on the political pulse, was heedful of every sign that suggested fulfillment of the promise of bounty tracts; he felt justified in reproving a complainant, "as my shoulders had supported the whole weight heretofore; and inasmuch as I might add without much arrogance that if it had not been for my unremitted attention to every favorable circumstance, not a single acre of Land would ever have been obtained."[116]

---

115 Butterfield, C. W., ed. — *The Washington-Crawford Letters* . . . 1877 1-2, 3, 25.
116 Washington — *Writings.* II:371. See also *Ibid.* 274 & 341-2 in this connection.

His *Journal of a Tour to the Ohio River 1770* with its shrewd comments on the nature of the soil assures us that when he later listed his possessions for sale as the cream of the country in which they were found, he spoke with certainty. As he made his inspection tour, meeting old acquaintances among the Indians, we wonder if he felt no sense of the incongruity of his position in view of his earnest speeches arousing the Indians against the French in 1754.

> "they speak well, promise fine things, but all from the lips only; whilst their heart is corrupt and full of the poison of the serpent. You have been their children, and they would have done everything for you, but they no sooner thought themselves strong enough, than they returned to their natural pride and drove you off from your lands, declaring you had no right on the *Ohio*. The English, your real friends, are too generous to think of using the Six Nations, their faithful allies, in such manner; after you have gone to the Governors of Virginia and Pennsylvania, they (at your repeated request) sent an army to maintain your rights, to put you again in possession of your lands, and to take care of your wives and children, to dispossess the *French*, to support your prerogatives and to secure that whole country to you, for these very ends are the English arms now employed; it is for the safety of your wives and your children that we are fighting; . . ."[117]

If so, he carefully refrains from expressing it; in the 1784 journal as he coolly discusses the economic possibilities of the Great Meadows there is no suggestion that he had ever seen the place before, not one word to link the Revolutionary hero with the enthusiastic young colonial officer.

> "Left Daughertys about 6 Oclock, — stopped awhile at the Great Meadows and viewed a tenament I have there, which appears to have been but little improved, tho capable of being turned to great advantage, as the whole of the ground called the Meadows may be reclaimed at an easy comparative expence & is a very good stand for a Tavern — Much Hay may

117 Washington — *Jour. . . . in 1754.* 111.

be cut here When the Ground is laid down in Grass & the upland, East of the Meadow, is good for grain.''[118]

Equally oblivious of incongruity is his attitude toward later ''Land Jobbers, speculators, and monopolizers'' whom he sees, as indeed they were, as a constant disturber of the Indian and menace to the peace of the country.[119]

Although we cannot but be amused by the difference in Washington's attitude when his own and others' interests were affected, there is no doubt that he tried to be fair in all of his dealings, no doubt, too, that his own large investment in the interior helped to make him the shrewd statesman and expansionist he was. Throughout the Revolution we find him giving instructions relative to his property, and to his interest in the western front and the knowledge of border warfare gleaned in his youth, his correspondence with Irvine alone is a sufficient witness. Almost immediately after his return to private life, he made his tour of 1784, designed chiefly to secure his western lands but in part ''to obtain information of the nearest and best communication between the Eastern & Western Waters; & to facilitate as much as in me lay, the Inland Navigation of the Potomach,''[120] a project he pushed steadily for both commercial and political reasons. His attitude toward the control of the Mississippi was somewhat singular; he realized, however, the gravity of the situation with the settlers beyond the mountains standing ''as it were upon a pivot — the touch of a feather would almost incline them any way.''[121] And all through his presidency his early knowledge of, and experience in the West with his clear vision of a unified American state, did much to solve the perplexing problems of Mississippi navigation, the Whiskey Insurrection, and Indian unrest. Though he decided finally that ''distant property in land'' was ''more pregnant of perplexities than profit,'' resolving to sell all he held on the western waters if he could obtain the prices which he conceived ''their quality, situation, and other advantages'' would authorize him to expect, his

118 Hulbert, A. B., ed. — *Washington & the West* . . . 1905. 41-2.
119 Note, for example, his *Writings* X:303 ff.
120 Hulbert — *Washington & the West.* 28-9. See also Mrs. Corra Bacon-Foster's *Early Chapters in the Development of the Patomac Route to the West,* 1912, & A. B. Hulbert's *The Great American Canals.* I. 1904.
121 Washington — *Writings.* X:408.

faith in the hinterland never left him. He saw in it the best opportunity for the "young man, just preparing to begin the world," or for one "advanced in life" but with "a family to make a provision for." To him as to many philosophers it offered solution, also, for the miseries of Europe.

> "I wish to see the sons and daughters of the world in Peace and busily employed in the more agreeable amusement of fulfilling the first and great commandment—*Increase and Multiply*: as an encouragement to which we have opened the fertile plains of the Ohio to the poor, the needy and the oppressed of the Earth; anyone therefore who is heavy laden or who wants land to cultivate, may repair thither & abound, as in the Land of promise, with milk and honey:—the ways are preparing, and the roads will be made easy, thro' the channels of Potomac & James river."[122]

Franklin never grew lyric about the West in just this fashion, but he did frequently discuss the opportunities of America for the downtrodden of Europe, giving in an account of his tour through Ireland and Scotland a most interesting presentation of the advantages of the Natural State, an idea he several times stressed.

> "Had I never been in the American Colonies, but was to form my Judgment of Civil Society by what I have lately seen. I should never advise a Nation of Savages to admit of Civilization: For I assure you, that, in the Possession & Enjoyment of the various Comforts of Life, compar'd to these People every Indian is a Gentleman: And the Effect of this kind of Civil Society seems only to be, the depressing Multitudes below the Savage State that a few may be rais'd above it."

During the French and Indian troubles he was zealous in preparing the province for defence, he himself giving us in his *Autobiography* the clearest and simplest account of his pamphlet *Plain Truth* and the voluntary military organizations which it encouraged. Adviser of the governor and council, a delegate to the Indian treaty-making, purveyor to Braddock, of whose

---

122 Letter to the Marquis de Lafayette, 25 July, 1785. Washington—*Writings* X:476 ff. There are a number of papers discussing Washington's interest in land chief among them the one by Prof. H. B. Adams. *Johns Hopkins Univ. Stud. in Hist & Pol. Sci.* 1885. III.

defects he gives a most interesting portrayal, defender of the frontier, he in Pennsylvania like Washington in Virginia was one of the foremost in securing the disputed territory for the English. With him, however, unlike Washington the pen was mightier than the sword. When he had carried through the House without much difficulty his bill "for establishing and disciplining a voluntary militia," he tells us,

> "To promote the association necessary to form the militia, I wrote a dialogue stating and answering all the objections I could think of to such a militia, which was printed, and had, as I thought, great effect."

Like Washington he was alert to all possibilities of danger, his discussion of the Germans in Pennsylvania showing that even he, the level-headed Franklin, could be a bit of an alarmist.

> "In short, unless the Stream of their Importation could be turned from this to other Colonies, as you very judiciously propose, they will so soon outnumber us, that all the advantages we have, will not in my opinion be able to preserve our Language, and even our Government will become precarious. The French, who watch all advantages, are now themselves making a German settlement back of us, in the Illinois Country, and by means of these Germans they may in time come to an understanding with ours; and, indeed, in the last War, our Germans showed a general Disposition, that seemed to bode us no good."

Like Washington, too, he was sensible of the need of right regulation of the Indian trade, this point like defence of the frontiers being touched upon in his hints for a union of the colonies. His project for barrier colonies was one that, as he indicates, received a good deal of attention.

> "There is one Mr. Hazard, who, happening to see last Fall a Paper of mine on the Means of settling a new Colony westward of Pensilvania (drawn up to divert the Connecticut Emigrants from their design of Invading this Province and so induce them to go where they would be less injurious and more useful) and picking out something farther from me in Conversation, has publish'd a Scheme for that purpose in my Ab-

sence, wherein he has added some Things and left out others, and now (like your Fire Hearth Man) calls it his own Project. He aims at great Matters for himself, hoping to become a Proprietor like Mr. Penn etc., and has got, they say, a great Number of Settlers engag'd to go with him, if he can get a grant of the Land from the Crown. It is certain that People enough may be had, to make a strong English Settlement or two in those Parts. I wish to see it done, and am almost indifferent how or by whom it is done; yet I think this Man not the fittest in the World to conduct such an Affair."

Much of Franklin's work like Washington's with the bounty grants was subterranean, however, accomplished only by hours of waiting in statesmen's anterooms, shrewd wirepulling, attention to every veering of the political wind. To some of this patient diplomacy his letters bear testimony.

"If this should be the case, possibly most of our advantages may be given up again at the Treaty, and some among our great Men begin already to prepare the Minds of People for this, by discoursing, that to keep Canada would draw on us the Envy of other Powers, and occasion a Confederacy against us; that the Country is too large for us to people; not worth possessing, and the like. These Notions I am every day and every where combating, and I think not without some Success. The Event God only knows. . . . To this I add, that the Colonies would thrive and increase in a much greater Degree, and that a vast additional Demand would arise for British Manufactures, to supply so great an extent of Indian Country, etc. with many other Topics, which I urge occasionally, according to the Company I happen into, or the Persons I address. And on the whole, I flatter myself that my being here at this time may be of some service to the general Interest of America."

*The Interest of Great Britain Considered with Regard to Her Colonies and the Acquisitions of Canada and Guadeloupe to which are Added Observations concerning the Increase of Mankind, Peopling of Countries &c.* (London. 1760) by Franklin and Richard Jackson is a more open contribution, one of the most informing of the many pamphlets of its type. And to his interest in the negotiations there could be no more striking testimony than his enthusiastic note of congratulation to Strahan "on the glorious Peace you have made, the most advantageous for the British Nation in my Opinion, of any your Annals have recorded."

The earnestness and diligence of Franklin's efforts to promote unity between the mother country and its protesting offspring in the troubled years before the Revolution must be left to the general historian. Passages describing his labors in behalf of the Walpole Grant, greatest of the land schemes, and the colonization of the West in general are, however, of direct interest to us.

> "I waited next morning upon Lord Clare, and pressed the matter of the boundary closely upon him. He said they could not find they had ever received any letters from Sir William concerning this boundary, but were searching farther: agreed to the necessity of settling it; but thought there would be some difficulty about who should pay the purchase money; for that this country was already so loaded, it could bear no more. We then talked of the new colonies. I found he was inclined to think one near the mouth of the Ohio might be of use in securing the country, but did not much approve that at Detroit."
>
> ". . . I shall wait on Lord H. again next Wednesday, on behalf of the sufferers by Indian and French depredations, to have an allowance of lands out of any new grant made by the Indians, so long solicited, and perhaps still to be solicited, in vain."

For a long time, of course, Franklin was credited with a great personal victory over Hillsborough by causing the Walpole petition to be granted over the latter's negative, thus indirectly bringing about the minister's resignation. This triumph has been transferred by later scholarship from him to Wharton, but no matter who its author, the victory brought no tangible results for the interested financiers, as Franklin suggests humorously in two of his letters to Galloway.

> "The Affair of the Grant goes on but slowly. I do not yet clearly see Land. I begin to be a little of the Sailor's Mind

when they were handling a Cable out of a Store into a Ship, and one of 'em said: ' 'Tis a long, heavy Cable. I wish we could see the End of it.' 'D — n me,' says another, 'if I believe it has any End; somebody has cut it off'."

"P. S. The Ship Ohio still aground."

The Revolution naturally put an end to all negotiations with the British, but not to the hopes and plans of the speculators as is proved by the pamphlets they issued such as *View of the Title to Indiana* (by Wharton and Edward Bancroft, 1776) and *Plain Facts* (by Samuel Wharton, 1781), on the latter of which Franklin comments to Richard Bache.

"I have read Mr. Wharton's Pamphlet. The Facts, as far as I know them, are as he states them. Justice is, I think, on the side of those who contracted for the Lands. But moral and political Rights sometimes differ, and sometimes are both subdu'd by Might."

Neither did the Revolution put an end to Franklin's interest in the West. Worn as he was by disease and his heavy labors in behalf of the new nation he yet found a spark of youthful fire with which to write to John Jay in 1780 concerning the negotiations with Spain.

"Poor as we are, yet, as I know we shall be rich, I would rather agree with them to buy at a great Price the whole of their Right on the Mississippi, than sell a Drop of its Water. A Neighbour might as well ask me to sell my Street Door."

And again to Robert Livingston in 1782 he waxes as indignant about the Spanish attempt to lay claim to the West as he did about the Quaker indifference to the French encroachments in his early days of combat. In denunciation of the slaughter of the Moravian Indians near Pittsburgh he re-echoes his earlier heartfelt protest at the Lancaster massacre, and in his satiric account of the captured bundles of scalps (*Supplement to the Boston Independent Chronicle*) he strikingly pillories the British atrocities, resentment of which burns through numbers of his letters. His advice to emigrants is in many ways sound and helpful. In short through all his maturer years he devoted the best of his thought, the majority of his time to the ideal in which he firmly believed — "America, the Land of Labour" and "by no means what the English call *Lubberland*, and the French *Pays de Cocagne*."[123]

Unlike Washington and Franklin, Jefferson had no financial interest in the development of the West, a point which he emphasized to the former in discussing the navigation project and which he made clear to Madison in 1784. His *Notes on Virginia* with its famous description of the Potomac bursting through the Blue Ridge and its account of Logan's speech so provocative of discussion, although it was probably the most important of the early books of its type, deals with the Trans-Alleghany region only incidentally, and the whole treatise was, of course, only the half accidental result of the French questionnaire. Nevertheless throughout his public life, as Governor of Virginia, as United States Minister, as Secretary of State, as Vice-President, and President, Jefferson's letters and state papers testify to his eagerness for expansion of the American Union as well as to his clear vision of the problems involved in such a program. The question of the Indian lands, the border disputes, the making of new states, the navigation of the Mississippi, all these he touches upon again and again. He aided in so far as was in his power Clark's conquest of the Northwest, and in his appeal for support to the border counties as early as 1781 brought out the need of co-operation which he always emphasized — "We are all embarked in one bottom, the Western end of which cannot swim while the Eastern sinks," — reiterating this idea throughout the whole controversy with the Spanish. In 1789, for instance, he wrote from Paris,

> "I was pleased to see the vote of Congress of Sep. 16, on the subject of the Mississippi, as I had before seen with great uneasiness the pursuits of other principles which I could never reconcile to my own ideas of probity or wisdom, and from which, and my knolege of the character of our Western settlers, I saw that the loss of that country was a necessary consequence. I wish this return to true policy may be in time to prevent evil."

123 *The Writings of Benjamin Franklin ed. by A. H. Smyth.* 1906. I:407; III:140 (see also 43, 72 Ibid.), 265-6; IV:7-8, 191; V:68, 117; VI:33-4, 197; VIII:304, 144, 607.

No one realized more than he the gravity of the Spanish intendant's closing of New Orleans as a place of deposit; the rumor of the cession to France filled him with alarm. In the crisis he acted with promptness and decision and with full consciousness of the issues.

> "The suspension of the right of deposit at New Orleans, ceded to us by our treaty with Spain, threw our whole country into such a ferment as imminently threatened its peace . . . our circumstances are so imperious as to admit of no delay as to our course; and the use of the Mississippi so indispensable, that we cannot hesitate one moment to hazard our existence for its maintenance. If we fail in this effort to put it beyond the reach of accident, we see the destinies we have to run, and prepare at once for them."

Although Jefferson's first idea at this time was to secure only a place of deposit, a letter to Archibald Stuart from Paris, January 25, 1786, shows that he early formulated a vast vision of empire.

> "Our confederacy must be viewed as the nest from which all America, North & South is to be peopled. We should take care too, not to think it for the interest of that great continent to press too soon on the Spaniards. Those countries cannot be in better hands. My fear is that they are too feeble to hold them till our population can be sufficiently advanced to gain it from them piece by piece. The navigation of the Mississippi we must have. This is all we are as yet ready to receive."

And when Napoleon offered the vast purchase that made the new nation masters of the Prairie, that realized at last the early dreams of a dominion stretching to the Western sea, no one rejoiced more than the President at the success of the negotiations.

> "The acquisition of New Orleans would of itself have been a great thing, as it would have ensured to our western brethren the means of exporting their produce: but that of Louisiana is unappreciable. . . ."[124]

---

124 *The Writings of Thomas Jefferson* ed. by P. L. Ford. 1892-9. II:453. V:63-4; VIII:204-205; IV:188-189; VIII:261.

# CHAPTER IV

## THE LOUISIANA PURCHASE AND NON-IMAGINATIVE TREATMENTS TO 1870

Of the magnitude of the purchase and the unparalleled opportunities it offered for national expansion and economic development, not even the president had adequate conception; certainly the nation at large was woefully ignorant. The negotiations were conducted with extreme caution; the evils of annexation and the extravagance of the payment were fervently denounced by opponents of the administration's policy.[1]

Jefferson was not slow, however, in preparing to enlighten the public,[2] reviving his long cherished plan of exploration to the Pacific, naming his private secretary, Meriwether Lewis, leader, and giving his personal attention even to minor details. The part that he played in securing a full and clear transcript of the expedition is particularly important. It was he who issued detailed instructions as to the manner in which observations should be made and preserved; he who desired that such of the men as should be able to write, would, like the leaders, keep journals; he who steadily urged publication; he who wrote a commendatory memoir of Lewis ending with the regret that the latter's death lost "to the nation the benefit of receiving from his own hand the narrative now offered them of his sufferings and successes, in endeavoring to extend for them the boundaries of science and to present to their knowledge that vast and fertile country which their sons are destined to fill with arts, with science, with freedom and happiness." And even after the publication of the "travelling journal" he wrote to Clark for an order for the note-

---

1 *State Papers & Correspondence Bearing upon the Purchase of the Territory of Louisiana* were issued by order of the 57th. Congress at the time of the Centennial Celebration. See also *The Louisiana Purchase in Correspondence of the Time. Annals of Iowa.* VI:401.

2 Various early publications answer the early demands for information as *Account of Louisiana, Being Abstracts of Documents Transmitted to President Jefferson & by Him Laid before Congress.* 1804. The same year *A Summary Description of the Lead Mines in Upper Louisiana . . .* by Moses Austin was issued & J. Scott's *Geographical Dictionary of the U.S. of N.A. . . .* (1805) contains "a succinct account of Indiana and Upper & Lower Louisiana."

books, hoping "the part I have had in this important voyage will excuse the interest I take in securing to the world all the beneficial results we were entitled to expect from it, and which would so fully justify the expences of the expedition incurred by the United States in that expectation."[3]

Yet, stimulating as his zeal must have been, the men associated with the Lewis and Clark expedition were of a type to leave to posterity their best endeavors even without the inspiration of the executive. The project itself made for greatness — the severing for years of familiar ties; the thrusting forth into the heavily forested bottoms and boundless plains of the Northwest; the laborious conquest of mighty rivers, the passage of the snow-capped mountains first sighted by Vérendrye, and then at last the vision of the hoped-for Western Sea. The record as a whole leaves the impression of individual endurance, of intense loyalty atoning for corrected fault, of good fellowship, and above all of unqualified devotion to a common ideal. This devotion was so strong, indeed, that it was felt by a man as remote from the actual achievement as Nicholas Biddle, the young lawyer who, putting aside his own interests, consecrated himself whole-heartedly to the difficult task of preparing and publishing the book.[4]

Financially the undertaking resulted in a deficit; but fortunately from the more enduring point of view of fame, both literary and historical, the results were more happy. The little band of sturdy men who with so little public notice, "hoisted Sail and Set out in high Spirits for the Western Expedition,"[5] who, two eventful years later, hurried down the Missouri, had in the interim made history. Theirs is undoubtedly one of the most noteworthy feats in our long line of achievement. For us the exploring tour opened up the Northwest; to our struggling nation it revealed superb visions — the fertile, flower-splashed meadows of the lower Missouri, the infinitude of the buffalo plains to the North, the murmurous pine solitudes of the coast. Its course offered wonder; its details, adventure; its accomplishment, inspiration. Of its power yet today we need no other testimony than the long line of books treating various phases of the expedi-

3 Coues, E., ed. — *Hist. of the Exped. under the Command of Lewis & Clark . . .* 4v. 1893. I:XLII, XCV.
4 For extracts from the Clark-Biddle Correspondence see *Ibid.* LXXXII ff.
5 Thwaites, R.G. — *Orig. Jour. of the Lewis & Clark Exped.* VII:30.

tion from the children's story of *The Bird Woman* (1905) to Olin D. Wheeler's careful tracing of *The Trail of Lewis and Clark 1804-1904* (2v. 1904).

That it has gained for itself so conspicuous a place must be due in part to the fluent, easily comprehended prose of the young Philadelphian, who used the first person so skilfully that undoubtedly most people have failed to realize that they were not reading the narrative of the leaders. Under his guidance we toil up the river; we cower in the rude cabins during the biting blizzards of Dakota; we thrill at the moment when "after ascending the highest summit of the hills on the north side of the river, Captain Lewis first caught a distant view of the Rock Mountains—the object of all our hopes, and the reward of all our ambition"; we exult with the man who "in a fit of enthusiasm, with one foot on each side of the river, thanked God that he had lived to bestride the Missouri"; we face the return journey with "the whole stock of goods on which we are to depend, for the purchase either of horses or of food, during the long tour of nearly 4,000 miles . . . so much diminished that it might all be tied in two handkerchiefs." For Biddle not only shaped the material, avoiding its repetitions, paring its excrescences, clarifying its obscurities; he shared the emotion and in many cases helped to make it articulate. On the whole, his work is suprisingly free from pedantry, with the simplicity of language and the continuity of effect that alone could do justice to the subject. Coues might well call this 'our national epic of exploration, conceived by Thomas Jefferson, wrought out by Lewis and Clark, and given to the world by Nicholas Biddle.'"[6]

And if this be the national epic of exploration, certainly we may consider the original journals the shorter lays, from the reworking of which it arose. These, gathered from their various places of deposit, were "upon the Hundredth Anniversary of the Departure of the Trans-Mississippi Expedition of Lewis and Clark" published by Dodd, Mead and Co. "in full and exactly as written" under the able editorship of Dr. Reuben Gold Thwaites.[7] The value of the records from a scientific, historical,

---

[6] Coues — *Hist. of the Exped. under the command of Lewis & Clark.* I:328, II:484, III:902, I:VI.

[7] The Journals of Lewis & of Sergeant Ordway discovered later were edited by M. M. Quaife. *Wis. Hist. Coll.* XXII.

and literary standpoint it is scarcely possible to estimate. To us they give barehanded contact with reality, emotion in the raw. They are the direct outgrowth of experience, the immediate impressions of men under strain. Absolute departure into the unknown dictated the terse, "this is the Last Setelment of whites on this River"; streaming sweat, aching muscles conditioned Floyd's "water verry Strong So Hard that we Could Hardley Stem it";[8] triumphant solution of unforeseen difficulties, Lewis's exultant details. Crude they all are to be sure, yet inescapably virile; indeed in their very crudity is their power. First savor of their pungency whets the appetite for more; experience of the blunt compactness and peculiar suggestiveness of Whitehouse or Floyd intensifies the longing for the unglossed narrative of Gass. Most emphatically Coues' figure was happy, more happy than he knew; unquestionably the relation of journal to finished narrative is the relation of fragmentary lay to rounded epic. Both have their values, and we should no more give up for Biddle's easy prose the rude daily jottings than we should cast aside for the more civilized *Nibelungenlied* or Morris's ornate modern poem, the tenseness and superb compression of the Volsung lays that have come down to us.

But whatever the form in which the trip is portrayed, the same feeling is expressed with regard to the prairie. In spite of the long tenancy of the Mississippi, once the band had left St. Charles and Bonhomme Creek, save for a few abandoned traders' huts or outlying cabins, the country they traversed was still that region of enchantment that had enraptured the earliest explorers. The description is limited, but through the toilsome phrasing — "a Butifull pint Between the two Rivers," as "handsom a prarie as ever eney man saw," we feel all the reverence for the peaceful flowering places felt by the man whose destiny it was soon to sleep among them. Whitehouse is more vivacious, assuming in his narrative rather amusingly the air of a man of the world; yet even he amid the bevy of proper names with which he dazzles the reader, condescends to elaborate a little concerning the "handsom prarie" which contained "the hill of little Devills," and the lavishness displayed by nature on the banks of the river, "Rice was pleanty Groeing . . . Straberyes,

8 Thwaites — *Orig. Jour. of the Lewis & Clark Exped.* VII: 5, 15.

Rosies, Red And White.'' Clark's enthusiasm leads him to unwonted detail.

> ''from the top of the highest of those Mounds I had an extensive view of the Serounding Plains, which afforded one of the most pleasing prospect I ever beheld, under me a Butifull River of Clear Water of about 80 yards wide Meandering thro: a leavel and extensive meadow, as far as I could See, the prospect much enlivened by the fiew Trees & Srubs which is bordering the bank of the river, and the Creeks & runs falling into it. The bottom land is covered with Grass of about 4½ feet high, and appears as leavel as a smoth surfice, the 2d bottom [the upper land] is also covered with Grass and rich weeds & flours, interspersed with copses of the Osage Plumb, on the riseing lands, Small groves of trees are Seen, with a number of Grapes and a Wild Cherry . . . ''[9]

Ordway comments ''their is Beautiful high Good praries on the South Side pleasantest place I have ever Seen.''[10] Even the schoolmaster who polished Gass's narrative gives repeated mention of a ''handsome prairie,'' or laconic praise like, ''We passed through a handsome country, with a rich soil, and the praries rising beautifully on both sides of the river,'' although he insists on straining the soldier's admiration through his own stilted diction.[11]

Yet as we read of conferences with the Indian chiefs or of messengers breaking their way to the Mahas ''through grass, sunflowers, and thistles, all above ten feet high and interspersed with wild pea,''[12] we see in these things only the prelude to change. The signal fires on the prairie announce not the visit of friendly tribes but the invasion of the white men. Lands are viewed always with an eye to their present beauty but with especial emphasis on their possibilities for future development. Ordway calls one prairie ''the Smothest prittyset Place for a Town I ever Saw'';[13] of ''the Littel River platte . . . it is Sayed that thare is a nomber of falls on it fitting for mills.'' Indeed even

---

9 Thwaites — *Orig. Jour. of Lewis & Clark.* VII:7, 11, 52, 41, I:75.
10 *Wis. Hist. Coll.* XXII:86.
11 Gass, Patrick — *Journal of the Lewis & Clark Exped.* . . . Repr. of the ed. of 1811 . . . Ed. by J. K. Hosmer. 1904. 23, 80.
12 Coues — *Hist. of the Exped. under the Command of Lewis & Clark.* I:75.
13 *Wis. Hist. Coll.* XXII:103.

during the explorers' progress up the river and their sojourn beyond the mountains, the influx of eddying life begins. Their return is very different from that first launching into the unknown; not only do they recognize familiar spots, but they observe "the remains of a house which had been built since we passed up";[14] near the Osage they "saw on the banks some cows feeding, and the whole party almost involuntarily raised a shout of joy at seeing this image of civilization and domestic life."[15] Equally significant are the meetings with the traders from whom the wanderers eagerly receive news; the Missouri had become in the two years of their absence an artery of commerce.

Meanwhile in the upper reaches of the Mississippi Zebulon Pike had set out on another governmental exploration. Of it, however, and all the later official surveys, the Lewis and Clark expedition may be taken as the forerunner and representative, the tangible embodiment to the American people of their spirit of tumultuous expansion and of their power of achievement. There were many more narratives, for, as the amazing resources of the new acquisition were revealed to the nation, the government realized and met the need for adequate information. Expedition after expedition went out to explore, and, as the great tide of emigration rolled over the Alleghanies, more and more territories were secured from the Indians, more and more surveyors were sent out to prepare for opening the great tracts, more and more agents were appointed for steadily increasing and more specialized functions. Yet, whether they were Indian commissioners or geologists, men with a literary gift or humdrum souls whose records are painfully stupid, in them the tendencies already noted are more or less apparent. They were the forerunners of settlement; in their work is reflected the country in a stage of transition — not yet dotted by homesteads, but its bison alarmed taking refuge westward, its scarce deer snuffing warily, its Indian hunters also departing in pursuit of their prey, or remaining to exhibit the debilitating effects of communion with the whites. Only the land appears comparatively unchanged, a few more trails over it, perhaps, a few more tiny saplings spared by the cessation of the annual fires, the characteristics of the oak

14 Thwaites — *Orig. Jour. of Lewis & Clark.* VII:14, V:372.
15 Coues — *Hist. of the Exped. under the Command of Lewis & Clark.* III:1211

opening beginning to break the smooth sward of the prairie. But none of these could diminish, rather they enhanced, the physical loveliness of the region. Indeed there could be no greater tribute to its charm than the reaction it produced in these men of science and business. Routine reports that read like the journal of a dilettante traveller today, forced confinement to statistics finding relief in a poetical peroration — these characterize the government documents of the early half of the century.

In those unrestricted days, too, men more distinctly litterateurs often accompanied for information or sport these official expeditions or joined for safety the parties of the fur-traders. Of such a nature were the tours of Irving and of Latrobe and part of the explorations of the posturing Beltrami. Peculiarly interesting examples of the type are the *Travels in the Interior of America in the years 1809, 1810, and 1811* of the naturalist John Bradbury, who accompanied to the Arikara villages the overland Astorians, and the *Journal of a Voyage up the Missouri* (1811) by Henry Marie Brackenridge, traveller, author, statesman, jurist. To each other the books form valuable supplement, for although the writers were close friends and the general content is the same, the tone, conclusions, and the details often differ decidedly. Both sketch the turbulent Missouri with its frequent obstructions; both revel in a country abounding in game; both vibrate responsively to the historical and legendary associations. Yet Bradbury is pre-eminently the scientist. It is he who foresees the future extinction of the swift-skimming deer and the countless bison herds, he who describes in detail the ferocious combats of the latter. And in spite of the fact that Brackenridge states that both men have come to the same conclusion about the Indian, "that the world would lose but little, if these people should disappear before civilized communities,"[16] Bradbury lets his disillusionment mar his judgment no more than the idyllic conceptions formulated in Europe, his description of the various tribes being distinctly valuable from an ethnological standpoint. He reasons calmly concerning the use of the prairie.

"In an agricultural point of view, the vast tract of prairie extending through all these regions, is an important object of

16 *E. W. T.* VI:128.

consideration. Amongst intelligent Americans, the question of — whether it can or cannot be peopled by civilized man? has often been agitated. Accustomed, as they are, to a profusion of timber, for buildings, fuel, and fences, they are not aware of the small quantity of that article that may be dispensed with, in a country abounding in another substance for fuel; nor can they conceive, that fences, and even buildings, may be constructed with the application of a very small portion of timber. Under these impressions, the belief in America is, that the prairie cannot be inhabited by the whites; even Mr. Brackenridge says it cannot be cultivated. My own opinion is, that it can be cultivated; and that, in process of time, it will not only be peopled and cultivated, but that it will be one of the most beautiful countries in the world."[17]

Brackenridge, on the other hand, a more impetuous type, ignorant of the changes soon to be wrought by the steamboat, is unable to conceive of the region as anything else for decades to come than the Arabian Nights solitudes of luminous sky and atmosphere so clear that animals move "across this stilly scene, like the shadows of the phantasmagoria, or Ossian's Deer made of mist."[18] In still another way the two narratives offset each other. For the cut-throat methods of the fur-traders and the ever present menace of the savage fanned jealousy and the fear of treachery into flame. Either side looks black to the loyal chronicler of the other. And in the bitterness caused by the death-fear of strong men and in the moments portentous of conflict the two records form interesting introduction to the succeeding struggle, of which Brackenridge was to be one of the clearest and most popular historians.

For the many-sided warfare of 1812 had nowhere more terrors than on the western frontier. To the constant threat of Indian depredations, rendered easy by weapons and ammunition gained from the British, were added the horrors of a "holy war." Tecumseh, whose ability was excelled only by Pontiac, and his fanatic brother, the Prophet, had bound together the despairing tribes in a coalition which in the earlier period of colonization would have checked for some years the whites. British tales of

17 *E. W. T.* V:266-7. See also 294-5.
18 *E. W. T.* VI:34.

Yankee weakness, unfortunately given credence by the effortless surrender of Hull, temporary inability of the Americans to transport stores and to whip into shape undisciplined troops, non-restraint of their allies by the English, all combined to lay open the settlements to atrocities, the horrors of which not even the stiff legal phraseology of affidavits presented to the Congressional investigating committee could in the slightest degree diminish.[19] Indeed the very terseness of these and other statements often render more lurid their records of strife — the Indians sating their blood lust on the frightened cattle at Mackinac, the narratives of the massacre at the River Raisin.[20] For long years the natural meadows were a background for the wily creeping of savages, the awkward marching of militia, midnight assaults, capture and burning, then the slow whitening of bones amid the luxuriant weed covert. For long years, too, the war formed a subject for writers. All phases of it were described from the naval battles on the Great Lakes to the siege of New Orleans, in productions equally varied — attacks on, and defences of Hull, the contemporary satire *The War of the Gulls*, children's readers, reports of combatants such as Atherton's *Narrative of the Suffering and Defeat of the Northwestern Army* . . . (1842). Too seldom, however, do these approach the pungency of Corporal Stubbs' similes[21] or the fullness of McAfee's *History of the Late War in the Western Country* . . . (1816), for us to treat them in detail. They are, nevertheless, one more passage in the portrayal of the prairie in literature, a passage that was to attain emphasis, however crude, in the beginning works of fiction and poetry.[22]

With the ending of the war was let loose once more the great flood of emigration, which had been increasing steadily throughout the first decade of the century. Travellers reveal clearly the

19 *Barbarities of the Enemy, Exposed in a Report of the Committee of the House of Representatives*, 1814.

20 Darnell, Elias — *A Journal* . . . *in the years 1812-13. Also Two Narratives by Men that Were Wounded in the Battles on the River Raisin and Taken Captive by the Indians.* 1854.

21 The homely and spirited narrative of the backwoodsman is one of the most picturesque we have. See Heartman's Hist. Ser. No. 5. *A Compendious Account of the Most Important Battles of the Late War, to which is added, the Curious Adventures of Corporal Stubbs* . . . Orig. pub. 1817.

22 Severance states whimsically, "A considerable shelf, perhaps five feet long, could be filled with stories of the War of 1812. My studies of American history have well nigh convinced me that the war was fought, not to maintain our rights on the high seas, but to stimulate the development of American letters by supplying picturesque material for budding romancers." *Buf. Hist. Soc. Pub.* XV:84.

bustling enterprise of the new regions, the mushroom villages, the economic development.[23] Yet so immense is the immigrant tide beginning about 1815 that the preceding changes seem a mere preface to progress. Roving spirits too long dammed up by the trouble on the frontier, cultivated families ruined in fortune by the financial depression of the war, English farmers strained to the limit by the unjust corn laws, German and Irish peasants, all these crowded together in the narrow mountain valleys. Comment upon them is ceaseless and impressive.

> "Nothing so strongly indicates the superiority of the western country as the vast emigration to it from the eastern and southern states . . . I was informed by an inhabitant of Cayuga, in April, 1816, that more than fifteen thousand wagons had passed over the bridge at that place within the last eighteen months, containing emigrants to the western country."[24]
> "All America seems to be breaking up and moving westward. We are seldom out of sight, as we travel on this grand track, towards the Ohio, of family groups, behind and before us."[25]

Fortunately among all these people, welded together by homogeneity of destination yet varying to all possible degrees in other respects, were still more of the scientists, business men, and writers, whose records have already been so valuable in a study of the western country, and to the publication of whose journals widespread interest offered incentive. In their unstudied lines we may experience again today that exultant passage of the mountains — by the Cumberland Gap where the yellow waters of the Potomac burst through the rounding slopes of the Blue Ridge, along the brawling Juniata's wooded valley and the steep

---

23 See *E. W. T.* III, IV, Jervase Cutler's *Topographical Description of the State of Ohio, Indiana Territory, & Louisiana* . . . 1812, etc. Among the best reports of the region at this period are those of the home missionaries. J. F. Schermerhorn & S. J. Mills in *A Correct View of that Part of the United States which Lies West of the Alleghany Mts.* . . . (1814) give statistics as to the population and land and add that in all probability the territory "should peace be restored, will fill up with unexampled rapidity." p. 11. *Report of a Missionary Tour through that Part of the United States which Lies West of the Alleghany Mountains; Performed under the Direction of the Massachusetts Missionary Society* by S. J. Mills and Daniel Smith (1815) states that "Indiana, notwithstanding the war, is peopling very fast. Its settlements are bursting forth on the right hand and on the left." and concludes of Illinois "that settlers will now begin to flock in, especially if the war should soon terminate." 15, 16-7. The events of the war and the soldiers' descriptions of the land tended to turn attention to the West as did the accounts of the bounty lands such as N. B. Van Zandt's, *A Full Description of the Soil, Water, Timber, & Prairies . . . of the Military Lands between the Mississippi and Illinois Rivers.* 1819.

24 *E. W. T.* V:296.

25 Birkbeck — *Notes on a Jour. in Amer.* 1818. 31.

sides of Laurel Hill. Treacherous paths make perilous our progress; vociferous taverns intensify the loneliness of the outer darkness; hailstones pelt down on our rude wayside camps. Yet always impulse resistless urges us onwards, and always stirs round us ambitious life. Beyond the mountains there is, if possible, even greater excitement. Pittsburgh and Wheeling, the chief ports of the West, teem with the immigrants. Frugal countrymen lament at the base profiteering; impetuous youths yearn for adventure; careful leaders barter for boats and for pilots. For barks are scarce; navigation is difficult; and until the invention of the steamboat travellers were often held up for weeks by the ice or high water.

Yet not even all this activity was to settle immediately the prairies. The distrust of the open places that had caused the first Kentucky pioneers to name their smiling meadows *The Barrens* and to clear their farms in the depths of the forest was now transferred to the grass lands of the north and west.[26] According to Birkbeck, "The inhabitants of the old states are profoundly and *resolutely* ignorant of the advantages of our prairie country";[27] and to the common prejudice even as shrewd an observer as Cuming gives emphatic expression.

> "The land is here the worst I had seen since I had left the banks of the Ohio; it had been gradually worse . . . and for the last two miles before we come to Marshons it had degenerated into natural prairies or savannas, with very little wood, and none deserving the name of timber, but well clothed with brush and low coarse vegetation."[28]

---

26 There are, of course, obvious reasons for the pioneers' delay in settling the prairie country well summarized by a contemporary. "The advantages of settling on the prairie are offset by certain disadvantages. In the first place there is a lack of good water. There are no acorns and nuts for the hogs. The subsoil is impervious clay. There is no building material. Prairie fires destroy the grass and endanger the human habitations." *Mo. Hist. Rev.* XVII:343. The early settlers made claims "'cordin' to wood 'n water." Note Regan's description of "A Select Farm" — *The Western Wilds of Amer.* 2d. ed. 1859. 57-8. A Methodist circuit rider tells of a community where in the absence of all other law the families met and permitted each man to take up 40 acres of timber and as much prairie as he pleased. *Wis. Hist. Coll.* XV:277. There are countless early passages showing the changing attitudes toward the prairie and many later studies such as B. Shimek's *The Pioneer & the Forest . . . Proc. of the Miss. Vall. Hist. Assoc.* III:96; ch. I & II in J. Schafer's *A Hist. of Agriculture in Wis.* & his *The Yankee & the Teuton in Wis., Wis. Mag. of Hist.* VI:125 ff.; W. V. Pooley's *The Settlement of Illinois from 1830 to 1850.* (*Univ. of Wis. Bull. — Hist. Ser.* I. 4); H. H. Barrows' *Geography of the Middle Illinois Valley* (Ill. St. Geol. Survey — *Bull.* no. 15) ch. V., etc.

27 *E. W. T.* X:150

28 *E. W. T.* IV:208.

Indeed to those men who had literally hewed their way through the unbroken forests, conception of a fertile treeless area was almost impossible. The woods to them were a part of their being; the gloomy shades had unconsciously sombred their characters as the dense solitudes had abbreviated and knotted their speech; one old pioneer gave as his reason for change that it was time for him to move when he could no longer fell a tree so that its branches would reach his front doorstep. Accessibility, too, was an important factor, and heavy timber lined most of the rivers, darkening the rich bottoms.

Too often wretched settlers found on these bottoms not only crude habitations but, from the prolific life of the newly turned soil, those banes of the immigrant — ague and chills. Unquestionably these diseases were due not only to the rankness of the vegetation, for centuries unchecked, but to malnutrition and to pestilential vapors from stagnant pools, near which the cabins were usually built and of which the waters were too frequently drunk. Only a few men realized this, however, and those few the scientists, whose book-words, for most of the denizens of the frontier, meant nothing. And so there arose a gaunt specter of disease — embodiment of fever, "shakes," the hideous ague-cakes of the lower Mississippi — a specter which to the pain-racked dwellers of the swampy places nevertheless brought comfort; for, whatever his tortures, the real disease centre, the sufferer knew, lay on beyond. The danger was said to lurk particularly on the prairie, now no longer enticing but sullen and grim. Unquestionably there was in this spectre a basis of truth;[29] nevertheless its exaggeration was for some time a factor in the ill repute of the prairie.

Certainly it constituted one of the most formidable weapons wielded by the English critics of the region, the attacks and answers of whom form a curious chapter. For in the controversy were involved not only the question of the utility of the prairies but the character of the Americans, the value of their body politic, their cultural contributions, and their relations to Europe. The strife dissolved itself ultimately into attempted overthrow of the Tory domination by the Radicals, whose watchwords were manhood suffrage, repeal of the corn laws, abolition of the ruin-

29 See, for instance, *E. W. T.* IX:130, 175, 184, 187, 189.

ous privileges of the upper classes, and the sharing of benefits; and although its ever widening ripples almost obscured it, primarily into the purchase by Morris Birkbeck and George Flower of a large tract of land in southeastern Illinois, as a protest against the ruinous conditions of the homeland and as a means of escape from oppression.

In the scheme for such a colony there is, of course, nothing new. From the days of the Greek philosophers we find visions of ideal states; after Columbus' momentous discovery these naturally centered in the new regions of America. The novelty came in the fact that Birkbeck and Flower were men of substance and resolution sufficient to put into execution their plan once they were fired by it; the importance resulted from the overwhelming reaction. Whatever the opinions of the wisdom of the move or the success of the project, no one can doubt the absolute sincerity of its promoters; and, now that the dust of conflict has cleared away, no one can accuse them of wilful beguilement of others. Birkbeck's *Letters from Illinois* (1818) and his *Notes on a Journey in America* (1817), Richard Flower's *Letters from Lexington & the Illinois* (1819) and his *Letters from the Illinois* (1822) form, indeed, some of our most intelligent pictures of conditions for the immigrants. Both writers were too clear-sighted to expect to find in America a second Utopia; neither had any expectation of changing the universe or even of reforming individuals. As Birkbeck says, "Emigration to the extreme limits of this western America will not repair a bad character";[30] and "the wilds of Illinois will yield no repose to perturbed spirits."[31] They warned families of the difficulties to be encountered; they gave sound advice to farmers and to laborers; and they wished none to emigrate "without serious and due consideration of their own circumstances."[32] They pictured the prairies so lovely "as to seem like the creation of fancy, gardens of delight in a dreary wilderness," but it requires only the designation of the Seven Miles' Prairie as a "spot charming to the eye, but deficient in surface-water" to show that such admiration did not mar their agricultural acuteness.[33] To be sure they made er-

30 Birkbeck — *Letters from Illinois.* 96.
31 *Ibid.* VI.
32 Flower — *Letters* . . . *E. W. T.* X:148
33 Birkbeck — *Notes of a Journey in Amer.* 120, 128.

rors of judgment and failed to allow for economic depression, but by such mistakes they themselves as well as others suffered. Their attitude, indeed, as the following will indicate was unwontedly generous — ebullient happiness eager to share with others its privileges.

> "As to the reward of his industry, every farmer who can stock a farm in England, may here become the proprietor of his own soil with that capital which affords him only a tenant's station, a precarious subsistence in his own country; an inducement, I should think, sufficient to make thousands follow our steps, and taste the blessings of independence and the sweets of liberty." [34]

Unfortunately for them, but fortunately for us, they did not receive from their opponents such generosity as they manifested. The indefatigable William Cobbett immediately took up the cudgels, and in his *A Year's Residence in the United States of America* (1818) after asserting "it would not have been proper to omit saying something of the *Western Countries*, that Newest of the New Worlds, to which so many thousands and hundreds of thousands are flocking, and toward which the writings of Mr. Birkbeck have, of late, drawn the pointed attention of all those Englishmen, who, having something left to be robbed of, and wishing to preserve it, are looking toward America as a place of refuge . . ." proceeded to deal heavy blows against "this Transalleganian romance," and the folly of the long journey westward for land.[35] At the time Cobbett was credited with being in the pay of real estate dealers near New York and Philadelphia, a charge which has been permitted to stand. Other writers, however, sided in the quarrel; residents of the new country aided in the controversy till the prospective immigrant must have been unutterably bewildered. Nevertheless, the hard-headed old farmers, who wished to share in the milk and honey of the prairies, were not to be deceived by the flourishes of hostile pens. And so there arose in this epoch of exodus, the custom of inspection of pro-

34 *E. W. T.* X:102-3

35 Cobbett — *A Year's Res.* 441, 552. For passages suggesting his alliance with eastern real estate dealers see *Ibid.* 83-4, 552, & his *Emigrant's Guide.* 1830. 98. E. E. Sparks' in *The English Settlement in Illinois* (1907) prints answers to Cobbett supplementary to the reprints given by Thwaites. See also George Flower's *Hist. of the English Settlement* . . . 1882. For another very hostile pamphlet see Wm. Savage — *Observations on Emigration to the U. S. of Amer.* . . . 1819.

spective purchases either in person or by proxy; and as a result of such inspections books and still more books appeared to magnify the already swollen torrent of emigrant literature.[36]

These at their worst, irritating even today, were unspeakably annoying to a generation still feeling the effects of the war and already angered by English superciliousness; at their best they present a view, honest and sane, of what would otherwise have been a little known side of the developing West. Of the first class Faux furnishes a typical example. His purpose, ostentatiously announced in his title, is to show "Men and Things as they are in America," he having a "strong desire to ascertain the naked truth, in all particulars relating to emigration to that land of boasted liberty"; his method, apparently, to repeat or enlarge every malicious rumor. Nothing seems to suit him — even the low cost of living including "game, fine prairie hens like grouse, and turkeys in sickening abundance." Not only is he a ridiculous snob, but a thorough cad, unctuously flattering during his stay at the "abode of the emperor of the prairies," but seizing his first opportunity to gloat over the Flower-Birkbeck quarrel, and assuring a discouraged young Devonshireman on his way to Albion that "he had better settle here. They of the Prairie were proud, and wanted only high-bred English." Jealousy, apparently, was at the root of his insinuations. Even such extreme statements, however, as, "I hate the prairies, all of them; insomuch that I would not have any of them of a gift, if I must be compelled to live on them. They are all without water except what is too muddy and distant for use," or his conclusion that "The west is fit only for poor men, who are the only proper pioneers of the wilderness," have value as reflection of contemporary prejudices.[37]

From this scandal monger, it is a relief to turn to the unprejudiced account of the frugal and contented Woods, who primarily the farmer, goes straight to his destination, chronicling appreciatively his journey, and who, arrived at Wanborough,

---

36 See, for instance, H. B. Fearon's *Sketches of America. Narrative of a journey of five thousand miles through the eastern and western states of America; contained in eight reports addressed to the thirty-nine English families by whom the author was deputed in June 1817, to ascertain whether any, and what part of the United States would be suitable for their residence. With remarks on Mr. Birkbeck's "Notes" and "Letters."* 3d. ed. 1819.

37 Faux, Wm. — *Memorable Days in America* . . . (1818-20). *E. W. T.* XI & XII, XI:25, 255-6, 264, 244, 214, 192.

purchases land and settles down contentedly to improve his possessions. His remarks are of especial value to the cultivator; he finds the prairie a pleasant relief from dense woods; admiration does not blind him, however, to the difficulty of a first plowing. But in spite of the fact that he refuses to commit himself as to the propriety of any person's leaving England, he convinces us of his satisfaction with his lot; his sturdy common sense and cheerful spirit augur well for his future on the prairie.[38]

To quote additional writers would be to indulge in that prolixity and repetition so wearisome in even the briefest survey of the immigrant manuals. Detailed treatment has been rendered obligatory, however, by the wide-spreading influence, too little realized today, of the English Settlement. At a time when, according to Fordham, such terrible stories of the West were in circulation that many of the inhabitants of the seaboard feared to cross the mountains, Kentucky seeming to them to be "the verge of the habitable world,"[39] and when General Thomas A. Smith called his prairie estate "Experiment,"[40] men of influence and means demonstrated the potentialities of the open places. Into the region inhabited as yet mainly by squatters and indolent hunting farmers, they introduced the careful methods of the English husbandman. The reader of today would scarcely accept Ferrall's breezy attribution of the gentler qualities of the population of Illinois to the leaven of the English, but their example must have made for refinement. And if the description of Welby is to be relied upon, their varied company must have produced a real high light upon the prairie.

> "The strange heterogeneous mixture of characters which are collected hither by the magic pen of Morris Birkbeck is truly ludicrous. Among many others, a couple now attend to the store at Albion who lately lived in a dashing style in London not far from Bond-street; the lady brought over her white satin shoes and gay dresses, rich carpets, and every thing but what in such a place she would require, yet I understand that they have accomodated themselves to their new situations, hand out

38 Woods, John — *Two Years Residence in the Settlement on the English Prairie . . . E. W. T.* X.

39 Fordham, E. P. *Personal Narrative of Travels & of a Residence in the Illinois Territory . . .* 1817-1818. Ed. by F. A. Ogg. 1906. 131.

40 *E. W. T.* XIV:151, f.n.

the plums, sugar, whiskey, &c., with tolerable grace, and at least 'do not seem to mind it.' "[41]

That they were early prominent in work for the common good the mention by Faux of Birkbeck's return from a convention to discuss the drainage of the state affords proof; and in the struggle against slavery the sturdy devotion of the English to their ideals had much to do with keeping the state free.

It is this latter service — the fight for freedom in the country of adoption — that proclaims the significance of the settlement in the island of Britain. For in those troublous days when the exactions of the upper classes pressed ceaselessly more intolerable burdens on the backs of the peasantry, when farms lay desolate and villages were wrecked for preserves, when the mechanization of industry forced thousands from employment, when Poor Laws were unable to cope with the overwhelming wretchedness, soul-sick, dreamers turned to the fruitful places of the West. There, they felt, want and misery need exist for no one; to the industrious a bountiful nature offered food, shelter, and raiment; an unselfish government encouraged the accumulation of property; an untrammelled society abolished false class distinctions. And of all of these things the English Colony afforded a symbol. No wonder its name became to the conservative anathema, its achievement, a rallying cry for the liberal. For the young literary man it partook of the glamor of Coleridge's and Southey's dream of a "pantisocracy" on the banks of the Susquehanna;[42] to the free thinker it became an object of pilgrimage. One of these, Miss Frances Wright, from the letters of two American acquaintances gives a clear picture of the colony;[43] another, Thomas Hulme, gives us its emotional connotation. The very plainness of the words of this self-made master-bleacher when they were stripped of the insinuations with which Cobbett enmeshed them make the more intense his passion of feeling. Come

41 Welby, A. — *A Visit to North America & the English Settlements in Illinois . . . E. W. T.* XII: 258-9.

42 Note Peacock's comment. "Birkbeck's *Notes on America* have fixed the public attention on that country in an unprecedented degree. . . . Multitudes are following his example, even from this neighborhood . . . He is a man of vigorous intellect, who thinks deeply and describes admirably. The temptation to agriculturists with a small capital must be irresistible; and the picture he presents of the march of cultivation and of population beyond the Ohio is one of the most wonderful spectacles ever yet presented to the mind's eye of philosophy." Thomas Love Peacock — *Letters to Edward Hookham & Percy B. Shelley . . .* ed. by R. Garnett. 1910. 78.

43 Wright, F. — *Views of Society & Manners in America . . .* 1821. 260-4.

to America himself to avoid leaving his children slaves to the "great insolent families," he found in the West as in the East "ease and happiness and a fearless utterance of thought everywhere prevail."[44] Yet his happiness was tinged with unavoidable bitterness, regret that these good things which everywhere abounded were to be found only away from old England. His emotion was, indeed, not unique; the successful emigrant put the matter to Mackay more crudely.

> "Eh man, if the poor Paizla weavers, that are starvin' at home, only kent what they could do here, wi' a little industry and perseverance, it's mony's the ane o' them would come awa' frae that recky, poverty-stricken hole, which would leave it a' the better for sic as were left behind."[45]

And Harriet Martineau gave it most forceful expression.

> "The prospect of agriculture in the States northwest of the Ohio are brilliant. The stranger who looks upon the fertile prairies of Illinois and Indiana, and the rich alluvions of Ohio, feels the iniquity of the English corn laws as strongly as in the alleys of Sheffield and Manchester. The inhuman perverseness of taxing food is there evident in all its enormity. The world ought never to hear of a want of food, — no one of the inhabitants of its civilized portions ought ever to be without the means of obtaining his fill, while the mighty western valley smiles in its fertility. If the aristocracy of England, for whom these laws were made, and by whom they are sustained, could be transported to travel, in open wagons, the boundless prairies, and the shores of the great rivers, which would bring down the produce, they would groan to see from what their petty, selfish interests had shut out the thousands of half-starved laborers at home. . . . The landlords of England do not go and see the great western valleys; but, happily, some of the labourers of England do. Far off as that valley is, those labourers will make themselves heard from thence, by those who have driven them there; and will teach the brethren whom they left behind where the blame of their hunger lies. Every British

44 Hulme, T. — *Journal Made during a Tour of the Western Countries of America . . .* (1818-1819). *E. W. T.* X:25, 26.

45 Mackay, Alex — *The Western World; or Travels in the United States in 1846-7 . . .* 3v. 4th ed. 1850. III:81. See similarly, John Regan's *The Western Wilds.* Wm. Oliver's *8 mos. in Ill.* 1843 is inscribed to the labouring men of Roxburgh.

settler who ploughs a furrow in the prairie helps to plough up the foundation of the British Corn laws.''[46]

That strange complex, however, of philosophical benevolence, hard-headed farming, pamphleteering distortions, and fiery idealism, denominated the English Settlement, presents the nub of the matter. By it the Middle West was brought into direct contact with the internal affairs of Great Britain; through it the great spirits of the age who like Carlyle [47] in *Past and Present* turned to the early monastic rule or who like Ruskin and Morris found relief in the mediaeval craft guilds, the nebulous but alluring wonderlands of the past, were faced with another solution of their problems — a solution to be found on the flowering fields, the pleasant pastures of the midland, only a few years before the haunt of Indian and bison.

And that this was true not only of England but of the continental countries we have numerous testimonies. Cabet's *Voyage en Icarie* (1842), the usual extravagant vision of an ideal republic, which had an extraordinary influence among the workmen of Paris and elsewhere, resulted in the establishment of a Fourier colony at Nauvoo, Illinois, where the deserted Mormon dwellings, the petty restrictions, and most of all the internal dissensions formed saddening contrast to the magnificent amusement places, the palatial hotels, the serene and well-ordered life of the imaginary state.[48] Germany furnished an even more extraordinary example of the influence of America in the Sturm und Drang period. There again the discontent of the workers at their meagre lives, the demand for greater privileges resulting from the Revolution in France, the unfortunate political and economic conditions all combined to make masses of the people singularly

---

46 Martineau, H. — *Society in America*. 2d. ed. 2v. 1837. I: 307.

47 It is interesting to note that Carlyle frequently alludes to America as a Land of Promise in his correspondence with Emerson in passages such as " . . . blessed are you where, what jargoning soever there be at Washington, the poor man . . . shoulders his axe, and walks into the Western Woods, sure of a nourishing Earth and an overarching Sky! It is verily the Door of Hope to distracted Europe; which otherwise I should see crumbling down into blackness of darkness." I:71.

48 There are a number of Icarian documents and later studies describing the American communities. The high hopes that were formulated at first are well revealed by Major William Williams' *Journal of a Trip to Iowa in 1849*. "The Mormons have all left. Sold out all their property to a French Company who will no doubt make it a great place. He tells me they are establishing all Mechanical branches. about 700 have arrived in all there. there is to be 25,000 made up of French and Germans from the Rhine. they are buying Lands all around Nauvou on the Illinois Side." *Annals of Iowa*. 3d. ser. XII:246.

open for suggestions of betterment, a suggestion that came like an electric spark with the publication of Gottfried Duden's book, *Bericht über eine Reise nach den westlichen Staaten Nord-Amerika's* . . . and that was to provide impulse for the great tide of immigration that flowed from Germany to America during the middle years of the century.

Duden was convinced that most of the crimes he was called upon to prosecute in Germany were due to poverty, the direct result of an excess of population. He, therefore, determined to discover the best place for emigration and to test for himself the difficulties of making a comfortable establishment. His book is designed chiefly for agriculturists; however he gives a variety of suggestions for merchants and artisans. As a matter of fact his rosy pictures of the mildness of the Missouri climate, the fertility of the soil, and the comforts of the life acted like a magnet on all classes from a cultured youth like Lenau, to whom America was a wondrous and as yet almost untouched source of poetic inspiration, to peasants desirous of meat three times a day. The majority of the readers, overlooking Duden's account of the swarms of mosquitoes and other discomforts, centered their attention instead on such passages as the following.

> "Many a time I have said to myself and to my traveling companion (whom I leave behind in the happiest circumstances), people in Europe will not and cannot believe how easily and pleasantly one can live in this country. It sounds too strange, too fabulous. Belief in the existence of such places has too long been banished to the fairy world. The inhabitants of the Mississippi territories, on the other hand, consider reports of the misery in Europe exaggerated. That there are so many white men there who in spite of the greatest exertions can scarcely obtain in a year as much meat as is thrown to the dogs in a few weeks here, that many families without the assistance of others would starve or freeze in winter is doubted by the inhabitants and even by their slaves so much that they are accustomed to consider such statements only as flattery of America. Occasionally one hears, however, the statement, 'Yes, my grandfather has told us that conditions were very bad there.' "[49]

49 Duden — *Bericht,* 1829. 233-4. For abstract and partial translation by Prof.

As a result numbers were greatly disillusioned and Duden became the centre of many bitter attacks. In his own defence he published in 1837 his *Self-Accusation,* "as a Warning against Further Indiscreet Emigration." Bitterly he said his work was intended for intelligent beings. His defence was rather ineffective, however, in spite of his citation of other authorities, and the attacks have continued down to our own day. On the other hand, his farm long remained an object of pilgrimage for those who owed to him happiness and prosperity.

One of the most alluring of the projects touched upon by Duden was that of a centre for German culture in the West. This, particularly attractive to the university men and radical leaders who controlled the thought of the folk and who often took refuge in America, comes up again and again throughout the century. The Zweiunddreiszigers or "Die Grauen," as the earlier immigrants were called, soon scattered and forgot their desire to establish freedom in Germany; the Achtundvierzigers or "Die Grünen" revived it, however, planning to Germanize the United States, first intellectually through their own superiority, second through the establishment of political leavens, centres of Teutonic government which would gradually bring the surrounding territory under their sovereignty.[50] To discuss further these dreams and ill-starred attempts is futile; they did bring to the midland, however, an impetuosity of aspiration which caused sometimes decidedly violent reactions; they did import a thrifty stock which was a potent factor in the development of prosperity; and they did add to the literature of Germany and America a series of such mutually interesting volumes as Gert Göbel's *Länger als ein Menschenleben in Missouri,* (1877) or the *Memoirs of Gustave Koerner, 1809-1896* (2v. 1909). These, primarily treating of the Teutonic settlers in the United States, supplement the accounts of the travellers like Paul Wilhelm, Duke of Würtemberg, or the Duke of Saxe-Weimar; the immigrant manuals or *Ratgeber* such as Rauschenbusch's *Einige Anweisungen für Auswanderer nach den westlichen Staaten von Nordamerika und Reisebilder* (3d. ed.

Bek see *Mo. Hist. Rev.* XII & XIII. In XIV *Ibid.,* he begins an important series of articles and translations. *The Followers of Duden.*

50 This is based largely upon T. S. Baker — *Lenau & Young Germany in America.* 1897. See also Beck — *The German Settlement Society of Philadelphia and its Colony, Hermann, Mo.* 1907, and his *A German Communistic Society in Missouri. Mo. Hist. Rev.* III:52 ff.; 99 ff.

1848) and the romantic and realistic novels, poems, and plays, the importance of which is being only gradually realized.

There was probably a larger body of literature dealing with America in Germany than in any other country save England. Interesting records from almost every nation in northern Europe can be quoted, however. A good example of a Welsh pamphlet is *Yr American* by the Rev. B. W. Chidlaw, who says, "Young people, sober, industrious, and faithful; maidservants and men-servants; together with ordinary mechanics, active and skillful, are the fit persons to go to America . . . Far away in the West, in Ohio, Indiana, Illinois, and the new states of Iowa and Wisconsin, is found the best land for the least money."[51] Ole Rynning's *True Account of America* reveals the exaggerated hopes of Europeans.

> "It is a general belief among the common people in Norway that America was well populated a few years ago, and that a plague — almost like the black death — has left the country desolate of people. As a result they are of the opinion that those who emigrate to America will find cultivated farms, houses, clothes, and furniture ready for them . . ."[25]

Similar fantastic beliefs are suggested in the diary of one of the original colonists of New Glaurus.

> "Food is cheap in Pittsburgh. Hogs' heads could not be seen laying in the street as some of us had been told at home, but we could buy them smoked in the shops for 4 cents a pound."
> [Apropos of hardships when the boat went aground] "Who would have imagined such things at home. We imagined golden mountains with air castles built upon them."

He pays tribute, however, to the plenty of the country.

> "If I could wish all the wood I see stranded on the sand bars, into the parishes of Diessbach, they would have no need for many years to distribute their Beech parcels. Likewise if I could distribute to our poor at home all of the food that is thrown away on the steamers, we would need no poorhouse or poor act. . . ."
> "Our road led us through regions that would rejoice the eye

51 Hist. & Phil. Soc. of Ohio — *Quar. Pub.* VI: No. 1. 34.
52 *Minn. Hist. Bull.* II:244.

of the most despondent, many miles over the Prairies on which countless herds of cattle could have bathed in the thick rich grass.''[53]

A similarly sensible view is taken by the author of *Eene Stem uit Pella* (1848), which gives a very fair picture of conditions in America, stating that those who liked work found it "while others who had formed of America a picture such as children have of Cocagne were less fortunate in finding what they did not seriously seek.''[54] Little has been said here of the religious colonies, which as a matter of fact were often combined with the national groups. The Rapp community, however, mentioned by almost every visitor to the English Settlement, formed a pleasant old world note on the prairie as do the Amanas today; and when it was purchased by Owen for his communistic experiment it brought together a number of most interesting scientists and artists.[55]

The attitude of the valley dwellers toward these visionaries would be an interesting study. Sometimes it flared into melodrama as in the riots of the "know-nothings" at the Louisville polls; usually, however, the feeling, unless the colonists willed otherwise, seems to have been one of neighborliness or at worst indifference. Americans themselves, of course, formed on the prairie communities which preserved the atmosphere of the old home state much as did the English Settlement; radicals among them took part in the celebrated Owen experiment; religious enthusiasts banded together for new and strange rites. These latter, indeed, form some of the weirdest annals of the prairie. Emotional fervor, as always on the frontier, inhibited from normal vents by the repressive conditions of existence, burst with fanatic violence through the narrow and often distorted channel of supernatural experience. Itinerant preachers, some noble and inspiring, others unfortunately incapacitated for their high mis-

---

53 *Wis. Hist. Coll.* XV:317, 318, 323, 327.

54 *Ia. Jour. of Hist. & Pol.* IX:534.

55 See *E. W. T.* for many references to New Harmony, also later studies such as J. Snack & R. Owen — *Hist. of New Harmony, Ind.* (1890), J. A. Bole — *The Harmony Soc.* (Pa. diss.), W. A. Hinds — *Amer. Communities*, etc. For the diaries of several members of the Owen group see *Ind. Hist. Coll.* I:536ff., V:360ff., *Ind. Hist. Soc. Pub.* IV no. 1. Lesueur, for a time a member of the Owen colony, has left us some of the most interesting sketches of the Mississippi Valley at this period. These have been preserved in the Museum at Havre and a number of them have been made accessible to the ordinary reader in a pamphlet by Mme. Adriene Loir. (1920).

sion by ignorance and unbridled zeal, followed from the woods and mountain fastnesses their uncouth flocks; the influence of the Kentucky camp meetings, occasionally vibrant with the ecstasy of a thousand naked souls, more often a Saturnalia intolerably painful, spread even west of the Mississippi. Mormons in throngs journeyed to Mount Zion, the new Jerusalem, situated near Independence, Missouri, or worshipped under Joseph Smith in the great tabernacle at Nauvoo. The macabre Pilgrim band with their rent and filth-rotted garments, their terrifying mortifications, the twanging jerk of their "Praise God! Praise God!" preached and tortured their way from the Canadian border down the Mississippi's green banks.[56] Such perversions of emotion seem, however, insignificant in comparison with the sombre phantoms and the grim imaginings of the New England forest. So in spite of Alexander's assertion that "On the banks of the Ohio are found fanatics possessed with the wildest possible conceits,"[57] the tendency seems to have been generally wholesome. Certainly the bustle of life in the valley was a check to wide-spreading contagion and gave a freedom of thought unparalleled save in the Far West. The average Anglo-American although occasionally he arose in his might to expel the Mormons from their strongholds[58] or to pluck from the Pilgrims the emaciated bodies of children, seems to have had to a pronounced degree the attitude of Laissez-faire, an attitude shared by the business-like traveller. As for the romantic traveller — to his melancholy-tinged spirit we owe preservation of the strange austerities, the weird rites, the Trappist silences, the solemn joys that wove mystic fibres in the emotional fabric of the Middle West.

For over the great valleys of the Ohio and the Mississippi hovered in those early days an ineffable lustre. The vast regions, descriptions of which had kindled successively the imaginations of Spanish grandee and French priest, Breton seafarer and Canadian habitant, English governor and American pioneer, now

---

56 Flint, T. — *Recollections of the Last Ten Years in the Valley of the Mississippi.* 275, See also *E. W. T.* XIII:294.

57 Alexander, J. E. — *Transatlantic Sketches* . . . 2v. 1833. II: 129.

58 *Early Days on the Grand River & the Mormon War* by R. J. Britton. *Mo. His. Rev.* XIII: 112ff. & the following articles should be consulted in this connection. Gerstäcker treats the expulsion of the Mormons in one of his stories. Des. of the relations of the Mormons with their neighbors in Ill. may be found in *Annals of Ia.* 3d. ser. XII:244, & Caswell, H. — *The City of the Mormons; or 3 Days at Nauvoo, Ill. in 1842.* 1842 & *Jour. of the Ill. St. Hist. Soc.* VIII: 281ff.

tempted with alluring vistas the romantic youths of the East. The exultation after the war, the increasing spirit of nationalism, the soaring desire for achievement, blended with, and were enhanced by, the West's superb vision. And, although unlike the English singers, whose full-throated outpourings were so richly melodious a prompting, American rhapsodists had behind them no long poetic tradition, no folk heroes refulgent with centuries of fame, no ripe classical culture, they did have a past of unqualified heroism, they did have a travel literature of extraordinary richness. And so much of the fervor that in the mother country was responsible for one of the most gorgeous webs of English poesy, in the new world was expended on celebration of the purchase. The mighty works of the mound builders offered impressive testimony to the power of past nations; the bitter struggles for possession, fields fertile in legend. And, although Maximilian criticized sharply American neglect of the aborigines' history,[59] even at the time that he wrote the increasing security of the West and the transportation of the tribes beyond the Mississippi tended to lessen the hatred and to throw about them the glamour of a vanishing race.

Yet so completely had the Indians themselves dropped from the life on the Ohio and Mississippi that it seems best to leave consideration of them to the other sections. Romantic attention centered instead on the picturesque French sketched at the moment of their submergence by the on-pressing Saxon. To the portraits afforded by the practical traveller of squatters and hunting farmers, these joyous childlike people in their low, balconied dwellings offer a most colorful contrast. Their chroniclers were numerous, but the one who most fully responded to the languorous appeal of their life was the young poet, novelist, journalist, and playwright, Edmund Flagg, who in Childe Harold spirit rode through the West. With a mind steeped in the picturesque lore of the valley he unites an abounding sympathy, an exceptional capacity for emotional connotation. Effortlessly he re-creates the peaceful routine of the past; yet clearly he etches the signs of decay; the rude tenements, their whitewashed walls stained by age, are crumbling, the trees, gnarled with years; every object,

59 Maximilian, Prince of Wied — *Travels in the Interior of North America* . . . *E. W. T.* XXII — XXIV. XXII:70-1.

the very soil even, seems moss-grown and hoary. More poignantly, too, than any other writer he lines in the changed conditions for the French — precarious subsistence, abridgement of former immunities, futile competition with superior industry. His low-eaved, grass-laned villages, half-hidden in a century's vegetation and their rustling common fields, are at once a culmination and a decline; they shine in the sunset glow radiant with the glories of the past yet wistfully shadowed by the troubles of the future.

And just as he immortalized the decaying charm of the French, so Flagg crowned triumphantly the loveliness of the prairies, "the most remarkable feature of the Western world."[60] The flowering meadow lands he displays vividly; over them "endless thickets of the wild plum and the blackberry" are "interlaced and matted together by the young grape-vines streaming with gorgeous clusters"; "the balmy thyme, the burgamot, and the asters of every tint and proportion" throw forth "their gaudy sunburnt petals upon the wind, until the whole meadow seems arrayed in the royal livery of a sunset sky." Yet in his book the cloying sweetness of such vegetation is mingled with vigorous life — a troop of cavalry winding with glittering bayonets over the prairie, white military tents on the moon-frosted grasses, round the fires of tired immigrants oxen hungrily browsing. As he traversed the Looking-Glass Prairie, "rosy sunbeams were playing lightly over the pleasant country seats and neat farm-houses . . . imbowered in their young orchards and waving maize fields"; and at Pekin he even encounters a "monkey-show which had wound its way over the mountains into the regions of the distant West and reared its dingy canvass upon the smooth sward of the prairie." Of all the tributes to the pictorial beauty of the midlands, his description, though slightly rococo, is richest and most suggestive.[61]

And in still one more way Flagg was to contribute — to the intoxicating beauty and pulsating life that had its source in the rivers. The vividness of re-creation that emotionally glorified his ride through the French villages was equally a factor in his passage on the Ohio, Illinois, and Mississippi. Before him un-

60 Latrobe, C. J. — *The Rambler in North America 1832-1833.* 2v. 1835. II:160.
61 Flagg — *The Far West* . . . (1836-7) *E. W. T.* XXVI-XXVII. XXVII: 69, XXVI: 286, 252, 130.

rolled not only the magnificent bluffs, the pendant isles and heat-shimmered flags, but the panorama of the past — the long extinct Moundbuilders, the enthusiastic voyageur entering a "paradise upon earth." His waters flash always in the crisp radiance of the morning or mellow into milky lustres in the riper splendor of the moonlight; his boat glides as smoothly among the clustering phantoms of past ages as the sparkling vistas of the present, its monotonous engine throbbing now keyed to the fairy echoes of the Canadian chansons, now exulting in that most thrilling of all pastimes — a steamboat race upon the western waters.

Yet no one man could sum up the Romance of the Rivers. For in it was the essence of the life of many people; it embodied the imaginings of several generations. The wind-capped ripples of the Ohio and the resistless torrent of the Mississippi not only provided perpetual novelty for the dwellers on their banks; they transported produce; they afforded communication; they conditioned existence. They developed distinct character types; in brief they epitomized the drama of progress. For in the change that took place from the time the first cumbrous broad-horn wabbled down the Ohio to be peppered by lurking Indians, perhaps wrecked in mysterious cross-currents, or still more from the time that the fleeting native canoe alone startled the kingfisher till the Mississippi steamers became synonyms for luxury are exemplified the changes of the tributary countries. Of this fact Timothy Flint gave one of the most interesting demonstrations. As he journeyed, the second great flux to the West was taking place; the heavy forests of the sacred hunting grounds were in most places levelled; prosperous cities like Cincinnati were already endeavoring to promote art and polite literature; the ease and opulence of life in Kentucky had long given the minister his famous peroration (that Heaven was a Kentuck of a place). In like manner the river craft had enormously developed. The emigrant arriving at Pittsburgh or Wheeling had almost limitless choice of conveyance — the stately barge, the keel-boat, the Kentucky flat, the "covered sleds" and Alleghany skiffs, the laboriously hollowed-out pirogues. The uses of these crafts were as various as their structure. Not only did they carry families with their flocks and household possessions in patriarchal fashion to the promised land;[62] they made with the abundant supplies of the new West the long trip to New Orleans; and by the Yankees they were ingeniously devised for the purpose of livelihood. Down the Mississippi drifted a large tinner's establishment where articles were manufactured and sold by wholesale and retail; floating dry goods stores and groceries were more frequent than in the Spanish and French regime; a complete blacksmith's shop and a grist mill were described; Tyrone Power even chronicled a floating theatre run by a former Covent Garden actor, Elder Chapman, to whom he whimsically wished "the undisputed sovereignty of the Mississippi circuit."[63] Invention changed, too, the means of locomotion; bucket wheels and horse power were utilized to lessen the toil of the passage. "Indeed," Flint concludes, "every spring brings forth new contrivances of this sort, the result of the farmer's meditations over his winter's fire."[64]

Inevitably under such conditions there developed a peculiar life — a pleasant picaresque one where families pitched camp for a while by the side of the stream, then, wearying of continuous residence and having their eyes always on a better land in the West, embarked kin and goods upon the capacious bosom of the flat. Those were the days when to the inexperienced traveller the *Pittsburgh Navigator* was the surest aid;[65] days when by the lonely dwellers in forest and champagne, diversion was found in the hails of passing barks. And reading today of the aimless descent with the current, while the smoke of breakfast fires coiled lazily into the ascending mists of the hillsides and the amorous lisp of the wavelets lulled to repose, or of the dancing to scraping fiddles mingled with the badinage of fleeting sweethearts, we find suggestion in plenty of the seductiveness of the river. To the stripling along the banks the silver, leaping bugle was challenge; its sounding, a promise; its high call, adventure.

62 Hall, Judge James — *Letters from the West* . . . 1828. 87-8.

63 Power — *Impressions of America* . . . (1833-5). 1836. II: 210.

64 Flint, Timothy — *Recollections of the Last Ten Years* . . . *in the Valley of the Mississippi* . . . 1826. 105. Latrobe — *Rambler in N.A.* I:93-4 gives a good condensed description of the various types of vessels as do many other travellers. For illustrations see Dunbar, Seymour — *Travel in America,* 4v. 1915. and contemporary sketches such as Lesueur's and Lewis's.

65 River guides were compiled under various titles, running through many editions. At first they were designed to be an aid to the voyager descending the river in his own craft; later they became a sort of tourists' guide. There were many obstacles to navigation, the chief being snags, sawyers, and sand-bars. According to Lewis dwellers by a riffle resembled farmers by a mud-hole at present. *Wis. Hist. Coll.* XXII:33.

And so we find thousands responding as boatmen — Irishmen, Germans, Kentuckians, backwoodsmen of all sorts, who by their swarms quite submerged their Canadian forerunners.[66] Theirs was the breed "half-horse, half-alligator with a cross of the wild-cat," whose picturesque boasts were the joy of the artist, but whose profligacy drew upon them the wrath of the godly. Variously and superlatively they were denounced — the most depraved creatures in human form whose "habits and education seem to comprehend every vice,"[67] "the most riotous and lawless set of people in America,"[68] "coarse and ferocious caricatures of the London bargemen" whose "chief occupation seems to consist in drinking, fighting, and gambling."[69] Undoubtedly much of this invective was thoroughly deserved. The terrific strain of their labors (according to Flint, "No life is so slavish, none so precarious and dangerous")[70] brought equally intense dissipations. The escape from lurking snags where the turbid waters sucked greedily, the frequent early contests with river pirates, the blackguarding of rival boat crews conspired to produce characteristic exaggerations; the long waits in port encouraged dissipation; flyting matches degenerated into fights with their attendant horrors of biting, kicking, stabbing, and gouging. According to one traveller, "At New Orleans where many boats' crews meet together, they are the terror of all the peaceable inhabitants;"[71] the vice of the Natchez they made proverbial throughout America.[72] Indeed at this time and through the influence of these roisterers arose much of the unsavory aroma that clouds sinisterly even today the name river town.

Yet at the very moment of the boatmen's wildest revelry entered the factor that was to set at naught most early predictions of settlement and that was to change incredibly the history of the Middle West. "It was in the year 1811," according to Flagg, who gives the most effective summary, "that the steam-

---

66 Alexander Wilson gives a vivid conception of the numbers of these boatmen, whom he met returning from New Orleans along the Natchez Trace. See his *Poems & Literary Prose* ed. by Grosart. 1876. For other statistics see R. S. Cotterill — *The Natchez Trace, La. Hist. Quar.* V:259ff.

67 Trollope, Mrs. Frances E. — *Domestic Manners of the Americans.* 2v. 1901. 23,

68 Ferrall, S. A. — *A Ramble of 6000 Mi. through the U. S. of Amer.* 1832. 245.

69 Murray, C. A. — *Travels in N. A.* . . . . (1834-6) 2v.. 1839. II:73.

70 Flint, T. — *Recollections.* 16.

136.

71 Blane, W. M. — *Excursion through the U. S. & Can.* . . . 1822-23. 1824.

72 Ashe, Thomas — *Travels in America performed in 1806* . . . 1809. 317.

engine commenced its giant labours in the Valley of the West . . . Many events . . . united to render this year a most remarkable era in the annals of Western history. The spring-freshet of the rivers buried the whole valley from Pittsburgh to New-Orleans in a flood; and when the waters subsided unparalleled sickness and mortality ensued. . . . The magnificent comet of the year . . . was beheld blazing along the midnight sky, and shedding its lurid twilight over forest and stream; and when the leaves of autumn began to rustle to the ground, the whole vast Valley of the Mississippi rocked and vibrated in earthquake-convulsion! . . . All this was the prologue to that mighty drama of *Change* which, from that period to the present, has been sweeping over the Western Valley; it was the fearful welcome-home to that all-powerful agent which has revolutionized the character of half a continent; for at that epoch of wonders, and amid them all, the first steam boat was seen descending the great rivers, and the awe-struck Indian on the banks beheld the *Pinelore* flying through the troubled waters.''[73]

With unparalleled rapidity the steamboat changed the course of civilization in the valley. The cumbersome flat boat and the redolent rafts of pine were still used for heavy freighting;[74] the swaggering boatman still drew the admiration of small boys, but gradually he was being supplanted in their affections by the lordly pilot, the dignified captain, even the sweat-begrimed fireman or the majestic waiter.[75] The fitful rhythms of the deck hand, the port and lading chants of the negro laborer now sounded above the interminable ballads of the backwoodsmen as they in turn had surmounted the carols of the French. The lordly settler, the eternal small town loafer no longer darted forth at the call of the bugle; instead they were stirred by the jangling of steamer bells, the monotonous soundings of the leadsmen. For steadily the number and speed of the steamboats increased. River dwellers watched at regular hours for these graceful passers in the mist, which, even from the sophisticated traveller, elicited the comparison of fairy castles; the crews gained proud friends at

---

73 *E. W. T.* XXVI:62-4. See also Latrobe — *Rambler in N. A.* I:88 ff.

74 Note for instance N. P. Willis's description of the flat boats in his *Health Trip to the Tropics.* 1850. 382.

75 It is said the river trade was so important in the commerce of the day that cloth was woven for the pilots' trousers representing the course of the Mississippi. *Mo. Hist. Coll.* III:415-16.

every port; favorite boats had enthusiastic backers, and strained every boiler to out-distance a competitor or to establish a new record. The passage from Pittsburgh to New Orleans and back which thirty years before, according to Tudor, had "occupied as much time as *three voyages across the Atlantic* . . . is accomplished within a shorter period *than a single average passage from New York to London or Liverpool.*"[76] Immense areas, which, because of the difficulties of ascending the stream, observers had prophesied would be for a century uninhabited, were divided almost over night into corn fields and town sites. Deck passengers thronged into the empty places; cabin passengers exultingly proclaimed the magnificent panoramas, the natural wonders, and the possibilities of the West.

For as a result of the new invention and the consequent ease and comfort of travel, there came visitors of a new type — cultivated men and women who sometimes for business, sometimes for pleasure, floated up and down the river and recorded their experiences. Almost always they pay tribute to the vessels and their fittings although Mrs. Trollope searingly qualifies her praise of the handsome carpet by the remark that its condition was worthy the pen of a Swift, and although the conduct in the dining halls calls for general censure. Almost always, too, there is found praise of the river. It is the "leviathan artery of the North American continent,"[77] a stream incomparable for "magnificence and utility," which affected both the prosaic traveller and the sensitive actor, Power, as he lay dreaming over the rushing midnight loveliness beyond the orgies of Natchez. And as these tourists passed from the cool green shades of the North, by the bearded forests of Red River where dizzying swarms of mosquitoes droned over alligators half buried in the swamp's viscous puddles, to emerge at last into the honeyed fragrance of the great plantations with their gleaming sugar fields, their rich clusters of oranges, they reflect successive stages in the transformation of the country. Dreary wood-cutters' huts peer on staggering piles through the dense vegetation; towns staked out by ambitious promoters spring up, magic beanstalk growths; more

---

76 Tudor — *Narr. of a Tour in N. A.* II:36. Flint summarizes well the effect of the steamboat. *Hist. & Geog. of the Miss. Val.* 2v. 1832. I:156.

77 Murray, Hon. H. A. — *Lands of the Slave and the Free* . . . 2v. 1855. I:212.

and more frequent are the tiny landing places, more and more costly, the hold-filling cargoes.

Those were the golden days of the South — days when the healthy new settlements coined through her their produce, when to her there thronged all sorts of romantic adventurers. In New Orleans' crescent-shaped harbour swayed the vessels of a thousand ports; in her narrow-balconied streets blended the folk of many nations. Never had she been so prosperous; slaves worked until late in the night amid the flickering fire-shadows of the levee; planters, merchants, mariners crowded the gambling hells, theatres, and race tracks. As to morals, "the word is obsolete," cries one shocked traveller;[78] "Here broad indeed is the road to ruin," laments Evans;[79] "A modern Sodom," protest still others while the scenes of desperation and distress yearly arising from the high play caused even the cosmopolitan Power to praise the legislative restrictions. But on the surface all is color, gaiety, fragrance — sun-warmed stuccoes not yet elbowed out by the garish red of Yankee brick; cloying, waxen-petalled magnolias dripping their sweetness into the moonlight; glittering ballrooms; brilliantly caparisoned horses — a foaming, frothing tide of life, the rainbow sheen of which even the terror-filled days of the yellow fever epidemics could only enhance; a tide mounting higher and higher till the desolation of the war, the terrors of carpetbagger supremacy, and the increasing competition of the railroads combined to break the bright bubble.

Perhaps even more striking illustration of the changes taking place may be found up the river — at Natchez, for instance, the "Vide Poche" of the French, with its well-plotted upper town, its chivalric society. There is exemplified the increase of material prosperity as in its disreputable lower section is evidenced the increase of order and law. For although Power chronicles barrooms, dance halls, and faro banks or roulette tables in full operation most of the day, he was permitted to prowl about unmolested; according to his own comment, "at Natchy-under-hill, manners, if not morals, are improving. Murder is not nigh so common here as it was a few seasons back."[80] Mackay even records a wholesale lynching at Vicksburg "of the gamblers, and

78 Knight, H. C. — *Letters from the South & West.* 1824. 125.
79 *E. W. T.* VIII: 336.
80 Power — *Impressions.* II:156.

blacklegs, who had made Natchez too hot to hold them."[81] This latter is perhaps the most notable example of the work of the regulators; steadily, however, the development of community consciousness goes on. In instance after instance is recorded the passing of the riffraff that inevitably congregates on the border and of which the early travelers gave evil report. Texas instead of the Yazoo becomes the favorite refuge of desperadoes; slovenly justice is treated to a taste of the medicine it had been loath to administer; men bringing their families are determined to stabilize their surroundings. On the steamers themselves emerge not only clear types but distinct changes in character. The vessels, for instance, long carry these subtle-fingered gentry, whose profession it was, according to Mrs. Trollope, to "drill the fifty-two elements of a pack of cards to profitable duty,"[82] and glimpses of their skill, their coolness, their unflinching determination long make dramatic bits in the annals of the river; but even in them there is change — from the dirk-flashing brawler of the out-places to the low-voiced, gentlemanly villain that Bret Harte has immortalized. Captains with less frequency are obliged to intervene between braggart Kentuckians and hot-blooded Creoles; fewer stops are made to isolate obstreperous or way-beating passengers; pleasant steamboat acquaintanceships develop. It is a stirring life, an inspiring one, — a restless, never-ceasing ebb and flow in the valley — the harnessing of a giant, the begetting of territories, the migration of peoples — an epoch too soon passing, an epic not yet sung — the triumphantly pulsating Romance of the Rivers.

Meantime the invention of the steamboat had had another effect — that of diverting to the north the immigrants who long had choked the passes of the Alleghanies into Kentucky, Tennessee, Ohio, and West Virginia.[83] The lake country had, of

---

81 Mackay, Alex — *The Western World; or Trav. in the U. S. in 1846-47* . . . 3v. 4th. ed. 1850. III:337. See also Murray, *Trav. in N. A.* II:79-80, Bremer, F. — *Homes in the New World* II:185-6. The "cleaning up of Keokuk" is described in Curtiss, D. S. — *Western Portraiture & Emigrants' Guide* . . . 1852. p. 329.

82 Trollope — *Dom. Man. of the Amer.* 259.

83 The opening of the Erie Canal is, of course, of great importance in this connection. For a helpful survey see Lois K. Matthews — *The Erie Canal & the Settlement of the West. Buf. Hist. Soc. Pub.* XIV:189 ff. T. L. McKenney in *Sketches of a Tour to the Lakes* . . . 1827 states, "It is not possible for me to convey any adequate idea of the wealth which floats upon the canal; nor of the advantages which are experienced from it by the people who live upon its borders, and those more remote settlements throughout the entire region of the northwest. The truth is the canal is in everybody's mouth." p. 59. The arguments for and against the canal

course, been visited and described to a certain extent. Evans, for instance, in his "close dress consisting of buffalo skins" had tramped over it, jumbling in his amusing fashion "rich and spacious flats," tooth-aches, wolves, and habitants.[84] Shirreff, coming down from Canada, in spite of the urging of friends who represented the country to the junction of the rivers Missouri and Mississippi "as a pestilential swamp, inhabited by demi-savages and dangerous animals," had spaded up and tested by vinegar the much-discussed soil, concluding of the prairie in question that "it was of small size, very picturesque, and not likely to repay the expense of draining," a remark typical, by the way, of his standards for description.[85] A steadily increasing number of lonely dwellings were thus revealed and routes were established along the lake shores; but it was not until the late twenties and thirties, the time Shirreff traveled, that the advance guard of speculators and the great throng of homeseekers began to press in. With them came the writers — economists, adventurers, sportsmen, and dreamers — through whose work we have preserved the Titanic awakening of the northwestern frontier.

Again in their reaction there is wonder — not the first childlike ecstacy of the old French explorers, not the bold admiration of the Kentucky pioneers, not the Utopian visions of the social reformers, not even the rapture of the youthful Flagg. They breathe of romance, romance tingling and virile, with a marvellous mingling of elements, the stamp of assured achievement yet the melancholy of decay. These narratives show us once more the Indians, not the filthy, besotted creatures that crave alms in the market at New Orleans, not the fierce and confident warriors who long made Kentucky in truth a "bloody ground," but tribes in a transitional state, still a factor to be reckoned with, yet being steadily, irresistibly shoved from their last strongholds near the Mississippi. At Chicago as Shirreff and Latrobe visit it, thousands of Pottawattomies are gathered to feast at government

---

such as C. G. Haines' *Considerations on the Great Western Canal* . . . (1818) were very important in directing attention toward the Northwest. According to Bradford in his *Notes on the Northwest* (1846) the region around and beyond the Great Lakes, "was almost unknown to geographers twenty years ago." p. 1. C. Colton in his *Tour of the Amer. Lakes* . . . *in 1830* (2v. 1833) says Green Bay was "commonly reckoned the end of the world." I:34.

84 Evans, E. — *A Pedestrious Tour of 4000 Miles through the Western States & Territories* . . . 1818 . . . *E. W. T.* VIII:103.

85 Shirreff, Patrick — *A Tour through North America* . . . 1835. 244, 206.

expense, stippling the prairies with blankets, rag-surmounted tepees, racing ponies, wolfish dogs, whooping children, and grave conclaves of chieftains. Within the village there is equal confusion, — "emigrants and land-speculators as numerous as the sand . . . horse-dealers and horse-stealers,— rogues of every description, white, black, brown, and red — half-breeds, quarter-breeds, and men of no breed at all; — dealers in pigs, poultry, and potatoes; — men pursuing Indian claims, some for tracts of land, others, . . . for pigs which the wolves had eaten; — creditors of the tribes, or of particular Indians, who know that they have no chance of getting their money, if they do not get it from the Government agents; — sharpers of every degree; pedlars, grog-sellers; Indian agents and Indian traders of every description, and Contractors to supply the Pottawattomies with food." Betting and gambling are the order of the day; casks of whisky lie for sale under the very eyes of the Commissioners; everything is "in a state of most appalling confusion, filth, and racket," a disgraceful commentary, in short, on the way too many of the Indian treaties were consummated.

Latrobe's description of the council where after Indian dawdling the Commissioner indulges in Jacksonian threats is also typical, not only of the treaty-making itself but of the whole problem of races — on the countenance of the whites as they face the West, the glorious beams of the setting sun falling full, "while the pale light of the East hardly lighted up the dark and painted lineaments of the poor Indians whose souls evidently clave to their birth-right in that quarter."[86] Throughout all the description of the region this note of defeat is sounded. Harriet Martineau writes of the "poor helpless squalid Potawatomies" restricted within a narrow territory so surrounded by whites that the game is sure soon to disappear and sadly troubled by squatters;[87] Hoffman traversing the winter woods which only six months before were alive with Indians finds only a few intoxicated stragglers and near the settlements a forlorn, half-frozen, half-starved little band. Over and over again we find lingering pathetically aged Indian exiles; the reluctance of the followers

86 Latrobe, C. J. — *Rambler in N.A.* II:152-3, 155, 158. See also De Tocqueville — *Democracy in America* I:295, 342 ff.
87 Martineau, H. — *Soc. in Amer.* I:244.

of Black Hawk to leave their ancient homes was responsible for one of the most tragic episodes in middle western history.[88] Only around the stately walls of Fort Snelling, the foaming rapids of Sault Ste. Marie, and the fairy isle of Michilimackinac hover reminiscences of the natives' primitive glory. There by vivid, spurting rolls of birch-bark the Indians spear fish in the night-tarnished depths of the lake, hunt in their wild rice thickets with their former independence, realize, in short, the travellers' "ideas of the wild and lordly savage." There the Indian dandies retain their original beautifully quilled and beaded costumes instead of donning the European incongruities that disfigure the less isolated tribes; there in the Elysian beauty of the summer nooning the warriors honor their guests by their barbaric dances. There the old bloody feuds still burst out in spite of government prohibition. There to the kissing of wavelets, the fluting of balsam, gentle Chippeway mothers croon lullabies; the tribal ancients ponder their primitive wisdom. Yet these are fleeting glimpses, the more poignant as we realize the rapidity of their passing and the infrequency of their occurrence. For instead of them we find usually even in the work of men as dashing as Oliphant, as open minded as Latrobe, as theatrical as Beltrami, sketches of the filth, the degradation, the wretchedness, and squalor, almost inevitable accompaniments of the savage life, especially after the encroachments of the whites checked the former freedom of movement and hastened the native decline. The attitude of these northwestern travellers is, on the whole, a remarkably fair one; what criticism there is of the government seems to be deserved; comprehension is shown of the anger of the frontiersman as well as righteous indignation at his extremes of vengeance; sharp complaints of the ignorant and doctrinaire mis-

88 *Life of Ma-Ka-Tai-Me-Me-She-Kia-Kiah or Black Hawk* . . . 1833 is a dispassionate but moving indictment of the selfishness and injustice of the whites that continually pushed the red men to the west. The greed for land was almost universal. Edwin James in his edition of *A Narrative of the Captivity & Adventures of John Tanner* (1830) gave one of the few contemporary protests against the treatment of the Indians. When they tried to resist, the soldiers who punished them brought back reports of the land which increased the influx of settlers. An interesting illustration of the way feeling was fomented against the natives and the literature of the captivities, adapted to suit the interests of the hour is found in the *Narrative of the Captivity and Sufferings of Mrs. Hannah Lewis, & her 3 Children, who were taken prisoners by the Indians, near St. Louis, . . . 1815 . . .* (1817) which was reprinted as *Nar. of the Cap. & Providential Escape of Mrs. Jane Lewis . . . made prisoners . . . by a party of . . . of the tribes of Sacs & Foxes commanded by Black Hawk.* 1833.

sionaries are balanced by tributes to the self-sacrifice of their solitary lives and sympathy for the comparatively small results which they achieve; the continental sentimentality, long so warping a factor in the Indian problem, loses its potency in the face of reality. The general attitude seems summed up in Latrobe's few sentences:

> "Even though convinced of the necessity of their removal, my heart bled for them in their desolation and decline. Ignorant and degraded as they may have been in their original state, their degradation is now ten-fold, after years of intercourse with the whites; and their speedy disappearance from the earth appears as certain as though it were already sealed and accomplished."[89]

The pictures of them are tinctured with the pathos of their passing; to the idealization that had from the beginning surrounded their existence with idyllic glamour succeeds a pensive comprehension no less romantic.

In much the same spirit are described the French Canadians. Of these the most conspicuous, perhaps, are the voyagers or crapauds, who, long outnumbered on the highway of the lower river, yet retain in the north their ancient supremacy. Flint they had dragged laboriously up the Mississippi, entertaining him at night as they lolled by the fragrant fire of red cedar with gorgeous tales of their conquests in love and in battle; Oliphant they shoot deftly over the rapids; Marryat they disgust by their gorging of raw pork; Latrobe they furnish both care and amusement. In his lively pages, indeed, we find our fullest sketch of the type — rogues all — "born without consciences," and with never a chance of acquiring them since, "men who would dance from night to morning at a Gombo ball — sing profane or pastoral French songs hour after hour on the water, — drink and smoke, — cheat their creditors, live for months in the woods, — work like slaves without grumbling when they could not help it — swim like otters, — maintain their French gaiety of character on most occasions, but grumble incessantly when they had nothing to grumble about."[90] Their laziness when unsupervised; their glut-

89 Latrobe — *Rambler in N.A.* II:158.

90 *Ibid.* 199; 200-1. See *Mich. Pion. & Hist. Coll.* XXXIX:245 for a very similar description of a voyageur's life by one of them.

tony that drove Marryat and his companions from regaling them with salt pork and whiskey to dealing out a diet of salt fish and a broomstick; their exorbitant pay demands when they thought their employers were trapped; all these cast on them most unfavorable lights. Yet they are withal most engaging rascals "with that Troubadour air, or gaieté de coeur," which Schoolcraft best summarized when he said, "To conquer distance and labor, at the same time, with a song, has occurred to no other people."[91]

Akin to them, of course, are the fur-traders who yet hold forth at Mackinac and Chicago — "a swarthy scowling race evidently tinged with Indian blood, speaking the French and Indian languages fluently, and much addicted to swearing and whiskey."[92] Picturesque, too, are the habitants near Detroit, with their one-horse carts which the bad roads render necessary, their sturdy ponies, and, in the winter, their gayly trimmed fur robes, and orange, green, and red capotes. Like their fellows to the South, "They go on exactly as their ancestors did a century ago, raising on their rich fertile lands just sufficient for a subsistence, wholly uneducated, speaking only a French *patois,* without an idea of advance or improvement of any kind, submissive to their priests, gay, contented, courteous, and apparently retaining their ancestral tastes for dancing, singing, and flowers."[93] Like their fellows, too, they are not only forced to rapid adjustment but threatened with engulfment, extermination at least of their distinctive society.

Momentarily, however, their old charm lingers; momentarily, too, the life of the incoming races is as darkly iridescent, as foamy-crested as any of the lake waves that break on the rock reefs of Michigan. Those were the mining days of the upper Mississippi, days when the metals for which Le Sueur and others had sought, which the Indian squaws and old men had dug and

---

91 Schoolcraft, H. R. — *Summary Narr. of an Explor. Exped. to the Sources of the Mississippi River, in 1820* . . . 1855, 124. See Barbeau & Sapir — *Folk Songs of French Canada* (1925), for some of the old canoe songs.

92 Shirreff — *Tour.* 228. One of the most vivid accounts of their life is given in *Letters on the Fur Trade 1833* by Wm. Johnston, a half breed brother-in-law of Schoolcraft. *Mich. Pion. & Hist. Coll.* XXXVII:132 ff. The documents on the fur trade are, of course, too numerous to go into. v. 19 & 20 of the *Wis. Hist. Coll.* give, for instance, much valuable material. See also Perrault's *Narrative. Mich. Pion & Hist. Coll.* XXXVII:508 ff.

93 Jameson, Mrs. — *Winter Studies & Summer Rambles in Canada.* 2v. 1839. II:64.

sold by the hundred pounds to the traders, were the prey of adventurers. From all over the world they came, "the most wonderful mixture of humanity that ever I beheld," according to Murray, "but chiefly from Ireland, Derbyshire, Cornwall and Germany. Besides the emigrants from the above and other places, there are fugitives from law and justice, from every part . . . thieves, pirates, deserters."[94] Belted coats of Kentucky jeans rub against fringed hunting frocks, the broadcloth of the investor, the supple finery of the Winnebago chieftains. High wages cause the men according to contemporary report, to work little more than half their time, and spend the remaining half chiefly in drinking, gambling, quarreling, dirking and pistolling one another; one journalist wrote, "The laws they carry in their pockets and are ready to read a chapter on the slightest occasion."[95] The life, although now almost forgotten, was as high-pressured, as extravagant, as contradictory, as swaggering, in short, as that of any California mining camp celebrated by Bret Harte.

And even of that far western life there was strangely enough here in the Northwest reminiscence. For as Oliphant and his companions "galloped over the grass, flushing prairie chickens," they passed a solitary California traveller, with his slashed and button-bedecked jacket, his many-daggered girdle, his high-peaked saddle, such a specimen as one would suppose to be extant only "in museums of Spanish curiosities." And amid the medley of ambitious Yankees and stolid Germans, that sprawl snoring in the wind-swept loft of the embryo Superior's only hotel, lank-haired, unkempt men quarrel by guttering candle light over the faro that they have brought with them from the diggings.[96] The recoil that Flint had anticipated had already be-

94 Murray — *Trav. in N.A.* II:78. In 1810 the Indian agent at Prairie du Chien reported that the Indians about the lead mines had largely abandoned the chase and turned to the manufacture of lead, which they sold to the traders. In 1825 there were about 100 white men in the lead region, and by 1829 they numbered into the thousands.

95 *Ia. Hist. Record.* XV:548. For other accounts of the riotous life see Schultz, Christian, *Travels on an Inland Voyage* . . . 2v. 1810. II: 52-3. *Wis. His. Coll.* XV:287-8, 358, 365, 379, 382. Early accounts of the mines are given *Ibid.* XV: 331-2, 338, 345, V: 317, VI: 271, XIII: 271, etc. Bradford in his *Notes on the N. W.* (1846) estimates the output as worth a million and a half annually. p. 154. For contemporary quotations on less spectacular phases of settlement see D. E. Clark — *The Westward Movement in the Upper Mississippi Valley during the Fifties, Miss. Vall. Hist. Soc. Proc.* VII: 212.

96 Oliphant, Laurence — *Minnesota & the Far West.* 1855. 302. 303, 162-3.

gun.[97] Much of it must be attributed, of course, to the lust for adventure, the luring lottery of speculation that, once the excitement of the gold rush had died away, led men to the newly opened territories. Yet, reading of the men who having made a stake in California returned to settle down on a middle western farm, we wonder if the desire for physical well-being was the only reason for their return. We like to think that as the forty-niners hastened feverishly past the fronding goldenrod, the brilliant clumps of black-eyed Susans, the beauty of the flowering meadows sank in more deeply than they knew; that during the gasping labor after straining oxen where eyeless buffalo skulls, dismantled schooners bleached on the hot sands, there mingled with the usual desert chimeras recollections of the cool waters and pleasant pastures far in the background.

Certainly there was beauty enough in all these yet unsettled regions to draw anyone back — even over the craggy steeps of the mountains, the parching terrors of the desert. And of them all perhaps most luscious is the region of Michigan, Minnesota, and Wisconsin. There in the winding channels of the upper lakes, creamy fields of water lilies open golden centres to the morning; jewel-like islands, rock-ribbed, moss-piled, hover luminous in the glory of the sunset. The stark whiteness of the dunes contrasts with the heavy thickets of the northern woods where great chunks of pure copper dazzle the investor. Everywhere there is the charm of infinite variety; everywhere, the sense of illimitable loveliness, far-stretching meadows, lustrous, perfume-breathing, "where no hand ever reaps, no finger ever culls, and but few feet ever tread."[98] An old New England farmer decided on White Pigeon Prairie as the place where Adam and Eve resided;[99] of the wilderness of trailing roses, enormous white convolvulus, scarlet lilies, and ground ivy, Harriet Martineau remarks, "Milton must have travelled in Michigan before he wrote the garden parts of 'Paradise Lost.' "[100] The world is one vacant for the most part of its old inhabitants, unscathed as yet by the new.

97 Flint, T. — *Recollections.* 206. "In the generations to come, when the tide of immigration shall have reached the western sea, and the recoil shall begin to fix the people of these open plains in Illinois and Missouri, on their prairies, then they will plant these naked, but level and rich tracts; . . ."

98 Latrobe — *Rambler in N.A.* I:41.

99 Shirreff — *Tour.* 219.

100 Martineau — *Soc. in Amer.* I:241.

Already intangibly it seems marked out for one of the play places of the continent — a delight to the hunter and fisher, a haven for the summer cottager. Marryat compares the flatness of the prairie to a billiard table;[101] as a game preserve the old keeper estimates the possibilities of the Fon-du-lac region. Flapping lake trout delight the fisherman near Mackinac; the stately muscallonge glides through the sun-splotched lakes of Wisconsin. The officers of Fort Snelling pursue all sorts of game in the season; after witnessing the amazing abundance of wild-fowl, bears, and deer, McKinnon concludes that, "With proper dogs, the sport on the western prairies would greatly surpass any afforded on the best moors in Scotland."[102]

And through all the annals of settlement this play spirit continues. "Le vin, le jeu, les belles" are the order on the steamers; desolate as are the shores on which the immigrants are dumped with their huge rolls of bedding, their clattering household utensils, resorts are always near, such as that at Sault Ste. Marie with tourists "doing the agreeable to the ladies" who "with pink and white complexions, black ringlets, bright dresses, and thin satin shoes, reclined gracefully upon carpet bags and presided over pyramids of band-boxes."[103] The growth of Chicago seems a pageant — the "little upstart village" with "frame and clapboard houses springing up daily under the active axes and hammers of the speculators,"[104] and "a negro, dressed up in scarlet" announcing the hours of sale;[105] the laying out of St. Paul, a game where Mr. Cook, "whose industrious wife attended to the affairs of the hotel, did little else than mark and name new streets, avenues, squares and parks."[106] In a spirit of play the Red River settlers make rendezvous in the new territory; boisterous merrymaking marks most of the descriptions. There were hardships, to be sure (no frontier was without them), stern facing of difficult tasks such as Harriet Bishop and other pioneers chronicle. Yet the same volume that relates the debauches of drunken Indians and the difficulty of establishing schools and churches, describes

---

101 Marryat, Capt. F. — *A Diary in America.* II:46.
102 Mackinnon, Capt. R.N. — *Atlantic & Transatlantic Sketches* . . . 2v. 1852. I:253.
103 Oliphant — *Minn. & the Far West.* 133, 103.
104 Latrobe — *Rambler in N.A.* II:149. 154.
105 Martineau — *Soc. in Amer.* I:259.
106 Peyton, J. L. — *Over the Alleghanies & across the Prairies* . . . 1869. 242.

the exploration by a holiday party in a specially chartered steamer of St. Peter's River, the light-heartedness which they made decision that the land must be obtained from the natives being characteristic of the region.[107] Over and over again this note is sounded. Not the numbing cold of the plain-sweeping winds, not the frigid monotony of the blinding snow expanses, but the gaieties of the winter absorb Hoffman's attention — the frontier ball at Chicago, the furiously racing carioles on the river, the game of prairie loo as the sleigh glides over the glittering crust, or "that most exciting of all sports, a wolf-chase on horseback."[108]

Very different from all this is the settlement of the Kansas-Nebraska region, Kansas especially being a storm centre. New Englanders and opponents of slavery in the other sections were urged to make the state free in an abolitionist crusade; according to Williams, a representative of the southern point of view, they "poured men and arms into the territory regardless of expense."[109] In the South feeling was equally intense; companies were organized and "war-funds" raised to win the state; Gladstone pictures the slaveholders as bent on "driving back at the point of the bayonet the nigger-stealing scum poured down by Northern fanaticism";[110] Missourians from "uttering prophecies, born of their desires, that the 'northwesters' would blow the Yankees away" soon organized systematically volunteer companies as the Kickapoo Rangers, Platte County Rifles, and Shot-Gun Militia for election frauds, pillage, and general terrorism, with the motto of "Ball to the muzzle, knife to the hilt!"

---

107 Bishop, H. — *Floral Home* . . . 1857. 285.

108 Hoffman, C. F. — *A Winter in the West.* 2v. 1835. I:247.

109 Williams, R. H., Sometime lieutenant in the Kansas rangers . . . *With the Border Ruffians* . . . 1907. 82. See also N. H. Parker — *The Kan. & Neb. Handbook.* 1857. 51. Eli Thayer's history of *The Kansas Crusade* was published 1883. For reminiscences of a settler drawn by the crusade see *Kan. Hist. Soc. Pub.* II: 11ff. W. H. Carruth discusses *The New England Emigrant Aid Company as an Investment Society* . . . *Kan. Hist. Coll.* VI: 90ff. For Gov. A. H. Reeder's plan of help for Kansas see *Kan. Hist. Soc. Pub.* I:30. Emerson's speech at a Kansas Relief meeting is given in his *Miscellanies. Complete Wks.* XI:241 and gives a good idea of contemporary feeling.

110 Gladstone, T. H. — *Englishman in Kansas: or, Squatter Life & Border Warfare.* 1857, 6. Williams' book cited above is particularly valuable since most of the narratives are from the northern side. For the reminiscences of another Southern participant see A. Morrall — *Pro-slavery Soldier in Kansas, Kan. Hist. Coll.* XIV:123ff. W. L. Fleming in *The Buford Expedition to Kansas* (*Trans. of the Ala. Hist. Soc.* IV: 167ff.) gives an excellent account of feeling and activities in the South. See also J. C. Malin's *The Pro-slavery Background of the Kansas Struggle, Miss. Val. Hist. Rev.* 10:285ff., Mary J. Klem's *Missouri in the Kansas Struggle M.V.H.A. Proc.* IX:393ff., E. L. Craik's study of southern attempts to induce emigration to Kansas, *Documents illustrating the Troubles on the Border, 1858 and 1859. Mo. Hist. Rev.* I:198.

And so to the territories that Lewis and Clark had described yet untenanted by the white man are brought new and strange elements.[111] Steamers ascend the Missouri now with the most motley of passengers and freights; United States troops, mountain men, negroes jamming the steerage; officers, Santa Fé traders, gamblers, speculators, Mormon elders, Eastern ministers and college men thronging the cabin. Kansas City is in a state of rapid development that causes building lots to be "selling at almost fabulous prices" and wages for all kinds of mechanics and laborers to be "fifty per cent higher than in the East"; Lawrence, the free-staters' stronghold, is a mushroom growth on the prairie; Franklin, West Point, and other pro-slavery towns have sprung up as rival camps; swaggering marauders swarm into the district. Of these and other changes we have exceptionally full record. For many years voyagers up the Missouri had sketched the lovely vistas of its banks; overland travellers, portrayed the places they passed; with the opening for settlement the usual flood of guide-books and immigrant manuals such as Boynton and Mason's *A Journey through Kansas* . . . (1855) or Greene's *Kansas Region* . . . (1856) chant the charms of the country.

These are, however, the conventional rhapsodies. The distinctive feature of this frontier is the strife between parties, a strife that was to equal in terrors the atrocities of savage warfare and that was to foreshadow in its tendencies the great national conflict. Of it the first note worthy our notice, perhaps, is Edward Everett Hale's *Kansas and Nebraska* . . . (1854) which, a careful compound from many sources, discusses the history, nature, tribes, routes of travel, and political development of the region "from a wish to share in the great enterprise of settling Kansas at once." More stirring is Mrs. Robinson's *Kansas; its Interior and Exterior Life,* a book almost as influential in its way for a time as *Uncle Tom's Cabin.* Written "amid all the inconveniences of tent life" at Lecompton where her husband was a state prisoner, it pours out all the pent-up bitterness of long

111 W. O. Lynch in his *Popular Sovereignty & the Colonization of Kansas, Miss. Val. Hist. Assoc. Proc.* IX:380ff shows that the effect of the struggle in peopling the region has been over-emphasized. His article brings out, however, the point that is made here — that a vast amount of advertising was given to Kansas. A. D. Richardson in his *Beyond the Mississippi* (1867) said that Kansas was already famous historically. C. C. Hutchinson in *Resources & Development of Kan.* (1871) says it was regarded "as a pandemonium of savage Indians and border ruffians."

months of outrage, "the daily news of some friend made prisoner or butchered with a malignity more than human, — the devastation of burning homes, by the connivance of the Governor, under the eye of the troops." Yet it has a tenderness for the new land, in spite of all its hardships, that dates back to a child's speculation on the semi-circular lines in fine letters, "Great American Desert, inhabited only by savages and wild beasts." In it are made articulate new complexes on the prairie — a childlike delight after coming from "the bleak and hilly north" in the rioting blossoms, a feeling of deep insignificance beneath a mighty creative power. The essence of the life is different; snowy linens, vases of flowers, pictures and engravings contrast with the dirt floors and slab furnishings of the oft-moving squatter; white churches with heaven-pointing spires overlook the rolling prairie; a bookstore, circulating library, and Unitarian parish library give choice of reading at Lawrence; military suppers, melon parties, drives, and calls provide recreation. Yet the very tranquillity of such outward observances makes the more intense the real spiritual agony. Ever present is the strain of ruffian invasions, imprisonment of men whose sin it is to be free-staters, tumultuous searching of houses, ferocious murders. Sabres flash now on the prairie; entrenchments are thrown by flickering torch light around the threatened city; little boys march in martial array; "hurrying bands of horsemen, brutal in their aspect" blot the fair landscape. Yet however wanton the outrages, however fraudulent the elections, however unjust the decisions, the resolution remains unchanged; if anything it is deepened. The fixed conception that, "This country, than which the sun shines upon no fairer, . . . was never to be cursed with the blackest of all villainies, the bitterest of all evils — human slavery," dominates all else.[112]

No other book could so adequately portray the ardor of the free-staters; *Six Months in Kansas* presents, however, an interesting contrast. The writer, "a Lady of Boston," cheerful as she is in the face of the domestic difficulties of a one room log cabin, good Samaritan as she shows herself in the frequent cases of sickness, proves not the stuff of which martyrs are made. The Missourians, she laments, "shoot at defenceless people with as

112 Robinson, Sara T. L. — *Kansas*. 7th. ed. 1857. III,III, 1, 240, 6.

much cool indifference as they would at partridges or prairie chickens." But these are things that her "poor woman's head does not pretend to sift, or unravel." "Heart-sick at all this fuss," she determines to go back to Massachussetts "for the present," and where Mrs. Robinson's book ends with the assurance that Lawrence "will come forth from its early burial clothed with yet more exceeding beauty," the Boston lady's is tolled out to the requiem — "Lawrence is dead. Lawrence is dead." Perhaps because of this very evident softness of fibre, the accounts of the settlers' hardships impress the more — winds from the Rocky Mountains rocking the cabin like a cradle, water congealing upon the stove hearth, the freezing of women's feet as they went about their housework.[113]

Unfortunately both her emotion and her diction are often stilted, the latter fault being found, also, in the record of a clergyman constantly harassed because of the complaint that he was "not sound on the goose." Valued glimpses as the writer gives of the scattered "foundations," the makeshift furniture, or such primitive modes of agriculture as chopping in seed with an axe on thirty-five acres, his book has too many statements about territorial government and politics to be a stimulating personal narrative, and is too lacking in unity and too poorly organized to give a satisfactory view of the Kansas trouble. Its chief value is its presentation of the toilsome and unrewarded life of a missionary; its author, a homely and inadequate hero, is yet revealed a fine contrast to the blustering and slave-supporting head of the Shawnee mission and to too many illiterate itinerants.[114]

But these are narratives of participants. Illuminating from other points of view are the volumes produced by outsiders. Prominent among these latter are the newspaper correspondents — Brewerton, the representative of the New York Herald, who in his *Wars of the Western Border* . . . (1857) describes with considerable humor and verve the trials of ramshackle wagons, squalid, icy taverns, rut-ploughed roads; Phillips, who from "the seat of war" sent information to the New York *Tribune* and who in his *Conquest of Kansas by Missouri and her Allies* (1856)

113 Ropes, Mrs. — *Six Months in Kansas.* 1856. 208, 208, 230. For the quotation from Mrs. Robinson see her *Kansas.* 348.

114 *Three Years on the Kansas Border* (1856). Advocates of slavery were considered "sound on the goose." For an excellent account of the "foundations," i.e. the devices for marking claims, see p. 175.

presents not only a clear statement of events and many vivid characterizations, but valuable documents, newspaper extracts, and letters from Pro-Slavery as well as Free-State forces; Gladstone, who as an *Englishman in Kansas* (1857) sketched with remarkable fairness his impressions for *The Times*. For us their interest is, of course, the human one, the glimpses of that seething caldron of society that made up the Kansas of the fifties.

Unquestionably outstanding are the border ruffians, "that eccentric class of Western men, who, being persons of terrible experiences, claim to 'scream louder, jump higher, shoot closer, get more drunk at night, and wake up more sober in the morning than any other human this side of the Rocky Mountains, and 'ef you don't believe it,' it's 'I'm easy to whip, stranger, I *am*, just pitch in, will yeou, and don't stand on ceremony,' with, mayhap, a flourish from a horn-handled bowie-knife to second the invitation.'"[115] The type at its purest is worthy successor to the Mississippi boatmen, of whom, indeed, the borderers furnish reminiscence not only in their oft-quoted boasts but in the epithets applied to them. In their uncouthness they glory; dribbling tobacco juice, earth-stained flannel shirts, unquotable oaths, these seem their concomitants. At the first hint of trouble they congregate in such numbers as to make one writer wonder whence come "all the hard customers on the Missouri frontier." In other writers is found the answer. According to Phillips, "most of them have been over the Plains several times, — if they have not been over the plains, the probability is, they have served through the war in Mexico, or seen a 'deal of trouble in Texas'; or, at least, run up and down the Missouri river often enough to catch imitative inspiration from the cat-fish aristocracy, and penetrate the sublime mystery of euchre or poker."[116] Others report bands of men marching from the far-off Carolinas, partly "because they wish to uphold slavery," mainly because "it is the prevalent kind of rascality." Of them there are all shades from the whiskey-guzzling boaster to the gentlemanly judicial type. For all of them, however, the title is a source of pride: "I am a border ruffian, I am; none of your city-raised

115 Brewerton, G. D. — *Wars of the Western Border*. 73.

116 Phillips, Wm. — *Conquest of Kansas*, 28. Col. Eldridge gives a similar explanation. "Politics substituted for trade, the plainsman developed into the border ruffian and in due time graduated with the degree of bushwhacker." *Kan. Hist. Soc. Pub.* II:31.

Down-easters." For their adherents, too, the name is a standby; Gihon reports it painted in flaming capitals on an omnibus; Gladstone records it given to a steamboat, a favorite horse or dog, and used as a sign for a grocery. From him, too, comes the story of a Missouri belle at a Kansas ball declining the hand of a Free-soiler on the ground that "she was a border-ruffian, and could not be seen dancing with an Abolitionist." [117]

Gladstone ends his description by the statement, "There is romance, therefore, even in ruffianism," a conclusion that all might echo if by romance we mean gaudy colors, flaring high lights, picturesque scenes, turbulent life. Certainly of these there is no lack. The swarming crowds on the ferries, the wagons inscribed with boasts and threats, the filibusters' flags, the revellers' camps, the one, for instance, where "a swarthy-looking disciple of Paganini, in homespun pants, and dirty blue shirt, was perched on a log, playing on the fiddle, while a group of wild-looking tipsy men were dancing round him, and cutting all kinds of capers," [118] all furnish a striking medley of elements. Crude songs develop from the adventurous life; anecdotes smacking of the lawlessness of the outrages, the earthiness of their perpetrators, collected would fill many an audacious page. The election frauds present amusing features; the tarred and feathered Abolitionists are set adrift in the river with wickedly clever inscriptions affixed to their craft; there is decided piquancy in the very directness with which one borderman upon inquiry as to whether he wished to see the member from Fort Scott enunciated, "Fort Hell!— I wish to see the member from Lafayette County, Mo."

Yet these are after all surface manifestations which, interesting as they are to us today, must not lead us any more than their contemporary chroniclers, to forget the almost daily tragedies, the very terrible sufferings that went in their wake. For being a non-participant did not restrain men from indignation; rather it seemed to increase their bitterness, causing visitors to describe the outrages more ghoulishly than the victims. Governor Geary's secretary, for instance, John H. Gihon, who, going to Kansas with all his proclivities on the side of slavery, was forced unwillingly to change, pencils in his brief review, *Geary and Kansas*

117 Gladstone — *Eng. in Kan.* 129. See also Mrs. Robinson's account of another girl's pride in the title. *Kansas.* 294.
118 Phillips — *Conquest of Kansas.* 181.

(1857), horrible things — "the mutilated bodies of murdered men, hanging upon the trees, or left to rot upon the prairies or in the deep ravines, or furnish food for vultures and wild beasts"; "a man writhing apparently in the agonies of death on one side of the street, the groggeries opposite . . . filled with loungers too unconcerned to take any special notice."[119] The newspaper correspondents and other writers, although they quote with meticulous care southern affidavits and editorials, practically all espouse violently the cause of the Free-Staters; practically all brand on the memory such pictures as John Brown, Jr. made a maniac by his treatment in captivity, lashing "his chains in fury till the dull iron shone like polished steel,"[120] or the ruffian bearing, for the sake of a pair of boots, a bloodied scalp in triumph round the town. These are the sensational aspects; even more poignant are the more intimate revelations — the funeral trains winding over the prairie; the famine days when with bread earners away, fighting or imprisoned, the fields trampled and desolate, one family, for instance, subsisted four weeks on wolf meat. Not romance this, but the stark stuff of tragedy, accompaniments of all war, inevitable, inescapable.

And it was war in Kansas! For, as the outrages continued, Robinson's policy of non-resistance gave way among the younger of the Free-Staters to the organization of military bands of their own. Raids were made on the strongholds of both sides; weapons of all kinds were shipped in by stealth, giving rise to stories like that of the plucky feminine ammunition carriers worthy to be placed on a par with Revolutionary legend. Systematic blockade of the river was undertaken by the Missourians, forcing all suspected abolitionists to take the roundabout route through Iowa and Nebraska. Heavy taxes to carry on the crusade were raised by Clay County and others; government troops rendered the situation a triangular one. The main issues, however, were between slave and free-soil forces, issues as sharply defined, as bitterly fought, as those of the great Civil War of which they were the prelude. Tomlinson in his *Kansas in Eighteen Fifty-eight* describes leaders of armed troops on both sides; and although in

119 Gihon — *Geary & Kansas.* 91, 122.
120 Phillips — *Conq. of Kan.* 333. *The Thrilling Narrative of Dr. John Doy, of Kansas . . .* 1860 portrays his own sufferings after capture by the Missourians and the New Eng. movement to people Kansas.

chapter seventeen he records the disbanding of Montgomery's men and the beneficial effects of the peace, the truce was but a temporary one, broken even then by the unprovoked attacks of some Missouri ruffians. The martial songs, of which he gives examples and which seem to have displaced the crude ballad effusions mentioned earlier, were soon to resound in the formal lines of marching men; the renowned Titus band and other similar organizations were again to have opportunity for looting unrestrained. Undoubtedly many of the crimes that stain the Civil War annals of Missouri, the guerrilla tactics that brought terror throughout the South and West, owe their extent in large part to the lawlessness arising with the invasion of Kansas.[121]

And to the development of the midland this great national conflict gave the most eloquent testimony. Already in the narratives of the travellers there had been many striking tokens. Boynton and Mason, for instance, the committee from the Kansas league, chronicle an amusing ignorance concerning their destination in Cincinnati, worthy of the effete East.

> "Some seemed to have no more definite notion of the position of Kansas, than of the distance of the fixed stars. They thought of it as indefinitely remote — somewhere 'out west' towards the Pacific Ocean. One individual placed it two thousand miles from Council Bluffs; another brought it within two thousand miles of Cincinnati, while an Irish friend inquired if it was indeed a newly discovered continent."[122]

Other wayfarers recorded increase of sophistication in still more remote sections. Journeying beyond the Mississippi was no longer "travelling beyond the Sabbath"; forms of law and order as well as conventions of religion had crossed the Great River. A network of rails now shimmered over the flat lands; the raucous screech of the locomotive now startled the scarce game.[123] The century-old forests and the amazingly high grass of the prairie with its snarl of creepers and weeds, its profusion of blos-

---

121 Williams — *With the Border Ruffians.* 118. Hildegarde R. Herklotz makes this point in her *Jayhawkers in Missouri. Mo. Hist. Rev.* XVIII: 64ff. See, too, Capt. N. L. Levering's *Bushwhacking in Missouri. Ia. Hist. Rec.* VI:553, and especially W. E. Connelley's *Quantrill & the Border Wars.* 1910.

122 C. B. Boynton & T. B. Mason — *A Journey through Kansas. . . .* 1855. 1-2.

123 The railroads' attempts to dispose of their land grants further advertised the prairie country, the Illinois Central Railroad, for instance, issuing for years a series of tracts containing valuable information.

soms had yielded acre by acre to the shock-dotted cornfield, the golden oat-stubble, the pungent fragrance of clover. The lop-sided cabin, alone in the landscape, had made way for the comfortable farm-house, the frequent cluster of villages; neighborhood gatherings for elections, patriotic celebrations, jollifications of all kinds replaced the months-long isolation of the pioneer families.

And when at the outbreak of the war, the call for volunteers went forth, thousands of boys and men responded from the sunny prairies of Iowa, the far coulees of Wisconsin, the lake shores of Michigan, only a few years before a vast stretch of wilderness. Women, no longer condemned to spend most of their lives without female companionship, gathered to make garments and bandages, waiting for news from the front with straining intensity; the splendid crops, the abundant food-stores of the midland flowed forth to give comfort. And in the struggle that was waged for the last time in the valley, undoubtedly the lusty life and the immense natural resources of these new states were a dominant factor. Of the changes that resulted from the conflict; of the warfare that made Vicksburg a cave city and that provided such picturesque incidents as Morgan's raid to the Ohio; of the carpetbagger supremacy that terrorized New Orleans more effectually than the plague and that stripped from the gleaming crescent all the frivolity of its charm, the details heroic or terrible that furnished the chief conversation as late as Mark Twain's memorable visit, it is not our province to take stock. It is sufficient to note that for the period we have been discussing the Civil War is the culmination; that the struggle which united men on both sides of the Alleghanies in devotion to an ideal of political unity was to stamp with finality what the War of 1812 had already indicated — the comparative insignificance for nationality of the mountainous barriers. The long years of fighting shoulder to shoulder, of common effort expended and suffering endured, welded indissolubly the western states with the eastern. The contributions of the newer regions to the victory already gave decided evidence of attainment; with the passing of the weary reconstruction years was to come a new era of achievement.

And as the war marked the close of the era of settlement, so it indicated, too, the climax of the literature of travel, in the yellowed pages of which we have traced the advancing frontier. Travellers were still to record their impressions of the Midlands—Stevenson, crossing the plains in an emigrant coach, to find in Ohio, Indiana, Illinois, and Iowa "a sort of flat paradise," which, however, he fears, apropos of a "fever and ague morning," is not unfrequented by the devil; Arnold Bennett visiting the literary Indianapolis and Chicago's sprawling industry, to register amaze; miniaturists like Reed in *The Dune Country* to exploit unappreciated charms. The emphasis, however, had changed; henceforth increasingly the prairie is to depend for its interpretation on fiction, drama, or poetry. Up to this time journals of exploration and personal reminiscence had blazed the way. A vast number of expository volumes of every conceivable style had made known to the world the characteristics of the Great Valley. Their value varies decidedly, of course, the chief tribute to some of them as well as the best testimony to the interest that prevailed in the region being the fact that they were ever printed at all, others combining with a knack for telling detail a real charm of composition. There is inevitably, too, enormous repetition. Yet in the most barren of the dusty volumes is apt to lurk some fascinating bit; the whole forms a collection of amazing richness and of hitherto unrecognized significance in the formation of our literature.

By such books is portrayed most fully the life of the great basin now long blotted out. The pushing back of the aboriginal inhabitants, a process early begun and in this era remorselessly extended, is in their pages laid bare. But although the Indians' vanishing from the regions of which they had once been the unquestioned owners is typified by their constantly lessening place in the travellers' annals, on the whole they receive fair treatment. Both the tribes in their primitive state and those bedraggled by the scourings of the white men are clearly etched in; and the basis is laid for the really thoughtful appreciation of the tribal rites and legends which of late years has presented us with many beautiful and lasting memorials. In the same way, too, on the cessation of rivalry the real brilliancy of the Creole life is sketched, yet with equal distinctness, its dangerous element of decay. And as the Indians and the Latin races lose their control we find revealed the successive waves of immigration, the progressive evolution of society — from the isolation of the pioneer's log-cabin, abandoned at the first sign of approaching civilization, through the roistering existence of the hunting farmer, to the stability and comparative comfort that come with the capitalist and the sturdy land-tilling stock, bases of our modern communities.[124] The distinctive traits of each region are suggested, the shifting elements of the life, the development of commerce, industry's humming advance. Ever dominant, however, is the rich note of romance, the triumphant attainment of new territories, the dazzling promise of fortune, life tumultuous and vociferous, yet startlingly picturesque, an ebullience of spirit, a soaring greatness of conception, a deep breathing of freedom, of all of which the first narrative we have quoted — that of Lewis and Clark is pre-eminently the symbol. The whole travellers' output is, however, an always-changing, never-breaking, richly-colored panorama, in the inland spaces of the continent, of the vitally significant, ceaselessly stirring drama of progress.

Even more important for literature, perhaps, at any rate a more tangible and easily traceable feature are the types projected forth on this background. Leading, of course, as they led in the march over the mountains are those products of the wilderness — the forest-hewing pioneers, men keen-eyed, rawboned, almost born with a rifle, who found in Kentucky their Elysium but who, when the number of their followers became too great, were compelled to exchange their woodland shades for the sun-steeped, echoless spaces of the prairie. Partaking of their features in a measure, a sort of mongrel, down-at-the-heel version, are the squatters and their shrewish wives who crouch upon the forested bottoms and hamper the prospector. Others might be mentioned — the exhorters and circuit riders or the omnipresent Yankee, unforgettable source of infinite crude border anecdotes. More interesting, however, are those that emerge from the memory-clouded past, distinctive contributions of the middle western frontier, the habitant with his hundred years or more of settled residence, the voluptuous Creole, the gambling Mississippian. Some of these like the bee-hunter, the river-

---

124 The change in the nature of the settlers is stressed by Lieut. A. M. Lea in his *Notes on the Wisconsin Territory. 1836*, repr. *Annals of Iowa*, 3d. ser. XI:115 ff. For ref. see 129.

wrecker, or the pilot have attained in imaginative literature recognition; most of them were depicted first in a few chance lines of a diarist's pages. Such are the miners of the upper Mississippi or the raw and awkward volunteers who make up Irving's border rangers. But whether the rolling region gave them birth or whether it merely ripened tendencies already implanted makes little difference. The significant thing is that in such figures is mirrored the development of the Middle West and that through them America makes to traditional stores contribution.

To mention the lavish praises of the section by practically all who traverse it seems at this time almost futile. There is a certain intrinsic interest, however, in noticing the way superlatives are heaped upon it. "The Missouri territory boasts the best land in the country";[125] "the celebrated 'American Bottom,' a tract of country which, for fertility and depth of soil, is perhaps unsurpassed in the world";[126] "I consider the Wisconsin territory as the finest product of North America . . . the whole of this beautiful and fertile region appears as if nature had so arranged it that man should have all difficulties cleared from before him, and have little to do but take possession and enjoy";[127] "The valleys of Ohio and Illinois comprise, perhaps, the finest region in the world."[128] "The valley of the Mississippi above Cairo . . . embraces probably the greatest tract of fertile land on the surface of the globe."[129] " 'For all agricultural purposes, Iowa is perhaps as fine a region as ever the sun cherished by its beams.' "[130] "The valley of the Mississippi is, upon the whole, the most magnificent dwelling-place prepared by God for man's abode."[131]

These are all, of course, mere variants of the crescendo of praise which, beginning with the first explorers of the valley, is repeated in different keys throughout its successive periods of ownership. So, too, the more extended descriptions re-echo notes early struck. The tribute "a good poor man's country; for, in truth, the clus-

125 *E. W. T.* XII:12.
126 *E. W. T.* XXVI:181.
127 Marryat — *Diary.* II:73.
128 Darby, Wm. — *The Emigrant's Guide to the Wesetrn & Southwestern States.* 1818. 187.
129 Caird, James — *Prairie Farming in America.* 1859. 31.
130 Jacob Ferris — *States & Territories of the Great West.* 1856. 243.
131 Tocqueville, Alexis de — *Democracy in America* tr. by H. Reeve. 2v. 1889. I:17.

ters are clusters of Eshcol, the land foams with creamy milk, and the hollow trees trickle with wild honey''[132] is only a slightly more orthodox conception of the mediaeval notion of the Earthly Paradise; while the following paragraphs by C. W. Dana at the beginning of his *Garden of the World* suggest nothing so much as the exuberances of the Mississippi Bubble pamphleteers.

> ''The *Land of Promise,* and the *Canaan* of our time, is the region which, commencing on the slope of the Alleghanies, broadens grandly over the vast prairies and mighty rivers, over queenly lakes and lofty mountains, until the ebb and flow of the Pacific tide kisses the golden shores of the El Dorado.
>
> ''With a soil more fertile than human agriculture has yet tilled; with a climate balmy and healthful, such as no other land in other zones can claim; with facilities for internal communication which outrival the world in extent and grandeur,—it does indeed present to the nations a land where the wildest dreamer on the future of our race may one day see actualized a destiny far outreaching in splendor his most gorgeous visions.''[133]

Small wonder that with such rhapsodies concerning the newly opened regions, the Americans were constantly selling out or, even without such formality, packing up for the West. Small wonder, too, that the Mississippi Valley possesses today a firm conviction of its resources and achievement, a deep and lasting sense of its own potentiality. Such feeling had its origin at the moment of discovery; its roots struck deep through the centuries of settlement.

Naturally as the material prosperity of the country advanced and as the increase of culture created the sensitiveness to criticism, so marked a characteristic of America at the period, there grew in all sons of the West, either adopted or native, a burning desire to make others realize its advantages. And so there de-

---

132 Knight — *Letters.* 89.

133 *Garden of the World* . . . 1856. 13. Of course the extravagant praises of the region were ridiculed. One author tells of hearing as a child stories of turkeys running about ready to eat. *Western Emigration. Narrative of a Tour to, and One Year's Residence in "Edensburgh." (Illinois) by Major Walter Wilkey* (1844), a satire on the paper cities and unbridled laudations of the region, was probably prompted by an interest in Eastern lands. Its lesson is summed up in the following couplet.

"Who have a *good* home and don't *realize* it,
A trip to the *West* will teach them to *prize* it!"

Frontispiece of Wilkey's *Western Emigration* illustrating the narrator's statement that as a result of a year's residence in the "highly extolled country of Illinois" he had "a *broken* down wagon — a *broken* winded horse! — a *broken* hearted wife! — a *broken* legged dog; — and . . . the irreparable *broken* constitution" of his "three *Fever and Ague* sons."

veloped a rich sectional literature, treating in detailed fashion tendencies already noted. Of this movement Schoolcraft, Timothy Flint, and Judge Hall may be named as the leaders. Schoolcraft is the Indian specialist, the agent who for many years won the respect of his charges and all visitors, whose collections of native myth, song, and tribal lore were foremost in the field. Of his long period of duty his *Personal Memoirs of a Residence of Thirty Years with the Indian Tribes . . .* (1851) in spite of its cumbersome method, affords a fair general notion, and his various books of exploration deal in detail with specific aspects of his labor. The young minister Flint, whose *Recollections of the Last Ten Years . . . in the Valley of the Mississippi . . .* (1826) we have frequently quoted and whose work pleases always by the unaffectedness of his enthusiasm as well as the singular sweetness of his personality published an interesting early life of Daniel Boone (1833). His *Indian Wars of the West* (1833), reveals also our debt to the past. Of the interest that inspired these his *Condensed Geography and History of the Western States* (2v. 1828) offers the most extensive testimony, a work which with the usual amount of quotation and statistics combined so much personal observation and description that within a few years it went through several editions and, as one contemporary complained, it was too interesting for reference. James Hall, a man exceptionally prolific considering his legal and editorial duties, combines the interests of both of these others. His early *Letters from the West* (1828) have as the most prominent feature a severe attack on the misrepresentations of the English critics; his later books fortunately devote themselves less to censure and more to constructive work. His *Notes on the Western States* (1838) sets forth clearly the resources of the land beyond the mountains; his biographical sketches laud several of its distinguished figures; even his significantly named *Western Reader* (1833) with its extracts from *Long's First Expedition,* Neville's *Reminiscence of the Scioto Valley,* and John Russel's *Spectre Hunter* tucked in among the conventional pictures of Franklin's entry into Philadelphia or Washington's *Farewell Address,* the whole delightfully reminiscent of the frontier school child on the backless wooden bench of long ago, betrays his desire to promote intelligent appreciation of the country of his adoption. It was he who provided the text for an elaborately illustrated work on the American Indians, he who collected indefatigably legends, both aboriginal and pioneer, he who summed up all these interests in his suggestive volume *The Romance of Western History* (1857).

To discuss fully the types of work which the output of these men represents is obviously impossible. They are distinguished both by quality and quantity; contemporaries and later writers produced, however, countless volumes, only the bare nature of which we can indicate. The old travel narrative originating either in exploration or an expedition definite in purpose evolves into a record of vacation wanderings; the guide book, continuing with greater variety and fecundity than ever before is specialized, also, into such productions as Bill's discussion of Minnesota as a health resort or Strickland's *Old Mackinaw* (1860), ostensibly a description of "the Fortress of the Lakes and its Surroundings," but also a sojourner in the realm of statistics and commerce. Of the treatment of single places Drake's *Picture of Cincinnati* is an early example as his *Pioneer Life in Kentucky* is of the autobiographical record. Although neither of these latter really belongs to the prairie any more than does Brackenridge's *Reminiscences of Persons and Places in the West* (1834) with its attractive sketches of the tiny French village, all such backward surveys tend to bring out the exuberant vitality, the impetuous change of the middle valley at this period. The importance of individuals and classes in the transformation is also given recognition early; McConnell in his *Western Characters* . . . (1853) sketches with a varying degree of adequacy such successive groups as the Indian, the voyageur, the pioneer, the justice of the peace, the schoolmistress, and the politician; R. P. Nevin in his *Black Robes* . . . (1872) typifies the evolution that had taken place in the clergy; and, by the close of the period, it is pleasant to think, Mrs. Ellett was paying tribute to *The Pioneer Women of the West* (1873), figures so heroic in their massive outlines of self-sacrifice that they lift to their own level their biographer's usual pinched expression.[134] Books like Harriet Bishop McConkey's *The Dakota War-Whoop* (1863) reveal the frightful-

[134] Note, also, Frost's *Pioneer Women of the West; or, Daring & Heroic Deeds of American Women.* 1859.

ness of the Indians' last outrages; writers like Mrs. Howitt boil down into irritating pabulum for children the life and history of the West. Indeed by 1870 in almost all branches of non-imaginative literature the Mississippi Valley had received full expression.

# CHAPTER V

## EARLY ROMANTIC TREATMENTS

Meanwhile slowly, steadily, throughout the centuries the English-speaking races had, with the pushing of their physical boundaries into the wilderness, extended their material for artistic interpretation. The sea-life, the tropic islands that had first captured the imaginations of the Elizabethans, the rocky reefs of the coasts were rivaled in fascination by the interior of the continent. Minds repelled by the witch-haunted darkness of the New England forests turned with relief to the inland where park-like glades, vine-shadowed vales, satisfied the regular tastes of the eighteenth century composer. The blue summits, the fleecy cloud-puffs of the Alleghanies, at first a barrier to achievement, soon lured with romantic vistas the literary as they had the actual explorer. Traders brought back from their daring pilgrimages glowing reports; narratives of captives and the raids of the savages on the unprotected frontier focused attention on their retreats; the French wars furnished another incentive. And so hillside by hillside, river by river, poetry and fiction crept along the stump-dotted trail of the settler and soldier.

To trace consistently the advance among the English is a study in itself; *The History of the Life and Surprising Adventures of Mr. Anderson. Containing his Strange Varieties of Fortune in Europe and America,* may be taken, however, as indicative of the interest aroused by the published reports, as well as of European conceptions of the interior. Tom, the kidnapped hero, is sold from a Virginia plantation to Mr. Mattewson, a wealthy trader, who later adopts him; and in the heart of the Creek country not only gains a fortune but, as a ranger, shares in many thrilling conflicts. For our purposes it is important to note the colonists' "terrible apprehensions of a visit from the French," the analysis of the latter's territorial aims together with a plaint over the English laxity, and the underlying hostility to "that base and perfidious people." But even more important is the vagueness of the geography. All prisoners from Moville, for instance, are conveyed to Quebec, the account of Tom's trip thither being particularly amusing. "They were three weeks in the journey to *Canada*, partly by land, and partly upon the navigable lakes, which the enterprising *French* had everywhere made to communicate with each other."[1]

Amusing in another way and even more conventional in its description is *The Adventures of Emmera, or the Fair American* (1767), the key to the contents of which is found in the sub-title *Exemplifying the Peculiar Advantages of Society and Retirement.* The hero, having been perpetually entertained on all sides with accounts of the "romantick beauty of the back country on the great lakes and rivers," embarks upon "the grand tour of North America." In the midst of an "enchanting landscip" on Lake Erie he finds a tiny house, the "happy refuge from the barbarous attacks of fortune" of an old man and his child. The father conveniently dies, lamenting his daughter's fate. "Here she existed innocent and happy — but what a change if her pure mind, unguarded against the vile practices of the world should now be open to its snares." In reality, however, the child of nature proves quite equal to the subtle logic of the English nobleman. They spend some time on the farm in "a feast of reason and a flow of soul"; then after the kidnapping of Emmera and the rescue by the Indians of their "queen," they attempt life à la Trianon on an English estate. The gambling quarrels of the fashionable callers who find Chetwyn "in a fustian frock, digging in the farm, and my dear Emmera, quite in dishabille, hoeing a bed of carrots," and the whipping of a deserter clinch Emmera, however, in her determination "to leave this detestable country with all speed." They marry, and

[1] *Hist. of the Life & Surpris. Adven. of Mr. Anderson.* 1799. 118, 124. (1st. ed. 1754.) It is interesting to note that in *The History & Remarkable Life of the Truly Honorable Colonel Jacques Commonly Called Colonel Jack* Defoe makes the crew, wrecked near the Mississippi, wander "among savages and the more savage French, who plundered and stripped them, instead of relieving and supplying them in their long wilderness journey over the mountains till they reached the S. W. parts of South Carolina, a journey which, indeed, deserves to have an account to be given of it by itself." Ed. by G. H. Maynadier. 2v. 1904. II:201. (1st. ed. 1722.)

with two shiploads "of every possible convenience . . . in the farming life, and a variety of common necessaries with noble presents . . . for the Indians." return to the scene of their former happiness, the husband thoroughly convinced by the arguments for the simple life. "My wife and my little farm are the world to me."[2]

Peculiar interest is found in the theory that Smollett's picture in *The Expedition of Humphrey Clinker* (1771) of the immortal Lismahago was prompted by Robert Stobo, hostage from the troops commanded by Washington. Aside from the narrative of his adventures in America and his marriage with a Miami squaw the book does not concern us, however; and these few examples of the many that might be given must suffice to suggest the manner in which place names and historical incidents were caught up to give a North American coloring to a tissue of melodramatic adventure, the application of formal ideas of scenery and conduct to the American hinterland and its denizens, and the localization there of sentimental advocates of the return to nature. Since these are tendencies, also, of the French treatment of the Midlands, attention may more profitably be centred on the emergence of the Mississippi Valley in the literature of America, an emergence paralleled, as a matter of fact, by that of the literature itself. As modern readers now recognize, Sidney Smith's famous question "In the four quarters of the globe, who reads an American book?" had its origin in the truth.[3] For America in general Cooper's *Spy* (1821) marks the beginning of really first-rate fiction as his *Prairie* (1827) does for the flat lands which his title celebrates.

Yet for more than a quarter of a century before that there had been tiny straws indicative of the way the current was tending, hints of the West that fascinate in the midst of their frequently barren setting. Brackenridge's *Modern Chivalry* (1792-3-7), said to be the first book printed on the far side of the Alleghanies, presents a whimsical sketch of such crudities of the new republic as stump oratory which prevailed by reason of the liquid refreshments rather than the merit of the compet-

---

2 *Adventures of Emmera or the Fair American* . . . 2v. 1767. I:21, 22, 23, 28, 28, II:178, 188, 191, 196.

3 For a good discussion of the circumstances under which this was written see *The Centenary of a Question* by Brander Matthews *Scrib. Mag.* LXVII:41 ff. Jan. 1920. The original article was published in the *Edinburgh Review* for January, 1820.

itors, random appointments to office, and backwoods justice, the whole being an interesting frontier adaptation of the picaresque formula.

Imlay's *Emigrants,* of 1793, is important not only because of its popularity in England and America but because of its close relation to the author's expository volume that was to mark so much of the early romantic literature. Chronicling their emotions at the rugged scenery, the field of Braddock's defeat, and the rapidly growing Pittsburgh in a manner early familiarized by the diarists, the ruined English family cross the mountains to seek a home in the West, already a haven for the unfortunates of all nations. The sentimental cult of nature is emphasized, of course; the married sister compares "the simple and sincere manners of the people of your hemisphere, with the studied ceremony of European customs," and laments that she is not "enjoying the charms of those Arcadian regions"; Captain Arlington proposes to look in the "wilds of this extensive region for that peace of mind which Caroline . . . has for ever destroyed," winding up in a fine frenzy, "Come, my friend, let us together explore the country until we find the sources of the Mississippi, and the limits of the more impetuous and extensive Missouri; for I will live in this uncultivated, and uncivilized waste, until my person shall become as wild as my senses." And even more specifically the prairies themselves are interwoven with the action. The desperate hero crossing "the immense Buffalo plains" meets and rescues the unfortunate Caroline, now a captive of the Indians. Her image "so fair and beauteous" rendered a scene which "seemed to be enchantment, Paradise itself," and in the "wild regions" of the Illinois "where the sweetened breezes attune the soul to love, and nature exuberant, in her extensive lap, folds the joyous meads which enraptured smile around" his proposal brings happiness. It is also significant that Arlington determined to establish his ideal society on the Ohio. The book is indeed a culmination with its scene in the midlands of the rococo description and the pastoral idealization that in the old country marked the literature of the century.[4]

---

4 Imlay, G. — *The Emigrants* . . . 3v. 1793. II:121, 121, III:3, 3, 29, 51, 51, 83-4.

Brackenridge was, of course, a pioneer lawyer of Pittsburgh, the shrewdest of observers of what went on about him, and Imlay, one of the most influential of the early writers of travel. Such specific knowledge of the life and people of the interior was, however, rare at the time. Writers such as there were on the coast were still unaware of the resources of their country; and there had not yet developed beyond the mountains that sectional pride that was responsible early in the history of the Ohio Valley for countless ephemeral periodicals. Consequently the *Female Review* (1797), a resumé of the career of the girl soldier, Deborah Sampson, seems much more typical. Mann, her biographer, apparently considering participation in the Revolution an inadequate achievement adds various extraneous incidents, prominent among them being an account of a tour to the Ohio "partly to contemplate the country and partly to discover the minerals." [5] Exhibiting the most stilted absurdities of diction and equally ridiculous absence of reality, these adventure-packed pages yet illustrate the growing interest in the interior as well as its importance as a setting for romance, an attitude which Charles Brockden Brown first consciously formulated.

In the preface of his *Edgar Huntly* (1799) he points out that for "calling forth the passions and engaging the sympathy of the reader . . . the incidents of Indian hostility, and the perils of the Western wilderness, are far more suitable" than "puerile superstition and exploded manners, Gothic castles and chimeras," [6] a theory he combines with Godwinian tragedy. His background with its rather abstract stressing of wild and romantic elements adds nothing to the early versions of the French, nor for that matter does it differ from the settings of the European school. His Queen Mab, however, the squaw of the Lenni-lennapee who had refused to retire with her tribe to the banks of the Wabash and Muskingum, is a really picturesque and individualized figure; her tragedy was one constantly repeated; while the raids of the Indians from over the mountains and the incidents of the border warfare recall all too vividly the

5 *Mag. of Hist.* Extra no. 47, p. 141.
6 Brown — *Edgar Huntly.* IV.

horrors which were the toll of our forefathers' approach to the prairies.

The Pennsylvania frontier, indeed, was second only to Kentucky in its annals of strife. Such a sentimentally sensational tale as *The Betrothed of Wyoming* (1830), numerous romances and poems find in the Susquehanna Valley inspiration, the most important for us being N. M. Hentz's *Tadeuskund, the Last King of the Lenape.* Melodramatic in plot, it nevertheless portrays with fidelity the wrongs on both sides and sketches fully figures already famed on the border or destined to develop into stock characters in the sensational novel. Rogers with his scalped head and vow of destruction to the whole red race, although his motives are complicated by his early passion for Burton's wife, typifies the frontiersman like Wetzel; the affected young hero has the usual continental yearning for liberty in America; Burton, who early made misanthropy a guide through the forest, hoping to find in the Indian "the romantick purity and golden-age virtues" which his "young imagination had formed,"[7] emerges during the main action in one of the most effective portrayals of the peace-loving Quaker. The motley-garbed border troop, the wild prophet Wancomand, the French in Indian disguise, the beautiful Elluwia, helper of the whites and, as is revealed at the end, the long lost daughter of Burton — all these were to reappear again and again in the half century following.

McHenry's *The Wilderness; or the Youthful Days of Washington, A Tale of the West* advances still further the track over the mountains. Gilbert Frazier, an Ulster immigrant carried by the Indians near the present Pittsburgh, clears a farm and raises his family and the lovely Marie, whose father, frenzied by his wife's death, had disappeared at her birth. This "flower of the Wilderness" presents a notable contrast to the fair Emmera, for "as she advanced in years," her Indian tutor, Tonnaleuka, "drew up for her use a book which he entitled 'Wisdom for a Young Lady,' in which he laid down maxims for the regulation of her conduct in both a state of seclusion and society, but particularly the latter." As a result she was so

7 Hentz — *Tadeuskund* . . . 1825. 187.

"eminently qualified to delight and adorn the most polished society in civilized life" that she enchanted not only Charles Adderley and the passionate French commander but the youthful George Washington. This sensational portrayal of the gallant Virginian, who, in addition to penetrating the enemy's fort to rescue his beloved, won enduring fame in the field and accomplished countless last minute prodigies of valor, is apparently the first outgrowth of Cooper's *The Spy*. Her Shannoah majesty, Alliquippa, is in her way as romantic a figure as the father of his country; Tonnaleuka, who turns out to be the long lost father and an exiled adherent of the Stuarts, a fantastic variant of the Indian prophet; the vengeful savage mutters execrations like a Gothic villain; only in the resourceful trader Paddy and the humorous Irish servant do we find much tang of reality. The background is touched in with some detail; the Ohio Company's servants hack their way through the thickets; the luxuriance of the vegetation and the Indian-hiding forest is frequently suggested; yet in general the chief descriptive advance is in definiteness of locality.[8]

This latter point is particularly noteworthy in contrast with the novel *Logan* of the preceding year (1822) when the turbulence of John Neal's spirit seethes over space with the hissing impetuosity of a very active volcano. The charting of the hero's course would be a task as difficult as remembering the

---

8 Quot. are from the 3v. Lond. ed. of 1823. I:54, 57. The illustration portraying Washington enraptured by the Flower of the Wilderness is from J. Priest's *A History of the Early Adventures of Washington among the Indians of the West*. 1841, a plain steal from McHenry. The following quotation from *Truth; a New Year's Gift for Scribblers* (1831) pp. 47-8, gives an interesting contemporary reaction.

"O miracle! What next! The greatest owl
Alive salutes us with an Irish howl;
And with a screech of horrible distress
Proclaims the wonders of the 'Wilderness.'
Cease, cease, M'H-nry, # cease for Heaven's dear sake,
Thy other drugs are bad enough to take:

— — — — — — — — — — — — —

# *Peregrina est bellua*, This fellow is an Irishman and a physician. In one of his novels (the Wilderness) he brings George Washington on his knees before his heroine: 'Think of that, Master Brook!' He has lately sinned in another sort; *videlicet*, in rhyme.

— — — — — — — — — — — — —

Think of the infamy thy novels gained;
Think of the name of Washington profaned;
Proceed not thus, still adding crime to crime,—
What, what the Devil prompted thee to rhyme?
Beside, the fashion never was in vogue
To woo the Muses in the Munster brogue.
Put by the pen — enough is given to fame;
Or rather, sooth to speak, Big O, to shame."

He stood amaz'd! behind a tree conceal'd,
And lov'd the charms her beauties there reveal'd............See Page 36.

From Priest's *History of the Early Adventures of Washington among the Indians of the West*

Ornamental title page of one of the later editions of J. B. Jones' *Wild Western Scenes*

ramifications of the action; he passes from colonial town to French capital, from Indian wigwam to gay salon. And although Neal turns to "the boundless, immeasurable savannah" with its troops of wild horses "thundering round, from horizon to horizon"[9] in one of the most luxuriant of his rhapsodies, his conventionalized setting of tangled forest, gaping chasms, weary deserts, conveys no reflection, on the whole, of the increased knowledge of the interior.

Woodworth had given some years earlier, however, a fairly specific background in his *The Champions of Freedom* (1816), a most amazing attempt to combine a "complete History of the Recent War" with the sepulchrally warning figure of a mysterious Indian chief and the usual patchwork of villainous assaults on virtue, splendid entertainments, marvellous rescues, and despairing loves. In the seclusion of the major and the rearing of his children, we have some suggestion of the doctrine of nature; more important, however, are the traces of the development of the Great Lakes region. By this time the shore of Erie had become "pleasingly diversified with farms and cottages, leafy groves, and lengthened prairies, cornfields and orchards, hills and vallies"; the repast of the company "was moistened with some exhilarating American wine, from the vineyards of New-Switzerland, in the Indiana Territory, where the enterprising Swiss emigrants had been very successful in its manufacture"; the "immense" flow of folk to the Ohio was taking place; and the travels of Ashe were being already denounced, "a work calculated to give very erroneous impressions to the minds of foreigners, . . . a pitiful attempt, among many others, to arrest the current of emigration." Since all phases of the war were included in these exceedingly comprehensive volumes, the battle of New Orleans and the part of the Baratarian outlaws received their meed of attention. Woodworth's picture of them is the approved romantic one; they "had declared war against a world that had discarded them"; their leader Lafitte is "a paragon of generosity and magnanimity — a second Charles de Moor."[10]

In 1828 this blighted but chivalric being became the central

9 Neal, J. — *Logan, a Family History*. 2v. 1822. I:206, 207.
10 Woodworth, S. — *The Champions of Freedom*. . . . 2v. 1816. I:61, 62-3, 67, II:321, 321.

figure in another extended romance. Although Lafitte himself remained the picturesque victim of fate and although the love story is the usual startling one of languishing damsels, a jealous rival, and decidedly primitive passions, the book is notable for an increase of local color. In the old British sailor's grumbling as the boat leaves New Orleans about the faults of "this land of Frenchmen and mulattoes — Spaniards and Indians — Creoles and Negroes; and the cursed, quarrelsome Americans," we get not only glimpses of such customs as duelling, but of the hotly resented intolerance of the English.[11] Balize, too, long declared by the travellers one of the most desolate places on the face of the globe, now comes in for some rather effective description. On the whole, however, the stilted re-working of sensational materials makes us grateful that other aspects of the old Southwest than the chase of rakish piratical schooners on the blue waters of the gulf or drunken orgies in the stronghold of Barataria have already begun to occupy the attention of the novelist.

Mrs. Royall, for instance, whose *Tennessean* (1827) reveals early the shift of romance to the Spanish settlements and the plains,[12] had in the progress of the adventurers from the rendezvous at St. Louis pencilled the constant phenomena of the meadow lands, the abundance of game, prairies "covered with wild rye, higher than the tallest man's head, and so thick that you could not see a man, on horse-back, at five paces distant."[13] In a similar fashion Flint in the best of these minor novels, *Francis Berrian* (1826), although he makes his hero a "Mexican Patriot" presents many fascinating glimpses of the central valley. Acquaintance between narrator and hero is struck up on an Ohio River boat; Francis Berrian at once proclaims his belief in romance, really Flint's creed, vocalizing at the same time the dreams of the youth of the age.

> "I delighted in the position of Robinson Crusoe and his man Friday in their lonely isle. At another time I imagined my-

11 *Lafitte* . . . 1828. 4. See *La. Hist. Quar.* II:418 ff., for an account of *Lafitte, the Louisiana Pirate & Patriot.*

12 The author believes that one reason for the prevalence of realistic literature in the Mississippi Valley is that the Mexican War and the gold rush early directed attention to the Southwest and Far West, sections which have remained ever since favorites with the romancer. This point she expects to work out in detail in her book on the plains.

13 Royall — *Tennessean.* 34.

self situated with my father's family in one of the boundless prairies of the West. Instead of journeying through cultivated regions and populous districts, I should have preferred to float down from the head-spring of the Missouri to the ocean, or to follow the intrepid Clark and Mackenzie over the Rocky Mountains to the Western sea.''

His extravagant ideas as to the wealth and beauty of the Red River region and the Eden localized in the Spanish Territory again exemplify popular attitudes as does his delight in the whimsicalities of the boatmen, or the depression caused by the swampy forests of the lower river and the pestilential huts of the woodcutters. And in the following passage Flint gives one of the first expressions in fiction of the emotional effect of the prairies.

''It was not far from this garrison that my eye dilated, and my heart expanded, as we opened upon one of those boundless grassy plains that stretch beyond the horizon, and almost beyond the imagination. Such a view presents to me the image of infinitude and eternity still more strongly, than a distant view of the ocean.''[14]

The promise of this story is not, however, fulfilled in his other volume devoted to the Mississippi, *George Mason*. In the homesick New England family's revolt at the plantation crudities, the toilsome labors of clearing, the sufferings of ''seasoning,'' and the malicious gossip of the neighbors we feel undeniable reflection of Flint's own experience. Yet vivid as are such bits as these or as the felling of the bee tree where the chivalric swains vie in the calm endurance of stings and the witty presentation of the dearly procured honeycomb, the book as a whole entirely fails to convey the stirring life of the valley. Elephantine coyness in the love scenes, a stilted and didactic manner of writing, long moralizings, and a prig of a hero, all these are faults that hamper not only it but practically all of the early fiction.

Consequently it is with a relief as great as that with which we find Irving's journal among the work of the travellers that we take up at last the really artistic interpretation of *The Prairie* (1827). In it for the first time in American fiction the open

14 Flint, T. — *Francis Berrian*. I:19-20, 40.

places receive adequate interpretation. The description is not original — the old comparison to the sea, with more elaboration perhaps because of the author's naval experience, the suggestion of "an ancient country, incomprehensibly stripped of its people and their dwellings." But these form a background inextricably linked with the action; the prairie fire is no longer merely a superb spectacle but a device of the Indians to trap or kill the fugitives; the high and tangled grasses, an obstacle to progress, prove also useful hiding places. As a result new emotional connotations are given — the sinister hush of the moonlight with, across the bleak plain, the approaching beats of Sioux raiders; the placidity of the morning following the conflict, the prairie "like the heavens after the passage of the gust, soft, calm, and soothing," the howling desolation of the storm that brought Abiram's execution. And by these emotional connotations the picturesque qualities are heightened; unforgettable scenes flash upon us continually — the musing figure of the old trapper against the gaudy West, Ellen startled on her high rock by the spurting warning gun of Ishmael, the witch-like hags on the withered heath leaping and chanting their blood-song, the heavy-winged vultures circling screaming between the leaden sky and the dark, matted thicket that shrouded the cold body of Asa.[15]

In still another way, too, Cooper was influential. Flint in *George Mason* had revealed the illusive quality of the romances of Imlay and Chateaubriand; Mrs. Mason was "perfectly willing to resign to the disciples of Rousseau their admiration of savage and demi-savage life";[16] in McHenry's book the immortal Washington had proclaimed the dangers of the Wilderness. Yet for the first time for the midland as he had done most effectively for the eastern forests, Cooper was imaginatively to portray in detail the results of isolation. The Bush family were no singular phenomenon but the natural product of generations of life in the outlands, a folk that, steadily pushing west from the coast, had lost with the refinements of life all sense of kinship with society. The massive bodies and dull minds, the indolent humor easily stirred to ferocity, the hatred for codified law, the boasts of the frontier virago, all these are superlative

15 Cooper, J. F. — *The Prairie.* Mohawk ed. 424, 406.
16 Flint, T. — *George Mason* . . . 1829. 137.

promulgation of the squatter. Paul Hovey is, of course, the reckless, impetuous, concretely-minded Kentuckian, typical secondary growth of the border; Obed Bat, M. D., the caricature of the naturalists who had early become a butt for the crude jests of the frontiersmen. Cooper's Indians, too, although his conception of them is typified by such a sentence as the following,

> "Few words were necessary between men who were governed by the same feelings of glory, and who were so well trained in the principles of their romantic honor,"[17]

are no more idyllized than those sketched by the explorers, whose pages glow with tributes to the splendid physique, showy costumes, superb horsemanship, and general daring of these equestrian tribes of the plains. Inez and Middleton unfortunately share the mediocrity that seems incumbent upon most of Cooper's gentlefolk, yet their union provides interesting reflection of the fusion of races attendant upon the Louisiana Purchase. Cooper has, in short, made his volume not only a magnificent example of his own art but an almost final expression of the tendencies we have been studying. Technical assurance, freedom on the whole from stiltedness and sentimentality, dignity of character, exceptional intensity of mood, all cause this first real fictional interpretation of the prairie to remain one of the finest, as the *Pathfinder* continues yet today an almost unrivalled exploitation of the great fresh-water seas.

Unfortunately this mastery deserted Cooper in *Oak Openings* (1848), a novel treating the outbreak of the War of 1812 in Michigan. Lagging and improbable action, a sentimentality that causes the leading character, the bee-hunter, to forget entirely in his love for Blossom the nature of the Indians and that transforms Scalping Pete, an unheralded rival of Tecumseh, into a benign and pious Christian moralizer, to say nothing of the affected diction, long disquisitions, and the bitterly intolerant spirit that rendered unhappy the author's old age, all submerge such really vivid pictures as the midnight council in the wood, or such significant revelations of early thought as "Mr. Amen's" theory of the Lost Tribes of Israel or Le Bourdon's effective use of his profession for necromancy.

---

17 Cooper — *The Prairie*. 404.

Cooper's books show some dependence upon the explorers; the Indians' taking refuge from the prairie fire under a fresh hide has its basis, for instance, in an occurrence of the Lewis and Clark expedition, as does the device of the buffalo skin boats. Yet this use of stock materials reveals almost entirely the unconscious gatherings of a creative mind; the novelist has so subtly adapted himself to the frontier point of view that searching out of courses seems unwarranted. Paulding, however, who in his *Westward Ho!* attempts to "combine an important moral, with the interest of a series of incidents, and sketches of scenery, character, manners and modes of thought and expression such as he knows or imagines exist, or have existed, in particular portions of the United States," works in an entirely different manner, placing his chief reliance on Flint's *Recollections,* which he commends to his readers. Consequently in method as in content his book is an almost supreme illustration of the evolution we are discussing; in it we have the concrete embodiment of the changes in the Great Valley. Character types long abstractly blocked in now move before us with exuberant vitality; familiar features become animating forces in the action. So the fanatic preacher of hell-fire and damnation, terrifying exponent of the harsh creed nurtured by forest and mountain, shatters a mind already verging upon delusion, and only the kindly ministrations of the old curé afford alleviation; the Mammelles, mounds singled out for special attention by almost every visitant of St. Louis, are now background for a new kind of heartbreak. The Dangerfields' removal beyond the mountains was typical of many easy-going families of the Old Dominion; Captain Hugg's coarse story about Hall, of the resentment of the natives at the supercilious English travellers, whose snobbishness Paulding had already severely castigated. The bewildered dismay of the habitants at the changes wrought in their sleepy lives by the sale of Louisiana is admirably brought out in the landlord's harangues against the "cochon Yankees"; and of the half-cocked yet unswervingly confident manner in which the new regions were built up Zeno Paddock's experience is a humorous illustration.

"Truth obliges us to say, that on his arrival at the city of New Pekin, as it was called, he found it covered with a forest of trees, each of which would take a man a half a day to walk around; and that, on discovering the square on which all the public buildings were situated, he found to his no small astonishment on the very spot where the court-house stood on the map, a flock of wild turkeys gobbling like so many lawyers, and two or three white-headed owls sitting on the high trees listening with most commendable gravity. Zeno was marvelously disappointed but the founder of New Pekin swore that it was destined to be the great mart of the West, to cut out St. Louis, Cincinnati, and New Orleans, and to realize the most glorious speculation that was ever conceived by the sagacity or believed by the faith of man. Whereupon Zeno set himself down, began to print his paper in a great hollow sycamore, and to live on anticipation, as many great speculators had done before him." [18]

In passages like this Paulding is at his best. The suavity and ironic ease with which he disposes of his characters in the trying last pages, for instance, suggest his kinship with Irving. In the portrayal of the primitive personages, too, he is really distinguished. The "whoppers" of the boatmen, the inquisitiveness of Mrs. Paddock, the free and easy speech of old Bushfield, all furnish fit materials for the broader strokes of his genius. The politer members of the story suffer from the usual affectations, enhanced in the case of the hero by a Gothic shading, all tedious to us to-day even when the purpose is ridicule; the exaggeration, secret of the author's comic success, carries out to an intolerable degree the Edgar-like ravings of Rainsford; the structure is loose; the carelessness of composition, apparent even in such a matter as dialect where Paulding excels if he wishes. Yet all these defects cannot outweigh the very great virility, the fundamental wholesomeness of the two slender volumes, now unfortunately lost sight of as is the life they portray; Flint's indirect contribution to them is worth much more for fiction than his own pallid sketch of life on the "Big River."

A much more copious, as well as in certain directions, more influential chronicler of the valley than either Cooper or Paulding is the South Carolina novelist, William Gilmore Simms, whose

---

18 Paulding — *Westward Ho!* 1832. I:4, II:179.

youthful visit to his father in the Southwest bore dark and bitter fruit in his series of Border Romances. These, immensely popular at the time they were written, have been sharply criticized since because of the melodramatic nature of their action, the viciousness and bloodshed with which their pages were spattered. Some of the details must be attributed, of course, to the Elizabethan tragedy by which Simms was all his life powerfully moved. Yet in essentials in even the most horrible of these crimes, Simms was enlarging no whit upon reality, a point that, as a matter of fact, he stressed over and over again. His *Beauchampe; or the Kentucky Tragedy* (1842) and *Charlemont, or The Pride of the Village* (1856) are based upon a famous civil case used by many other writers in ballad, drama, and prose tale. Not only their direct inspiration, the Murrell gang, can be evinced for the general truthfulness of *Richard Hurdis* (1838) and *Border Beagles* (1840) but other equally elaborate organizations in Ohio, Indiana, Illinois, and Iowa which, frequently described by the travellers and a prominent feature in the work of Judge Hall, long terrorized the half-settled regions.[19] Simms' visit was made in one of the most turbulent times in the Mississippi's history — when the Yazoo was still the resort of outlaws of all sorts, when gamblers not only robbed by means of cards but by murderous attacks on the crowded steamers, when lower Natchez housed the dregs of civilization, when New Orleans became the resort for the wild dissipations of thousands. Naturally, on the mind of the impressionable youth such experiences and legends were indelibly stamped; equally naturally he turned to them to supply a public increasingly avid for sensationalism in fiction. His plots, however, are of comparative inconsequence; he makes contribution not by them but by his thorough understanding of frontier life and his powerful portrayal of the progeny of that life. Poor as are his *Beäuchampe* and *Richard Hurdis,* they contain details significant for the social historian; and their companion volumes are still more deserving of attention. *Charlemont* is particularly noteworthy

19 See H. R. Howard — *The History of Virgil A. Stewart & his Adventures in Capturing the 'Great Western Land Pirate' and his Gang.* 1836. There are numerous early narratives about this famous outlaw. Simms had many conversations with Stewart.

for its characterization; Stevens' adoption of a pious guise was a favorite trick of the scoundrels of the border; William Hinkley in his adherence to strict forms of religion is typical of the combination of bull-headedness and perverted faith so common on the frontier; John Cross in his distress at being called Mister, his unsophisticated belief in the cogency of his own eloquence, his horror at play books, lying stories, and other inventions of the devil does much to preserve a ministerial type almost passed away. The school-teacher, Mr. Calvert, loyal, honest Ned Hinkley with his unfailing remedy of a "lickin;" brilliant and disdainful Margaret Cooper also present interesting studies against, or of, their environment.

This environment Simms summarized not only in individuals but in generalizations unquestionably sound. His best concrete portrayal, probably, is *Border Beagles.* Instead of the bald statement of *Richard Hurdis* that the gang had fifteen hundred members in all stations of life, the detailed workings of the system are given, from the fraudulent complicity of the shirt-sleeved justice to the warning of Gideon Badger, one of the hypocritical scoundrels who hid utter rascality under oily piety. The frontiersman, Rawlinson, is one of the best examples of his wholesome type, neither debased nor heroic. William Badger with his lengthy grace and strict Methodism, whose pride and stern habits as soldier and magistrate force him to condemn his own son to death, is a border martinet, uncompromisingly real. Tom Horsey, although a caricature whose ranting and eternal quotation of the "immortal bard" grow exceedingly tiresome, must in his futile aspirations and his wastrel career at New Orleans, reflect many a stage-struck youth of the great valley. His father's questioning of the stranger Vernon is an epitome, certainly, and a vivid one, of the inveterate curiosity of the westerners, recorded by all travellers. Other reflections of the life might be mentioned — the excitement of court day, the horrible fights, the superstition that worked to the advantage of the outlaws, the coarse fabric, in short, of a shifting civilization. Yet these were unfortunately not the elements to be taken up by Simms' followers; instead later writers stress the magnetic villain, the jealous creole mistress, the absconding cashier, the marvellous rescue of lovely damsels, all the claptrap of villainy and sensual passion that Simms uses too much and that we to-day would gladly forget.

The same thing is true of his historical romance featuring the valley. For the youthful wandering that gave such clear insight into the crotchets of the homely border folk likewise suggested the splendid pageant of the past. Through the silent forest's stately aisles, plumed Indians, mailclad Spaniards marched before him. As a result his *Vasconselos* (1854), a story of De Soto's ill-fated expedition, portrays admirably the mingled pomp and harshness of the adventurers, while glorifying the natives as does Garcilasso de la Vega's chronicle. In other respects, however, the book is sheerest melodrama, Simms quite defeating his own ends by piling up horrors, and giving them all an added air of unreality by the ranting nature of much of the dialogue. On the whole a thrilling drama with many stirring moments, much of splendid spectacle and tragic passion, yet with a fundamental unwholesomeness like the swamp miasma, *Vasconselos* typifies the feverish brilliancy, the theatricality and the moral decay that characterized practically all the interpretations of the lower Mississippi.

A few other of the early romancers for various reasons deserve to be mentioned by name — Judge James Hall, James Weir, Robert Montgomery Bird, J. H. Ingraham, and Major John Richardson. The first three devoted themselves to the "dark and bloody ground," the interest in which Bird summarizes in his preface to *Nick of the Woods* (1837). All, of course, are chronicles mainly of the forest; all portray the spectacular aspects of the border life. Hall's *Harpe's Head* (1833) is, indeed, so poor a blending of diverse and sensational elements that we would scarcely need to touch upon it were it not for the importance of the author's other work in the beginning literature of the Midlands. The firing of a Virginia planter's home and the resultant impoverishment of his niece, wooden Indians, a pilfering "station" gang, and the murderous Harpes animated by a love of evil for its own sake and a settled hate for the whole human race, the usual thrilling rescues and rival loves are slapped together with almost no sense of novel structure, a conventionality of diction, and a passion for moralizing that almost blot out the author's occasional dry humor and that intensify the fantasy of the Caliban-like snake-killer, Hark Short.[20]

*Nick of the Woods* (1837) and Weir's *Simon Kenton, or the Scout's Revenge* (1852) and *The Winter Lodge* (1854) combine with better structure and style even more melodramatic elements. Both use a stolen will and a villain who wishes not only to secure broad plantation lands but a beautiful heiress; both when the noble lovers fly to Kentucky avail themselves of a white renegade for their evil ends. Bird's book is memorable mainly by virtue of his title character. Bloody Nathan, ostensibly the peace-loving Quaker, in reality the Jibbenainosay who long had scourged the Shawnees, although his qualms against fighting grow rather tiresome, remains, with his bundle of dried scalps and his faithful little dog, Peter, perhaps the most moving, certainly the most powerful of the depictions of the fanatic avengers that haunt the border. For the rest his Indians, Bird confesses in his preface, exhibit "hues darker than are naturally employed by the painters of such figures,"[21] and his hero attracts attention mainly by being one of the first of those self-sufficing and declamatory beings who refuse all advice and mar all escapes, making us wonder why their much enduring guides do not profanely leave them to the fate they apparently court and richly deserve. This unenviable distinction is to a certain extent shared by Roaring Ralph, the horse thief, who, the author would have us believe, "fights Indians like a wolverine," but who displays his prowess here chiefly by getting himself and the rest of the party into difficulties. Stackpole remains, nevertheless, a boisterously amusing although somewhat anachronistic attempt to link the Mississippi "alligator" with the border ruffian.

It is unfortunate that Weir cumbers himself as he does with the tawdriest of melodrama, for the literary quality of his book is somewhat above the average through the exoticism of some of its descriptions, and the striking quality of the figures and scenes in the stalactite brilliancy of the Mammoth Cave makes

20 This was published in London 1834 as *Kentucky*. See Otto A. Rothert's *The Outlaws of Cave-in-Rock* (1924) for historical background.

21 Bird, R. M. — *Nick of the Woods*. Burt. 1890[?] V. This novel was popular in Europe as well as in America, having been translated into German and Dutch. Its dramatization in 1838 by Louise Medina was also successful.

us quite disregard the question of probability. Incidentally in his description of the Great Prophetess of the Boundless Lodge, based upon Collins' *History of Kentucky,* Weir furnishes a good illustration of the artist's elaboration of authorities. His Simon Kenton, too, remains one of the most notable of the scout personifications of the child of nature, of whom Leatherstocking is the most famous, and of all of whom the features are well summed up in the following.

> "Notwithstanding he was well skilled in every species of woodcraft, an adept at following the trail of the wild beasts of the forest, and familiar with all the cunning tricks of the wily savage; yet, strange as it may appear he was the most credulous of men, and as simple as a child in what is naturally termed the 'ways of the world,' or, in other words, in tortuous windings of policy and hypocrisy, so often met with under the garb of civilization."[22]

Nevertheless, in spite of this naïveté, on his visit to his old friend whom he hoped "by his glowing descriptions of the flowing savannahs beyond the Blue Ridge, and of the wild freedom of the frontier life" to induce to return with him to Kentucky, he showed himself quite equal in his retorts to the keen-witted lawyers and judge, while his outburst on jails is worthy to be compared with the attack of the old Huron Adario. The real pungency of his speech, the spontaneous humor of the faithful negro, Titus, are again qualities too rare in most of this fiction not to make us wish that they rather than abysmal villainy might have proved models.

The romanticism that marked Weir as well as the criminal motives of his action are prevalent to an even greater degree in the work of J. N. Ingraham. His *Lafitte,* the most elaborate of the romances of the "Pirate of the Gulf," makes an impossible series of events pegs for luxurious upholstering, Spanish treasure troves, and Byronic ravings. Incidentally the author takes occasion to introduce at New Orleans an Indian "who was the

22 Weir, J. — *Sharp Eye* . . . 7, 6. (Eng. ed. of *Simon Kenton*). A much poorer novel by Weir, *Lonz Power or the Regulators* (1850), makes use of the second of the themes which the author considered the West offered to the pen of the romancer: "the first based upon the arduous and protracted conflict between the native savage and the Anglo-Saxon invader; the second, upon the discordant elements of civilized society in a primitive and unsettled condition." IX.

last of his name and race — with whom would expire the proud appellation, centuries before recognized among other tribes, as the synonyme for intelligence, civilization, and courage — THE NATCHEZ!"[23] Another novel of Ingraham's, *The Quadroon,* is even more absurd in its plot and its incongruous ornamentation. Truly Irving had much to answer for if his Spanish series was responsible for the perfumed fountains and marble chambers, the Moorish princesses and Oriental slaves that transport the social problem of the mixed races and the cession of New Orleans to the Spaniards, the main ingredients of the story, to the enchanted realms of the Arabian Nights. Than Ingraham's description of the coureurs-de-bois, gay youths of the town apparently a combination of cavalier, Robin Hood, and Spanish grandee, silken history could go no farther. The Canadian Richardson, on the other hand, could not be accused of softening the past since he chose always for his starting point the bloodiest of Indian massacres. Yet even his *Wacousta* (1832), a powerful "tale of the Pontiac Conspiracy," betrays the tendency to heighten by melodramatic machinery the frontier outrages, a tendency even more pronounced in some of his other and poorer volumes such as *Hardscrabble* (1850), or *Wau-nan-gee* (1852).

To elaborate further on writing of this type would be futile. Throughout the first three quarters of the century novelists followed with ever increasing degeneracy the paths we have indicated. Those were the days when cheap fiction flourished, when countless newspapers and magazines catered to the "blood and thunder" tastes of the public. Munroe and Beadle made famous the "Yaller Kivers." Emerson Bennett and Ned Buntline were the favorites of thousands. Naturally the Southwest and the Great Plains with their outlaw tribes, their alien civilization, and their hectic adventure were an ever-increasing lure for the romancer; scout and soldier, however, boatman and bandit, still lingeringly gave incentive to the chroniclers of the Mississippi. And whether the books were decorous cloth-bound

23 Ingraham — *Lafitte.* 2v. 1836. II:125. A detailed analysis of the absurdities of this story may be found in the *Complete Works of Edgar Allan Poe,* Crowell ed. IX:106 ff., the review originally appearing in the *Southern Literary Messenger,* Aug. 1836. The next review in the same volume of Poe's *Works,* 116 ff., is equally instructive, *Elkswatawa; or the Prophet of the West,* from the same magazine. For a good letter by Ingraham on Lafitte see *La. Hist. Quar.* III: 100 ff. Longfellow gives an interesting note about Ingraham. *Life* by S. Longfellow. II:35.

volumes or the much maligned ten-centers the result was about the same. To-day they are practically forgotten by the reading public or sought after only as the prize of collectors.[24]

In them the land is important almost wholly, of course, as a background for the action. Sometimes as in Mrs. Snelling's *Kabaoza, or the Warriors of the West* (1842) elaborate descriptions are given of "that portion of the western country where the poet and the philosopher, the adventurer, and the mere lover of Nature in her solitary beauty will alike find employment for the eye and instruction for the mind";[25] again as in Emerson Bennett's *Leni Leoti* the prairies "expand the soul" of their admirers and bear them "above the groveling thoughts of every day life,"[26] providing them with material for columns of "hifalutin" generalization. Yet neither in the didactic employment of old forms of description nor in the sentimentality that makes us long to shake the dreamers is there enough of artistry to repay attention.

The same thing is true, on the whole, of the characters. Adopted captives, miraculously recognized after many years by their families, impossible Indians, prominent among whom are the hopeless victims of love for whites of the opposite sex, carry on the melodramatic or sentimental tendency to such an extent that the most absurd of them, La-u-na, the Trembling Fawn in Jones' *Wild Western Scenes*, resembles a Christmas tree fairy or the principal of a musical extravaganza rather than any dark-skinned inmate of a wigwam. Scowling villains bear out the decadent tradition of the Gothic romance. Most amusing of all, however, are the devotees of nature — a motley conglomeration of trappers, secluded girls, deluded victims, and blasé men of the world. As illustration of the depths to which the Rousseau cult had fallen it might be worth while to quote one of the more extreme passages.

"But you don't know, Dave, what anxiety I suffer for the sake of my dear girl. I brought her with me because I

24 The most valuable treatment of *The Dime Novel in American Life* is given by Chas. M. Harvey. *Atlantic Mo.* 100:37 ff. Arthur Guiterman pays tribute to the spell of these "thrillers" in his *Ballade of Dime Novels*, repr. in Helen L. Cohen — *Lyric Forms from France*. 1922.

25 Snelling — *Kabaoza*. 212.

26 Bennett — *Leni Leoti* . . . 1850. 99.

thought she would be safer here than in a city. Ah, there are more terrible *dangers* lurking in the crowded city than ever threatened the dweller in forest solitudes! the blood-thirsty savage is not so much to be feared as the more polished villains who entrap the unwary feet of innocence. Yes, I have thought I would bring her up in these virgin wilds, where not even a rumor of vice would reach her — where, from the caroling birds and the purling streamlets and the unstrained sunlight, and the free breezes she could derive a purity of nature, like that of the wild violet on which heaven's own dew has fallen."[27]

In technical atrocities of this kind — the most hopeless caricatures for personages, the most stilted of dialogue, and the most creaking of machinery is found one of the main reasons for the decay of the genre. The fundamental one, however, is the misplacing of emphasis, for, in spite of the fact that many of the "thrillers" were excruciatingly moral, the offensive intrigues, the black crimes that drove the victims to the wilds and the stressing there of physical supremacy and violence could not fail to have their effect. *Border Beagles* redeems by its wild poetry and seething life the enormities of the Murrell gang; Bonney's *Banditti of the Prairies, or the Murderer's Doom*!! merely outlines the crimes and their punishment. And although even some of the most sensational of these publications possess a power of etching in men and of reflecting frontier psychology, books like Col. Chris Forrest's *The Outlaw's Bride* (1869) and its predecessor with their idealization of the leader of one of the guerrilla bands of Missouri reveal the real moral menace of the "shocker." Strangely enough, however, almost all of the purveyors of the sensational fiction were profoundly impressed with the seriousness of their mission. Time after time they apologize for their own inadequacy by the statement that they have at least done something to uncover the rich ore of American literary materials. And crude and misleading as many of their interpretations were, they unquestionably did much to turn to the Middle West the attention of readers who might otherwise never have dreamed of it.

---

27 Dod — *On-ma-non-tah.* [1870?] 36.

Unquestionably, too, they were an indirect factor in promoting other forms. The horrified opponents of the novel of intrigue and blood were compelled to guard against the pollution of youth by providing somewhat more edifying entertainment. Consequently authors of such uplifting tales as *The Berry Pickers of Wisconsin* (1867) and other Sunday School literature, localized their moralities amid the prairies and inland forests. At the same time, too, that the cheap romancers were making tawdry a glorious past the fireside novelists of the feminine gender were carrying on the sentimental manner of Mrs. Rowson. Their effusions, sloppy and conventionalized as they too often were, yet have distinct value in revealing the settlement and domestic life of the valley. Mrs. Caroline Lee Hentz, for instance, one of the most prolific and popular, centres her dramas of thwarted love, mercenary ambition, and overwhelming poetic justice, on the plantations of Kentucky or in the prosperous centres of Ohio, while the courageous and persevering hero of *Linda* has his virtue rewarded in being made ''Pilot of the Belle Creole'' by one of the wealthiest planters on the Mississippi. Mrs. Soule's *The Pet of the Settlement* (1859) also belongs to this group, being an interesting combination of melodrama (the kidnapping villain, the abandoned child, the grateful Indian) and of the more abiding elements of the border. Pioneer women are there, inquisitive, garrulous, uncouth, yet resourceful, courageous, and truly neighborly. A primitive wedding occurs with its mammoth feast; herb-devotees gather in the case of sickness with that community of interest fostered by isolation; and the prairie appears always, a source of supply, a comforting presence. To the beauty of its brilliant flowers and dipping butterflies the delicate girl of the East turns for relief from the rudeness of the cabins; by the changes in the land is measured the development of the territory.

Yet important as is the evolution of the homes on the prairie, the novel is emphatically one of the frontier; a book such as *Ethelyn's Mistake* (1869) by Mrs. Mary J. Holmes must be taken to represent the emergence at last of a fairly stable civilization as far west as Iowa. Less melodramatic than Mrs. Holmes' other volumes, it illustrates to a truly remarkable extent the fusion of tendencies. In its marital complications and its improbable reunion in the mansion on the Mississippi, as well as in such wordly figures as Mrs. Van Buren and her weak and selfish son, it uses material worn threadbare to provide "sob-stuff" for thousands. Yet in its essential motivation it catches, somewhat mechanically to be sure, the essence of the life in the new state. In the shrinking of Ethelyn from the unexpected crudities of her western home and the sadness of the rain-soaked prairie, it typifies not only the natural reaction of the cultivated East but its first failure of comprehension of the sturdy stock and blunt virtues of the great agricultural regions. And in the barrenness of that home, free as it is from material hardship, is revealed the spiritual poverty and the matter-of-factness of existence against which Hamlin Garland rebelled.

Here we come to the close of this first period of extended romance, for to go into the many other poor novels that use a pallid western background for a projection of slavery or anti-slavery sentiment or wishy-washy love would be vain repetition. Poor stuff, most of it is, superficial in its presentation of life, exaggerated in its emotions, pedantic in its style, as unreal in one direction as the dime novel became in another. The mid-landers themselves were almost as guilty in these respects as the writers on the coast; most frequently they turned for inspiration to distant lands, past ages; when they did confine themselves to the material at their gates, too often it was to import there old world villainy as in *Beyond the Breakers* (1870) by Robert Dale Owen, eldest son of the philanthropist. F. W. Thomas through his *East and West* (1836), which gave a vivid picture of frontier life, formed a happy exception to the rule, but he wrote other novels having no connection with the Mid-land. On the whole, save for the one brief flowering in the work of Cooper, Paulding, and Simms, fumbling and inadequate without question was the novel's interpretation of the overflowing vitality, the emotional surge, the stirring adventure and grim endurance which with countless other diverse elements made up the developing life of the valley. Yet tendencies were established; foundations were laid; on them even though they themselves crumbled were to be reared finer, more dignified structures.

In general, of course, the same tendencies hold true for the short story. Such tales as *The Black Patch* or *The Quadroon of Orleans* in Ingraham's *The American Lounger* (1839), *Queen's Story; or, Mrs. Desborough's Secret* in Mrs. Clack's *Our Refugee Houshold,* (1866) emphasize again the iridescence, the exoticism, and the creeping corruption of life in the Crescent City. Coggeshall in his *Stories of Frontier Adventure in the South and West* (1863), Watson, and others retailed, usually with considerable tedium and awkwardness of technique, heroic incidents in the early history of the trans-Alleghany region; Mrs. Dumont, first woman to achieve literary recognition in the Ohio Valley, produced the annoyingly formulized Fanny Fern type of fiction of which the chief ingredients are stern fathers, exiled sons, ministering angels, and starving poor, with a skim milk setting which might as well be London as Ohio.

Nevertheless, strangely enough considering that for the country at large the local color story was not yet in vogue, the Middle West early found in that form some of its finest and most flexible interpretation. Snelling, whose *Tales of the Northwest* (1830) were written to correct the popular idea of Indian character and manners, gives in his *Payton Skah,* a pleasant and fortunately credible picture of native devotion with a harmony between subject and style rarely found at the time, and in his *Pinchon,* an extraordinary account of the audacity, unscrupulousness, and strength of these early wood-rovers. Schoolcraft in his *Algic Researches* (1839) and the later revised edition *The Myth of Hiawatha* (1856) simplifies his usual formality and cumbersomeness of diction to accord with the naïveté and untutored imaginings of the Indian legends, preserving such widely varying material as the very delicate and charming Shawnee *Tale of the Celestial Sisters* or the fantastic exploits that cluster around the half human, half manitou, Manabozho, and presenting a new point of view, "from which to judge the race, and to excite intellectual sympathy." In the striking figures of the effervescent border life Morgan Neville found his inspiration, producing in his *Mike Fink* the classic among the tales that celebrate the love, exploits, and death of this "Last of the Boatmen" and that furnish a most interesting revelation of the process of legend.[28] William Leggett, of interest because of his connection

28 Pr. in *The Western Souvenir* (1829), the first annual issued beyond the Alleghanies. The latest treatment of Mike Fink is Neihardt's *The Three Friends.*

with the loco-foco movement and his friendship with Bryant, uses the formula of crime, conviction of an innocent man, and final solution in several border stories. The most important of these, *The Rifle,* used by Gerstäcker in his *Mississippi-Bilder* under the title of *Doktor Middleton* and dramatized in one of the early midland plays, gives an interesting revelation of the beauty of the prairie as well as of the traditions of unhealthiness; *The Squatter* pictures the meadow lands; and all of the stories in spite of the fact that their characterization is rather stilted and their technique clumsy present distinctive types of the frontier.[29]

Judge James Hall's work is the most noteworthy of all. Although certain stories like *The Backwoodsman* display the digressions, poor structure, and unreal dialogue that mar his novel and although his *Pete Featherton* begins somewhat long-windedly and uses in parts an unfortunately declamatory diction, it has, in its account of the way the streams turned back and the shadows danced at the hunter's approach, a fantastic Irving-like quality, approaching in ease and mood *Rip Van Winkle.* His *Michel de Coucy* and *Legend of Carondelet* are among the most delicate interpretations that have ever been given of the original, light-hearted, happy-go-lucky life of that tiny French village, already as Hall writes dwindled into an obscure and ruinous hamlet remarkable only for its outlandish huts and lean ponies. Most fascinating of all is *The Dark Maid of Illinois,* in its record of the barber and the Indian princess a really supreme interpretation of the dapper buoyancy with which the Gallic adventurers penetrated the wilderness. All the tales have a suavity, a gentle irony, and easy grace comparable only to the charm of vers de société, inimitably right for the shimmering stuff of the past.

In all of these writers is brought out, of course, the change in emphasis we are recording; in the work of all we find shifting glimpses of the prairie and its people. Mrs. Dumont at times sketches backwoods characters, the give-and-take of the frontier elections in a way that shows she could have done much had she cared to devote herself more concretely to the region about her;

29 See *Tales & Sketches by a Country Schoolmaster* (1829) for *The Squatter & The Rifle, Tales of Glauder Spa* (1844) II for *The Block-House.* See Whittier's *Old Portraits & New Sketches* for a tribute to Leggett.

Alphonso Wetmore in *Gazetteer of the State of Missouri* (1837), Gilman in *Legends of a Log Cabin* (1835), Drake in *Tales and Sketches from the Queen City* (1838), Hall, and Neville furnish us a gallery of types from the English immigrant who "determined to study agriculture, and immediately purchased 'Speed the Plough,' 'The Farmer's Boy,' 'The Cotter's Saturday Night,' and 'The Shepherd of Salisbury Plain,' " to the renowned "Doctor Jeremy Geode, the seventh son of a celebrated Indian doctor," who "would cure all diseases, by means of the wonderful Hygeian Tablet, a Kickapoo Panacea, of which he was sole proprietor." The American Bottom with its century-old, rustling common-fields receives its customary praise; spontaneous expressions of wonder and delight burst forth at sight of "the greatest natural curiosity and the most attractive scenic exhibition of our Western hemisphere," the *prairie*; its flame-pitted horizon suggests purgatorial torments to the terrified barber-explorer; and in the picturesque native legends it furnishes a basis for heaven.[30]

The most distinctive feature in the literary evolution of the Middle West is found, however, in a newer, cruder form — the colloquial sketches of the humorists of the Great Valley. Product of the frontier they are unmistakably, fruit of the story-telling seed first planted in the lazy camp-fire vigils, sprouted in the marvels told to visitors by loungers at the posts, matured in the tale-swapping evenings at the "doggery," on court days, or during the listless drifting down the river. Exaggerated in their general tendencies, racy in their characterization, redolent of the soil in their speech, they smack indubitably of the teeming forests and mould-piled bottoms, the boisterous life and bare cabins, the free and easy manners and rude habits of the pioneers of civilization. Sometimes as in *How Mike Hooter Came Very Near "Walloping" Arch Cooner* the humor lies in facetious elaboration of the gawkiness and boastfulness of the rustics, sometimes in slap stick burlesque as in *A Tight Race Considerin'* where the pious "circus rider" and the old woman whose father once owned a race horse indulge in a thrilling contest winding up at the meeting house. Practical jokes are a favorite source of amusement, witness *A Millerite Miracle* where the negro in ascen-

30 Hall — *Legends of the West*, 372, 297, 388.

sion robes is assisted heavenward by means of a rope attached to his belt; frequently reliance is placed on the process of "stuffing," of which *The Big Bear of Arkansas* furnishes a classic example.

> "Then look at my land — the government ain't got another such a piece to dispose of. Such timber, and such bottom land! why, you can't preserve anything natural you plant in it, unless you pick it young; things thar will grow out of shape so quick. I once planted in those diggins a few potatoes and beets: they took a fine start, and after that an ox-team couldn't have kept them from growing. About that time, I went off to old Kentuck on bisiness, and did not hear from them things in three months, when I accidentally stumbled on a fellow who had stopped at my place, with an idea of buying me out. 'How did you like things?' said I. 'Pretty well,' said he; 'the cabin is convenient, and the timber land is good; but that bottom land ain't worth the first red cent.' 'Why?' said I. ''Cause it's full of cedar stumps and Indian mounds,' said he, 'and *it can't be cleared.*' 'Lord!' said I, 'them ar "cedar stumps" is beets, and them ar "Indian mounds" ar tater hills.' "[31]

In all types, however, the method is the same — an exaggeration at its height in *The Steamboat Captain Who Was Averse to Racing*[32] where the narrator's hair stuck out so straight it was impossible for him to get his head "within six inches of the pillow," a primitive fecundity and force of metaphor, a general exuberance of fancy and cumulation of effect obvious even in the subtle ironies of Joseph G. Baldwin's *The Flush Times of Alabama and Mississippi* (1853). Fundamentally, too, the material is alike — the oddities of one stage of culture held up to the ridicule of another. Obviously in such a case there could be no glossing or romanticizing; rather pains is taken to emphasize the grotesqueness of character and the primitiveness of the life. Consequently whether the misspelled complaints of the much abused Southern democrats, the swamp-doctor's experiences, the

---

31 Haliburton, Thos. C. — *Traits of American Humour.* 3v. 1852. I:51-2. "Mike Hooter" & "A Tight Race Considerin'" are also to be found in this collection.

32 In *Col. Thorpe's Scenes in Arkansas.* 1858. 125 ff., as is a *Millerite Miracle.* 60 ff.

wit combats of budding lawyers, or the hunting reminiscences of the border-men form the theme, there is sharp illumination of idiosyncrasies, deficiencies of all sorts. The exposure is humorous, but it is pitiless nevertheless — of the absurdities of the motley crowd that hamper the log-cabin theatricals, of the artistically lying "dead-beats," of the high play and cheating on the steamers, of the inflation of credit and the smashing of the speculative bubble, of the lack of reticence entailed by the one-room dwellings, of the ignorance and squalor that shiftlessness developed. In it we have an important step toward the realism that has been the most distinctive outgrowth of life in the Midland.

These tales demonstrate, too, a new method applied to old materials and a fusion of local with national tendencies. From the time of John Josselyn's *New England's Rarities* (1672) "tall stories" have been a prominent feature of American humor; gross misspelling and emphasis on the illiteracy of the central figure are others. Over-sensitive at first concerning their cultural weakness, Americans in the nineteenth century realized its humorous aspect and, as a result, we have a whole crop of homely jesters and philosophers. In their effusions, also, the West receives frequent recognition. The facetious Doesticks has his college preparation in Michigan; he wanders in the state of Kentucky, "the land of good horses, poor jackasses, glorious corn-bread, and lazy darkies."[33] Petroleum V. Nasby's postmaster at Confedrit X roads flashes a white light on post-bellum conditions in Ohio, Kentucky, Tennessee, and New Orleans while the free state struggle receives vivid recognition in the vision of the hereafter where Frank Pierce who declined to enter the stream lined with devils "wuz immediately seezed, and on each leg wuz tied a weight labelled 'Kansas.'"[34] The Yankee, Sam Slick, who rendered Judge Haliburton famous, compared the Bay Country to the "Prair-i's of Illanoy . . . the top of the ladder with us," where food is so cheap you can live "for half nothin'"; by his account of Ohio crop gatherings he raps the Munchausens of the frontier; his ridicule of the English travellers is among the most biting of the many satires they

---

33 Thompson, Mortimer M. — *Doesticks. What He Says.* 1857. 201.
34 Locke, D. R. (P. V. Nasby) — *"Swingin' round the Cirkle."* 1867. 68.

excited; while his allegory of the Heavenly emigrants is the last word in parody of this sort.

> " 'Why,' said I, 'Governor, that landscape on the right, with a great white two-storey house in it, havin' a washin' tub of apple sarce on one side, and a cart chock full of punkin pies on t'other, with the gold letters A. P. over it, is intended to represent this land of promise, our great country, Amerika; and the gold letters A. P. initialise it Airthly Paradise.' 'Well,' says he, 'who is that *he* one on the left?' 'I didn't intend them letters H and E to indicate he at all,' said I, 'tho' I see now they do; I guess I must alter that. That tall, graceful figur,' says I, 'with wings, carryin' a long bowie knife in his right hand, and them there small winged figures in the rear, with little rifles, are angels emigratin' from heaven to this country. H. and E. means heavenly emigrants.' "[35]

In this bombastic humor the Middle West found a type peculiarly congenial — coarse, earthy, but rich, spontaneous, turbulently alive. The minor writers have long since dropped out of sight; nevertheless many are interesting in themselves in addition to their paving the way for Mark Twain, America's greatest exponent of their method and materials.

Equally interesting, even more varied, is the poetic literature of the Middle West, although for it no such systematic development can be traced. Rather it remains an integral part of the life, with filaments of song threading the border from the shrill vibrations of the Indian war chants, the gay refrains of the French to the lengthy and decidedly free ditties of the raftsmen. Many of the pieces were exotic, of course; negro slaves with the wagon companies from the South crooned plantation melodies;[36] lonely immigrants cherished lyrics of the homeland; psalm tunes of New England mingled with the choruses of professional entertainers. Probably many songs developed, however, as a result of the frontier life. The balladists celebrated military engagements as *The Battle of Point Pleasant* or *Sainclaire's Defeat* beginning respectively,

---

35 Haliburton, T. C. — *Sam Slick, the Clockmaker* . . . ed. by E. A. Baker. 125, 198.

36 Many of the negro songs from the Mississippi Valley have local touches of interest to us. See, for instance, E. C. Perrow — *Songs & Rhymes from the South. Jour. Amer. Folk Lore.* XXVIII:129 ff.

"Let us mind the tenth day of October,
Seventy-four, which caused woe,
The Indian savages they did cover
The pleasant banks of the Ohio."

* * * * * *

" 'Twas November the fourth, in the year of ninety-one,
We had a sore engagement near to Fort Jefferson;
Sainclaire was our commander, which may remembered be,
For there we left nine hundred men in t' West'n Ter'tory."[37]

Wagoners cheered their toilsome ascent of the Alleghanies by rhythmical accounts of their experiences; the river voyages and terminal sprees as well as the boatmen's triumphs in love were mirrored repeatedly;[38] the throngs surging to the West extolled the riches of the territory.

"My eastern friends who wish to find
A country that will suit your mind,
Where comforts all are near at hand,
Had better come to Michigan.

"Here is the place to live at ease,
To work or play, just as you please;
With little prudence any man
Can soon get rich in Michigan.

"We here have soils of various kinds
To suit men who have different minds,
Prairies, openings, timbered land
And burr oak plains in Michigan."[39]

* * * * * *

---

37 Many versions of these ballads may be found. See Louise Pound — *American Ballads & Songs.* 1922; Rufus King — *Ohio* . . . (Amer. Commonwealths) 1888. Ap. III, p. 409-11; *Ohio Hist. & Arch. Pub.* XV:377-8. The song about St. Clair's defeat is given in the appendix to Bunn's narrative, where it is attributed to him. Ludlow gives an interesting account of how *The Hunters of Kentucky, or the Battle of New Orleans* by Samuel Woodworth delighted the river men and other inhabitants of the valley. *Dram. Life as I Found It.* 237-8, 241, 251.

38 Somewhat later but very interesting are the songs developing on the Great Lakes. Among the fragments given by Lomax in his excellent article *Some Types of American Folk-Song, Journal Amer. Folk Lore,* XXVIII:1 ff. is the following.

"We left Duluth bout half past four,
A-loaded down with the red iron ore;
The wind was high and the stream was low,
And forty-two was the number of the tow."

39 More of this Michigan emigrant song is given *Mich. Pion. Coll.* III:265. The

"Come all you girls from New England that are unmarried yet,
O come along with us, and young husbands you shall get;
For there's all kinds of game besides the buck and doe,
To hunt with dog and rifle on the Ohio."

Inevitably by their very nature most of these doggerel verses have long since perished; their type is revealed, however, by fragments preserved by travellers or novelists such as Cherub Spooney's ditty with its swinging refrain of "All on the Ohio, boys"[40] or Gerstäcker's peasant song.

"In Amerika können die Bauern in den Kuts-chen fahren,
In den Kuts-chen mit Sammet und mit Se-i-de,
Und sie essen dreimal Fleisch und sie trinken Wein dazu,
Und das ist eine herrliche Freu-ih-de!"[41]

Of the universality of the rhyme-making instinct, too, whether of the group or individual, we find countless examples. Smith cites a song recounting the Black Boys' capture of the Indian goods;[42] Davy Crockett is fabled to have felt the need of bursting into poetry when he left for Texas; Jones of the Cane Hill murder case was seized by the regulators while roaring the first stanza of his much prized composition,

"On the wings of love I'll fly,
From doggeree to doggery!"[43]

Schoolcraft proclaimed in formal metre the discovery of Itasca

---

Toledo war songs are also interesting. They were occasioned by the forced cession to Ohio of a tract on the south, the upper peninsula being given as compensation.

"But now the song they sing to us
Is — trade away that land,
For that poor, frozen country,
Beyond Lake Michigan."

*Ibid.* VIII:146. See also *Ibid.* VI:60.

40 Paulding — *Westward Ho!* 1:76. A typical passage is the following from Hall's *Letters from the West*, 94, "in the meanwhile I bid you good night, in the words which the rowers are even now sounding in my ears, as they tug at the oar, timing their strokes to the cadence:

Some rows, up, but we rows down,
All the way to Shawnee town,
Pull away — pull away!"

41 Gerstäcker — *Nach Amerika* I:415. Note also Goebel's statement that "One revolutionary song of thirty-four stanzas, in which each of the German princes was remembered, and one kind of misfortune or another was wished upon him, was very popular among the immigrants." *Mo. Hist. Rev.* XVI:372.

42 *An Account of the Remarkable Occurrences in the Life & Travels of Col. James Smith.* 111-113.

43 Arrington — *Desperadoes of the Southwest.* 22.

Lake; Banvard recited an effusion of his, the *White Fawn*, in illustration of one of the scenes of his Mississippi panorama;[44] Colonel Arent Schuyler de Peyster, later commander of Burns' regiment at Dumfries, versified his experiences as commander at Michilimackinac to fill in his own time and to amuse some of his friends.[45] The War of 1812 gave rise to fervent petitions for success.

> "Lord, since we are compell'd to take,
> The implements of death, to check
> The savage rage of British charms,
> May we successful prove in arms!"[46]

And in the sub-literary work of a slightly later day we find crystallized into print a somewhat similar type of production. Newspapers published popular pieces like *The Little Old Sod Shanty on the Claim*, other newspapers taking them up and printing variants of, and answers to them. Song and dance artists, medicine shows, and above all the black-faced minstrels imprinted crude ballads so deeply in public favor that the Beadles and other publishing houses found much profit in issuing cheap song collections.[47] Numbers of these like the hymn books bear titles suggestive of the interior — *The Western Songster, The Harp of the West*; others even with such sophisticated names as *The Fifth Avenue*, or *The Grecian Bend Songster* contain numerous allusions to the hinterland. Among the most interesting of these are again the verses reminiscent of the river — *De Gospel Raft; Down the River; Boatman Dance or Go Home wid de Gals in de Mornin* with its broadly humorous closing stanza.

---

44 *Description of Banvard's Panorama of the Miss. Riv.* . . . 1847. 9.

45 See *Miscellanies by an Officer* (1813) ed. by J. Watts de Peyster. 1888. The relation between him and the Scotch poet is interesting. Burns sent a poem to his commander in response to the latter's inquiries as to his health; De Peyster's tribute to the greater poet strongly echoes some of Burns' own lyrics, etc. See also *Mich. Pion. & Hist. Coll.* XX:296 ff. The *Memoir of John Johnston* by H. R. Schoolcraft gives an account of another poet and man of affairs inspired by his western life. *Ibid.* XXXVI:53 ff.

46 Wm. Downs — *A New Kentucky Composition of Hymns & Spiritual Songs.* 1816. 13-4.

47 Dreiser's sketch *My Brother Paul* in his *Twelve Men* (1919) gives an interesting picture of early conditions. The following poems are taken mainly from the O'Brien collection at the New York Public Library and from that of Professor Edwin Ford Piper, who generously went over his pieces with me.

"A steamer load o' whiskey,
One day elapsed her flue,
She blowed up all de spirits,
And made de water blue.
De ole Ohio staggered,
Like a salt water snake,
It made de fishes dance as if
Dey cotch de bowel ache."

The Ohio is unquestionably the favorite among the streams; it forms the refrain for numerous grotesque or sentimental lyrics. *The Log Hut*. *The Mississippi Woodman's Wife* shows, however, that the Father of the Waters was not neglected; and *Betsy Baker* furnishes an amusing satire on the oft-described trip across the Alleghanies and down to New Orleans.

"At last arrived at Louisville,
We thought ourselves quite lucky
To get so far down our route,
And lodge safe in Kentucky:
My wife she wished to see the men;
Half horse, half alligator,
I fearful was that they might gouge
My lovely Betsy Baker." etc.[48]

*My Old Kentucky Home* has immortalized one very common type of piece. Its note of reminiscent melancholy pervades, however, such different songs as *Rosalie, the Prairie Flower, The Indian Hunter,* or the farewells of the emigrants. *The Western Trapper's Camp Song* is interesting in that it displays recognition of distinct character types; its stressing of the freedom of forest and prairie is repeated many times in such spirited stanzas as *Westward Ho!* and *To the West* or jeered at in the parody of the latter beginning,

"To the West! to the West, I once went, do you see,
And one visit, I'm sure, was sufficient for me;
Oh, the things that I saw there, they frightened me quite
And ever since then, sirs, I've scarcely been right.

[48] *Dixson's Oddities.* 20-3.

My children got sick every day, sirs, almost
And my wife took the chills, and got deaf as a post;
Oh, there's some may exult, but for me, sirs, I'm blessed
If I haven't as much as I want of the West.''[49]

Somewhat similar to these vaudeville and newspaper productions with their coarse burlesque and their jolting rhythm as well as their suggestion of the popular voicing of the phenomena of the hinterland from the most insignificant of its villages to the slums of a great city are the campaign songsters of the middle century. In them not only do the prairies constantly appear as boundary marks, established features of the landscape, but western traits are made the rallying cry for the candidates.[50] In the "singing campaign of Harrison," for instance, collections like the *Log-Cabin Song Book* present dozens of exaltations of Tippecanoe, his prowess in battle or his rural activities — *The Hero of the Thames, The Farmer of North Bend, The Gallant Old Backwoodsman.*[51] Sometimes the tendencies are combined as in the selection beginning,

"Hurrah for the father of all the green West!
For the Buckeye who follows the plough!
The foeman in terror his valour confest,
And we'll honour the conqueror now."

Of the style of all, however, this is a fair sample. In the prewar contests Kansas furnishes the leit-motiv. *Away with Kansas Folly, The Sale of Kansas, How the South Overreached Itself*, are typical titles; verses like the following illustrate the manner in which the wrongs on the frontier were dinned into the nation.

"Hurrah, hurrah! from hill and valley,
Hurrah, from prairie wide and free!

49 *Beadle's Dime Song Book.* 27. For a *Farewell to Illinois* in similarly sardonic vein see *Ill. St. Hist. Soc. — Journal.* XIV:332-5.

50 Besides the song books Horace Greeley's *Log Cabin* with its whig editorials, speeches, & songs should be noted. It attained an immense circulation and became the basis of the *Tribune*, founded in 1841.

51 A vivid picture of the great whig gathering at the battlefield of Tippecanoe, 1840, in which such songs and frontier floats played a large part is quoted from John Sutherland's Journal by Ella Lonn. *Miss. Val. Hist. Rev.* IV:362. *The Political Campaign of 1840. Mich. Pion. & Hist. Coll.* X:8 ff. is one of many similar articles.

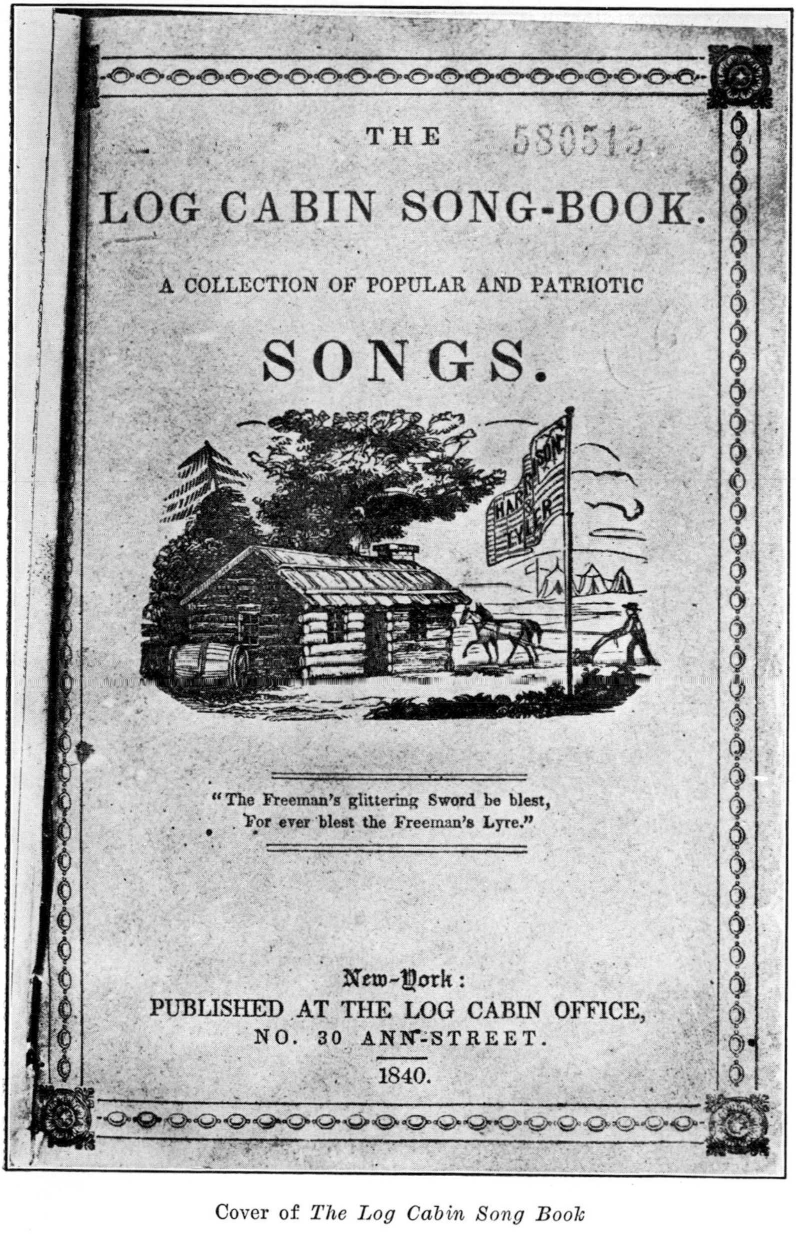


Cover of *The Log Cabin Song Book*

Around our glorious Chieftain rally,
For *Kansas* and for *Liberty*!"

* * * * *

"The wide rolling prairies of Kansas
Lay smiling in Liberty's light,
When the black Southern Serpent advances
Their promise of beauty to blight."

* * * * *

"Our brothers bold in the prairies cold,
In bloody shrouds are lying,
And their wives on high send the piercing cry,
And from burning homes are flying." [52]

It is the Middle West again that dominates the Lincoln campaign — its crudities, the attacks of his opponents; the sturdiness of its stock and the homeliness of its virtues, his supporters. Titles such as *Old Abe, the Rail Splitter* and *The Woodchopper of the West* are typical titles; *"Honest Abe" of the West* by Stedman presents a sectional figure against a national background.

"O hark! from the pine-crested hills of old Maine,
Where the splendor first falls from the wings of the morning,
And away in the West, over river and plain,
Rings out the grand anthem of Liberty's warning!
From green-rolling prairie it swells to the sea,
For the people have risen, victorious and free;
They have chosen their leaders, and bravest and best
Of them all is OLD ABE, HONEST ABE OF THE WEST!" [53]

Many more quotations might be given. These should suffice, however, to show the entrance of the frontier into the politics of the nation; mid the redolent smoke-wreaths of flambeaus, the clashing of cymbals, oratorical outbursts, and the hoarse cries of swaying thousands its features were chanted.

These are all more or less, however, developments of the com-

---

52 *Republican Campaign Songster: . . . Specially Prepared for the Friends of Freedom in the Campaign of Fifty-Six.* 1856. 5, 85, 98.

53 *Republican Campaign Songster.* 1860. 51. *Old-Time Campaigning & the Story of a Lincoln Campaign Song* is suggestive. *Ill. St. Hist. Soc. Jour.* XIII: 23 ff.

munity consciousness. Conceived in definite response to the ideals of a comparatively homogeneous body, or sensitive to the crises and emotions that pulse through the arteries of the multitude, they are either distinctively social in origin or become group possessions by virtue of spontaneous adoption. Removed from them, yet in certain respects influenced by them and paralleling their progress are the more definitely "literary" productions of the late eighteenth and early nineteenth century.

Noteworthy among these latter and most sharply illustrative of the cleavage between what might be called the "Volk" and "Kunst" poetry are the long elaborate epics that celebrate the deeds of hunter and warrior. Probably the earliest of these is *Ouabi; or the Virtues of Nature* (1790), which Mrs. Morton says she undertook from "an idea of being original" in her subject.

" 'Tis not the golden hill, nor flowing dale,
Which lends my simple muse her artless theme;
But the black forest and uncultur'd vale,
The savage warrior, and the lonely stream.

"Where MISSISSIPPI rolls his *parent flood*.
With hope impetuous to the surgy main,
The desert's painted chiefs explore the wood,
Or with thund'ring *war-whoop* sake the plain."

The romantic young exile, a familiar figure in the novels, forms the complicating character.

"On these far-extended plains,
Truth and godlike justice reigns!

. . . . .

Tired of scenes, where crimes beguile,
Fond of virtue's honest smile,
From perfidious vice I flee,
And devote my life to thee."

Having saved the Illinois warrior's wife, the white youth naturally falls in love with her, and after various marital adventures the noble chieftain celebrated in the title rises to the occasion and resigns Azakia, thus proving "the Virtues of Nature."

Daniel Bryan's *The Mountain Muse. Comprising the Ad-*

C Gullager Del.
Engravd by S.Hill.
Then amidst yon Chiefs retire,
Seated round the sacred fire,
Waiting for the warrior-feast,
Let them hail thee as their guest.


Frontispiece of Mrs. Morton's *Ouabi, or the Virtues of Nature*

*ventures of Daniel Boone; and the power of Virtuous and Refined Beauty* is in a similar vein. In it are featured the usual melodramatic elements — the adventurous nobleman who, disgusted "at the Perfidy, Corruption, Vice, and Parasitic meanness" of the courts, left

"The blazing clash of European WAR,
In the wild Forests of this Western World,
To seek the silent shades of bloodless PEACE;"

the robbers and their cave, "the hellish hoard of horrid Homicidal villainy," the fair and kidnapped daughter, the marvellously returning captive son. Nevertheless Boone's historic exploits are not forgotten; wandering amid the fruit and flower-brightened forest, the buffalo-pasturing savannahs,

"like the primary lord of Paradise
The Nomenclature of an opening world
He form'd;"

he aids Dunmore, combats the renegade Girty and the intrigues of the British and with all his own marvellous escapes and rescues of other prisoners finds time to philosophize. His importance as the founder of the Trans-Alleghany region is, of course, constantly emphasized, his dying son, for instance, exclaiming,

"Oh, Father! God preserve thy noble life
To see this lovely land I now must leave,
Become the happy Garden of the World." [54]

As to the style the quotations perhaps furnish a sufficient testimony. All of the faults, few of the virtues, of the eighteenth century are there. Banal invocations to the muses, prescribed emotions and sentimental reflections, tortured epithets and labored metre, the whole rattling machinery of the classical age present with singular incongruity the raw material of the West.

And to a lesser extent this is true of most of the poems of the type. Celebrated Indian chiefs are the favourite heroes, the exploits of Logan, Tecumseh, Black Hawk being repeatedly

54 Bryan — *The Mountain Muse.* 1813. 73, 66, 101, 144, 219.

celebrated. Richard Emmons is the author of an elaborate epic *The Fredoniad; or Independence Preserved* (1827);[55] and Wayne's battles are commemorated in Andrew Coffinberry's *The Forest Rangers* (1866).[56] Coloney's *Manomin* (1866) is a "rhythmical romance of Minnesota, the great rebellion and the Minnesota massacres"; the War of 1812 appears again and again in compositions like the *Heroes of the Lake* (1814) or *The Battle of New Orleans* (1825). Mitchell's *Indecision* (1839) deals with the fortunes of the immigrant; Butler describes *The Irish on the Prairie* (1874), glowingly forecasting a new Erin which will "plant all the joys of the Old Land amidst the bright scenes of the New"; *The Wyndott's Bride* treats of the romance of a missionary's daughter, near

> "The Sandusky River rolling outward into the lake:
> Mid leafy groves, and prairies bright with flowers."[57]

Humor, rather slighted in most of the poems, receives its due in *The Kansas War; or, the Conquests of Chivalry in the Crusades of the Nineteenth Century* (1856), which burlesques the material that Peacock tried to treat in a heroic manner in his *Rhyme of the Border War.*

Unfortunately the majority of these compositions are marred by a crazy-quilt patching of elements that forms a prominent source of structural weakness although it is occasionally responsible for giving us valuable details. Smith's *Ma-ka-tai-me-she-kis-kisk; or Black Hawk* (1894) shifts from the Mormons at Nauvoo to the speculation mania in Milwaukee like a lightning change artist; but the description of the copper diggings, the thousand wagons standing on the line for the opening of "the region joining on Des Moines," the great prairie hunt and feast under the liberty pole are distinctly suggestive. *Indecision* in its graceful *Song of the Prairie* furnishes a suggestion of the dreams of the immigrant with which the long sea voyage was beguiled; *Escalala* (1824) by Beach, with its absurd application of Arthurian customs to the fabled colony of the West furnishes a striking illustration of the wildness of the conjectures as to

---

55 Emmons is the author of an early play on Tecumseh.

56 See *The Pioneer Poet Lawyer* by N. B. C. Love. *Ohio Arch. & Hist. Soc. Pub.* X:305 ff.

57 *Ibid.* XV:182 ff.

the origin of the mounds. As a rule the time-worn and melodramatic elements already discussed in the novels predominate and with the mediocre verse demonstrate the reason for these productions being now mere literary curiosities.

Although in them the background is in no case etched with such distinction as to deserve detailed comment, there are a number of definite touches about the middle valley, and one poem *Mississippian Scenery* (1819) by Charles Mead, as the sub-title states, devotes itself largely to a description "of the interior of North America." The author asserts that the piece was chiefly written "while exploring some of those extensive regions which border the Mississippi River," and he makes a definite attempt to present the characteristic marks of the landscape.

"Where rosy plains in wild luxuriance lie,
And wat'ry glades reflect the azure sky;"

* * * * *

"Along the margin of each lucid stream,
Groves and savannas variegate the scene;
Majestic trees extend their leafy bow'rs,
And cast their shadows o'er the blushing flowers."

The rock hieroglyphics, the burial mounds, the relics of the mastodon, the control by French, Spanish, and by English, all these successively focus Mead's attention. Yet his innate poetic inspiration is so slight, his phraseology, so threadbare, and his reactions are so stereotyped, that the poem can have value for us today only as more evidence of the increasing interest in the West.[58]

The Indians of these long narratives as well as of the shorter poems that fill many worthless volumes, may well be treated together. At this time the cult of the red man developed to its highest extent; apparently each poetic aspirant felt it incumbent upon him to indite at least one effusion celebrating primitive virtues or retelling native legends. In numerous volumes, too, such productions form not only the title piece but

58 Mead — *Mississippian Scenery.* V, 13, 27. F. W. Thomas — *The Emigrant, or Reflections while Descending the Ohio* (1833) and Alexander Wilson — *The Pilgrim* (in his *Poems and Literary Prose*) are somewhat similar poems. Wilson's is further valuable for the realistic description it gives of the settlers along the banks.

the major portion of the contents. The general tendency is for them to be as indefinite in locality as they are improbable in substance. Ossian-like heroes float gracefully in a golden mist of romance; no vermin-infested, smoky wigwams offer them inadequate shelter; instead in a sort of happy hunting ground they woo beauteous maidens with cheeks like dusky petals and hair of silken sheen. From the petty ills of life they are immune; the tragic elements are designed solely to afford a splendid gesture — defiance of the whites, singing a death song as one floats placidly over the falls to rebuke an erring husband. Others combine similar ornamentation with a supposedly realistic setting and a historic or legendary basis. Such is Chivers' *Nacoochee; or, the Beautiful Star* (1837); this lady being a satin-gowned inhabitant of a fragrant heaven "beyond that wild-illimitable waste of unfenced prairie," the whole the author's embodiment of an old Creek legend given currency by Bartram. *Wakondah* (1841), a poem of the same type by Cornelius Mathews, illustrates interestingly, also, the transfer from the travel literature, for it quotes as a basis a passage from *Astoria* on the Black Hills. Many, of course, bring in even more definitely descriptions of the Middle West. The land is never so important, however, as its native inhabitants, the great point about their treatment being the increasing sympathy for them. Idealization goes to absurd lengths;[59] yet the very desire to make the average warrior, and particularly the chiefs, a combination of a Greek statue, Demosthenes, Alexander, and Sir Philip Sidney reveal the tardy recognition of the heroic qualities of the natives together with a desire to do justice to the tribes still cruelly wronged. Certainly in *Indian Melodies*, a typical collection of 1830, there is striking insistence upon this note, from *Geehale*, an Indian's lament over his family all destroyed by the race from "beyond the big seas" to *The Indian's Farewell to the Ohio Valley* or *The Chippewa Girl* beginning;

"They tell me the men with a white — white face,
Belong to a purer, nobler race,

[59] Dake, said to be the "author of the first volume of Nebraska poetry," an early teacher of literature in the university of that state, definitely propounds the theory that "A brutal savage is not a poetical object, and except under rare conditions, has no business in poetry," and that, "Every inducement, therefore, that could urge an ancient poet to portray prehistoric peoples as chivalrous and of a sustained dignity, should impel the writer of today to do likewise." *Nebraska Legends & Poems*. 1871.

But why, if they do, and it may be so,
Do their tongues cry 'yes' — and their actions 'no'?"[60]

Certainly, too, the beauty of the aboriginal myths, first brought out fully by Schoolcraft, inspired many imitators and retellers, ignorant and unskilled often, yet in their admiration unquestionably sincere.

Although the Indians formed one of the principal motifs, the shorter poems offer many other themes of interest to us. Rejoicings at individual victories in the War of 1812, especially that of New Orleans, prompt many effusions; first sight of the Mississippi is responsible for numerous sounding platitudes; the Barratarian receives the usual Byronic adulation; the pioneer of the Boone type soliloquizes in dignified verse; the mounds evoke weird guesses as to their origin and endless moralizings as to the brief career of man. For the stay-at-homes the accounts of travelers furnished inspiration for such productions; to the poets, on the other hand, the diarists and makers of handbooks turned for the enlivening of their pages. Curtiss, in his *Western Portraiture*, introduces Clement's *Hymn from the Prairies*, stating that "the fertile Prairies of the West seem to be as inspiring to poets, as they are attractive to the soil-tiller";[61] Parker quotes a Minnesota editor's explanation that Minnehaha is the Waterfall "after which Mr. Longfellow has named the interesting squaw described in his story of Hiawatha."[62] Of the combination of tendencies the long rhymed guide-book by Harriet Bishop McConkey *Minnesota; Then and Now* (1865) and the doggerel verse by Cordova, *The Prince's Visit* (1861) with its account of his tour on the prairies furnish almost perfect although artistically worthless examples, as *Dakota Land or the Beauty of St. Paul* (1868) by Col. Hankins does for the prose.

Inevitably in all this verse, mediocre as it usually is, is reflected the development of the territory. The prairie appears still the resort for the lover of the wild and the emotional exile,

"He has left the green valley for paths, where the bison
Roams through the prairies, or leaps o'er the flood;"[63]

---

60 *Indian Melodies.* 11, 16, 32.
61 Curtiss — *Western Portraiture.* 282.
62 Parker, N. H. — *Minnesota Hand Book* . . . 1857. 58-9.
63 Brainerd, J. G. C. — *Literary Remains, with a Sketch of his Life by J. G. Whittier.* 1832. 114.

again it is the goal for the wanderer or fortune-hunter,

"Talk not of the town, boys — give me the broad prairie,
Where man, like the wind, roams impulsive and free."

* * * * * *

"Droop not, brothers!
As we go
O'er the mountains
Westward Ho!"[64]

By the sentimental lyrist the populated midland is pictured,

"A home nest's mirrored on the 'Looking-Glass'
Like a small ark on emerald waves of grass,

"That summer winds break into flowery foam,
Creating a green sea, white-capped with bloom."[65]

For the religious enthusiast it furnishes a field for missionary enterprise.

"I've heard of vigorous men that ply
The oar, and those that urge the stream;
Whose toiling barques, adventurous, fly
O'er western lake and stream,—
Who mock at sense of sin and shame,
And flout and scorn their Maker's name."[66]

To it also resort the professional humorists such as Charles Godfrey Leland, maker of the *Breitmann Ballads.* In the reminiscences of the Kansas trouble such as the *Charge of the Border Ruffian Brigade,* Realf's *The Defense of Laurence* and *Kansas,* or Lucy Larcom's prize poem we find rhythmical interpretation of the struggle for freedom.[67] And from the earliest days the

---

64 From *Life in the West & Western Refrain.* G. P. Morris' *Poems.* 15th. ed. 1860. 80, 129. Morris is the author of a number of western poems — *The Prairie on Fire* (131-2), *O'er the Mountains* (97-8), *Fragments of an Indian Poem* (59-62).

65 From *Annie of Looking Glass Prairie* in Mrs. Anne M. Spaulding's *Poems.* 139.

66 From *The Boatmen of the West* in W. M. B. Tappan's *Poems.* 1836. 18.

67 In the spring of 1855 the secretary of the New England Emigrant Aid Company offered a prize of $50 for a Kansas poem. The prize winner *The Call to Kansas* is given in facsimile *Kan. St. Hist. Soc. Collections.* V:39. Realf is often called the poet of free-state Kansas. He was selected as secretary of state in the government John Brown expected to establish for the slaves he freed. See *Poems by Richard Realf Poet . . . Soldier . . . Workman, with a Memoir by Richard J. Hinton.* 1898, also *Richard Realf's Free State Poems . . .* 1900.

progress of the country was a favorite theme for the laudatory rhymester.

In another way, too, the literary evolution of the prairie is indicated — by the steadily increasing number of songsters on the western side of the Alleghanies, for the average reader best revealed and for our purposes best summarized by consideration of the anthologies of Gallagher (1841) and Coggeshall (1860). That the poets shared the tendency of the novelists to go far afield for inspiration or to rely on rather formal conceptions is clearly brought out by the contents of the first, for out of one hundred and nine poems only seventeen are really middle-western in subject, and the proportion in Coggeshall is about the same. For the most part these resemble verses already discussed. Some few, however, are worthy of particular notice. Gallagher, for instance, pays tribute in vigorous ringing lines to the heroic *Mothers of the West*, and in his *Miami Woods* gives some luscious descriptive touches in blank verse of a really commendable quality. Butler in his *The Boatman's Horn* bodies forth a little of the leaping magic of the river signal.

"O, Boatmen! wind that horn again,
For never did the list'ning air
Upon its lambent bosom bear
So wild, so soft, so sweet a strain!"

Some of his brother's gravity of mood combined with his perception of descriptive values is revealed by John H. Bryant in his *Senatchwine's Grave, Winter,* or *Indian Summer,* from which the following stanza is quoted.

"O'er the wide plains, that lie
A desolate scene, the fires of autumn spread,
And on the blue walls of the starry sky,
A strange wild glimmer shed."

*Lewis Wetzel* by Florus B. Plimpton is interesting as an example of the ballad technique applied to frontier materials; and close poetic analogy with the work of the middle western prose humorists is found in Finley's *The Hoosier's Nest.*

"I'm told, in riding somewhere West,
A Stranger found a Hoosier's Nest,

In other words, a Buckeye cabin,
Just big enough to hold Queen Mab in.
Its situation low, but airy,
Was on the borders of a prairie."

Very different from this unconventional and facetious bit are the somewhat formal poems of Micah P. Flint, which attract attention partly because he was the oldest son of Timothy, secondarily because of the localized nature of many of them. Most noteworthy, perhaps, is *The Silent Monks* celebrating the order whose monastery on one of the Indian Mounds near Cahokia had already attracted the attention of the travellers, a poem written with a sombreness of mood, a grim restraint thoroughly in harmony with the subject.

"Here, midst a boundless waste
Of rank and gaudy flowers, and o'er the bones
Of unknown races of the ages past,
They dwelt. Themselves knew not the deep, dark thoughts
Of their associates. . . .
Man's heart is made of iron, or 'twould burst
'Midst mute endurances of woes, like these.
I saw the sun behind the western woods
Go down upon their shorn and cowled heads.
No vesper hymn consoled their troubled thoughts.
Far o'er the plain the wolf's lugubrious howl,
The cricket's chirp, and the nocturnal cry
Of hooting owls, was their sad evening song." [68]

Certain work of a rather creditable character is barred for us, of course, by the nature of its subject. Yet the greater part of it has disappeared from sight not because of the content but because of the feebleness of the treatment. Sincere as was the poetic impulse that crowded the columns of the dingy old newspapers under such headings as the "Parnassiad" or "Seat of the Muses," and that turned out from the pioneer presses dozens of "home talent" volumes, it was productive of but little enduring verse.

---

68 Coggeshall, W. T.—*The Poets & Poetry of the West* . . . 1860. All poems cited are given here. For quot. see 173, 192, 83, 62-63. *The Hoosier's Nest* is printed *Ind. Hist. Soc. Pub.* IV no. 2. Gallagher's anthology was only one of a series he projected to display the culture of the West.

One volume at least is of marked value to the collector — the slender little *Poems of Two Friends* (1860) which is the first published book of William Dean Howells. In his contributions, however, in spite of the melancholy realism of *The Movers* and the affectionate description of *The Autumn Land* and *Evening Voices* there are few distinctive notes. And in spite of his later generous tribute to Piatt — that "in him the Middle West has its true poet,"[69] we find in the work of the latter not much more local color. In selections such as *The Pioneer Chimney* or *The Prairie Fires* sympathetic response to the heroic past is evident; his autumn poems give good pictures; *The Western Pioneer* attractively portrays the coming of the bees as predecessors of the whites.

"The Indian saw the moving Bees,
From flower to flower, in dream-like breeze
  Blowing their pilgrim way;
Or, deep in honey of the flower,
Hanging in sunshine hour by hour,
  Dream through the dreaming day.

"He saw the Future's garment gleam
O'er mounds of tribes and legends stream —
  O'er the sweet waste of flowers;
He saw his hunting ground — the Past!
Lit with the domes of cities vast —
  Glory of spires and towers!"[70]

But in the remainder of the volume as, in fact, in most of the collections of the Piatts, the pervading note is the tepid sentimentality of the period. Certainly only Howells's later reputation has prolonged the life of *Poems of Two Friends*.

Yet some of this early verse attained contemporary popularity, some has kept the name of its makers fresh down to our own day. The gentle voices of the Cary sisters, for instance, still hum low lullabies or sentimental ballads to the inmates of many a placid American household. Their chief contribution to poetry as to

---

69 Howells, W. D. — *My Literary Passions*. 1895. 58. See also his *Years of My Youth*. 1916. 79. For Howells' description of the reception of his first book see *My Lit. Pas.* 57.

70 *Poems of Two Friends*. 78-9.

prose — the portrayal of the domestic life of the Midlands — may be best brought out by comparison with another feminine favorite of the early half of the century — Mrs. Lydia Huntley Sigourney. In her facile and poorly constructed poems we find again the old romantic native elements, the whites, if introduced at all, being of the pioneer type as in *The Emigrant Mother* or the *Death of a Missionary at the West.* Most of her verse belongs, of course, to the forest or the mystic wonderland of the Indian; yet it displays the exaltation of the native, characteristic of the century; in the account of the massacre of the Christian Indians, it presents interesting historical material; and to the description of the prairie it contributes one truly lovely line,

"A sea at rest, whose sleeping waves were flowers,"

a line so far above the author's usual average, as a matter of fact, that she herself gave it praise in her *Lucy Howard's Journal.*

In contrast with her work the homely lyrics of the Ohio sisters reveal with doubled effect the transformation of the inland valley. The dark forests that once shrouded the pestilential soil are now levelled; the prairie grasses, clipped and unsnarled, save beside the roadbeds; in their stead ripple rustling corn-tassels, clover's spicy pink and white, the silvery sheen of timothy. The creaking of the loaded hay wagons, the mooing of cows, the shrill whistle of the freckled chore-boy replace the Indian war whoop, the crack of the lone hunter's rifle. Houses cluster together now without palisades; the ringing stroke of the blacksmith, the shouts of released school-children mark beginning community activities; neighborhood characters gain recognition. And although throughout such ballads as *The Prairie on Fire* or *The Lamp on the Prairie* there weaves a pronounced didactic and sentimental tendency, their core is sound. The tenderness, the lingering affection with which the Careys describe the "common flowers, with common names" and all the quaint, familiar surroundings of the home land give to the western landscape the domestic touch it long had lacked.

Decidedly different, infinitely more vigorous were the *Pike County Ballads* of John Hay, through which in the early period the middle western frontier gained its most adequate representation. They are, lifted to the level of literature, the successors of the river chanties and the rhymes of the crude border bards. In them are exemplified the coarser tendencies of the life — the careless morals, the ready cursing, the fighting and the gambling of men freed from restraint. In a ballad like *Jim Bludsoe of the Prairie Belle,* however, the poet penetrates beneath the rough exterior to the inherent manliness and generosity, redeeming features almost always in even the rudest of the borderers.

"He weren't no saint — them engineers
  Is all pretty much alike, —
One wife in Natchez-under-the-Hill
  And another one here, in Pike;
A keerless man in his talk was Jim,
  And an awkward hand in a row,
But he never flunked, and he never lied, —
  I reckon he never knowed how.

"And this was all the religion he had, —
  To treat his engine well;
Never to be passed on the river;
  To mind the pilot's bell;
And if ever the Prairie Bell took fire, —
  A thousand times he swore,
He'd hold her nozzle agin the bank
  Till the last soul got ashore."

Assuredly a simple creed but when the test came,

"He seen his duty, a dead-sure thing —
  And went for it thar and then;
And Christ ain't a-going to be too hard
  On a man that died for men."

And in the brief statement of such a code Hay did far more to make articulate the frontier than less gifted mortals in pages of exposition. In later life he himself tended to belittle his border pieces; and, as a matter of fact, *Little Breeches* and *Golyer* do verge dangerously on the sentimental. This is a tendency, however, throughout the whole period of romance and one that cannot be too seriously held up against them. All of the poems have a swinging vigor and a rough-hewn vividness that are exactly right for the life they portray. Through them, too, pulses a latent tenderness, lavished especially on the lovely land that begot them, *The Prairie.*

> "Far in the East like low-hung clouds
> The waving woodlands lie;
> Far in the West the glowing plain
> Melts warmly in the sky.
> No accent wounds the reverent air,
> No footprint dints the sod,—
> Lone in the light the prairie lies,
> Rapt in a dream of God."

And the blending of romantic wistfulness with sensuous abandon to the wild pinks' burst of crimson fire or the fennel's floods of flowery gold that marks the other stanzas and that allies Hay to a prose rhapsodist like Flagg were to find in General Albert Pike an even abler exponent. For on the dawn-flushed loveliness of the misted prairie he echoes the unadulterated beauty and the throbbing ectasy of a Keats or a Shelley. He emotionalizes the "thick Aeolian grass" of the Southwest with the fervor of the lyrist and with the intimacy that imperceptibly distills from days and months of brooding love; through his verse there trills "the merry mimic of the southern woods"; locust blossoms drip honeyed fragrance; the calm of a myriad stars rests upon the forest-buttressed prairie. And aside from such direct touches of description we like to feel the midland evasively inspiring the more exotic pieces—its jets of blossoms, for instance, the brilliant color of *Ariel,* said to have been written on the prairie while the author's horse fed by his side. Certainly in the same poem the flat country is linked with the rest of the continent most effectively before Whitman.

> "Broad fields spread inland, robed in green and gold,
> And waving with a mighty wealth of grain,
> From where the bear snarled at the Arctic cold,
> To the Mexique Gulf, and the Pacific Main;—
> Far South, in snowy undulations, rolled,
> With their white harvests many a treeless plain;

And where the Sierra westwardly inclines,
Gleamed a new Ophir, with its glittering mines."[71]

And in so exquisitely rapturous a chant as *Love* or the elaborate tracery and rich melody of the *Hymns to the Gods* this dweller on the crude frontier avails himself not only of the golden haze of the English romanticists, really too much his masters, but of the surpassing splendor of the far-off classic age.

Yet Pike's audience is even today an undeservedly small one; the entrance of the prairie into the work of the better known of our poets is, therefore, significant. As early as Freneau we find allusions to the West. In *The Rising Glory of America* he speaks of Washington's gallant opposition to

"The bold invaders of his country's rights,
Where wild Ohio pours the mazy flood,
And mighty meadows skirt his subject streams,"

and prophesies mighty cities on that river and the Mississippi. *On the Emigration to America and Peopling the Western Country* also foreshadows the development of the region of our study.

"To western woods, and lonely plains,
Palemon from the crowd departs,
Where Nature's wildest genius reigns,
To tame the soil, and plant the arts—
What wonders there shall freedom show,
What mighty states successive grow!"[72]

*On the Symptoms of Hostilities, 1809, On a Celebrated Performer on the Violin,* and *The Newsmonger* all reflect political events on the western frontier.

In spite of numerous other allusions to the Middle Valley, however, it is not until we reach the distinguished New England

---

71 Pike, A.—*Hymns to the Gods & Other Poems.* 1916. 86.

72 *The Poems of Philip Freneau, Poet of the American Revolution* ed. for the Princeton Historical Association by Fred Lewis Pattee. 3v. 1902. I:65, II:280. This latter poem was first printed in Bailey's *Pocket Almanac* for 1785. *The Midnight Consultations* as early as 1775 prophesied a future happy time,

"When one vast cultivated region teems
From ocean's side to Mississippi streams,
While each enjoys his vineyard's peaceful shade,
And even the meanest has no foe to dread." I:181.

group that we find really notable interpretations of the West. Bryant's response to the Midland we expect to be peculiarly interesting; in his prose works it is, nevertheless, decidedly disappointing. His journal *Illinois Fifty Years Ago* uses as uninspired details and as monotonous a style as the productions of the least literary of the travellers; *The Early Northwest* is better written and presents well chosen material, yet even it produces a distinctly sketchy effect. Stories in which early in his career, he treated subjects from the interior are also inferior technically — *The Whirlwind,* the tale of a Baptist itinerant; the *Skeleton's Cave,* an account of a narrow escape from burial alive near a "French settlement in the western region of the United State"; and *The Marriage Blunder,* which might have been an interpretation of the ancient debatable ground of France and Spain as deft as Hall's charming tales of the habitant villages, had Bryant possessed the requisite play of wit and delicacy of touch. The latter story does have several realistic characters and does give one impassioned passage on the prairies of the Southwest. In general, however, Bryant holds true to his statement about Illinois, "What I have thought and felt amid these boundless wastes and awful solitudes I shall reserve for the only form of expression in which it can be properly uttered."[73]

And in this mode of expression, the natural one for him, the loftiest for all, he does react nobly to the charm of the blossoming lawns of the west. His short pieces are rather orthodox in theme — *The Hunter's Serenade, The Hunter of the Prairies, The Painted Cup*; naturally, too, somewhat unoriginal in detail; yet they do blend attractively the products of the prairie — the slim papaya's yellow fruit, the rustling hazels, the blue-bright clusters of the bordering vines; they do exult in the pastures "measureless as air"; they do contribute to Bryant's mystic doctrine of nature. It is in his long poem of *The Prairies,* however, that his interpretation reaches its height. There is chronicled his first emotion.

> "These are the gardens of the Desert, these
> The unshorn fields, boundless and beautiful,
> For which the speech of England has no name —

73 Bryant, W. C. — *Prose Writings* ed. by P. Godwin. 1884. I:223. II:22.

The Prairies. I behold them for the first,
And my heart swells, while the dilated sight
Takes in the encircling vastness."

There is given most dignified expression to the deeply religious awe of the New Englanders, so prominent a factor in the annals of Kansas. There is impressed the mortality of man, a thought inspired in all by the towering monuments of the past but peculiarly pregnant to Bryant's melancholy disposition. He expresses no new strain in all this, but he does give the most haunting suggestion of the tragic past that we have so far found, and, in the graceful close, the most charmingly vitalized representation of the present as well as a serene and kindly promise for the future.

"Still this great solitude is quick with life.
Myriads of insects, gaudy as the flowers
They flutter over, gentle quadrupeds,
And birds, that scarce have learned the fear of man,
Are here, and sliding reptiles of the ground,
Startlingly beautiful. The graceful deer
Bounds to the wood at my approach. The bee,
A more adventurous colonist than man,
With whom he came across the eastern deep,
Fills the savannas with his murmurings,
And hides his sweets, as in the golden age,
Within the hollow oak. I listen long
To his domestic hum, and think I hear
The sound of that advancing multitude
Which soon shall fill these deserts."

And because of the fact that Bryant did use thoughts, details, emotions long familiarized, he emphasized most powerfully the transition we have been discussing; his verse did for the prairies what poetry does for all life — summarized enduringly its tendencies, intensified its moods, ennobled its expression, a fitting task for America's first notable nature poet.

With Whittier the emphasis is very different. In his verse the prairie entered incidentally — as boundary marks, as natural phenomena in such pieces as *The Shoemakers* or *Kenoza Lake*;

its golden grain formed one of the cargoes of *The Ship-builders*; an eagle's quill from Lake Superior gave occasion for a survey of its features and a vivid suggestion of the drama of progress — the rocking pines of the North, the wild rice eaters' threshing, the far-off voyager's horn, the advance of the Yankee.

> "Behind the scared squaw's birch canoe,
> The steamer smokes and raves;
> And city lots are staked for sale
> Above old Indian graves.
>
> "I hear the tread of pioneers
> Of nations yet to be;
> The first low wash of waves, where soon
> Shall roll a human sea."

Nevertheless his main contribution is not to direct interpretation of the prairie but to the struggle that formed one of its darkest chapters. The intense feeling that made him the foremost poetic opponent of slavery involved him inevitably in the Kansas conflict. In *Le Marais du Cygne* he portrays one of the most sensational episodes in that struggle.

> "A blush as of roses
> Where rose never grew!
> Great drops on the bunch-grass,
> But not of the dew!
> A taint in the sweet air
> For wild beasts to shun!
> A stain that shall never
> Bleach out in the sun!
>
> "Back, steed of the prairies!
> Sweet song-bird, fly back!
> Wheel hither, bald vulture!
> Gray wolf, call thy pack!
> The foul human vultures
> Have feasted and fled;
> The wolves of the Border
> Have crept from the dead."[74]

[74] Several articles about this massacre have been published by the Kansas State Historical Society. See the *Coll.* XIV:208, 224, *Trans.* VI:365.

Tragic as is the prompting of its bitter lines, however, it lacks the ringing fervor, the martial swing that immortalized immediately *The Kansas Emigrants.*

"We cross the prairies as of old
The pilgrims crossed the sea,
To make the West, as they the East,
The homestead of the free!

. . . . . . . . . . . . . . .

"We're flowing from our native hills
As our free rivers flow;
The blessing of our Mother-land
Is on us as we go.

"We go to plant her common schools
On distant prairie swells,
And give the Sabbaths of the wild
The music of her bells.

"Upbearing, like the Ark of old,
The Bible in our van,
We go to test the truth of God
Against the fraud of man."

Chanting it the free-staters jolted across the frost-rutted prairies, ploughed in the contested corn fields, threw up ramparts against the invaders. The song was unquestionably Whittier's most lasting contribution to the literature of the midland.

With Lowell, of course, the West counted little. Yet, that even to him it served as a symbol for freedom is revealed in the first stanza of *The Pioneer.*

"What man would live coffined with brick and stone,
Imprisoned from the healing touch of air,
And cramped with selfish landmarks everywhere,
When all before him stretches, furrowless and lone,
The unmapped prairie none can fence or own."

Even to him, who found his chief inspiration in the rich literatures of the past, there came poetic prompting, grim yet stately, for *A Chippewa Legend* in Schoolcraft's account of *Sheem, the Forsaken Boy, or the Wolf Brother.*

And these native materials, barbarically picturesque, elementally emotional, were to find in another purveyor of European culture to the new world, their most popular exponent. Longfellow after long pondering over the Indian materials in Schoolcraft decided "to weave together their beautiful traditions into a whole,"[75] centering the series on the many-sided hero, Manabozho, but knotting in the cradle songs transcribed by the ethnologist and using incidentally such detached legends as *The Stone Canoe or Mon-daw-min.* His background, of course, is the forest and the prairie, "the great lakes of the northlands," the retreats of the Dacotahs. To them he brings not only the intuitive response of the native but the translucent haze steeping the Indian regions for the civilized story tellers. He creates the acme of wonder — the far-off golden age of the Indian, the animal-speaking fairy-land of a child. Yet all this idealization is flavored by reality — the soughing of pine-trees, the lone hoot of the owl, the chirring of locusts; at night fireflies flit through the darkness; the pale spirits' Death-Dance flares in the heavens. And the nature phenomena intensifying the background penetrate the language, now vivifying it in great splotches like the warring braves' paint, now tincturing it with the smoke of burning meadows, now deepening it with the wild fowls' "clangorous pinions." In the poem the red man's prairies obtain most complete symbolization.

In it, too, is carried farthest the idealization of the native. In a way this is permissible, since it is the half man, half god that prevails, the ordinary mortals being relegated to the background. Yet Hiawatha displays much the same freshly laundered qualities that Schoolcraft speaks of in the second edition of his tales; the malignancy, the low cunning of Manabozho that pervade so strongly such legends as that of his fight with his father, the West Wind, are all carefully ironed out; instead of a Loki, Longfellow's hero becomes a Prometheus. He is the peace-weaver, the teacher, the inventor of writing. He it is that slays the Magician, sender of fever from the marshes and the pestilential vapors; he who welcomes the black-robed stranger;

---

75 Longfellow, Samuel — *Life of Henry Wadsworth Longfellow with extracts from his Journals & Correspondence.* 2v. 1886. II:248. See also Stith Thompson — *The Indian Legend of Hiawatha. M. L. A. P.* XXXVII:128 ff. For additional references see Samuel Longfellow's book.

he who in a vision foresees the coming of the white men and the scattering of his own weakened, warring nations.

Similarly iridescent with a milky, mother-of-pearl lustre is Longfellow's portrayal of the Creole life of the valley. For to the weary love-quest of the Canadian Dorothea the midland furnishes a background in its way as idyllized as that for the aboriginal hero. Neither in the placid village of Grand-Pré nor the flower-girdled home of the blacksmith is there any hint of wrong on the part of the Acadians; the indolence and shiftlessness that aroused the resentment even of their French contemporaries here are refined away; wholly charming is the life of Opelousas; entirely virtuous are the impulses of the characters. In spite of the ever-present aching void the lonely years for Evangeline slip along with some of the monotonous and resistless ease of the flood of the great river. This effect is due in part, of course, to the smoothness of the hexameters; in larger measure, however, it is caused by the nature of the poet's images. With him is stressed always the peacefulness of the "limitless prairie." Even over the "terrible war-trails" of the tribes of "Ishmael's children" the sky "like the protecting hand of God is inverted." This lofty, almost religious conception of the land ennobles, too, the lover's passion. As of old the prairie is the retreat for the wretched; Gabriel, weary with waiting, unhappy and restless, sought in the western wilds oblivion of self and of sorrow; the moonlight upon the garden inundated the soul of Evangeline with indefinable longings. Yet even in her feverish pursuit across the wondrous wastes of the West enters none of the guilty pining of René, the sensual intoxication of a Manon. Every element that could give to her patient love purity, holiness is adopted by the poet — compassion for the Shawnee woman who, too, had her tale of love "with its pleasures, and pains, and reverses," submission to the guidance of the Jesuit father, likening of the faith in her soul to the "compass-flower, that the finger of God had suspended . . . to direct the traveller's journey over the sea-like, pathless, limitless waste of desert." And in this transformation of the love motif is demonstrated as forcibly the adoption of the Gallic romantic elements in the yet somewhat Puritanic literature of America as is the transfer of details from such works of fact as Darby's guide to Louisiana in the luxuriant descriptive passages based upon it and Banvard's panorama.[76] The idyll is, like so many of the landmarks of this early literature, at once a summary and a promise; in it are adapted the elements of Chateaubriand and Prévost; by it were determined later American portrayals. For the lovely chronicle of the Acadian maiden has done more than any other thing not only to promote the study of the Nova-Scotian exiles but to inculcate the romantic tradition of the early inhabitants.

Yet because in both these longer poems Longfellow, like the majority of his predecessors and contemporaries, turned to remote events, because the Middle West was as yet largely an isolated region of story, we are glad to have for the full flowering of the first period of romance the poet who is still preeminently the interpreter of the prairies, who first penetrated beneath surface phenomena to the fundamental significance of the land and its people, who, the Chanter of Democracy, found in the Great Valley its fruition. For in the Old Gray Poet, from his Long Island childhood inured to the vast harmonies of the sea, the broad swells of the prairie sounded a chord profoundly responsive. A reporter in New Orleans during the "rattling" days of '48, he gained a vague perception of the contributions of the Latin races to American nationality in the South and Southwest, but, as he himself confesses, his acquaintance among the Creoles was slight; with his quaintly tropic surroundings he was obviously not en rapport; for complete community of sympathy with the magic city of the delta we must turn to that later strangely gifted reporter, himself an exotic, Lafcadio Hearn. Whitman's journal of his voyage up the Mississippi and across the Great Lakes, portions of which he quoted many years afterward, is also disappointingly commonplace. The trans-

76 Longfellow's diary is interesting in this connection. [Dec. 17, 1846] "I see a panorama of the Mississippi advertised. This comes very *à propos*. The river comes to me instead of my going to the river; and as it is to flow through the pages of the poem, I look upon this as a special benediction." [Dec. 19] "Went to see Banvard's moving diorama of the Mississippi. One seems to be sailing down the great stream, and sees the boats and the sand-banks crested with cottonwood, and the bayous by moonlight. Three miles of canvas, and a great deal of merit." *Ibid.* 67-8. (The best idea of the nature of these panoramas may be obtained from H. Lewis — *Das Illustrirte Mississippithal.* Lange repr. of Rare Americana.) [Jan. 7th, 1847] "Went to the Library and got Watson's *Annals of Philadelphia* and the *Historical Collections of Pennsylvania.* Also, Darby's *Geographical Description of Louisiana.* These books must help me through the last part of Evangeline, so far as facts and local coloring go. But for the form and the poetry — they must come from my own brain." *Ibid.* 74.

continental trip of '79, however, thrilled him to the depths of his being. The "bread-raising" fields of Indiana and Illinois, Kansas "flat as a floor," all these interminable and stately prairies were for him entirely "freeing, soothing, nourishing . . . to the soul." They gave Lincoln and Grant — "vast-spread, average men — their foregrounds of character, altogether practical and real, yet (to those who have eyes to see) with finest backgrounds of the ideal." Food granaries of the world, key to the "real geographic, democratic, indissoluble American Union," they are also promoters of "those grandest and subtlest element emotions;" in theirs and the Rockies' "pure breath, primitiveness, boundless prodigality and amplitude, strange mixture of delicacy and power, of continence, of real and ideal," he sees the basis for America's great poetry, its original and lasting art. "Even their simplest statistics" are to him "sublime."[77]

And in his own poetry he unconsciously does his best to carry out his theories. For him "these immense meadows — these interminable rivers" are a symbol — of the vast resources, the latent power, the inherent dignity of the republic. On them in his disembodied wanderings through space he touches again and again, emphasizing them more than the phenomena of any other section, with the possible exception of his own beloved Manhatta.

"Other lands! interlink'd, food-yielding lands!
Land of coal and iron! Land of gold! Lands of cotton, sugar, rice!
Land of the spinal river, the Mississippi, and of the Alleghanies! Ohio's land!
Land of wheat, beef, pork! Land of wool and hemp! Land of the apple and grape!
Land of the pastoral plains, the grass-fields of the world!
Land of those sweet-air'd interminable plateaus!"

His view is ever the panoramic one, now linking the Mississippi with the "long river-stripes of the earth," again passing from the brilliant sunlight of the Gulf to the heavy pine forests of the North, from the teeming streets of New York to the crests of the Rockies or the blue billows of the Pacific, but always

77 Whitman — *Complete Prose Works*. 1897. 149, 141-2, 143, 152, 150.

resting contentedly over the broad spaces of the Midland. In part it is the fruitfulness of the West that seems to attract him.

> "Thou lucky Mistress of the tranquil barns!
> Thou Prairie Dame that sittest in the middle, and lookest out upon thy world, and lookest East, and lookest West!"

More profoundly, however, the calm power of the meadow-lands seems to move him.

> "Give to me fresh corn and wheat — give me serene-moving animals, teaching content;
> Give me nights perfectly quiet, as on high plateaus west of the Mississippi, and I looking up at the stars."

His conception of the central valley's primal sanities seems, moreover, to dominate Whitman's attitude toward its inhabitants. For him it is "always the West, with strong native persons." The women with their attempts to ape their sisters of the East displease him, yet he ceases not to sing

> "Of future women there — of happiness in those high plateaus ranging three thousand miles, warm and cold;
> Of mighty inland cities yet unsurveyed and unsuspected . ."

What he calls the natural persons ever attract him — hunter, trapper, flat-boatman, farmer, the butcher in the slaughter-house, the builder in the city — men simple, sure, slow-moving, common. To such a one he compares the momentous year 1861; in part for their embodiment of the type he admires Grant and Lincoln. In their midland home he finds his most picturesque and dignified figures of the present; and in *The Prairie-Grass Dividing* he expresses his high hopes for the future. To the West he awards the leadership in the march of democracy in his *Pioneers! O Pioneers!* To the men of the outlands belongs the task of building up a new and perfect state, the old, old dream of the explorers of the Midlands. Just how his vision is to be realized Whitman never questions; he is content that he is in a new and unspoiled world amid a nation strong and buoyant, almost every activity of which calls for rejoicing. Of his attitude, mystic, uncritical, the following lines are entirely typical.

"Americans! conquerors! marches humanitarian;
Foremost! century marches! Liberatad masses!
For you a programme of chants.
Chants of the prairies;
Chants of the long-running Mississippi, and down to the Mexican sea;
Chants of Ohio, Indiana, Illinois, Iowa, Wisconsin, and Minnesota;
Chants going forth from the centre, from Kansas, and thence, equi-distant,
Shooting in pulses of fire, ceaseless to vivify all." [78]

And his own chants he would have the clue for the poet of the future. Unconsciously, perhaps, he adapted his own rhythms to the gentle prairie swells, the shifting immensity of the horizon, the billows of the sea. Consciously, however, and repeatedly he proclaimed the need of new and artistic forms for the artists to come thereafter. As he travelled through the West, he could not help feeling,

"Grand as the thought that doubtless the child is already born who will see a hundred millions of people, the most prosperous and advanc'd of the world, inhabiting these Prairies, the great Plains, and the valley of the Mississippi, . . . it would be grander still to see all those inimitable American areas fused in the alembic of a perfect poem, or other æsthetic work, entirely western, fresh and limitless — altogether our own, without a trace or taste of Europe's soil, reminiscence, technical letter or spirit." [79]

His is the most superb vision of the new literature of America.

Because of all these things — his insistence upon the elemental verities, his stressing of the strong and simple life, the breadth of his vision and the fervor of his chant, Whitman has become not only the increasingly lauded herald of a new art in America,

---

78 Whitman, W. — *Starting from Paumanok* (in *Leaves of Grass.* 1900.) 25-6; *A Carol of Harvest, for 1867,* 416; *Give me the Splendid Silent Sun* 263, *American Feuillage* 152, *Songs of Parting* 338, *Starting from Paumanok* 17-18.

79 Whitman — *Specimen Days* in *Complete Prose Works.* 149. The same thought is repeated in the *Phantom by Ontario's Shores & Marches Now the War is Over.*

but the most influential exponent abroad of the western continent's aspirations. Among the sophisticated readers of Europe he comparatively easily gained the acclamation his own country denied him. And in the recognition thus accorded is found only another evidence of the development we have been tracing. Europe was not at the time of publication of *Leaves of Grass* overwhelmingly cordial toward American offerings, and its critics were not exceptionally penetrating. But from the moment that Columbus proclaimed his discovery to the present what Mr. Lippmann designated as the twin complexes of *The Crude Barbarian and the Noble Savage* [80] have alternated or combined in European conceptions of America, and into these Whitman fits better than the majority of our writers.

Survey not only of the reception accorded him but of foreign literatures shows that a surprising amount of attention has been devoted by the "intellectuals" to the phenomena of the new land. Even in the classic age exotic bits such as Voltaire's *Alzire,* Pope's "Lo, the poor Indian," or Mrs. Aphra Behn's *Oroonoko,* bear testimony to the almost unsounded fascinations of the western hemisphere. And with the casting off of conventional fetters and the lunge into Romanticism, America's allurements were incalculably multiplied. Like the splendid pageantry of the Middle Ages, the heroism of the northland, the glamour of the supernatural, it offered for the dreamer a refuge from reality; its watchword of freedom, its proud vaunting of the stars and stripes, made it like France, a rallying point for the liberal, although it suffered with that country from the revulsion of feeling engendered by the excesses of the Revolution. Its countless travel volumes formed with other voyages into the unknown the favorite reading of thousands; and in its "storied past," its unique character types, were available materials yet untarnished by long handling. In short its influence in the Romantic Revival and other epochs of European literature is a factor even yet too little appreciated.

This penetration of European thought and expression is, of course, characteristic of the new world as a whole, yet specific

80 *The New Republic* XXV:70, Dec. 15, 1920. The article prompting Mr. Lippmann's, *America, Listen to Your Own* by D. H. Lawrence, *Ibid.* 68 is a good portrayal of the European attitude.

traces of the region we have been studying may be indicated. The English treatments are particularly noteworthy for the reliance that they show upon the accounts of the travellers. The advertisement of *Gertrude of Wyoming*, for instance, unquestionably the most popular of the many romantic interpretations of the Pennsylvania massacres, cites book testimony for the events although Byron's charge that it is "full of grossly false scenery"[81] and Willis's longing to see Campbell's "fine face while the *real* displaced the *ideal* valley of his imagination"[82] express early the modern reader's desire that the poet had relied more upon authentic sources for the landscape rather than the conventional pastorals. Moore, too, in spite of the fact that he visited America surrounds himself with a formidable row of authorities. The epistle "To the Lady Charlotte Rawdon describing the St. Lawrence and the Great Lakes," alone contains references to nine works on the new continent from Lafitau to Morse's *American Geography*. Allowances must be made, of course, for the passion of Moore's generation for footnotes, but interesting as are the allusions he gives to Indian superstitions and customs, we cannot help wishing he had spared a little of the time he spent in attacking American institutions for personal observation of the scenery. Southey, on the other hand, although his youthful dream of a Pantisocracy was never carried out, conceived it from his reading — Rousseau, the ancients, and Cowley, whose "favourite intention" it was "to retire with books to a cottage in America, and seek that happiness in solitude which he could not find in society."[83] And from books he obtained the material for his exotic pieces, the most important of which for us are *The Huron's Address to the Dead* and his long poem *Madoc*, which is based upon two well established traditions, that of the white Indians and that of the Welsh colonies in America.[84] Byron, too, we should find worthy of mention if for

81 Byron — *Letters & Journals*. 1904. V:166. *Coll. Poems*. I:430.
82 Willis, N. P. — *Rural Letters* . . . 1849. no. 13. p. 117.
83 Southey — Letter to Horace Bedford Nov. 13, 1793. *Life & Letters* ed. by Denis. Other comments by Shelley on his plan are to be found. *Ibid*. 87-8, 91-5.
84 Catlin, who spent much time among the Mandans and was greatly influenced by them, believed the impression that they were descended from Madoc's colony well founded. Southey in the preface to his poem written 1805 gives extended discussion of the tradition, in 1815 adding this note, "That country has now been fully explored, and, wherever Madoc may have settled, it is now certain that no Welsh Indians are to be found upon any branches of the Missouri."

no other reason than the fun that he poked at the Tory Laureate's youthful Utopian vision and the epic, *Madoc*.[85] As a matter of fact, however, Byron's ardor for freedom always provided a link with America, one which the admiration which his works there excited served to link closer.[86] And in his narrative poems we find evidence that he himself was personally interested in this new territory that exalted him. To the ninth edition of his *Corsair* was appended a long note demonstrating the probability of Conrad's characterization by an account of Lafitte from an American newspaper, a particularly interesting use of the Barratarian material since Byron's own work was to stamp strongly the legend, then only in the making, of the Pirate of the Gulf. The famous settlement of Rapp came in for some of the banter of *Don Juan*;[87] and in the same poem is given perhaps the crowning picture of the child of nature among the British writers of the century, the semi-whimsical tribute to Daniel Boone that interrupts for a moment the siege of the Moslems in the eighth canto.[88]

> "Of all men, saving Sylla the man-slayer,
>   Who passes for in life and death most lucky,
> Of the great names, which in our faces stare,
>   The General Boone, back-woodsman of Kentucky,
> Was happiest amongst mortals anywhere;
>   For killing nothing but a bear or buck, he
> Enjoy'd the lonely, vigorous, harmless days
>   Of his old age in wilds of deepest maze.
>
> "Crime came not near him — she is not the child
>   Of solitude; Health shrank not from him — for
> Her home is in the rarely-trodden wild."

We might comment, too, upon the work of Wordsworth, in which Professor Lane Cooper has found numerous traces of the poet's reading of travels.[89] In *Ruth*, for instance, the descrip-

85 Byron — *Vision of Judgment*. XCVII. *Don Juan*. Canto III, st. 93. For the reference to *Madoc* see *English Bards & Scotch Reviewers*.

86 See Byron's entry in his Diary for Dec. 5, 1813. "Dallas' nephew . . . tells Dallas that my rhymes are very popular in the United States. These are the first tidings that have ever sounded like fame to my ears — to be redde on the banks of the Ohio."

87 Byron — *Don Juan*. Canto XV st. 35-37.

88 *Ibid*. Canto VIII st. 61-67.

89 Cooper, Lane — *Methods & Aims in the Study of Literature*. . . . 1915. 96 ff.

tions of Bartram are directly responsible for the lovely stanzas about the faithless lover's carefree life in the West.

> "The youth of green savannahs spake,
> And many an endless, endless lake,
> With all its fairy crowds
> Of islands, that together lie
> As quietly as spots of sky
> Among the evening clouds."

*The Excursion* near the end of the Third Book affords an interesting reaction to the cult of nature.

> "Let us, then, I said,
> Leave this unknit Republic to the scourge
> Of her own passions; and to regions haste,
> Whose shades have never felt the encroaching axe,
> Or soil endured a transfer in the mart
> Of dire rapacity. There, Man abides,
> Primeval Nature's child. A creature weak
> In combination, (wherefore else driven back
> So far, and of his old inheritance
> So easily deprived?) but, for that cause,
> More dignified, and stronger in himself;
> Whether to act, judge, suffer, or enjoy.
> True, the intelligence of social art
> Hath overpowered his forefathers, and soon
> Will sweep the remnant of his line away;
> But contemplations, worthier, nobler far
> Than her destructive energies, attend
> His independence, when along the side
> Of Mississippi, or that northern stream
> That spreads into successive seas, he walks;
> Pleased to perceive his own unshackled life,
> And his innate capacities of soul,
> There imaged: . . . . . . . . . . . . . . . . .
> So, westward, toward the unviolated woods
> I bent my way; . . . . . . . . . . . . . .
> *But that pure archetype of human greatness,*
> *I found him not.* There, in his stead, appeared
> A creature, squalid, vengeful, and impure;

Remorseless, and submissive to no law
But superstitious fear, and abject sloth.
Enough is told!"

And these are only a few among many striking interpretations.

In France mention of the Midland falls into two distinct channels, each an interesting but one a decidedly feeble carrying on of tradition. On the romantic songsters of the nineteenth century the Chateaubriand influence impressed itself strongly. One might, indeed, trace out a whole genealogy for favorite incidents such as his account of an Indian mother's depositing her dead child in the flowering branches of a tree, used by M. de Saint Victor, by Millevoye in his *L'Amour Maternal,* and the young Hugo in his *La Canadienne.*[99] Even more obvious in method as well as in materials is the debt of de Vigny displayed in the luxuriant comparison of *Éloa*[91] or the picturesque narrative of *La Sauvage.* The latter poem is noteworthy for its revocation of the Rousseau cult in the words of the severe yet upright young Anglo-American.

"Hommes à la peau rouge! Enfants, qu'avez-vous fait?
Dans l'air d'une maison votre coeur étouffait,
Vous haïssiez la paix, l'ordre et les lois civiles,
Et la sainte union des peuples dans les villes,
Et vous voilà cernés dans l'anneau grandissant.
C'est la Loi qui, sur vous, s'avance en vous pressant.
La Loi d'Europe est lourde, impassible et robuste,
Mais son cercle est divin, car au centre est le Juste.

. . . . . . . . . . . . . . . . . . . . . . . .

Elle dit, en fondant chaque neuve cité:
'Vous m'appelez lo Loi, je suis la Liberté.' "[92]

90 *Oeuvres Complètes de Millevoye* . . . 1823. III:54-5. In the notes p. 102 ff. are quoted the related passages from Chateaubriand and M. de Saint-Victor.

91 "Ainsi dans les forêts de la Louisiane, Bercé sous les bambous et la longue liane, Ayant rompu l'oeuf d'or par le soleil mûri, Sort de son lit de fleurs l'éclatant colibri;" etc. Oeuvres Complètes de Alfred de Vigny. Poëmes . . . ed. by M. Fernand Baldensperger. 1914. 18.

92 "J'ai voulu prouver, écrit le poète à Mlle. Maunoir le 31 janvier 1843, que la *civilisation* pouvait être chantée ainsi que la *raison* et que les races sauvages étaient *coupables* envers la famille humaine de n'avoir pas su vénérer la Femme, la culture, l'hérédité, former une société durable, et qu'il était juste que l'Europe les forçât d'en recevoir une. Quoique j'aime J. J. Rousseau, ma conscience m'a forcé de prendre le thème contraire au sien." *Ibid.* 369. For the quotations from the poem see 205-7.

In the stately address, however, to the solitudes of the new world with which the piece opens and in the appeal of the Osage woman with her two helpless children are found elements more conventional and more filled with local color.

> "Les Hurons, cette nuit, ont scalpé
> Mes frères; mon mari ne s'est point échappé;
> Nos hameaux sont brûlés comme aussi la prairie.
> J'ai sauvé mes deux fils à travers la tuerie;
> Je n'ai plus de hamac, je n'ai plus de maïs,
> Je n'ai plus de parents, je n'ai plus de pays."

In writers like Baudelaire or Leconte de Lisle on the other hand, the Chateaubriand influence is blended with that of his American successor. Baudelaire, for instance, calls his "Le Calumet de Paix" an imitation of Longfellow, and in the mellow lines of the poem is found a dignified although rather colorless representation of the gathering on the prairie convened by the Great Spirit, decidedly allied in spirit with *Hiawatha.*

> "Par le chemin des eaux, par la route des plaines,
> Par les quatre côtés d'où soufflent les haleines
> Du vent, tous les guerriers de chaque tribu, tous,
> Comprenant le signal du nuage qui bouge,
> Vinrent docilement à la Carrière Rouge
> Où Gitche Manito leur donnait rendez-vous."

It is of Longfellow again that the opening of *Le Calumet du Sachem* reminds us. The fauna display the variety that the French always delighted in, but we are given a specific touch about the region in which we are interested.

> "Ses guerriers dispersés errent dans les prairies,
> Par delà le grand Fleuve où boivent les bisons.
> Loin du pays natal aux riches floraisons,
> Comme le vent d'hiver fait des feuilles flétries,
> L'exil les a chassés vers tous les horizons."

The whole has, moreover, a delicacy of finish, a certainly pensiveness of mood, peculiarly appropriate for the account of the old sachem returned to die in the territory of his fathers, and decidedly characteristic of the Gallic interpretations. This pensiveness prevails, too, in the description of *La Prairie* itself in spite of the quick beat of the ponies, the moans of the wounded, the cries of the hunters that for an instant spurt across it.

> "Dans l'immense Prairie, océan sans rivages,
> Houles d'herbes qui vont et n'ont pas d'horizons,
> Cent rouges cavaliers, sur les mustangs sauvages,
> Pourchassent le torrent farouche des bisons." [93]

In prose unfortunately the interpretations are not so artistic, for the French novels and short stories of the West rapidly equalled and even excelled as thrillers the dime novels of America. The leader of this blood and thunder school is unquestionably Gustave Aimard, whose name was sufficient to thrill the hearts of all school boys for a generation and who attained among adults equal popularity. In spite of the fact that he was alleged to have been in turn squatter, hunter, trapper, and miner, and to have "seen the mode of life of all the adventurers who traverse the Indian deserts," much in his books is an obvious compound of his predecessors' details. Whole paragraphs of his description are lifted from Chateaubriand; character types, situations, motifs, even names long familiarized by romancers he uses repeatedly. In the plains of the new world over which they wander trustingly the heroes' eyes are opened to the truth and wonder of the universe and they repudiate the falsehoods of civilization; the Gothic traits of overpowering ambition, black villainy, and the seeking of blood vengeance reappear again and again; polished chiefs whose ambition it is Pontiac-like to exterminate the whites, Canadian guides with the childlike faith of a Leatherstocking, impressionable maidens, diplomatic squatters, all have value only as a revelation of the conceptions of the time. Yet in his blending of tendencies there remains distinct interest. The *Missouri Outlaws*, for instance, absurd as are the descriptions of the luxurious homes and elaborate gardens in the wilds of the upper river, the hissed warnings and unreal dialogues and the accumulation of harrowing details, impresses by its declamatory denunciation of Spanish rule in the West, by its accounts of the policy of

93 *Oeuvres de Leconte de Lisle. Poèmes Tragiques*, 147, *Derniers Poèmes*. 68.

Bonaparte, and its reminiscence of the Reign of Terror which sends to be leader of the desert outlaws the son of the grim judge, Maillard. The very flagrant violation of geographical probability that locates palms and magnolias hundreds of feet high among the stunted shrubbery of the upper Missouri is after all a significant revelation of the extent to which Chateaubriand had inculcated in the minds of the reading public the conception of a tropical America.

But to go further in work of this sort would be useless. We might better turn to the similarly melodramatic but more accurate and historically valuable tales of the German visitors to America, especially Gerstäcker, Sealsfield, and Möllhausen. Probably the least influential of these for our purposes is the latter. A member of several exploring expeditions in the Far West, he first chronicled his travels in *Tagebuch einer Reise vom Mississippi nach den Küsten der Südsee* (1858), a narrative that his scientific training made valuable. This was only the first, however, of a long series of volumes, over one hundred and fifty of fiction alone, in which as a mere enumeration of titles would testify, he made lavish use of frontier materials. Although most of these display considerable knowledge of the West and its types, they are written, as might be expected, in too facile a manner, and the lurid plots of old world intrigue of which he often availed himself as in *Der Fahrmann am Kanadien* weaken his vivid pictures of the various phases of border life. Much of his work deals with a region too far West for our study.

More influential and more worth while in many ways is Friedrich Gerstäcker, that indefatigable wanderer over two hemispheres, who used the middle valley of the United States as the scene for several of his exotic narratives. Like Möllhausen he presented his experiences in a simple autobiographic account — *Streif und Jagdzüge durch die Vereinigten Staaten Nord-amerika's* (1844), then composed various tales with the material he had gleaned. Since the West was at the time he visited it in an extremely unsettled state, it was but natural that he should be impressed by the more violent phases of border life. Both *Die Flusspiraten des Mississippi* and *Die Regulatoren in Arkansas* deal with organized robbery and violence, criminal passion such as we have already discussed in the work of Simms and others. His *Mississippi Bilder, Aus Zwei Welttheilen,* and other shorter tales are, however, much more subdued in tone, a series of rather effective sketches presenting types and customs of the frontier. The main drawback to his work from a literary point of view is the unwieldiness of the German language in portraying the rough and ready life of the border, a difficulty of which Gerstäcker himself seemed conscious. As an author who had a tremendous vogue both in Germany and America and as one of the first of the German novelists to use to any great extent the Mississippi Valley life, his importance cannot be overlooked.

More artistic than either of the above mentioned authors, perhaps, in spite of the staccato and fragmentary nature of many of his sketches and equally important for the student of social history is the Austrian Charles Sealsfield (Karl Postl), who proudly dubbed himself Bürger von Nord-amerika. The range of life he depicts is wide, varying from the slave-holding Kentuckians to the exiled Creeks and the Barratarian outlaws in *Der Legitime und die Republikaner.* He is at his best, however, in the depiction of the Creoles of the Southwest. So vivid is his portrayal of their domestic life, so thorough his understanding of their attitude toward politics and the bustling Anglo-Saxon world, and above all so charming are his sketches of the sunlit meadows of the lower valley that we cannot wonder at Longfellow's fondness for him.[94]

These three are the most prolific of the German story-tellers dealing with the middle valley. There are a number of other rather copious writers who might be mentioned, however, since they touch upon it at intervals. Otto Ruppius, for instance, himself a political refugee in America, in his short story *Bill Hammer* shows the joy of the Secessionist rowdies in Missouri at a chance to get even with the Germans for their opposition to slavery; *Eine Spekulation* uses the rather common device of deliberate blowing up of a Mississippi steamboat to bring together the two lovers; *Der Erste Ball in Milwaukie* reveals a crude state of society that we today have almost forgotten; *Auf*

94 [Jan. 23d. 1847] ". . . F. read our favorite Sealsfield. His descriptions of the Southwest are very striking. The Creole Ball quite life-like, and the passage through a cypress-swamp terrible." Longfellow, S. — *Life of Henry Wadsworth Longfellow*. II:77.

*Regierungslande* portrays the lawlessness to which the desire to make fortunes in land gave rise; *Mary Kreuzer* by its account of the experiences in Iowa of this orphaned daughter of an "acht und vierziger" suggests the friction that arose in the early days between the foreign born and English speaking groups; and *Waldspinne* depicts with real vividness border life in the Southwest; indeed it is one of the best of stories about the sharpers that caused untold suffering by their fleecing of guileless land purchasers. Valuable as are the studies of American and German life from a social standpoint, however, Ruppius' characters are too bloodless, his plots are handled with too little technical assurance or reality for him to be an outstanding writer. More distinguished by far is Auerbach who touches lightly upon various phases of Mississippi Valley life in *Das Landhaus am Rhein* and who introduces a rather original note in *Der Tollpatsch aus Amerika* where the prosperous son returns to seek a wife in the village from which his father, the original *Tollpatsch*, had fled to forget his disappointments in the Ohio country.

Certain other writers attract attention not so much by the frequency of their allusions to America, but by single volumes noteworthy for one reason or another. Such is Waldow, whose very title *Das Paradies am Ohio* serves to suggest one of the most important of the European concepts. Schefer's fantastic rhapsodies about freedom and the escape so ardently desired by all classes from the hardships and oppressions of Europe, his amazing geography which places Mt. Vernon and Washington's grave in Kentucky, and his equally fantastic account of the negro uprising in New Orleans, the hundreds of slaves with their arms lopped off as the punishment for revolt, and the richly jewelled young widow who almost threw herself in the arms of the narrator in *Die Probefahrt nach Amerika* (1837) do much to explain Kürnberger's hostility to the visions of the young radicals.

The book which immediately shaped his protest, however, was Ernst Willkomm's *Die Europamüden* (1838), probably the most exaggerated propaganda by the devotees of "free America." The first volume devotes itself almost entirely to exposition and elaboration of the title, Europe and particularly Germany being portrayed as the grave of all hopes. Nevertheless the romantic concept of America crops up continually — in the plan of the insane egoist, Casimir, to write a prairie drama, in the comparisons of its young and virile society with the worn and poisoned organism of Europe. The dreams of the new world come to a head with the decision to emigrate, described in the rhapsody of Sigismund which closes the first book and which reveals more clearly than any other single passage, perhaps, the Chateaubriand-like nature of the vision. In the second volume the continental dreams of the new world are revealed in even greater detail, an American traveller affording in addition a shining example of the independence, uprightness, and generosity of the free-born son of nature. Not only are the preparations of the central characters described but a typical group of peasants is revealed seeking prosperity overseas. The last words are those of Sigismund, a promise to write from the bank of the Mississippi. Valuable as the book is today as a revelation of contemporary feeling, its characters are so exaggerated, its whole tone is so morbid and neurotic, that we cannot wonder at the rebellion it excited among some contemporary critics.

For the novelist, thus, the emigration of the peasants to America, the dreams of the philosophers of finding there a refuge from the evils of old world society, and the wild life of the border formed the most prolific themes. Various other factors which do not concern us entered in early, of course; the part played by the Hessians in the Revolution produced its effect in literature; the influence of religious as well as political idealism may be traced; and the Rousseau cult was no less powerful in Germany than in the other countries of Europe in spite of Fanny Lewald's and Grillparzer's satires. Indeed this practice of idealizing the savage and of depicting in colors as glowing as those of Chateaubriand the scenery of the new world forms the most pronounced notes in the poetic interpretations. Many of these again are eliminated from our consideration by their locality or lack of it as Seume's famous poem *Der Wilde* or the majority of Lenau's and Chamisso's Indian pieces, which bitterly attack the aggressiveness and faithlessness of the whites. Yet we find astonishingly frequent allusion to the tribes and places we are considering. Schiller's *Nadowessische Totenklage* (1797), for instance, is an interesting early example of the stimulus of

Carver's travels. Freiligrath, translator of *Hiawatha,* some of Walt Whitman, and several short Indian compositions by various authors, in his own early poems illustrates almost all the different romantic tendencies. His address *An Audubon von Freiligrath* beginning,

"Mann der Wälder, der Savannen!
  Neben rother Indier Speer,
An des Mississippi Tannen
  Lehntest du dein Jagdgewehr!"

is an almost perfect illustration of the continental idealization of the red men, whom he advises to free themselves from the yoke of the whites.

"Nadowessier, Tschippawäer,
  Heult den Kriegsruf, werft den Speer!
Schüttelt ab die — Europäer!
  Schüttelt ab das Raupenheer!"

So perfect was it indeed that it brought forth indignant answer from America, emphasizing the terrors of Indian vengeance and winding up with the amusing exhortation,

"Willst du nicht? Nun so verschwinde!
  Doch da drüben hüte dich!
Dass dich dort kein 'Indier' finde
  Zornroth — sonst skalpirt er dich."

The poem *Die Auswanderer* written in the summer of 1832 gives the dreamer's imaginings and questionings in response to this frequent sight. *Florida of Boston* (1833) reveals a Chateaubriand-like independence of geography in its account of the flamingo,

"Den scharlachfarbigen, als er von Sanct Domingo
Gen Norden zum Ohio flog."

*Der Ausgewanderte Dichter. Bruchstücke eines unvollendeten Cyklus* emphasizes a number of important exotic threads, and *Die Steppe* furnishes an interesting fragment dealing with our section.

"Sie dehnt sich aus von Meer zu Meere;
Wer sie durchritten hat, den graus't.
Sie liegt vor Gott in ihrer Leere,
Wie eine leere Bettlerfaust.
Die Ströme, die sie jach durchrinnen;
Die ausgefahrnen Gleise, drinnen
Des Colonisten Rad sich wand;
Die Spur, in der die Büffel traben:—
Das sind, vom Himmel selbst gegraben,
Die Furchen dieser Riesenhand."

Elisabeth Kulmann, that very brilliant and talented young poet whose ability early attracted the attention of the literary world, uses American materials, also, one of her most interesting pieces for us being *Der Mississippi-Strom,* which traces with delicate fantasy the course of the great river and its tributaries.

"Der Wälder kühle Schatten,
Der nahen Indier Spur,
Unabsehbare Wiesen,
Louisiana's Götterflur, . . ."

And Anastasius Grün in his *Cincinnatus,* part of the volume *Schutt* which went through several editions in the 1830's, illustrates again almost all phases of the romanticist's concept—comparison by "a son of America" of the external beauties but fundamental tyrannies of Italy, typical of the old world, with the new, which he enthusiastically addresses,

"Gewalt'ge Ströme, drauf des Dampfschiffs Wolke
Durch Urwaldwüsten und Savannen steigt
Und, wie die Säule Rauchs einst Jacobs Volke,
Die Bahn zu neuem, schönrem Eden zeigt!"

luxuriant pictures of the interior,

"Sei mir gegrüsst, Ohio schöner Strom,
Der im gebetesstillen Urwaldsdom
Auf neuer Städt' unheil'gen Marktlärm stösst,
Hier Goldsaat tränkt, dort Felskolosse flösst!

"Ein Bild der Zeit, begegnen sich auf dir
Der Riesenbaum, den Sturm entwurzelt, hier
Und dort des Dampfschiffs wandelnder Palast,
Des Wilden Kahn, gebaut aus einem Ast!

"Hier hörtest du des Briten feilschend Wort;
Des irren Indianers Wehruf dort
Und lauschest jetzt des Deutschen ernstem Lied,
Das auf dem Strom der Sehnsucht heimwärts zieht!"

the departure of emigrants,

"die fern an Westens Strand
Jetzt suchen, was sie fliehn: ein Vaterland!"

escape from the toils and passions of the Old World; comfort in the new.

Goethe himself showed keen interest in the new world. He remarked that if he were twenty years younger he would go to America and atoned for his European residence by exotic reading, the influence of which upon his *Novelle* has been traced. His *Wilhelm Meisters Wanderjahre* is, of course, the most philosophical of the treatments of migration, a direct incentive, as Schefer testified, to many of the pilgrims in that era of exodus.

But our discussion cannot be confined to the old country. In America itself from the time Pastorius founded the first German settlement at Germantown (1683) to the present a quaint literature in the mother tongue has borne testimony to the spread of the Teutons in America. This, originally confined almost entirely to Pennsylvania, has for us early interest in the verses of Count Zinzendorf who, attended by one or two of the Moravians and the faithful Conrad Weiser, on the Shawnee flats of the Wyoming Valley, engaged in preparing supplements to the hymns then in use among the brethren. These beginning, "Ich bin hier in der Wüsten, und lauer auf Wilde wie sie auf die wilden Thiere" and subscribed, "Aus dem Zelte vor Wayomick, in der grossen Ebene Skehandowana, im Canada, am 15 October 1742" have a touching realism in their portrayal of the surroundings and work of the missionary.

"Wir dachten an die Hirtentreu
  Des Jesuah Jehovah,
In der betrübten Wüsteney
  Mit Namen Shehandowa.

* * * * * * *

"Allein der Schmerz, der Seelenschmerz,
  Den wir in diesen Landen
Um so manch Indianer Herz
  Im innern ausgestanden —

* * * * * * *

"Doch lindert uns kein *Hurons*herz
  Die Kirch voll *Mohikaner*,
Noch einzelner *Chikasi* den Schmerz
  Um diese Floridaner.

* * * * * * *

"Gedenke nicht an unsern Schweiss,
  Gedenk an Jesu Narben,
Der diesen Lohn für seinen Fleiss
  Nicht lange mehr kann darben."

In general, however, there is little local color in the verse of the cultured German Americans, although the great immigration to the interior after 1800 brought rapid development of the foreign language literature of the Mississippi Valley. Too many of the newspaper pieces or the slim volumes of verse that form their chief creative output are pallid in tone, consisting for the most part of conventional love lyrics, reminiscences of the fatherland or rather general praises of the new home. Not until near the end of the century do we find collections more native in their tendencies such as B. Brühl's ("Kara Giorg") *Poesien des Urwalds* (1871) with its sympathetic tributes to the German pioneers and its Indian legends. Anthologies contain many interesting earlier bits, however, and volumes such as Schults *Lieder aus Wisconsin* (1848) can be found illustrating the affiliations of the Teutons with almost every middle western state. These can be adequately studied, however, only when there are more collections to make accessible the scattered news-paper and periodical material and when there is a greater realization on the part of our libraries of the historical value of some of the foreign language treatments of America.

A still more interesting foreign language development in America is the French creole literature of the nineteenth century. Plays, novels, and poems, although strongly influenced by modes of the mother country, reveal the growth of a respectable body of native literature. Peculiarly interesting are those which treat the glowing events of the Latin past, many of them inspired as a matter of fact by Gayarré's brilliant histories. It is worthy of note that this writer himself produced a couple of novels giving descriptions of Louisiana — *Fernando de Lemos* (1872) and its sequel *Aubert Dubayet* (1882). Garreau in his *Louisiana* (1845) conscientiously painted the old days of the colony; Oscar Dugué in *Mila ou le Mort de La Salle* (1852) wove a romantic love plot around the figure of the explorer. Charles Testut narrated the picturesque exploits of Saint Denis (1845) and treated the runaway German Princess, *Die Prinzessin von Wolfenbüttel* celebrated by Zschokke and a favorite subject for other romancers, in his *Calisto* (1849), the name under which, according to him, the abused lady smuggled herself to Louisiana. D'Artly's *Le Soulier Rouge* (1849) was, like the earliest Louisiana play *Poucha Houmma*, inspired by contact with the Choctaws. Inevitably there was an account of the Barratarians *Michel Peyroux ou l'histoire des Pirates en Amérique* (1848), and equally inevitably tribute to the noble Frenchmen who led the Revolution of 1768, A. Lusson's play *Les Martyrs de la Louisiane* (1839) and Canonge's more imaginative drama *France et Espagne* (1850)[95] We might mention also the two treatments of slavery — Testut's revelation of abuses, *Le Vieux Salomon* (written 1858, pub. 1877) and Dr. Alfred Mercier's *L'Habitation St. Ybars* (1881), which paints the Old South more attractively but which also reveals the dangers of the system. An interesting reminiscence of Chateaubriand is Father Adrien Rouquette's *La Nouvelle Atala* (1879), in which the heroine, prompted by romantic reading and mediaeval devotion, leaves her home and retreats to the forest to worship and die in seclusion.[96]

---

95 A similar English play by Judge T. Wharton Collins was performed and published in 1836.

96 A flattering review of this book by Lafcadio Hearn is quoted by E. L. Tinker — *Lafcadio Hearn's American Days*. 1924. 145. Hearn also paid tribute to *Les Comptes Rendus de l'Athénée Louisianais*, in which many of the imaginative treatments of Louisiana appeared. *Ibid.* 261.

Father Rouquette's poetry like his novel shows the influence of Chateaubriand, to whom he paid tribute in *Les Savanes* (1841). This early book reflects the restlessness of his youth; *L'Antoniade ou La Solitude avec Dieu* (1860), the placidity of his later life as a missionary. In both volumes, however, the themes are the same. Frequent tributes to Boone and the naturalist, Audubon, glorification of the child of nature and disparagement of the city, praises of the natural beauty of the Mississippi country show the trend of his thoughts. Passages like the folowing are found constantly.

> "Oh! qui n'a pas rêvé, dans les villes fiévreuses,
> Ces savanes en fleurs, ces plaines onduleuses,
> Ces temples verdoyants, où Dieu nous parle encore,
> Et d'où l'âme, en repos, prend un sublime essor?
> Pour fuir des froids salons l'enervant esclavage,
> Quel homme n'a pas rêvé de se faire Sauvage?
> Oui, j'irai me bâtir, dans un coin reculé,
> Dans les vierges forêts de l'Ultima Thulé,
> Au milieu des Tribus de ton Grand Territoire,
> J'irai, pour y rester, construire un oratoire!"

A brother Dominique Rouquette was also a poet and picturesque figure. He, too, in *Les Meschacébéennes* (1839) and *Fleurs d'Amérique* (1856) treated the beauty of the lower valley in a romantic manner, being fortunate enough to win the approval of Hugo and other writers in the mother country. Mercier's *Erato* (1842) also contains a number of lyrics on love and Louisiana; in narrative poetry, however, the French seem less fortunate. Chief among the longer pieces are celebrations of the battle of New Orleans—Urbain David's *Les Anglaise à la Louisiane en 1814 et 1815* (1845) and Tullius Saint-Céran's *Mil Huit Cent Quatorze et Mil Huit Cent Quinze* (1838), a very conventional and colorless piece.

It is to be regretted that the difficulty of getting material as well as lack of space makes impossible more extended survey. Most of the work is mediocre in quality, much of it disappointingly colorless; nevertheless distinct glamour is attached to these treatments of Louisiana by the heirs of the Latin spirit that endowed its life with its unique flavor. Unquestionably, too, all these romantic treatments of the Midland have a value for the social historian hitherto almost entirely neglected. Melodramatic as many of them were, annoyingly conventional in their adherence to established forms and motifs, they yet depicted actual though spectacular phases of border life, they presented an enormous gallery of western scenes and western types. From the point of view of the literary historian they are equally important. Probably not one of the literatures of Europe was left untouched by the influence of the new continent. From the moment of its discovery it focused aspiration, suggested new visions. Naturally the attention of the writer was drawn to the distinctive phases of its life, chief among them the frontier where an abundance of cheap land lured the immigrant and where the conflict of races and the majesty of primeval nature endowed with unique dignity the latest phase of the westward migration of the whites. This advance line of civilization moving across America as it had moved across the fens and forests of the old world, for a couple of centuries lodged in the Mississippi Valley. And in turn the Valley's most distinctive feature, the Prairies, together with the forests and rivers and the life they produced formed a distinct thread in the romantic literature of America and Europe. They with the rest of the frontier created a new and rich storehouse of materials for literary interpretation.

# CHAPTER VI

## THE REALISM OF THE MISSISSIPPI VALLEY

Yet this romantic literature, abundant as it remains and popular as it was in its own epoch, does not represent the most distinctive contribution of the prairie. For romance is always fleeting, evanescent; the glamour of the unknown, the lure of the path beyond the horizon. And as the sturdy pioneers pushed further and further into the great plains, as the exiled Indian hunter, the dismayed herds of bison, the scout and outlaw found their last refuge among the monotonous sage brush and cactus, amid the hills of the north, or on the many-colored sands of the Southwest, romance staked out there its supreme stamping-ground in America, a domain it holds yet today although irrigation, intensive culture, and modern business methods have practically banished the bold bad man, the prospector, and the cowboy who in their turn long held sway.

The Middle West was too quickly civilized, too closely allied to the everyday life of the East long to make appeal. It early became the food purveyor of the nation, the provider of raw products, the absorber of finished ones, all useful functions but to the ordinary view unpoetic. Nevertheless the tilling of the earth, the earliest and most stable factor in the section's wealth, has been one of the most frequent themes in the literature of mankind. Naturally, therefore, the meagerness of lowly lives spent close to the soil that in Europe formed the basis for *La Terre, Sussex Gorse*, or *The Peasants* was in America responsible for a similarly pitiless realism.

True the bounteous new areas did not involve the killing toil on small and outworn plots, too often for tyrannical masters, that had crushed the peasantry of Europe for generations. Yet existence was complicated at the same time it was simplified by elements for the most part insignificant or submerged in more settled regions. The labor of clearing, the task of cleaving the tough, tangled roots of the prairie, diseases resulting from privation and lack of acclimatization, caused hardships which were enhanced in the transition period when the game, either wastefully slaughtered or driven away, no longer afforded an easy living and when lack of transportation facilities left the most industrious with little market for their produce. The coarseness and shiftlessness of some of the types engendered by the border were important for a realistic literature; infinitely more tragic, however, were the maladjustments on the frontier. The passing of the older inhabitants and the monuments of extinct races inspired a certain melancholy; but sadder than the suggestion of the past to those who could see the materialism resultant on the daily struggle for existence, was the outlook for the future.

The mental bias of the observer did much, of course, to determine his reaction to the frontier. To many, especially the traveller from abroad, it was the rawest, most uncouth manifestation of a crude and braggart republic. Of this attitude Dickens in his *American Notes* gives probably the most famous manifestation. To him the prospect was unrelievedly gloomy. Dreaming, as he set out upon his excursion to the interior "of cities growing up, like palaces in fairy tales, among the wilds and forests of the west," bad travelling conditions inspired in him immediate disillusion. His disparagement of American customs in general is too well known to be discussed. In no place, however, is his pessimism more striking than in his description of the much-vaunted Midland. The huddled stumps of the clearings to him resemble "earthy butchers' blocks"; the American Bottom is "an ill-favored Black Hollow"; the Mississippi, "an enormous ditch, sometimes two or three miles wide, running liquid mud, six miles an hour." The track to the Looking Glass Prairie, which provided Ole Bull with a gorgeous lark, succeeded only in arousing in Dickens compassion for others besides himself; the Monks' Mound and the old village of Carondelet had for him none of the charm that delighted more imaginative travelers; even the prairies were to him a source of disappointment.

"Looking towards the setting sun, there lay stretched out before my view, a vast expanse of level ground; unbroken, save by one thin line of trees, which scarcely amounted to a scratch upon the great blank; . . . . . . . . . . . . . . . . . . . . . . . . . . There it lay, a tranquil sea or lake without water, if such a simile be admissible, with the day going down upon it: a few birds wheeling here and there: and solitude and silence reigning paramount around. But the grass was not yet high; there were bare black patches on the ground; and the few wild flowers that the eye could see were poor and scanty. Great as the picture was, its very flatness and extent, which left nothing to the imagination, tamed it down and cramped its interest. I felt little of that sense of freedom and exhilaration which a Scottish heath inspires, or even our English downs awaken. It was lonely and wild, but oppressive in its barren monotony. I felt that, in traversing the Prairies, I could never abandon myself to the scene, forgetful of all else: . . . ''[1]

And these desolate pictures by the great novelist were only the most famous among dozens of similar ones by foreigners and Americans.[2] The first object of scorn is the squatter, the sentiments of several generations being summed up in the oft-quoted words of irascible old Dr. Dwight.

''A considerable part of all those, who *begin* the cultivation of the wilderness, may be denominated *foresters,* or *Pioneers.* . . . These men cannot live in regular society. They are too idle; too talkative; too passionate; too prodigal; and too shiftless; to acquire either property or character. They are impatient of the restraints of law, religion, and morality; grumble about the taxes, by which Rulers, Ministers, and School-masters, are supported. . . . After displaying their own talents, and worth; after censuring the weakness, and wickedness, of their superiours; after exposing the injustice of the community in neglecting to invest persons of such merit with public offices; in many an eloquent harangue, uttered by many a kitchen fire, in every blacksmith's shop, and in every

1 Dickens, Charles — *American Notes.* Illus. Cabinet ed. Dana Estes Co. 184, 232, 258, 249, 264-5.

2 The Indian, for instance, is portrayed as a filthy disgusting outcast, the writers apparently agreeing with Irving that "the Indian of poetical fiction is, like the shepherd of pastoral romance, a mere personification of imaginary attributes." Irving, Washington — *A Tour on the Prairie* in *The Crayon Miscellany.* Hudson and Geoffrey Crayon ed. 53.

> corner of the streets; and finding all their efforts vain; they become at length discouraged; and under the pressure of poverty, the fear of a gaol, and the consciousness of public contempt, leave their native places, and betake themselves to the wilderness."[3]

The lack of education on the frontier is scathingly portrayed, even the professional men being pilloried as examples of illiteracy; and the personal habits of the border dwellers are described as disgusting, the women slovenly, with weathered skin, straggling hair, and a single stained and sack-like garment, the men brutal and quarrelsome. The ill-managed farms, the lack of privacy and cleanliness in the taverns, the indolence which served to render almost intolerable the crowded life in a one-room cabin, all receive repeated and deserved condemnation.

Although it is obvious that in such criticisms the heroic aspects of the life are neglected, it is not sufficient to conclude easily as does one of the combatants in the War of the Reviewers that these are misrepresentations so enormous that they are "adapted only to the palate of the knight in Pantagruel, who could swallow a chimera for his breakfast, provided it was cooked by a critic."[4] Many of the passages reveal both fairness and penetration. Unquestionably, too, many residents of the backwoods, such as Hall in *The New Purchase,* painted conditions in sombre colors.[5]

Yet to combat the old, old assertion that such statements are false or distorted, it might be well to quote from the travellers unquestionably romantic in their tendencies. Flagg, for instance, in spite of the beauty of the Illinois River scenery "wonders not at the sallow complexion, the withered features, and the fleshless, ague-racked limbs, which, as he passes, peer forth upon him from the luxuriant foliage of this region of sepulchres; his only astonishment is, that in such an atmosphere the human constitution can maintain vitality at all." Even he, picturesque as he makes the dwellings of the habitants, realizes their incon-

---

3 Dwight, Timothy — *Travels; in New-England and New-York.* 4v. 1821. II:459. A number of interesting early descriptions of the pioneers both favorable and unfavorable are cited by Shambaugh, *The Hist. of the West & the Pioneers. Wis. Hist. Proc.* 1910. 132 ff.

4 Davis, J. — *The American Mariners* . . . VI.

5 Hall's disappointment according to his own statements seems to have been due to the unduly poetic expectations he had formed of the frontier. See Hall, B. R. — *The New Purchase* . . . ed. by J. A. Woodburn. 1916. 1, 39, 51-2, etc.

veniences, exclaiming, "Prairie du Pont is one of the dampest, filthiest, most disagreeably ruinous of all the old villages I have ever visited."[6] Indeed the domestic life on the frontier seems almost always to introduce a depressing element. Flint, beginning an excellent discussion in his *Recollections of the Last Ten Years,* states that, "The first few months of the life of a family that seats itself in these remote solitudes, have a charm of romance thrown over them, which alas! more intimate acquaintance is but too sure to dispel."[7] Thompson testifies to the hardships of the journey.

> "These emigrants have a hard life of it. Poor fare and exposure to the elements, on the open deck of the boat, often engender disease among them, and break up families before they reach their destined home."[8]

Countless diarists picture the forlorn situation of the settlers, alone on the swampy banks as the boat steams away; seekers of fortune, such as Percy G. Ebbutt in *Emigrant Life in Kansas* (1886), portray the hardships brought about by fires, crop failures, and cold winters.

Not only the constant fight for a livelihood but the landscape itself had its saddening aspect. For gorgeous as was the prairie's flower-strewn expanse in the brilliance of noonday, when the sunlight disappeared and the mist and grey clouds shut down, the wide prospect became inexpressibly sombre. Blane comments on the melancholy appearance of the seared grasses;[9] Thompson experiences a strong feeling of desolation "in the midst even of harvests that might feed the world";[10] Brewerton describes in detail the discomforts of the winter prairie;[11] even Hoffman, romantic as is in general his account of *A Winter in the West,* concludes of the snow-covered Savannah that "A prospect more bleak and lonely, when night is closing in, and you press towards some distant grove, whose tree tops cannot yet be discovered above the monotonous plains, is inconceivable."[12]

The chief note, of course, in all these descriptions is the ever

6 *E. W. T.* XXVI:127, XXVII:117.
7 Flint, Timothy — *Recollections of the Last Ten Years* . . . 200.
8 Letter quoted by Curtiss, D.S. — *Western Portraiture.* 1852. 318.
9 Blane, W. N. — *Excursion through the U.S.* . . . *1822-23.* 1824. 190.
10 Curtiss — *Western Portraiture.* 339.
11 Brewerton, G. — *Wars of the Western Border.* 129, 240, etc.
12 Hoffman, C. F. — *A Winter in the West.* I:290.

recurring one of the loneliness of the prairie. The majesty of the midland scene with its green swells, its clear rivulets, and its shadowing tree clumps served, as we have noted in the annals of Kansas, to impress the devout New Englander with a sense of the greatness and imminence of the Creator; the poet it usually filled with rapture. Yet on those less exalted the effect was often unwontedly depressing. Harriet Martineau and Fredrika Bremer, great as was their delight in the beauty of the flowering meadows, felt keenly the solitude; Flagg is similarly sensitive; Irving gives the mood detailed analysis.

> "To one unaccustomed to it, there is something inexpressibly lonely in the solitude of a prairie. The loneliness of a forest seems nothing to it. There the view is shut in by trees, and the imagination is left free to picture some livelier scene beyond. But here we have an immense extent of landscape without a sign of human existence. We have the consciousness of being far, far beyond the bounds of human habitation; we feel as if moving in the midst of a desert world."[13]

And Birkbeck drives it home most effectively of all with his suggestion of the woman "quite overcome with 'lone' "[14] — the representative of incalculably many home-weary and heartsick frontier wives.

Inevitably if these analyses of the emotions produced by the prairie had in them any shadow of truth, the effect upon the character of the settlers must have been profound, McConnell, for instance, stating in his *Western Characters* that, "whatever the pioneers may have been before their migration, they soon become meditative, abstracted, and taciturn."[15] It is difficult, of course, to rely on such generalizations. Naturally, however, emphasis on the physical side of life, unavoidable in a newly settled and rapidly developing country, would develop, outwardly at least, a practicality of attitude, which, although a great asset to the economic advance of a country, would be nevertheless a distinct hindrance to its spiritual development. This menace brought out very clearly by two talented women — Fredrika

13 Irving, Washington — *A Tour on the Prairies.* 204-5.
14 Birkbeck, Morris — *Notes on a Journey in America.* 127.
15 McConnell, J. L. — *Western Characters, or Types of Border Life in the Western States.* 1853. 28.

Bremer and Margaret Fuller — obtains in their pages particular force since both of them are acutely responsive to the romantic possibilities of the territory. Miss Bremer who revels in the beauty of the prairies, and finds charming people wherever she goes, concludes that Chicago "is one of the most miserable and ugly cities which I have yet seen in America, and is very little deserving of its name, 'Queen of the Lake'; for, sitting there on the shore of the lake in wretched dishabille, she resembles rather a huckstress than a queen. . . . And it seems as if, on all hands, people came here merely to trade, to make money, and not to live." Ending her trip, she feels obliged to give up the beautiful dreams with which she began.

> "The western land of the New World will not produce anything essentially different from the eastern. The New Paradise is nowhere to be met with on earth. It will probably never be obtained in this world, and upon this earth!"[16]

Margaret Fuller, too, tries to be just in attitude.

> "I come to the west prepared for the distaste I must experience at its mushroom growth. I know that where 'go ahead' is the only motto, the village cannot grow into the gentle proportions that successive lives, and the gradations of experience involuntarily give. . . . The march of the peaceful is scarcely less wanton than that of warlike invasion. The old landmarks are broken down, and the land, for a season, bears none, except of the rudeness of conquest and the needs of the day, whose bivouac fires blacken all the sweetest forest glades. I have come prepared to see all this, to dislike it, but not with stupid narrowness to distrust or defame. On the contrary, while I will not be so obliging as to confound ugliness with beauty, discord with harmony, and laud and be contented with all I meet, when it conflicts with my best desires and tastes, I trust by reverent faith to woo the mighty meaning of the scene, perhaps to foresee the law by which a new order, a new poetry is to be evoked from this chaos, . . ."[17]

Yet on the boat her disillusionment begins, and as she travels

16 Bremer, F. — *Homes of the New World.* I:605, II:137.
17 Fuller, Margaret — *Summer on the Lakes in 1834.* 1844. 28.

through the outlying settlements her consciousness of destructive ugliness and of engrossing materialism grows. Her sympathy and her enthusiasm never blind her to defects; with the philosopher's thoroughness, she estimates not only the disheartening features of the present but the prospects for the future. Hers is in many ways an excellent summary of the possibilities and deficiencies of the exuberant West.

Inevitably even the wildest of the romantic literature had been obliged to take some cognizance of the drawbacks of the frontier; indeed the main value of much of it comes from its casual setting forth of plain, unglorified facts. James Handasyd Perkins, whose stories are artistically worthless, deserves comment only for the faithfulness with which he touches in the background — the farm in the Miami Valley, for instance, with its "dirty, noisy, gabbling, companionable, gossiping ducks; the sleepy dog with his eyes wide awake, the all-sweeping, all-scolding, all-spanking mother."[18] Read, too, although he includes in his *New Pastoral* (1855) all the favorite scenes and situations of the romancers, warns against the hardships of the border.

> "Some shake the doubtful head — the older these —
> And tell of labours long to be endured —
> The battle with the forest, and the stern
> Privation to be borne, where oft the call
> Of chill necessity affrights the soul;"[19]

Leggett, depicting in detail the beauty of the prairies, reveals also their unhealthfulness. In the rambling reminiscences of old Zabet in *Fernando de Lemos* we get occasional glimpses of the ugly foundation on which some of the gaudy display of New Orleans was built up.

> "Why, why, dear gossip, his grandfather was a convict, who, harnessed like a horse, used to pull the government's barge up the river."[20]

William Gilmore Simms, aside from the homespun reality in the novels we have mentioned, gives valuable material in many of

---

18 *Memoir & Writings of James Handasyd Perkins* ed. by W. H. Channing. 2v. 1851. I:469.
19 Read, T. B. — *New Pastoral.* 1855. 116-7.
20 Gayarré, Chas. — *Fernando de Lemos.* 1871. 298.

his short stories, in the preface to *The Wigwam and the Cabin* (1845-6) vouching for the accuracy of his portrayal of the border history of the South. A similarly truthful aim is found in other of the authors whom we mentioned earlier. Snelling writes in opposition to the story-book Indian whom he criticizes sharply, stating that "No man can learn much of the character of the aborigines of America unless by personal observation." [21] Mrs. Caroline A. Soule asserts that the incidents upon which *The Pet of the Settlement* is founded were related by an aged pioneer and that she felt competent to handle them only after "four years of actual pioneer life in the valley of the Upper Des Moines, of emigrant life in a cabin on the prairie" had given her "experience enough in Western scenery and Western character, to delineate, with at least tolerable accuracy and fidelity, the events." [22].

Yet that no one of these is distinctively realistic has already been demonstrated. To discover a true promulgation of the realistic formula or an explanation of its dominance in middle western literature we need to turn elsewhere. Our main clues it seems probable that we can find, as we find the basis for much of the romance, in the history of the region. Professor Turner, pioneer investigator of the political significance of the frontier, feels that the value of the Mississippi Valley in American history has lain partly in the fact that it was a region of revolt.

> "Here have arisen varied, sometimes ill-considered, but always devoted, movements for ameliorating the lot of the common man in the interests of democracy. Out of the Mississippi Valley have come successive and related tidal waves of popular demand for real or imagined legislative safeguards to their rights and their social ideals. The Granger movement, the Greenback movement, the Populist movement, Bryan Democracy, and Roosevelt Republicanism all found their greatest strength in the Mississippi Valley. They were Mississippi Valley ideals in action. Its people were learning by experiment and experience how to grapple with the fundamental problem of creating a just social order that shall

21 Snelling, W. J. — *Tales of the Northwest.* V.
22 Soule, Mrs. C. A. — *The Pet of the Settlement.* 1859. III.

sustain the free, progressive, individual in a real democracy."[23]

And from this region of economic and political revolt, there issued, too, some of the earliest and most emphatic literary challenges to the theory, universally proclaimed since the discovery of America, that the unsettled expanses of the new continent offered a solution for all the evils of society, — a potential successor to the Golden Age, an embryonic Utopia.

Appropriately enough the first writer adequately to portray in fiction the discouraging aspects of the frontier was a woman — Mrs. Caroline Mathilda Kirkland. For it was the woman who suffered most profoundly in the great movement of peoples that populated the wilds. They dreaded most the breaking of old ties; they yearned in secret for the homes and friends behind them; they were compelled to labor beyond their strength in the weary days of "breaking" or "clearing"; they had the task of rearing a family far from civilization. Theirs were the weary night vigils with the ever-present fear of Indian marauders or wild beasts; theirs, the long months of loneliness, resulting frequently in melancholia. Unquestionably an existence such as theirs created some splendid heroic figures — true Mothers of the West — superb in physique, abounding in vitality, with a resourcefulness, a rude cheer that no difficulties could vanquish. Equally unquestionably, however, the wandering life begot also unkempt slatterns, retaining in their appearance almost no vestige of femininity, shiftless in their housekeeping, shrewish in temper. Unquestionably, too, although generations of such existence rendered its participants oblivious of its defects, such coarsening was as unfortunate as the sufferings of those with more delicate sensibilities who dreamed of better things in the past or whose hopes were wistfully centered on the prospects for their children in the future.

It was by those latter types that Mrs. Kirkland was particularly stirred. She starts, however, with much of her own experience in the volume, *A New Home — Who'll Follow.* Having formed her conception of the frontier from various "elegant sketches of western life" which had fallen under her notice and

23 Turner, F. J. — *The Frontier in Amer. Hist.* 1920. 203-4.

having "dwelt with delight on Chateaubriand's *Atala*, where no . . . vulgar inconvenience is once hinted at," her "floating visions of a home in the woods were full of important omissions and always in a Floridian clime, where fruits serve for *vivres*." The mudholes and corduroy roads of the West early forced reality upon her, however, as did baking and ironing over an open fire on a sultry August day, an uneven puncheon floor which permitted snakes and toads to crawl up between its cracks, and clouds of mosquitoes and gnats that compelled evenings of darkness in the cabins. She praised the stalwart virtues engendered by the frontier but she could never be blind to the equally stalwart defects. Everywhere around her the struggle for existence had over-emphasized the physical. The spirit of intense practicality prominent throughout the country at large, she feels, is especially marked in the new regions. There she can find almost no trace of idealism, almost no yearning for beauty. The mark of progress to the settler is girdling every tree in sight; an offering of geranium slips to one practical dame brings the remark that " 'she never know'd nobody make nothin' by raisin' sich things' "; lectures on horticulture produce the sniffing comment, " 'Taters grow in the field, and 'taters is good enough for me.' " The boasted equality of the border wishes always to level down, never up; and the Golden Rule is there so interpreted as to be largely give on one side, largely take on the other.

Nevertheless Mrs. Kirkland's heart goes out always to the poor and oppressed. It is of the destitute families in the little clearings that she thinks when the wildcat bank bubble bursts and the hoarded notes prove useless; it is the tattered state of the wife that flashes before her eyes when one noble specimen of humanity sacrifices two days of labor to do his duty by his country and go to the polls and vote. Familiar as the sight is to her, she can never become indifferent to the devastation wrought by the ague; nor forgetful of the ignorance and superstitious prejudice that causes much of the suffering. Neither can she ever become reconciled to the false pride that permits several grown daughters to lounge slipshod around a dirty cabin rather than lower their status by going out to service. It is in the depiction of sordid scenes, in the analysis of the most forlorn and shiftless families in the community that her work is memorable.

It must not be supposed, however, that her pages are confined to them. Her sense of humor, and her sharpness of tongue, usually well held in check, make her an admirable painter of such types as Mrs. Campaspe Nippers, the village information bureau, or Mrs. Titmouse who alone on the blunt frontier seems "to have paid her devoirs at Castle Blarney." Such varying groups as the hunting farmers, the English immigrants, or the fraudulent land speculators are analyzed, and the ambitions and prejudices of the border as well as its characters and life are brought before us. *A New Home* is, in short, an excellent record of a typical Michigan village — from its start under the land boom through its varying stages of progress.[24]

Of course Mrs. Kirkland shared the fate of all realists. In her second volume *Forest Life,* largely a series of essay-like disquisitions, she finds it necessary to defend her preceding sketches, "ingenious malice" having been "busy in finding substance for the shadows which were called up to give variety to the pages of *A New Home,*" and some of the more enthusiastic of the Western patriots finding "something treasonable in exhibiting the settlers of a new country as deficient in some of the amenities of life and language." In her *Western Clearings* (1845) she vouches for the general authenticity of plot and character in the individual stories; and in all of her work she had strength enough in spite of criticism to rebel against convention and to portray as she saw them "the forest, — the pioneers, — the settlers, — the people who, coming here of their own free will, — each with his own individual views of profit or advancement, — have, as a mass been the mighty instrument in the hands of Providence of preparing the way for civilization, for intelligence, for refinement, for religion."[25]

---

24 Kirkland, — *A New Home.* 1839. 83, 135, 139, 195. See Edna Twamley's *The Western Sketches of Caroline Mathilda (Stansbury) Kirkland. Mich. Hist. Coll.* XXXIX:39-124. The contemporary tribute of Poe is interesting and easily accessible in *The Literati of New York City. Complete Wks. of Edgar Allan Poe* ed. by J. A. Harrison. XV:84 ff.

25 Kirkland — *Forest Life.* 2v. 1842. 3-4, 4, 5. In the preface of her *Western Clearings* she gives the key to her work in her statement "that these are *Western* stories — stories illustrative of a land that was once an El Dorado — stories intended to give more minute and life-like representations of a peculiar people, than can well be given in a grave, straightforward history." VI.

Her shrinking from the free and easy manners and makeshift housekeeping of the frontier is duplicated in the homely pages of *Western Border Life; or, What Fanny Hunter Saw and Heard in Kanzas and Missouri* (1856). Mrs. Stowe's famous chronicle *Uncle Tom's Cabin* (1852) has its main scenes in sections of the Mississippi Valley long consecrated to the romancers — the comfortable estate of the Shelbys in Kentucky, the tropical luxury of the St. Clare home in New Orleans, the dismal cypress swamps of the Red River. Its characters, too, are of a type long favored — the selfish Creole beauty, Marie; the indolent and graceful Southern gentleman, her husband; the passionate exotic, Cassie; the bullying planter. It represents the romanticist's challenge to the problem of slavery, its sentimental pages forming a direct contrast in almost every way to the realistic annals of Fanny Hunter in the Middle West's most tragic section. Yet to us the latter book presents a valuable because a comparatively unfamiliar social study — a record from the point of view of a New Englander in Missouri of the Kansas invasion. Not at all spectacular in its exposé of evils, its denunciation is nevertheless crushing. The slipshod methods and the waste of the Catell housekeeping, the careless indifference to the welfare of the slaves, the contempt felt for the poor whites, the generally low level of culture, and the spirit of mob-violence quickly engendered by the blunted sensibilities of a slave-holding community, all serve to explain the slow advance of a state like Missouri. Stilted and unskilled as is the technique of the narrative, the drab details of life in a border farm serve as most valuable supplement to the high lights of Mrs. Stowe; the two books together form a striking protest from the Midland against the black blight of the South.

This spirit of revolt early found expression in Europe, also, two German novels being in this respect most typical. *Der Amerika-müde* by Ferdinand Kürnberger represents a more or less artificial reaction, the answer of the conservative to the wild dreams of the radical. Moorfeld, whose impassioned address to America opens the volume, is a typical continental visionary, modelled, it is thought by some, upon the unfortunate young poet Lenau.[26] His disillusionment begins, of course, the

[26] A good paper on this debated topic by G. A. Mulfinger, *Ferdinand Kürnbergers*

moment he sets foot in New York. With his experiences there we have little concern, save that they present one of our most illuminating pictures of the frauds of the land speculators and that they made him resolve to seek speedily his Utopia in the heart of the continent.

The course that he took to the Ohio was the usual one. But how different were his reactions from those of an Imlay! Notice, for instance, the description of a prairie near Pittsburgh:

> "I rode over a seemingly endless grassy plain; there was nothing on it, absolutely nothing. The air burned as in a blast furnace. Far and wide there was not a bird, not a butterfly, not the cry of an animal, not the hum of an insect; everything that was not a salamander seemed to be dead."

In the midst of this desolate waste the traveller discovers a tiny hut in which a fever-parched sufferer cries vainly for water. In the experiences of this woman — the daughter of a Marburg professor — and her husband, the "the handsomest and most brilliant student" of her father, Kürnberger feels is summed up "the whole of the German emigration. In part one deceives oneself, in part one is deceived; the result, total ruin!" Incidentally the hero finds in the barren cabin "a fine collection of law books together with German and English classics, Chateaubriand's Natchez, Duden's Missouri, and other such fairy-like accounts of America, all covered thick with dust."

And this is only the first of many similar sketches, dark enough to shatter the most tenacious conceptions of Hinterwaldspoesie. His intellectual loneliness Moorfeld bears pretty well; his nonproductiveness in his coveted isolation he long hopes to overcome; but the strange workings of border justice which rules that possession is nine points of the law, barring him from his own home, and the insanity of Annette, the heroine of his American forest idyl, brought about by the violent denunciation of the camp-meeting exhorter — these make him retreat in despair from his deceptive land of promise.

The very purpose of this volume is inevitably its main source

---

*Roman "Der Amerikamüde," dessen quellen und Verhältnis zu Lenaus Amerikareise,* is to be found in *Ger. Amer. Annals.* New Ser. I. 1903. See also T. S. Baker's *Lenau & Young Germany in America.* p. 31 ff.

of weakness. There are far too many such vitriolic comments as this:

> "We read the newspapers concerning America far too superficially in Europe. Otherwise we would speak not of the United States but simply of piratical states." [27]

Künberger's situations and characters in many cases are unpardonably exaggerated; his judgment is on the whole warped; he has been accused of many plagiarisms; his technique is often poor, there being, for instance, far too many fortuitous meetings. Yet the book has elements of truth and strength. The vision of the pestilence rising from the catacombs of the Ohio and Mississippi is a powerful passage; desolation of mood in individual or landscape is portrayed very well; at times rather striking situations are precipitated. In general the book furnishes an excellent antidote to the romances which, according to Carlyle, soar "on bold pinions into the thundery regions of *Atala, ou les Amours de deux Sauvages.*" [28]

Superior from the standpoint of both information and art, indeed the best of all the German novels touching upon the Midland, is Friedrich Gerstäcker's *Nach Amerika.* In it we have none of the author's usual thrilling stories of adventure; instead a very careful study of the great emigrant flood that rolled across the Atlantic. *Nach Amerika*! — it is the rallying cry for the unfortunate, the motto of the ambitious, the source of comfort for the oppressed — a world of promise condensed in four syllables, an *Open Sesame* that unlocks the Ali Baba Cavern of the western hemisphere. Everywhere in Germany we hear the cry; everywhere in Germany we see the consequences — long trains of emigrants marching along the road:

> "Day after day it goes on so; band after band come down over the mountain with bag and baggage, with wife and child — and all are emigrating, all are emigrating";

groups in the taverns discussing the wondrous letters from abroad,

> "Here children are a blessing, not a curse as for many a poor man in Germany";

---

27 Kürnberger, F. — *Der Amerika-müde.* 1855. 293, 295, 269.
28 Carlyle, Thos. — *German Romance.* Scribner ed. 1898. I:2.

timid inquirers at the steamboat offices. In the picture of the emigration agent, by the way, we get an extraordinarily effective account of one of the most crying evils of the period — the commercialism which led the companies to display marvellous lithographs, to issue page after page of deceptively glowing description; the agent's unscrupulous desire to obtain "a dollar a head" that made his laudation of America "a slow poison, which he injected in many a peaceful and contented family," the greed that prompts him to sell water covered lots as well cultivated farms, to change the complaints of one victim into honeyed praise that will inveigle other prey. All classes we find gathered through his ministrations at the little seaport town — the unscrupulous American adventurer with his innocent German bride; the unsuccessful Professor's family; the Jewish accordion-player with his ill-treated boy singer; Black Stephen and his wretched wife, whom he has torn from their children; the youthful deserter; George, the faithful son, leaving home to make a fortune for his family. The delays to which the voyagers were subjected, the conditions on shipboard, the games and songs and stories with which the weary hours were beguiled, all these are well portrayed.

But the greatest interest comes with the landing in the account of the inevitable disillusionment that one of the characters amusingly sums up when he remarks,

> "Since we have been roaming about here on the levee, it has seemed very strange to me. I thought at first we would not be able to set foot on land without the Americans coming up to us and asking us what wages we would take by the day or month, and now not a single human soul concerns himself about us and the people act as if we did not exist."

To the weary immigrants the golden crescent appears no gaily tinted city of enchantment but a heartless monster that drives them to despair. It is truly an appalling picture of hardship that Gerstäcker draws — seventeen ships of Irish and Germans docking at New Orleans in one week — hundreds of starving families crouched on the levee while the men seek vainly for work. Nevertheless although Gerstäcker feels keenly the need of organized relief for the destitute, although he makes an impassioned plea for the immigrant, he is no blindly partisan critic. He realizes that some of the keenest sufferings of his countrymen are due to the rascality of their compatriots or to their own wilfulness. The negro porter, for instance, to whom the baggage is carelessly intrusted may in an unguarded moment steal it, but the German landlord bleeds his victims by slow degrees, extorting to the limit his pound of flesh, and regardless, as long as his own coffers are enriched, of whether by padded board bills or fraudulent land deeds he drives his fellows to beggary or suicide. The Red River settlers may be an illiterate, uncouth group, but they come valiantly to the rescue of the sick and weary drudge whose aristocratic husband has by his gambling and brutality dragged her down to the lowest stratum of civilization. Hundreds and hundreds of immigrants may have been swindled by land-sharks, but the Professor owes his financial collapse to his own pig-headedness — his refusal to adopt new ways, his squandering of his capital on ambitious projects such as a summer house before the necessary farm building were completed.

The varying threads of his action Gerstäcker weaves together with a good deal of adroitness, in the development of his plot using a number of rather prominent middle western scenes and situations. Young George has an opportunity to display his heroism as a result of an explosion on a Mississippi steamboat; in the Teutonic city of Milwaukee Henkel swindles the landlord; Maulbeere's contact with the camp-meetings of the West suggests to him an easy way of obtaining a living; a yellow fever epidemic in New Orleans is well described; on the ocean-like expanses of the Illinois prairie George makes friends with a prosperous German family from his old neighborhood; there, too, he is informed of the financial straits of the Professor.

Yet the main value of the book lies not in the presentation of familiar elements like these but in its realistic treatment of the theme that its title suggests. In spite of the fact that it verges dangerously in places upon the sentimental; in spite of the fact that poetic justice rewards most of the good people and punishes the bad, the predominating impression is sobering. In the book's clear-sighted depiction of the evils attendant upon the great influx of poverty-stricken Europeans, in its sane portrayal of conditions in the new land, it is more valuable than a dozen of the immigrant manuals.[29] To-day as when it was written it serves as a most excellent counterpoise to the rainbow bubbles of the romancers, unintentional sources of infinite misery.

Coming back to America, we find in Edward Eggleston, also, a protest — at the constant imitation of foreign models and at the sensational fiction and cheap biographies of men like Murrell which spread broadcast misleading conceptions of the interior and which he holds responsible for the ruin of such weaklings as Walter Johnson in his *Hoosier Schoolmaster.* Combined with this he has the student's desire to "describe life in the back-country districts of the Western States."[30] This project, he continues, had been in his mind ever since he was a Hoosier boy.

> "It used to be matter of no little jealousy with us, I remember, that the manners, customs, thoughts, and feelings of New England country people filled so large a place in books, while our life, not less interesting, not less romantic, and certainly not less filled with humorous and grotesque material, had no place in literature. It was as though we were shut out of good society. And, with the single exception of Alice Cary, perhaps, our Western writers did not dare speak of the West otherwise than as the unreal world to which Cooper's lively imagination had given birth."

He himself wished to make his "stories of value as a contribution to the history of civilization in America."[31] That he succeeded in fulfilling his ambition is obvious in the most superficial scrutiny of his cycle of tales. His *Hoosier Schoolmaster* (1871) and its inferior companion *The Hoosier School-Boy* (1883) reveal the drawbacks to education in the Indiana backwoods; *The End of the World* (1872), a story of the Ohio Valley, centres around the Millerite prophecies that set the western world agog in the eighteen-forties; *The Mystery of Metropolisville* (1873) reveals the trickery and fraud pervading a typical boom town of Minnesota; ***Roxy*** (1878) gives a vivid picture of

29 I have been told that a condensed version of the book was used as an immigrant manual in France, but I have never seen a copy of it. For quotations see *Nach Amerika.* I:36, 42, 85, 86, 437. A somewhat similar novel by Johann Bojer *The Emigrants* has appeared in translation as this goes through the press. It is an admirable treatment of the departure of a group of Norwegians for America and of their creation of a new saga on the prairies of the Northwest.

30 Eggleston — *The Hoosier School Master.* Pref.

31 Eggleston — *The Mystery of Metropolisville.* Pref.

homespun politics in Indiana; *The Graysons* (1888) artistically introduces Abe Lincoln as a young lawyer in Illinois; *The Circuit Rider* (1874) exalts the rude heroism, the splendid enthusiasm of the type named in the title.

Even more valuable, however, than the scope of his projects is the minute detail with which Eggleston fills them in. We know that the elections of the hinterland were the source of constant ridicule to the travellers; only when we read a novel like *Roxy,* however, can we effectively visualize the barbecues, the torch-light processions, and the shrewd "mixing" tactics of a dyed-in-the-wool politician like Major Tom Lathers. Historians have told us of the Know-nothing movement; Eggleston shows us concretely the persecution of honest men like Gottlieb Wehle. For our twentieth century rationalism it is somewhat hard to comprehend the torrential power of the massed religious fervor in the early revivals and camp-meetings until we read of conversions resulting in such heroic abnegation of self as Little Kike's, or the "jerks" with which even so unrepentant a scoffer as Captain Lumsden was affected. And so we might continue enumerating striking situations and motives Eggleston makes us experience, which form an integral part of the rough-hewn life of the frontier.

Sometimes, to be sure, this historical bent, which in his later life caused Eggleston to abandon fiction, became a source of weakness. For it led him into long didactic disquisitions on manners and customs, which although they were occasionally reminiscent, in their smoothness and ease, of the informal essay, as a rule, weighted down the dialogue and hampered the free development of the plot. On the whole, however, in its strength and its weakness, Eggleston's method resembles most nearly that of the early humorists. They "aired" the crudities of the middle western civilization to excite the laughter of a more sophisticated public; in the idiosyncrasies of the border types that surrounded them they found a literary soil, rich, deep, and uncultivated as that of the Mississippi bottoms. In exploiting such material the chief danger, of course, was that of caricature — a danger that Eggleston himself evidences in his vain and shallow Mrs. Plausaby, his chronic invalid, Mr. Minorkey, his reminiscent New Englander, Miss Matilda Hawkins, or his Backwoods Philosopher. The strength of the humorists' characterization lay largely in their ability to reproduce awkward but virile and good hearted types; their strength Eggleston excelled in his portraits of bashful Bud Means with his cumbersome body and inarticulate desire to put in his "best licks" for Christ; of the crotchety cobbler; or of herculean, indolent, adventurous, and faithful Bob McCord, successor to the stalwart pioneers who first braved the fastnesses of the Great Valley. Moreover our author himself possessed a rich vein of humor which made such characters as the stage-driver, Whiskey Jim, the hired man, Jonas, with his shrewd observation and quizzical comments, or the Irish schoolmaster, Brady, real triumphs of their sort.

In his portrayal of background as well as of types Eggleston resembles the humorists. They made no attempt to redeem the squalor of the frontier cabins; indeed the very paucity of the resources therein supplied them with some of the most pungent of their story materials. Eggleston, his desire for truth always pre-eminent, in no degree brightens reality. His picture of the Hoosier metropolis of Bonamy's day is enough to make present Indianapolis dwellers grow hoarse in protest; the Broad Run grocery and the dwelling of Jake Hogan, head of the lynchers, furnish an unexcelled study of shiftlessness and sloth; while his sod-tavern with its indigestible, badly prepared food produces on us the same repellent effect that it did on the young student, Charlton. Yet the novelist was too true an artist to give only the dark portions of the picture. With the same detail that he used to reveal the deficiencies of the "poor-whiteys'" huts, he portrays the plainly furnished but homelike kitchen of the Graysons. The volume that depicts the ignorance and vulgarity of many of the itinerants pays tribute to the cultivation and unostentatious devotion of a preacher-physician like Dr. Morgan; the man who denounces lip Christianity and the fruitless rivalry between religious sects can find in every village unassuming Samaritans like Miss Nancy Sawyer or the one-legged old basket-maker, Pearson. Sensitive himself to the beauty of the misted hills, the great tulip trees and flowering bushes of the Ohio, the rolling prairies of Minnesota and Illinois, he manages to make them a delicately impressive background to the action. The banks of the Beautiful River subtly reflect the minister's happiness; the monotony of the great flocks of swift-flying wild pigeons blends perfectly with the numb despair of the desolate wife Roxy. Shy Julia Anderson and her German lover, August, find companionship in the charm of the countryside, yet by the majority of the farm dwellers, Eggleston realizes, the landscape is really unseen. Indeed in his treatment of the setting as in all other phases of his work he endeavors to live up to the ideal he promulgated in the preface to *The Circuit Rider.*

> "But no man is worthy to be called a novelist who does not endeavor with his whole soul to produce the higher form of history, by writing truly of men as they are, and dispassionately of those forms of life that come within his scope." [32]

As a result of his adherence to this code, it is particularly interesting to note his treatment of the stock romantic materials. In part these cause very pronounced weaknesses in his work — the melodrama of the *The Mystery of Metropolisville,* for instance, where the tender-hearted village maid is cast away upon a cheap city "sport." In general, however, the sanity of his outlook brings to earth many a motif of the "thrillers." The dapper Mississippi gamblers lose much of their gloss when we realize that they live by preying off "greenies" like Norman Anderson and that the stately captains protect them in return for a share of the "swag"; the highwaymen are no longer dashing cavaliers, but sleek hypocrites like Dr. Small or petty thieves who enrich themselves on the side by brutally defrauding the paupers in their charge. Instead of the picturesque figures of Simon Kenton or Daniel Boone we get the backwash of that great movement over the southern mountains in the "poor-whiteys." The Indian country remains still a refuge, but it is revealed unmistakably as the resort for outlaws, men who are compelled to flee the processes of justice. And in more pleasant ways adjustments are shown — the Swiss family Lefaure with their laughing daughter, Twonnet, no longer objects of curiosity but one of the most attractive features of the county seat of Luzerne; the New England minister, Whittaker, although an alien on the border, a zealous and quiet worker, whose education furnishes a

32 Eggleston, Edward — *The Circuit Rider.* 1910 ed. VII.

valuable element amid the untutored forces that surrounded him. Altogether in spite of numerous technical weaknesses Eggleston is a distinctly important figure in literary history and one whose vivid stories of the West have fallen into undeserved oblivion.

His significance may perhaps be best estimated by contrast with William Dean Howells. Born the same year in somewhat similar circumstances, both men spent their early life in the West; both were largely self-educated; both through newspaper work turned to literature as a profession; both did their important creative writing in the East. Yet there the likenesses cease. During the wanderings of his boyhood and his youthful endeavors as a circuit-rider Eggleston apparently never failed to collect "these sharp contrasts of corn-shuckings and camp-meetings, of wild revels followed by wild revivals; these contacts of highwayman and preacher, this mélange of picturesque simplicity, grotesque humor, and savage ferocity, of abandoned wickedness and austere piety" that enabled him to write with "photographic exactness."[33] In his adherence to the literary possibilities of the frontier materials he never wavered; his technique, too, partook largely of the qualities of the border; according to Professor Pattee, "From Harte came the first conception of a new and powerful literature of the West. Eggleston was the directing hand that turned the current of this new literature into the channel of realism."[34]

Howells, on the contrary, won his first extended recognition in prose through his travel volumes of Italy and based the greater number of his novels upon New York and New England. The reason for this is not far to seek. Howells' fictional creed was that of a realist; his life in the West was that of a romanticist. His picture of *A Boy's Town*, for instance, is almost wholly idyllic, a charming, golden-hued representation of the sports and fancies of a very happy boy. And in his other autobiographical volumes this same atmosphere prevails — *Years of My Youth, My Year in a Log Cabin, My Literary Passions.* According to his own confession the youthful Howells, affectionately dubbed "The Dreamer" by his similarly minded father, saw much of the outer world through a veil of fancies quivering like an au-

33 Eggleston, E. — *The Circuit Rider.* Pref. V.
34 Pattee, F. L. — *Hist. of Amer. Lit. since 1870.* 1915. 98.

tumn haze between him and its realities, softening their harsh outlines, and giving them a fairy coloring.''[35] And so we have not only in the whole life of the ''Dean of American Letters'' but more specifically in his attitude toward, and use of the Middle West that slow and steady evolution from romance to realism evidenced for us most strikingly in the contrast between his early sketch *My Year in a Log Cabin* and the chronicle published not many years before his death, *New Leaf Mills.*

Reviewing in after life the work of his apprentice days, he, of course, tried to unearth the seeds of his later literary creed. Speaking of his liking for history, he states that ''Perhaps there was already in my early literary preferences a bent toward the reality which my gift, if I may call it so, has since taken'';[36] he is glad to think that the first poem he ever offered an editor ''dealt with so humble a fact as a farmer's family leaving their old home for the West.''[37] In spite of the terrible blow dealt by the failure of his first story, he confesses,

> ''. . . I must for several years have been working in stolen moments at another story of village life, which I vainly offered to the *Atlantic Monthly* and the *Knickerbocker Magazine,* and after that for many years tried to get some publisher to bring out as a book. The manuscript must still somewhere exist, and I should not be surprised, if I ever found it, to find myself respecting it for a certain helpless reality in its dealing with the conditions I knew best when I began writing it.''

He mentions, too, a kindly editor's carrying away ''one of the minutely realistic sketches in which I had begun to practice such art as I have been able to carry farthest,'' and there is the further suggestion of local projects which any student of the Middle West will wish could have been fulfilled.

> ''With its four hundred inhabitants less Jefferson was so much more than Ashtabula a village; and its young gaieties welcomed us and our little force of printers to a social liberty and equality which I long hoped some day to paint as a

---

35 Howells, W. D. — *A Boy's Town.* 1890. 240.
36 Howells, W. D. — *Years of my Youth.* 1916. 20.
37 Howells. — *My Literary Passions.* 1895. 45-6.

> phase of American civilization worthy the most literal fidelity of fiction."
>
> * * * * * *
>
> "I have sometimes thought that I would write a novel, with its scene in our capital at that supreme moment when the volunteering began, but I shall never do it, and without the mask of fiction one cannot give the living complexion of events."[38]

Yet on the whole passages like these are the exception rather than the rule. More frequently we find statements of this sort.

> "One night's round of the police stations with the other reporters satisfied me that I was not meant for that work, and I attempted it no farther. I have often been sorry since, for it would have made known to me many phases of life that I have always remained ignorant of, but I did not know then that life was supremely interesting and important. I fancied that literature, that poetry was so; and it was humiliation and anguish indescribable to think of myself torn from my high ideals by labors like those of the reporter."[39]

In that day, of course, romanticism was still at the flood. Thomson, Byron, Scott, Moore — the poems of these the boy heard most frequently at home; they with De Quincey, Hazlitt, Wordsworth, Coleridge filled the book-shelves of the village drug-store; one morning as a treat to a busy editor, a state senator, later to be President Garfield, read Tennyson aloud; in the printing offices tramp compositors "spouted" Shakespeare. And this romantic fervor, inculcated by every phase of the boy's reading, found equal nourishment in the thought and deeds of his own family. Apparently all except the older brother and mother were exceptionally emotional and idealistic. The grandfather, an unrecognized follower of Rousseau, had "settled his family in a log-cabin in the Ohio woods, that they might be safe from the sinister influences of the village where he was managing some woolen mills."[40] The father was one of

---

38 Howells — *Years of my Youth.* 209-10, 96, 81, 233.
39 Howells — *My Literary Passions.* 165-6.
40 Howells — *My Literary Passions.* 3.

those charming wistful spirits, pathetic misfits on the frontier, devoted to literature, interested in every aspect of nature and life, affectionate, incurably optimistic, capable of doing most things except to make money. And to prove that on the mother's side, too, the life was romantic we need only mention that the boy's uncles were eager participants in that most glorious pageant of the river.

Almost inevitably with such relatives and such reading, the lad's head was stuffed with wondrous visions. "In the older West," he says, "the woods called to us with a lure which it would have been rapture to obey; the inappeasable passion for their solitude drove the pioneer into the forest, and it was still in the air we breathed."[41] When the family moved in 1850 to their clearing on the Little Miami, to the father it was like renewing the wild romance of his boyhood; and it was the fond dream of his sons "to realize the trials and privations which he had painted for them in such rosy hues. . . ."

> "The winter, which was so sore a trial for my mother in the log-cabin, and was not, perhaps, such a poetic rapture for my father as he had hoped, was a long delight to their children."

Howells gives only one hint of discomfort in the account of their sojourn.

> "Life in the log-cabin had not become pleasanter with the advance of the summer; we were all impatient to be out of it."[42]

And the rainbow imaginings that transfigured the rude dwelling by the mill were equally powerful in in the other childhood homes. The little village of Ashtabula, for instance, "was all that we could have imagined of simply and sweetly romantic in the moonlight, and when the day came it did not rob it of its charm." Idyllic pictures adorn every page of the past — fellow printers reading poetry to the orchestral accompaniment of the rippling streams and soughing woods; tramps through the forest where the flocks of wild pigeons rose in fright "like the upward leap of fire, and with the roar of flame";[43] tranquil days on the river.

---

41 Howells — *Years of my Youth.* 33.
42 Howells — *My Year in a Log Cabin.* 1893. 2, 23, 40.
43 Howells — *My Literary Passions.* 62, 180.

Small wonder then that Howells hugged to himself these precious memories and that he painted them in tenderly reminiscent volumes. Of course the West is not an unknown factor in his novels. *The Kentons* (1902) represent an early type of middle-western family; the heroine of *A Chance Acquaintance* (1873) is the daughter of a Kansas martyr; in *The Rise of Silas Lapham* (1885) Irene takes refuge from her troubles in Dubuque; there are situated the mills, transfer of which attests Rogers' rascality; there, too, is projected one of the many communities of English dreamers. The denunciation of Bartley Hubbard by Squire Gaylord in the tobacco-stained Indiana court-room is unquestionably the most dramatic scene in *A Modern Instance* (1882); Kinney, the philosophical cook, one of the direct agents in the catastrophe, had taken part in the "Border Ruffian War of Kansas." Nevertheless, in spite of the fact that Howells in this latter volume philosophizes interestingly over the destiny of the Midland, most of these incidental allusions are such as might be made by any well-read or observant traveller. Certainly the study of the natural gas millionaires in New York — that old theme of the humorists, conflicting stages of culture, productive this time, however, not of boisterous buffoonery but of vulgar tragedy — is made entirely with the attitude and art of the cosmopolite.

Just how profoundly Howells' early life in the West impressed his later thought it is difficult to estimate. Much of the time it seems to be closed in a separate compartment, yet we are tempted to trace scattered strands. Reading, for instance, such passages as the following, one wonders if the real seed of his humanitarian visions like *A Traveller from Altruria* is not to be found in his experiences in the Ohio Valley instead of in his reading in Tolstoi.

> ". . . when I think of it [the hopeless burden of debt under which his father was staggering], and of the wide-spread, never-ending struggle for life which it was and is the type of, I cannot but abhor the economic conditions which we still suppose an essential of civilization."[44]

*　　*　　*　　*　　*　　*

[44] Howells — *Years of my Youth.* 41.

> "In that village there was a social equality which, if not absolute, was as nearly so as can ever be in a competitive civilization. . . ."[45]

Certainly *A Hazard of New Fortunes* (1889) seems a connecting link between the Middle West and Altruria. The true charity of young Conrad, incomprehensible to his fellows; the sordid degeneration of the elder Dryfoos; Lindau's bitter denunciation of this "oligarchy of traders and tricksters, this aristocracy of railroad wreckers and stock-gamblers and mine-slave drivers and mill-serf owners"; March's ironic musing on "our civilization, the battle we fight in, the game we trick in"; his objections to "this economic chance-world"; to say nothing of the situations and other characters of the book, furnish a grim indictment of our present social system through mouthpieces primarily of the West.[46]

And as we read *New Leaf Mills* the tie between later Utopian visions and earlier experiences seems to become more pronounced, this time in the ideals of the father whom Howells has painted full length as Owen Powell. The book itself is a remarkable feat — the re-creation from a different point of view of the year's stay in the woods, the cue to which is found in a single passage of *My Year in a Log Cabin.*

> "I try to give merely a child's impressions of our life, which was nearly all delightful; but it must have been hard for my elders, and for my mother especially, who could get no help, or only briefly and fitfully in the work that fell to her. What her pleasures were I can scarcely imagine."[47]

In the later volume the radiance of the child's outlook is stripped away; to it succeed the trials of the mother, the forced awakening to reality of the father. The physical ugliness of the farming community Howells here realized at last — "the huddle of neglected graves on the hilltop, with their sunken barrows and their slanting stones, and the miller's pigs rooting for the mast among the dead leaves"; the "large, lop-eared, liver-colored hounds." The limitation of the natives' mental horizons is

---

45 Howells — *My Literary Passions.* 127.
46 Howells — *A Hazard of New Fortunes.* I:255-6, II:251.
47 Howells — *My Year in a Log Cabin.* 41-2.

equally conspicuous; "a fierce religiosity, choosing between salvation and perdition, was the spiritual life which an open atheist here and there sweepingly denied"; save for a few rural festivals and gatherings where "neighborly help was given for neighborly hospitality," "the farmers dwelt apart on their wide acreages in a solitude unbroken from Sunday to Sunday for their wives."

The emotions of Ann embody the shuddering distaste of refined women at all times for retrogression in the civilized scale.

> "For her it was all a reversion to the barbarism of the new country where her childhood was passed, and which she had so gladly escaped from to the civility of the towns where she had lived ever since she had left the farm with her young husband. Now, when they were both middle-aged people, she seemed to have been dragged back to conditions worse than those of the backwoods."

But her husband's experiences bring out more forcibly the sordidness of life in such an environment. His is the sad fate of most idealists whose actual farm experiences give the lie to their town-made visions; his whole year is one of progressive disenchantment warranted to embitter utterly any less optimistic individual. At the beginning of his venture he is forced to see his cabin "with the unsparing eyes of his wife, which robbed it of the glamour it had worn to his retrospective vision"; the saw-mill sent him "home to his meals with aches and pains unfelt during the years of his town life, but now ungrudgingly recognized as experiences of his rustic past"; very early, too, he realized that the neighbors were not exactly the nature's noblemen he had pictured waiting to be inspired. Yet he leaves after the unsuccessful experiment only a little saddened, not at all disillusioned.[48]

Apart from the portrayal of the family the book runs rather thin. Miller Overdale's surly resentment and the simple gratitude of Bellam are well done, but more might have been made of Elder Griswell who held the latter in peonage and of the other neighbors. Also, the incident of Rosy and Captain Bickler rather fails of conviction, remaining somewhat extraneous. On

48 Howells — *New Leaf Mills.* 1913. 35, 22, 22, 22, 23, 24, 21, 36.

the whole the book is most interesting as a sort of literary tour de force — an author's doubling on his tracks and applying his approved realistic formula gained from literature to experiences, long sentimentalized, from life.

A somewhat similar criticism might be made of Howells' other middle western study *The Leatherwood God* (1916). The basis is, of course, that strange religious imposture best described by Judge Taneyhill in the *Ohio Valley Series,* the method, Howells' usual one of objective detail. In places his fictional elaboration results in rather striking dramatic situations — the proud girl, Jane, grovelling before the man who had abused and deserted her Aunt Nancy, the boy Joey's narration of the trip over the mountains and his father's drowning. In other places, however, the dependence upon another's version produces marked inequalities of technique. The representation of the cynical, free-thinking justice of the peace, Mathew Braile, is excellent; the use of the simple-minded Sally and Abel for expository and dramatic purposes is also most effective; the psychology of Dylke, interesting. Yet on the whole the book renders somewhat inadequately the flaming passion, the hysteric fervor of this squalid and pathetic travesty of the border. Howells can depict and analyze fanaticism; he could never, even imaginatively, be a fanatic. Consequently the story fails to move profoundly; consequently it lacks, too, emotional and technical unity. Moreover the romanticism that colored always the novelist's recollections of the West forbade him to push to its relentless consequences the tragedy. Poetic justice is satisfied; most of the characters end happily; on them as on their fertile valley rests the mellow light of the sunset; we see them through a golden and translucent haze.

Yet although the Middle West had to wait until almost the end of Howells' long life for extended realistic treatment, and although even then the result was a very ripe and kindly realism the product of alien cultural forces, his deficiencies in this respect are more than atoned for by his friend and follower Hamlin Garland. The latter wrote some of the most widely discussed of western short stories; he created the most complete and artistic portrayal of the epic lure that in three centurie drew the line of migration from the Atlantic to the Pacific he flung down the gauntlet to Eastern critics in his early volume of essays *Crumbling Idols*; in his work appears not only the fullest presentation but the most satisfying explanation of the ironic paradox that has caused the Middle West, a region celebrated since its discovery in the most hyperbolic terms — "a region of enchantment," "a terrestrial Paradise," "the Garden of the World" — to be the source of our harshest literary realism.

His artistic theories he promulgated early, the keynote to them being struck in the dedication to his volume of essays already mentioned:

> "To the men and women of America who have the courage to be artists."

There he promulgates the code of the realist, proclaiming the local novel as the most promising and sincere of the literary attempts of the day; there he suggests the possibilities of new fields in fiction; there he cries for an interpretation of our common life in painting and sculpture; there with true midland fervor he heralds Chicago as the coming cultural centre, prophesying the original nature of the literature resulting from the great interior spaces of the South and West; there he makes impassioned appeal to the "Sayer and Doers of this broad, free inland America of ours."[49]

Early as he formulated his creed, however, the explanation of his critical theory as of his best creative work is to be found in one of the latest and unquestionably the most significant of his many volumes — *A Son of the Middle Border*. The book reads like a saga of America's progress. Mr. Garland's first memories are of the heroic age — life on a coulee farm with the post-office town embodying the romance of the river and in the far distance the suggestion of the primeval forest. Splendid dauntless figures surrounded him there — the grandfather McClellan, "a mystic as well as a minstrel," his sturdy sons and handsome daughters, through all of whom ran a deep vein of poetry, of subconscious Celtic sadness. Theirs was the confidence begotten of physical vigor; in the spirit of sportsmen they and their neighbors bent to the task of taming the West. "With them reap-

49 Garland, Hamlin — *Crumbling Idols*. 1894. 161.

ing was a game, husking corn a test of endurance and skill, threshing a 'bee'."

But this lovely life in the valley was unfortunately fleeting. For in the boy's stern New England father flowed the blood of the pioneers; the land of promise was to him always the place where the sun went down; his desire was ever to advance, to embody in deeds the on-pushing spirit that excited the balladist's words,

> "Cheer up, brothers, as we go
> O'er the mountains, westward ho."

And so the boy's life is a record of change — removal to a Minnesota farm where the wood and prairie of the marching song did actually mingle; sale of that charming place to the "English duke" who came "to try farming in the American wilderness"; advance to the unplowed shelterless stretches of the Iowa prairie; and finally pilgrimage to the evanescent promise of the Dakotas. It is an epic progress — an expression of the effervescing restlessness of the border — a never-ceasing endeavor to overtake the shifting frontier — one family's part in the world movement that, begun by the tiny sailing vessels of the European refugees, continued by canoes, flat-boats, and canvas-covered wagons, in the land of the Straddle-Bug found its vehicle in the railroad, and today makes use of the automobile — that resistless urge of ambitious peoples to the free and bounteous spaces of the West.

And not only did Mr. Garland take part in that steady advance; he was a witness of, and agent in, the changes wrought by settlement. Entering the Big Prairie, he felt for the first time the poetry of the unplowed spaces.

> "The sky so big, and the horizon-line so low and so far away, made this new world of the plain more majestic than the world of the Coulee."

His uncle's first attack on the tough prairie sward induced a sense of lasting transformation.

> "I confess that as I saw the tender plants and shining flowers bow beneath the remorseless beam, civilization seemed a sad business, and yet there was something epic, something large-

> gestured and splendid in the 'breaking' season. . . .
> "At last the wide 'quarter-section' lay upturned, black to the sun and the garden that had bloomed and fruited for millions of years, waiting for man, lay torn and ravaged. The tender plants, the sweet flowers, the fragrant fruits, the busy insects, all the swarming lives which had been native here for untold centuries were utterly destroyed. It was sad and yet it was not all loss, even to my thinking, for I realized that over this desolation the green wheat would wave and the corn silks shed their pollen."

Increase of population hastened the process.

> "Day by day the settlement thickened. Section by section the prairie was blackened by the plow. Month by month the sweet wild meadows were fenced and pastured, and so at last the colts and cows all came into captivity, and our horseback riding ceased, cut short as if by some imperial decree. Lanes of barbed wire replaced the winding wagon trails, our saddles gathered dust in the grain-sheds, and groves of Lombardy poplar and European larch replaced the tow-heads of aspen and hazel through which we had pursued the wolf and the fox."

So that when the pest of the chinch bug came, producing unrest and bitterness among all the farmers, it was on a fairly old and settled community, one belonging to a past cycle of migration, that the Garlands turned their backs and set out once more for the West.

The Jim River Valley now was the focus; to it all America seemed surging. At Ordway "the street swarmed with boomers. All talk was of lots, of land. Hour by hour as the sun sank, prospectors returned to the hotel from their trips into the unclaimed territory, hungry and tired but jubilant, and as they assembled in my father's store after supper, their boastful talk of 'claims secured' made me forget all my other ambitions," Garland confesses.

> "I was as eager to clutch my share of Uncle Sam's bounty as any of them. The world seemed beginning anew for me as

> well as for these aliens from the crowded eastern world. 'I am ready to stake a claim,' I said to my father."
>
> And when at last, "far beyond the last claimant, we turned and looked back upon a score of these glittering guidons of progress, banners of the army of settlement, I realized that I was a vedette in the van of civilization, and when I turned to the west where nothing was to be seen save the mysterious plain and a long low line of still more mysterious hills, I thrilled with joy at all I had won."

For the youth as for the father romance was still in the West.

There had been hardships for him, of course, a primitive mode of life, in spite of Dave's dream of free lands needing "only to be tickled with a hoe to laugh into harvest" long hours of labor really beyond a lad's strength. Yet the prairie seemed almost an ideal place for boyhood, and no matter how heavy the tasks nature furnished compensation. Moreover, as the territory developed good prices had brought prosperity; the men were continually buying more land; improvements in farm machinery steadily lightened their burdens. Only the drudgery of the housewife remained, but mothers are uncomplaining and boys unthinking. Therefore, although the youth had achieved enough of a prejudice for the lowlier tasks of farm life to force his way through the academy and to conceive far-reaching ambitions, his plans were early tossed aside at the rainbow promise of the James River bubble. On the Dakota plain it required only one arid summer, one pitiless winter to convince the young Hamlin Garland of the futility of his return to the frontier. It required months of bitter brooding, however, a long stay in the East, and a second return to the West to make him fully comprehend the tragedy of life there for others.

To that epoch-making trip in the summer of 1887 may be attributed his emergence as a realist, the ripening of the seeds of revolt sown intermittently throughout his boyhood. The visit to Joseph Kirkland, son of Mathilda, who praised his western sketches and urged him to write fiction, gave him the impetus that he needed, and, as he rode past great stretches of timothy, rippling fields of grain, he throbbed with a new sense of kinship and power. This was his land; he understood it thoroughly, could make others know it. For the first time in his life he longed to put the Mississippi Valley into verse.

> "All that day I had studied the land, musing upon its distinctive qualities, and while I acknowledged the natural beauty of it, I revolted from the gracelessness of its human habitations. The lonely box-like farm-houses on the ridges suddenly appeared to me like the dens of wild animals. The lack of color, of charm in the lives of the people anguished me. I wondered why I had never before perceived the futility of woman's life on a farm.
>
> "I asked myself, 'Why have these stern facts never been put into our literature as they have been used in Russia and in England?' "

His mind in a tumult of revolt, every alert sense proffering him material, he began in his father's barren Dakota cabin to solidify his resentment into literature. A casual tale of his mother's gave him the theme of his first story known to us today as *Mrs. Ripley's Trip*; others shaped themselves easily.

> "No sooner did I reach my little desk in Jamaica Plain than I began to write, composing in the glow of a flaming conviction. . . . I had no doubts, no hesitations about the kind of effect I wished to produce. I perceived little that was poetic, little that was idyllic, and nothing that was humorous in the man, who, with hands like claws, was scratching a scanty living from the soil of a rented farm, while his wife walked her ceaseless round from tub to churn and from churn to tub. On the contrary, the life of such a family appealed to me as almost unrelievedly tragic futility." [50]

There is no question that Mr. Garland succeeded in producing his effect. His longer tales such as *A Little Norsk* or *Rose of Dutchers's Coolly* have flaws in structure and a sentimentality that weaken them decidedly; too many of his later books seem purely commercialized; but the stories that followed his epochal visit, collected for us in *Main-Travelled Roads* (1891), *Other Main-Travelled Roads* (1910), and *Prairie Folks* 1893, form next to the *Son of the Middle Border* his most significant work.

---

50 Garland, Hamlin — *A Son of the Middle Border.* 1917. 19, 21, 45, 79, 85, 104, 105, 144, 301-2, 302, 303, 62, 356, 375.

Almost all of them are unrelievedly gloomy. Shanty-like cabins, the inmates of which are crowded together much as in a New York tenement, with unplastered lofts, furnace-like bedrooms, small steaming kitchens — these are the settings. Buzzing flies swarm around almost always; crying children scuffle underfoot; outside reeks the barnyard, torrid in the sunlight, gluey with muck in a storm. In such habitations the toiling men and women sink at times almost to the level of the beasts. Warped with poverty and toil, they take on the labor mask of a Daddy Deering, the hideous outward semblance of a Lucretia Burns. But their physical ugliness is as nothing in the face of their spiritual degradation. A life of savage toil produces equally savage passions; absolute sway over one's beasts tends to produce a desire for equally absolute sway over one's fellows as is demonstrated in such tales as *William Bacon's Man* or *A Preacher's Love Story*; the lack of adequate recreation causes a petty question of property to bring about *A Division in the Coolly*; absence of the outward luxuries of life is intensified by the complete omission of its spiritual graces. The careless brutality of her husband, the nagging of her "in-laws" make Agnes Kinney's daily life a literal hell; years of unrecognized labor bring to Lucretia Burns dreadful rebellion at last. As Douglas Radbourn sums up the situation,

> "Men who toil terribly in filthy garments day after day and year after year cannot easily keep gentle; the frost and grime, the heat and cold, will soon or late enter into their souls. The case is not all in favor of the suffering wives and against the brutal husbands. If the farmer's wife is dulled and crazed by her routine, the farmer himself is degraded and brutalized."[51]

There are other brighter aspects of the picture, but they do not mitigate, rather they accentuate, its essential sombreness. Mr. Garland admits in his preface to *Other Main Travelled Roads* that "youth and love are able to transform a bleak prairie town into a poem, and to make of a barbed-wire lane a highway of romance";[52] yet, watching the merrymaking at the Grove School-

51 Garland, Hamlin — *Other Main Travelled Roads.* Border ed. 112-3.
52 Garland — *Other Main Travelled Roads.* VIII.

house, the gaiety of the racing drivers, the shy "coupling-off" in the intermissions of farm labor, we are confronted always by the question of how long the youthful love will last, how long before the rosy laughing girls will be transformed into gray and shapeless slatterns, the dashing youths, into surly brutes. The landscape, marred only by the habitations of man, loses no whit of the beauty it bore to the dreaming eyes of the prairie boy; but "how much of consolation does the worn and weary renter find in the beauty of cloud and tree or in the splendor of the sunset? — Grace of flower does not feed or clothe the body, and when the toiler is both badly clothed and badly fed, bird-song and leaf-shine cannot bring content." [53]

The most terrible thing about all the stories is the hopelessness of their outlook; most of the characters seem come to an absolute impasse. The hero of *A Stop-Over at Tyre* is literally forced by circumstances into a marriage that strikes the death-blow to all his ambitions. In *Up the Coolly* the inequalities of opportunity and environment make the brother who went to New York rich and successful, the younger who stayed behind and took up the father's burdens poor and oppressed with a bitter sense of failure. The tales are filled with scenes that are symbolic — poor Martha in *Before the Low Green Door* who doesn't care to live but who never thought she'd die so early and unsatisfied; Simeon Burns trying to puzzle out the situation over which Democrats and Republicans, Grangers and Greenbackers disputed while hard-working, discouraged farmers in bewildered and wordless resentment toiled on; the despair of poor Haskins after his years of killing and fruitless labor,

> "He was under the lion's paw. . . . He was hid in a mist, and there was no path out." [54]

The toilers are indeed of the Main Travelled Road — the road arid and brown with the choking dust of the summer; desolate with the dingy mud and stinging snow of the winter; the road long and wearisome, almost always ungracious to the laboring feet that traverse it.

The denuciation of the stories was immediate and bitter. "Editorials and criticisms poured into the office," says Mr. Gar-

---

53 Garland — *Son of the Middle Border.* 368.
54 Garland — *Main Travelled Roads.* Border ed. 216.

land, "all written to prove that my pictures of the middle border were utterly false." And, as a matter of fact, the charges of distortion and untruth persist yet to-day. Yet scene after scene, character after character in the much-maligned tales can be paralleled in the pages of the autobiographical volume. And after all the criticism availed little save to solidify the author's purpose; he had, he asserts, the confidence of truth behind him; and if ever he were tempted to waver he had but to think of his father and mother in the Dakotas. For on another visit he had found another dry year upon the land and the settlers deeply disheartened.

> "The holiday spirit of eight years before had entirely vanished. In its place was a sullen rebellion against government and against God. . . . Two of my father's neighbors had gone insane over the failure of their crops. Several had slipped away 'between two days' to escape their debts, and even little Jessie, who met us at the train, brave as a meadow lark, admitted that something gray had settled down over the plain."

On that same withered treeless plain, with no shade save that cast by the little cabin, the weary mother gave out at last; on that plain the resolute father unable to face crop failures year after year, although he still wanted to try irrigation in Montana, was persuaded to turn his back on the West, almost convinced of the elusiveness of the pot of gold at the foot of the rainbow.

> "After nearly a third of a century of migration, the Garlands were about to double on their trail, and their decision was deeply significant. It meant that a certain phase of American pioneering had ended, that 'the woods and prairie lands' having all been taken up, nothing remained but the semi-arid valleys of the Rocky Mountains. 'Irrigation' was a new word and a vague word in the ears of my father's generation, and had little of the charm which lay in the 'flowery savannahs' of the Mississippi valley. In the years between 1865 and 1892 the nation had swiftly passed through the buoyant era of free land settlement, and now the day of reckoning had come."[55]

[55] Garland — *A Son of the Middle Border.* 415, 398, 439.

For the realist the day of reckoning has been at hand ever since. True there were important figures before Garland who shadowed forth the tragedies found on the prairie. E. W. Howe, for instance, in *The Story of a Country Town* (1883) which contains as its main theme a love so intense and so thwarted as to rank it with the tremendous drama of passion that Emily Bronte projected on the moorlands of Britain, pictures a community where every individual and thought seem to give the sneer of disillusionment to the title of Fairview — where all the women are pale, meek, bowed down by their "cross," where all the men are poor, disgruntled, oppressed by their sombre creed, a bleak and shadowed community from which even the "movers" seem anxious to get away. In his *The Mystery of the Locks* (1885), too, he etches an unforgettable although indefinitely localized picture of a decaying river town, whence all the ambitious have departed, where there remain only the human flotsam and jetsam, the spiritual mud left by the great flood that swept over the Midland. Nevertheless, Howe has remained yet to-day a figure too little recognized, and what is perhaps more to the point, so dark are his imaginings, so complete his obsession with the tragedy of mismating that we feel the result would be much the same no matter what his environment.[56]

Joseph Kirkland, too, whose chief claim to fame lies in his *Zury* is prevented by his technical crudities from taking the place that he earned by his intelligent use of homely materials. In the single volume named we have a bridging even more complete than in Garland of the apparently incongruous gap between the glowing superlatives of the days of exploration and the pitiless realism of the days of settlement. For rich as may be the soil (and the location of the Prouders was of the best), mere zeal, even superhuman labor and self denial cannot build up a farm. Cash, too, is needed; and it was Zury's recognition of the fact that "money was life; the absence of money was death," driven in upon him by the unnecessary death of his petted little sister Shoog and by his twelve or fourteen hours of bitter daily toil in making profitable the section, that gained for him in later life the title of "The Meanest Man in Spring Coun-

56 *A Man Story* (c1888) also illustrates this tendency, an unhappy marriage forming the central theme, and the middle western background being only slightly suggested by mention of the Prairie and of the "Boomer."

ty." But that money is not the only good is demonstrated by the barrenness of his riches, the sordidness of his thought till development comes through his love for a daughter of the East, the school-teacher Anne McVey. The early conditions of his life were such as led Hamlin Garland to revolt; the fact that the majority of the men of Zury's type do not find an Anne McVey furnishes the key to the work of many of the later rebels. Yet in spite of the clear-sightedness with which Kirkland was able to trace out the evolution of the country, in spite of the valuable information he gives as to pioneer customs and types, his knowledge seems too often that of the student; he lacks on the whole the fusing imagination, the coherent structure, to give his creations lasting vitality. As he himself admitted, he began too late; and his work was too early forgotten. Yet on Hamlin Garland and indirectly through him on his followers, Joseph Kirkland's influence has been profound. His advice to Hamlin Garland, "the first actual farmer in American fiction,"[57] to *tell the truth* has been heeded since then by many types of men for the most varied kinds of material.

For in the realistic movement that stormed the critical outposts in the eighties and that down to the present day has produced some of the least ephemeral of our literature, it is unquestionably true that Middle Westerners have been the leaders. The explanation of this phenomenon is not, however, so simple. In part it was due to a world-wide reaction from romance; this would not explain, however, its centralization in one locality. Perhaps the absence of a stately past such as dignified the genteel decay of New England and the South pivoted attention on the raw realities of the present. The clear air and broad horizons of the prairie may have tended to sharpen the vision. More probably the absence of hampering tradition, the spur of the adventurous pioneer blood that won the frontier, continued to incite in literature as in politics to revolt — revolt as much against the blatant self-satisfaction of the western promoter as against the academic strictures of the Atlantic conservatives. Certainly no more striking manifestation of the insufficiency of mere material prosperity could be found than this pitiless blazon-

57 Garland — *A Son of the Middle Border*. 371.

ing forth of its deficiencies by this most prosperous section of the world's most prosperous nation.

Inevitably in a dominantly agricultural community a prominent part is played by chronicles of the farm. Mr. Garland, describing the revolt of the populist party, remarks,

> "How far away all this seems in these days of three dollar wheat and twenty-six cent cotton — these days of automobiles, tractor plows, and silos."[58]

Yet the rapid spread of the Non-Partisan league in the Dakotas and Minnesota, the agricultural bloc in Congress, the organized attack by the farmers on the Chicago board of trade, the numbers of rural coöperative associations reveal much discontent. And the frequent failures resulting from the rash and extensive purchase of high-priced lands during the war boom caused disappointments as keen as any that stirred Hamlin Garland. Even when there is unquestioned prosperity such as we find evidenced constantly by the comfortable farmsteads, the elaborate equipment, the blooded stock, the thousands of automobiles in the state of Iowa alone, — the prevalence of the one-room schoolhouse, the reluctance to vote appropriations for libraries and community improvements show still the narrowness of interests of which the story tellers complained. Probably all of these things combined to keep alive in the thinker the spirit of revolt. Certain it is that although a writer like William Allen White in *The Home-Coming of Colonel Hucks* portrays the winning of true happiness, it comes only through many stern and troublous years of struggle, and the same volume (*The Real Issue*, 1896) records in *A Story of the Highlands* a grim and complete defeat of the presumptuous mortals by the "Lorelei of the Prairies."

And this conception of man pitting himself at a terrible cost against the untamed forces of nature is a dominant one for the truth-teller in the portrayal of the pioneers. The title of Keene Abbott's story *The Wind-Fighters* suggests one of the powers against which man is arrayed; the drought which renders bitterly ironical White's story of *Aqua Pura,* another; but most menacing of all was the soil itself — sullen, sometimes quies-

---

58 *Ibid.* 423.

cently resistant, again apparently actively malignant. Even the old world hunger for land, bred in the race through generations of tenant living, found itself baffled by the enigmatic and ugly moods of the Prairie, a temporary defeat best demonstrated in Miss Willa Sibert Cather's epic *O Pioneers,* as is man's final wrenching of victory. John Bergen died leaving the land with which he had struggled eleven years unconquered; his daughter Alexandra studies it, comprehends it, wins from it prosperity, and loves it. She is a true daughter of the soil, strong, full-breasted, placid — with rich comprehension, courage, and poise rooted deep in the great mother. The whole book indeed is a saga of the earth; the land furnishes the figures for the descriptions of Marie's life; it forms Ivar's refuge from the annoyances of civilization; it had its little joke, according to Alexandra, pretending to be poor because nobody knew how to work it right,

> "and then, all at once, it worked itself. It woke up out of its sleep and stretched itself, and it was so big, so rich, that we suddenly found we were rich, just from sitting still."

It remains the abiding element throughout the changing generations of mankind. And yet even the Norwegian Alexandra, deep and true as is her reverence, profound as is her gratitude, there in the midst of her smiling country with its great grain fields, its laden orchards and trim hedges, feels somehow a lack.

> "We grow hard and heavy here. We don't move easily and lightly as you do, and our minds get stiff. If the world were no wider than my cornfields, if there were not something beside this, I wouldn't feel that it was much worth while to work."[59]

And if Alexandra felt the lack of mental stimulus in the midst of her fruitful homestead, how much more pronounced must be that lack in the small town or village. Originally huddles of bare pine structures dumped down on the prairie, only of recent years have some of them taken on grace through their thickening elms, their attractive homes. Others still and ever will remain desolate way stations with the sun-streaked red depot prominent

59 Cather, Willa — *O Pioneers!* 1913. 116, 124.

in the foreground, in the rear the nodding fronts of the one business street. Motley settlements they are — sometimes determined by the needs of the railroads, again ill-judged ventures of the boom times, combining the ugliness of a premature decay with the vulgar rawness of the new. But whatever the stunting of their growth, it is as nothing compared to their mental stagnation. For with the development of a specialized civilization and conflicting individual demands, the communal spirit of the pioneer settlement early disappeared. Classes of society became more or less fixed; the frontier sense of adventure soon died away; interests turned in upon themselves with the muddying effect of a torpid prairie stream choked by its own sediment. The physical limitations of the prairie village in the past have restricted much of its life; its leisure class, mainly retired farmers, are not such as easily to solve its social problems. The rebellion at its materialism and its intellectual limitations has blazed out fiercely within the last decade, perhaps the earliest significant note being sounded by Masters in his *Spoon River Anthology.* Through all the era of settlement it has smouldered, however. Even the good-natured laughter of Booth Tarkington at the uneventfulness of life in Plattville (see his *Gentleman from Indiana*), although he gives credit to its population for a customarily unrecognized kindliness of spirit, intensifies rather than conceals a multiple spiritual tragedy.

Less obviously sluggish, perhaps because more varied, but still materialistic is the life of the fair-sized town, emergence of which from the cocoon-like prairie village forms an interesting study. The best full-length portrayal is William Allen White's *A Certain Rich Man*, in which John Barclay and Sycamore Ridge go through their raw, gawky, ugly adolescence together.

> "But the miracle of growth passes not merely our understanding but our imagination. So though men tell us, and grow black in the face with the vehemence of telling, that the Sycamore Ridge of the sixties — a gray smudge of unpainted wooden houses bordering the Santa Fé trail, with the street merging into the sunflowers a block either way from the pump, — is the town that now lies hidden in the elm forest, with its thirty miles of paving and its scores of acres of wide velvet

lawns, . . . and with twenty-two thousand people whizzing around in trolleys, rattling about in buggies, or scooting down the shady avenues in motor-cars — whatever the records may show, the real truth we know; the towns are not the same; the miracle of growth cannot fool us. And yet here is the miracle in the making. Always in John Barclay's eyes when he closed them to think of the first years that followed the war between the states, rose visions of yellow pine and red bricks and the litter and débris of building. . . ."[60]

Octave Thanet with careful artistry catches one midland city in a transitional state (*Stories of a Western Town,* 1892), painting her adopted home with a kindliness of spirit and a pleasant homeliness of detail unusual amid the violent naturalism of middle western fiction.

But in a very little while her western *town* would have resented its title, for, as she hints in her later, more romantic books, it early expanded, the kindly paternalism of Harry Lossing's relations with his employees giving way to the hard-headed, grasping policy of Horatio Armorer, the gleaming waters of the Mississippi being darkened by the smoke clouds and gases from the factories of the Tri-Cities. Again in White we have a picture of such evolution, the change from the blue sky and prairie grass that the pioneers found to the greasy tenements and stunting conditions of an industrial city being the most valuable element in his *In the Heart of a Fool* (1918). In its plot the novel is only a melodramatic variation of *A Certain Rich Man*; it suffers, also, from a nebulousness of sociological theory and a maundering idealism of which post-war conditions have already demonstrated the futility. Sensationalism or sentimentality of plot seems an almost inevitable accompaniment of such transition novels, Booth Tarkington's *The Turmoil* (1915) and *The Magnificent Ambersons* (1918) suffering, too, from conventional and overdrawn love stories. Both, however, give vivid portrayals of the emergence of the midland metropolis, the former demonstrating the clamor and dirt of the city and the falsity of the new gods of Bigness and Wealth without, unfortunately, suggesting any positive remedy. The latter with

60 White, W. A. — *A Certain Rich Man.* 1909. 51.

delicious irony and meticulous detail contrasts the epoch following the Civil War, when the Ambersons reigned supreme, with the modern era of progress, in which the inventor and manufacturer, Eugene Morgan, is the symbol of success. George Minafer, bringing his mother from her cruel and unnecessary exile abroad, finds a changed town, a town in which the Amberson name is already forgotten, a town in which the comfortable homes of his childhood have degenerated into cheap boarding places; in which great apartment hotels and business blocks jut into the smoke-blotted sky, in which the people of all nations hurry and toil; a city thunderous with feverish, relentless activity.

And it is in such cities that the realism of the Midland like its civilization early found its culmination. Huge, boastful, all-engulfing in their amoeba-like advance over the prairie, with an amazing energy, a supreme consciousness of success, they typify the chafing force of the West, the emergence of the agricultural regions into the industrial struggle of America. Each has its individual drama of progress, each its own brand of achievement — the automobile factories of Detroit, the flour mills of Minneapolis and St. Paul, the great power-dam of Keokuk. Of many of them, the majority, in fact, the literary possibilities have not been realized; they are yet to receive portrayal by the artist. The greatest one of all, however, may be taken as typical. For on the flowering plain joyously traversed by the old French explorers, the scene of the horrible massacre of Fort Dearborn, in the early days of settlement a site for frenzied speculation, now the commercial vantage point for the midlands, sprawls the great port that most completely exemplifies the changes on the prairie. There of all the cities of the country, according to Norris, throbs the true life. Through it more than any other Mississippi Valley city is revealed the far-spreading power of these complex organisms of civilization.

"The Great Grey City, brooking no rival, imposed its dominion upon a reach of country larger than many a dominion of the Old World. For thousands of miles beyond its confines was its influence felt. Out, far out, far away in the snow and shadow of Northern Wisconsin forests, axes and saws bit the bark of century-old trees, stimulated by this city's energy. Just as far to the southward pick and drill leaped to the assault of veins of anthracite, moved by her central power. Her force turned the wheels of harvester and seeder a thousand miles distant in Iowa and Kansas. Her force spun the screws and propellers of innumerable squadrons of lake steamers crowding the Sault Sainte Marie. For her and because of her all the Central States, all the Great Northwest roared with traffic and industry; . . . ."[61]

In it there was early collected wealth undreamed of by its founders. Libraries, art galleries, theatres, splendid mansions, luxurious clubs — all these demonstrate the potentialities of the city. The reverse side, too, rickety tenements, some of the lowest and filthiest dives of the country, hideous plague spots of moral corruption, vie with and excel the dark places in the oldest capitals of Europe. And between these the homes of the great middle class — gaudy flats and apartment hotels, monotonous and seemingly endless lines of bare and cheaply built cottages — suggest the immensity of the hives of the workers. In the inequalities of such a background and even more in the inequalities of opportunity for the denizens thereof, in the hidden tragedies of these squalid and splendid streets, the realists find their incentive for literary reproduction.

It is in a distinctive growth of the American city, the skyscraper, that one of the most striking of these is centred — *The Cliff Dwellers* by Henry B. Fuller, a book that created a sensation in the nineties. From floor to floor of the eighteen-storied "Clifton" the thread of the story floats. The plot is commonplace and sordid enough. George Ogden is the modern type of immigrant from the East — a well-bred young man and a very helpless sort of lamb amid the thorns of the business and social thickets of Chicago. The dishonesty of his brother-in-law cheats him of his estate; the extravagance of his wife drives him to ruin; only the death of the banker, Brainerd, saves him from paying in the penitentiary for the father's mortified pride. He is unmistakably the victim in part of his own weakness, but more emphatically of circumstances, of the ethics and ideals of

61 Norris, Wm. — *The Pit.* 1903. 62.

his new environment. The whole atmosphere is unwholesome, materialistic, corrupting. Atwater sounds the practical code in his speech to his new draughtsman:

> " 'My dear boy, go in for mining or dredging, or build bridges, or put up railway sheds, if you must; but don't go on believing that architecture nowadays has any great place for the artist. There won't be another Fair until long after you are dead and gone.' "

Every facet of the Brainerd fortunes seems to reflect the evils attendant upon ill-gotten millions. They bar Ogden from his rightful choice, Abby; they are the source of the unfortunate marriage of Mary to the fortune hunter, Vibert; they bring about the ruin of the younger boy, Marcus, who, dragged through the dregs of vice, stabs his father and hangs himself; they vanish like melting snow under the rash ventures of the favored son Burt. McDowell, the real estate dealer, succumbs to the desire to fly too high in rash and unprincipled speculation; Jessie is an irresponsible product of her wealthy friends and her consuming social ambition. Yet contrary to the impression that might be given by so brief a summary Mr. Fuller is no doctrinaire exhorter; the book is strikingly objective, in its sardonic grimness so clean-cut that even the occasional symbolism seems almost an extraneous ornament. Typically the very restraint of the close magnifies its challenging force. Ogden from his place in the balcony recognizes in a radiant occupant of the boxes the cause of his own domestic unhappiness.

> "He knew that she was Cecelia Ingles, and his heart was constricted by the sight of her. It is for such a woman that one man builds a Clifton and that a hundred others are martyred in it."[62]

Contentment comes only when Ogden and Abbie, truly mated at last, sink into a neutral grayness of habit. The same lesson is enforced with, unfortunately, more moralizing in the Chicago novels of Robert Herrick — notably *The Common Lot* (1904) and *The Web of Life* (1900). In the former a young architect cheated, as he considers, out of his rightful share of his uncle's

62 Fuller, W. B. — *The Cliff Dwellers*. 1893. 97, 324.

millions, sets up in business for himself, his first large "job" being virtually a bribe to secure his silence concerning a contractor's failure to live up to specifications. The dishonest partnership thus established is maintained through many years, largely as a result of Hart's need of money to satisfy his "champagne appetite." To the outward marks of success — a home in a fashionable suburb, expensive clothing, his own horses — he sacrifices his professional standards, his uncle's trust, his own character, his wife. Awakening comes at last through his witnessing the terrible death by fire of the inmates of an apartment hotel that he and Graves had fraudulently erected. Encouraged by his wife, he makes what restitution he can and although he is condemned as a weak fool by the worldly, he regains his own manhood and wins the admiration of the discerning by his courageous return to his original employer and his honest sharing of *The Common Lot.* Incidentally the same clue to happiness is found by Venetia Phillips who leaves her own wealthy circle where ennui has made her the favorite topic of the gossips to marry the blunt and impecunious but brilliant Dr. Coburn.

With but slight variations the same formula is used in *The Web of Life.* Dr. Sommers, a brilliant young surgeon just entering upon his career in Chicago, disgusted by the heartlessness and emptiness of the newly rich circle to which he is introduced and by the organized commercialism of the prosperous office, cuts loose from all conventional ties to work out his own salvation. Graft, self-seeking, inefficiency prevail, also, however, in the much humbler stratum to which he drops. Even his complete surrender to love in his free union with Alves fails to bring satisfaction, a fact that with woman's quick perception she realizes more completely than he, and her voluntary death brings "the end of his little personal battle with the world, the end of judging and striving, the end of revolt."

> "Already Alves had bequeathed him something of herself. She had returned him to his fellow-laborers with a new feeling toward them, a humbleness he had never known, a desire to adjust himself with them." [63]

63 Herrick, Robert — *The Web of Life.* 315, 330.

And with the unspoiled and generous Louise Hitchcock whom he has made dissatisfied with her unearned riches, he, too, finds content in the modest but satisfying middle course.

The reverse side of the picture inevitably found its interpreters, too, Fuller in his *On the Stairs* (1918) giving one of the most ironic interpretations of the changing fortunes of the new age. Raymond Prince, early favorite of fortune, represents the decaying ideal of inherited wealth and culture. A dilettante dabbler, untrained, singularly futile, when he returns to Chicago it is to the bitter realization of his own inadequacy; to the bustling, self-made, self-satisfied representative of the new America he yields place and fortune, even wife and son. *Jerry the Dreamer* (1896) by Will Payne also suggests that love without money is not always happy. Petty misunderstandings; friction and worry; on Jerry's part, jealousy of the wealthier Bane; for Jerry's wife, lack of comprehension of his socialistic dreams and ideals; all these result apparently from a marriage out of one's class. Yet Payne accords with convention in suggesting that the money, chief source of Judge House's pride, is tainted; the nondescript editor of the *New Era*, Dillingham, with his sincere though nebulous idealism is on a far loftier plane than any of the more "successful" figures of the book; and the novel closes with a complete reconciliation and apparently deepened devotion between the two lovers.

The great tragedy of our civilization, however, lies in the experiences of those who in spite of their agonizing struggles can never attain to the middle lot. These are the protagonists of Upton Sinclair in the earliest and one of the most scathing of the indictments of our industrial organization. The packing plants of Chicago that later were to form a background for such brutally realistic dramas as Kenneth Goodman's *Back of the Yard* or Will Levington Comfort's story of the same title are the life-crushing, hope-subduing, all-absorbing monsters of the volume. The tide of immigration is still flowing across the Atlantic, but the Irish and Germans who early furnished the cheap labor to the Middle West have yielded to the influx of the Slavic races. Grandmother Majauszkiene who had come to America with her son at a time when so far as she knew there was only one other

Lithuanian family in the district describes the successive waves as evidenced by the inmates of the little house which the latest arrivals had trustingly purchased as new — Germans, Irish, Bohemians, Poles, Lithuanians, and Slovaks.

> "People said that old man Durham himself was responsible for these immigrations; he had sworn that he would fix the people of Packingtown so that they would never again call a strike on him, and so he had sent his agents into every city and village in Europe to spread the tale of the chances of work and high wages at the stockyards. The people had come in hordes; and old Durham had squeezed them tighter and tighter, speeding them up and grinding them to pieces, and sending for new ones. . . . Who there was poorer and more miserable than the Slovaks, Grandmother Majauszkiene had no idea, but the packers would find them, never fear." [64]

With, however, all the implicit confidence, the childlike hope of the first light-hearted explorers of the prairies, Sinclair's family ventures into the greedy maw of packing-town. Jurgis is strong and confident, Ona, young and trustful; both are very much in love; Jonas, Marija, old Antanas, Elzbieta, all are willing to work; the children are to go to school; through the murk of the factories the world lies bright before them. But the new country is different from the old; the young men after eating a fine dinner and drinking themselves sodden fail to give their share at the *veselija,* and the married life begins encumbered by debt. Jobs are hard to get and working conditions, horrible; before the all-encompassing graft and the unavoidable accidents Jurgis's confident remedy "I will work harder" proves impotent; one by one the family, even the children, are beaten out of human semblance and engulfed in the struggle. The rickety frame hut that has for many weary months sucked their life blood for rent, taxes, and interest, is torn from them by the octopus arms of the company; old Antanas coughs out his life in a consumption hastened by the atmosphere of the pickle rooms; little Antanas is drowned in the slush of the unpaved street; Ona after suffering constant insult, inconceivable degradation from the Irish boss, Connor, dies in horrible agony; Marija,

64 Sinclair, Upton — *The Jungle* 1906. 78-9.

all hopes of her own happiness snatched from her, pays with her body for the aunt and children still living. To attempt to suggest the long years of exhausting labor, sickening worry that make the tragedy is useless; the situation amounts simply to this: There is nothing so cheap as human life. Therefore extract all that is possible for as little as possible from a man and junk him. By the side of the financial interest of the packers nothing else matters — the ruin of thousands of simple lives, the cheating and poisoning of the public, the wholesale corruption of government. As well hurl oneself before the Juggernaut as lift puny voice against them! These are the facts that Sinclair iterates with sickening realism. Little Stanislovas being beaten to drive him to the factory on a snowy morning, Ona cowering shamed at the feet of her husband, Jurgis with the blood lust upon him — there are dozens of unforgettable pictures. Mr. Sinclair was writing from a partisan point of view, of course; some of the incredible details that he gives of the filth and mammoth fraud of the packers have the unreal, phantasmagoric quality of a nightmare; the latter part of the book loses artistic merit through its extended exposition of socialistic tenets; yet the whole remains a brutally vivid, a crushing indictment of "big business" in America.

All of these are novels matching one or more individuals against man-made forces — the industrial organism, the struggle for economic supremacy, the pressure of the race for conformity. In *The Pit*, however, the second of Norris's trilogy of the Wheat, we go a step higher. There man is opposed once more to the elemental forces of Nature herself — not in bare-handed, isolated contact as was the homesteader, but through the complicated modern medium of stock exchange buying and selling. Curtis Jadwin is the logical successor to the pioneer — a native of Michigan whose people were farmers, and who had invested fortunately in Chicago real estate. His background is appropriate — Chicago, already a city yet still homely and unsophisticated, a city in which people like the Cresslers still sit on their front doorsteps and visit.

So completely does the Wheat dominate the book, however, that such details seem mere matters of incident. The gossip of the Helmick failure permeates all Laura's first night at the opera; the chief impression of her drive home is the lighted windows of the brokerage district with the Board of Trade building black in the distance. The Stock Exchange again, "black, grave, monolithic, crouching on its foundations, like a monstrous sphinx with blind eyes, silent, grave —," forms her last impression of Chicago. Between the two drives past the dark, silent hulk is embodied one act of the drama of the Wheat. Jadwin, who early "conceived the notion of some great, some resistless force within the Board of Trade Building that held the tide of the streets within its grip, alternately drawing it in and throwing it forth," makes various small speculative ventures, mere dashes in a light canoe on the gentle outer ripples of the whirlpool. The success of these stimulates him like the success of a frontier scout's raid into the Indian country; return from one expedition causes plans for another; the lust for adventure, for power, grows upon him. And just after he has promised his wife to cease all speculation forever, he returns with renewed Titanic energy in the person of the Unknown Bull to the Stock Market. The lure of the pit it is now beyond his strength to resist.

Not now as an isolated raider but as the captain of modern finance, the Napoleon that Landry Court admiringly calls him, with all the vantage that a long train of trusted lieutenants, the costly paraphernalia of modern exchange, can afford, he returns to the conflict. Far-seeing shrewdness, deep-laid strategy, the enormous power that he wields, all these enable him to accomplish his purpose. He, Curtis Jadwin, gains a corner on wheat. He dictates the grain prices of the world. But at what a cost! In each daily paper he is extolled or vituperated. A deputation of wheat growers present him with a silver cup in token of the prosperity he has brought to their agricultural district; yet his name is hailed with execrations by the peasants of Europe where the wheat loaf had grown as small as the fist and as costly. For himself the corner brings not rest but more labor. At night his brain repeats maddeningly the refrain of the Wheat; by day he forces himself ever to more and more feverish activity. His home is made desolate; his wife, lonely and self-pitying, practically handed over to the artist Corthell; one of his best friends commits suicide after being caught in the corner; he himself is afraid to trust a doctor lest his own verdict of almost complete mental and physical collapse be confirmed. Yet, drunk with power, the confidence of his success, he refuses to heed the advice of his brokers, refuses to believe the reports of the enormous acreage that his own high prices had caused to be planted. He is above the words and deeds of men. The Wheat alone can make him at the same time that it breaks him.

> "Out of that hideous turmoil, he imagined, there issued a strange unwonted note; as it were, the first rasp and grind of a new avalanche just beginning to stir, a diapason more profound than any he had yet known, a hollow distant bourdon as of the slipping and sliding of some almighty and chaotic power.
>
> "It was the Wheat, the Wheat! It was on the move again. . . .
>
> "There in the Pit its first premonitory eddies already swirled and spun. If even the first ripples of the tide smote terribly upon the heart, what was it to be when the ocean itself burst through, on its eternal way from west to east? For an instant came clear vision. What were these shouting, gesticulating men of the Board of Trade, these brokers, traders, and speculators? It was not these he fought, it was that fatal New Harvest; it was the Wheat; it was — as Gretry had said — the very Earth itself. What were those scattered hundreds of farmers of the Middle West, who because he had put the price so high had planted the grain as never before? What had they to do with it? Why the Wheat had grown itself; demand and supply, these were the two great laws the Wheat obeyed. Almost blasphemous in his effrontery, he had tampered with these laws, and had roused a Titan. He had laid his puny human grasp upon Creation, and the very earth herself, the great mother, feeling the touch of the cobweb that the human insect had spun, had stirred at last in her sleep and sent her omnipotence moving through the grooves of the world, to find and crush the disturber of her appointed courses."

As a whole the book lacks the symbolism, the vein of delicate imaginative detail that makes so richly poetic the earlier California story *The Octopus*. Yet the greater restraint of *The Pit* is decidedly right. For it is the immense reserve power of the slumbering earth that Norris here chronicles — its almost limitless resources, its indifferent superiority to mortal's feverish striving.[65]

And this potency of the soil, here a dominant factor, in all the etchings of the city forms an underlying thread, a resuscitating, permanently vitalizing force. Jurgis when the deaths of his wife and child drove him to complete despair fled from his place of bondage to the country. There as he tramped over the fruitful land, the blue skies, the sunny landscape ever beckoning him onward, "his health came back to him, all his lost youthful vigor, his joy and power that he had mourned and forgotten!"[66] Alves Preston, penned up in her lonely cottage with the wreck that was once her husband, was glad of her exile to the school of last resort, for there she found some joy, some consolation in the prairie around her, man-marred though it was.

> "There were glorious sunrises from the lake and sunsets over the desolate marshes. The rank swamp grasses were growing long, covering decently the unkempt soil. At night, alone, she had comfort in the multitudinous cries from the railroads that ribbed the prairie in this outskirt of the city. The shrieks of the locomotives were like the calls of great savage birds, raising their voices melodiously as they fled to and fro into the roaring cavern of the city, outward to the silent country, to the happier, freer regions of man. As they rushed, they bore her with them to those shadowy lands far away in the sweet stillness of summer-scented noons, in the solemn quiet of autumn nights. Her days were beset with visions like these — visions of a cool, quiet, tranquil world; of conditions of peace; of yearnings satisfied; of toil that did not lacerate."[67]

Jackson Hart after the catastrophe that shakes his soul, that totters from its crumbling foundations the tower of his ill-earned conceit, turns for succor to the soil.

---

65 Norris, Frank — *The Pit*. 1903. 41, 79, 373-4.
66 Sinclair, Upton — *The Jungle*. 259.
67 Herrick, Robert — *The Web of Life*. 79.

"He was content to rest there on the warm earth, waiting and listening for the voice which should come from beyond, content to forget himself. . . . . . . . . The sun sank into the deepening blue haze of the heavens; the thin shadows of the trees faded from the brown earth; the south wind from the prairies began to rise, blowing strongly, scented by the breeding land over which it had come. And as the day drew to its close, the murmuring voices of re-created life ascended from all parts of the earth with a strengthened note. . . . . . . . . . An immense, powerful, impersonal life, the greatest Life of all, was going forward all about him. In the midst of this large mystery he felt that he was but an atom — an accident which counted for nothing." [68]

It is to the most ancient and greatest nurse of mankind — the nurse which the Celts revered in the rite of the earth-mothering — that in response to some primitive call, some deep-rooted instinct, the offspring of the modern city goes in time of supreme stress and tribulation.

The land's unshakable serenity, its brooding power, its inherent beauty form the truest possible measure, moreover, of the greatness of the city. Contrast Hoffman's picture of the dunes with the Illinois Central tracks that bar the sight of Lake Michigan. Compare the glinting waters of an unspoiled prairie stream with the black, caked, and oozy surface of the packers' "Bubbly Creek." Picture the miles of fly-covered, sour-smelling dumps, the tumble-down dwellings and rubbish-filled backyards that make the modern approach to the city, the street-darkening elevated roads of Chicago, the never-lifting pall of smoke and gas, with the flower-strewn expanse that Harriet Martineau pictured, and estimate the improvements of civilization on the prairie. Chicago, "The Ugly City," its boast its bigness, or the country unlittered by man — which is superior? The era of the wild land, of course, is past. The city is here to stay. The question is whether or not the best possible use has been made of the opportunities. How many of the Midland cities have approximated even roughly the projects of the speculators? Which is to be the true symbol — the fair flower of the

68 Herrick, Robert — *The Common Lot.* 336.

White City, the speedy destruction of which Herrick chronicled, or Chicago's flaunting Pageant of Progress, which the moment of its completion was stigmatized by graft?

The problem of civic responsibility, of course, is involved. Thinking back over the visions of Utopia projected on the prairie and contrasting them with the sordid realities clamoring at us from the newspapers, with Herrick's pictures of official betrayals of trust, with Sinclair's and Whitlock's revelations of travesties of justice that favor always the rich, of wholesale political corruption and organized vice, may well provide a sobering check for our vaunted Americanism. Considering fairly the golden dreams with which thousands of immigrant families embark for the United States and the disillusionment too many of them suffer, the self-seeking of each class, the colossal centering of power, we may be able adequately to weigh the soundness of our boast of making the world safe for democracy.

Or, looking at the matter from still another angle, we may estimate the progress of our civilization by the types that it has produced. How much do the brutality of the policemen in Harris's *The Bomb* (1909), the pathetic mummery of the War-Whoop League, the rat-like Mike Scully, or the other political bosses pictured by Booth Tarkington, Brand Whitlock, and Dreiser justify the reams of flamboyant rhetoric about the rights of the common man, the sacred power of the ballot, the unperverted voice of the people, that for generations have distinguished our oratory? Which is the nobler representative — John Barclay diluting his oatmeal with clay that he may the more speedily become one of the richest men in America or his father killed for preaching abolition from a wagon tongue as he hastened to do his part in making Kansas free? Unquestionably the most prominent and the most successful type produced by our modern era is the self-made rich man. Equally unquestionably, however, he is a demonstration of the fact that money alone does not bring happiness. On Jurgis's one expedition into the fairy land of wealth with the confiding Freddie he learns that old man Jones who so ruthlessly handles his thousands of workers has troubles of his own caused by his family's leanings toward musical comedy stars, impoverished nobles, and strong drink. Colonel Hitchcock in *The Web of Life* presents the rather pitiful picture of a man who has fought fair and hard and long only to be uncomprehending and resentful before the indifference and dissipation of his son whom he wished to be his successor. Of course, part of the trouble is due to the too rapid rise from the masses, the acquirement of wealth without the time for its contributing culture, a fact emphasized by the vulgarity of the promoter, R. Gordon Carson, the cold brutality of Brome Porter toward the Pullman strikers, or the weak frivolity of the younger generation. Yet even in the most wholesome of these earlier representatives of the type — Curtis Jadwin — the contrast with the artist Corthell seems to indicate that, although the making of money may be the royal road to material success, it provides no infallible guide for the truest and fullest enjoyment of life, a lesson that is driven home by the emptiness of coveted honors revealed in Herrick's *The Memoirs of an American Citizen* (1905), and by the disappointments that even Dreiser's traction king, *The Titan* (1914) encounters.

The very fact that this is true seems to give our greatest source of hope for the future. For the midland has developed more rapidly than almost any other section. As always the tendency has been to idealize the past. Careful scrutiny, however, such as is given by the writers treated in this chapter reveals flaws in the most idyllic concepts. In every stage there are imperfections, notably at the transition epochs and in periods like the present when business deals of all sorts assume a magnitude undreamed of in the past. Yet after all the swindling real estate company, of which Sinclair's Lithuanian family is the victim, is only a more highly organized successor of the cheating agents denounced as blood-suckers through all the period of settlement, and this same efficient modern specialization is probably in part atoned for by the laws designed to circumvent fraud. In fact our attitude of increased responsibility toward inequalities and misfortunes that in the past would have been regarded as irremediable is one of the most reliable indications of our progress. The captain of finance, the self-made man is only our modern parallel to the explorer like La Salle, the empire builder like Bienville. Less strong physically but intellectually acute, he raids the stock market, grabs up a railroad or two, arranges for some enormous industrial combine, in much the same spirit of audacious demonstration of prowess that pricked on to achievement the frontier imagination.[69] Does it not seem probable considering the Herculean energy that in a century has civilized the major portion of the West, that has piled up fortunes of a magnitude almost incredible, that the same force, directed to spending wisely and distributing fairly the money that hitherto it has been the main ambition to amass, will bring about a new and glorious era of achievement? The chief obstacle to such progress would be that boastful self satisfaction, chief bane of America, that scored by Dickens in *Martin Chuzzlewit* still forms a principal topic for our satirists. To such harmful complacency, such blatant egotism, the uncompromising stand of the realists forms the best antidote.

---

69 *The Autobiography of Gurdon Saltonstall Hubbard* . . . ed. by Caroline M. McIlvaine (1911) furnishes example of the transformation from Indian trader to modern commercial magnate.

# CHAPTER VII

## ROMANTIC TREATMENTS AFTER 1870

Even when the realistic cult flourished most strongly, however, the romantic spirit was not quenched. Rather in the latter part of the nineteenth century it attained results more noteworthy than ever before. In part this statement may be based solely on bulk — the enormous mass of ephemeral material that in a time of agricultural prosperity and industrial expansion catered to the tastes of a steadily increasing reading public.

The works of the favorite dime novelists such as Aikin, Aimard, Bennett, continued to be reprinted, and each year added a number of new titles such as *Captain Cool Blade; or The Man-Shark of the Mississippi* (1879), or *One-Armed Alf, the Giant Hunter of the Great Lakes* (1881). The religious publishing houses, however, continued to combat the plague of the "yellow covers" by productions of their own. Reminiscences of pioneer preachers, collections of sermons and hymns, discussions of western church history, — to these were added sober stories like the Reverend C. H. Pearson's *The Cabin on the Prairie* (1870) to edify old and young or to moulder away on the dusty shelves of the Sunday School library.

Numbers of these books went through several editions. The more moralizing juveniles could not, however, successfully compete with the tales of adventure. Mayne Reid, E. Sylvester Ellis, Kirk Munroe, W. O. Stoddard, and of recent years Altsheler, are among the most prominent authors of these latter concoctions, but it would be difficult to find many prolific writers for boys and girls who have not at one time or another ventured into the field of the Middle West. The contents of these productions are most varied in type. Earning a living by fishing on the Great Lakes forms the subject of one of the earlier volumes *Just His Luck*; Alger centres in the Great Valley his record of *Luke Walton; or, the Chicago Newsboy*; Amanda N. Douglas re-creates the life of Old St. Louis, New Orleans, etc. in her *Little Girl* series; adventures on the Mississippi form an attractive theme; but dominating all in popularity are pioneer experiences or bloody struggles either in the Indian campaigns, the War of 1812, or the civil conflict. The majority of these are so conventional in theme, so careless in treatment, or so obviously didactic in purpose, that they do not bear detailed inspection. Yet even the poorest have some value in focusing attention upon picturesque figures or facets of the past.

In some measure connected with the narratives of this type are the masses of Indian material that emerge continuously from the presses. The most valuable of these are the scientific studies of aboriginal life for which the government, various learned societies, and careful investigators have been responsible. Their range is too great, especially since their purpose is, as a rule, non-literary, for us to discuss them here. We may mention, however, that the reminiscent accounts of various missionaries continued as did the autobiographies, written or dictated by various chiefs and white captives. Most notable of all, George Bird Grinnell, Eastman, and other cultivated Indians performed generously their tasks of displaying to the world the culture of their people. The fictional representations of the natives continued popular, contemporary descriptions of them being as a rule confined, however, to such final warlike demonstrations of the one time owners of the continent as those chronicled by Captain Charles King in his *Campaigning with Crook* (1880) or *The Colonel's Daughter* (1883). The tribes that he represents are almost entirely the dashing horsemen of the plains; the haughty warriors and toiling squaws have been largely restricted to reservations; and more significant than either of the preceding points, the author's sympathies are entirely with the wearers of the blue. To him the natives are rebels against law and order, murderous outlaws who cause suffering and death to hundreds of loyal families; in his severe though dispassionate criticisms of the aborigines and the treacherous agents who supply them with ammunition King gives a striking reaction to the long idealization of the Indian.

To outline thus vaguely the enormous amount of work after

1870 is, however, comparatively futile, it being far more important to note that the period marks in general the attainment of a distinctly high level of literary achievement. The foundations of the romantic literature, unstably bedded as they were in the fetid swamps and trembling prairies of the lower valley, the turbid river eddies, the shimmering grasses of the natural meadows, charred and stained as they were with countless crimes and deeds of violence, yet proved firm enough to support fair superstructures. In numerous instances later authors are noteworthy not because of striking originality but by virtue of the fact that they have brought to full fruition their predecessors' feeble strivings.

So it is with the humorists. From their earliest emergence gifted members of the clan had secured for the newspapers to which they contributed more than local reputation; consequently, it was but natural that in the latter part of the century a man like Robert J. Burdette should give national eminence to the *Burlington Hawkeye*. For us so extended a fame is in a way unfortunate since it tended to make Burdette as unlocalized in his sketches as his fellow lecturer Artemus Ward. The majority of his anecdotes, although he designates Burlington as their breeding place, might be, and in fact were, adapted to dozens of different communities simply by change in nomenclature. His method, however, smacks of the West — humorous exaggeration combined with farcical irony; and in such skits as *Stuffing a Stranger*, where he indulges in a blood curdling account of the Indians around Burlington only to discover that his companion hails from there, or *Agricultural Afflictions*, in which he satirizes the farmers' grumbling, he gives interesting demonstration of his Iowa affinities.

Exactly the same tendency away from local color is notable in the work of Eugene Field, first of the great "colyumnists". His early satirical volume *Culture's Garland, being Memoranda of the Gradual Rise of Literature, Art, Music and Society in Chicago, and Other Western Ganglia* (1887) is, of course, a most valuable contribution to our satirical literature. The pork-packing, soap-manufacturing, rail-controlling nouveaux riches, who buy their libraries at so much per front foot, who go abroad expecting to patronize royalty, who in their eager quest for "articles of virtue" pay enormous sums for such rarities as an autograph of Dante on the flyleaf of one of Ella Wheeler Wilcox's volumes of verse, are his special objects of ridicule. Any undue assumption of importance or refinement serves, however, as a butt for his wit, he delighting particularly in riddling the western city's flaunting pretensions to being a literary, musical, and philosophical centre, and being entirely indifferent as to whether his shafts are launched at such dignified bodies as the Union League Club or at such leading citizens as the Markessy di Pullman. His method is that of the older humorists — an assumption of blissful simplicity and of a state of illiteracy that leads to the most amusing misstatements and the most amazing spellings. His subject matter, however, is strikingly indicative of the strides the Middle West had taken.

But, clever as this volume is, Field's publishers have not seen fit to preserve it in the collected edition of his works, and it remains today almost unknown. Such bits of it as are reprinted in *Sharps and Flats* as well as the political squibs and parodies of a purely local nature are quite obscured by the more romantic pieces. It is these, of course, that have won him his present fame — iridescent fairy fancies, the whimsical chat of a bibliomaniac, Horatian paraphrases, lyrics like *Little Boy Blue*. Noting, however, their number and their grace, so different from the bustling life about him, we wonder at Field's refusal to go farther east than Chicago lest he be hampered in his literary development. He may have considered himself pre-eminently a Westerner; the bulk of his work, if *Culture's Garland* and his mining camp poems are omitted, will not permit of our doing so. Nevertheless in all of its phases his output affords an interesting demonstration of the increasing sophistication of the Valley.

In the sentimentality that Field frankly confesses, he is somewhat akin to another popular favorite, Will Carleton, who, like so many of the early writers, followed the path of western journalism to literature. Field's lightness of touch saved him as a rule from mawkishness. Carleton's poetic crudities, however offer little to redeem the conventionality of his message or the exaggerated pathos of such poems as *Over the Hills to the Poor house.* Yet the very fact that he appeals lavishly to such elemental emotions as those of home and parenthood does much to explain the enormous circulation attained by *Farm Ballads* (1873) and his later volumes. In such pieces, too, as *The New Church Organ* or *Out of the Old House, Nancy* there is a rather appealing suggestion of memory's tenacious clinging to the homely realities of the past, particularly characteristic of the older generation in the rapidly developing West.

Of both these strains, humorous and sentimental, James Whitcomb Riley furnishes poetic culmination. The sweetly sorrowful flavoring that endeared Field and Carleton to a large public, in Riley was responsible for such effusions as *Little Mandy's Christmas Tree,* or *The Happy Little Cripple,* verses that permitted his audience to demonstrate the tenderness of their hearts by a few gentle tears, without producing any permanently depressing effects. He is distinguished from the ante-bellum humorists, in fact, by his unconquerable optimism and by his inability to realize the sordidness of much of life. They, as we have seen, inclined toward realism, delighting in the crudities of the border as heightening factors for their grotesquerie. Riley, on the other hand, although the stuff of his poems was the same, almost invariably lightened the effect, as may well be illustrated by his narrative *Coon-Dog Wess.* "Coon-Dog Wess" is a typical poor white, one of the squatting, hunting offshoots of the frontier that excited censure from the earliest period. His life is, however, far from the desolate one it would have been had Eggleston or Mrs. Kirkland been dramatizing it. Losing both his legs in his last coon hunt presents neither to him or Riley any insuperable affliction; instead it gives to the hunter and his wife opportunity for humbly heroic rôles inconceivable to most students of the genre.

"Had *his* nerve! — And nussed him through, —
  Neighbors he'pped her — all she'd stand. —
Had a loom, and she could do
  Carpet-weavin' railly grand!—
' 'Sides,' she ust to laugh and say,
'She'd have Wess, now, *night* and day!'

"As fer *him,* he'd say, says-ee,
'I'm resigned to bein' lame:—
They was four coons up that tree,
And hounds got 'em, jest the same!'
'Peared like, one er two legs less
Never worried 'Coon-Dog Wess'!"

And the romanticizing tendency that caused Wess's wife to hug and kiss him after the catastrophe instead of bursting into shrill rebuke is marked throughout all Riley's depictions of the Midlands. His was the fate — most exceptional for America — to be entirely satisfied with the region in which he was born. Not all of his later lecturing tours, not all of the adulation of the world at large could woo him from his first love for the flat lands of his birthplace. As a matter of fact not even the Indiana of later years could satisfy him. Like Howells he looked ever back with wistful eyes upon the enchanted playground of his youth. There the clouds were ever white and fleecy, and the sky was ever sunny. Clover crushed under foot; fruit trees bowed below heavy burdens, beckoning the passerby to partake. Under cool green brakes tiny streams slipped, now resting in hollows of darkness where the speckled fish loved to lurk, now widening and deepening into those pleasure spots of boyhood — the old swimming holes —, then foaming into the white of a mill-race. Plump squirrels chattered in the tree-tops; wild fowls and small game yearned to be caught; birds and insects blended in a drowsy song of summer, or in dwindling chorus emphasized the dropping nuts of the autumn. To this lovely land Riley pays constant tribute.

"On the banks o' Deer Crick! There's the place fer me!—
Worter slidin' past ye jes' as clair as it kin be: —
See yer shadder in it, and the shadder o' the sky,
And the shadder o' the buzzard as he goes a-lazin' by;
Shadder o' the pizen-vines, and shadder o' the trees—
And I purt' nigh said the shadder o' the sunshine and the breeze!
Well!—I never seen the ocean ner I never seen the sea.—
On the banks o' Deer Crick's grand enough fer me!"

No better proof can be given, indeed, of his yearning for the past than the frequency of such titles as *The Orchard Lands of Long Ago, The Old Days*, or *The Used-to-be.* But whether his Indiana is of the past or of the present, his alchemy performed for it very great service.

Such a world as Riley presents is primarily a boy's world, his reminiscent poems of youth representing some of his greatest popular successes — *The Old Swimmin' Hole, Out to Old Aunt Mary's.* Gifted with an intuitive knowledge of childhood, he gains universality chiefly because he reproduces exactly the pranks and reactions of his own boy life, playing hooky, raiding melon patches, giving circuses, all the healthy, happy existence of the middle western town. Even when he uses adults, they are the homely, wholesome, hearty types that he idolized in boyhood — the self-taught fiddler, Old Doc Sivers, the country editor, the bee-keeper, Fessler.

> "Oh, Home-Folks! you're the best of all
> 'At ranges this terreschul ball,—"

this thought chimes through all his verse. Unconscious of social cleavages, of sociological formulae, he is the idealizing poet of equality. To all of his work Howells' criticism of *A Child-World* seems applicable.

> "From beginning to end it moves through the world of childhood, the childhood of that vanished West which lay between the Ohio and the Mississippi, and was, unless memory abuses my fondness, the happiest land that ever there was under the sun."

It is as this luminous painter of a by-gone West that Riley is most valuable. In method he differs little from the older humorists. All the tricks of the trade are his — exaggeration (see *Thanksgiving Day at Hunchley's*), flippant parody (*That Other Maud Muller*), atrocious punning (*Lines on Hearing a Cow Bawl*), unexpected closing twists (*A Ballad with a Serious Conclusion*) —, and in a poem such as the Raggedy Man's *Grandfather Squeers* he combines them most effectively. Yet his purpose is generally serious. The earliest humorists had used dialect to emphasize the illiteracy of their sections and to make a coarse popular appeal. Such a debasing of it Riley in his introductory talks about *Old-Fashioned* Roses censured severely. Hay is said to have grown ashamed of his use of dialect; Riley, on the other hand, greets it as "a dear old-fashioned friend who comes to shake a hearty hand with us, and gossip of the good old days 'when you and I were young.'" To him it is the best means of satisfying the tastes of his people.

> "What We want, as I sense it, in the line
> O' poetry is somepin' Yours and Mine—
> Somepin' with live stock in it, and out-doors,
> And old crick-bottoms, snags, and sycamores:
> Putt weeds in — pizen-vines, and underbresh,
> As well as johnny jump-ups, all so fresh
> And sassy-like! — and groun'-squir'ls, — yes, and 'We,'
> As sayin' is,—'We, Us and Company!'"

In putting his best efforts into it Riley is being true not only to himself but to dozens of his unrecognized forebears, a fact that he himself explains in the preface of his earliest volume, *The Old Swimmin'-Hole.*

> "As far back into boyhood as the writer's memory may intelligently go, the 'country poet' is most pleasantly recalled. He was, and is, as common as the 'country fiddler,' and as full of good old-fashioned music. . . . . . . . . . . . . .
> 'And it is simply the purpose of this series of dialectic studies to reflect the real worth of this homely child of nature, and to echo faithfully, if possible, the faltering music of his song."

By realizing in literature the aspirations of these humble toilers, by making articulate the old settlers' emotions (or what he thinks are their emotions) *When the Frost is on the Punkin* or *When the Green Gits Back in the Trees*, Riley has performed a task of great value for the Midland.[1]

Enticing as was the region of his boyhood, however, it lacked the chief charm of Samuel Langhorne Clemens' home, the most

---

1 Riley — *Complete Works* ed. by E. H. Eitel. (6v. 1913) IV:160, III:290, V:141, IV:549, II:485, IV:232-3, II:535-6. For further descriptions applicable to his verse see *The Ginoine Ar-tickle* II:134 and *A Tale of the Airly Days* III:328-9.

important single factor in the humorist's literary production. For it is as the Chronicler of the River that Clemens will probably attain most permanent literary fame. Into almost every facet of his early thought and activity the Mississippi penetrated. Its broad surface furnished him an ever-changing panorama; on its swirling waters he found perpetual entertainment; from its followers he gained his knowledge of the world beyond the horizon; the landing of its steamers was the battery that galvanized his sleepy little town into action. And so when he became a professional writer, what would be more natural than that he should turn for material to the river, even, indirectly from his pilot's experience, glean his pseudonym, Mark Twain?

His *Life on the Mississippi* (1883) affords, indeed, our most racy summing up of the flush times of steamboating. In it we have depicted with Twain's inimitable humor the potent lure of the life — the permanency of each boy's ambition to be a steamboatman; the awe with which he, and in fact all other mere landsmen, regarded even the humblest satellites of the lords of the deep; the majesty of the pilots; the tightness of their combine; the thrills of the boat-races. With what irony he recounts his own blissful ignorance and his trials as a cub! With what yearning he strives to emulate the wondrous expletives of the mate. With what heartfelt admiration he echoes the visiting pilot's tribute to Mr. Bixby, " 'By the Shadow of Death, but he's a lightning pilot!' " With what joy after twenty-one years of absence he once more gets the wheel in his hands. It was a stirring life, a heroic one. No wonder Twain recalls with zest those by-gone days of magnificent toil and Gargantuan adventure!

In the latter part, however, the book is decidedly journalistic in tone, basically a fact chronicle of a rapidly fading phase of transportation. And for literature facts are important only when fused by the power of imagination into a unified and artistically pleasing whole. Much finer and more permanent in quality, therefore, are the two novels of the early West — *The Adventures of Tom Sawyer* (1876) and *Huckleberry Finn* (1884), both America's most masterly examples of what Riley was pleading for — the real boy in literature. Besides excitement enough to satisfy any youthful cravings, the former has a delicious irony that only an adult can altogether appreciate — Tom's troublesome adoration for Becky, his superb diplomacy in the matter of the whitewashing, the Sunday School's showing off before the distinguished visitors. In the blood-curdling figure of Indian Joe, the tracking of the robbers, and the redemption of Muff Potter there are introduced elements unfortunately melodramatic in spite of the fact that they are somewhat typical of the period. The majority of the characters are lifelike, however; and on the whole the book presents an extremely realistic picture of the ante-bellum Missouri village.

Yet even *Tom Sawyer* is distinguished by a series of vivid scenes rather than a continuously powerful plot. For the full unfolding of Mark Twain's genius we need to turn to his picaresque tale *Huckleberry Finn.* There he seems to be freed from the baffling conflict of tendencies that render so disappointing the exaggerations and contradictions of the *Gilded Age* (1874) and the grotesque mingling of elements in *Pudd'nhead Wilson* (1894). In it after years of fitful striving he settles down to a steady flood of narrative, as resistless, as effortless as the flow of the Mississippi, the supreme embodiment of the Romance of the River. In *Tom Sawyer* the glamour of the water is frequently suggested; in *Huckleberry Finn,* however, it is the dominant factor. The care-free quality of the life, the fights and the boasts of the raftsmen (cited in *Life on the Mississippi* chap. 3), the narrow escape from the steamer, — all these are characteristic. To the Robinson Crusoe appeal of the camp on Jackson Island or the securing of the plunder from the floating house and the stranded boat, the book adds such prose poetry as Huck's description of life on the raft in chapter nineteen when the days really "swum by, they slid along so quiet and smooth and lovely." Perfect calm, starry nights, the spreading paleness of the dawn, the peaceful rising of the mist, the sparkle of the open river, or the pungent coolness of the bankside; food to be had for the taking; music and companionship in abundance on the other water craft — no wonder the pioneers were ever ready to embark upon the river.

The shore life, too, had fascination. The Sheperdson-Grangerford feud that is responsible for the enacting of a Romeo and

Juliet tragedy in the Midland, the kindly hospitality of Tom Sawyer's relations, the devotion of the negro Jim, even the scoundrelly tricks of the King and Duke of rascals — all these are typical of that interesting place and time. Twain, although he loves to indulge in such unadulterated humor as the debate concerning King Solomon, in the essence of his work is serious, the observations of the unfettered child of nature forming a valuable social study of the middle western frontier. Indeed Twain furnishes an excellent example of that rather frequent anomaly where a writer, realistic in method, must by virtue of his material be classed with the romanticists.

The same thing is true to an even more striking extent of the chroniclers of New Orleans, that enchanted gateway for the valley's frothing life. Of these the most noteworthy is Lafcadio Hearn, strange fusion of Celtic and Hellenic impulses, who, emotionally thwarted throughout his youth, bowed by poverty and disease in London and New York, chilled in Cincinnati as much by the derision of his companions as the cold blasts from the North, in the Crescent City found for the first time partial satisfaction of his tropic yearnings. Of his stay there (beginning in 1877) the quaint *Letters from the Raven* (1907), edited by Milton Bronner, afford fascinating glimpses, for in them he sends to his faithful friend, Henry Watkins, his fleeting impressions, moods, and ambitions. In New Orleans he suffered some of the bitterest moments of his life — the utter desolation of poverty, jealousy, misunderstanding, venomous criticism, even pilfering of his work. He laments whimsically concerning the "frogs and bugs and the everlasting mosquitoes"; he criticizes bitterly the making of "all the preparations against fever possible, except the only sensible one of cleaning the stinking gutters and stopping up the pest holes"; "the heavy, rancid air of a Southern swamp in midsummer . . . dust that is powdered dung, — quaking ground that shakes with the passage of a wagon, — heat as of a perpetual vapor bath, — and at night, subtle damps that fill the bones with rheumatism and poison the blood" arouse in him strange despondency. Yet of his feeling for the delta his first letter seems to strike the keynote.

"The wealth of a world is here, — unworked gold in the ore,

one might say; the paradise of the South is here, deserted and half in ruins. I never beheld anything so beautiful and so sad. When I saw it first — sunrise over Louisiana — the tears sprang to my eyes. It was like young death, — a dead bride crowned with orange flowers, — a dead face that asked for a kiss. I can not say how fair and rich and beautiful this dead South is. It has fascinated me. I have resolved to live in it; I could not leave it for that chill and damp Northern life again.''[2]

And the emotions that Hearn thus describes are the dominating ones in the weird and luscious bits of prose that under the heading of *Fantastics* he contributed to the New Orleans *Daily Item* and the *Times-Democrat*. As he wandered through the quaint balconied streets of New Orleans, lingering in the musty bookshops, the strange foreign eating houses, or on the mast-fretted levee, at night stooping with his damaged sight over the sensuously lovely pages of the French romanticists or stray books from the Orient, all these mingled sights and fancies shaped themselves into hauntingly passionate brain flowers. The restrained and simple pathos of *The Little Red Kitten*, the rich, almost oppressively beautiful *Fountain of Gold,* most idyllic of the tales clustered around the fabled Fountain of Youth, the magic of the *River Reverie,* by which Hearn paid tribute to the former pilot and distinguished visitor Mark Twain, the fever images of *The One Pill Box,* the cruelty of *El Vomito,* all these reveal the multiplicity of the appeal of New Orleans. Yet through all the sketches breathes the twin idea of love and death, a common unity of tone that seems effluence of the long decomposed swamp mould, the harbor's opalescent waters, the twining, odorous blossoms, and the milky wonder of the Southern moon — an effluence that finds truthful expression alike in the pestilential oppression of *MDCCCLIII* or the awesome quiet of *The Vision of the Dead Creole.* Of them all Hearn's own sentence seems most descriptive.

''There are tropical lilies which are venomous, but they are more beautiful than the frail and icy-white lilies of the North.''[3]

---

2 Hearn — *Letters from the Raven,* 80, 52, 74, 42-3.
3 Hearn — *Fantastics.* 1914. 3.

One of these *Fantastics, The Post-Office,* uses material very similar to that of the long story which first won Hearn extended recognition, *Chita: a Memory of Last Island* (1889). If the writer was forced to get analogy for his *Fantastics* from floriculture, surely we, for description of this may turn to art. Nothing, certainly, but Hearn's own term *sun-paint* will do justice to the great splotches of color with which he pictures the steamer's winding path through the heavily shadowed bayou, past the gleaming wind-swept islands, over the "long, quivering, electrical caresses of the sea." The "whirling flower-drift of sleepy butterflies," the tremulous rainbow jellies of the deep, the monstrous growths on the emergent shore of the gulf — all these are levied upon to provide illumination for his pages. Strange harmony, too, blends the many voiced grumbling of the ocean, "the great Witch-call of storms," the moaning of the rising surf answering the wind "as if the rhythm of the sea moulded itself" after the rhythm of the chilling air, the stupendous crash of breakers, into the fearful music of that wild night when the wind waltzed with the sea for his partner and L'Ile Dernière was destroyed. The book is a marvelous mingling of moods from the terror of the storm to the bliss of Carmen at the Virgin's sending of the child or the last powerful scene of recognition, delirium, and death, all fluid, vibrant, shifting with the ease and invisible power of the sea waves, and heightened by a rhythmical, colorful style peculiarly Hearn's own. He more than any other man has succeeded in catching the impalpable essence, the imperishable charm of the South.[4]

In George Washington Cable we have another of the gracious chroniclers of the Crescent City, one, however, who busied himself not so much with the atmosphere of the place as with the character of its inhabitants — particularly those picturesque descendants of the original French and Spanish who have done so much to impart to New Orleans its charm. An obscure clerk fascinated by his surroundings, he haunted the French quarter and delved in ancient records until the life of the old world city had become his own. His collection *Old Creole Days* (1879)

4 Hearn — *Chita.* 27, 11, 19, 33. See *An American Miscellany* ed. by A. Mordell (2v. 1924), *Creole Sketches* ed. by C. W. Hutson (1924), *Gombo Zhebes* (1885), & *Lafacadio Hearn's American Days* (1924) by E. L. Tinker, for other examples of Hearn's work at this period.

occupies an exceedingly high place in American fiction, so appealing is its material, so deft and graceful its treatment. To appreciate fully the quality of his work we have only to compare it with that of his predecessors. That the tawdry exploits of the Lafitte school or that the oft-stressed tragedy of race fusion could produce so delicately rounded a masterpiece as *Madame Delphine* (1881) seems at first almost incredible. The fineness of Cable's place description, his keen appreciation of the aroma of the ancient city, the delicacy of his characterization, the emotional restraint that dignifies the tragedy *Jean-Ah Poquelin,* all are distinguishing factors in his work. The whole volume breathes a high-bred elegance peculiarly the property of a race whose position among the out-numbering Anglo-Saxons seems somehow symbolized by the light and merriment of Belles Demoiselles Plantation at the moment of its engulfment by the Mississippi.

This atmosphere also pervades Cable's early novel *The Grandissimes* (1880), the main action of which takes place in 1803 "when the Anglo-American flood that was presently to burst in a crevasse of immigration upon the delta has thus far been felt only as a slippery seepage which made the Creole tremble for his footing."[5] The author traces the histories of his rival families, however, back to the coming of the Casket Girls and the explorations of Iberville, vividly suggesting to us early Louisiana society. The dismay at, and disbelief in, the cession to the United States, the fear concerning the validity of land titles, are matters of temporary importance. In addition to them we have depicted such permanent factors as the terrors of the yellow fever, the high play which caused Aurore De Grapion's husband to stake his whole estate upon a last fatal card game; the pride that was responsible for Agricole Fusilier's impossible terms for the return of the property and the De Grapions' haughty refusal; the feudal life and clan loyalty; and dominating all, the terrible menace of slavery. Not the soft pastels of *Old Creole Days,* but the lurid reds and sulphur yellows of the terrible fate of the African king Bras Coupé or of Palmyre la Philosophe's vengeance prevail in *The Grandissimes.* There are lighter aspects, of

5 Cable — *Old Creole Days.* 179.

course, the playful tenderness of Aurore and Clotilde, the childlike simplicity and bewitching beauty of these Nancanou ladies, the humorous relief afforded by Frowenfeld's assistant, Raoul Innerarity, and his famous "pigshoe." Yet all are darkened by what Cable calls the Shadow of the Ethiopian, the working of the voudoo magic, the fears of a negro rising, the thwarted lives and spiritual isolation of Palmyre and Honoré Grandissime, Free Man of Color.

Various others of Cable's books touch upon life near the Gulf. *Strange True Stories of Louisiana* (1889) is almost as fascinating as *Old Creole Days. Dr. Sevier* (1885) emphasizes the troubles of strangers in New Orleans; *The Cavalier* (1901), a war romance, pictures the South during the Civil struggles; *Bonaventure* (1888) paints in a lyric way the pastoral region that earlier delighted Sealsfield and Longfellow, presenting to us also some quaint characters of the outlying communities and unforgettable glimpses of the havoc wrought by high water. It is rather uneven, however, and the majority of the later volumes have so diminished in power as to win consideration mainly by virtue of the author's earlier work. On *Old Creole Days* and *The Grandissimes* Cable's reputation must rest.

That the spell of New Orleans seems to lend itself most readily to miniature painting, such women writers as Grace King, Mrs. Chopin, and Ruth McEnery Stuart seem further to demonstrate. Miss King not only illustrated, but herself put into words our contention that, so poignant is the charm of the Crescent City, even the most rigidly realistic treatment must be classed with the romantic literature.

> "I am not a romanticist, I am a realist *à la mode de la Nouvelle Orleans.* I have never written a line that was not realistic, but our life, our circumstances, the heroism of the men and women that surrounded my early horizon — all that was romantic."[6]

Educated among the Creoles and herself with a tincture of their blood, she began to write, however, not because she was stimulated by the men we have discussed but because of her share

---

[6] Quot. from Pattee, F. L. — *Amer. Lit. since 1870.* 1915. 362. See *La. Hist. Quar.* VI:365 ff. for Miss King's account of the way she began to write.

in a common Southern feeling — that Cable's depiction of the Latin inhabitants of the South was untrue. Perhaps the most serious in her purpose of any of this group of writers, her work will long be of value for the faithfulness with which she depicts her surroundings. Lacking some of the subtle felicities of Cable's early polished style, she, at the same time, avoids the suggestion of exaggeration (due partly to his abuse of dialect) which becomes increasingly pronounced in his treatment of the Creoles. With a meticulous touching in of background, a constant dignity of tone, she succeeds remarkably in producing depth and richness of emotion. Usually the mood of her work is sombre — the monotonous daily privation of the girls at Bayou l'Ombre, the intense racial suffering of Mary Madeline, whose wish as a child had been to be left in the cemetery "with the good dead, with the white dead";[7] the tragedy of *The Little Convent Girl*; the fate of *La Grande Demoiselle*.[8] Yet contrasting always with the bleak desolation of the war and its aftermath, she reveals the opulent plantation life. A story like Bayou l'Ombre where the negresses in a Saturnalia of rejoicing at the coming of the Yanks abandon husbands, homes, and mistresses, may shatter the romantic traditions of slavery; but the story which follows in *Tales of a Time and Place* (1892), *Bonne Maman,* demonstrates most movingly the power of the old ties, and the graceful *Monsieur Motte* (1888) is almost a fairy tale, based solely upon the faithfulness of an old servitor.

Miss King's outstanding characters, too, are almost all in accord with the aristocratic tradition — the great heiress Idalie Sainte Foy Mortemart des Islet, who a month after her début held the refusal of half the beaux of New Orleans; Madame Lareveillère, head of the fashionable Institute St. Denis; Bonne Maman, true *grande dame* of the old regime. The irony of their situation in the world of commerce and common sense she realizes with more intensity than any other story-teller; on the contrast between the two ideals her early story *A Drama of Three* depends; it is the basis for a bitter indictment in *The Pleasant Ways of St. Medard* (1916). In Miss King's early tales the dispassionateness of her attitude heightens her effect. She suggests,

7 King — *Tales of a Time and Place.* 1892. 138.
8 These are in *Balcony Stories* (1893).

refrains with a true Gallic ellipsis; this latter book, however, really a loosely connected series of sketches, is unfortunate in its tone, whatever the provocation. As a whole the tale is markedly, inferior to her earlier, essentially artistic studies.

Although Miss King's favorite and most fruitful theme is the portrayal of the great lords and ladies of the feudal South, she does not disdain its humble workers as her moving *The Story of a Day* demonstrates. Kate Chopin, however, is far more democratic. Indeed her main sources of strength are her lack of established prejudices and her interest in the individual. Our old acquaintance, the Acadian, she presents, for instance, without the sneers of the early travellers, without the romantic idealization of a Longfellow, but with the sympathy born of her varied ancestry, her years of residence in remote sections, and her own full experience. Many plantation owners ruined by the war appear in her pages, but their tragedies are always presented with tolerance, never with the note of vehement accusation. Charming relations between black servants and white master are revealed in stories like *Beyond the Bayou*; yet, without the anti-slavery bias of Cable, Mrs. Chopin makes evident in such little masterpieces as *La Belle Zoraïde* or *Desirée's Baby* the cruel wrongs almost inevitably engendered by the system. Perhaps it is her impartiality, her interest in the event rather than the thesis that gives her work its freshness and spontaneity. Some of her tales are mere sketches, some longer narratives that make contact through common characters with still others of the group. Whatever the theme, however, she attains with a French simplicity of means a French poignancy of effect. Her studies in *Bayou Folk* (1894) are entirely realistic in tone, yet partake of that witchery inherent since the very earliest days in the Southwest's pastoral life.

Less extended in her range and less skilled in her technique than the other two women, Mrs. Ruth McEnery Stuart yet deserves attention for the simple charm as well as the number, of her portrayals of Louisiana. As a rule she is at her best in her characterizations of the negro — such human oddities as the healer Uncle 'Riah Washington in *Holly and Pizen* (1899), who takes upon himself the diseases of others, or the resourceful, cheery George Washington Jones, a *Christmas Gift that Went a Begging* (1903). All of this latter group of tales uphold the romantic tradition — patriarchal masters and mistresses, black servants who cling passionately to the memories of ancient grandeur, whose personal ambitions are entirely sunk in their loyalty to their "great family," Mrs. Stuart's favorite formula being the long separation and joyous reunion of such a group. In her most ambitious story of this type, *The River's Children* (1904), she weaves as well a very charming idyl of the Mississippi. The volume opens with the feverish labors of the floodtime, thence switching by a natural transition to the tragedy of Harold Le Duc who, according to the graphic description of the Creole, has returned "from de war, already robbed, to find *all* gone — home, wife, child, family, servants, *all* obliterate', an only de river's mark, green mold an' mildew, on de walls above de mantel in de house. . . ."[9] Although the author digresses unduly here about the splendors of Brake Island, Le Duc's secluded domain among the bayous, the dominant feature of the book is that of the river. Its alarm songs vibrate through the pages; the most frivolous of Creoles regard it with pagan awe; devout old Aunt Hannah holds with its "mericle mystery" communion. Temporary destroyer of Le Duc's happiness, it in time brings him to his child; serene, resistless, it offers the answer to the faithful old couple's prayer, that, their trust fulfilled, they may pass out together.

In her affection for these old colored servants and these cunning darky boys, and her appreciation of the unique relation existing between the two races, Miss Stuart resembles the dialect poet Edwin Russell. The latter's poems, collected after his early death, are few in number, but, according to Joel Chandler Harris, there can be found no "happier or more perfect representation of negro character." The gay charlatanry, the suave flattery with which the old farmer tries to palm off a stone-weighted bale of inferior cotton, the injured innocence with which another old servant resents the attempt to punish his borrowing from his master's woodpile, do much to uphold the traditional depiction of the negroes as mischievous but light-hearted and lovable children.

9 Stuart — *The River's Children.* 20.

Their attitude toward their masters is excellently represented in *Mahsr John,* that vivid epitome of the change brought by the war in the planter's estate. Most interesting to us are the poems about the river, *Precepts at Parting,* which gives a glimpse of caste distinctions upon one of the great steamers, and especially that portion of *Christmas Night in the Quarters* in which the story of Noah and the flood is recited in terms of the Mississippi.

"Dar's gwine to be a' oberflow," said Noah, lookin' solemn —
Fur Noah tuk the 'Herald,' an' he read de ribber column—
An' so he sot his hands to wuk a-cl'arin' timber-patches,
An' 'lowed he's gwine to build a boat to beat the steamah *Natchez.*

* * * * * * * *

"Now, Noah had done cotched a lot ob ebry sort o' beas'es —
Ob all de shows a-trabbelin', it beat dem all to pieces!
He had a Morgan colt an' sebral head o' Jarsey cattle —
An' druv 'em 'board de Ark as soon's he heered de thunder rattle.

"Den sech anoder fall ob rain! — it come so awful hebby,
De ribber riz immejitly, an' busted troo de lebee;
De people all wuz drowned out — 'cep' Noah an' de critters,
An' men he'd hired to work de boat — an' one to mix de bitters.

"De Ark she kep' a-sailin' an' a-sailin' *an'* a-sailin';
De lion got his dander up, an' like to bruk de palin';
De sarpints hissed; de painters yelled; tell, whut wid all de fussin'
You c'u'dn't hardly hear de mate a-bossin' 'roun' an' cussin'.

"Now, Ham, de only nigger whut wuz runnin' on de packet,
Got lonesome in de barber-shop, an' c'u'dn't stan' de racket;
An' so, fur to amuse he-se'f, he steamed some wood an' bent it,
An' soon he had a banjo made — de fust dat wuz invented."[10]

Athough Russell died in New Orleans, he must be reckoned

10 See Talley, T. W. — *Negro Folk Rhymes.* 1922. p. 44. for a slightly different folk version.

a Mississippi poet. That Louisiana reigns first among the states we are considering in the romantic storehouse of the Old South may be proven, however, not only by the merit of the authors we have discussed but by the numbers of writers who put forth such works as *The Octaroon; or, the Lily of Louisiana, The Blonde Creole; a Story of New Orleans,* or *Toward the Gulf; a Romance of Louisiana* to say nothing of the stray short stories which pay tribute to the charm of the Crescent City. Interpretations of Arkansas, a state which also ranks high in the number of tales it inspired, divide curiously enough into two distinct classes—rather simple realistic studies such as Mrs. Stuart's tales of Simpkinsville or some of Octave Thanet's stories of the canebrakes, and such melodramatic narratives as Opie Read's *Len Gansett* (1888). The latter author, who at one time or another wrote of almost every Southern state, is most closely associated with Arkansas; but although some of his books like *The Arkansas Planter* (1896) show sympathy for nature and grasp of the contrasts between poor white and lordly planter that marked the state, he has in general too little literary merit to deserve much attention. Type characters, conventional material, pronounced unevenness of style, make him worthy of attention mainly as a monument of the popular tastes of the past.

Kentucky deserves a section all its own. Popular as were the episodes of its early history, once its dark forests were levelled, it assumed a newer, lighter, even more fascinating character. Its wealthy planters, largely émigrés from Virginia, brought with them the Old Dominion's traditions of stately country places, lavish hospitality, gentlemanly amusements, and beautiful women. Add to these elements the blooded stock that the richness of the soil and the Kentucky blue grass brought to peculiar perfection, and the interest in horse-racing that marked the latter portion of the century, and we have the essentials for one of the concoctions describing Kentucky. For a time there was a fad for blue grass fiction resulting in such titles as *Tilting at Windmills; a Story of the Blue Grass Country* (by Emma M. Connelly, 1888), *A Blue Grass Beauty* (by Gabrielle E. Jackson, 1903), or *A Blue Grass Thoroughbred* (by Tom Johnson, 1889). Most of these books are already forgotten, however, Kentucky in the literary world being for the average person represented by the work of James Lane Allen.

One of the most studious of the writers with whom we deal, Allen like Howells brought to his work not only wide reading in various languages but a careful critical theory, his first tales *Flute and Violin* (1891) being as a result a really distinguished collection. Ripened, polished, grave in tone, they seem to distill the essence of the aristocratic tradition, the blue blood, the gentle breeding of Kentucky. In them are reflected some of the finest of her types — the struggling, pathetic cleric, whose sole comfort was the magic flute; the colonel and his faithful Peter, admirable representatives of the old regime; Pauline Cambron, last descendant of "one of those sixty Catholic families of Maryland that formed a league in 1785 for the purpose of emigrating to Kentucky without the rending of social ties or separation from the rites of their ancestral faith."[11] In them, too, are apparent in varying degrees practically all of the traits that marked Allen's later works.

That the majority of these deal with his native state we may prove by a brief survey of the most important. *The Blue Grass Region of Kentucky* (1892) contains a series of thoughtful social studies, originally intended to accompany the preceding group of tales; *The Choir Invisible* (1897), an enlargement of the earlier *John Gray* (1893), turns back to pioneer days; *A Kentucky Cardinal* (1894) and *Aftermath* (1895) form a charming lyric unfolding of the love of a Kentucky naturalist; *The Reign of Law, a Tale of the Kentucky Hemp Fields* (1900) presents in its portrayal of a boy whose anthropocentric faith is wrecked by his perusal of the works of Darwin and other scientists, a study of peculiar interest to us in view of the recent controversy concerning evolution. In all of these books Kentucky is a dream region, from which Allen's art purges away all that is dross. In *The Choir Invisible*, for instance, the dominant note is not that of the swaggering, arrogant frontier but almost a cathedral mood — solemn silences, light subdued, enriched by slow filtration through the jeweled panes of rainbow windows.

In part this tendency is due to Allen's unconscious affection

11 Allen — *Flute and Violin.* 188.

for pleasant surroundings, gentle folk, upright characters, spiritual victories. To a more pronounced extent, however, we may attribute it to the philosophizing habit that not only slowed up his action but governed his conceptions of nature and of man. To him as to the school teacher John Gray the Indian battles of the past offer moral lessons for the present; unlike the average historical novelist he sees in the wilderness road not the opportunity for stirring adventure but a thought-inspiring link with antiquity, reminder of the prehistoric denizens of the midlands, the early Saxon advance over Europe. Nature, always beautiful but sometimes terrible, is not only a generally beneficent power, purveyor of life, but a teacher and comforter, the revelation of the Omnipotent. Naturally, therefore, Allen's depiction of the outer world, in such a story as *Sister Dolorosa* a finely etched concomitant of the action, enhancing the mood, in *The Kentucky Cardinal* inseparably a part of the bird lover's wooing, becomes steadily more luxuriant, delaying the plot to exhibit a mass of intricately lovely detail, elaborating in *The Reign of Law*, for instance, the description of the hemp to provide a parallel for our development. This mystic, allegorical tendency is perhaps most marked in *A Summer in Arcady* (1896), a book that in a way forms a transition between two groups of novels. In it the two young lovers drift helpless, uncomprehending as two quick-fading butterflies. Nature, golden, oozing sweetness, blooming with the ripe perfection of the summer, yet is a terrible, dominating force, using all her lush charm to drug the intellect, to intoxicate the sense, to make plastic and subordinate her creations to the resistless, the primal surge of mating. In it Allen's two themes — nature and love — are inextricably combined. The later novels, however, notably *The Mettle of the Pasture* (1903), *The Bride of the Mistletoe* (1909), and *The Doctor's Christmas Eve* (1910) neglect landscape description to centre on the thwarting tragedies of sexual passion. The dreamer, the nature lover becomes primarily the preacher. Although he still uses his native state for a background, the action and characters might be satisfactorily set in almost any locality. It is the universal aspect of his men and women that appeals to him now — their common weaknesses, their common struggles.

By both interests his artistry has suffered — in the first case by undue elaboration of description, in the second by rather tedious emphasis on ethical problems. The latest books, too, such as *The Sword of Youth* (1915) are unfortunately suggestive of empty husks — carefully wrought out literary formulae, familiar material, but an absence of any vital urge, any spontaneous prompting. Consequently Allen's fame will probably rest upon his polished early work. By it he has given Kentucky a high place in the local color movement of the nineteenth century.

And the service that the novelist did for the state in prose, Madison Cawein tended to render in poetry. Like Allen, Cawein lavished a wealth of affection on the rustic scenery around him, and like Allen he reproduced it in words with a voluptuous fidelity of detail. The budding beauty of the springtime, the desolation of the winter, the barbaric coloring, autumn's announcement of decay, and above all the splendors of the summer, furnished the dominating themes of his poetry. On almost every page one may find suggestion of the stately beechwoods, the crowding may-apples, the flowering dogwood, the flitting dragon flies, the melancholy whip-poor-wills, in short, of the thousand and one birds and plants, insects and trees, that go to make up the landscape of Kentucky. Nature was to him not only a rapture to the sense but a comforter and a source of intellectual and ethical inspiration. In poem after poem like *Longings, Epiphany, Field and Forest Call,* he described the lure of the country; in Nature he found the basis for his Platonic creed of evolution; repeatedly he echoed the Shakespearian concept of sermons in stones. Since in his philosophy there is nothing new or profound, however, his work must stand because of the delicacy and the vibrant fervor of his woodland portrayals, the mellowing love for the out-of-doors which interested Howells in the poet and which early brought tribute from Riley.

Yet even in this there is a lack that apart from questions of technique, would prevent Cawein from being truly the creator of the New Song of which he dreamed. His work was not merely the product of his environment, but too much an inspiration of that old world romance which long dominated the South. Not any segment of the Kentucky landscape but most frequently one with a sentimental flavoring—a deserted house, a lonely grave, an old mill stimulated his fancy. Even when he abandoned himself most completely to the languorous appeal of the summer noontide, the balmy fragrance of the night, the Kentucky background did not sufficiently content him; to it he felt obliged to import the classic deities. In a way this may be regarded as an indication of the fineness of Cawein's tastes; in a way it is rather a pathetic linking of the "dark and bloody ground" with the Grecian groves and vales in which jocund nymphs and satyrs danced during the golden morning of the world. Yet that, in a region so rich in heroic lore, Cawein should have had to turn for dream figures to European realms of fancy seems to argue a fundamental lack. It is the same factor that, in the few cases when he used the red man made him turn to the South American races, the factor that has steadily hampered the writers of the Midland, a reliance for inspiration upon the stock materials of the past.

This lack of originality we find demonstrated repeatedly in the period of later romance. The lusty call of Whitman died unheard; until comparatively recent years poetry offered nothing to compete with the notable studies of the realistic novelists. Instead old materials, old metres, were used again and again. The storied history of the Indians still attracted many as is demonstrated by such poems as Eli W. Huggins' *Winona; a Dakota Legend* (1891) or W. P. Norris's *Calumet of the Coteau* (1883). The Kansas and Missouri outrages received their meed of attention in such short poems as W. H. Babcock's *Bushwhacker Ben* (in *Lord Sterlings Stand*, 1880) or longer narratives like Thomas Brower Peacock's weakly Byronic *Rhyme of the Border War* (1880), which won for its author contemporary fame. Mary Ashley Townsend in *Down the Bayou* (1881) and Arthur Wentworth Eaton in *Acadian Ballads and De Soto's Last Dream* (1905) convince us that the lower stretches of the river had not lost their poetic glamour although the development of the cities was at the same time being commemorated in such pieces as Lillian B. Fearing's *In the City by the Lake* (1892) and some of the Ben King's humorous verse. Numerous titles suggest their author's allegiance to the flat lands — Ellen P. Allerton's *Poems of the Prairies* (1889), W. R. H. Dunroy's *Tumbleweeds* (1901), Minnie Gilmore's *Pipes from Prairie-Land* (1886), *A Prairie Idyl* (1882) by Amanda T. Jones; and occasional western pieces are scattered through countless other collections near the turning point of the century. The isolated nature of most of these makes impracticable any attempt at survey. In general the limited capacity of most of the hinterland's aspirants to fame, as well as the conventionality of their treatment and theme, renders comparatively valueless any discussion save an indication of the channels which they followed. Certain of them, of course, produced some charming pieces; but on the whole the middle western verse may be regarded as important only for state literary histories. The few poets who, apart from Riley, attained national fame, the chief of them, of course, Moody, produced work essentially non-local in character.[12] Therefore we must regard the poetry in this period of later romance as quite eclipsed by the short story, temporarily the most important of the genres as we have seen, although the novel presents various interesting features.

In the field of the short story one other distinguished writer must be mentioned, Miss Constance Fenimore Woolson, whose early volume *Castle Nowhere* (1875) opened up a field even yet strangely untilled — the fascinating region surrounding America's great inland seas. A rude Lake Superior mining settlement forms the background for the pathetically heroic struggles of *Peter the Parson*; an equally rough camp of trappers, the scene for the missionary endeavors and tragic love of the *Lady of Little Fishing*; the plenty and placidity of an Ohio Separatist community intensifies the spiritual hunger of *Solomon* and *Wilhelmina*.[13] In all of these stories Miss Woolson's treatment is realistic, betraying fearlessness and strength, a knowledge of dramatic and emotional values, but lacking the delicate perfection and polish of the Louisiana group. Both her *Jeannette* and *The Old Agency*, however, are vibrant with the primeval charm of Mackinac, and her *St. Clair Flats*, that tale of religious fanaticism amid the tremulous loveliness of the water lilies, reeds,

---

12 Attention may be called to Moody's *Ode in Time of Hesitation*, stanza III of which gives practically his only poetic mention of the prairie states.

13 *The Separatist Society of Zoar* is described by E. O. Randall, *O. Arch. & Hist Soc. Pub.* VIII:1 ff.

and clear waters of the straits, is lyric in its charm. For her truthful preservation of picturesque early phases of the lake country we owe Miss Woolson much. Yet in spite of her success she early deserted the site of her pioneering, in most of her later volumes treating her adopted home, the South. For the mass of her work and her influence on others Mrs. Mary Hartwell Catherwood is much more important.

Stimulated by her reading of Parkman, the latter woman, a native of Ohio, early began to make the domain of the French in America her own. With the ambition that marked the Gallic advance into the wilds, she seized upon their outposts, shifting her scene from the Atlantic seigniories, constant scenes of conflict with the English, to the Canadian strongholds of Quebec and Montreal, the whirling rapids of Sault Ste. Marie, Tonty's fort among the Illinois, and the tangled verdure of the Mississippi. Upon this background she projects a gallery of picturesque figures — dauntless La Salle, faithful Tonty, and the other leaders in the conquest; saintly recluse, self-abnegating missionary, the much loved parish priest; hale and carefree voyageur, half-breed fisher and trapper, prosperous trader, post coquette, exiled court lady. Unfortunately she adds to the authentic figures of history creations of her own to heighten the effect, a customary device of the historical novelist, but unwarranted in one who makes Mrs. Catherwood's pretensions to accuracy. Unfortunately, too, her strength does not lie in long narration, her *Story of Tonty* (1890) being markedly uneven, and her *Lazarre* (1901), a poorly articulated tale of the dauphin in America based upon the fantastic pretensions of Eleazer Williams.[14] Even her attractive little volume *Old Kaskaskia* (1893) is a series of vivid sketches notable for its depiction of the life of the ancient village and such individual portraits as the renegade dancing friar, Father Baby, rather than for its plot. In her short stories such as *The Windigo* or *The Kidnapped Bride* or *Mackinac and Lake Stories* (1899) she demonstrates unquestionably her ability to reproduce primitive moods and to vitalize the most widely varying characters. The latter volume, indeed, is the epitome of a century of lake history, beginning with the idyllic *Marianson,*

---

14 For an account of this individual by W. W. Wight see *Parkman Club Papers* V. 1. no. 7.

an episode of the War of 1812, passing deftly over the quarrels and festivities of the voyageurs, the expulsion of the Mormons from Beaver Island,[15] and ending with a sophisticated love story typical of the Mackinac of fashion resort, all tinctured and made lambent by her own fusing imagination and the glamour that is associated indissolubly with the annals of the French.

And Mrs. Catherwood is only the first of a long line of romancers. Partly in reaction to the simple but detailed studies of contemporary manners and customs, a movement led abroad by Stevenson, partly in satisfaction of the natural yearning for dramatic love and adventure, there grew up during the latter part of the nineteenth century a whole school of rococo novelists. To a certain extent this school treated of distant countries and past ages in the fashion that so long hampered American literary development, witness General Lew Wallace's *Ben Hur* (1884), Mark Twain's *Personal Recollections of Joan of Arc* (1896), Booth Tarkington's *Monsieur Beaucaire* (1900), Charles Major's *When Knighthood Was in Flower* (1898), all of these popular favorites, it is interesting to note, being by Middle Westerners. The contemporary factors that contributed to the vogue of the historical novel, however, a sense of workaday comfort and security that centered attention on the historic past, and a national pride stirred to patriotic expression by the war with Spain, tended to further the use of native materials. Old times in Virginia and Revolutionary exploits formed perhaps the most prolific themes; the Middle West, nevertheless, came in for its share of attention. William Carruthers had early described Governor Spotswood's expedition over the mountains in his *Knights of the Horseshoe* (1845); now Maurice Thompson popularized the achievements of Clark in his *Alice of Old Vincennes* (1900); Emerson Hough defended Law in his explanation of the blowing and breaking of *The Mississippi Bubble* (1902); Mrs. Dye in *The Conquest* (1902) gave a most faithful chronicle of the United States' gaining of the West. To attempt to analyze all of these historical novels would be useless; it is interesting, however, to note how certain early themes repeat themselves again and again. The

15 In this connection see M. M. Quaife's *Polygamy at Beaver Island, Mich. Hist. Mag.* V:333 ff and a number of articles in *Mich. Pion. & Hist. Coll.* XVIII, XXXII, etc.

Kansas slavery struggle, for instance, gives rise to such varied productions as Mary A. Humphrey's stilted *The Squatter Sovereign* (1883), William R. Lighton's philosophical *Sons of Strength* (1899), or Margaret Hill McCarter's sentimental effusions. Mary Devereaux adds to the already long list another *Lafitte of Louisiana* (1902), which bears in an only slightly improved form all the earmarks of the earlier piratical biographies. The Indian wars furnish an ever reliable source for narrow escapes and thrilling adventures as is indicated by the repeated appearance of celebrated chieftains in such lively tales as Mary C. Crowley's melodramatic *The Heroine of the Strait* (1902) or Randall Parrish's *Sword of the Old Frontier* (1901). The French occupation of the valley never ceases to charm, there being an abundance of such narratives as Mrs. Marah Ellis Ryan's *Flower of France; A Story of Old Louisiana* (1894) or Sheppard Stevens' *In the Eagle's Talon* (1902). After 1870, too, we have in the struggles of the Civil War and of the reconstruction period a whole new field for romance, a field that so far has found its most noteworthy popular expression in Winston Churchill's interesting chronicle *The Crisis* (1901), but that is responsible for a host of lesser volumes such as Millard F. Cox's *The Legionaries* (1899), even indirectly for S. Weir Mitchell's tragic study *Constance Trescott* (1905). Besides these large groups there are dozens of comparatively isolated volumes — Edward Everett Hale's *East and West* (1892), portraying the New England emigration to Marietta, C. F. Pidgin's *Blennerhassett* (1901), which, primarily a defense of Burr, incidentally pictures that western island paradise referred to by almost all the travellers who descended the Ohio; Zane Grey's *The Spirit of the Border* (1906), which, culminating in the destruction of the Moravian missions, shows comprehension of the wrongs done by both red men and white; Frederic Isham's picturesque tale *The Strollers* (1902), portraying the tour of an early theatrical company. Even the middle western communities find interpretation in Katherine Blake's *Heart Haven* (1901), which deals with the Rappite colony, Katherine Brown's *Diana* (1901), centering in the Icarian settlement on the Mississippi, or the first part of C. F. Goss's *The Redemption of David Corson* (1900).

The treatment of these romances is as varied as their themes, running the gauntlet from as careful a reliance upon sources as we find in Dr. John C. Parish's *The Man with the Iron Hand* (1913) to so frank a shading of history as William Dana Orcutt's *Robert Cavalier* (1904). A few are simple, ostensibly autobiographical accounts, aiming to give a faithful concept of life in the early West; in the majority, however, the chief interest is the plot. If they are true to form, they contain a bewitching maiden won by a conquering hero, and various black, black villains—tyrannical British officers, bloodthirsty Indians, Civil War profiteers, or monkish conspirators. A series of border merry-makings, narrow escapes, and closely fought battles usually winds up with cheers of victory and the ringing of wedding bells. Naturally with such a formula there can be no place for the ugly, shiftless squatters depicted by the practical travellers. Famous American leaders, picturesque and kindly scouts, debonair French habitants, and aristocratic heroines; attractive homes and historic army posts — these make up a striking panorama.

In it the land is necessarily a subsidiary factor, yet we do have frequent glimpses of the water-covered flats over which George Rogers Clark made his historic march, of the park-like meadows which gave Law his faith in the West, of the fertile bottoms and foaming torrents of the western rivers, all enriched and made meaningful by their human centres. It is in this latter fact, indeed, that we find the chief significance of the historical novelists. The majority of the early romancers, although they drew largely upon their imagination, had some personal contact either direct or indirect with the events and types of which they wrote. The later school, however, had to reconstruct after minute study of historical records the daily life of the fugitive past. That the Midland is considered so rich in tradition as to be worthy of such investigation is one of the most reliable indications we have of its rapid development.

In numerous other ways, however, its increasing complexity is to be traced. In the detective stories, for instance, that proved a popular type near the end of the century, we find, with the exception of numerous annals of the James brothers, almost none of the chronicles of large robber bands that we noted earlier; instead predominate titles like *Chicago Sensations; or Leaves from the Notebooks of a Chicago Reporter and Detective* (1885), *Ned Backman, the New Orleans Detective* (1887), *Lured to Death; or, the Minneapolis Murder* (1895). And in the twentieth century even those literal transcripts of crime become too crude for the mystery-loving public. Now we demand strange happenings plus a beautiful girl plus a handsome and courteous criminal investigator with solution of the plot and a wedding ceremony going hand in hand, such Chicago tales as Bannister Merwin's *The Girl and the Bill* (1909) fitting the assignment perfectly. The detective story like the historical romance, is, of course, a descendant of the dime novel; the sentimental tale and the religious books, early bidders for favor against the "shockers," show, moreover, exactly the same tendencies.

As in the realistic literature the most striking feature is the dominance of the city, and again as in the realistic literature *the* city is Chicago. Various events in its history of national importance explain in part this focusing of attention, the mere fact that the great Chicago fire served as the climax of E. P. Roe's *Barriers Burned Away* (1872) tending, for instance, to give it a wide vogue quite aside from its sickly sentimentality and its moralizing tendency. The Chicago World's Fair, too, the most successful affair of its kind, roused the interest of the nation, Clara Louise Burnham's *Sweet Clover* (1895) being the most notable example of the way in which the makers of fiction enlarged their sales by availing themselves of the fame of the White City. Such outstanding events alone cannot, however, explain the glamour of Chicago.

The most varied, even the most ordinary factors of its daily life find treatment in books. To take the place of the circuit rider we have a famous Chicago preacher in Dixon's *The One Woman* (1903); the development of our modern agencies of social welfare is reflected in the romance of a Chicago probation officer, "*Just Folks*" (1910) by Clara Laughlin. Instead of tales of high play on the Mississippi River boats there is listed *The Gambler; a Story of Chicago Life* (by Franc B. Wilkie, 1888); *Street Types of Chicago* are given attention by S. Kransz; Frank Hutcheson put forth a collection of *Barkeep Stories; Originally*

*Published in the Chicago Daily News* (1896). A saloon-keeper, too, the white-aproned Mr. Dooley, forms our most famous modern oracle on all social, economic, and political problems.

The pieces by Dunne even more than the columns of Field mark a new stage in middle western humor. Like the early writers Dunne uses dialect and the monologue, Mr. Dooley drawling out the most ironic observations with apparent guilelessness. Yet his position is in no way comparable to that of the isolated postmaster at Confederate Cross Roads or to the awkward Irish servant who from the time of Brackenridge is a familiar figure in midland fiction. As autocrat not only of his bar-room but of his ward, as newspaper reader and shrewd thinker on contemporary problems, he is truly representative of the immigrants of his race, who, early furnishing necessary common labor for digging canals and extending railroads, soon congregated in the cities, becoming our most powerful bosses, our most numerous and resourceful political henchmen.

George Ade in his *Fables in Slang* (1899), *Breaking into Society* (1904), and the other similar volumes advances a step further. If the exaggerations and coarse jests of the early humorists were, as we have suggested, fruit of the lonely life in the outlands, Ade's skits are unquestionably a resultant of the crowded existence of the city. The sharp wit of the street gamin, the retorts (not courteous) that bawled from window to window furnish one of the chief amusements of the tenement quarter, the superficial smartness of the young man about town, the cynical patter of the vaudeville comedian and the newspaper funmakers, all these blend to form an essentially urban product. His style, slangy, condensed, clever in a hard and chiselled fashion, irreverent, and above all sophisticated, is in a rudimentary way, the style of O. Henry, Edna Ferber, Fannie Hurst, Jack Lait, and all the other literary exploiters of our great white ways. Ade's subject matter, too, is aptly designated by his oft-repeated subtitle *A Story of the Streets and Town* — the expanding ambitions of the self made man, the worldly wisdom of the débutante, the ludicrous fate of the commuter, the perils of the bucket-shop patron, the efforts of the social climber. Even the make-up of his work — the illustrations by McCutcheon, the abundant use of capitals — are suggestive of the city, of jazz music and grinding cars, of crowded cafés and cheap theatres, of feverish activity, of a determination to get an effect no matter what aids are necessary.

In their satire on contemporary modes and ideals and their shrewd common-sense observations, Dunne and Ade belong with the realists. It is interesting, however, to bring them in here as a foil to those literary panders who regard our modern pursuit of wealth and social prestige not with irony but with reverence and who have utilized descriptions of great wealth in their books to gain for themselves rich financial rewards. So-called kitchen-maid fiction has always served to brighten the lives of the masses. What more natural, then, than that, as the fortunes of the midland merchant princes, industrial monopolizers, and financial jugglers swelled and swelled, there should develop a new source of material? To the kidnapped children, the betrayed heiresses, and the strawberry-marked noblemen of the Ouida school there succeed the representatives of the new American moneyed aristocracy; the mansions along Lake Shore Drive, palatial summer homes, luxurious clubs, displace the English estates and the fairy-like splendors of the plantations before the war. There is not much place description, of course, only enough to give a sense of showy magnificence, of hothouse luxury, enough, in short, to suggest the marvelous transformation that has been effected since the breaking of the prairie. Neither is there much endeavor to make the characters individual. The typical family group contains a money-getting father absorbed in his business; a portly mother hectically engaged with dressmakers, beauty doctors, masseuses, and hair dressers in an attempt to preserve the fast-fleeting illusion of youth; a lovely willowy creature, graduated from a fashionable boarding school but devoid of interests save her clothes, her amusements, and her masculine conquests; and a conventionally handsome and blasé son who, having distinguished himself on the field of sport and having made the best club in an eastern university, naturally finds himself unable to pass his academic courses or to soil his hands with his father's business. Then to make matters more interesting there is usually a penniless nobleman in pursuit of a dowry and a noble American youth who puts all to shame by his virtue, industry, and charm. A rough course of love with all happy in the end and much description of fashionable entertainments and wardrobes are enough to guarantee a certain financial remuneration for the author. After a brief vogue, however, quickly gone into the limbo of forgotten things, the novels would scarcely be worth mentioning were it not that their essentially romantic material has been taken up by the thinker and the reformer.

Winston Churchill and Robert Herrick, for example, in a *Modern Chronicle* (1910) and *One Woman's Life* (1913) both make middle western social climbers centres of full length studies. Honora Leffingwell, brought up simply in St. Louis by her unworldly aunt and uncle, is heir to her spendthrift father's charm and her equally thoughtless mother's beauty, the combination making her bewitch all males with whom she comes in contact and gain fashionable triumphs even in Newport's most exclusive circles. Two unsatisfactory marriages, however, and virtual banishment from society as a result of her divorce serve merely to throw her back into the arms of the self-made St. Louis lawyer who has always loved her, Churchill's thesis apparently being that only by suffering can she be stripped of her early flatteries and affectations and brought to a true understanding of greatness. His heroine is somewhat of an abstraction; Herrick gives us in his social butterfly a much more real and unpleasant picture Nevertheless he like Churchill, although he satirizes the fashionable set's amusements and aspirations, fails to indicate any underlying significance in these hot-house growths on the prairie.

Henry B. Fuller, however, with the penetration he displayed in *The Cliff Dwellers* analyzes social progress in his *With the Procession* (1895). In it for the first time the fashionable triumphs of the middle western women are placed on a par with the business successes of their men. If the captain of industry is the successor of the frontier explorer and conqueror, surely the modern social dictator is akin to the dauntless pioneer mother. How pitiful Eliza Marshall, "a kind of antiquated villager . . . a house-keeper cumbered and encompassed by minute cares largely of her own making," appears by the side of the active, keen-minded, generous, undaunted Sue Bates — partner in her husband's success, assured mistress of her home, excellent mother, and leader in the city's activities. Surely she deserves the tribute that Fuller pays her when he declares Jane Marshall feels herself "with one of the big, the broad, the great, the triumphant." There is something a trifle pathetic but infinitely more splendid about her rise in the social scale, her adaptation to new conditions. She is not mercenary nor petty but magnificent. We cannot but thrill with her pæan of triumph.

> "'There!' she said; 'you've seen it all.' She stood there in a kind of impassioned splendor, her jeweled fingers shut tightly and her fists thrown out and apart so as to show the veins and the cords of her wrists. 'We did it, we two — just Granger and I. Nothing but our own hands and hearts and hopes, and each other. We have fought the fight — a fair field and no favor — and we have come out ahead. And we shall stay there, too; keep up with the procession is my motto, and head it if you can. I *do* head it and I feel that I'm where I belong. When I can't foot it with the rest, let me drop by the wayside and the crows have me. But they'll never get me, never!'"

In portraying this achievement of the carpenter's daughter to whom princes later became as thick as blackberries, Fuller has done a unique thing; with firm lines he has drawn the feminine parallel of the victorious and irresistible ascent of the self-made rich man, the heiress of the spirit that won the frontier.[16]

The fundamentally practical nature of the Middle West that has made gentlemen of leisure only of certain of the second and third generation forbids that much time be given to the essentially social novel even though its chief protagonists be women, its motifs and methods being most frequently combined with those two absorbing interests — politics and business. Of the latter the literary ramifications are various, one of the most popular formulae being a combination of love and sociology such as is used by Octave Thanet in her *The Man of the Hour* (1901) or George Cram Cook in *The Chasm* (1911), both blending the social life of a Mississippi manufacturing town, the Russian

16 Fuller — *With the Procession.* 5-6, 51, 69-70. *The Log-Cabin Lady* (1922), "an anonymous autobiography," shows the same development.

nobility, beautiful women, successful business men, and labor agitations and agitators into most thrilling concoctions. Merwin and Webster in *Calumet "K"* (1901) and *The Short Line War* (1899) get hold in a much more significant way of the true romance of our modern America — its bitter struggles, its driving energy, its unwillingness to permit any obstacles, either natural or human, to block the course of its gigantic projects. In both novels, however, the love story is a rather forced and feeble element, the plots, especially in the better book *Calumet "K,"* standing by virtue of their spirited presentation of modern conceptions of efficiency. Among the most distinctive of these business books, two that had a great deal of influence in their decade, are G. H. Lorimer's *Letters from a Self-Made Merchant to His Son* (1902) and the sequel *Old Gorgon Graham* (1904). Both epitomize the rugged humor, the shrewd common-sense, and the obstinate will that, according to the modern fairy-tales, make financial magnates of all adherents of the ancient motto "Early to bed, early to rise." Together they form the most complete fictional exposition of our philosophy of "getting-on." As a rule, however, it is only in the realistic novel that the makers of our modern fortunes receive much attention, a decidedly more approved hero being the young master whose father's death forces him into the business that in the course of a few short months effects a marvellous transformation. Although the plot is capable, of course, of infinite elaboration, its most distinguished treatment is again an encroachment on realism — David Graham Phillips' *The Second Generation* (1907).

The fault of overstatement that marks most of the novels of business is equally prominent in those the dominating force of which is politics. Here the plots spring from a definite urge for reform; as in the business novels, however, the results are too speedy and too happy to be entirely convincing. Experience has made us skeptical as to the ultimate success of the poor but honest lawyer's fight against entrenched graft and as to the probability of his marriage to the millionaire's daughter who lurks admiringly in the offing. The romantic formula is a contagious one, however, so contagious that although Booth Tarkington in his collection of short stories *In the Arena* (1912) offers some cynical variations upon it, and although a strong thinker like Brand Whitlock holds out against it in *The 13th District* (1902) it dominates practically all of our novels of politics save those which devote themselves to a fascinated analysis of the character of a "Boss."

Since politics and business differ in various localities only in degree, each of these types of novels belongs to both the city and the small town. Inevitably, however, the prevalence of the small rural communities throughout the Middle West, before the invention of telephones, automobiles, radios, and other modern means of communication rendered each almost a suburb of the nearest city, developed a peculiar type of fiction. According to one view, the secluded, intimate life where everyone knew all about the other inhabitants from the amount of their incomes to the number of their correspondents, where almost every venture was coöperative from buying a new church carpet to organizing a uniformed fire company, resulted in a peculiar idyllic life compounded of all the virtues. Such is the famous *Friendship Village* of Zona Gale. Another, perhaps the approved formula, recognizes the snobbishness, the petty jealousy, and hypocrisy which the stagnant life of the small town engenders, but instead of denouncing rather welcomes them as heightening factors in the melodrama. An almost perfect example of the type is Booth Tarkington's *The Conquest of Canaan* (1905), in which two ugly ducklings, really pariahs among the local aristocracy, leave their place of humiliation and after years of adventure abroad, appear transformed to astonish the natives, reveal the deficiencies of the leading citizen, and finally to marry with the community at their feet. Charles Tenney Jackson, who in *The Midlanders* (1912) introduces new and valuable elements in the portrayal of the political and agricultural progressiveness of the college-trained farmers of the young generation and of the efficient county superintendent, representative of the new woman, shows himself unable to realize them effectively, relying in his rather wandering narrative upon stock situations like Tarkington's, with the plot of the nameless girl's rise to fame and union with the community's matrimonial prize even more than ordinarily highly colored.

Hamlin Garland's rebellion against the farm in the nineties seems to have effectively quenched most of the comic opera representations of pretty milkmaids and singing plowboys against which he protested. However, the return to nature movement that is one of the resultants of the increasing congestion in our cities inevitably finds a certain reflection. O. Henry made his *Gentle Grafter* (1908), that appealing predecessor of Get-Rich-Quick Wallingford, take profitable refuge among the prosperous farmers of the Mississippi Valley, constant boon for gold-brick men and wild-cat stock vendors; and Mrs. Gene Stratton Porter in her saccharine love stories embodied for thousands the lure of the open. She, almost alone among these later romantic writers of the West, paid much attention to background, nature in her tales forming not merely an attractive setting but a dominating factor in the action. The luxuriance of her pictures of wild life is approached, if at all, only by Allen and Cawein; futhermore she had the power, unknown to the others, of so sugar-coating her descriptive pill that her audience not only absorbs it instead of skipping, but cries greedily for more. Her characters, especially *Freckles* and *The Girl of the Limberlost,* may be regarded as the modern prototypes of the philosophical child of nature, who in the person of the lovely Atala or the fair Emmera dominated the earliest novels of the West. Brought up in isolation, companion to the birds and flowers, they emerge from their cocoon-like existence, lovely, unspoiled creatures who win all hearts. The blissful change in their estate has the power of inspiring readers with dreams of their hitherto unsuspected potentialities for fame; and since Mrs. Porter added to her fairy tale elements of good fortune, edifying morality and gushing sentimentality it is no wonder that she was for years on the list of best sellers.

For one other thing this period may be noted, for almost the first notable treatments of the Midland in the theatre. We have numbers of interesting anecdotes of the time when the phrenologist and the actor were about on a par, when the little companies floated down the Ohio and Mississippi or made comfortless journeys overland, performing at barns, log-taverns, on flat-boats, or at rare intervals in a regular playhouse; when the audiences' lack of sophistication gave rise to many humorous or grotesque incidents such as N. M. Ludlow records in *Dramatic Life as I Found It* (1880) and Sol Smith in *Theatrical Management in the West and South for Thirty Years* (1868). The reminiscences of famous actors like Joseph Jefferson throw various side lights on the picture, and not only autobiographies like that of William Dean Howells but novels from Simms' *Border Beagles* to *Huckleberry Finn* reveal the allurement all sorts of "shows" and "show-people" bore for the youth of the valley. Yet in spite of the fact that amateur theatricals flourished fairly early and that various larger towns maintained stock companies, there was apparently singularly slight conception of the value of native materials, Kotzebue's dramas, Shakespeare, some mediocre and melodramatic English plays seeming the favorites. Occasionally are found bits of local color as when real Indians were used with rather disastrous consequences in a performance of Sheridan's *Pizarro.* Imitation of a Louisville negro brought extraordinary success to the pioneer minstrel Thomas D. Rice; another darkie "Old Corn Meal" was copied on the New Orleans stage. Several plays dealing with the Crescent City were given there — a parody of the operetta *Cinderella* using for an opening scene the swamps of Louisiana; *Le Commerce de Nuit,* a creole comedy; *L'Écossais à la Louisiane,* etc. The annals of the German theatre in St. Louis record the production of a local Scherzspiel called *Liebeleien in Cincinnati, Neckereien in St. Louis und Foppereien in Carondelet*; there as in New Orleans J. M. Field was responsible for a number of local pieces. For the most part, however, little can be found to distinguish the early theatre of the West from that of the rest of the country save its crudities and the hardships undergone by the actors.

On the seaboard we find comparatively early the writing of plays revealing the advance to the interior as had prose fiction and poetry. Some of these as *The Paxton Boys* (1764) are technically entirely unsuited to the stage; others by one chance or another remained unproduced. Among the most important in the latter group is *Ponteach; or the Savages of America* (1766) attributed to Major Robert Rogers. The famous chief and the other Indians are here the usual conventionalized figures —

Philip, the black, black villain who betrays his brother's love and his father's and country's cause for private revenge, Ponteach and Chekitan, the noble red men who philosophize with lofty diction on the encroachments of the whites. The painting of the darker side of frontier life has, however, extraordinary vividness. The opening scene between the two traders whose fundamental maxim is "That it's no crime to cheat and gull an Indian" reveals without exaggeration the tricks that were so often the cause of strife — false weights, watered brandy, etc.

> "He like an honest Man, bought all by Weight,
> And made the ign'rant Savages believe
> That his Right Foot exactly weighed a Pound;
> By this for many Years he bought their Furs,
> And died in Quiet like an honest Dealer."

Scene II by the conversation of the hunters reveals another of the sinister stains upon the border, the spirit of revenge and unreasoning hate that led to the indiscriminate slaughter of all Indians.

> "Curs'd Heathen Infidels! mere savage Beasts!
> They don't deserve to breathe in Christian Air,
> And should be hunted down like other Brutes."

No class is spared in the indirect denunciation of the insolence and injustice that so embittered the tribes against the English; scene III contrasts the blustering of the officers and summary dismissal of the Indian claims with the tactful promises of the French; and the following section reveals the theft of a large portion of the gifts for the Indian treaty-making by the significantly named governors Sharp, Gripe, and Catchum. The treachery of the priest, who perverts his spiritual teaching to serve his own pleasures and who reveals Ponteach's plans after the dream of using him as a tool for the French is shattered, completes the indictment, revealing as well some of the religious prejudice of the time; and Chekitan's speech to Monelia gives direct expression to the old cult of the natural man.

> "Would you compare an Indian prince to those
> Whose Trade it is to cheat, deceive, and flatter?

Who rarely speak the Meaning of their Hearts?
Whose Tongues are full of Promises and Vows?
Whose very Language is a downright Lie?
Who swear and call on Gods when they mean nothing?
Who call it complaisant, polite good Breeding,
To say Ten thousand things they don't intend,
And tell their nearest Friends the basest Falsehood?
I know you cannot think me so perverse,
Such baseness dwells not in an Indian's heart,
And I'll convince you that I am no Christian."

Indeed the whole play with its emphasis on the vices of the conquering race makes us wonder not why there was so much strife upon the border but why there was so little.

Another besides Rogers probably had a hand in the play; certainly it seems more in accord with the continental tradition than with the sentiments and actions of the average frontiersman.[17] Its idealization of the Indian chief was to be repeated many times in the century and a half that has intervened with but slight variations in plot and nomenclature but with the same emphasis on the noble qualities of the red man. The fact that Doddridge, the chronicler of the border wars, wrote a dialogue, *Logan,* which hinges upon the chieftain's famous speech, is worthy of notice. R. Emmons' *Tecumseh; or, the Battle of the Thames* (1836) is interesting for its reflection of early attitudes;[18] A. H. Quinn calls *De Soto, the Hero of the Mississippi* (1852) one of the most appealing of the Indian plays; *Catharine Brown, the Converted Cherokee* (1819), really a missionary appeal in dialogue form, is suggestive for its mention of the unhealthfulness of the Southwest and of the ambition of the more farsighted Indians to learn white men's ways before they were entirely blotted out. In spite of its stilted and pedantic speeches and its faulty structure, *Tango-ru-a,* printed by Peterson in 1856 presents valuable material in its depiction of the title character torn between his

17 *Ponteach* was originally published in 1766. The best edition is by Allan Nevins (1914); the most accessible reprint is in M. J. Moses' *Representative Plays by American Dramatists.* I. 1918. Another drama on this theme was published in 1835 by General Alexander Macomb, *Pontiac, or The Siege of Detroit.*

18 A similar English play was published a few years later — George Jones' *Tecumseh and the Prophet of the West* (1844), an elaborate attempt to embody the old theory of a Jewish origin for the Indians.

red birthright and his white training; the old Moravian missionary; and the quarrels between Quakers, governor, and borderers at the time when the dissatisfaction of the natives at the land frauds and the aggressiveness of the French created great excitement throughout all Pennsylvania.

All of these early plays, poor as they are technically, possess a certain interest in their treatment of historic materials. The conventional Indian of the stage, however, naturally gave rise to many absurdities. Without regard for tribal differences or limitations of locality, the dramatists projected the race of god-like beings already familiarized to us by the story tellers and poets, members as Mark Twain wittily remarked of "an extinct tribe which never existed" and chiefly distinguished by an unlimited capacity for splendid posturing, heroic action, and classic declamation. Of course they were parodied, Brougham's *Pocahontas, or the Gentle Savage* (1855) proving a remarkable stage success and *Hiawatha; or Ardent Spirits and Laughing Water* (1856) in the hands of C. M. Walcot degenerating into musical extravaganza. Much as we may ridicule his presentation, however, unquestionably the Indian was the most potent early factor in bringing native color to the stage and in turning the attention of the audience toward the frontier.[19]

Stalking close at his heels we find the scouts that pursued him so closely in real life. Hutton names Paulding's *The Lion of the West* (1831) as the leader in the border school, the part of Colonel Nimrod Wildfire in it being later put into a drama *The Kentuckian* by Bayle Bernard. *Daniel Boone* and *Simon Kenton* are examples of the way in which the valor and self-reliance of these hunters and Indian fighters appealed to their sensation loving descendants. The more successful of the border novels such as *Wacousta* (1833, 1834, 1852) and *Nick of the Woods* (1838) were dramatized, and for many years busy playwrights found a rich mine in frontier materials till they were driven to their last stronghold in the Bowery and other ten cent theatres, finally to be supplanted even there by the movies.

---

19 An excellent discussion of the Indian and Border Drama is found in L. Hutton's — *Curiosities of the American Stage*. 1891. For an account of the slap stick way in which one of the western dramas was put together see *Life & Adventures of "Ned Buntline"* by F. E. Pond. 1919. 86 ff.

It must not be supposed, however, that the romantic phases of a disappearing race and of the settlement of Kentucky alone represented the hinterland. *Evangeline* was dramatized (1860) as was Woodworth's *The Champions of Freedom* under the title of *The Mysterious Chief, or the Heroes of 1812* (1851). *The Battle of New Orleans* was triumphantly celebrated in the theatre; *The Battle of Tippecanoe* gave birth to plays as well as to many campaign songs (1840); McCarty's *The Golden Horseshoe* demonstrated the perennial fascination of the Spotswood expedition; the New York Public Library possesses the manuscript copy of an operetta ententaining for its very absurdities, *The Buccaneers of the Gulf; La Fitte* was celebrated in a series of adaptations (1836 & 1838); William H. Rhodes in *Theodosia, the Pirate's Prisoner* links Burr's daughter, mysteriously lost, with the famous outlaw.

> "... when she comes,
> Announce to her that I, Lafitte, Lafitte,
> The Pirate of the Gulf; and 'Scourge of God,'
> Face to face would speak with her."[20]

Gayarré used the dramatic mode not for entertainment but reform in *The School for Politics* in which he attacked political degradation in Louisiana. *Murrell, the Land Pirate* was played in 1847; it should be noted, too, that the killing of Colonel Sharp, which prompted two of Simms' novels, gave rise to various plays one of which, *The Sybil*, according to the pioneer actor, Krone, almost prompted a second feud.[21] *The Gamblers of the Mississippi* (1850), *The Louisianian*, and *The Pirates of the Mississippi* (1856), are other titles which suggest the popularity of the region of our study, their effect on the early audience being excellently described by Brand Whitlock.

> "I remember that long years ago, when as a boy I used to frequent the gallery of the theatre, I sat rapt afar in the mystery and romance of life on the Mississippi while gazing on the scenes of Bartley Campbell's melodrama, 'The White Slave.' I can call back now, with only a little effort of the imagination

20 Rhodes — *Indian Gallows & Other Poems.* 1846.
21 *Mo. Hist. Coll.* III:426-7.

and the will, that wonderful pageant — the *Natchez,* the *Robert E. Lee,* the great steamboats I knew so well from Mark Twain's book, the plantation hands, the darkies singing on the levee, the moonlight and the jasmine flower — and there was no David Belasco in those days to set the scene either, nor, for the imagination of youth, any need of one!"[22]

Naturally in the years preceding the Civil War as the question of slavery agitated the country more and more the stage, as Whitlock's description suggests, like the magazines and newspapers reflected the prominence of this problem. Treatment of it in a manner that would not arouse the hostility of some part of the audience was difficult. By its tact as well as its really effective dramatic qualities the play *The Octaroon* (1859) by the prolific Irish playwright, actor, and manager, Dion Boucicault, far overshadows all others. Based upon a novel by Mayne Reid, *The Quadroon* (pub. in New York in 1856, dramatized in London, and played at the City of London Theatre), it introduces many new characters and situations, for us being chiefly important in that it is localized in Louisiana. The chief tragedy is the fatal one of the black drop, especially poignant in the Gulf state where the ranks of the *gens de couleur* embraced so many beautiful and cultured women. As a secondary problem, however, we find the bankruptcy precipitated by the dishonesty of one overseer and the extravagance of another. The whole play well suggests the lavishness of expenditure, the easy hospitality, and the pleasant relations between masters and slaves prevailing on the better class of plantations in the days before the war.

After the war we find such titles as *Ku-klux-klan; or, the Carpet-baggers in New Orleans* portraying the troubles of the Reconstruction era. The more sensational melodramas seemed, however, to decline for a time in favor, giving way to local color comedies, such as *Down in Injianny,* or sentimental effusions of the Old Home type where the pastoral virtues and native idiosyncrasies of one section are displayed for the entertainment of the others, pieces which it is difficult to find today and which, as a rule, but slightly reward our quest. One of the best known of the type is Augustus Thomas' *In Mizzoura,* a good acting play

22 Whitlock — *Forty Years of It.* 1914. 271.

which made use of background and character types comparatively new to the theatre.

One drama about this time needs to be considered by itself *The Prophet: A Tragedy* by Bayard Taylor, which was printed in 1874. Apparently a chronicle of the Mormon settlement at, and expulsion from Nauvoo, it unfolds the psychological factors entering into this strange creed with a fullness unknown to the more melodramatic narratives based upon it. The prophet's youth is shown, the fact that he feels himself set apart, and the signs that cause him to be acclaimed as one of the Lord's anointed. Next we find David with his wife and child migrating to the West where the believers have preceded him.

> "The signs of heaven are fair; the earth believes
> In them, and, glad as any living thing,
> Smiles far and wide. The sky is larger here,
> And brighter; other life is in the winds;
> The grass is lost beneath a waste of flowers:
> It is our promised land."

The second woman that attracts the Prophet here enters — the gifted Livia Romney, whose dupe David becomes when through his love for her he adopts her suggestion of polygamy. With the development of the religious settlement, however, the development of the vacant lands around keeps pace.

> "The world is pressing on us: right and left
> New colonies have passed the prairie lands,
> To settle on the river-bluffs, and build
> Some cabin-city they believe shall be
> A centre of the world . . . . . . . . . .
> . . . With all the priest's freemasonry
> To keep the usage secret, here and there
> Are leaky souls; the raftsmen, as they pass
> The landing; firemen, wooding up their boats;
> Or peddling agents, prowling through the land,—
> Catch hints of it, and bear disfigured forth."

The suspicions grow; dissatisfied ones within the colony league with officials outside; violence against one of the malcontents is the brand that sets all aflame; the neighbors band together for the attack that causes the death of the Prophet and the expulsion of his followers, who leave for "another Eshcol in the West." The historic interest attaching to this portrayal of misdirected mysticism on the prairie, however, is really subsidiary to the analysis of the motives and emotions of the three central characters. David is more to be pitied than censured; in Rhoda's cry of triumph at his death, "He is all mine at last," we find a striking revelation of feminine suffering.[23]

Such a play, of course, had little if any effect on stage history, the annoying thing about the American drama before the twentieth century being the fact that the pieces that were printed were rarely acted, while those that ran for months on the stage were often entirely lost save for their records in play bills or an occasional prompt book. Within the last couple of decades, however, the two types seem to have come together more closely than ever before. William Vaughn Moody's *The Great Divide* is perhaps the best example we could have of this union. His middle-western play, *The Faith Healer,* interesting as his interpretation of the psychological effect of the prairie is to us and realistic as are his characters, because of its mystical tendencies did not have wide appeal in the theatre. Augustus Thomas' *The Copperhead* has also attracted extensive attention in both ways. Its linking of the troubled war days of the West when the League of the Golden Circle was a blighting factor[24] with the post-bellum bitterness, and the restraint of the humble hero whom Lincoln himself had called to his dangerous mission make numerous effective dramatic situations, while the verisimilitude of the characters and background permits the slower and more detailed analysis of reading.

Various things account for this phenomenon of our dramatic writing, chief among them, perhaps, being increasing technical dexterity on the part of the playwrights and increasing interest on the part of the reading public. Two special developments are of significance for us — the first the widespread interest in com-

---

23 Taylor — *Dramatic Works.* 1880. 40, 105, 106, 162, 164.

24 Mayo Fesler's *Secret Political Societies in the North during the Civil War. Ind. Mag. of Hist.* XIV:183 provides background for this. An early novel or two used this theme.

munity pageantry which tends to emphasize always the romantic and heroic aspects of the past and the distinctive physiography and life of the region featured. The most elaborate example was the St. Louis pageant and masque with the book of the former by Mr. Thomas Wood Stevens displaying "the more local and historic meanings of human life, as that life has been enacted by successive generations on or near the locality of St. Louis," and the latter by Mr. Percy Mackaye selecting "only such elements of local history as take on national and world significances."[25] The Omaha pageant, also rather elaborate, seems to have become an annual affair, presenting artistically the facts of prairie life; and in various other places in the Great Valley such communal enterprises are illuminating legend by poetry, tableaux, music, and dancing. In combination with individual productions like Lily Long's *Radisson* (1914) they are performing great service in familiarizing the picturesque phases of our history.

The Little Theatre movement, too, must be credited with doing much to stimulate interest in local drama. Of its aspirations the opening prospectus of The Prairie Playhouse (Galesburg, Illinois) may be taken as expression.

> ". . . the Prairie Playhouse hopes to create in and about Galesburg an interest in the work of the theatre strong enough to assemble a group of players and to stimulate the dramatization of the life of this section. There is a rich vein of dramatic material, as yet untouched in the life of the Upper Mississippi Valley. We have had dramas of the Golden West and of the Great Divide; of the New England homestead; of the Southern Plantation; but no one has attempted plays dealing with the life of the great corn and harvest fields, the coal mines, or the quaint settlements along the river banks of the Middle West. The Prairie Playhouse sees in such variety of occupation and environment the possibility of a group of 'Galesburg Plays.' "[26]

The Hull House Theatre, the Little Country Theatre in Fargo, and the Indianapolis and Kansas City organizations, all may be cited as having done good work in the encouragement of local

25 Mackaye — *Saint Louis*, 1914. XI.
26 Mackaye, Constance — *The Little Theatre in the United States*. 1917. 131.

dramatic talent and in the production of work by such men as Dreiser, Goodman, and Hecht which might not easily have found harborage on the professional stage. Two of the strongest one act plays the Little Theatre has produced for us, *The Clod* given by the Washington Square group and *Trifles,* by the Provincetown, portray the tragedies produced by tyrannical husbands and the dulling monotony of farm routine; *The Medicine Show* by Stuart Walker gives an interesting character study in the debate on the banks of the Ohio by the two poor whites and the doctor who learned his profession from the Family Medicine Book; *Mansions* by Hildegarde Flanner deals with the blight of family pride; *Only in America* shows the anomaly of social distinctions on the prairie; Zona Gale's *Neighbors* dramatizes the spirit of her *Friendship Village;* William Ellery Leonard's *Glory of the Morning* poetically represents what must have been an oft-repeated tragedy in the days of temporary unions between red men and white. And these are only a portion of the titles that might be cited to suggest the multiplicity of phases of middle western life interpreted in this movement.

The criticism is frequently made, of course, that the one act play, the form chiefly favored by the Little Theatre, like the short story appeals only to a limited number of people and that it is incapable of portraying any very extended character development or action. Not all the plays the Little Theatre produces are of one act, however, witness the *Inheritors* (1921). The author, Susan Glaspell Cook, who had already done notable work in her novels like *The Glory of the Conquered* and her shorter plays like *Trifles,* here gives one of the most striking single portrayals of the change in life, thought, and character on the prairie. Act I shows without sentimentalizing the noblest manifestations of the pioneer life — the generosity and uncomplaining bravery of the grandmother, the fineness of Fejevary, refugee from Hungary because he fought for freedom in 1848, the sympathy of Silas for the Indians despoiled of their territory, his feeling for the soil, his vision for the hill, that there be a "college in the cornfields—where the Indian maize once grew—" to "wake things in minds — so ploughin's more than ploughing" and so the world will be a better place to live in than he and

Black Hawk knew. The second act reveals tragically the working out of his dream or rather its failure — the snobbishness, silliness, and narrow-mindedness of the callow undergraduates, the checking for the sake of material expansion of whatever of the original idealism still persists. The play ends, however, with a gleam of hope. Madeline Morton, her hard youthful veneer scratched by an emergence of the old feeling, from her warped and half-crazed father conceives, too, a vision — the world a moving field with nothing to itself. It involves leaving that "runt on a high hill," meeting new problems in a new way, but reader and she feel that she is carrying on, that maybe she like Silas can lie under the same sod with her forerunners and not be ashamed; that the things of which he dreamed are not wholly unattainable.[27]

The basic thing that the play emphasizes just as the one thing the whole study of the prairie emphasizes is the continuity of its aspirations, the sweep of its life and character, the part of its struggle in the age-old, often apparently almost futile climb toward richer, nobler life, a fuller realization of ultimate truth and beauty. The drama has been slower, even more imperfect than the other genres in portraying the Mississippi Valley's part in this vista. The signs of the present seem to indicate, however, that it will not only increasingly depict the surface manifestations of background and characters but that it will more sincerely interpret the underlying truths of the Midland's life.

---

27 Glaspell — *Inheritors.* 1921. 30, 153. A number of recent Broadway plays have their settings in the Middle West. Since they make no attempt to treat distinctively the life of that section, they are not considered here although they furnish an interesting illustration of its increasing prominence. Several of Zona Gale's books have been dramatized; *The Square Peg, The Goose Hangs High, Hospitality,* are other examples.

# CHAPTER VIII

## RECENT TENDENCIES

Since the beginning of the twentieth century and particularly in the last decade, the interpretations of Middle America have seemed in many respects more distinctive than ever before. Old veins of material have been consistently worked; new ones are constantly being uncovered. Romance, relying as it does upon the kindly veil of the past, naturally tends to change little in type; and at present it suffers from the present enormous craze for light reading. It is interesting, however, to note the wide scope of its offering. The picaresque tale, in spite of the fact that emulation of *Huckleberry Finn* seems hopeless, is a special favorite, varying from boys' records of adventure like Father Finn's *Cupid of Campion* (1916) to frivolous love stories like Emerson Hough's *The Lady and the Pirate* (1913) or stirring compounds of mystery and melodrama such as Randall Parrish provides in his tale of the pearl fishers, *Don MacGrath* (1919). The popularity of the river is evinced as much, moreover, by the number of authors who treat it as by the variety of its phases. George Washington Cable, of course, uses it often, *Gideon's Band* (1914), a tale of Mississippi steam boat rivalry in the days before the war, being perhaps his most extended, although a very mediocre, portrayal. Miss Murfree, deserting her Tennessee mountains, makes the floods an important element in her *Fair Mississippian* (1908) and *The Story of Dulciehurst* (1914); Vaughan Kester in his interesting although somewhat colorless *Prodigal Judge* (1911) goes back to the early part of the nineteenth century, availing himself of such stock materials as the Murrell gang. In general the same criticism is applicable to all of these books. Presenting picturesque facets of the old river life or interesting developments of the new, they yet fail to grasp the essential charm of the water. Too many threads in the story, too conventional a plot, and a general feebleness of style are debilitating factors in most of the river volumes; and such defects are not outweighed even by the vividness of the portrayal of the life of the shanty-boaters in R. S. Spears' *The River Prophet* (1920) or by the interest inherent in his description of such specialized water craft as the dancing and gambling resorts. Only Charles D. Stewart's *The Fugitive Blacksmith* (1905) with the loneliness of the prairie driving the wanderer ever back within sound of the steamer bells, and his whimsical *Partners of Providence* (1907) satisfactorily represent the picaresque romance. *Partners of Providence* lacks the lyric grace of Mark Twain's volume, which it resembles in its method of narration and certain of its episodes, but it is perhaps even more completely saturated with the spray of the river. The boy's devotion to the "Big Muddy" and the old slip, the detailed description of the "conjiners," the lucid exposition of past methods of transportation, the constant reliance upon steamboat life even for speech figures, all furnish fascinating vistas. *Partners of Providence,* as we might expect, winds up in New Orleans; *The Fugitive Blacksmith,* too, gives glimpses of the Crescent City. In general, however, the mediocrity characterizing most of the river yarns is even more pronounced in the tales of the delta, none of them even bearing comparison with the distinguished work of the nineteenth century.

In the same way the numerous annalists of youth, who, following in the trail blazed by Howells, Riley, and Mark Twain, have made the Middle West seem the ideal location for the real boy, produce a sense of only partial success. Booth Tarkington's *Penrod* (1914) and *Seventeen* (1916) both lean too heavily on the side of farce; Ellis Parker Butler's *Swatty* (1920) lacks sufficient distinction to raise it to the plane of *Tom Sawyer*. Masters in *Mitch Miller* (1920) and Robinson in *Enter Jerry* (1921) have given detailed and serious studies of boyhood in the upper portions of the Mississippi Valley, and Merwin in his *Temperamental Henry* (1917) has made apparent the trials of adolescence. None of these books is a truly outstanding production, however.

To analyze mediocrity in detail is both discouraging and useless. Unquestionably, however, the romantic literature of the

Middle West is suffering from over-emphasis upon the financial rewards attendant upon production of a best seller or of successful serialization in the popular magazines. Survey of the portrayals of the rural community reveals a discouraging number of peaceful villages, beautiful girls, unfortunate youths, charming old ladies, and sweetly sentimental love stories, just as the records of the town suggest on the part of many authors entire obliviousness of the fact that the majority of the inhabitants sometimes do something besides frequent cabarets, smoke and talk in dilettante studios, don elaborate costumes, indulge in hilarious parties at country clubs, or run ticker tape through nervous fingers. The effusions thus described are, of course, nation-wide as are the demands that create them. It is well to recognize, nevertheless, that catering to the "tired business man" or the blasé woman can produce no more distinctive results in the novel or short story than it can in the musical comedy. Writers who indulge in it, even though, like Meredith Nicholson, they pride themselves on remaining loyal to their native regions, create tales amazingly detached and annoyingly thin, for the most part unworthy of their serious efforts.

The fact that each year's output from the presses reveals a heightened consciousness of the possibilities of middle western material is, however, an encouraging factor. John Taintor Foote's *The Look of Eagles* (1916), for instance, attracts because it is so complete a summing up of the Kentucky racing tradition. In the historical novel, though the swelling of the Lincoln legend by such books as Irving Bacheller's *Man for the Ages* (1919) is perhaps the most striking feature of recent years, Hugh Pendexter's *Kings of the Missouri* (1921) dealing with the fur trade or Frederick Russell Burton's *Redcloud of the Lakes* (1909), a portrayal of the Ojibway Indians through three generations, suggests a commendable branching out of attention. The Great Lakes, of course, have filled too small a niche in literature to permit much comparison. Richard Matthews Hallet's *Trial by Fire* (1916), however, a drama wrought out in the inferno of the boiler room, contrasting with real power the world of the toilers with the world for which they toil, and William MacHarg's and Edwin Balmer's *Indian Drum* (1917) make us long for more voyages in these uncharted waters. The latter book in its strength and its weakness, is entirely typical of the present. Centering around the rivalry of important competing lines at a time when the modern era of consolidation and enormous capital was just beginning, it gives immensely interesting material in its account of the lake trade and the men who have shaped it. There is fascination, too, in its description of the north country, in former centuries the site of the missionary endeavors of the Jesuits, still a haven for the Indian and half breed, although fast becoming a resort for the summer cottager. But in the conventionality of the love story and the melodrama of the Indian drum, the book falls to the level of the ordinary thrillers, the fate of far too many of the romances of the Midland.

Besides this increasing consciousness of the richness of middle western material, there is, moreover, an increasing technical dexterity that needs to be taken into consideration. Occasionally it hampers the writer as in *Bodbank* (1916) where the O. Henry formula has so firmly grasped the author, Richard Washburn Child, in its toils that he makes all the story tellers in his old river town use exactly the same mannerisms. His kindred interpreters of the city also suffer in that they seem to prize a rather cheap and showy type of cleverness above all other virtues. Jack Lait, however, in *Beef, Wine, and Iron* (1916) through the mouth of Charlie the Wolf, Omaha Slim, and other philosophers of the pavements, presents exceptionally penetrating and condensed sketches of the city, and Edna Ferber in *Girls* (1921) has produced a really valuable contribution to middle western literature, depicting the advance toward freedom and the changing standards of women in the three generations of Charlotte Thrifts, the muddy pioneer village, the city after the World's Fair, and the sprawling Chicago of to-day forming their flamingly different cultural backgrounds.

In general, of course, this stressing of literary skill is increasingly advantageous. To it Cobb's *Old Judge Priest* (1916) undoubtedly owes his superiority over Mrs. Obenchain's *Aunt Jane* (1907), another kindly oracle of Kentucky; by it *Bertram Cope's Year* (1919), although the book is not up to the standard of its author, Fuller, lifts the western colleges, hitherto limited to such standardized narratives as Cuppy's *Maroon Tales* (1910) or to the deliciously ironic buffoonery of *Petey Simmons at Siwash* (1916), up to a new plane of seriousness. Henry Kitchell Webster uses somewhat sensational materials, but he increases fairly steadily the depth and thoughtfulness of his characterizations through his various volumes — *The Painted Scene* (1916), stories of a small Chicago theatre, *The American Family* (1918), presenting the familiar problem of capital versus labor, *Mary Wollaston* (1920), a society study, and *Joseph Greer and his Daughter* (1922). Mrs. Mary Watts, in spite of the fact that her novels have a certain unanalyzable lack, has a thorough knowledge of Ohio life throughout the nineteenth and twentieth centuries and possesses assured control of the tools of her profession, these two attributes combining to produce a number of rather brilliant but superficial social studies, and in *Nathan Burke* (1910) one of the most distinguished examples of our American historical fiction. Herbert Quick, whose *Brown Mouse* (1915) presented a good deal of constructive propaganda concerning the rural school problem, in *Vandemark's Folly* (1922) has painted a very attractive picture of the settlement of the Iowa prairies. In his description of the boy's stay on the canal boat when "California, the Rockies, the fur-trade, the Ohio Valley, the new cities up the Lakes and the new farms in the woods back of them, and some few tales of the prairies — all these voices of the West kept calling . . . more loudly and plainly every year," he vitalizes a new and hitherto neglected field of activity. His reproductions of the land-agent's "spiels" and of the old man's protest that going to a place "where it's all ready for the plow" is "trying to dodge God's curse on our first parents," his accounts of the town rivalries, the bandits, the queer types of the border, and his tribute to the loveliness and sublimity of the unbroken prairie all reveal thorough and sympathetic knowledge of the land of his childhood and make us look forward to the other books of the trilogy.[1]

---

1 Quick — *Vandemark's Folly*. 50, 97. This chapter was written several years ago; consequently books published since January, 1923, have not been included. *The Hawkeye* (1923) carries on effectively the record of the settlement and stabilizing of Iowa, but the third book, *The Invisible Woman* (1924) is distinctly inferior to its predecessors, being a poorly proportioned and badly digested combination of politics and melodrama.

This stressing of the land, particularly of a hitherto neglected phase of it, is a still more important factor in Margaret Lynn's *The Stepdaughter of the Prairie* (1914). In its portrayals of childhood the book is akin to the Tom Sawyer annals we have already mentioned. The emphasis, however, is different. The vital thing in Miss Lynn's account is the girl's adjustment to the prairie. Early a lover of books and book phrases, a seeker of romance beyond the horizon, she first found mystery and loveliness in the prairie during a long night ride, a runaway journey to the wild meadows beyond the last dreary farmhouse completing her enchantment. Daily loiterings on the way to school in a quarter-section of yet unbroken prairie increased her loving comprehension of each flower and berry on it, each seasonal shading of tints in its luxuriant wild grasses. And when the strictures of a visitor from the East made her first a conscious partisan of the rolling country, when the cultivation of the last stretch of wild land was rumored, with a sense of joyous possession she rode to take farewell, analyzing the prairie moods with a delicacy and understanding that few other writers have exhibited.

From Miss Lynn's account of her simple, wholesome childhood with its democratic training in the little country school, its pleasant family relationships, its old-fashioned reading, it seems a far cry to Katherine Keith's *The Girl*, published only a year or so afterward (1917). In Miss Keith's limpid sketches, rather Gallic in type, we find response to the prairie, but it is a prairie frequently littered by the débris of the city, its red sunsets pencilled by the smoke wreaths of the factories. The naturalness with which the Kansas children regard the process of getting an education contrasts strikingly with Miss Keith's difficult adjustment to the fashionable school, but even more striking is the farm child's reluctant but irrevocable farewell to her imaginary suitor once the accidental overhearing of a love scene had made it seem rather silly, in contrast with the city girl's passionate and deep-rooted drama with Jim. Even making all possible allowances for differences in individuals, the conclusion seems inevitable that the divergences between the types is in part a reflection of their environment, that the somewhat morbidly introspective and neurotic tendencies of Miss Keith are increasingly characteristic of the life of our cities while the extreme normality on the part of Miss Lynn is already as rapidly passing as her natural meadows. Taken together the two semi-autobiographical volumes form a most interesting demonstration of the evolution on the prairie. In its life as in its literature we find an increasing note of sophistication.

In poetry much thc same conditions prevail as in the prose — a more multitudinous prompting to rhythmical expression, a greater conscientiousness in the resultant word-weaving. Since there is inevitably, however, a certain amount of repetition involved, we can mention but a few of the more outstanding productions. One of the most striking publications in recent years is the tastefully decorated volume issued by Boni and Liveright in 1918, containing George Cronyn's anthology of songs and chants from the Indians of North America, *The Path on the Rainbow*. Most of the translations had already appeared in various magazines, books, and learned publications, as had the majority of the interpretations. Nevertheless their grouping here according to the region of their creation, the appreciative introduction by Mary Austin, the number of writers whose interest in the aborigines made the collection possible, and above all the fact that the book was designed for the general public, not the specialized student, all serve to make this a distinguishing mark in the history of our literature.

As Mrs. Austin explains, poetry to the Indian is the Path on the Rainbow by which the soul climbs. Always originating in a strongly emotional state on the part of the Indian, frequently it is genuinely mystic in tone. It may condense in a few brief phrases a whole cycle of Indian imagining; for its effect it depends not only on words but on melody and dance movement. As a result, for the average reader Lew Sarett's little volumes of Wilderness Poems, *Many, Many Moons* (1920) and *The Box of God* (1922) are probably more suggestive than the comparatively literal transcripts in Cronyn. Forest ranger, guide, adopted member of an ancient tribe, he is peculiarly fitted to interpret the imaginative consciousness of the red men. It is not, however, the originally proud inhabitants of the lovely lake region that Sarett portrays, but a broken band of exiles whom a paternal government wishes to push still farther from their ancient strongholds into the barren lands of the north, whose original territories have been so greedily seized that Sarett makes one of his wise men cry with sarcasm at the council:

> "How can Eenzhun be good farmer! Ugh?
> He got-um land all over lake!
> He got-um land all under lake!
> For Eenzhun be good farmer
> Eenzhun should be good for walking under water!
> Should be plow hees land wit' clam-drag!
> For Eenzhun be good farmer
> Eenzhun should be fish!
> Ugh!"[2]

Today the pungence and color of the early nature imagery is tinctured with allusion to the thought and speech of the whites much as the ancient ceremonial costume is supplemented by the bedraggled finery of civilization. Yet as Sarett explains, by his artistic expression the Indian still has power to sing his soul out of his rags back for a moment to the old glory of the wild days. To the luscious tenderness of the *Chippewa Flute Song,* the pictorial quality of *Red Rock, the Moose-Hunter,* the terse suggestion of the tragedies of the winter famine and the summer drought in the *The Blue Duck* and the *Rain Song,* it is difficult to pay appropriate tribute. In the dignity and bitterly accumulated irony of the Council oratory, we have interesting refutation of the sceptic's cry that the aborigine's power of speech is but a figment of the story-tellers, and both collections demolish the theory of his non-responsiveness to nature. *The Squaw Dance* and one or two other pieces seem to suggest too much the influence of Lindsay. In general, however, Sarett's work carries out well his announced purpose, conjuring up a vivid reflection of a romantic past, presenting a tawdry and pathetic but still gorgeous present.

Of interest in connection with these shorter poems are the long narratives *The Song of Hugh Glass* (1915) and *The Song of Three Friends* (1919) in which the red man appears still a

2 "Little Caribou Makes Big Talk" in *Many Many Moons.* p. 61.

menace to the advance of the whites. Both of the poems are localized in the region of the upper Missouri and the Yellowstone; so important are their characters and their plan, however, for the history of Mississippi Valley literature that they must be given attention here. The crawl of Hugh Glass is one of the most incredible of those feats of endurance by which trappers and scouts extended the outposts of the West; about Mike Fink, famed as "the Last of the Boatmen," hover numerous diverting legends. Mr. Neihardt, dubbed by the state legislature "the poet laureate of Nebraska," is one of the first versifiers to recognize the fact of which Frank Norris complained, "that we have neglected our epic."[3] He asserts rightly that "the four decades during which the fur trade flourished west of the Missouri River may be regarded as a typical heroic period" and that the expedition of the Ashley-Henry men embodied true saga stuff.[4] Unfortunately, however, although his material is excellent, his treatment is too ornate, really too lyric in tone, to give the effect of an epic. He lacks the terse vigor, which would harmonize his lines with his themes. Yet for the sincerity of his effort and the fact that he is really a pioneer in the field his work is memorable.

Vachell Lindsay is a confusing sort of person. If Neihardt's cycle be regarded as an approach to an American epic, Lindsay may perhaps be classified as a modern minstrel. A prophet clothed in corduroy, a jongleur in a swallow-tail, he tramped through the country preaching the gospel of beauty, and still on the lecture platform recites his interpretations. Like the bard of old he celebrates the great figures of the past — Johnny Appleseed, long a favorite for romancers, patriarchal Old John Brown, the sad figure of Lincoln brooding at midnight. The vanished Red Man, also, awakens his sympathies; Pocahontas he visions as our spiritual progenitor; in the *Ghosts of the Buffaloes* he is transported one black midnight to the land of dreams where

> "Ghost-kings came headlong, row upon row,
> Ghosts of the Indians, torches aglow."

---

3 Norris — *Responsibilities of the Novelist.* 1903. 62.
4 Neihardt — *Song of Three Friends.* VII.

Then

> "Buffaloes, buffaloes, thousands abreast,
> A scourge, an amazement, they swept to the west."

To describe *An Indian Summer Day on the Prairie* he uses the nature figures of the aborigines. Merely for its intrinsic interest we should mention his graceful tribute to Mark Twain and the immortal charm of Huck Finn in *The Raft* where re-embodying the characters of the King, the Duke, and Christian Jim, as well as the glamour of the water, he sees in the chief character and his creator an underlying significance.

> "This Huckleberry Finn is but the race,
> America, still lovely in disgrace,
> New childhood of the world, that blunders on
> And wonders at the darkness and the dawn,
> . . . . . . . . . . . . . . . . . .
> The bad world's idol;
> Old Mark Twain!
> He takes his turn as watchman with the rest,
> With secret transports to the stars addressed,
> With nightlong broodings upon cosmic law,
> With daylong laughter at this world so raw." [5]

For all Lindsay's tributes to the past, however, he is even more romantic in his outlook for the future. In him we have an echo of the dreamers of the Victorian era. Like them he abominates machinery; like them he finds a healing power in the land; like them he sees the promise for the future in "the eminent village," "the lonely country neighborhood."[6] Reading his *Proclamations* at the close of his *Adventures while Preaching the Gospel of Beauty* (1914) we might well conclude that we had in hand a later version of *News from Nowhere*. According to him a new Renaissance is coming, a new New England, with its roots deep in the soil. Yet that the change is not to be wrought at once, he makes clear in his poem on the *Building of Springfield*. His theories are interesting, especially for their optimism as contrasted with the attacks of the realists. Both groups are alike,

5 Lindsay — *Collected Poems*. 1923. 79, 80, 260.
6 Lindsay — *Adventures*. 177-179.

however, in their yearning for a new, more spiritual civilization. It is a sad irony that the war came so quickly to shatter Lindsay's bright vision.

In spite of the originality of his work, however, and in spite of the variety and conscientious craftsmanship of many of these romantic writers, the conclusion is inescapable that the most significant work of the last few years has been again that of the realists. That the trend of the valley literature is in this direction may be attested rather strikingly by the number of writers who, beginning their careers with markedly sentimental viewpoints, shift in purpose and method to a blunt and depressing naturalism. With a writer like Winston Churchill the change from the freshness and optimism of his early historical fiction to the rather ponderous and labored formulas of such later problem novels as *The Inside of the Cup* (1913) seems to indicate merely a desire to keep up with the procession, a catering to present day interests and standards. But when Zona Gale struggling through the chaos and emotional and physical waste of *Birth* (1918) achieves the stripped and convincing aridity of the life of *Miss Lulu Bett* (1920), there is evident distinct triumph for the new school of fiction. Miss Gale was the most prolific and the most saccharine of the Friendship Village laureates; she most clearly formulated the idealistic creed concerning "the real little home towns, their kindly, brooding companionship, their doors to an efficiency as intimate as that of fairy fingers."[7] Booth Tarkington, too, whose plunges into sentiment greatly weakened the real power of his portrayal of the modern city in *The Turmoil* (1915) and *The Magnificent Ambersons* (1918) and filled one with a sense of the non-realization of his potentialities, in *Alice Adams* (1921) has produced a genuine middle class tragedy. In its directness, its basic reality, its analysis of certain American types, unquestionably it is, for Tarkington, a triumph.

Naturally, however, more significant objects of study than these men and women who, apparently against their natural leanings, have been forced into realism are those writers who have whole-heartedly abandoned themselves to it, for whom it has

---

7 Gale — *Friendship Village.* VII.

summed up their literary creed. And, it is interesting to note, there are certain sturdy figures who, prominent in the literary world to-day, serve to link the violent outcries of the present with the detailed and plain-spoken studies that aroused such a storm of protest near the close of the last century. Foremost of these is Dreiser who bulks among two generations in the same immovable, colossal way as the unwieldy mass of his novels does among the picture papers and light fiction of the day. Although his broad experience has made him more cosmopolitan in scope than most Middle Westerners, although his method is continental, and although he has never shown any desire to ally himself with the local color school, his harking back to the prairie in most of his long books — *Jennie Gerhardt* (1911), *Sister Carrie* (1900), *The Genius* (1915) — as well as in such short tales as are contained in his *Free and Other Stories* (1918) reveals constantly his affinity with his birthplace. His influence, too, on the young Midland writers of the day has been probably more profound than that of any other single American.

Another interesting link is formed by E. W. Howe, a man who after the sombre thwartings of his early experiments, *The Mystery of the Locks* and *A Moonlight Boy*, and the tremendous spiritual tragedy of his *Country Town* for many years abandoned fiction, giving his literary, or at least his published, energies wholly to his papers the *Globe* and the *Monthly*, work which is given permanent form in his travel volumes or in such a collection of penetrating aphorisms as his *Ventures in Common Sense* (1919). In *The Anthology of Another Country Town* (1920), however, apparently in part a response to Masters, in part a return in a different spirit to the community of his youth, he combines very interestingly new and old tendencies, suggesting, also, a rather striking mental transformation. In its sparseness of treatment the book furnishes reminder of the author's long drill at the writing of epigram; in its freedom from grossness it represents the reticence of the nineteenth century. It portrays the narrowness and malignant gossip of village life and particularly the limitation of interests for the women; it even touches on Howe's old theme of the blighting effects of unhappy marriage. And yet somewhat sardonically it reveals a kindliness in the village that in the earlier books was minimized, even the most cutting exposés being somehow without bitterness. It is as if the author, having climbed triumphant through the morbidity and spiritual catastrophes of his early years, had emerged on a new plane of understanding, a man who, still conscious of human frailties and injustice, is without resentment, who, having passed through the bitter slough of despond, is devoting his mature years in detachment to seeing life clearly and seeing it whole.

Such a viewpoint is, however, impossible for most of the realists of the present. They are the young writers of the young West, akin to their predecessors mainly in their spirit of revolt. The industrial transformation, the agrarian hardships that in the eighties were the most prolific sources of protest they take in general as an accepted fact. The bloating of the cities, the curious methods of accretion by which the urban centres writhe over the prairie, sucking into their ever yawning vortices races and products from the ends of the earth, interest them but slightly. Instead, their cultural background is best suggested by one critic's apt phrase — The Revolt from the Village. They are in rebellion at society, its smugness and hypocrisy, its restricting conventions. The snobbishness and commercial ratings of our modern caste system, its spiritual desiccation, its imperviousness to ideas, its standardized reactions, its lip morality, all these they assail mercilessly and shrilly. No longer is their hero the self-made man of affairs. Instead it is the impractical visionary and radical — the Moon Calfs, the Carol Kennicotts of our civilization. No longer does the central character appear in the first chapter poor but ambitious and wind up in the last rich and famous, an inspiration to the young, an object of adoration by the multitude. Instead, except for the rose-colored background Dorothy Sheridan's portrait may be taken as the symbol.

> "Painted with an exquisite and mordant irony — with stick and cigarette, uncertainly halting, as if in front of life, the head tilted with a quirk of inquiry, the face curious and evasive with something that was almost boldness in the eyes, something that was almost courage in the chin — Felix Fay, observant, indecisive, inadequate."[8]

8 Dell — *The Briary Bush.* 258.

One trait all these dreamers have in common. They talk — endlessly. In their studios, their garrets, their foreign eating-houses, their office cubby-holes, — at their work, at their play, in all-night sessions, — about men, about places, about pictures, about books, and, above all, about Life. Never on the verge of a solution of their own, they indefatigably rail at the formulas of others, undauntedly attack again and again the enigma of existence. And in theory at least, though inconsistently in practice, they remain ever true to their watchword of Freedom.

In the movement three men of the Central West may be designated as leaders — Sinclair Lewis, Floyd Dell, and Sherwood Anderson. Mr. Lewis, who in his early stories such as *The Trail of the Hawk* (1915) presents certain interesting phases of life in the northern part of the central valley, occupies his present commanding position by virtue of the enormous vogue of his recent volumes. *Main Street* (1921), perhaps the most widely debated novel of recent years, is the culmination of numerous minor attacks on the narrowness, smugness, and intellectual apathy of the prairie village. Carol Kennicott, throughout her lifetime conscious of certain indefinable yearnings, goes to Gopher Prairie, determined for her husband's sake to like it and for her own to elevate it. Instead of being recognized as an emissary of sweetness and light, however, she finds herself ridiculed by some, by others barely tolerated. Her hired girl, Bea, the radical outcast, Miles Bjornstam, and Guy Pollock, a lawyer infected by the village virus, represent almost the only companionable souls; the others are blind to any need for improvement, or in a few cases want aid for their own material interests. Her efforts at "uplift" come to naught; the hypocrisies, the narrow and timorous conventionality, the prying curiosity concerning the most intimate details of her life, press ever closer upon her until in despair she flees Gopher Prairie. Yet consistently she refuses to give up her fight, to admit her belief in the "favorite American myth that broad plains necessarily make broad minds, and high mountains make high purpose." Growing in comprehension and realizing that the Northwest "for all its fat richness . . . is a pioneer land," that small towns in all countries throughout all times have a tendency to be much the same, she yet insists on the menace of such a standardized, mechanical, and complacently materialistic civilization attempting to dominate the world. Recognizing the magnificent possibilities for the future of the Mississippi Valley's fertile acres, she yet refuses to be bullied by the faith that the future is already here in the present. She accomplishes no definite reform; she goes back to Gopher Prairie fully aware that before the Midland realizes its potentialities "a hundred generations of Carols will aspire and go down"; but she dauntlessly maintains her rebellion against Main Street standards, concluding, "I may not have fought the good fight, but I have kept the faith."[9]

*Main Street's* successor *Babbitt* (1922) applies the same formula of satirical flagellation and exposure to another prairie town, this time "Zenith, the Zip City," noted for its "Zeal, Zest and Zowie," the symbol of rapidly growing municipalities all over the country, but especially prominent in the ambitious West. Babbitt is the typical middle class booster, energetic, fairly cheery, and relentlessly standardized, — in his family life, his social relaxations, his business, his politics, his religion. Yet in his regular scheme of things he becomes aware of a curious lack — a lack that he tries in vain to satisfy by an acutely self-conscious "devilling" with women, exceedingly hilarious and "wet" evenings with the "Bunch," a half shamefaced defence of certain radicals. The pathos of the book lies in the fact that, once conscious of his discontent, Babbitt has no resources with which to combat it. His mind is as destitute of thought as his speech is empty; his half venture into liberalism is due solely to his meeting in a moment of dissatisfaction a former college-mate, now beyond the conservative pale; once he has asserted his independence he is almost hysterically grateful for a chance to return to the conventional fold without loss of self respect. Unlike Carol Kennicott he has not the courage to remain true to himself; like her, however, he finds his hope in the next generation.

Babbitt is, of course, simply a symbol for the whole standardized world of today, representative as he proudly admits, of "the new generation of Americans; fellows with hair on their chests

9 Lewis — *Main Street.* 343, 24, 450, 451.

and smiles in their eyes and adding-machines in their offices." His praise of the business-like and prosperous artist, for instance, is only a minor illustration of the type of thinking that leads Chum Frink to assert that "Culture has become as necessary an adornment and advertisement for a city today as pavements or bank-clearances," and that "The thing to do then as a live bunch of go-getters, is to *capitalize Culture*, to go right out and grab it." In its conservatism, its varying degrees of snobbishness, its imperviousness to ideas, its materialism, Zenith, too, is a symbol; in spite of its complacent despair over the "hickyness" of its small neighbors it is simply a glorified Main Street, and each dusty (or rather oiled) Main Street, as it proudly recognizes, has in it the germ of a Zenith.[10]

Like *Main Street* this latest book is exaggerated. Babbitt's speech is even more incredibly vulgar and slipshod than Dr. Will Kennicott's. No Rotary or Commercial Clubs are so blatant or inane as the gang that Lewis portrays. The parallel of the McKelveys' entertainment by the Babbitts and the dinner offered the latter by the forlorn Overbrooks is so obvious that it must have penetrated even the realtor's thick hide. Yet the very grotesquerie of the volume may heighten its final effect. Babbitt has excellent qualities, many of them, smothered as they are beneath the mechanical formulas of his existence until they tend to become vices rather than virtues. On these sensitive readers may pride themselves while thanking their lucky stars that they have escaped his absurdities. The bass drum pounding on what are undoubtedly evils of the day will awaken many to thought whom a more subtle treatment would leave unaffected. And, after all in the very vigor of the things that Lewis's brilliant satire censures, are there not significant currents which, directed into the right channels, may be productive of much good? Even he, for instance, can praise the office architecture that the generation of Babbitts has brought forth.

In sharp contrast to Sinclair Lewis's preoccupation with the evils of our village and city organization is Floyd Dell's manner of making these a minor issue in his detailed biographical studies *Moon Calf* (1920) and *The Briary Bush* (1921). He brings in,

---

10 Lewis — *Babbitt*. 160, 183, 261, 261.

to be sure, much valuable social background — the patriarchal rule of Old Jimmy Fay that won for him and his six sons their broad acres, the difficulties of adjustment to village life for the young Jimmy after his dare-devil Civil War exploits, Vickly, "the stepmother city of the surrounding city, unlovely and unloved,"[11] to which ambitious boys came though they dreamed of Chicago, again the Tri-Cities. Yet all the persons and all the places that the author includes are important not for themselves but as they affect Felix Fay. The Mississippi is significant only as it enchants the dreaming boy; Port Royal, as, through its cultural leaven of New Englanders and Germans, it forms a fit site for the apprenticeship of an embryo poet; the budding rebel Stephen Frazer with his youthful pride in atheism, the librarian, the socialistic chiropodist Wheels, whose talk was like a bitter tonic, the sympathetic rabbi, the novelist Tom Alden, are individualized only as they aid in the development of Felix. Even Chicago is seen with the wondering eyes of the country lad as we stand by him on the steps of the Public Library looking over the moist brightness of Michigan Boulevard. "There was something odd about this. Chicago seemed beautiful!"[12]

*The Briary Bush,* to be sure, is advertised as a study of marriage, but it concerns itself not fundamentally with marriage in general, but with the emotions, adjustments, and problems of that complex and unstable organism, Felix Fay. And it is in this aspect that we find the chief importance of the volumes — the fact that on the bounteous fields of the Central Valley, a century ago the grazing place of the bison, the hunting heaven of the Indian, there emerges this study of groping artistic evolution, roughly a parallel to the Jean Christophes of the older civilizations. The impulse that is responsible for it is illustrated in another way in the bald statement of Rose Anne, as she classifies the youth as a fellow-freak, that "Chicago is beginning to realize that it needs us. Chicago wants to be a metropolis. And all the stock-yards in the world won't make a metropolis. Enough of us, given a free hand — can. And Chicago knows it. Just now we are at a premium here. We can be as crazy as we like!"[13]

11 Dell — *Moon Calf.* 95.
12 Dell — *The Briary Bush.* 28.
13 Ibid. 34. For an earlier record of artist life in Chicago, see H. B. Fuller's *Under the Skylights.* 1901.

The horde of young reporters who are also poets, Don's and Roger's eager quest of background, Doris Pelman's artistic tea, the studio apartments, a hang-over from the fair — all bear witness to the fact that the West, having mastered the land, having fought its way to the top in industry, is now throwing its hat into the ring as announcement of its entry into the everlasting pursuit of Culture. Felix Fay is only the latest type in the gallery of missionary, trader, scout, and captain of affairs, by means of which literature at every stage has shadowed the development of the Midland.

This social evolution on the prairie Sherwood Anderson portrays in a different and even more significant way, he more than most of the writers of the present being concerned with the effects of the growth of industry. His early novel *Windy McPherson's Son* (1916) follows the old plan of picturing the self-making of a rich man, introducing new notes, however, by Anderson's clear vision of the dishonesty and brutality of most of "the dollar men" and still more by Sam's distaste for the life he had made for himself and his fantastic quest for truth. *Marching Men,* published the following year, is also akin to the realism of the eighties in that it represents the protest of labor. Neglecting, however, the immediate evils of a certain industry, presentation of which formed the main asset of theorists like Upton Sinclair, Mr. Anderson tries to go deeper, to show "how men, coming out of Europe and given millions of square miles of black fertile land, mines and forests, have failed in the challenge given them by fate and have produced out of the stately order of nature only the sordid disorder of man." His hero's early hatred of mankind is changed into sympathy at the death of his mother; the swinging into step of miners behind the funeral bier crystallizes his impressions of the powerful effect of organized militia; and his vision falls into words.

> " 'Some day a man will come who will swing all of the workers of the world into step like that. . . . He will make them conquer, not one another but the terrifying disorder of life.' "

His later years McGregor devoted to the working out of his project. Nevertheless in spite of a weird beauty inherent in the picture of the marching thousands, and the haunting, irregular chant of the song that, brought from the Russian steppes, seemed on the American prairies to express the very soul of labor, the book is uneven, unconvincing, and certainly more immature than the others of Anderson.[14] To it *Poor White* (1920) is much superior.

One of the most distinctive features of *Windy McPherson's Son* is the way Anderson avoids partisanship in his denunciation. The rich speculators, members of Sam's crowd, swoop upon the public and each other like vultures; when, however, Sam tries vainly to save valuable water power for the people, he finds on the part of the small contractors and even the day laborers an equal disregard for the rights of others, a concern only for immediate and personal gain. In a strike he is prevented from winning by the petty jealousies and hampering restrictions of the local union leaders and parlor socialists; he seeks vainly for guidance or inspiration amid the common mass of people. In short his amassing of money with no regard save his own interest is looked upon as no isolated phenomenon; Anderson links up his characters with the spirit of their age as does no other contemporary American writer.

> "He was in business, and young in business, in a day when all America was seized with a blind grappling for gain. The nation was drunk with it, trusts were being formed, mines opened; from the ground spurted oil and gas; railroads creeping westward opened yearly vast empires of new land. To be poor was to be a fool; thought waited, art waited; and men at their firesides gathered their children around them and talked glowingly of men of dollars, holding them up as prophets fit to lead the youth of the young nation."[15]

And the power of this new spirit that sweeps all but the very exceptional man before it is demonstrated even more forcibly in *Poor White*, practically the entire book being devoted to exposition of the changes it produced. Possibly Mr. Anderson idealizes the past too much; at any rate his conceptions are stimulating.

"In all the towns of mid-western America it was a time of

---

14 Anderson — *Marching Men.* 63, 148-9.
15 Anderson — *Windy McPherson's Son.* 139-40.

waiting. The country having been cleared and the Indians driven away into a vast distant place spoken of vaguely as the West, the Civil War having been fought and won, and there being no great national problems that touched closely their lives, the minds of men were turned in upon themselves. "A sense of quiet growth awoke in sleeping minds. It was the time for art and beauty to awake in the land. Instead, the giant, Industry, awoke."

"A vast energy seemed to come out of the breast of earth and infect the people . . . Without music, without poetry, without beauty in their lives or impulses, a whole people, full of the native energy and strength of lives lived in a new land, rushed pell-mell into a new age."

And these changes affect alike all the inhabitants of the village. The carpenter gives up his leisurely, friendly manner of doing business, hurriedly builds many cheap houses, and exacts huge toll on the materials. The journeyman harness-maker lords it over the owner of the shop, a bewildered representative of the early age of handicraft. The farm boys rush from the field to the factory only to find too late that the work there is equally exhausting and more prolonged. Yet practically all are enchanted with the new era; the newspapers laud it; the manufacturers, puffed by their own importance, journey like princes among their slaves. Only the inventor, Hugh McVey, moved by the attack of the crazed harness-maker and by the complaints of the boy whose painful toil in the cabbage fields had inspired his first invention, begins to question the formula that all growth is good, begins to wonder whether the giant whose bonds he had loosed is altogether kindly.

"Unconsciously and quite without intent he had come into a new level of thought and action. He had been an unconscious worker, a doer, and was now becoming something else. The time of the comparatively simple struggle with definite things, with iron and steel, had passed. He fought to accept himself, to understand himself, to relate himself with the life about him. The poor white, son of the defeated dreamer by the river, who had forced himself in advance of his fellows along

> the road of mechanical development, was still in advance of his fellows of the growing Ohio towns. The struggle he was making was the struggle his fellows of another generation would one and all have to make.''

He is feverishly eager to believe that he has lightened the labors of men; seeing the drabness of the towns scattered over the flat lands, he longs for them to be shot with color and light as are the tiny stones he has picked up on the lake shore. Providing color and light, we are led to assume, is to be the task of the Hugh McVeys of the future.[16]

The need of these ingredients is reiterated again and again in Anderson's books of short stories, *Winesburg, Ohio* (1919) and *The Triumph of the Egg* (1921). In these, contradicting his idyllic pictures of the middle western village at the close of the Civil War, he devotes himself to searching out the passions, the hidden tragedies, the bitter futilities of existence. Not the progress of the country, not the problems of the industrial age, but individual misunderstanding, disappointment, sorrow — these are his themes. Against the peaceful background of the meadows, the ordered quiet of the corn rows, he projects these evidences of constant unhappiness, of misspent, unfilled lives. Misunderstandings in families, the nonfulfillment of unvoiced, unanalyzable longings, the brutalities of early farm life, the gossip of the villages, the loneliness of the cities, all these he stresses constantly. His method is sketchy, individual, on the whole objective, producing a drabness of effect, a grim hopelessness of outlook that makes life seem comparable only to the sodden monotony of the winter prairie. It may with justice be asserted that his tales concern themselves almost exclusively with only one side of life. The later collection, however, *The Triumph of the Egg,* shows a profound gain both in subject matter and technique over *Winesburg, Ohio.* Both volumes strike an unfamiliar note in middle western fiction.

Certain similarities in effect to these short stories of Anderson's may be found in Eunice Tietjen's *Jake* (1921). Like most of Anderson's characters, Jake has the capacity for good, but like them he is caught in a trap of circumstances and personality —

---

[16] Anderson — *Poor White.* 46, 132-3, 130, 364.

an unfortunate marriage, a selfish mother, perpetual strife between his two women dependents, and an essential weakness, both physical and moral, that prevented him from holding his own against either. A lover of gaiety, a man filled with tenderness, it was his fate to be surrounded ever by a sense of tightening doom, to suffer till his mind clouded. Against the background of the Midland, the flooding Mississippi, the suburbs of Chicago, the tawny wonder of the dunes, Mrs. Tietjens tries to trace out the agony of his spirit.

Most of the realists of today, however, combine this drama of the perpetual corroding of the soul with some immediate wordly problem. Newton Fuessle, for instance, who in *Gold Shod* (1921) shows the attempt of worldly wives for three generations to mould their husbands' artistic yearnings into the ambitions and achievements of the successful business man, in *The Flail* (1919) gives one of the most valuable studies we have of the assimilation of the immigrant. Many writers like Mulder in his tales of the Dutch in Michigan or Waldo in *Stash of the Marsh Country* (1921) have shown the foreigners a race apart; but Fuessle is one of the first to dramatize the struggles for comprehension, the hurts and alien loneliness of those Germans whose exodus we chronicled in the earlier chapters, and to trace the fate of their inherited traits amid the jarring contacts of the new land. The father, a stern, devout, neurotic man, is early a victim of the commercialism of Chicago's West Side, for as his mother had opposed his being a soldier, so his German-American wife opposes, because of the small salary, his ministry, in which like so many of the pioneers he had found vent for his emotional ardor. The son, Rudolf, the central figure of the book, filled with distaste for the crudities of Bleeker Street life, the stolidity and earthiness of the German peasant congregation, has from his childhood desired to be an American. Yet for long years he remains an alien, uncomprehended, uncomprehending,—throughout his public school course and his work as a brokerage office boy, even throughout most of his career at the University of Chicago. Gradually, however, the spirit of America, or rather of American business, grows upon him. His "abashed, incomprehensible, artistic impulses" which in the Loop "flared in vivid, luminous, hidden jets'' are harnessed to the grind of a great advertising agency. The lust for authority, gain, eminence, first stirred in him by the prosperous business district of Chicago, grows with his success, the Prussian traits of his father aiding him in the struggle. And when finally he attains commercial mastery he attains as well an insight that is yet lacking in America, realization that ''the very traits of ruthlessness and self-esteem that we damn in the Hun are the traits that score the biggest success in American business.'' His survey of his career reviews the career of many an alien in a manner distinctly worthy of notice.[17]

A very different phase of our international relations is touched upon by Mary Borden in *The Romantic Woman* (1920), for, instead of vitalizing the bewilderment of the European peasant thrust into our bustling America, she reveals the impotency of the youth of our nation amid the sophistication of the older civilizations of Europe. The narrator was a child of the first generation of the prairie-rich, as is indicated by her playing on the streets with the ''Hot Push'' when Iroquois (a thinly veiled Chicago) ''big as it was, had still something of the country town.''[18] No matter when she was born, however, she would be still *The Romantic Woman,* and it is to be doubted whether any débutante of today would be any less dazzled than she by the background and accessories of a Binky. Of the futility of such infatuations there could be afforded no better demonstration than the dearly bought comprehension of this world-weary woman. Miss Borden's book is an extraordinarily strong summing up of two contrasting civilizations — as powerful a presentation of the virtues as well as the vices engendered by a thousand years of aristocratic tradition as it is of the cruder types, the consciously showy society in the mushroom city on the lake. To estimate the advance made in insight, seriousness, and technique by the modern realistic novel, we have but to compare this striking version of a much worn theme with the tawdry early treatments of the international marriage.

Yet while the most wealthy of the prairie offspring are win-

17 Fuessle — *The Flail.* 93, 93, 292.
18 Borden — *The Romantic Woman.* 23.

ning the world's superficial acclaim if not their own happiness, it is well to remember that in outlying regions the old, old tragedy of the narrow, hardening life on the farm is still being enacted. In *Dust* (1921) Mr. and Mrs. Haldeman-Julius almost exactly echo the fundamental theme of one of the earliest of the Midland's realists — Joseph Kirkland. Like Zury's, Martin Wade's parents come to the West practically penniless. In each case a child dies for lack of the bare essentials of existence; in each case even the very meagre payments for the land are gathered together only by the most unremitting efforts; in each case the boy becomes practically a slave of the soil. Each sacrifices his emotions to the lust of accumulating property; neither has any conception of how to enjoy his wealth. Zury's redemption is brought about finally by the school teacher, Anne McVey. The woman Martin marries is too weak and affectionate for the task, and Rose, her niece, the one person whom he ever really loved, weighs lighter in the balance than his material possessions. The last touches of irony are given to the sordid struggle by the Haldeman-Juliuses; Martin's death comes about through infection from one of the pure-bred cows which he has prized above his own son; the farm for which his mother, his father, his brother, and his children have died is left in the possession of the woman he never really loved; the mammoth barns, the great silos are torn down to make way for a new city addition; and the book closes with the splendid plant which he had once fondly hoped would be a monument for generations, returned to the thick velvety dust from which he had by superhuman toil extracted it.

The objection may be made that the book is not typical. Certainly women like Rose Conroy in this feministic age are becoming rare, as the authors seem to imply in the defensive lavishness of analysis they give to her character. Certainly, too, the passionate devotion to the soil is most common among the immigrants of peasant stock who for generations have been tenants or among the pioneers who can never forget their early privations. And fortunately the day of the great barns and the little house is practically everywhere passing. Yet there are almost as many farmers who today like Martin Conroy do not really know how to live as there are who, like him, have introduced modern improvements and scientific methods. The book is a significant reminder of what is yet to be accomplished in the prairie regions of America and an interesting linking of early and later realism.

In poetry the same conditions prevail as in the novel — an insistence upon truth-telling, a wrenching free from convention. In spite of the numerous and careful craftsmen like Nelson Antrim Crawford, Lewis Worthington Smith, Arthur Davison Ficke, writing in or of the Midland today, unquestionably its most widely known and significant interpreters are those belated followers of Whitman, Edgar Lee Masters and Carl Sandburg.

The former's first book, *The Spoon River Anthology* (1915) fired, as is well known, the first gun in the so-called Revolt from the Village.[19] So terrific were the detonations it aroused and so heavy the counter attack that it seems scarcely worth while to analyze the volume again in detail. Certainly this passionate utterance from the grave of the warped and saddened souls that once walked the streets of Spoon River forms a most searing indictment of our present social organism, the more so as we recognize the prevalence of the types that are described — that whited sepulchre Deacon Rhodes, the big man of the community, who escapes unscathed from the ruins of the bank he has gutted while he drags down to destruction the poor puppets, his underlings; Cooney Potter, who, by working his family mercilessly from dawn until dark, has increased his father's legacy of forty acres to two thousand; Minerva Jones, the village poetess, who in spite of her heavy body and cock eye hungers so tragically for love and for life. Spirits like these last are the most pitiable — born with a longing for beauty whose frail wings have been unable to bear them. Occasionally there are gleams of light — the happiness of blind Lois Spears; the exquisite love message of *Charles Webster*; the gay-hearted fiddler; Father Malloy, who by his broadmindedness, Griffy the Cooper, Seth Compton, or Harry Goodhue, who by their intellect, transcend the narrow hypocrisies of the village. On the whole, however, the sordidness of the picture of corruption, cruelty, deception, and gloom forms

19 For a study of the book in its historical aspects see *The Spoon River Country* by Josephine C. Chandler. *Jour. of the Ill. State Hist. Soc.* XIV:252 ff.

a most uncompromising snatching away of the veils of romance that long enshrouded the rural regions.

Masters goes farther than a mere denunciation of Spoon River, however, for even in this early volume he makes clear that the vices of the village are but the epitome of conditions that prevail throughout the country, that the weaknesses of a small group of men and women represent the weaknesses of a generation.

"And these grand-children and great grand-children
Of the pioneers!
Truly did my camera record their faces, too,
With so much of the old strength gone,
And the old faith gone,
And the old mastery of life gone,
And the old courage gone. . . ." [20]

In *Songs and Satires* (1916) "The Loop" is a powerful presentation of the wretched inequalities of the modern city that give all thinking people pause; "Cities of the Plain" in *Towards the Gulf* (1918) is one of his most violent denunciations of

"the cabalists, the insidious committees,
The panders who betray the idiot cities
For miles and miles toward the prairie sprawled"; [21]

*Domesday Book* (1920) hopes to gather a store of truth for the development of

"laws, instructions, systems
For saving and for using wasting spirits:
So wasted in the chaos, in the senseless
Turmoil and madness of this reckless life." [22]

*Starved Rock* (1919) is symbolic of the spiritual thirst throughout the whole adjacent territory to-day. The very violence of these denunciations weakens the poet's case and would at times entirely discredit it, were it not that his hope for the future in its fervency almost equals his despair for the present. *The Great Valley* (1916) presents both phases fully, it being the

20 Masters — *Spoon River Anthology*. 200.
21 Masters — *Towards the Gulf*. 14.
22 Masters — *Domesday Book*. 18.

most interesting of the later volumes by virtue of its historical perspective. Picturing the region at the entrance of the white men, it gives some basis by which to judge the changes they have wrought; exalting the career of a Lincoln, it visualizes with doubled irony through the eyes of the man who freed the negro, industrial slavery; recognizing the generations of the past who have contributed to the present, it summarizes the labor of each in the slow evolution of a democracy.

"A hundred years ago
Marquette, La Salle, scarce housed and poorly fed
Gave health and life itself to find the way
Through icy marshes, treacherous swamps and forests
For this Fort Dearborn, where tonight we sit
Warming ourselves against a roaring hearth.
And what's our part? It is not less than theirs.
And what's the part of those to come? Not less
Than ours has been!
. . . to strive
For men to be, for cities, nobler states
Moving foreshadowed in your dreams at night,
And realized some hundred years to come.
When this Fort Dearborn, you and all of you,
. . . shall be dust —
Our triumphs, sorrows, even our names forgotten."[23]

This preoccupation with social and political problems, which forms for us the main value of Masters' work, is also, strikingly enough, his chief source of weakness. His absorption in his teaching makes him unmindful of his art and renders even his free verse at times unpardonably prosaic. *Domesday Book* is especially long-winded and tedious; in a number of other poems dealing with modern problems, however, the rabidity of his invective obscures dignity and fitness of phrasing, and the ironic nuances which made many of the closing couplets of Spoon River cut like the flick of a whip are unfortunately lost in his hysterical later castigations.

Carl Sandburg, who shows the same humanitarian sensing of

---

23 Masters — *The Great Valley*. 11-12.

the tragic and ironic contrasts of our civilization, writes with somewhat finer sensibilities and more poetic skill. Occasionally he strikes a mellow chord reminiscent of the romantic past — a Mississippi steamboat pushing "up the night river with a hoo-hoo-hoo-oo" . . . and the green lanterns calling to "the high soft stars," *Buffalo Dusk*. As a rule, however, his work is of the present, being distinguished like Sherwood Anderson's by equal responsiveness to the secret places of the city and the unspoiled loveliness of the country. Indeed he pits the two in perpetual contrast. In a number of his pieces like *Prayers of Steel* he forges out some of the beauty of our new industrial civilization which Joseph Husband was feeling for in his prose sketches *America at Work* (1915). More often, however, he shows in contrast to the clean-cut lines of the skyscrapers the mutilated shapeless lines of men — by the flaring light of the foundry fires in the title poem of *Smoke and Steel* (1920), in the dusk that enshrouds the *Psalm of Those Who Go Forth before Daylight*. Epigrammatic epitomizer of the city as he is,[24] he never becomes oblivious of the toiling masses that compose it. He can make articulate the grief of a stockyards hunky whose job it is all day long to "keep on shoving hog blood ahead of him with a broom"; he can comprehend the tragedies of the Great White Way's butterfly questings for happiness. In the town of Abraham Lincoln he finds prominently displayed in a store window the *Knucks* that feature the property conflicts of our civilization; with merciless compression he outlines the inequalities that most shamefully stigmatize it.[25] His *I Am the People, the Mob,* demonstrates his faith in the ultimate achievements of the mass. Until the millennium comes, however, he seems to seek refuge from the injustices of the city, the "dish water drab" of the smaller towns in that old place of refuge — the grassy levels of the prairie.

With it he seems always in the most intimate contact. Of it he paints gorgeous pictures — the *Tawny* days of the autumn, the *Rusty Crimson* of sunsets, Mississippi Valley ghosts riding in the light of the "silver papoose moon in the Indian West." Prairie waters make a litany through his pages; young bullfrogs

---

24 See his *Omaha* and *Chicago*.
25 See his *Graceland, Onion Days, A Fence.*

render the summer night tremulous with beaten cadences; blizzards boom in the storm strife of winter. On the prairie before him rise the faces of dead men, then other faces — the unborn, the future.

> "Yesterday and to-morrow cross and mix on the skyline
> The two are lost in a purple haze. One forgets. One waits." [26]

In *Baltic Fog Notes* he blends an Illinois cornfield with a mountain graveyard in Norway, the swells of the Atlantic. And more completely even than Whitman in the first poem of *Cornhuskers* (1918) he shadows the prairie's evolution.

> "Out of prairie-brown grass crossed with a streamer of wigwam smoke — out of a smoke pillar, a blue promise — out of wild ducks woven in greens and purples —
> Here I saw a city rise and say to the peoples round world: Listen, I am strong, I know what I want.
> Out of log houses and stumps — canoes stripped from treesides — flat boats coaxed with an ax from the timber claims — in the years when the red and white men met — the houses and streets rose.
> A thousand red men cried and went away to new places for corn and women: a million white men came and put up skyscrapers, threw out rails and wires, feelers to the salt sea: now the smokestacks bite the skyline with stub teeth.
> In an early year the call of a wild duck woven in greens and purples: now the riveter's chatter, the police patrol, the song-whistle of the steamboat." [27]

These transitions on the prairie that Sandburg shadows are shown in greater detail by a newer poet, Edwin Ford Piper. A Nebraskan like Miss Cather, like her he goes back for his subjects to the early days of settlement; like her he depicts the gradual filling up and cultivation of the grassy meadows. *The Last Antelope* and *Once on a Time* both trace the passing of the game; *Dry Bones* emphasizes the squalid travesty of our destruction of our immense animal wealth.

---

26 Sandburg — *Smoke and Steel*. 229.
27 Sandburg — *Cornhuskers*. 6.

"So ends the buffalo. Five years since he tossed
In great earth-shaking herds his shaggy mane;
Now not one calf. Once furious bulls did roar
The challenge moving terribly to fight.
Dry bones — the price one dollar for a ton."

Before the advancing civilization, however, even the tame herds must give way, a fact that *Barbed Wire* commemorates.

"Hail to barbed wire!
It broke the free range, sent the cowman west, —
Cowboys in dimmer distance, riding, riding
Into rich sunset light whence lingering notes
Drift over dusky distances of trail."

And once they are gone, we find rapidly increasing traces of settlement — *The Movers, The Settler, Breaking Sod, The Sod House, The Well.* The motley array of immigrants from all states and many countries, as a group

"Scarce matched in vigor and resource the first
Old pioneers who set adventurous feet
In lonely wildernesses."

Yet in their humdrum, daily, never-ending toil occur tragedies not less poignant although less spectacular than those that from the beginning made lurid the frontier — a boy's drowning at the swollen ford, another burned while rescuing his horse from a prairie fire, women going insane from loneliness. Bitter memories strengthen the picture of *The Drought,* make us realize the meaning of *Ten Cents a Bushel* and *Three Per Cent a Month,* emotionalize the devastation of *The Grasshoppers.*

"Three years ago that clinging, hopping horde
Made the earth crawl. With slobbery mouths,
All leafage, woody twig, and grain, and grass,
They utterly consumed, leaving the land
Abominable . . .
. . . Afterwards,
A jest to strangers — charity — cattle hungering —
Women and children starving!"

The whole collection is valuable as a poetic treatment of that heretofore neglected and homely but epic theme — the settlement of the prairies.[28]

Sherwood Anderson in his one volume of verse *Mid-American Chants* (1918) turns to the epoch he analyzes in most of his novels where agriculture has yielded, in emphasis at least, to industry. His formless Whitmanesque effusions strike no particularly new notes — a rather futuristic symbolism in his stressing of the creative and nutritive aspects of the prairie; constant allusion to the corn; reiterated praise of the old men of the West; sincere dreams for the future; an insistence upon the grotesquerie, the confusion, the clangor, the brutalities, and the grime of our modern manufacturing cities. In his vision for the poetry of years to come Anderson is more engrossed even than his master. Meanwhile in practically every piece he suggests the choked yearnings for self expression that characterize the present; in Middle America, he feels, men are awakening and hungering for song; for his own book of chants he asks that it be allowed to stand stark against the background of his own place and generation.

As Anderson's preface unmistakably demonstrates, neither the realists' poetic nor prose interpretations are to be regarded as in any sense masterpieces, merely as typical products of a new and highly significant stage in the literary evolution of the prairie. Their themes are the subject of violent debate, their technique suffers from undoubted crudities. They hover indiscriminately over the multitudinous sights and sounds of the outer world, the thoughts and emotions of the inner, much as the lackadaisical heroes do before life. They tend to lack coherence, concentration, grasp; they seem obsessed with sex. Yet curiously enough some of their weaknesses are indications of their strength. Their lack of selection from their frequently wearisome abundance of material serves as an important reminder of our present-day complexity. Their objective depiction of persons and events, their comparative detachment, their lack of definite formulas, all force their readers face to face with the realities of the present. Breathing restlessness, discontent,

28 Piper — *Barbed Wire & Other Poems*. 1917. 3, 13, 77, 32.

they somehow make articulate the smouldering discontent of the mass, or better still stir to questioning the smug complacency of the many. And, without going into a comparison with other sections, we may admit that the Mississippi Valley can profit by the shock *Spoon River* and *Main Street* have given it. Without the conflict precipitated by these books, the reverberations of which are still heard, it might be content to rest important years in lethargic self-satisfaction on its material laurels, content with statistics as to the productivity of its black loam, its buried mineral wealth, its rapid increase in population.

The fact that there are, however, so many voices crying aloud to prevent such a catastrophe, the fact that the emphasis in literature has changed from adulation of the merchant prince to patient chronicling of the doubts and despair of the artist and dreamer, the dissatisfied rich man, the fact that the attractiveness of a city is coming to be regarded as more significant than its size, serve, however, to suggest that the centuries old vision of the promoters of the Midland is coming a step nearer to fruition. No longer are the happiest interpretations of the prairie by such visitors from the East as Bryant or Whitman; instead natives lavish upon it sympathetic appreciation. No longer do promising young journalists make Western pilgrimages for travel volumes upon which to build their fame, or, carrying press and type, go forth into the outlands to build up a paper with the country. Instead to an appreciably increasing extent, the leaders in our publishing centres are men who have come from the West to the East. Not without significance is the *Literary Digest's* poll of critics concerning the "leading American literary stars that have risen above the horizon in the past ten years," in which almost one fourth of the total number receiving votes are prominent in the making of middle western literature, and almost an equally large number, though their literary interests have led them afield, are identified with that section by birth or in a few cases by long residence. Not without significance, too, is H. L. Mencken's placing of the literary centre of America in the hinterland.

> "It is, indeed, amazing how steadily a Chicago influence shows itself when the literary ancestry and training of the present-

day American writers are investigated. The brand of the sugar-cured ham seems to be upon all of them. With two exceptions, there is not a single American novelist of the younger generation — that is, a serious novelist, a novelist deserving a civilized reader's notice — who has not sprung from the Middle Empire that has Chicago for its capital."[29]

Any estimates of this kind are dangerous, of course, the more since we of the West have always been too prone to boast, too ready to feel that youth excuses our deficiencies, and above all that roughness is the sign of virility. The fact that of all of the novelists of the Midland Miss Willa Sibert Cather stands almost solitary, that only in her firm, sure, carefully thought-out volumes, serene with the brooding melancholy of the empty land she portrays, dignified by the restraint of the artist, do we have a really notable fictional interpretation of the conquest of the prairie, serves more than any other to suggest the distances we must yet traverse. And even Miss Cather's books lack that fine and artless unity that knits Knut Hamsun's *Growth of the Soil* or Louis Hémon's *Marie Chapdelaine* apparently indissolubly to the earth they portray.

Her structural weaknesses seem due mainly to a fault we have already mentioned — that of having too much material. For the evolution of the western prairie was not that simple "making of land" that renders the Canadian girl's life largely an extension of the efforts of the first habitants, nor even that steadfast process of growth that causes the development of the Norwegian homestead to be inevitable as the expansion of a prairie-dog colony. Instead of Hamsun's peasants, as close to the soil, as natural in their physical and mental processes as the beasts that surround them, we find gathered on the rusty wastes of the buffalo grass, a sad colony of misfits, who must not only adjust themselves to the wrench from old homes and old friends, but to new language, new customs, new methods of farming, and new machinery, to, in short, an economic and social revolution compressed in one lifetime, which in the European countries

29 "The Literary Capital of the United States" in *On American Books* ed. by Francis Hackett. 1920. 35. Since this chapter was written, Mr. Mencken laments that "Chicago produces next to nothing" although he "guesses" that the best writing of the next fifty years in America will come out of the Middle West with the South pushing it closely. *Lit. Dig.* May 2, 1925, p. 31-2.

would have taken centuries. And confronted as Miss Cather is by this medley of persons and things, by a thousand vivid memories of her own youth, she, in spite of her conscientious labor, shows herself unable sufficiently to eliminate non-essentials. She has understanding and sympathy — almost too much, in fact; a sense of style rare in America; an exceptional power of portraying the moods of the prairie. Yet almost every one of her novels (*The Song of the Lark, My Antonia, One of Ours*) breaks in the middle for having not one, but at least two central themes besides minor digressions.

In the main, however, the other writers suffer not so much from this defect, although it plays its share with each of them, as from failure to realize adequately the need of good craftsmanship. In part the critics themselves are responsible for this state of affairs, since throughout the centuries they have cried loudly not only for border themes but for border technique. Just as in the accounts of the intersectional contests that have taken place in the last few years, the sports writers have racked their brain and vocabularies for epithets sufficient to differentiate the "corn-fed" and brawny West from the vitamine-nourished and brainy East, the critics have insisted the artists rack theirs for a new and fitting mode of treatment. Undoubtedly the European vogue of Whitman was due to the fact that in his fluid lines there was felt to be a new and original beat — a barbaric rendition of barbaric materials. Little polish was expected from the frontier; therefore little polish was insisted upon, and we to-day are confronted by such anomalies of past criticism as high praise of Peacock's *Rhyme of the Border War*, which technically could scarcely be worse.

The tendency throughout the centuries, in short, has been to insist that the chronicler of the new land be primarily a reporter, a herald of strange things in distant places, only secondarily an interpreter, a prophet, an artist. This European inclination we Americans have taken up in an intense consciousness of our own individuality, in our stressing of sectionalism and local color. Forgetful of the lessons given by the great literatures of the past, negligent of the fact that the most permanent expression in any art is that which most completely embodies our common humanity, we have laid our emphasis upon transient idols, we have sought constantly to differentiate, to isolate. Dazzled by the changes we created in this great continent of ours, stupefied by the swiftness with which we filled up its empty places, awed by the wealth we so rapidly amassed, the skyscrapers we reared, the iron monsters with which we supplemented slower hand labor, like Aladdin unable to comprehend the power we called forth, it is only recently we have begun to ponder and question.

And perhaps now that some few of us at least have taken breath and begun to wonder, perhaps now that the war has jarred us out of some of our complacency, that the wonders of the industrial age are losing some of their enchantment, we may be on the road to a new era of progress. Philosophers tell us that an age of doubt, disillusionment, and turmoil heralds nearly always a new plane of aspiration and achievement, a plane in which the old dream of a perfect state will be approached from a new angle. Chronological study of the Midland unquestionably drives home to us the continuity of mortal hopes and ambitions. Equally unquestionably it demonstrates the futility of hopes for their sudden realization. Each age brings forth new remedies, each remedy involves new evils; the race advances only by a continual reaching out toward inaccessible patterns. Our lack of perspective, a defect to which America is particularly prone, makes us exaggerate the blemishes from which we suffer, and, forgetful of the great blots on the pages of the past, see only its bright gildings which enhance our depravity. As a matter of fact our situation is not at all hopeless; it would be as interesting to write a paper on our realized as on our unrealized Utopias. Certainly to overthrow by any violent revolution the structure we have been so many years in building would be deplorable, for the Midland colonies have shown the impossibility of realizing fully any idealistic scheme as long as human nature remains imperfect. It would be equally deplorable, however, to settle back in the stupor of content toward which for a few years we seemed to incline and to feel that, if there were restless elements to disturb us, our sacred constitution and our legislative and judicial systems, for which we felt no particular personal responsibility, would soon put a stop to the annoyances. Such an attitude of complacency, as we have already suggested, is best safeguarded against by the constant clamor of our realists.

To forecast the future of a literature is as rash as to forecast the destinies of a nation. Of one thing we may be sure, provided the experience of the past avails anything, that the prairie literature of the years to come will reflect the life of the prairie people. The extent to which changes in our thought and experience have been paralleled by our written records is really extraordinary. Already the pastoral life that Miss Cather chronicles is that of an almost bygone epoch. With the passing of the era of free land, the overcoming of the natural obstacles, is tolled the knell of the pioneer; the self-made rich man or the captain of industry has been obliged to give way as the shoddiness of certain of his methods and ideals has been revealed and as the public have found that the amassing of gigantic fortunes by the few does not appreciably better the individual condition of the many. At present the tendency seems to be to reflect our state of doubt and dissatisfaction, of which Ben Hecht's *Erik Dorn* (1921) furnishes an outstanding example.

Brilliant as have been few figures in the Midland gallery, cynical, sure of himself, the editor stands aloof from life, seeing it through the windows of his newspaper with a clarity that flattered him.

> "A tawdry pantomime was life, a pouring of blood, a grappling with shadows, a digging of graves. 'Empty, empty,' his intelligence whispered in its depths, 'a make-believe of lusts. What else? Nothing, nothing. Laws, ambitions, conventions — froth in an empty glass. Tragedies — comedies — all a swarm of nothings. Dreams in the hearts of men — thin fever outlines to which they clung in hope. Nothing . . . nothing . . .'"

A man of phrases, he screens himself by this inexhaustible fountain of ironic comment from the fundamental emotions of life. His epigrams furnish entertainment, awaken the interest of Rachel, for a time conceal his desire. But once his love grows too strong, the exhausted vocabulary collapses; "he who had stood with his head thrust through the sky'' is on a level with the most ordinary of mortals.

> ''In the back of his brain the city tumbled — an elephantine grimace, a wilderness of angles, a swarm of gestures that beat at his thoughts. But before his eyes there were no longer the precise patterns of another day. He was no longer outside. He had been sucked into something, the something that he had been used to refer to condescendingly as life.''

His course is the usual one of the day. He leaves his wife and follows Rachel, only to have his original ecstasy wear itself out, the way of epigram and peace returning once more. Wanderings through the war-stricken countries of Europe, a few more amorous adventures, companionship with that kindred soul Von Stinnes, ''a Don Quixote of disillusion,'' phrases, more phrases, and he returns to a changed Anna, a dead Erik, and the making of his own epitaph as he lays a cigarette stub on the table.

> '' 'Yes, that's me. Life has had its lips to me blowing smoke and fire out of me. And now a table top on which to glow reminiscently for a moment. And cool into ashes. Apologies to Laura Jean, Marie Corelli — and God.' ''

Certainly Dorn provides no model for life any more than the ''poor boob'' Babbitt. The coruscating and cynical qualities of his wit, however, the broken, staccato style of the major portion of the book, even though Hecht sometimes drops into such lusciousness of lyric description as the account of Erik's and Rachel's walk in the park are simply the culmination of that type of writing and thought to which we have already referred as being outgrowths of the city. The fact that so gifted a man shows himself as helpless as the most ignorant or stupid among us in the face of the fundamental problems of existence serves more than anything else to enhance our sense of bewilderment and futility; the whole book serves as an admirable index of present tendencies.

Tesla summarizes Dorn best when he says, '' 'he can write in a big way. But he isn't a big man.' ''[30] What we are feeling

30 Hecht — *Erik Dorn*. 18, 147, 403, 291.

for to-day are the truly big men, men who know not only how to kill Indians or make money, but how to live. At present we are too uncertain to hazard anything more than tentative heroes, figures who, we think, may be able to solve the problems that oppress us — the artist, the writer, the dissatisfied rich man, the organizer of labor. Every indication suggests, however, that what we crave are leaders — men who, as has been suggested, will teach us not how to support life, but how to make life supportable. Not only the types that our authors project, but almost every manifestation of our thought and activity today — our political dissatisfaction, our criticisms of pettiness in our churches, our experimenting in our educational systems, our popular cultural movements, serve to emphasize our wide-spread seeking for betterment, our pathetic faith in legislation, also our insistent neglect of the one remedy which is possible for all of us—the consistent and conscientious practice of the Golden Rule.

The type of background which will be used most in the Midland literature of the future, it is also impossible to prognosticate, Country, city, and small town, alike have been harshly criticized and glowingly praised, alike have been the centre of attention for varying periods. The development of modern commerce and invention, the reaching out of the city into the country, and the closer contact of the country with the town may well serve to minimize if not to abolish past distinctions. The increased intercourse between different portions of the nation, the increased communion between different nations of the world will undoubtedly, moreover, make for steadily developing cosmopolitanism. Again for this Erik Dorn, who goes from Chicago to New York, from there to Europe, and then back to Chicago, may be taken as a symbol, or the hero of *One of Ours,* who finds in France a happiness his own land has denied him.

Certainly the era of intense sectionalism in literature as in politics seems past. In part this attitude was forced upon the West by the seaboard's consistent refusal to see anything but barbarism beyond the Alleghanies. The Civil War put an end to any idea of separation of the western states from the eastern. In spite of the great men, the great inventions, the great wealth of the Midland, the Atlantic coastal states still refused, however, to relinquish their innate sense of superiority. Seeing is believing, however; and now that transcontinental travel has enormously increased, now that leadership in many lines is being furnished by the West, that section may be permitted to become less aggressively assertive of its claims for recognition. It is too early as yet, of course, to evaluate the culture which is being actively promoted by the Babbitts, but in spite of our sneers at their "bally-hoo" methods they may be able to give it a vitality which in the hands of certain of its more rigid and emotionless exponents it has lacked.

One thing is certain, Middle America is no longer a frontier. Its attractive cultivated landscape and its physical resources will always give it a certain individuality. Just as the felling of forests, the breaking of the prairie, have made the Central West of today resemble fairly closely the fields of the level sections at the East, however, so the life is becoming steadily more sophisticated. Common prosperity, common language, common customs, common thought, all these have united indissolubly various regions. Throughout the advance of the frontier a gigantic process of fusion has taken place which will undoubtedly continue even more rapidly — and let us hope more intelligently — now that the dangers of non-assimilation have been revealed by the war and now that the value of alien contributions to our civilization is beginning to be appreciated. The Valley's thought and the Valley's literature will always be tinged by certain elements due to the country, but it will probably be increasingly conscious of the universality of human problems and emotions, increasingly conscientious about the manner of presentation. We are rightfully the heirs, not only of America's but of Europe's past; for us to cast aside its experience, to evolve a completely new type of literature or of life would be a thing as impracticable in attempt as impossible in achievement.

Meantime the value of the former stress upon sectionalism cannot be over-emphasized in a survey such as this. It is to be regretted that lack of space prevents as complete a paralleling as would be possible of the tendencies of the past and the present — the balancing of Jane Addams' *Twenty Years at Hull*

*House* (1910), for instance, with the records of the pioneer missionaries; the comparison of Meredith Nicholson's *Valley of Democracy* (1918) or Arthur E. Bostwick's *The Different West* (1913) with one of the early celebrants like Hall; the enthusiasm of George's *Hail Columbia* (1921) with the sneers of a Faux; analysis of the pathetic yet cheering difference between the disillusionment, tolerance, and hard-won knowledge that our progress for the present must depend upon makeshifts of that fine fighter for democracy, Brand Whitlock, in *Forty Years of It* (1914) and the quickly collapsing bubbles of the early idealists.

And yet the shift in emphasis from biography, travel, statistics to prose fiction, drama, and poetry, serves as effectively as anything to demonstrate the advance of the Midland — the transformation in the Mississippi Valley from the wide flowering meadows over which the Indian hunted through the cultivated luxuriance of the French common fields, the magnificence of the Spanish land grants, the fenced in pastures of the acquisitive Americans and the foreign land seekers to the present striking panorama of high priced and well tilled farms running to the very edge of smoke-blurred cities or busy mine; the change in population from the aboriginal red man to the present world mixture; the development of habits of work and thought through a national, almost a racial evolution. The hunting life, the pastoral, the agricultural, the industrial, all these are epitomized in the development we have traced with dozens of human types illustrating its complexity, with a consequent constant refining and elaboration of description. In a survey of the literature we find truly a revelation not only of the Prairie but of the Making of Middle America.

# APPENDIX

## APPENDIX A

Highly indicative of the scorn with which the ambitious schemes for the Mississippi were regarded is a long poem of 1717 *La Compagnie d'Occident.* The following extracts from it are taken from Raunié's *Chansonnier Historique* II:244ff.

Célébrons l'établissement
De la compagnie d'Occident,
  Lon lan la deriretté,
Autrement dit Missisipi,
  Lon lan la deriri.

Pour lui donner plus de crédit,
On met à la tête un proscrit,
Qu'on voulait pendre en son pays.

. . . . . . . . . . . . . .

Le pays n'est pas habité,
Il sera bientôt fréquenté;
Peut-être dans cent ans d'ici.

Des filles on y enverra,
Et d'abord on les mariera,
Si l'on y trouve des maris.

Les mines l'on y fouillera,
Car sans doute on en trouvera,
Si la nature y en a mis.

Nos billets vont être payés,
Car les fonds en sont assurés,
Sur l'or qu'elles auront produit.

Crozat, qui n'aime plus l'argent,
Crainte d'être opulent,
A laissé là Mississippi.

Pour policer ce grand pays,
On va bien faire des édits,
On en défera bien aussi.

. . . . . . . . . . . . . .

Pour premier établissement,
Envoyons-y le Parlement,
Qui ne sert de rien à Paris.

Un collège on y fondera,
Le Latin on enseignera,
Aux enfants de Missisipi.

Notre habile duc d'Orléans
Ira lui-même être régent,
En sixième à Missisipi.

Une académie y aura,
De beaux jetons on donnera
Faits d'argent de Missisipi.

La Force veut y présider
Et prendre le soin d'épurer
La langue du Missisipi.

. . . . . . . . . . . . . .

De Pascal on ne parlera,
Ni ses Lettres on ne lira;
Elles causeraient trop d'ennui.

Le beau cardinal de Rohan,
Chargé de soins plus importants,
Peuplera le Missisipi.

Nul janseniste on n'y verra,
Mais les enfants de Loyola
Iront réformer le pays.

. . . . . . . . . . . . . .

Monsieur le Duc, fort peu content,
De chasser dans ce continent,
Veut chasser à Mississippi.

. . . . . . . . . . . . . .

On envoie à Missisipi
Toutes les p. . . de Paris,
  Lon lan la derirette.
Adieu, duchesse de Berry!
  Lon lan la deriri.

. . . . . . . . . . . . . .

Les beaux-arts on cultivera
Et des prix on proposera
  Landerirette,
Aux savants du Missisipi,
  Landeriri.

Des loteries on ouvrira,
Et les billets on brûlera,
Pour en maintenir le crédit.

Des conseils on établira,
Et le commerce y fleurira,
Tout ainsi qu'en France il fleurit.

Les maltôtiers y pilleront,
Et les juges les taxeront
Pour avoir leur part du profit.

Enfin tout y prospérera,
Et la France on desertera
  Landerirette,
Pour peupler le Missisipi,
  Landeriri.

Louis Antoine Pardaillan,
Jadis marquis, duc à présent,
  Landerirette,
Présidera dans ce pays,
  Landeriri.

Comme il est intègre et prudent,
Il gouvernera le dedans
Des États du Missisipi.

Il ordonnera des Palais
Si beaux, que l'on n'en vit jamais
Semblables en aucun pays.

L'on y verra des monuments,
Des édifices surprenants,
Et des arcs de triomphe aussi.

Un nouveau Louvre il plantera,
Et sans doute il l'achèvera
Dans deux ou trois siècles d'ici.

## APPENDIX B

Significant in connection with *Manon Lescaut* are the songs about the sad fate of the rôtisseur Quoniam, who was deported to the Mississippi because of the admiration of a great man for his wife. A few typical stanzas are the following.

O vous tous, messieurs les maris,
Si vos femmes ont des favoris,
Ne vous mettez martel en tête:
Vous auriez fort méchante fête.
Si vous vous en fâchez, tant pis
Vous irez à Mississippi. Raunié III: 20-1

* * * * * * *

Maris, prenez bien garde à vous;
Bannisez cet esprit jaloux;
Ne songez plus qu'à vos boutiques,
Si vous n'aimez pas l'Amérique.

Quoniam, se grand fricasseur,
Va faire le gain des farceurs.
Pour avoir été trop rigide,
Il est parti pour la Floride. *Ibid.* 23.

* * * * * * *

La charmante rôtisseuse,
Pour son ami,
Envoie, pour se rendre heureuse,
Son homme à Mississipi.

. . . . . . . . . .

Il faut être plus commode,
Mes chers amis,
Il vaut mieux être à la mode
Que de voir Mississippi. *Ibid.* 23-4.

## APPENDIX C

Typical of the interest aroused in France by the war in America is the song of 1755 entitled *La Défaite de Braddock* (Raunié — *Chansonnier Historique*, VII:249-250).

Braddock avait toujours dit
Qu'il viendrait, chose bien sûre,
Pour attaquer Pécaudit,
Turelure,
Et renverser la clôture,
Robin turelure lure.

Dumas avec Ligneris
Ont voulu voir sa figure,
Et l'ont mis même au défi
De soutenir la gageure.

Aussitôt deux mille Anglais
Se sont mis tous en posture;
Mais nos Hurons et Français
Ont fait voler leur coiffure.

Quinze cents sur les chemins
Ont trouvé la sépulture,
Les Outtawaïs algonkins
Leur ont donné la tonsure.

Ils ont laissé après eux
Fusils, poudre sans mesure,
Ainsi nous les attendons,
Avec leur propre armure.

Ils nous ont abandonné
Leurs chariots et leurs montures.
S'ils reviennent en ces lieux,
Nous leur paierons leurs voitures.

Nous annonçons à Vaudreuil
Cette triste déconfiture;
Il leur en marque son deuil,
Turelure,
A la point de la chevelure,
Robin turelure lure.

# BIBLIOGRAPHICAL NOTES

"Do you know *Bartram's Travels*? This is of the Seventies (1770 or so); treats of *Florida chiefly*, has a wonderful kind of floundering eloquence in it; and has grown immeasurably old. All American libraries ought to provide themselves with that kind of book; and keep them as a future *biblical* article." *Carlyle-Emerson Correspondence.* II:228.

Since *The Prairie and the Making of Middle America* is in itself a sort of descriptive bibliography, no attempt has been made to include here the books named in the text. The edition used is there indicated in brackets, and the bibliography like the footnotes is devoted largely to additional material throwing light on the subject matter.

BIBLIOGRAPHIES — Chapters I-IV. There is no really adequate bibliography for this section, the best being the lists given in Justin Winsor's *Narrative and Critical History of America* (8v. 1884-9). State bibliographies such as S. J. Buck's *Travel and Description, 1765-1865* (Ill. St. Hist. Lib. — *Coll.* IX. 1914) and P. G. Thompson's *Bibliography of the State of Ohio* (1880) are also helpful. Other bibliographies of varying value are the following: A. L. Boimare — *Notes Bibliographiques et Raisonnées sur les Principaux Ouvrages Publiés sur la Floride et l'ancienne Louisiane depuis leur Découverte jusqu'à l'Epoque Actuelle* (1855, repr. *La. Hist. Quar.* I:10ff.); T. L. Bradford — *Bibliographer's Manual of American History* (5v. 1907-1910); E. Channing, A. B. Hart, & F. J. Turner — *Guide to the Study and Reading of American History* (Rev. ed. 1912); N. E. Dionne — *Québec et la Nouvelle France, Bibliographie. Inventaire Chronologique des Ouvrages publiés à l'étranger en diverses langues sur Québec et la Nouvelle France* . . . (1906); D. C. Durrie — *Bibliography of Wisconsin* (*Hist. Mag.* 1876. VI.); P. L. Ford — *Check List of Bibliographies, Catalogues, Reference Lists, & Lists of Authorities on American Books and Subjects* (1889); A. P. C. Griffin — *Discovery of the Mississippi; a Bibliographical Account* (repr. from the *Mag. of Amer. Hist.* Mar. & April 1883) and *Bibliography of American Historical Societies* (2d ed. rev. and enlarged. Pr. as Amer. Hist. Assoc. *Annual Report.* 1905. II); Philéas Gagnon — *Essai de bibliographie Canadienne.* . . . (1895); Henry Harrisse — *Notes pour servir a l'histoire, à la bibliographie, et à la cartographie de la Nouvelle France et des pays adjacents, 1545-1700* (1872); Adelaide Hasse — *Reports of Explorations Printed in the Documents of the United States Government* (1899); Kan. St. Hist. Soc. — *List of Books Indispensable to a Knowledge of Kansas History and Literature* (1916); J. N. Larned — *Literature of American History, a Bibliographical Guide* (1902); H. E. Ludewig — *The Literature of American Local History; a Bibliographical Essay* (1846); T. M. Owen — *A Bibliography of Mississippi* (Amer. Hist. Assoc. — *Annual Report.* 1899. I:633-828); Obadiah Rich — *Bibliotheca Americana Nova; or, a Catalogue of Books in Various Languages, relating to America, Printed since the Year 1700* (2v. 1835, 1846); F. B. Streeter — *Michigan Bibliography.* . . . (2v. 1921); H. T. Tuckerman — *America and her Commentators.* . . . (1864); F. J. Turner & F. Merk — *List of References on the History of the West* (Rev. ed. 1922); J. F. Williams — *Bibliography of Minnesota* (1880. Also in Minn. Hist. Soc. — *Coll.* III: 13ff.); *Writings on American History* (an annual compilation, the 1902 volume being by E. C. & A. E. Richardson, the 1903 by A. C. McLaughlin, W. A. Slade, & E. D. Lewis, & most of the later ones by Grace G. Griffin).

In addition to these somewhat miscellaneous bibliographies attention may be called to those on special topics such as *Narratives of Captivity among the Indians of North America. A List of Books & Manuscripts on this Subject in the Edward E. Ayer Collection of the Newberry Library* (1912) or T. W. Field's *Essay towards an Indian Bibliography* (1873). Catalogues of libraries rich in Americana such as *Bibliotheca Americana. Catalogue of the John Carter Brown Library in Brown University, Providence, Rhode Island* (1919. Earlier ed. 1865-71 & 1875-82) and sales catalogues of Americana are also helpful. Attention may be called to the bibliographies of Travel and History in the *Cambridge History of American Literature* (I:363-380, 380-385, 468-490, II: 488-499, IV: 681-728, 728-742). The standard histories such as McMaster's or Channing's, special reference books, and recent reprints of rare old volumes, many of which are cited elsewhere, will be found rich in bibliographical aids. Joseph Sabin's *Dictionary of Books relating to America, from its Discovery to the*

*Present Time* (1868-1892) unfortunately goes only to the Smiths. To it the travel bibliography now being compiled under the auspices of the American Historical Association should prove an invaluable supplement.

GENERAL REFERENCE BOOKS — CHAPTERS I-IV. *The American Nation. A History*, ed. by A. B. Hart (27v. 1905-8); Henry Adams — *History of the United States of America 1801-1817* (9v. 1889-1891); George Bancroft — *History of the United States, from the Discovery of the American Continent* (10v. 1834-75); A. P. Brigham — *Geographic Influences in American History* (1903); H. E. Bolton & T. M. Marshall — *The Colonization of North America 1492-1783* (1920); Edward Channing — *History of the United States* (1905-); E. Channing & M. F. Lansing — *Story of the Great Lakes* (1909); *Chronicles of America*, ed. by Allen Johnson (50v. 1918-21); Thos. Donaldson — *The Public Domain, its History*. . . (1884); John Fiske — *Colonization of the New World* (1902), *Discovery of America* (2v. 1892), *Mississippi Valley in the Civil War* (1900), *New France & New England* (1902); *Handbook of North American Indians* (Bur. of Amer. Ethnology — *Bull.* no. 30); B. H. Hibbard — *History of the Public Land Policies* (1924); B. A. Hinsdale — *The Old Northwest; the Beginning of Our Colonial System* (1899); J. K. Hosmer — *A Short History of the Mississippi Valley* (1901); A. B. Hulbert — *Historic Highways of America* (16v. 1902-5); C. J. Kappler, ed. — *Indian Affairs; Laws and Treaties* (2v. 1904); R. M. McElroy — *Kentucky in the Nation's History* (1909); J. B. McMaster — *A History of the People of the United States from the Revolution to the Civil War* (8v. 1883-1913); Charles Moore — *The Northwest under Three Flags, 1635-1796* (1900); J. W. Monette — *History of the Discovery and Settlement of the Mississippi by the Three Great European Powers, Spain, France, and Great Britain* (1846); W. A. Mowry — *Territorial Growth of the United States* (1902); F. A. Ogg — *Opening of the Mississippi; a Struggle for Supremacy in the American Interior* (1904); A. E. Parkins — *The Historical Geography of Detroit* (1918); Francis Parkman — *History of the Conspiracy of Pontiac and the War of the North American Tribes against the English Colonies after the Conquest of Canada* (1851. 8th ed. enlarged 1875), *France & England in North America* (9v. 1865-1892). *The Pioneers of France in the New World, The Jesuits in North America, The Discovery of the Great West*, pub. 1879, 11th ed. as *La Salle and the Discovery of the Great West, The Old Regime in Canada, Count Frontenac and New France under Louis XIV, A Half Century of Conflict, Montcalm and Wolfe*); *The Pageant of America. A Pictorial History of the United States* ed. by R. H. Gabriel (1925-); F. L. Paxson — *History of the American Frontier 1763-1893* (1924) & *The Last American Frontier* (1910); M. M. Quaife — *Chicago and the Old Northwest 1763-1835*. . . (1913); Theodore Roosevelt — *Winning of the West* (4v. 1889-96); James Schouler — *History of the United States of America, under the Constitution* (rev. ed. 7v. 1894-1913); Ellen C. Semple — *American History and its Geographic Conditions* (1903); Cyrus Thomas — *Indians of North America in Historic Times* (1903); J. F. Turner — *The Frontier in American History* (1920) and his *Character and Influence of the Indian Trade in Wisconsin* (Wis. Hist. Soc. — *Proc.* 1889. 52ff. & Johns Hopkins Univ. — *Stud. in Hist and Pol. Sci.* Ninth ser. no. XI-XII. 1891); Justin Winsor — *Cartier to Frontenac. Geographical discovery in the Interior of North America, in its Historical Relations, 1534-1700* (1894), *The Mississippi Basin. The Struggle in America between England and France, 1697-1763* (1895), *The Westward Movement. The Colonies and the Republic West of the Alleghanies 1763-1798* (1897), *Narrative and Critical History of America* (8v. 1884-9); Clark Wissler — *The American Indian, an Introduction to the Anthropology of the New World* (2d. ed. 1923).

## CHAPTERS I-II

REFERENCE BOOKS. General reference books of value for the first two chapters are E. G. Bourne — *Spain in America* (*Amer. Nat. Ser.* III. 1904); L. J. Burpee — *The Search for the Western Sea* . . . (1908) & *Pathfinders of the Great Plains; a Chronicle of La Verendrye and His Sons* (*Chron. of Can.* XVIII. 1914); T. J. Campbell — *Pioneer Priests of North America* (1908-) & *Pioneer Laymen* (2v. 1915); J. H. Finley — *The French in the Heart of America* (1915); Pierre Heinrich — *La Louisiane sous la Compagnie des Indes 1717-1731* (1908); Woodbury Lowery — *Spanish Settlements within the Present Limits of the United States, 1513-1561* (1901); le P. Camille de Rochemonteix — *Les Jésuites et la Nouvelle France au XVIIe Siècle*. . . (3t. 1895-6); J. D. G. Shea — *History of the Catholic Missions among the Indian Tribes in the United States* (1855); F. H. Severance — *An Old Frontier of France. The Niagara Region and Adjacent Lakes under French Control* (2v. 1917); R. G. Thwaites — *France in America* (*Amer. Nat. Ser.* VII. 1905).

A large number of western state histories have been printed dealing chiefly with the period of French and Spanish control. Prominent examples of such studies are the following: C. W. Alvord — *The Illinois Country 1673-1818* (*The Centennial History of Illinois.* I. 1922); F. L. Billon — *Annals of St. Louis in its Early Days under the French and Spanish Dominations* (1886); T. J. Chapman — *French in the Allegheny Valley* (1887); J. F. H. Claiborne — *Mississippi as a Province, Territory & State . . .* (1880); Silas Farmer — *History of Detroit and Michigan* (1884); Alcée Fortier — *History of Louisiana* (I. *Early Explorers and the Domination of the French 1512-1768.* II. *The Spanish Domination and the Cession to the United States 1769-1803.* III & IV. *The American Domination*); C. E. A. Gayarré — *History of Louisiana* (New ed. 1903, v. I & II dealing with the French domination, v. III with the Spanish, & v. IV with the American); Peter Hamilton — *Colonial Mobile 1519-1821* (1897); Louis Houck — *A History of Missouri from the Earliest Explorations and Settlement until the Admission of the State into the Union* (3v. 1908); Louise P. Kellogg — *The French Regime in Wisconsin and the Northwest* (1925); J. H. Lanman — *History of Michigan* (1839); F. X. Martin — *History of Louisiana from the Earliest Period* (2v. 1827-1829); E. O. Randall & D. J. Ryan — *History of Ohio* (5v. 1912); Mrs. Electra M. Sheldon — *Early History of Michigan from the First Settlement to 1815* (1856); Jos. Wallace — *The History of Illinois & Louisiana Under the French Rule. . .* (1893).

Various special monographs have also been prepared by historical workers which furnish aid to the student. Because of their number and their accessibility only a few are named as indicative of the nature of the many. C. W. Butterfield early prepared accounts of some of the pioneers of the West, his *History of Brulé's Discoveries and Explorations 1610-1626. . .* (1898) and his *History of the Discovery of the Northwest by John Nicolet in 1634* (1881) being among the earliest in their field. Ernest Gagnon's *Louis Jolliet, Decouvreur du Mississippi et du Pays des Illinois, Premier Seigneur de l'île d'Anticosti* (1902), Henri Gravier's *L'Oeuvre de d'Iberville à la Louisiane 1698-1707* (1899), H. E. Legler's *The Man with the Iron Hand* (1896), and Grace King's *Jean Baptiste Le Moyne, Sieur de Bienville* (1892) are later examples of the biographical study. A book of the same type revealing popular interest is Agnes C. Laut's *Pathfinders of the West* (1904). Monographs of a different sort are P. J. Carayon's *Le Banissement des Jesuites de la Louisiane* (1865). Edward Dunn's *Spanish & French Rivalry in the Gulf Region of the United States 1678-1702* (*University of Texas. Bull., Studies in Hist.* no. 1. 1917), and J. H. Deiler's *The Settlement of the German Coast of Louisiana & the Creoles of German Descent* (1909). Undoubtedly the most prolific topic in the period is the Law Bubble, J. C. Horn in *Jean Law. Ein finanzgeschichtlicher Versuch* (1858), A. Cochut in *Law, Son Système et son Époque* (1853), and Adophe Thiers in his *Histoire de Law* (1858) being only three of the many writers who have treated this fiasco. Henri Gravier's *La Colonisation de la Louisiane à l'époque de Law, Octobre 1717-Janvier 1721* (1904) should also be noted.

RECENT ARTICLES. Some of the most valuable research of recent years has appeared in the form of short articles in the various historical publications. Among the most illuminating for our period are the following: Jane M. Berry — *Indian Policy of Spain in the Southwest, 1783-85* (*M. V. H. R.* III: 462); H. E. Bolton — *The Location of La Salle's Colony on the Gulf of Mexico* (*M. V. H. R.* II: 165ff.); Vera L. Brown — *Anglo Spanish Relations in America in the Closing Years of the Colonial Era* (*Hisp. Amer. Rev.* Aug. 1922); Pierre de Coubertin — *L'Amérique Française et le centénaire de la Louisiane* (*Revue des deux Mondes, April,* 1904); Wm. E. Dunn — *Search for La Salle's Colony 1685-1689* (*Southwestern Hist. Quar.* XIX:323 ff.; Archibald Henderson — *Isaac Shelby and the Genet Mission* (*M. V. H. R.* VI: 451-469); J. A. James — *Spanish Influence in the West during the American Revolution* (*M. V. H. R.* IV: 193ff.); *Louisiana as a Factor in American Diplomacy.* (*M. V. H. R.* I: 44); Louise P. Kellogg — *The Fox Indians during the French Regime* (Wis. Hist. Soc. — *Proc.* 1907. 142ff.); E. C. Mason — *The March of the Spaniards across Illinois* (*Mag. of Amer. Hist.* XV: 457ff.); F. P. Renaut — *La Question de la Louisiane, 1796-1806* (*Revue de l'Histoire des Colonies Françaises* 1918. Repr. separately); F. L. Riley — *Spanish Policy in Mississippi after the Treaty of San Lorenzo* (Amer. Hist. Assoc. — *Annual Report* 1897, p. 175 ff.); Wm. G. Shea — *Account of the Voyage of the Ursulines to New Orleans in 1727* (*U. S. Cath. Hist. Mag.* I, 1887); W. R. Shepherd — *The Cession of Louisiana to Spain* (*Pol. Sci. Quar.* XIX: 439ff.) and his *Wilkinson and the Beginnings of the Spanish Conspiracy* (*Amer. Hist. Rev.* IX: 490ff.); F. J. Teggart — *Capture of St. Joseph, Michigan, by the Spaniards in 1781* (*Mo. Hist. Rev.* V: 214); F. J. Turner — *The Policy of France toward the Mississippi Valley in the Period of Washington and Adams* (*Amer. Hist. Rev.* X: 249ff.) & his *The Origin of Genet's Proposed Attack on Lousiana and the Floridas* (*Ibid.* III; 650ff.).

CONTEMPORARY SOURCES. Important books and papers not treated specifically in chapters I and II are Barbé-Marbois — *Histoire de la Louisiane et de la Cession de cette Colonie par la France aux États-Unis de l'Amérique Septentrionale* (1829 tr. 1830); Brissot et Clairière — *De la France et des États-Unis* (1787); *Journal de la*

*Guerre du Micissippi contre les Chicachas, en 1739 et finie en 1740. . .* ; le Père Lafitau (S. J.) — *Moeurs des Sauvages Amériquains* (2v. 1724); le Père Laval, S. J. — *Voyage de la Louisiane, fait par ordre du roi en l'année mil sept vingt. . .* (1728); Gabriel Sagard-Theodat — *Histoire du Canada* (1836. New ed. 4t. 1865-6); Talleyrand — *Essay upon the Advantages to be Derived from New Colonies in the Existing Circumstances* (1806); Vergennes — *Mémoire Historique et Politique sur la Louisiane. . .* (1802). Typical of the continued interest in Louisiana in France or possibly of Napoleon's endeavors to popularize his policy is *Mémoires sur la Louisiane et la Nouvelle Orléans accompagnés d'une dissertation sur les avantages que le Commerce de l'Empire doit tirer de la stipulation fait par l'article VI du Traité de cession du 30 avril, 1803, suivi d'une traduction de diverses notes sur cette colonie, publiés aux États Unis peu de temps après la ratification du Traité* (1804). A book from which Villiers du Terrage quotes extensively and which he says is very rare is Laussat's *Mémoires sur ma vie à mon fils pendant les années 1803 et suivantes que j'ai rempli des fonctions publiques, savoir: à la Louisiane en qualité de commissaire du gouvernement français pour la reprise de possession de cette colonie et pour sa rémise aux États-Unis. . .* (1831). In N. D. Mereness' *Travels in the American Colonies* (1916) Diron d'Artaguiette's *Journal* is particularly valuable for its account of the hardships suffered by the concessionnaires as a result of the inefficiency of the Company, testimony borne out by the *La Hist. Quar.* II: 164ff. and offering illuminating contrast to the criticisms of Father Poisson. The magazine just mentioned, the *Louisiana Historical Quarterly* prints a number of letters, documents, etc., throwing light on the social history of the period. The *Journal* of the Société des Américanistes de Paris includes a number of interesting reprints as well as articles bearing on our field. Among the former are *Extrait d'un Journal de Voyage en Louisiane du Père Paul du Ru (1700)* publié par le Baron Marc de Villiers (n.s. XVII: 121ff.), *Notes sur les Chactas d'après les Journaux de Voyage de Régis du Roullet (1729-1732)* by the same scholarly writer (n.s. XV: 223ff.), *Les Indiens du Texas et les Expéditions Françaises de 1720 et 1721 à la "Baie Saint-Bernard"* by him and P. Rivet (XI:103ff.) and *L'Établissement de la Province de Louisiane, Poème inédit* described by de Villiers (New ser. II: 35ff.).

MANUSCRIPT SOURCES. Documentary sources aside from those reprinted by Margry and states like New York, Wisconsin, and Michigan have not been extensively used and consequently are not listed. For information on the struggle between English and French in the Ohio Valley and the West the *Colonial Records of Pennsylvania* (16v. 1838-1853), particularly V-VIII, and the *Calendar of Virginia State Papers* (9v. 1875-1890), particularly I, are very valuable; S. Car. Hist. Soc. — *Coll.* (5v. 1857-1897) portray conditions in the South; and each year more documents are made accessible to the average reader. Other collections of value for this period are *Collection de Manuscrits contenant Lettres, Mémoires et autres Documents Historiques Relatifs à la Nouvelle France. . .* (ed. by J. Blanchet. 4v. 1883-5), and *Collection de Documents Inédits sur le Canada et l'Amérique* (3t. 1888-90). Further references may be found in Alvord, Thwaites, etc.

In addition to the reprints so frequently cited in the text and those given in the preceding section special mention should be made of the pioneer work of Wm. G. Shea —*Discovery and Exploration of the Mississippi Valley* (1852, repr. 1903) & his *Early Voyages up and down the Mississippi* (1861, repr. 1902); of R. Thomassy's *Géologie Pratique de la Louisiane* (1860); of *Exploration of the Great Lakes, 1669-1670 by Dollier de Casson & de Brépant de Galinée* tr. & ed. by J. H. Coyne (Hist. Soc. of Toronto — *Papers & Records* v. IV. 1903); of J. A. Robertson's *Louisiana under the Rule of Spain, France, & the United States, 1785-1807* (2v. 1911); and of Louise P. Kellogg's *Early Narratives of the Northwest 1634-1699* (*Orig. Narr. of Early Amer. Hist.* 1917).

A number of documents concerning the French attempts to secure Louisiana near the close of the eighteenth century are now available. See *Selections from the Draper Collection . . . to Elucidate the French Expedition under George Rogers Clark against Louisiana, in the Years 1793-94* (Amer. Hist. Assoc. — *Annual Report* 1896. I: 930ff.), *The Mangourit Correspondence in respect to Genet's Projected Attack upon the Floridas, 1793-94* (*Ibid.*, 1897. 569ff.), *Seventh Report of the Historical Manuscripts Commission. Correspondence of the French Ministers to the United States, 1791-1797* (*Ibid.*, 1903. II), and additional documents on the same problem *Amer. Hist. Rev.* II: 474ff. & III: 490ff.

The student will find valuable J. A. Robertson's *List of Documents in Spanish Archives relating to the History of the United States which have been printed or of which transcripts are preserved in American libraries* and the *Calendar of Documents in the French Archives relating to the Mississippi Valley* which has been in preparation for some years under the direction of W. G. Leland.

REFERENCES ON THE LITERATURE. Authority on the literature of the period is Professor Gilbert Chinard, his books *L'Amérique et le Rêve Exotique dans la Lit-*

*térature Française au XVIIe et au XVIIIe Siècle* (1913) and *L'Exotisme Américain dans la Littérature Française au XVIe Siècle* (1911) being particularly valuable. His *L'Exotisme Américain dans l'Oeuvre de Chateaubriand* (1918) is perhaps the most compete survey of the debated work of the French novelist, Professor Joseph Bedier's article in the same field published in his *Études Critiques* (1903, pp. 127-294) being notable in that it prompted Professor Chinard's investigations. A good recent article which lists many others is *La Louisiane de Chateaubriand* — by Baron Marc de Villiers (Société des Américanistes — *Journal* t. 16. 1924). See also Armstrong — *Chateaubriand's America* (*M. L. A. P.* XXII: 345-370). The various biographies of Prévost devote considerable space to his *Manon* and early Louisiana, and several articles on *Manon* are given (*La Hist. Quar.* II: 307ff.). Margry has an interesting discussion of the influence of the early voyages upon Rabelais in his *Les Navigations Françaises et la Révolution Maritime du XIVe au XVIe Siècle.* . . (1867, 332-341).

## CHAPTER III

REFERENCE BOOKS. Later research has dealt with many phases of this unsettled period. The following are some of the more important of the monographs, biographical studies, etc.: G. H. Alden — *New Governments West of the Alleghanies before 1870* (Univ. of Wis.— *Bull. Hist. ser.* v. II. no. 1. pp. 1-74. 1897); J. A. Barrett — *Evolution of the Ordinance of 1787; with an Account of the Earlier Plans for the Government of the Northwest Territory*; (Univ. of Neb. — *Dep. of Hist. & Econ. Seminary Papers* no. 1. 1891); A. P. Brigham — *From Trail to Railway through the Appalachians* (1907); Jacob Burnet — *Notes on the Early Settlement of the Northwestern Territory* (1847); C. W. Butterfield — *History of the Girtys.* . . (1890) and his *Historical Account of the Expedition against Sandusky under Col. William Crawford in 1782.* . . (1873); J. S. Corbett — *England in the Seven Years War; a Study in Combined Strategy* (2v. 1907); I. J. Cox — *The West Florida Controversy, 1798-1831. A Study in American Diplomacy* (1918); C. E. Carter — *Great Britain and the Illinois Country 1763-1774* (1910); J. H. Deiler — *Zur Geschichte der Deutschen am unteren Mississippi. Das Redemptionssystem im Staate Louisiana* (1901); W. H. English — *Conquest of the Country Northwest of the River Ohio 1777-1783.* . . (2v. 1896); J. T. Faris — *On the Trail of the Pioneers* (1920); Berthold Fernow — *The Ohio Valley in Colonial Days* (1890); T. M. Green — *The Spanish Conspiracy.* . . (1891); Henry Howe — *Historical Collections of Ohio* (2v. 1888); A. B. Hulbert — *The Ohio River, a Course of Empire* (1906); Archibald Henderson — *Conquest of the Old Southwest.* . . (1920); Alice M. Keyes — *Cadwallader Colden, a Representative Eighteenth Century Official* (1906); W. F. McCaleb — *The Aaron Burr Conspiracy.* . . (1903); E. I. McCormac — *Colonial Opposition to Imperial Authority during the French and Indian War* (Univ. of Cal. — *Pub. in Hist.* v. I. no. 1, 1911); W. A. Pusey — *The Wilderness Road to Kentucky, its Location and Features* (1921); P. C. Phillips — *The West in the Diplomacy of the American Revolution* (Univ. of Ill. — *Stud. in the Soc. Sciences.* II. nos. 2 & 3); W. M. Sloan — *The French War and the Revolution* (1893); C. E. Slocum — *The Ohio Country between the Years 1783 & 1815.* . . (1910); W. L. Stone — *Life & Times of Sir William Johnson, Bart.* (2v. 1865); L. S. Shimmell — *Border Warfare in Pennsylvania during the Revolution* (1901); P. J. Treat — *The National Land System, 1785-1820* (1910); R. G. Thwaites — *How George Rogers Clark Won the Northwest & Other Essays in Western History* (1903); A. T. Volwiler — *George Croghan and the Westward Movement 1741-1782* (1926); J. S. Walton — *Conrad Weiser and the Indian Policy of Colonial Pennsylvania* (1900); G. W. Ward — *Early Development of the Chesapeake and Ohio Canal Project* (*Johns Hopkins Univ. Stud.* XVII, nos. 9-10-11. 1899).

ARTICLES. Articles of value for this period are: C. W. Alvord — *Virginia and the West* (*M. V. H. R.* III: 19-38) and his *Conquest of St. Joseph, Michigan, by the Spaniards in 1781* (*Mo. Hist. Rev.* II: 195ff. See *Ibid.* V: 214ff. for J. F. Teggart's article on the same topic); V. Crane — *The Tennessee River as the Road to Carolina: Beginning of Exploration and Trade.* (*M. V. H. R.* III: 3); E. C. Dawes — *The Scioto Purchase in 1787.* (*Mag. of Amer. Hist.* XXII: 470-482); M. Farrand — *The West and the Principles of the Revolution.* (*Yale Review.* XVII. 44); F. Harrison — *The Virginians on the Ohio and Mississippi in 1742* (*Va. Mag. of Hist.* XXX: 203); A. Henderson — *Richard Henderson and the Occupation of Kentucky* (*M. V. H. R.* I: 341-363); J. A. James — *Significant Events during the Last Year of the Revolution in the West* (Mis. Val. Hist. Assoc. — *Proc.* VI: 239ff.), *To What Extent Was George Rogers Clark in Military Control of the Northwest at the Close of the American Revolution?* (Amer. Hist. Assoc. — *Annual Report.* 1917. 313-329), *Significance of the Attack on St. Louis, 1780* (M. V. H. A. — *Proc.* 1908. 212ff.);, *G. R. Clark and Detroit* — (M. V. H. A. — *Proc.* III: 291), *Last Year of the Revolution in the West.* (*Ibid.*, VI: 239), and *Pittsburgh a Key to the West during the Amer. Rev.*

(*O. Arch. and Hist. Quar.* Jan. 1913); W. F. McCaleb — *The Aaron Burr Conspiracy and New Orleans* — (Amer. Hist. Assoc. — *An. Rep.* 1903, p. 131ff.); A. J. Morrison — *Virginia Indian Trade to 1673* (in *William and Mary College Quarterly*. Oct. 1921 and later nos.); W. Notestein — *Western Indians in the Revolution* (*O. Arch. & Hist. Quar.* XVI: 269); P. C. Phillips — *American Opinions regarding the West 1778-1783* (M. V. H. A. — *Proc.* 1913-4, VII: 286ff.); F. L. Riley — *Transition from Spanish Rule* (Miss. Hist. Soc. — *Pub.* III: 261); W. H. Siebert — *The Loyalists in West Florida and the Natchez District* (*M. V. H. R.* II: 465ff.) and *The Tory Proprietors of Kentucky Lands* (*O. Arch. & Hist. Quar.* XXVIII: 48ff.); W. E. Stevens — *Organization of the British Fur Trade 1760-1800* (*M. V. H. R.* III: 172-202); Wm. M. Thornton — *Spotswood's Expedition of 1716*. (*Nat. Geog. Mag.* VII: 265ff.); F. J. Turner — *Western State Making in the Revolutionary Era.* (*Amer. Hist. Rev.* I: 70-87, 251-269) and his *Diplomatic Contest for the Mississippi Valley*, (*Atlantic Mo.* XCIII: 676-691, 807-817); J. Viles — *Population and Settlement in Missouri before 1804.* (*Mo. Hist. Rev.* V: 189); S. B. Weeks — *General Joseph Martin and the War of the Revolution in the West.* (Amer. Hist. Assoc. — *Annual Report* 1893. 401-477).

EARLY SOURCES. So many and so varied are the books bearing on the interior in this period that only an indication of their nature such as was given in the text can be attempted. Among the more valuable recent reprints of contemporary material may be mentioned R. G. Thwaites' and Louise P. Kellogg's *Revolution on the Upper Ohio, 1775-1777* (1908), *Frontier Defense on the Upper Ohio, 1777-8* (1912), *Frontier Advance on the Upper Ohio* (1916), and *Frontier Retreat on the Upper Ohio* (1917), also N. D. Mereness' *Travels in the American Colonies* (1916), which contains a number of narratives depicting relations with the Indians in the South and *Colonel William Fleming's Journal of Travels in Kentucky, 1779-1780.* The most accessible representative of the many pamphlets dealing with the French and English disputes about territory in the West is Wm. Clarke's *Observations on the Late and Present Conduct of the French. . . .* (1755) reprinted in the *Magazine of History*, Extra no. 62. Also easily obtained is *The Journal of Nicholas Cresswell 1774-1777* (1924), the author of which shared the current dreams of making a fortune rapidly in western lands. After long neglect Peter Wraxall's *Abridgment of the Indian Affairs . . . Transacted in the Colony of New York, from the Year 1678 to the Year 1751* has been ably edited by Chas. H. McIlwain (*Harvard Historical Studies* XXI. 1915), who feels that the historical value of Wraxall's work excels that of Colden's to which it forms valuable supplement. Illinois State Historical Society — *Collections* X (*The Critical Period, 1763-1765*), XI (*The New Regime, 1765-1767*), and VIII & XIX (*George Rogers Clark Papers*), and *Mississippi Provincial Archives, 1763-66. English Dominion I* are state collections valuable in addition to those hitherto mentioned.

Very numerous are the records of captivity and warfare. In addition to the collections cited in the text — John A. McClung's of 1832, Joseph Doddridge's of 1824, and Withers' of 1831, mention should be made of Samuel G. Drake's *Indian Captivities* (1850), of W. L. Stone's *Life of Joseph Brant. . . .* (1838) and his *Border Wars of the American Revolution* (2v. 1845), and of that rarest of books of American Indian history — Archibald Loudon's *Selection of Some of the Most Interesting Narratives of Outrages Committed by the Indians in their Wars with the White People* (2v. 1808-11, repr. 1888). The interest in the narratives of Indian warfare is also illustrated by their inclusion in the Appendices of many such books as Henry Trumbull's *History of the Discovery of America. . . .* (1810). Disappointment at the outcome of some of the campaigns directed against the Indians resulted in such publications as *A Narrative of the Manner in which the Campaign against the Indians in the Year One Thousand Seven Hundred and Ninety One was Conducted, by Major General St. Clair, together with his Observations on the Statements of the Secretary of War . . . and the Reports of the Committees Appointed to Inquire into the Causes of the Failure Thereof* and *Proceedings of a Court of Inquiry Held at the Request of General Josiah Harmon* (1791). Lt. Boyer's *Journal of Wayne's Campaign* (1866) is a well known source.

J. F. Turner prints documents showing *English Policy toward America in 1790-1791* (*Am. Hist. Rev.* VII: 706ff., VIII: 78ff.) and *Documents on the Blount Conspiracy, 1795-1797* (*Amer. Hist. Rev.* X: 574ff.). *Narrative of the Transactions, Imprisonment and Sufferings of John Connolly, an American Loyalist and Lieutenant-Colonel in his Majesty's Service* (1783) presents a glimpse of conditions at Pittsburgh during the Revolution. The second edition of 1780 of the *Narrative of Mr. John Dodge during his Captivity at Detroit* has been reprinted with an introduction by Burton (1909). Among the best known records of this period is the *Narrative of the Perils and Sufferings of Dr. Knight and John Slover among the Indians during the Revolutionary War, with Short Memoirs of Colonel Crawford and John S. Slover, and a Letter from H. Brackenridge on the Rights of the Indians. . . .* (1867).

*A Plain Narrative of the Uncommon Sufferings, and Remarkable Deliverance of*

*Thomas Brown, of Charlestown, in New England; who Returned to his Father's House the Beginning of January 1760* . . . (1760, repr. *Mag. of Hist.* Extra no. 4) concerns itself chiefly with the experiences of the captive who was taken by his Indian masters down the Ohio to the Mississippi; the penetration of the Ohio country is evidenced by the *Narrative of the Incidents Attending the Capture, Detention, and Ransom of Charles Johnston, of Botetourt County, Virginia, who was Taken Prisoner by the Indians, on the River Ohio, in the Year 1790.* In addition to the Braddock references given in the text notice might be taken of *The Expedition of Major General Braddock to Virginia; with the Two Regiments of Hacket & Dunbar.* . . *Being Extracts from an Officer to his Friend in London Describing the March and Engagement in the Woods* . . . (1755), of the letter of Orme on Braddock's Defeat in the *Hist. Mag.* (VIII: 353ff.), of *Letter to a Friend, Giving a Concise but Just Account, according to the Advices Hitherto Received of the Ohio Defeat* (1755), of *The Life, Adventures, and Surprising Deliverances of Duncan Cameron, Private Soldier in the Regiment of Foot, Late Sir Peter Halket's* (3d ed. 1756), and of the fact that A. B. Hulbert's *Braddock's Road* (1903) gives copious extracts from the early accounts. An earlier pamphlet somewhat similar to Thomson's is James Parker's *The Importance of Gaining and Preserving the Friendship of the Indians to the British Interest, Considered* (1751).

Miscellaneous sources are so numerous and varied that it is impossible to indicate the nature of all of them. *Affairs at Fort Chartres, 1768-1781,* letters by Ensign Butricke reprinted by Munsell (1864) from the *Hist. Mag.* (VIII. no. 8), like Pittman's better known work, give praise of Illinois, "the finest country in the known world." Lewis Evans' *Geographical, Historical, Political, Philosophical and Mechanical Essays.* . . (ser. 1 & 2, 1755) written to accompany his map were very well known and are significant for their praise of the western lands, their censure of governmental neglect, and their plans for settlement. Inasmuch as they were printed by Franklin they may be regarded indirectly as another one of his efforts for the winning of the West. *Memoirs of Robert Stobo* ed. by N. B. Craig (1854) are interesting in that Stobo is supposed to have been the model for Smollett's Lismahago. Charles Beatty's *Journal of a Two-Months' Tour; with a View of Promoting Religion among the Frontier Inhabitants of Pennsylvania, and of Introducing Christianity among the Indians to the Westward of the Alegh-geny Mountains* . . ., (1768), which gives some interesting information about the Delaware Indians, may be taken as another example of the missionary narrative. Indicative of contemporary interest is *A Voyage to North America, Perform'd by G. Taylor, of Sheffield, in the Years 1768 and 1769; with an Account of his Tedious Passage* . . *Manner of Trading with the Indians* . . . *his Setting Sail from Philadelphia to New Orleans* . . . *and Other Matters Worthy of Notice* . . . (1771). Lezay-Marnézia's *Lettres Écrites des Rives de l'Ohio* (1801) are very disappointing, for, passing rather lightly over the misfortunes he experienced through the Scioto Company, the author devotes most of his energy to romantic rhapsodies urging Bernardin de Saint Pierre to become the leader of a new republic in the heart of America "dirigée suivant les loix de la Nature."

Additional early publications throwing light on the land companies are *New England Mississippi Land Company; Articles of Association,* etc. (1797) and *Memorial of the A. E. Mississippi Land Company to Congress; with a Vindication of Their Title* (1804). Of interest in connection with the Spanish Conspiracy are Major General James Wilkinson's *Memoirs of My Own Times* (1816) and Daniel Clark's *Proofs of the Corruption of General James Wilkinson* (1809). The excitement about the closing of the Mississippi is reflected in various contemporary publications *The Mississippi Question Fairly Stated and the Views and Arguments of Those who Clamor for War Examined* . . . by Camillus [Wm. Duane] (1803) and *Mississippi Question. Report on Certain Resolutions concerning the Violation of the Right of Deposit in the Island of New Orleans* (1803). Of special interest because of the author's literary fame is Charles Brockden Brown's *Address to the Government of the United States on the Cession of Louisiana to the French; and on the Late Breach of Treaty by the Spaniards; including the Translation of a Memorial on the War of St. Domingo, and Cession of the Mississippi to France, Drawn up by a French Counsellor of State* . . . (1803).

## CHAPTER IV

REFERENCE BOOKS. *American Commonwealth ser.* ed. by H. E. Scudder; R. B. Anderson — *First Chapter of Norwegian Immigration (1821-1840)* (1895); F. W. Billon — *Annals of St. Louis in its Territorial Days, from 1804 to 1821* (1888); K. C. Babcock — *Scandinavian Element in the United States* (Univ. of Ill. Stud. 1914); A. C. Boggess — *The Settlement of Illinois, 1778-1830* (Chic. Hist. Soc. — *Coll.* V. 1908); H. J. Desmond — *The Know-Nothing Party* (1905); A. B. Faust — *The German Element in the United States* (2v. 1909); G. N. Fuller — *Economic and Social Beginnings of Michigan* . . . (*Mich. Hist. Pub. — Univ. ser.* 1); G. P.

Garrison — *Westward Extension, 1841-50* (1906); C. L. Goodwin — *The Trans-Mississippi West (1803-53). A History of its Acquisition and Settlement* (1922); J. K. Hosmer — *History of the Louisiana Purchase* (1902); Ida A. Johnson — *The Michigan Fur Trade* (1919); G. M. Stephenson — *The Political History of the Public Lands from 1840 to 1862, from Pre-emption to Homestead* (1917); F. J. Turner — *Rise of the New West 1819-1829* . . . (*Amer. Nat. Ser.* XIV. 1906) and the *United States 1830-1850* (In preparation); Jacob Van der Zee — *The Hollanders of Iowa* (1912); R. G. Wellington — *Political and Sectional Influence of the Public Lands, 1828-1842* (1914); D. E. Willard — *Story of the Prairies; or, The Landscape Geology of North Dakota* (1902).

ARTICLES — R. S. Cotterill — *The Natchez-Trace* (*La. Hist. Quar.* V: 259ff.); F. Carney — *Geographic Influences in the Development of Ohio* (*Pop. Sci. Mo.* LXXV: 479); Samuel M. Davis — *Some of the Consequences of the Louisiana Purchase* (Amer. Hist. Assoc. — *Annual Report.* 1897. 149-160); R. Gittinger — *Separation of Nebraska and Kansas from Indian Territory.* (*Mis. Valley Hist. Rev.* III: 442); O. G. Libby — *The Lead and Shot Trade in Early Wisconsin History* (*Wis. Hist. Coll.* XIII: 293-374); Harlow Lindley — *Western Travel, 1800-1820* (*M. V. H. R.* VI: 167-191); Isaac Lippincott — *Industrial Influence of Lead Mining in Mo.* (*Jour. of Pol. Economy.* XX: 695-715); O. H. Marshall — *Early Notices of the Copper Regions* (In *Amer. Rev.* IV: 347-350. Repr. in *Historical Writings of the late O. H. Marshall,* p. 333-342); Moses Meeker — *Early History of the Lead Region of Wisconsin* (in *Wis. Hist. Coll.* VI: 271-296); Louis Pelzer — *Economic Factors in the Acquisition of Louisiana* (M. V. H. A. — *Proc.* VI: 109ff.); B. F. Shambaugh — *Frontier Land Clubs or Claim Associations* (Amer. Hist. Assoc. — *Annual Report.* 1900. I: 67-84); Wm. M. Sloane — *The World Aspects of the Louisiana Purchase* (Amer. Hist. Assoc. — *Annual Report.* 1903. I: 85-103); E. E. Sparks — *The Influence of the Ohio River in Western Expansion* (*Ohio Arch. & Hist. Quar.* Jan. 1913); R. G. Thwaites — *Early Lead Mining in Illinois and Wisconsin.* (Amer. Hist. Assoc. — *Annual Report.* 1893. 189-196, and a fuller article in *Wis. Hist. Coll.* XIII: 271-292 and in *How George Rogers Clark Won the Northwest*); F. J. Turner — *The Colonization of the West, 1820-1830* (*Amer. Hist. Rev.* XI: 303ff.)

EARLY SOURCES AND RELATED MONOGRAPHS. Greater than ever before is the flood of descriptive literature on the West appearing in the nineteenth century. A sketch of the life and districts therein portrayed and an outline of the types of material available have already been given; various other contemporary accounts and later studies are listed below.

One of the most interesting of the books produced by the War of 1812 for its comments on the prairie and for its plan of a military settlement is Samuel R. Brown's *Views of the Campaigns of the Western Army* . . . (1814). Another account, very rare, is Adam Walker's *Journal of Two Campaigns of the Fourth Regiment of U. S. Infantry, in the Michigan and Indiana Territories, under the Command of Col. John P. Boyd and Lt. Col. James Miller during the Years 1811 & 1812* (1816). Dissatisfaction with the various campaigns is reflected in such publications as James Foster's *Capitulation, or a History of the Expedition Conducted by William Hull, by an Ohio Volunteer* (1812) and H. A. S. Dearborn's *Defence of Gen. Henry Dearborn against the Attack of Gen. William Hull* (1824).

An early history of the Black Hawk struggle is J. A. Wakefield's *History of the War between the United States and the Sac and Fox Nations . . . in 1828, 1831 and 1832* (1834). The famous *Life of Black Hawk, Ma-Ka-Tai-Me-She-Kia-Kiah* (1833) has been attractively edited by M. M. Quaife (1916). Later treatments of that struggle are given by R. G. Thwaites in *Wis. Hist. Coll.* I: 64-85 and in *How George Rogers Clark Won the Northwest* (1903), by F. E. Stevens in *The Black Hawk War, including a Review of Black Hawk's Life* (1903), and by P. A. Armstrong in *The Sauks and the Black Hawk War* (1887).

Some of the latest of the Indian outrages are described in Mrs. Abigail Gardner Sharp's *History of the Spirit Lake Massacre and Captivity of Miss Abbie Gardner* (1885) and I. V. D. Heard's *History of the Sioux Wars and Massacres of 1862 and 1863* (1863). A later treatment of the Sioux War is given by M. P. Satterlee in Minn. Hist. Soc. — *Coll.* XV: 349-370. No reference to the natives could be complete without reference to one of the most popular books that ever dealt with them — George Catlin's *Letters and Notes on the Manners, Customs and Conditions of the North American Indians* (1841). A very reliable source is Jedidiah Morse's *Report to the Secretary of War of the United States, on Indian Affairs, Comprising a Narrative of a Tour Performed in the summer of 1820, under a Commission from the President of the United States for the Purpose of Ascertaining, for the Use of the Government, the Actual State of the Indian Tribes in Our Country* (1822). Annie H. Abel gives an admirable *History of Events Resulting in Indian Consolidation West of the Mississippi* (Amer. Hist. Assoc. — *Annual Report* 1906. I: 233-450) and

*Proposals for an Indian State, 1778-1878* (*Ibid.*, 1908. I: 87-104). Also to be commended for its account of the government's Indian policy is Lucy E. Textor's *Official Relations between the United States and the Sioux Indians* (Leland Stanford Junior Univ. — *Pub. Hist. & Economics.* II. 1896). A glimpse of the life of the soldiers who patrolled the border is found in Louis Pelzer's *Marches of the Dragoons in the Mississippi Valley* . . . (1917) and Marcus Hanson's *Old Fort Snelling, 1819-1858* (1918) and Mrs. John H. Kinzie's *Wau-Bun, the "Early Day in the Northwest"* (1856). The influence of the soldiers in promoting settlement is well illustrated by the following passage from the Kan. Hist. Soc. — *Pub.* (IV: 251), "In the winter of 1854, Major Woods, who had been stationed at Fort Leavenworth, came to New Paris and gave such glowing accounts of Kansas that a number of families who were holding property as before described determined to make Kansas their home as soon as the government would treat with the Indians."

Among other glimpses of the river life may be mentioned G. H. Devol's *Forty Years a Gambler on the Mississippi* (1887, repr. 1926) and *Fifty Years on the Mississippi; or Gould's History of River Navigation* (1889). A novel narrative and one indicative of the way the efforts of the home missionaries shifted with the development of new routes to the West is M. Eaton's *Five Years on the Erie Canal: An Account of Some of the Most Striking Scenes and Incidents during Five Years' Labor on the Erie Canal and Other Inland Waters* (1845). Also typical of the shift in interest from the river routes is S. A. Storrow's *Narrative of a Tour in the Summer of 1817 on the Shores of Lake Superior and Other Northern Lakes of the United States* . . . (1818). The influence of the Erie Canal in peopling the West is well suggested in the immigrant song quoted by Silas Farmer in his *History of Detroit and Michigan,* I: 335-6.

> "Then there's the State of New York, where some are very rich;
> Themselves and a few others have dug a mighty ditch,
> To render it more easy for us to find the way,
> And sail upon the waters to Michigania."

Later, somewhat related papers are George Geddes — *Origin and History of the Measures that Led to the Construction of the Erie Canal* (1866) and William Hodge's *Papers concerning Early Navigation upon the Great Lakes* (1883).

The immigrant guides, travellers' narratives, etc., are so numerous that it is impossible to attempt to cite more of them than are given in the text. Zerah Hawley's *Journal of a Tour through Connecticut, Massachusetts, New York, the North Part of Pennsylvania and Ohio, including a Year's Residence in that Part of Ohio, Styled New Connecticut or Western Reserve* . . . (1822) is noteworthy among the American descriptions, however, because like Hall and some of the English travellers the author feels it his duty "to undeceive the community, respecting a portion of the western country which has been represented as an *Earthly Paradise,* where every thing necessary, every thing convenient, and almost every thing which is considered as a luxury, might be had almost without care, labour or exertion."

Although the Mormons will be treated more fully in the book on the plains mention might be made of several books treating their colonies in the Middle West: W. Aitken's *Journey up the Mississippi River from its Mouth to Nauvoo, the City of the Latter Day Saints* (2d ed. 1843); Wm. Swartzell's *Mormonism Exposed, Being a Journal of a Residence in Missouri* . . . (1840); J. P. Greene's *Facts Relative to the Expulsion of the Mormons or Latter Day Saints from the State of Missouri* . . . (1839); P. P. Pratt's *Late Persecution of the Church of Jesus Christ, of Latter Day Saints* (1840); J. A. Little's *From Kirtland to Salt Lake City* (1890); Henry A. Brown's *History of Illinois* (1844). *The Journal of Heber C. Kimball, an Elder of the Church of Jesus Christ of Latter Day Saints* (1840), one of the first imprints of the Mormon press at Nauvoo, includes an account of his missionary journeys in the West. J. J. Strang's *Ancient and Modern Michilimackinac* (1854, repr. 1894) includes an account of the Mormon controversy in Michigan. Among the many later studies of this sect the following may be named as of special interest here: O. F. Berry — *The Mormon Settlements in Illinois* (Ill. St. Hist. Soc. — *Tran.* 1909); J. H. Kennedy — *Early Days of Mormonism; Palmyra, Kirtland, and Nauvoo* (1888); D. L. Leonard — *Mormon Sojourn in Ohio* (O. Church Hist. Soc. — *Papers,* 1890. I: 43); Jacob Van der Zee — *The Mormon Trails in Iowa* (*Ia. Jour. of Hist.* Jan. 1914); *Michigan Pioneer & Hist. Coll.* XXII.

More conservative missionary work is outlined in J. L. Batchelder's *The United States, the West, and the State of Ohio as Missionary Fields* (1848). The various communal experiments on the Prairie are mentioned frequently by the travellers. Among the outstanding accounts of New Harmony are the Duke of Saxe Weimar's *Travels through North America, Travels in the Interior of North America, 1832-1834* by Maximilian, Prince of Wied, who describes it after Owen's ownership (*E. W. T.* XXII: 163ff.); S. A. Ferrall's *A Ramble of Six Thousand Miles* (1832), which discusses the cause of the failure of the Owen scheme; Paul Brown's *Twelve Months in New Harmony* (1827), which is distinctly bitter in tone; and the charming historical novel *Seth Way* (1917) by Caroline Dale Snedeker. One of the members of the Owen colony is responsible for some of our best sketches of the early West. See Mme. Adrien Loir's *Charles-Alexandre Lesueur, Artiste et Savant Français en Amérique de 1816 à 1839* (1920) and the account of his work in the *Journal* of the Société des Américanistes.

The dissolution and other phases of the Harmony Society are treated in some feeble poems by C. F. Straube — *The Rise and Fall of Harmony Society — Economy, Pennsylvania* (1911). Studies of the Rapp band are found in J. A. Bole's *Harmony Society* (1904); G. B. Lockwood — *The New Harmony Communities* (1902) and G. B. Lockwood's and C. A. Prosser's *New Harmony Movement* (1907). *The Swiss Settlement of Switzerland County, Indiana*, has been described by Perret Dufour (1925). That the bond of a former home was felt even by the Americans is shown in the description of the Vermontville Colony (*Mich. Hist. Coll.* XXVIII: 197ff.

Early accounts of the massed religious phenomena of the West are found in Richard M'Nemar's *The Kentucky Revival; or, a Short History of the Late Extraordinary Outpouring of the Spirit of God in the Western States of America* . . . (1807) and Adam Rankin's *Review of the Noted Revival in Kentucky* (1803); later studies are D. L. Leonard's *Kentucky Revival of 1799-1805* (Ohio Church Hist. Soc. — *Papers* V: 44-71) and Catharine C. Cleveland's *The Great Revival in the West, 1797-1805* (1916).

Almost no phase of the settlement of the West was productive of as much controversial writing as that of Kansas. Not only were there dozens of such contemporary articles and books as those described in the text designed to stir up feeling in the North or the South, but there were factions within the Free-Soil and Slavery parties who after the main issues were settled gave their personal feelings full vent. Unpleasant because of this bias are Charles Robinson's *The Kansas Conflict* (1892) and *Reminiscences of Governor R. J. Walker; with the True Story of the Rescue of Kansas from Slavery* by George W. Brown (1880). Bound in with the preceding and written by the same author is *False Claims of Kansas Historians Truthfully Corrected* (1902), chiefly directed against those who have lauded John Brown. The latter storm centre has been alternately sanctified and reviled; readers will find a number of books attempting to gain their adherence to one extreme view or the other. One of the most notable of the biographies is Oswald G. Villard's *John Brown, 1800-1859, a Biography Fifty Years After* (1910). Similar to the books discussed in the text are Mrs. Miriam D. Colt's *Went to Kansas: Being a Thrilling Account of an Ill-fated Expedition to that Fairy Land and its Sad Results* . . . (1862); T. H. Webb's *Information for Kansas Immigrants* (1857); T. W. Higginson's *Ride through Kansas* (1856. See also *Kansas & John Brown* in *Cheerful Yesterdays*, 1898); W. P. Montgomery's *Report of Exploration to the Members of the Presbyterian Colonial Association, and Facts regarding a Location in Kansas Territory* (1860). The *Organization, Objects, & Plan of Operations of the Emigrant Aid Company* were set forth together with *A Description of Kansas for the Information of Emigrants* (1854); in a later year (1862) was published a *History of the New England Emigrant Aid Company. With a Report on its Future Operations. Lays of the Emigrants, as Sung by Parties for Kansas on the Days of their Departure from Boston* (1855) suggests Apollo coming to the aid of Mars. Among the later studies may be mentioned W. E. Connelley's *James Henry Lane, the "Grim Chieftain" of Kansas* (1899); W. E. Miller's *Peopling of Kansas* (1906), and L. W. Spring's *Kansas, the Prelude to the War for the Union* (1885). A later phase of Kansas life is described in E. J. Jenkins' *The Northern Tier; or, Life among the Homestead Settlers* (1880). A condensed account of the *Buford Expedition to Kansas* by W. H. Fleming is available in the *Amer. Hist. Rev.* VI: 38ff. Other articles are J. W. Isely's *The Sharps Rifle Episode in Kansas History* (*Amer. Hist. Rev.* XII: 546ff.) and *A Chapter in the Life of Charles Robinson, the First Governor of Kansas* (Amer. Hist. Assoc. — *Annual Report*. 1894. 213-226).

It should be noted that just as Judge Hall rebelled at the strictures of the English travellers so Mann Butler, Kentucky historian, issued an *Appeal from the Misrepresentations of James Hall, respecting the History of Kentucky and the West.* (1835). A useful state collection is Lindley, Harlow, ed. — *Indiana as Seen by Early Travelers. A Collection of Reprints from Books of Travel, Letters and Diaries prior to 1830* (*Ind. Hist. Coll.* 1916).

## CHAPTERS V TO VIII

### BIBLIOGRAPHIES

Some of the bibliographies such as Sabin's listed for the preceding chapters will be found useful here. No duplication of titles has been attempted, however; and the following are recommended as being chiefly valuable for the chapters dealing primarily with the imaginative literature: *American Catalogue, The.* Ed. by F.

Leypoldt & others. Covers a period from July, 1876, to 1910. Title varies after 1886. Supplemented later by the *Publishers Weekly; Catalogue of Copyright Entries of Books and Other Articles Entered in the Office of the Librarian of Congress* 1891-; *Cumulative Book Index, The,* 1898 to date; E. K. Crews — *Illinois in Modern Literature* (Ill. St. Hist. Soc. — *Jour.* III:26ff.); Elsie Dershem — *Outlines of American State Literature* (1921); A. N. De Menil — *Literature of the Louisiana Territory* (1904) and *A Century of Missouri Literature* (*Mo. Hist. Rev.* XV:74 ff.); C. Evans — *American Bibliography. A Chronological Dictionary of All Books, Pamphlets & Periodical Publications Printed in the United States from the Genesis of Printing in 1639 down to and including the Year 1820* (only 9 vols. down to 1794 pub. to date); H. S. Fiske — *Provincial Types in American Fiction* (1903); W. M. Griswold — *Descriptive List of Novels and Tales dealing with the History of North America* (1895) and *Descriptive List of Novels and Tales dealing with American Country Life* (1890); Emma A. Hawley — *Bibliography of Wisconsin Authors* . . . (1893); J. G. Johnson — *Southern Fiction Prior to 1860* . . . (Va. diss. 1909); James Kelly — *The American Catalogue of Books. 1861-1871* (2 v. 1866-1871); Sophia J. Lammers — *A Provisional List of Nebraska Authors* (1918); Alice Marple — *Iowa Authors and their Works* (1918); F. L. Mott — *Literature of Pioneer Life in Iowa* (1923); *Poole's Index to Periodical Literature* 1802-1907; Meredith Nicholson — *The Hoosiers* (1900); *Reader's Guide to Periodical Literature* (1900-); O. A. Roorbach — *Bibliotheca Americana. Catalogue of American Publications including Reprints and Original Works from 1820 to 1852* . . . (1852). Supplements 1855, 1858, 1861; F. A. Sampson — *A Bibliography of Missouri Authors* (1901); J. W. Townsend — *Kentuckians in History and Literature* (1907) & *Kentucky in American Letters 1784-1912* (2 v. 1913); Nikolaus Trübner — *Trübner's Bibliographical Guide to American Literature: A Classified List of Books Published in the United States of America during the last Forty Years (1817-1857)* Pub. 1859; *United States Catalogue, The. Books in Print Jan. 1, 1912* (1912). Supplements 1918, 1921, 1924, 1925.

In addition to the preceding bibliographies attention is called to the full and helpful lists given in the *Cambridge History of American Literature* edited by W. P. Trent, John Erskine, S. P. Sherman, and Carl Van Doren (4 v. 1917-1921). Because of their accessibility the bibliographies in this section are much briefer than in the preceding. Attention is called to sections particularly valuable in connection with the chapters that follow, and further bibliographical references are given there.

## GENERAL REFERENCE BOOKS — CHAPTERS V TO VIII

The most valuable single reference work is the *Cambridge History of American Literature* cited above. In addition the following may be recommended: O. F. Adams — *A Dictionary of American Authors* (1897. 5th ed. rev. & enlarged 1905); S. A. Allibone — *A Critical Dictionary of English Literature & British & American Authors* (3 v. 1882. Sup. 2 v. by J. F. Kirk 1891); E. A. & G. L. Duyckinck — *Cyclopedia of American Literature* (2 v. 1855. Sup. 1866. Rev. ed. by M. L. Simons 1875); R. W. Griswold — *The Poets & Poetry of America* (1842) & *The Prose Writers of America* (1847); Leon Kellner — *American Literature* (Rev. 1915); J. A. Macy — *The Spirit of American Literature* (1913); Brander Matthews — *An Introduction to the Study of American Literature* (1896); F. L. Pattee — *A History of American Literature* . . . (1896. Rev. ed. 1918) & *The Development of the American Short Story; an Historical Survey* (1923); Bliss Perry — *The American Spirit in Literature* (*Chron. of Amer.* XXXIV); A. H. Quinn — *A History of the American Drama from the Beginning to the Civil War* (1923); W. P. Trent — *A History of American Literature 1607-1865* (1903); M. C. Tyler — *A History of American Literature during the Colonial Time 1607-1763* (2 v. 1878. New rev. ed. 1897) & *The Literary History of the American Revolution 1763-1783* (2 v. 1897); Carl Van Doren — *The American Novel* (1921); Barrett Wendell — *A Literary History of America* (1900).

## ANTHOLOGIES

In addition to the large general compilations familiar to all students of American literature, the following special collections may be mentioned: Mrs. W. J. Arnold — *The Poets & Poetry of Minnesota* (1864); C. G. Blanden & Minna Mathison — *Chicago Anthology; a Collection of Verse from the Work of Chicago Poets* (1916); W. H. Carruth — *Kansas in Literature* (2 pts. 1900); J. H. Combs — *All That's Kentucky* (1915); T. W. Herringshaw — *Poets & Poetry of Iowa* (1894) & *Local & National Poets of America* . . . (1890); Hattie Homer — *Collection of Kansas Poetry* . . . (1891); *Michigan Poets & Poetry* (1904); Brander Matthews — *Poems of American Patriotism* (rev. ed. 1922); Thomas M'Caleb — *The Louisiana*

*Book* . . . (1894); B. S. Parker & E. S. Heiney — *Poets & Poetry of Indiana* . . . (1900); B. E. Stevenson — *Poems of American History* (1908); Emerson Venable — *Poets of Ohio* (1909); Minnie Williams — *Indiana Authors, a Representative Collection for Young People* (1916).

The following German lyrical anthologies are useful: G. A. Neef — *Vom Lande des Sternenbanners* (1905); Konrad Nies — *Deutsch-Amerikanische Dichtung* (1888-90); H. A. Ratterman — *Deutsch-Amerikanisches Biographikon und Dichteralbum* (3 v. 1911); G. A. Zimmerman — *Deutsch in Amerika. Beiträge zur Geschichte der Deutsch-Amerikanischen Literatur. 1. Epischlyrische Poesie.* (Hrsg. vom "Germania Männerchor" in Chicago. 2d. ed. 1894.)

## CHAPTER V

Probably the most valuable single reference book for this chapter is W. H. Venable's *Beginnings of Literary Culture in the Ohio Valley* (1891). Unfortunately this has long been out of print; however R. L. Rusk's *Literature of the Middle Western Frontier* (2 v. 1925) is largely a reproduction of the material given by Venable, with some additions, chiefly concerning the drama. Various smaller monographs have been prepared such as Mary M. Atkeson's *Study of the Local Literature of the Upper Ohio Valley with Special Reference to the Early Pioneer and Indian Tales* (O. State Univ. — *Bull.* XXVI. *Contrib. in Eng.* 2. 1921); O. A. Rothert's *Local History in Kentucky Literature* (1915); & Isabel Jamison's *Literature & Literary People of Early Illinois* (Ill. St. Hist. Soc. — *Pub.* no. 13. 1909).

FICTION. A very helpful guide is Lillie D. Loshe's *Early American Novel* (1907); Oscar Wegelin's *Early American Fiction, 1774-1830* (1902. Rev. ed. 1913) should also be noted. In addition to Carl Van Doren's book, *The American Novel*, his chapters on American Fiction in the Cambridge History (I:284-325) and the corresponding bibliography (I:525-546) should be noted. Biographical accounts of the various fiction writers are helpful — W. P. Trent's *William Gilmore Simms* (1892), J. E. Kirkpatrick's *Timothy Flint, Pioneer, Missionary, Author, Editor, 1780-1840* . . . (1911), V. L. O. Chittick's *Thomas Chandler Haliburton ("Sam Slick"), a Study in Provincial Toryism* (1924), and P. L. James' *Judge James Hall, a Literary Pioneer of the Middle West* (O. Arch. & Hist. Soc. — *Pub.* XVIII:468 ff.). As yet unpublished studies on James Kirke Paulding by Prof. Herauld and on Charles Brockden Brown by Professor Clark should also be helpful. A monograph on Judge Hall is being prepared by Professor F. W. Scott; I note that a biography of Charles Fenno Hoffman also seems to be in preparation.

The dreams of the speculators satirized in the passage quoted from Paulding are also treated in greater detail in David Ross Locke's *A Paper City* (1878) and other later volumes. A mania for speculation in land is used for the ruin of one of the central characters in *Ellen Woodville; or, Life in the West* (1844). As typical of the poetical satires the following passage may be quoted:

"Lithographic towns
In western wilds, where yet unbroken ranks
Of thrifty beavers build unchartered 'banks,'
And prowling panthers occupy the lots,
Adorned with churches on the paper plots!"

There were numerous publications about the outlaws of the border which gave Simms the inspiration for his *Richard Hurdis* and *Border Beagles.* The substance of all is well summed up in the elaborate title of one by A. Q. Walton — *A History of the Detection, Conviction, Life and Designs of John A. Murel, the Great Western Land Pirate. Together with his System of Villainy, a Plan of Exciting a Negro Rebellion. And a Catalogue of the Names of Four Hundred and Forty-five of his Mystic Clan, Fellows and Followers, and their Efforts for the Destruction of Mr. Virgil A. Stewart, the Young Man who Detected Him. To which is added a Biographical Sketch of Mr. Virgil A. Stewart* (1835). A similar but later account is J. R. S. Pitts' *Life and Bloody Career of the Executed Criminal, James Copeland, the Great Southern Land Pirate Leader of a Devastating Clan Ranging over a Great Portion of the Nation, particularly the Gulf States, Spreading Terror and Insecurity Everywhere. Mystic Alphabet of the Clan, for their Secret Correspondence, Giving a List of all the Members throughout the Union, with an Appendix of Profound Research, Bringing to Light More of Crime, Corruption and Dissimulation, Unveiling the Many Ways in which Talent, Wealth and Influence Have Given Assistance.* (2d. ed. 1874.) Exploits of such criminals next to the struggles of Indians and scout formed the most popular theme in the early fiction; that their popularity still persists is shown by Herbert Quick's depiction of such a band in his Iowa trilogy, by the numerous narratives about the James brothers, and by the frequent use of the latter band in the early moving pictures. O. A. Rothert in his *Outlaws of Cave-in-Rock* has shown the correlation of history and literature in this respect.

The best collection of dime novels is *The Beadle Collection of Dime Novels* given to the New York Public Library by Dr. F. P. O'Brien and catalogued in 1922. In addition to the references cited in the text, a helpful discussion of the dime novel is given in the preface of a recent reprint of Sylvester Ellis's *Seth Jones* and a brief account in E. L. Pearson's *Books in Black or Red* (1923).

Among the early chap books showing interest in the West should have been included *A Wonderful Discovery of an Old Hermit, Who Lived Upward of Two Hundred Years* (1786).

It is unfortunate that Gallagher was unable to carry out his design of making a volume of "Selections from the Polite Literature of the West," but some of the best of these, the stories of Judge James Hall, are fairly accessible. His *Legends of the West* was first published 1822 (2d ed. 1833), *The Soldier's Bride and Other Tales*, 1833, *Tales of the Border*, 1835, and *The Wilderness and the War Path*, 1846. Selections from these are included in C. S. Baldwin's *American Short Stories* (1904), Alexander Jessup's *Representative American Short Stories* (1923), and other collections. Several of the early western stories are included in Mary Russell Mitford's *Lights and Shadows of American Life* (1832). She praises the majority of them including Flint's *The Young Backwoodsman* for their "unvarnished picture" of native scenes and manners, adding that "one or two of the Stories, especially 'The Squatter' and 'The Last of the Boatmen' seem to me fuller of individuality and power than any American Sketch that I have ever met with." (*Ibid.* IV.)

The best general reference for the short story is the book by Professor Pattee already cited, *The Development of the American Short Story* (1923). Will D. Howe's chapter on the *Early Humorists* in the *Cambridge History of American Literature* (II:148-159) and the accompanying bibliography (*Ibid.* 503-511) should be noted. Worthy of special mention in connection with the humorists are J. L. Ford's *A Century of American Humor* (*Munsey's Mag.*, July, 1901); H. C. Lukens' *American Literary Comedians* (*Harper's Mag.*, April, 1890); Stephen Leacock's *American Humour* (*Nineteenth Century*, Aug., 1914); W. P. Trent's *A Retrospect of American Humour* (*Century Mag.*, Nov., 1901). *Humour and Satire* (Ch. V of *The American Mind*) by Professor Bliss Perry, the article on American Humour in Brander Matthews' *The American of the Future* . . . (1909), and a Columbia dissertation *Cracker Box Philosophers* should also be noted.

POETRY. Bibliographical aids of special value for this section are the following: J. C. Frank — *Early American Poetry 1610-1820. A List of Works in the New York Public Library* (1917); *Index to American Poetry and Plays in the Collection of C. Fiske Harris* (1874. Rev. by J. C. Stockbridge. 1886); Oscar Wegelin — *Early American Poetry . . . Issued during the Seventeenth and Eighteenth Centuries* (1903) & *Early American Poetry 1800-1820* . . . (1907). In addition the following chapters and bibliographies in the *Cambridge History* will be found useful: *The Beginnings of Verse, 1610-1808* (I:150-184, 457-467); *Bryant and the Minor Poets* (I:260-283, 517-525); *Whittier* (II:42-54, 436-451); *Longfellow* (II:32-41, 425-436); & *Whitman* (II:258-274, 551-581).

Biographical and bibliographical data about the various poets may be found in the local literary histories listed at the beginning of this secton, also scattered through historical magazines in such articles as the following: *Wisconsin's First Versifiers* (*Wis. Mag. of Hist.* I:65 ff.); *Mary Elizabeth Mears. "Nellie Wildwood."* (Wis. Hist. Soc. — *Proc.* 1916. 254 ff.); *The Pioneer Poet Lawyer* (*O. Arch. & Hist. Soc. Pub.* X:306 ff.); *High Lights in Ohio Literature* by E. O. Randall (*Ibid.* 255 ff.), *An Illinois Poet, Elijah Whittier Blaisdell* (Ill. St. Hist. Soc. — *Jour.* III:95 ff), *Some Poets of Illinois* by Stuart Brown (Ill. St. Hist. Soc. — *Journal* XIV:330 ff.). A series of articles *Song Writers of Ohio* appeared in Ohio Arch. & Hist. Soc. — *Pub.* XIV.

In addition to the long poems mentioned in the text we may cite *The Kansas War; or the Conquests of Chivalry in the Crusades of the Nineteenth Century* (1856), one of the few long burlesque poems found during the period, *The Ojibway Conquest, a Tale of the Northwest*, by Kah-ge-ga-gah-Bowk, or G. Copway, Chief of the Ojibway Nation (1850), worthless as verse but interesting because of the position of the author and Eli Lewis's *St. Clair's Defeat* . . . "A Tale which strongly claims the pitying tear, And every feeling heart must bleed to hear." (1792.)

The anthologies cited in the text furnish the best idea of the early western verse. An interesting article by W. H. Venable, *William Davis Gallagher* (O. Arch. & Hist. Soc. — *Pub.* I:358 ff.), shows the ambitious plans of the latter for displaying the achievements of western writers. A good example of the fervor of the requests that Middle Westerners devote themselves to interpretation of their section is found in

*An Address Delivered on the Sixth Anniversary of the Erodelphian Society of Miami University; September 27, 1831,* by Benjamin Drake (1831). Typical collections of the shorter poems are John Finley's *The Hoosier's Nest and Other Poems* (1860); Micah P. Flint's *The Hunter & Other Poems* (1826); William R. Wallace's *The Battle of Tippecanoe . . .* (1837); D. R. Arnell's *Fruit of Western Life; or, Blanche & Other Poems* (1847); C. H. Jones' *The Outlaw . . .* (1835). Of interest in connection with the French and Indian Wars is Stephen Tilden's *Poems on Divers Occasions Chiefly to Animate and Rouse the Soldiers* (1756). *The Poems of Charles Fenno Hoffman* (1873) show some of the same appreciation of the romantic aspects of border life that made his *Winter in the West* so attractive.

The most representative collection of American ballads is Louise Pound's *American Ballads & Songs* (1922) although there are numerous other suggestive compilations such as *Folk Songs of the South,* ed. by J. H. Cox (1925). Smaller collections and interesting discussions are, of course, scattered through such publications as the *Journal of American Folk Lore.* Typical of such articles are Mrs. L. D. Ames' *The Missouri Play-Party* (*J.A.F.L.* XXIV:295-318), Phillips Barry's *Native Balladry in America* (*J.A.F.L.* XXII:365-373), Mrs. Annie L. Ellis's *O Bury Me Not on the Lone Prairie* (*J.A.F.L.* XIV:186), Edwin F. Piper's *Some Play-Party Games of the Middle West* (*J.A.F.L.* XXVIII:262-289). H. G. Shearin & J. H. Combs published *A Syllabus of Kentucky Folk Songs* (1911), and H. G. Shearin read a paper *The Historic Value of Kentucky Folk Songs* before the Ohio Valley Historical Association in 1913. Miss Pound's chapter *Oral Literature* in the *Cambridge History* (IV:502-516) and its accompanying bibliography (*Ibid.* 799-802) should be noted.

Illuminating for the ballads is C. B. Galbreath's *The Ballad of "James Bird." Its Authorship* (*O. Arch. & Hist. Quar.* XXVI:52 ff.) and his *The Battle of Lake Erie in Ballad and History* (*Ibid.* XX:415 ff.). A number of contemporary songs are found in Thwaites and Kellogg's *Documentary History of Dunmore's War.* For the negro melodies H. E. Krehbiel's *Afro-American Folksongs, a Study in Racial and National Music* (1914) should be noted, also T. W. Higginson's article *Negro Spirituals* in the June, 1867, *Atlantic Monthly.* For some of the river songs see Lafcadio Hearn's *Levee Life. Haunts and Pastimes of the Roustabouts, Their Original Songs and Peculiar Dances* (in *An American Miscellany* ed. by Albert Mordell. I: 147-170).

FOREIGN INTERPRETATIONS AND FOREIGN LANGUAGE TREATMENTS IN AMERICA. Of distinct value for English treatments of America is Dr. Benjamin Bissell's monograph *The American Indian in English Literature of the Eighteenth Century* (*Yale Studies in English.* LXVIII. 1925). I am indebted to Dr. Bissell for an opportunity to read his study while it was still in manuscript. Professor Chauncey B. Tinker's series of lectures *Nature's Simple Plan, a Phase of Radical Thought in the Mid-Eighteenth Century* (1922) throws light on the phase of the romantic movement in which America was most prominent as do Professor Lane Cooper's studies on Wordworth's reading, etc. An interesting tract of 1787 by George Burden on the supposed *Welch Indians* who formed the basis for Southey's *Madoc* has been reprinted in the *Mag. of Hist.* Extra no. 78. As indicative of the wide-spread interest in them two other tracts issued near the close of the eighteenth century may be cited — John Williams' *An Enquiry into the Truth of the Tradition concerning the Discovery of America by Prince Madog ab Owen Gwynedd, about the Year 1170 . . .* (1791) and *Further Observations . . .* by him (1792).

Professor Gilbert Chinard has in preparation a study of the influence of America on the later French romanticists, which should prove as illuminating as his earlier ones have been. Professor Bernard Faÿ's *L'Esprit Révolutionnaire en France et aux États-Unis à la fin du XVIIIe Siècle* (1925) is interesting in this connection. Almost any good study of French literature such as C. H. C. Wright's *History of French Literature* (1912) or of the romantic movement such as Irving Babbitt's *Rousseau and Romanticism* (1919) should give background for the reader unfamiliar with the cult of nature. The most earnest students of French literature in America were M. Édouard and M. Alcée Fortier. Not only the former's article in the *Cambridge History of American Literature* (IV:590-598, 820-822) should be noted but his study *Les Lettres Françaises en Louisiane* (*Mémoires du Premier Congres de la Langue Française au Canada.* 1915). The latter was the author of a *History of Louisiana* (1904), of *La Litterature Française de la Louisiane,* of *Louisiana Studies: Literature, Customs & Dialects, History & Education* (1894), of *Louisiana Folk Tales in French Dialect and English Translation* (1895), besides numerous other works which concern us less intimately.

The *Comptes Rendus* of L'Athenée Louisianais, a society for the encouragement of the French language and literature, contains much of the foreign language literature of Louisiana that is most worth while. It is interesting to note that Lafcadio Hearn praised the publication. It like the native poems, plays, etc. which have been published as separate volumes are exceedingly difficult to procure. Apparently only in New Orleans can a student work with any ease. Mr. W. H. Beer, librarian of the Howard Memorial Library, and several other collectors are said to have excellent private libraries, to which they welcome earnest workers. It is to be hoped that the *Louisiana Historical Quarterly* will continue the excellent work it has done along other lines by making accessible some of the best of these pieces to residents of other sections.

The Louisiana French writer who seems to have attracted most attention is the Abbé Adrien Rouquette. A good article about him by G. W. Nott appeared in the *Louisiana Historical Quarterly* (VI:388 ff.) and he is the subject of a short biographical study by Mrs. Susan Elder (1913). He is also pictured in *Lafcadio Hearn's American Days* by E. L. Tinker.

For the German literature of and in America the best aids are the article and bibliography by Professor A. B. Faust in the *Cambridge History of American Literature* (IV:572-590, 813-820). A large amount of excellent investigation has been done along this line, the series of monographs on the German stage in various cities putting to shame, for instance, our neglect of our dramatic history. One of the most prolific investigators is Preston A. Barba who has issued a series of excellent monographs — *Friedrich Armand Strubberg* (*Ger. Amer. Annals*, new ser. X, nos. 5-6, XI, nos. 1-4), *Emigration to America Reflected in German Fiction* (*Ger. Amer. Annals*, new ser. XII, no. 6), *Balduin Möllhausen, the German Cooper* (*Americana Germanica Monograph* ser. no. 17), *The American Indian in German Fiction* (*Ger. Amer. Annals*, new ser. XI, nos. 3-4), *Cooper in Germany* (*Ind. Univ. Studies*, 1914). Sealsfield has been especially well treated by posterity, Professor Faust having published *Charles Sealsfield's Place in Literature* (*Americana Germanica* I, no. 1) and *Charles Sealsfield (Carl Postl); Der Dichter beider Hemisphären. Sein Leben und Seine Werke* (1897), Paul Schultz having discussed *Die Schilderung exotischer Natur in deutschen Roman mit besonderer Berücksichtigung von Charles Sealsfield* (Münster diss., 1913) and B. A. Uhlendorf, *Charles Sealsfield, Ethnic Elements and National Problems in his Works* (originally in "*Deutsch-Amerikanische Geschichts-Blätter.*" *Jahrbuch der Deutsch-Amerikanischen historischen Gesellschaft von Illinois.* 1920-1. XX-XXI, reprinted 1922). The fact that that excellent publication *The German American Annals* as well as the yearbooks of local societies is always open to such contributions suggests that more avenues of publication would result in more studies of our native literature.

As with the Creole literature it was sometimes difficult to procure the books desired. I was able, for instance, to read only a few of the books of Möllhausen although inquiry for them was made at most of our larger libraries. *Der Leuchtturm am Michigan* (1883) would seem peculiarly interesting for our study. *Die Einsiedlerinnen* (1873) by the same author deals with Missouri life, *Wildes Blut* (1886), with the love of a medicine man for a Kaskaskia maiden, etc. Many of the German poems and stories are scattered through various magazines and newspapers and are therefore unavailable although anthologies such as those cited earlier have brought together a number of interesting pieces and useful biographical information. *Wisconsin's Deutsch-Amerikaner*, v. II, chapter 2, *Poesie und Prosa*, gives an account of a number of these Teutonic writers with extracts from their works; H. E. Legler's *A Wisconsin Group of German Poets; with a Bibliography* (*Wis. Acad. of Sciences, Arts, & Letters.* Pub. XIV) and Gottlieb Betz's *Die Deutschamerikanische Patriotische Lyrik der Achtundvierziger und ihre Historische Grundlage* (*Americana Germanica*, no. 22. 1916) should also be noted.

## CHAPTER VI

For this and the following chapters Professor F. L. Pattee's *American Literature since 1870* (1915) is exceedingly valuable. J. C. Underwood's *The Literature of Insurgency* (1914) should also be noted. In the *Cambridge History* the chapter *The Later Novel: Howells* (III:66-95) and the accompanying bibliography (*Ibid.* IV:656-671) is of value. Various magazine articles present material of value — J. W. DeForest's *The Great American Novel* in *The Nation* (Jan. 9, 1868, pp. 27-29), J. S. Perry's *American Novels* (in the *No. Amer. Rev.*, Oct., 1872, pp. 366-378), and Harold Waldo's *Old Wests for New* (in the *Bookman*, June, 1920, v. LI, pp. 396-400).

Realistic novels showing the tragedies of the underlings in our civilization that might be mentioned in connection with Sinclair are Isaac K. Friedman's *Poor People* (1900) and *By Bread Alone* (1901), both of which are localized on the prairie.

*The Cabin in the Clearing* (1887) may also be mentioned in connection with this chapter inasmuch as the author Benjamin S. Parker devotes many of his verses to depiction of the hardships of the early pioneers.

## CHAPTER VII

In addition to Professor Pattee's book *American Literature since 1870* and the other more general reference books already cited, the following chapters and bibliographies in the *Cambridge History* are valuable: *The Short Story* (II:367-395, 616-631), *Mark Twain* (*Ibid.* III:1-20, IV:635-639), *Minor Humorists* (III:21-30, IV:639-644), *Later Poets* (III:31-65, IV:644-656), and *The Later Novel: Howells* (III:66-96, IV:656-671).

In connection with the historical novel the following guides are useful: E. A. Baker's *History in Fiction* (2 v. 1907) and his later and more complete *Guide to the Best Historical Fiction* (1914); H. C. Bowen's *Descriptive Catalogue of Historical Novels & Tales, for the Use of School Libraries and Teachers of History* (1882); Zella Z. Dixson's *Comprehensive Subject Index to Universal Prose Fiction* (1897), and Jonathan Field's *Guide to the Best Historical Novels & Tales* (1911).

Magazine articles helpful for this chapter are: *Two Views regarding Historical Fiction* (*Hist. Teachers' Mag.*, Oct., 1916); Floyd Dell's *Chicago in Fiction* (*Bookman*, Nov., Dec., 1913); P. L. Ford's *The American Historical Novel* (*Atlantic Mo.*, Dec., 1897); W. S. Harwood's *New Orleans in Fiction* (*Critic*, Nov., 1905); Robert Herrick's *The Background of the American Novel* (*Yale Review*, Jan., 1914), & *The American Novel* (*Ibid.* April, 1914); W. D. Howells' *Certain of the Chicago School of Fiction* (*No. Amer. Rev.*, May, 1903); I. F. Marcosson's *The South in Fiction — Kentucky and Tennessee* (*Bookman*, Dec., 1910); Ruth McEnery Stuart's *American Backgrounds for Fiction — Arkansas, Louisiana, & the Gulf Country* (*Bookman*, Aug., 1914); Marie Thérèse de Solms Blanc ("Th. Bentzon") *Le Roman Historique aux États-Unis* (*Revue des Deux Mondes*, April, 1906).

A number of poems as well as plays and novels celebrating the Spotswood expedition may be found — among them R. A. Stewart's *Knights of the Golden Horseshoe & Other Lays* (1909). Illustration of the perennial interest of the old historic figures is afforded also by Walter Malone's long poem *Hernando de Soto* (1914). Denton J. Snider, whose *St. Louis Movement* (1920) furnishes an interesting chronicle of cultural development in the Middle West wrote a series of long poems centering around Lincoln; he was also fascinated by the figure of Johnny Appleseed, writing *Johnny Appleseed's Rhymes* (1894), an interesting combination of border eccentricity and German philosophy, and an autobiographical novel *The Freeburgers* (1889), in which Johnny Appleseed appears as one of the central figures.

As an interesting supplement to the "Blue-grass" fiction, W. L. Visscher's *Blue Grass Ballads* (1900) may be noted. An immensely popular Louisville bard of the Will Carleton class was William Shakespeare Hays whose *Poems and Songs* passed through many editions. Another description of the *Society of Separatists in Zoar, Ohio,* used by Miss Woolson as the background of a couple of her short stories, is given in the *Annual Report* of the American Historical Association, 1898, pp. 163-220. One aspect of the Prairies much stressed by the travellers, that is, the pleasure they afforded to the sportsman, is brought out in Isaac McLellan's *Haunts of Wild Game; or, Poems of Woods, Wilds & Waters* (1896) and his *Poems of the Rod & Gun; or, Sports by Flood & Field* (1886).

An unfortunate attack by Adrien Rouquette *Critical Dialogue between Aboo and Caboo on a New Book or a Grandissime Ascension* (1880) reveals the bitterness aroused by Cable's pictures of American life. Fortier says his "types of the Creole gentleman and lady are utterly incorrect. They are misrepresentations of an honorable and chivalric race, and have excited the just indignation of every Louisianian of the Latin race and of many of the Anglo-Saxon." (*La. Studies*, 117.) Further illumination of the sojourn of Lafcadio Hearn in New Orleans may be found in Elizabeth Bisland [Wetmore's] *Life and Letters of Lafcadio Hearn* (2 v. 1906), *Leaves from the Diary of an Impressionist* (ed. by Ferris Greenslet. 1911), & Nina Kennard's *Lafcadio Hearn* (1911).

The best survey of the early drama is that provided by Professor Quinn's excellent book *A History of the American Drama, from the Beginning to the Civil War* (1923). The chapters and bibliographies on the drama in the *Cambridge History* should also be noted (I:215-232, 490-507, III:266-298, & IV:760-774). Other helpful bibliographies are the private catalogue of the F. W. Atkinson collection of American plays, now in the library of the University of Chicago, *Becks Collection of Prompt Books in the New York Public Library* (*Bull.*, Feb., 1906); *Index to American Poetry & Plays in the Collection of C. Fiske Harris* (1874, rev. by J. C. Stockbridge, 1886); D. C. Haskell — *A List of American Dramas in the New York Public Library* (1916); Oscar Wegelin — *Early American Plays, 1714-1830 . . .* (Dunlap Soc. *Pub.* Ser. 2, v. X. 1900, rev. ed. 1905); R. F. Roden — *Later American Plays, 1831-1900* (Dunlap Soc. *Pub.* Ser. 2, v. XII. 1900); & *Dramatic Compositions Copyrighted in the United States, 1870 to 1916* (2 v. 1918).

Much information is given in M. J. Moses' *Representative Plays by American Dramatists. 1765-1917* (3 v. 1918-1926) and A. H. Quinn's *Representative American Plays* (1917). Reminiscences of actors and managers such as Joseph Cowell's *Thirty Years Passed among the Players in England and America* (2 pts. 1844) throw much light on early theatrical conditions; for certain types such as the minstrel shows or border dramas Laurence Hutton's *Curiosities of the American Stage* (1891) is very valuable. In this connection several articles by Professor Brander Matthews are very valuable — *The American on the Stage* (*Scribner's Mo.*, XVIII, July, 1879, pp. 321-333); *The Banjo and the Bones* (*Lond. Sat. Rev.* 1884); *The Decline & Fall of Negro Minstrelsy* in a *Book about the Theatre* (1916).

In connection with the little theatre in the West A. G. Arvold's *The Little Country Theatre* (1922) should be noted. John Gainsford has published an account of *The Drama in New Orleans* (1849), which, however, was of little value for this study; and helpful studies have been made of the German theatre in various western cities such as A. H. Nolle's *The German Drama on the St. Louis Stage* (*Ger. Amer. Annals*, new ser. XV, nos. 1 to 4. 1917). Among the shorter monographs and articles P. I. Reed's *The Realistic Presentation of American Characters in Native American Plays prior to Eighteen Seventy* (O. St. Univ. *Bull.*, XXII. *Contrib. in Lang. & Lit.*, I. 1905) and Oscar Wegelin's *An Early Wisconsin Play* (*Wis. Mag. of Hist.*, I:307) should be noticed.

## CHAPTER VIII

The best aids to study of the recent writers are provided in the critical and popular magazines, to which *The Reader's Guide* forms a helpful index. An illuminating picture of many of the writers discussed is found in Harry Hansen's *Midwest Portraits, a Book of Memories and Friendships* (1923). Carl Van Doren's *Contemporary American Novelists, 1900-1920* (1922) should also be noted, especially the section called *The Revolt from the Village* and parts of his *Many Minds* (1924). Some material is afforded by Carl and Mark Van Doren's *American and British Literature since 1890* (1923). Many of the novelists treated in this chapter are giving valuable autobiographical records of their life and work — notably Anderson and Dreiser. For treatment of the aboriginal literature of the red men see Mary Austin's chapter in *The Cambridge History* (IV:610-634, 826-827).

Note: Dr. Paul Weber's survey of the treatments of America in the German literature of the first half of the nineteenth century should have been included on p. 449. I am indebted to Dr. Weber for an opportunity to read in manuscript his monograph, which has just been issued by the Columbia University Press.

# INDEX

DATE DUE

| | | | |
|---|---|---|---|
| | | | |
| | | | |
| | | | |
| | | | |
| | | | |
| | | | |
| | | | |
| | | | |
| | | | |
| | | | |
| | | | |
| | | | |
| | | | |
| | | | |
| | | | |
| | | | |
| | | | |
| | | | |
| GAYLORD | | | PRINTED IN U.S.A. |